EDITORIAL
Project Directors: Kathleen Daniel, Mescal Evler
Executive Editors: Juliana Koenig, Kristine E. Marshall
Manager of Operations and Planning: Bill Wahlgren
Managing Editors: Marie Price, Mike Topp
Manager of Editorial Services: Abigail Winograd
Senior Product Manager: Don Wulbrecht
Editorial Staff: Jane Archer-Feinstein, Rob Giannetto, Mikki Gibson, Annie Hartnett, Sean W. Henry, Julie Barnett Hoover, Tressa Sanders, Errol Smith, Amy Strong, Suzanne Thompson, Michael Zakhar
Copyediting Manager: Michael Neibergall
Copyediting Supervisor: Mary Malone
Copyeditors: Christine Altgelt, Joel Bourgeois, Elizabeth Dickson, Emily Force, Anne Heausler, Julie A. Hill, Julia Thomas Hu, Jennifer Kirkland, Millicent Ondras, Dennis Scharnberg
Project Administration: Lori de la Garza, *Editorial Operations Supervisor;* Elizabeth LaManna, *Editorial Finance Manager*
Editorial Support: Renée Benitez, Louise Fernandez, Christine Han, Mark Holland, Ruth Hooker, Bret Isaacs, Marcus Johnson, Laurie Muir, Joie D. Pickett, Margaret Sanchez, Kelly Tankersley, Tom Ver Gow
Editorial Permissions: David Smith, Carrie Jones

Index: Alana Cash

ART, DESIGN, AND PRODUCTION
Director: Athena Blackorby
Senior Design Director: Betty Mintz
Design: Fred Yee, Rich Colicchio, Peter Sawchuk
Design and Electronic Files: Kirchoff/Wohlberg, Inc.; Preface, Inc.
Photo Research: Kirchoff/Wohlberg, Inc.; Omni–Photo Communications, Inc.
Photo Researcher: Richard Benavides, Image Acquisitions
Art Buyer Supervisor: Michelle Rumpf, Image Acquisitions
Production Manager: Catherine Gessner
Production Coordinator: Joseph Padial
Production Assistant: Myles Gorospe

2005 Printing

Acknowledgments appear on pages 752–753, which are an extension of the copyright page.

Printed in the United States of America

ISBN 0-03-056492-1

7 8 9 048 06 05

ii

First Course

HOLT
Literature
&Language
Arts

 Mastering the California Standards
Reading · Writing · Listening · Speaking

 HOLT, RINEHART AND WINSTON

A Harcourt Classroom Education Company

Austin · New York · Orlando · Atlanta · San Francisco · Boston · Dallas · Toronto · London

Program Authors

Kylene Beers established the reading pedagogy for Part 1 of *Holt Literature and Language Arts* and wrote the lessons in the Reading Matters section of the book. A former middle school teacher, Dr. Beers has turned her commitment to helping readers having difficulty into the major focus of her research, writing, speaking, and teaching. A clinical associate professor at the University of Houston, Dr. Beers is also currently the editor of the National Council of Teachers of English journal *Voices from the Middle*. She is the author of *When Kids Can't Read: The Reading Handbook for Teachers Grades 6–12* and co-editor of *Into Focus: Understanding and Creating Middle School Readers*. She has served on the review boards of the *English Journal* and *The Alan Review*. Dr. Beers currently serves on the board of directors of the International Reading Association's Special Interest Group on Adolescent Literature.

Lee Odell helped establish the pedagogical framework for Part 2 of *Holt Literature and Language Arts*. Dr. Odell is Professor of Composition Theory and Research and, since 1996, Director of the Writing Program at Rensselaer Polytechnic Institute. He began his career teaching English in middle and high schools. More recently he has worked with teachers in grades K–12 to establish a program that involves students from all disciplines in writing across the curriculum and for communities outside their classrooms. Dr. Odell's most recent book (with Charles R. Cooper) is *Evaluating Writing: The Role of Teacher's Knowledge About Text, Learning, and Culture*. He is Past Chair of the Conference on College Composition and Communication and of NCTE's Assembly for Research. Dr. Odell is currently working on a college-level writing textbook.

Special Contributors

Flo Ota De Lange and **Sheri Henderson** helped plan and organize the program and played key roles in developing and preparing the informational materials.

Flo Ota De Lange is a former teacher with a thirty-year second career in psychotherapy, during which she studied learning processes in children and adults. These careers have led to her third career, as a writer.

Sheri Henderson brings to the program twenty years of experience as a California middle-school research practitioner and full-time reading and language arts teacher at La Paz Intermediate School in Saddleback Valley Unified School District. She regularly speaks at statewide and national conferences.

Since 1991, DeLangeHenderson LLC has published forty-three titles designed to integrate the teaching of literature with standards requirements and state and national tests.

Writers

John Malcolm Brinnin, author of six volumes of poetry that have received many prizes and awards, was a member of the American Academy and Institute of Arts and Letters. He was a critic of poetry and a biographer of poets and was for a number of years Director of New York's famous Poetry Center. His teaching career, begun at Vassar College, included long terms at the University of Connecticut and Boston University, where he succeeded Robert Lowell as Professor of Creative Writing and Contemporary Letters. Mr. Brinnin wrote *Dylan Thomas in America: An Intimate Journal* and *Sextet: T. S. Eliot & Truman Capote & Others.*

John Leggett is a novelist, biographer, and teacher. He went to the Writer's Workshop at the University of Iowa in the spring of 1969, expecting to work there for a single semester. In 1970, he assumed temporary charge of the program, and for the next seventeen years he was its director. Mr. Leggett's novels include *Wilder Stone, The Gloucester Branch, Who Took the Gold Away?, Gulliver House,* and *Making Believe.* He is also the author of the highly acclaimed biography *Ross and Tom: Two American Tragedies* and of a biography of William Saroyan, *A Daring Young Man.* Mr. Leggett lives in California's Napa Valley.

Joan Burditt is a writer and editor who has a master's degree in education with a specialization in reading. She taught for several years in Texas, where her experience included work in programs for readers having difficulty. Since then she has developed and written instructional materials for middle-school language arts texts.

Madeline Travers Hovland, who taught middle school for several years, is a writer of educational materials. She studied English at Bates College and received a master's degree in education from Harvard University.

Richard Kelso is a writer and editor whose children's books include *Building a Dream: Mary Bethune's School; Walking for Freedom: The Montgomery Bus Boycott; Days of Courage: The Little Rock Story;* and *The Case of the Amistad Mutiny.*

Mara Rockliff is a writer and editor with a degree in American civilization from Brown University. She has written dramatizations of classic stories for middle-school students, collected in a book called *Stories for Performance.* She has also published feature stories in national newspapers and is currently writing a novel for young adults.

Program Consultants

SENIOR PROGRAM CONSULTANT
Carol Jago is the editor of CATE's quarterly journal, *California English.* She teaches English at Santa Monica High School, in Santa Monica, and directs the California Reading and Literature Project at UCLA. She also writes a weekly education column for the *Los Angeles Times.* She is the author of several books, including two in a series on contemporary writers in the classroom: *Alice Walker in the Classroom* and *Nikki Giovanni in the Classroom.* She is also the author of *With Rigor for All: Teaching the Classics to Contemporary Students* and *Beyond Standards: Excellence in the High School English Classroom.*

CONTENT-AREA READING CONSULTANT
Judith L. Irvin served as a reading consultant for the content-area readers for *Holt Literature and Language Arts: The Ancient World; A World in Transition;* and *The United States: Change and Challenge.* Dr. Irvin is a Professor of Education at Florida State University. She writes a column, "What Research Says to the Middle Level Practitioner," for the *Middle School Journal* and serves as the literacy expert for the *Middle Level News,* published by the California League of Middle Schools. Her several books include the companion volumes *Reading and the Middle School Student: Strategies to Enhance Literacy* and *Reading and the High School Student: Strategies to Enhance Literacy* (with Buehl and Klemp).

ADVISORS
Dr. Julie M. T. Chan
Director of Literacy
   Instruction
Newport-Mesa Unified
   School District
Costa Mesa, California

Cheri Howell
Reading Specialist
Covina-Valley Unified
   School District
Covina, California

José M. Ibarra-Tiznado
ELL Program Coordinator
Bassett Unified School
   District
La Puente, California

Dr. Ronald Klemp
Instructor
California State
   University, Northridge
Northridge, California

Fern M. Sheldon
K–12 Curriculum and
   Instruction Specialist
Rowland Unified School
   District
Rowland Heights,
   California

CRITICAL REVIEWERS
Stacy Kim
Rowland Unified
   School District
Rowland Heights,
   California

Mary Alice Madden
Lathrop Intermediate
   School
Santa Ana, California

Carol Surabian
Washington
   Intermediate School
Dinuba, California

FIELD-TEST PARTICIPANTS
Kate Baker
South Hills Middle
   School
Pittsburgh,
   Pennsylvania

Linda Lawler
Arcadia Middle School
Rochester, New York

Cindy MacIntosh
Seven Hills Middle
   School
Nevada City, California

Tim Pail
South Hills Middle
   School
Pittsburgh,
   Pennsylvania

Mathew Woodin
Martha Baldwin School
Alhambra, California

Part 1

Mastering the California Standards in Reading

Vocabulary Development, Reading Comprehension (Focus on Informational Materials), and Literary Response and Analysis

Part 2

Mastering the California Standards in Writing, Listening, and Speaking

Writing Workshops and Listening and Speaking Workshops

Resource Center

PART 1

Chapter

Mastering the California Standards in Reading
Structures:
Clarifying Meaning

"Once upon a time, they lived happily ever after."

Standards Focus

Vocabulary Development 1.3 Clarify word meanings through the use of definition, example, restatement, or contrast.

Reading Comprehension (Focus on Informational Materials) 2.1 Understand and analyze the differences in structure and purpose between various categories of informational materials (for example, textbooks, newspapers, instructional manuals, signs).

Literary Response and Analysis 3.2 Identify events that advance the plot, and determine how each event explains past or present action(s) or foreshadows future action(s).

Characters: Living Many Lives

 Standards Focus

Vocabulary Development 1.2 Use knowledge of Greek, Latin, and Anglo-Saxon roots and affixes to understand content-area vocabulary.

Literary Response and Analysis 3.3 Analyze characterization as delineated through a character's thoughts, words, speech patterns, and actions; the narrator's description; and the thoughts, words, and actions of other characters.

Chapter

Themes Across Time

Standards Focus

Vocabulary Development 1.1 Identify idioms, analogies, metaphors, and similes in prose and poetry.

Vocabulary Development 1.2 Use knowledge of Greek, Latin, and Anglo-Saxon roots and affixes to understand content-area vocabulary.

Reading Comprehension (Focus on Informational Materials) 2.3 Analyze text that uses the cause-and-effect organizational pattern.

Literary Response and Analysis 3.4 Identify and analyze recurring themes across works (for example, the value of bravery, loyalty, and friendship; the effects of loneliness).

Chapter

4

Point of View: Who's Talking?

Standards Focus

Vocabulary Development 1.3 Clarify word meanings through the use of definition, example, restatement, or contrast.

Reading Comprehension (Focus on Informational Materials) 2.4 Identify and trace the development of an author's argument, point of view, or perspective in text.

Literary Response and Analysis 3.5 Contrast points of view (for example, first and third person, limited and omniscient, subjective and objective) in narrative text, and explain how they affect the overall theme of the work.

**Mastering
the Standards**

Worlds of Words: Prose and Poetry

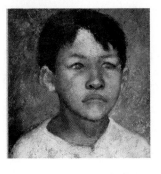

 Standards Focus

Vocabulary Development 1.1 Identify idioms, analogies, metaphors, and similes in prose and poetry.

Vocabulary Development 1.3 Clarify word meanings through the use of definition, example, restatement, or contrast.

Literary Response and Analysis 3.1 Articulate the expressed purposes and characteristics of different forms of prose (for example, short story, novel, novella, essay).

Chapter

Where I Stand: Literary Criticism

Standards Focus

Vocabulary Development 1.2 Use knowledge of Greek, Latin, and Anglo-Saxon roots and affixes to understand content-area vocabulary.

Reading Comprehension (Focus on Informational Materials) 2.6 Assess the adequacy, accuracy, and appropriateness of the author's evidence to support claims and assertions, noting instances of bias and stereotyping.

Literary Response and Analysis 3.6 Analyze a range of responses to a literary work, and determine the extent to which the literary elements in the work shaped those responses.

Chapter

Reading for Life
by Flo Ota De Lange and Sheri Henderson

 Standards Focus

Reading Comprehension (Focus on Informational Materials) 2.2
Locate information by using a variety of consumer, workplace, and public documents.

Reading Comprehension (Focus on Informational Materials) 2.5
Understand and explain the use of a simple mechanical device by following technical directions.

Sheri Henderson

Informational Materials

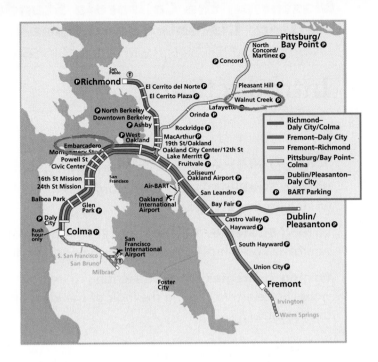

Informational Materials Following Technical Directions

Reading Matters by Kylene Beers 508

PART 2   **Mastering the California Standards in Writing, Listening, and Speaking**

Introduction

 Standards Focus

Writing Strategies 1.0 Students progress through stages of the writing process as needed.

Writing Strategies 1.3 Use strategies of note taking, outlining, and summarizing to impose structure on composition drafts.

Writing Strategies 1.7 Revise writing to improve organization and word choice after checking the logic of the ideas and the precision of the vocabulary.

Calvin & Hobbes copyright 1987 Watterson. Distributed by Universal Press Syndicate. Reprinted with permission. All rights reserved.

Workshop 1 — Narration

Standards Focus

Writing Applications 2.1 Write fictional narratives.
Speaking Applications 2.1 Deliver narrative presentations.

Mastering the Standards ▷

Workshop 2 — Response to Literature

Standards Focus

Writing Applications 2.2 Write responses to literature.
Speaking Applications 2.2 Deliver oral summaries of articles and books.
Listening and Speaking Strategies 1.8 Analyze the effect on the
viewer of images, text, and sound in electronic journalism; identify the
techniques used to achieve the effects in each instance studied.

Mastering
the Standards

Workshop

3

Persuasion

Standards Focus

Writing Applications 2.4 Write persuasive compositions.
Speaking Applications 2.4 Deliver persuasive presentations.

Mastering
the Standards

Workshop

Research

 Standards Focus

Writing Applications 2.3 Write research reports.
Speaking Applications 2.3 Deliver research presentations.

Workshop

Writing to Learn

Standards Focus

Writing Strategies 1.6 Create documents by using word-processing skills and publishing programs; develop simple databases and spreadsheets to manage information and prepare reports.
Writing Applications 2.5 Write summaries of reading materials.

Mini-Workshops

 Standards Focus

Writing Strategies 1.5 Give credit for both quoted and paraphrased information in a bibliography by using a consistent and sanctioned format and methodology for citations.
Writing Applications 2.0 Students write narrative, expository, and descriptive texts.
Writing Applications 2.3d Document reference sources by means of footnotes and a bibliography.
Listening and Speaking Strategies 1.8 Analyze the effect on the viewer of images, text, and sound in electronic journalism.

Writing

Media

Resource Center

SKILLS

Literary Response and Analysis Essays

Reading Matters: Strategy Lessons

Literary Skills

Reading Skills for Literary Texts

 Reading Skills for Informational Texts

Vocabulary Skills

STANDARDS

Review Standards from Earlier Grades

Vocabulary Development

Reading Comprehension

Literary Response and Analysis

You Can't Soar If You Can't Fly the Plane

by **Kylene Beers**

He was eighty-five years old when he stood in front of the younger man who was wearing a T-shirt that said "A-One Flyers." He told the flight instructor again, "I'm not leaving until you sign me up for flying lessons." The flight instructor said, "Sir, I just don't understand why, at eighty-five, you want to learn how to fly." The old man crossed his arms and said, "I'll never be able to soar if I can't fly the plane."

The man had a point, a good point: *Wanting* to soar wasn't enough to make the soaring happen. He had to know how to fly the plane if he really wanted to climb the clouds.

Think about the things you want to do—all the ways you want to soar. If you want to soar with your favorite computer games, you've got to know all the rules. If you want to soar with sports, you've got to practice. If you want to soar with your grades, you've got to study.

You Can't Soar If You Can't Read

Perhaps more than anything else in life, reading has the potential for letting you soar. With reading you can learn to do just about anything—from building an ark to repairing your zither (or even figuring out what a zither is). With reading you can step back in time, go forward in time, and travel to new lands. With reading you can meet characters who are just like you or as far removed from you as you can possibly imagine. Sometimes books act as mirrors, showing us characters who remind us of ourselves. At other times, books act as windows, showing us characters and situations that take us far beyond ourselves.

Sometimes we need lessons to help us accomplish all the things a skilled reader can do. This textbook is your manual for soaring—it's your pilot's lesson plan for helping you soar as high as you can.

Using the Standards to Set the Standard

This book is designed to help you master the skills you need to be a strong reader *and* writer. The California standards are your tour guide. They will lead you through this book, helping you learn the literacy skills you'll need for this year, for your remaining years in school, and for your life as a member of society.

Everyone who worked on this book—the people who chose the reading selections, the people who wrote the activities, the people who chose the artwork—continually asked themselves, "How do we create a book that not only meets the California standards but also *sets* the standard when it comes to helping students become readers and writers?" We think that as you read through this book, you'll find that we answered that question by providing you with

- interesting selections to read
- powerful models to help you learn to write
- lots of opportunities to practice new skills
- specific information about each

standard—so that you will always know what is expected of you
- the kinds of topics and art that middle-schoolers have told us interest them

In this book, then, you'll get practice in all kinds of language skills.

You will read all kinds of material, from ads to odes, from stories to Web pages.

You will learn better ways to talk, listen, and write.

You will understand more, sound better, and be more confident about what you know and understand.

What's in This Book?

Holt Literature and Language Arts has three parts:

- Part 1 covers reading of all types—literature and informational texts.
- Part 2 covers writing, speaking, and listening.
- The last part of the book is a reference section, full of special activities and information you might need as you work through Parts 1 and 2.

Part 1

The chapters in Part 1 begin with an essay that explains the key standards you'll be mastering in the chapter. Then you'll read several literary selections. Following almost every literary selection, you will find some interesting readings, called informational texts. These might be newspaper or magazine articles, Web pages, interviews, signs, maps, or other documents. All of these informational texts relate to the piece of literature. For example, following the story "Rikki-tikki-tavi," about a little mongoose that faces two deadly cobras in India, you'll find an informational article on cobras and pages from a geography textbook about India. Along the way you'll find a lot of help in acquiring new words.

Here is a diagram showing how a chapter in Part 1 might look:

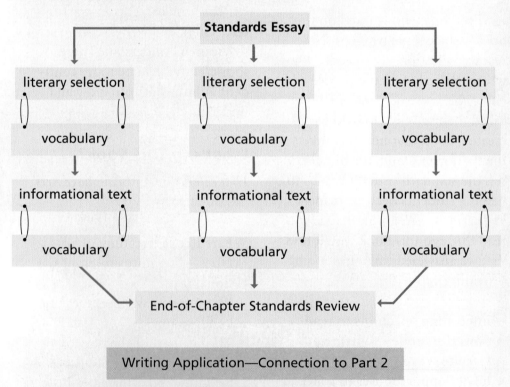

Part 2

Part 2 is a series of big and small workshops that will help you *write*. Here are workshops on writing narratives, essays, research reports, responses to literature—all the writing skills required by the California standards. Part 2 also includes workshops in listening and speaking. All of Part 2 will help you practice the writing, listening, and speaking skills that you are required to master by the end of this school year.

Part 3

Need help with a literary term? Could you use some tips for taking tests? Do you want to find out where to go for help in identifying the main idea of an informational text? Turn to Part 3. Part 3 includes a section called Test Smarts, with tips for test taking. Part 3 includes definitions of literary terms and of reading and informational terms. Part 3 includes a glossary and extensive indexes. Part 3 is your Resource Center.

A Book with a Big Idea

This is a book with a big idea—that you are going to learn a lot about your language.

This book came together because of the efforts of lots of people—writers, editors, artists, teachers, and even students like you.

Now it's time for us to hand the book to you, the reader. We hope you'll use it as a key to life-time literacy and as a guide to lifetime reading. Enjoy!

 At our Internet site you can discover much more about the stories, poems, and informational materials in this book. You can look at how professional writers work. You can even submit your own writing for publication on an online gallery. As you use *Holt Literature and Language Arts* to master the standards, look for the very best online resources at **go.hrw.com**.

GO TO: go.hrw.com
KEYWORD: HLLA

PART 1

Mastering the California Standards in Reading

vocabulary

informational materials

literature

Chapters

Structures
Clarifying Meaning

CONFLICT

PLOT

CONTRAST

TEXTBOOK

TELEPLAY

MANUALS

NEWSPAPERS

SIGNS

California Standards

Here are the Grade 7 standards you will study for mastery in Chapter 1. You will also review standards from earlier grades.

Reading

Word Analysis, Fluency, and Systematic Vocabulary Development

1.3 Clarify word meanings through the use of definition, example, restatement, or contrast.

Reading Comprehension (Focus on Informational Materials)

2.1 Understand and analyze the differences in structure and purpose between various categories of informational materials (for example, textbooks, newspapers, instructional manuals, signs).

Grade 5 Review
2.2 Analyze text that is organized in sequential or chronological order.
2.3 Discern main ideas and concepts presented in texts.

Literary Response and Analysis

3.2 Identify events that advance the plot, and determine how each event explains past or present action(s) or foreshadows future action(s).

Grade 5 Review
3.2 Identify the main problem or conflict of the plot, and explain how it is resolved.

Grade 6 Review
3.7 Explain the effects of common literary devices (for example, symbolism) in fictional texts.

KEYWORD:
HLLA 7-1

Plot *by* John Leggett
A STORY'S BUILDING BLOCKS

Plot is what happens in a story. Plot consists of a series of related episodes, one growing out of another. Most plots have four parts, which are like building blocks.

1 The first part of a plot tells you about the story's **basic situation:** Who are the characters, and what do they want? This is usually where you find out about the conflict, or problem, in a story. A **conflict** is a struggle between opposing characters or opposing forces. In an **external conflict** a character struggles against another person, a group of people, or a force of nature (a tornado, a bear, an icy mountain path). An **internal conflict** takes place in a character's mind (he struggles with shyness; she struggles to accept a death). Here is the introduction to a new version of a tale you know well:

"Hi there, Red," said a wolf to a little girl in a red velvet hood. "How'd ya like a ride on my motorcycle?"

"Thank you, sir, but I can't," replied Little Red Riding Hood. "As you can see, I'm carrying this basket of ginger cookies to my grandmother, and I can't be late."

"Tell you what, Red. You just hop on the back, and I'll run you over to Granny's in five seconds flat."

"My grandmother lives way out at the end of Lonely Road," Red protested. "It's miles and miles."

"This here motorcycle eats miles."

"No, thank you," said Little Red Riding Hood. "I've made up my mind."

To make us feel suspense, storytellers give us clues that **foreshadow,** or hint at, future events. Maybe you felt a shiver of fear when you read that Granny lives on Lonely Road. Bad things can happen on lonely roads. Could this foreshadow trouble for Little Red?

2 In the second part of a plot, one or more of the characters act to resolve the conflict. Now a **series of events** takes place that makes it very hard for the character to get what he or she wants. (Sometimes these events are called **complications.**)

"Suit yourself," chuckled the wolf, who had thought of a wicked plan. He would go alone to the end of Lonely Road, gobble up Red's grandma, and then, when the little girl turned up, he would gobble her up too.

So, arriving at the last house on Lonely Road, the wolf raced his engine, scaring Grandma out her back door and under the woodshed. The wolf was puzzled to find the house empty, but he put on Grandma's nightcap and nightshirt and climbed into the bed to wait for Red.

Reading Standard 3.2 Identify events that advance the plot, and determine how each event explains past or present action(s) or foreshadows future action(s).

3 Now comes the **climax,** the story's most emotional or suspenseful moment. This is the point at which the conflict is decided one way or another.

It was nearly dark when Red arrived, but as she approached her grandma's bed, she sensed something was wrong.

"Are you all right, Granny?" Red asked. "Your eyes look bloodshot."

"All the better to see you with," replied the wolf.

"And your teeth—suddenly they look like fangs."

"All the better to eat—" the wolf began, but he stopped at the sound of his motorcycle engine thundering in the front yard. "Wait right there, Red," said the wolf, bounding from the bed.

The wolf was startled to find Grandma sitting on the motorcycle.

"Hey!" he shouted. "Stop fooling with my bike." As he lunged for her, Grandma found the gearshift, and the cycle leapt forward, scooping the wolf up on its handlebars and hurling him into a giant thorn bush—which is where the police found him when they arrived.

4 The **resolution** is the last part of the story. This is where the loose ends of the plot are tied up and the story is closed.

The wolf was brought to trial and sent to prison. Granny became a popular guest on talk shows. Red lived happily ever after.

Practice

The main events of a story's **plot** can be charted in a diagram like the one below. Think about a story you know well—maybe a movie or a TV show or a novel. See if you can show the story's main events on the diagram.

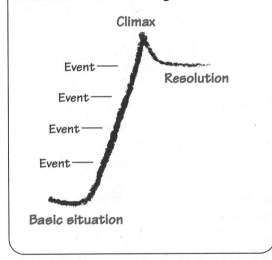

BONUS QUESTION

What parts of the plot has the writer below left out?

"*Once upon a time, they lived happily ever after.*"

Duffy's Jacket

Literary Focus
Foreshadowing

Stories are made up of a series of events that advance the plot and keep you guessing about how things will turn out. However, not all events are part of the present action of a story. Sometimes the writer tells you about events from the past, such as something that happened to a character in childhood. When a writer tells you about past actions, you can expect that those actions will **foreshadow,** or hint at, what will happen later in the plot.

Reading Skills
Making Predictions

Try a skill called **making predictions** to see if you can determine what's going to happen next in this story about a boy named Duffy. Duffy's actions reveal a certain characteristic that might alert you to the outcome of the story. As you read, you'll find this little open-book sign at certain points in the story: . Stop at these points, and jot down what you think will happen as the plot advances and the story unfolds.

Reading Standard 3.2 Identify events that advance the plot, and determine how each event explains past or present action(s) or foreshadows future action(s).

Make the Connection
Quickwrite 🖉

All of us have little failings, or flaws. We forget to put the lid on the peanut butter. We leave our clothes on the floor of the closet. We forget to feed the cats. We trip over our own two feet. We talk too much. Write a few sentences describing one of your minor failings. How do other people feel about this problem? How does it affect your life?

Vocabulary Development

Don't forget! These are words you'll be learning as you read this story:

fumigating (fyo͞o′mə·gāt′iŋ) v. used as n.: cleaning out by spraying with chemical vapors. *Andrew's room was so cluttered with junk that it needed a good fumigating.*

sentinel (sent′′n·əl) n.: watchful guard. *Duffy could have used a sentinel to help him keep track of his stuff.*

sabotage (sab′ə·täzh′) v.: obstruct or destroy. *Duffy didn't want to play Monopoly anymore, so he decided to sabotage the game.*

huddled (hud′′ld) v.: nestled close together. *When the creature scratched at the door, the children huddled close to one another.*

Duffy's Jacket

Bruce Coville

If my cousin Duffy had the brains of a turnip it never would have happened. But as far as I'm concerned, Duffy makes a turnip look bright. My mother disagrees. According to her, Duffy is actually very bright. She claims the reason he's so scatter-brained is that he's too busy being brilliant inside his own head to remember everyday things. Maybe. But hanging around with Duffy means you spend a lot of time saying, "Your glasses, Duffy," or "Your coat, Duffy," or—well, you get the idea: a lot of three-word sentences that start with "Your," end with "Duffy," and have words like *book, radio, wallet,* or whatever it is he's just put down and left behind, stuck in the middle.

Me, I think turnips are brighter.

But since Duffy's my cousin, and since my mother and her sister are both single parents, we tend to do a lot of things together—like camping, which is how we got into the mess I want to tell you about.

Personally, I thought camping was a big mis-take. But since Mom and Aunt Elise are raising the three of us—me, Duffy, and my little sister, Marie—on their own, they're convinced they have to do man-stuff with us every once in a while. I think they read some book that said me and Duffy would come out weird if they don't. You can take him camping all you want. It ain't gonna make Duffy normal.

PREDICTING

1. Make a guess about how Duffy's forgetfulness could affect this camping trip.

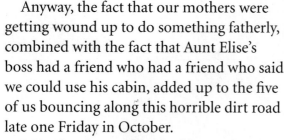
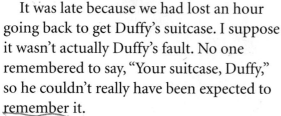

Anyway, the fact that our mothers were getting wound up to do something fatherly, combined with the fact that Aunt Elise's boss had a friend who had a friend who said we could use his cabin, added up to the five of us bouncing along this horrible dirt road late one Friday in October.

It was late because we had lost an hour going back to get Duffy's suitcase. I suppose it wasn't actually Duffy's fault. No one remembered to say, "Your suitcase, Duffy," so he couldn't really have been expected to <u>remember</u> it.

"Oh, Elise," cried my mother, as we got deeper into the woods. "Aren't the leaves beautiful?"

That's why it doesn't make sense for them to try to do man-stuff with us. If it had been our fathers, they would have been drinking beer and burping and maybe telling dirty stories instead of talking about the leaves. So why try to fake it?

Anyway, we get to this cabin, which is about eighteen million miles from nowhere, and to my surprise, it's not a cabin at all. It's a house. A big house.

"Oh, my," said my mother as we pulled into the driveway.

"Isn't it great?" chirped Aunt Elise. "It's almost a hundred years old, back from the time when they used to build big hunting lodges up here. It's the only one in the area still standing. Horace said he hasn't been able to get up here in some time. That's why he was glad to let us use it. He said it would be good to have someone go in and air the place out."

Leave it to Aunt Elise. This place didn't need airing out—it needed <u>fumigating</u>. I never saw so many spider webs in my life. From the sounds we heard coming from the walls, the mice seemed to have made it a population center. We found a total of two working lightbulbs: one in the kitchen and one in the dining room, which was paneled with dark wood and had a big stone fireplace at one end.

"Oh, my," said my mother again.

Duffy, who's allergic to about fifteen different things, started to sneeze.

"Isn't it charming?" asked Aunt Elise hopefully.

No one answered her.

Four hours later we had managed to get three bedrooms clean enough to sleep in without getting the <u>heebie-jeebies</u>—one for Mom and Aunt Elise, one for Marie, and one for me and Duffy. After a supper of beans and franks we hit the hay, which I think is what our mattresses were stuffed with. As I was drifting off, which took about thirty seconds, it occurred to me that four hours of housework wasn't all that much of a man-thing, something it might be useful to remember the next time Mom got one of these plans into her head.

Things looked better in the morning when we went outside and found a stream where we could go wading. ("Your sneakers, Duffy.")

Later we went back and started poking around the house, which really was enormous.

Vocabulary
fumigating (fyoo′mə·gāt′iŋ) v. used as n.: cleaning out by spraying with chemical vapors.

That was when things started getting a little spooky. In the room next to ours I found a message scrawled on the wall. "Beware the Sentinel," it said in big black letters.

When I showed Mom and Aunt Elise they said it was just a joke and got mad at me for frightening Marie.

Marie wasn't the only one who was frightened.

We decided to go out for another walk. ("Your lunch, Duffy.") We went deep into the woods, following a faint trail that kept threatening to disappear but never actually faded away altogether. It was a hot day, even in the deep woods, and after a while we decided to take off our coats.

When we got back and Duffy didn't have his jacket, did they get mad at him? My mother actually had the nerve to say, "Why didn't you remind him? You know he forgets things like that."

What do I look like, a walking memo pad?

Anyway, I had other things on my mind— like the fact that I was convinced someone had been following us while we were in the woods.

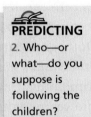

PREDICTING

2. Who—or what—do you suppose is following the children?

I tried to tell my mother about it, but first she said I was being ridiculous, and then she accused me of trying to sabotage the trip.

So I shut up. But I was pretty nervous, especially when Mom and Aunt Elise announced that they were going into town—which was twenty miles away—to pick up some supplies (like lightbulbs).

"You kids will be fine on your own," said Mom cheerfully. "You can make popcorn and play Monopoly. And there's enough soda here for you to make yourselves sick on."

And with that they were gone.

It got dark.

We played Monopoly.

They didn't come back. That didn't surprise me. Since Duffy and I were both fifteen they felt it was okay to leave us on our own, and Mom had warned us they might decide to have dinner at the little inn we had seen on the way up.

But I would have been happier if they had been there.

Especially when something started scratching on the door.

"What was that?" asked Marie.

"What was what?" asked Duffy.

"That!" she said, and this time I heard it, too. My stomach rolled over, and the skin at the back of my neck started to prickle.

"Maybe it's the Sentinel!" I hissed.

"Andrew!" yelled Marie. "Mom told you not to say that."

"She said not to try to scare you," I said. "I'm not. *I'm* scared! I told you I heard something following us in the woods today."

Scratch, scratch.

"But you said it stopped," said Duffy. "So how would it know where we are now?"

"I don't know. I don't know what it is. Maybe it tracked us, like a bloodhound."

Scratch, scratch.

Vocabulary

sentinel (sent'ʼn·əl) *n.:* watchful guard.

sabotage (sab'ə·täzh') *v.:* obstruct or destroy.

"Don't bloodhounds have to have something to give them a scent?" asked Marie. "Like a piece of clothing, or—"

We both looked at Duffy.

"Your jacket, Duffy!"

Duffy turned white.

"That's silly," he said after a moment.

"There's something at the door," I said frantically. "Maybe it's been lurking around all day, waiting for our mothers to leave. Maybe it's been waiting for years for someone to come back here."

Scratch, scratch.

"I don't believe it," said Duffy. "It's just the wind moving a branch. I'll prove it."

He got up and headed for the door. But he didn't open it. Instead he peeked through the window next to it. When he turned back, his eyes looked as big as the hard-boiled eggs we had eaten for supper.

"There's something out there!" he hissed. *"Something big!"*

"I told you," I cried. "Oh, I knew there was something there."

"Andrew, are you doing this just to scare me?" said Marie. "Because if you are—"

Scratch, scratch.

"Come on," I said, grabbing her by the hand. "Let's get out of here."

I started to lead her up the stairs.

"Not there!" said Duffy. "If we go up there, we'll be trapped."

"You're right," I said. "Let's go out the back way!"

The thought of going outside scared the daylights out of me. But at least out there we would have somewhere to run. Inside—well, who knew what might happen if the thing found us inside.

We went into the kitchen.

I heard the front door open.

"Let's get out of here!" I hissed.

We scooted out the back door. "What now?" I wondered, looking around frantically.

"The barn," whispered Duffy. "We can hide in the barn."

"Good idea," I said. Holding Marie by the hand, I led the way to the barn. But the door was held shut by a huge <u>padlock</u>.

The wind was blowing harder, but not hard enough to hide the sound of the back door of the house opening, and then slamming shut.

"Quick!" I whispered. "It knows we're out here. Let's sneak around front. It will never expect us to go back into the house."

Duffy and Marie followed me as I led them behind a hedge. I caught a glimpse of something heading toward the barn and swallowed nervously. It was big. Very big.

"I'm scared," whispered Marie.

"Shhhh!" I hissed. "We can't let it know where we are."

We slipped through the front door. We locked it, just like people always do in the movies, though what good that would do I couldn't figure, since if something really wanted to get at us, it would just break the window and come in.

"Upstairs," I whispered.

We tiptoed up the stairs. Once we were

> **PREDICTING**
>
> 3. What do you think will happen to Andrew, Duffy, and Marie?

in our bedroom, I thought we were safe. Crawling over the floor, I raised my head just enough to peek out the window. My heart almost stopped. Standing in the moonlight was an enormous, manlike creature. It had a scrap of cloth in its hands. It was looking around—looking for us. I saw it lift its head and sniff the wind. To my horror, it started back toward the house.

"It's coming back!" I yelped, more frightened than ever.

"How does it know where we are?" asked Marie.

I knew how. It had Duffy's jacket. It was tracking us down, like some giant bloodhound.

We <u>huddled</u> together in the middle of the room, trying to think of what to do.

A minute later we heard it.

Scratch, scratch.

None of us moved.

Scratch, scratch.

We stopped breathing, then jumped up in alarm at a terrible crashing sound.

The door was down.

We hunched back against the wall as heavy footsteps came clomping up the stairs.

I wondered what our mothers would think when they got back. Would they find our bodies? Or would there be nothing left of us at all?

Thump. Thump. Thump.

It was getting closer.

Thump. Thump. Thump.

It was outside the door.

Knock, knock.

"Don't answer!" hissed Duffy.

Like I said, he doesn't have the brains of a turnip.

It didn't matter. The door wasn't locked. It came swinging open. In the shaft of light I saw a huge figure. The Sentinel of the Woods! It had to be. I thought I was going to die.

The figure stepped into the room. Its head nearly touched the ceiling.

Marie squeezed against my side, tighter than a tick in a dog's ear.

The huge creature sniffed the air. It turned in our direction. Its eyes seemed to glow. Moonlight glittered on its fangs.

Slowly the Sentinel raised its arm. I could see Duffy's jacket dangling from its fingertips.

And then it spoke.

"You forgot your jacket, stupid."

It threw the jacket at Duffy, turned around, and stomped down the stairs.

Which is why, I suppose, no one has had to remind Duffy to remember his jacket, or his glasses, or his math book, for at least a year now.

After all, when you leave stuff lying around, you never can be sure just who might bring it back.

Vocabulary
huddled (hud″ld) *v.*: nestled close together.

Bruce Coville

A Word Wrangler

Bruce Coville (1950–   ) grew up in a rural area north of Syracuse, New York, around the corner from his grandparents' dairy farm. Before becoming a full-time writer, he worked as a gravedigger, a toy maker, a magazine editor, an elementary-school teacher, and a cookware salesman. About his writing he says:

> For years I have been maintaining that I can't really write short stories, that they are just something that happen to me by accident every now and then. . . . 'Duffy's Jacket,' on the other hand, was pure joy. The idea came to me while I was walking in the woods with some friends. When we got back to the house, I excused myself, went upstairs, and typed it in a single sitting, the words seeming to fly from my fingers. . . . If only it were always that easy! But I figure a quarter century of word wrangling entitles you to at least one story that comes fairly quickly.

For Independent Reading

You can read more of Coville's unusual and highly entertaining stories in *Oddly Enough* and *Odder Than Ever.* You might also check out his wildly popular longer works: *My Teacher Is an Alien, Jennifer Murdley's Toad,* and *Jeremy Thatcher Dragon Hatcher.*

Literary Response and Analysis

Reading Check

1. Use the following story map to outline the main parts of this story's **plot.**

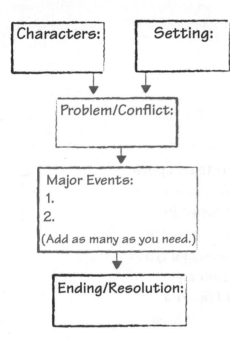

Characters:

Setting:

Problem/Conflict:

Major Events:
1.
2.
(Add as many as you need.)

Ending/Resolution:

Interpretations

2. What is the first sign that **foreshadows** trouble for the campers?

3. How do Duffy's past actions **foreshadow** what happens in the story?

Evaluation

4. Think about the way the plot was **resolved.** Did you feel cheated? What did you predict (or hope) would happen? Can you think of a better ending?

5. The narrator makes several comments about "man-things" and "man-stuff." Find his comments, and tell how you feel about them.

Writing

The Dreaded Sentinel Speaks

The narrator of this story has a sarcastic sense of humor. Find some of his comments about the family and their camping trip that you think are funny. If this story were told by the dreaded Sentinel itself, how would the voice change? What would you know that you don't know now? Let the Sentinel speak and tell its side of the story. Remember to write in the first person, using *I.*

Writing a Story Outline

Think back to the minor failings you wrote about in your Quickwrite on page 6. After reading "Duffy's Jacket," do you see any story possibilities in them? If you do, jot down some notes on the settings, characters (will you develop your own version of the Sentinel?), and events you might use. Save your ideas for the story you'll write for the assignment called "Minor Failings" in the Writing Applications on page 101.

BONUS QUESTION

Could the Sentinel be one of the mothers in disguise? Think about it.

Reading Standard 3.2 Identify events that advance the plot, and determine how each event explains past or present action(s) or foreshadows future action(s).

Vocabulary Development

Clarifying Word Meanings: Restatement

Writers sometimes help readers understand difficult words by providing definitions, examples, contrasts, or restatements. A writer who uses **restatement** makes the meaning of a word clear by stating it in different words. It's not difficult to understand the meaning of *hurricane* in this passage, since it's explained by the phrase *powerful tropical storm.*

> The <u>hurricane</u> hit the U.S. mainland at about midnight yesterday. This <u>powerful tropical storm</u> battered coastal villages and vacation homes for more than twelve hours before winds began to die down.

Words or phrases that restate the meaning often appear near the difficult word.

Word Bank

fumigating
sentinel
sabotage
huddled

PRACTICE

Make a three-column chart for the words in the Word Bank, like this one:

Word Bank Word	Similar Word	Similar Phrase
fumigating	disinfecting	cleaning out with chemicals

Then, fill in the blank in each sentence below with words or phrases that restate the meaning of the underlined word.

1. Duffy's room was so dirty it needed <u>fumigating</u>, or _____.

2. The <u>Sentinel</u>, or _____ , of the woods was never seen; it was only heard.

3. The narrator's mom thought he was trying to <u>sabotage</u>, or _____ , the trip.

4. The children were <u>huddled</u> together when the Sentinel knocked. They were _____.

Reading Standard 1.3
Clarify word meanings through the use of restatement.

Yeti-like Monster Gives Staid Town in Illinois a Fright

Structure and Purpose of Informational Materials: Newspapers

One of the easiest ways of getting information is through newspapers. They're inexpensive, printed every day, and cover just about any topic you can think of. Compared with television news and news-related portals on the Web, newspapers provide us with some of the best up-to-date coverage of developing situations all over the world. You can also fold them up and put them in your book bag. Try doing that with your TV.

The most important thing a news story tells us is what happened. That's its main **purpose,** and that's why we keep up with the news. To be clear about what happened, it helps to understand how newspaper stories are **structured,** or put together. Reporters spend a lot of time trying to make sure that they explain very clearly what happened. To do this, they often explain the events in **chronological order.** That is, they tell the events in the order in which they occurred.

Here are some tips for **analyzing news stories** that are organized in chronological order:

- Look for the date the story was printed or another date or time within the story to establish the exact time of the events.
- Ask yourself, "When did each important event happen? What happened *before* that event? What happened *after*?"
- Look for words and phrases like *first, next, during, later, at that point, at last,* and *finally,* which signal when events happened.

Vocabulary Development

Before you read what happened in Illinois, you should learn these words. They'll be appearing in the news story that follows.

staid (stād) *adj.:* settled; quiet. *With the arrival of the monster, the staid lives of the people of Murphysboro were changed.* [Word appears in title of the article.]

eternity (ē·tur′nə·tē) *n.:* very long time; forever. *The massive creature seemed to hold us in its gaze for an eternity.*

amplified (am′plə·fīd′) *v.* used as *adj.:* increased in strength. *The narrow walls of the cliffs echoed with the creature's amplified cry.*

elusive (ē·lōō′siv) *adj.:* hard to detect. *Though the monster is nearly eight feet tall, it has remained elusive: People with cameras and video equipment have not caught sight of it.*

commotion (kə·mō′shən) *n.:* disturbance. *Just the mention of a sighting of the monster creates a commotion.*

Grade 5 Review Reading Standard 2.2 Analyze text that is organized in sequential or chronological order.

Reading Standard 2.1 Understand and analyze the structure and purpose of informational materials (for example, newspapers).

Yeti-like Monster Gives Staid Town in Illinois a Fright

by **Andrew H. Malcolm**

MURPHYSBORO, Ill., Oct. 31—Mrs. Nedra Green was preparing for bed in her isolated farmhouse near here the other night when a shrill, piercing scream came from out by the shed.

"It's it again," she said.

Four-year-old Christian Baril was in his backyard chasing fireflies with a glass jar. He ran in the house. "Daddy, Daddy," he said, "there's a big ghost out back."

Randy Creath and Cheryl Ray were talking on her darkened porch when something moved in the brush nearby. Cheryl went to turn on a light; Randy went to investigate.

At that moment it stepped from the bushes.

Towering over the wide-eyed teenage couple was a creature resembling a gorilla. It was eight feet tall. It had long shaggy matted hair colored a dirty white. It smelled foul like river slime.

Silently, the couple stared at the creature and the creature stared at the couple, fifteen feet apart. Then, after an eternity of perhaps thirty seconds, the creature turned slowly and crashed off through the brush back toward the river.

It was the Murphysboro Monster, a strange creature that has baffled and frightened the police and residents for weeks now in this southern Illinois town on the sluggish Big Muddy River. . . .

Such monster sightings are bizarre indeed for an old farm county seat where brightly colored leaves fall on brick streets and high school majorettes practice baton twirling for the Red Devils' upcoming football game with Jonesboro's Wildcats.

"A lot of things in life are unexplained," said Toby Berger, the police chief, "and this is another one. We don't know what the creature is. But we do believe what these people saw was real. We have tracked it. And the dogs got a definite scent."

It all began shortly before midnight June 25. Randy Needham and Judy Johnson were conferring in a parked car on the town's boat ramp down by the Big Muddy.

At one point the couple heard a loud cry from the woods next to the car. Many were to describe the sound as that of a greatly amplified eagle shriek.

Mr. Needham looked out from the front seat. There, lumbering toward the open window was a light-colored, hairy, eight-foot creature matted with mud.

Vocabulary

staid (stād) *adj.:* settled; quiet. [Word appears in title of the article.]

eternity (ē·tʉrʹnə·tē) *n.:* very long time; forever.

amplified (amʹplə·fīdʹ) *v.* used as *adj.:* increased in strength.

At that point, the police report calmly notes, "complainant left the area." He proceeded to the police station and filed an "unknown creature" report. . . .

Later, as Officer Jimmie Nash inspected some peculiar footprints fast disappearing in the oozing mud left by the receding river, he became a firm believer.

"I was leaning over when there was the most incredible shriek I've ever heard," he said. "It was in those bushes. That was no bobcat or screech owl, and we hightailed it out of there."

Officers searched the riverbank for hours, following an <u>elusive</u> splashing sound like something floundering through knee-deep water. They found nothing.

Plains folk hereabouts do not excite easily. So the next day on page three, *The Southern Illinoisan* published a two-hundred-word account of the "critter." That presumably was the end of the case.

But the next night came young Christian Baril's encounter and the experience of Cheryl Ray and Randy Creath, the seventeen-year-old son of a state trooper, who drew a picture of the creature.

That did it for Chief Berger. He ordered his entire fourteen-man force out for a night-long search. And Jerry Nellis, a dog trainer, brought Reb, an eighty-pound German shepherd renowned for his zealous tracking.

With floodlights, officers discovered a rough trail in the brush. Grass was crushed. Broken branches dangled. Small trees were snapped. On the grass Reb found gobs of black slime, much like that of sewage sludge in settling tanks on a direct line between the river and the Ray house.

Reb led Mr. Nellis and Officer Nash to an abandoned barn on the old Bullar farm. Then, at the door, the dog yelped and backed off in panic. Mr. Nellis threw it into the doorway. The dog crawled out whining. The men radioed for help. Fourteen area police cars responded, but the barn, it turned out, was empty.

It Came to the Carnival

Ten days later the Miller Carnival was set up in the town's Riverside Park, not far from the boat ramp. At 2 A.M., July 7, the day's festivities had stopped and the ponies that walk around in circles with youngsters on their backs were tied to bushes.

Suddenly they shied. They rolled their eyes. They raised their heads. They tried to pull free. Attracted by the commotion, three carnival workers—Otis Norris, Ray Adkerson, and Wesley Lavander—walked around the truck and there, standing upright in the darkness was a three-hundred- to four-hundred-pound creature, hairy and light colored and about eight feet tall.

With no menace, but intent curiosity, the creature was watching the animals. . . .

—from *The New York Times*

Vocabulary
elusive (ē·lo͞o′siv) *adj.*: hard to detect.
commotion (kə·mō′shən) *n.*: disturbance.

Reading Informational Materials

Reading Check

1. When was this news story printed?

2. When was the Yeti-like creature first sighted?

3. Who saw it, and what happened during that first sighting?

4. When was the creature spotted for the second time?

5. How many days went by before the foul-smelling monster was seen for the third time?

6. Who were the last people to see the creature?

Test Practice

Yeti-like Monster Gives Staid Town in Illinois a Fright

1. Even though there are four sightings of the creature, the news story begins with the —

   A most recent sighting

   B second sighting

   C third sighting

   D least recent sighting

2. *This news story explains what happened when a small Illinois town encountered an eight-foot, hairy creature.* This statement describes the news story's —

   F structure

   G purpose

   H plot

   J theme

3. Which of the following words or phrases would *not* help you determine if a news story is structured in **chronological order**?

   A Yesterday

   B Next

   C Fortunately

   D A month ago

4. This reporter tells a story chiefly by using —

   F eyewitness accounts of the monster

   G statistics about monsters

   H experts' opinions about monsters

   J his personal experience with the monster

Grade 5 Review Reading Standard 2.2 Analyze text that is organized in sequential or chronological order.

Reading Standard 2.1 Understand and analyze the structure and purpose of informational materials (for example, newspapers).

Vocabulary Development

Clarifying Word Meanings: Restatement

When you are unsure of the meaning of a word, check the text to look for clues. Sometimes a writer will restate a passage in a way that explains the meaning of the unfamiliar word. Here is an example of a restatement that gives you a clue to the meaning of *staid*:

> Murphysboro, in Illinois, was a staid town. It was very settled and old, and nothing unusual ever happened there.

Here is an example that tells you what a Yeti is:

> The Murphysboro monster seemed like a Yeti, a large, hairy creature that has been seen in the mountains of Tibet. Sometimes it has been called the Abominable Snowman.

Word Bank

staid
eternity
amplified
elusive
commotion

PRACTICE

Below are sentences using the Word Bank words. Fill in the blanks with words that restate the meaning of the underlined words.

1. The monster stared at them for what seemed to be an eternity, or _____.

2. The monster's amplified, or _____, shriek was echoed by the cliffs.

3. The monster has remained elusive, that is, _____.

4. The police investigated a commotion, or _____, in the barn.

Reading Standard 1.3 Clarify word meanings through the use of restatement.

Rikki-tikki-tavi

Literary Focus
Conflict

All stories are built on some kind of **conflict.** Usually a conflict results when a character wants something very badly but has a hard time getting it. Think of the stories in movies and on TV, and you'll be able to find a conflict in every one of them. Conflict is worked out in the series of related events called **plot.**

Reading Skills
Retelling

Try a strategy called **retelling** to identify the events that move this plot forward. Here is how it works: As you read this story, you'll see little open-book signs alongside the text. At those points, stop and jot down notes that retell what has just happened. As you do your retelling, focus on the important events that keep the plot moving.

Make the Connection
Quickwrite

Conflict is part of our real lives. For example, most people face bullies at some time in their lives. If you were facing a bully, what would you do? Would you fight? Would you run away? Would you try to negotiate? In your journal, describe how you think you would react.

Background

This story takes place in India many years ago, when the British ruled that huge country. The family in this story lives in a cantonment (kan·tän′mənt), which is a kind of army base. The father is in the British army. This story is about a conflict that takes place between two deadly snakes and a brave little mongoose—a creature that looks something like a weasel or a large squirrel.

Vocabulary Development

Every time you read, you have a chance to add words to your vocabulary. The words that follow are underlined and defined in the story. See if you can use each one in a sentence of your own.

immensely (i·mens′lē) *adv.:* enormously. *Rikki is immensely brave. The snakes are immensely powerful.*

cowered (kou′ərd) *v.:* crouched and trembled in fear. *Darzee, who is a coward, cowered before the snakes. Rikki cowered before no one.*

valiant (val′yənt) *adj.:* brave and determined. *Rikki is a valiant hero. Would other snakes think Nag and Nagaina are valiant too?*

consolation (kän′sə·lā′shən) *n.:* comfort. *Snakes get no consolation from Rikki. Rikki's consolation comes from a safe, peaceful garden.*

impotent (im′pə·tənt) *adj.:* powerless. *With all but her last egg destroyed, Nagaina felt impotent against Rikki.*

Rikki-tikki-tavi

Rudyard Kipling

Inch by inch rose up the big black cobra . . .

A bungalow in India.

This is the story of the great war that Rikki-tikki-tavi fought single-handed, through the bathrooms of the big bungalow[1] in Segowlee cantonment.[2] Darzee, the tailorbird, helped him, and Chuchundra, the muskrat, who never comes out into the middle of the floor but always creeps round by the wall, gave him advice; but Rikki-tikki did the real fighting.

---

1. **bungalow** *n.*: in India, a low, one-storied house, named after a type of house found in Bengal, a region of South Asia.
2. **Segowlee** (sē·gou′lē) **cantonment:** British army post in Segowlee (now Segauli), India.

He was a mongoose, rather like a little cat in his fur and his tail but quite like a weasel in his head and his habits. His eyes and the end of his restless nose were pink; he could scratch himself anywhere he pleased with any leg, front or back, that he chose to use; he could fluff up his tail till it looked like a bottlebrush, and his war cry as he scuttled through the long grass was *Rikk-tikk-tikki-tikki-tchk!*

One day, a high summer flood washed him out of the burrow where he lived with his father and mother and carried him, kicking and clucking, down a roadside ditch. He found a little wisp of grass floating there and clung to it till he lost his senses. When he revived, he was lying in the hot sun in the middle of a garden path, very draggled[3] indeed, and a small boy was saying: "Here's a dead mongoose. Let's have a funeral."

"No," said his mother; "let's take him in and dry him. Perhaps he isn't really dead."

They took him into the house, and a big man picked him up between his finger and thumb and said he was not dead but half choked; so they wrapped him in cotton wool and warmed him over a little fire, and he opened his eyes and sneezed.

"Now," said the big man (he was an Englishman who had just moved into the bungalow), "don't frighten him, and we'll see what he'll do."

It is the hardest thing in the world to frighten a mongoose, because he is eaten up from nose to tail with curiosity. The motto of all the mongoose family is "Run and find out," and Rikki-tikki was a true mongoose. He looked at the cotton wool, decided that it was not good to eat, ran all round the table, sat up and put his fur in order, scratched himself, and jumped on the small boy's shoulder.

"Don't be frightened, Teddy," said his father. "That's his way of making friends."

"Ouch! He's tickling under my chin," said Teddy.

Rikki-tikki looked down between the boy's collar and neck, snuffed at his ear, and climbed down to the floor, where he sat rubbing his nose.

"Good gracious," said Teddy's mother, "and that's a wild creature! I suppose he's so tame because we've been kind to him."

"All mongooses are like that," said her husband. "If Teddy doesn't pick him up by the tail or try to put him in a cage, he'll run in and out of the house all day long. Let's give him something to eat."

They gave him a little piece of raw meat. Rikki-tikki liked it immensely, and when it was finished, he went out into the veranda[4] and sat in the sunshine and fluffed up his fur to make it dry to the roots. Then he felt better.

"There are more things to find out about in this house," he said to himself, "than all my family could find out in all their lives. I shall certainly stay and find out."

He spent all that day roaming over the house. He nearly drowned himself in the bathtubs, put his nose into the ink on a writing table, and burnt it on the end of the big man's cigar, for he climbed up in the big man's lap to see how writing was done. At nightfall he ran into Teddy's nursery to watch how kerosene lamps were lighted, and when Teddy went to bed, Rikki-tikki climbed up too; but he was a restless companion, because he had to get up and attend to every noise all through the night and find out what made it. Teddy's mother and father came in, the last thing, to look at their boy, and Rikki-tikki was awake on the pillow. "I don't like that," said Teddy's mother; "he may bite the child." "He'll do no such

> **PLOT**
>
> 1. Before you read about how Rikki explores his new home, retell the events that brought him here.

---

3. **draggled** v. used as adj.: wet and muddy, as if from being dragged around.

---

4. **veranda** (və·ran′də) v.: open porch covered by a roof, running along the outside of a building.

Vocabulary
immensely (i·mens′lē) adv.: enormously.

thing," said the father. "Teddy's safer with that little beast than if he had a bloodhound to watch him. If a snake came into the nursery now—"

But Teddy's mother wouldn't think of anything so awful.

Early in the morning, Rikki-tikki came to early breakfast in the veranda riding on Teddy's shoulder, and they gave him banana and some boiled egg; and he sat on all their laps one after the other, because every well-brought-up mongoose always hopes to be a house mongoose someday and have rooms to run about in; and Rikki-tikki's mother (she used to live in the General's house at Segowlee) had carefully told Rikki what to do if ever he came across white men.

Then Rikki-tikki went out into the garden to see what was to be seen. It was a large garden, only half cultivated, with bushes, as big as summerhouses, of Marshal Niel roses; lime and orange trees; clumps of bamboos; and thickets of high grass. Rikki-tikki licked his lips. "This is a splendid hunting ground," he said, and his tail grew bottlebrushy at the thought of it, and he scuttled up and down the garden, snuffing here and there till he heard very sorrowful voices in a thorn bush. It was Darzee, the tailorbird, and his wife. They had made a beautiful nest by pulling two big leaves together and stitching them up the edges with fibers and had filled the hollow with cotton and downy fluff. The nest swayed to and fro as they sat on the rim and cried.

"What is the matter?" asked Rikki-tikki.

"We are very miserable," said Darzee. "One of our babies fell out of the nest yesterday and Nag ate him."

"H'm!" said Rikki-tikki, "that is very sad —but I am a stranger here. Who is Nag?"

Darzee and his wife only cowered down in the nest without answering, for from the thick grass at the foot of the bush there came a low hiss—a horrid, cold sound that made Rikki-tikki jump back two clear feet. Then inch by inch out of the grass rose up the head and spread hood of Nag, the big black cobra, and he was five feet long from tongue to tail. When he had lifted one third of himself clear of the ground, he stayed balancing to and fro exactly as a dandelion tuft balances in the wind, and he looked at Rikki-tikki with the wicked snake's eyes that never change their expression, whatever the snake may be thinking of.

"Who is Nag," said he. "*I* am Nag. The great God Brahm[5] put his mark upon all our people, when the first cobra spread his hood to keep the sun off Brahm as he slept. Look, and be afraid!"

He spread out his hood more than ever, and Rikki-tikki saw the spectacle mark on the back of it that looks exactly like the eye part of a hook-and-eye fastening. He was afraid for the minute; but it is impossible for a mongoose to stay frightened for any length of time, and though Rikki-tikki had never met a live cobra before, his mother had fed him on dead ones, and he knew that all a grown mongoose's business in life was to fight and eat snakes. Nag knew that too, and at the bottom of his cold heart, he was afraid.

"Well," said Rikki-tikki, and his tail began to fluff up again, "marks or no marks, do

---

5. **Brahm** (bräm): in the Hindu religion, the creator (also called Brahma).

Vocabulary
cowered (kou′ərd) *v.*: crouched and trembled in fear.

you think it is right for you to eat fledglings out of a nest?"

Nag was thinking to himself and watching the least little movement in the grass behind Rikki-tikki. He knew that mongooses in the garden meant death sooner or later for him and his family, but he wanted to get Rikki-tikki off his guard. So he dropped his head a little and put it on one side.

"Let us talk," he said. "You eat eggs. Why should not I eat birds?"

"Behind you! Look behind you!" sang Darzee.

Rikki-tikki knew better than to waste time in staring. He jumped up in the air as high as he could go, and just under him whizzed by the head of Nagaina, Nag's wicked wife. She had crept up behind him as he was talking, to make an end of him; and he heard her savage hiss as the stroke missed. He came down almost across her back, and if he had been an old mongoose, he would have known that then was the time to break her back with one bite; but he was afraid of the terrible lashing return stroke of the cobra. He bit, indeed, but did not bite long enough, and he jumped clear of the whisking tail, leaving Nagaina torn and angry.

"Wicked, wicked Darzee!" said Nag, lashing up as high as he could reach toward the nest in the thorn bush; but Darzee had built it out of reach of snakes, and it only swayed to and fro.

Rikki-tikki felt his eyes growing red and hot (when a mongoose's eyes grow red, he is angry), and he sat back on his tail and hind legs like a little kangaroo, and looked all round him, and chattered with rage. But Nag and Nagaina had disappeared into the grass.

📖 **PLOT**

2. Retell what happens when Rikki first meets the snakes.

When a snake misses its stroke, it never says anything or gives any sign of what it means to do next. Rikki-tikki did not care to follow them, for he did not feel sure that he could manage two snakes at once. So he trotted off to the gravel path near the house and sat down to think. It was a serious matter for him. If you read the old books of natural history, you will find they say that when the mongoose fights the snake and happens to get bitten, he runs off and eats some herb that cures him. That is not true. The victory is only a matter of quickness of eye and quickness of foot—snake's blow against the mongoose's jump—and as no eye can follow the motion of a snake's head when it strikes, this makes things much more wonderful than any magic herb. Rikki-tikki knew he was a young mongoose, and it made him all the more pleased to think that he had managed

"I am Nag. . . . Look, and be afraid!"

to escape a blow from behind. It gave him confidence in himself, and when Teddy came running down the path, Rikki-tikki was ready to be petted. But just as Teddy was stooping, something wriggled a little in the dust and a tiny voice said: "Be careful. I am Death!" It was Karait, the dusty brown snakeling that lies for choice on the dusty earth; and his bite is as dangerous as the cobra's. But he is so small that nobody thinks of him, and so he does the more harm to people.

Rikki-tikki's eyes grew red again, and he danced up to Karait with the peculiar rocking, swaying motion that he had inherited from his family. It looks very funny, but it is so perfectly balanced a gait[6] that you can fly off from it at any angle you please; and in dealing with snakes this is an advantage. If Rikki-tikki had only known, he was doing a much more dangerous thing than fighting Nag, for Karait is so small and can turn so quickly that unless Rikki bit him close to the back of the head, he would get the return stroke in his eye or his lip. But Rikki did not know; his eyes were all red, and he rocked back and forth, looking for a good place to hold. Karait struck out, Rikki jumped sideways and tried to run in, but the wicked little dusty gray head lashed within a fraction of his shoulder, and he had to jump over the body, and the head followed his heels close.

Teddy shouted to the house: "Oh, look here! Our mongoose is killing a snake," and Rikki-tikki heard a scream from Teddy's mother. His father ran out with a stick, but by the time he came up, Karait had lunged out once too far, and Rikki-tikki had

sprung, jumped on the snake's back, dropped his head far between his forelegs, bitten as high up the back as he could get hold, and rolled away. That bite paralyzed Karait, and Rikki-tikki was just going to eat him up from the tail, after the custom of his family at dinner, when he remembered that a full meal makes a slow mongoose, and if he wanted all his strength and quickness ready, he must keep himself thin. He went away for a dust bath under the castor-oil bushes, while Teddy's father beat the dead Karait. "What is the use of that?" thought Rikki-tikki; "I have settled it all"; and then Teddy's mother picked him up from the dust and hugged him, crying that he had saved Teddy from death, and Teddy's father said that he was a providence,[7] and Teddy looked on with big, scared eyes. Rikki-tikki was rather amused at all the fuss, which, of course, he did not understand. Teddy's mother might just as well have petted Teddy for playing in the dust. Rikki was thoroughly enjoying himself.

PLOT

3. Retell what happens in Rikki's conflict with Karait.

That night at dinner, walking to and fro among the wineglasses on the table, he might have stuffed himself three times over with nice things; but he remembered Nag and Nagaina, and though it was very pleasant to be patted and petted by Teddy's mother and to sit on Teddy's shoulder, his eyes would get red from time to time, and he would go off into his long war cry of *Rikk-tikk-tikki-tikki-tchk!*

Teddy carried him off to bed and insisted on Rikki-tikki's sleeping under his chin.

---

6. **gait** (gāt) *n.:* way of walking or running.

7. **providence** (präv′ə·dəns) *n.:* favor or gift from God or nature.

Rikki-tikki was too well bred to bite or scratch, but as soon as Teddy was asleep, he went off for his nightly walk round the house, and in the dark he ran up against Chuchundra, the muskrat, creeping round by the wall. Chuchundra is a brokenhearted little beast. He whimpers and cheeps all night, trying to make up his mind to run into the middle of the room; but he never gets there.

"Don't kill me," said Chuchundra, almost weeping. "Rikki-tikki, don't kill me!"

"Do you think a snake killer kills muskrats?" said Rikki-tikki scornfully.

"Those who kill snakes get killed by snakes," said Chuchundra, more sorrowfully than ever. "And how am I to be sure that Nag won't mistake me for you some dark night?"

"There's not the least danger," said Rikki-tikki, "but Nag is in the garden, and I know you don't go there."

"My cousin Chua, the rat, told me—" said Chuchundra, and then he stopped.

"Told you what?"

"H'sh! Nag is everywhere, Rikki-tikki. You should have talked to Chua in the garden."

"I didn't—so you must tell me. Quick, Chuchundra, or I'll bite you!"

Chuchundra sat down and cried till the tears rolled off his whiskers. "I am a very poor man," he sobbed. "I never had spirit enough to run out into the middle of the

"Be careful. I am Death!" It was Karait. . . .

room. H'sh! I mustn't tell you anything. Can't you *hear,* Rikki-tikki?"

Rikki-tikki listened. The house was as still as still, but he thought he could just catch the faintest *scratch-scratch* in the world—a noise as faint as that of a wasp walking on a windowpane—the dry scratch of a snake's scales on brickwork.

"That's Nag or Nagaina," he said to himself, "and he is crawling into the bathroom sluice.[8] You're right, Chuchundra; I should have talked to Chua."

He stole off to Teddy's bathroom, but there was nothing there, and then to Teddy's mother's bathroom. At the bottom of the smooth plaster wall there was a brick pulled out to make a sluice for the bathwater, and as Rikki-tikki stole in by the masonry[9] curb where the bath is put, he heard Nag and Nagaina whispering together outside in the moonlight.

"When the house is emptied of people," said Nagaina to her husband, "*he* will have to go away, and then the garden will be our own again. Go in quietly, and remember that the big man who killed Karait is the first one to bite. Then come out and tell me, and we will hunt for Rikki-tikki together."

---

8. **sluice** (slo͞os) *n.:* drain.
9. **masonry** *n.:* something built of stone or brick.

"But are you sure that there is anything to be gained by killing the people?" said Nag.

"Everything. When there were no people in the bungalow, did we have any mongoose in the garden? So long as the bungalow is empty, we are king and queen of the garden; and remember that as soon as our eggs in the melon bed hatch (as they may tomorrow), our children will need room and quiet."

"I had not thought of that," said Nag. "I will go, but there is no need that we should hunt for Rikki-tikki afterward. I will kill the big man and his wife, and the child if I can, and come away quietly. Then the bungalow will be empty, and Rikki-tikki will go."

Rikki-tikki tingled all over with rage and hatred at this, and then Nag's head came through the sluice, and his five feet of cold body followed it. Angry as he was, Rikki-tikki was very frightened as he saw the size of the big cobra. Nag coiled himself up, raised his head, and looked into the bathroom in the dark, and Rikki could see his eyes glitter.

"Now, if I kill him here, Nagaina will know; and if I fight him on the open floor, the odds are in his favor. What am I to do?" said Rikki-tikki-tavi.

Nag waved to and fro, and then Rikki-tikki heard him drinking from the biggest water jar that was used to fill the bath. "That is good," said the snake. "Now, when Karait was killed, the big man had a stick. He may have that stick still, but when he comes in to bathe in the morning, he will not have a stick. I shall wait here till he comes. Nagaina—do you hear me?—I shall wait here in the cool till daytime."

There was no answer from outside, so Rikki-tikki knew Nagaina had gone away.

Nag coiled himself down, coil by coil, round the bulge at the bottom of the water jar, and Rikki-tikki stayed still as death. After an hour he began to move, muscle by muscle, toward the jar. Nag was asleep, and Rikki-tikki looked at his big back, wondering which would be the best place for a good hold. "If I don't break his back at the first jump," said Rikki, "he can still fight; and if he fights—O Rikki!" He looked at the thickness of the neck below the hood, but that was too much for him; and a bite near the tail would only make Nag savage.

"It must be the head," he said at last, "the head above the hood; and when I am once there, I must not let go."

Then he jumped. The head was lying a little clear of the water jar, under the curve of it; and as his teeth met, Rikki braced his back against the bulge of the red earthenware to hold down the head. This gave him just one second's purchase,[10] and he made the most of it. Then he was battered to and fro as a rat is shaken by a dog—to and fro on the floor, up and down, and round in great circles, but his eyes were red and he held on as the body cartwhipped over the floor, upsetting the tin dipper and the soap dish and the flesh brush, and banged against the tin side of the bath. As he held, he closed his jaws tighter and tighter, for he made sure[11] he would be banged to death, and for the honor of his family, he preferred to be found with his teeth locked. He was dizzy, aching, and felt shaken to pieces, when something went off like a thunderclap just behind him; a hot wind knocked him senseless and red fire singed his fur. The big

---

10. **purchase** *n.:* firm hold.
11. **made sure:** here, felt sure.

man had been wakened by the noise and had fired both barrels of a shotgun into Nag just behind the hood.

Rikki-tikki held on with his eyes shut, for now he was quite sure he was dead; but the head did not move, and the big man picked him up and said: "It's the mongoose again, Alice; the little chap has saved *our* lives now." Then Teddy's mother came in with a very white face and saw what was left of Nag, and Rikki-tikki dragged himself to Teddy's bedroom and spent half the rest of the night shaking himself tenderly to find out whether he really was broken into forty pieces, as he fancied.

> **PLOT**
>
> 4. Retell what happens when Rikki sees Nag poke his head into the bathroom.

When morning came, he was very stiff but well pleased with his doings. "Now I have Nagaina to settle with, and she will be worse than five Nags, and there's no knowing when the eggs she spoke of will hatch. Goodness! I must go and see Darzee," he said.

Without waiting for breakfast, Rikki-tikki ran to the thorn bush, where Darzee was singing a song of triumph at the top of his voice. The news of Nag's death was all over the garden, for the sweeper had thrown the body on the rubbish heap.

"Oh, you stupid tuft of feathers!" said Rikki-tikki angrily. "Is this the time to sing?"

"Nag is dead—is dead—is dead!" sang Darzee. "The valiant Rikki-tikki caught him by the head and held fast. The big man brought the bang-stick, and Nag fell in two pieces! He will never eat my babies again."

"All that's true enough, but where's Nagaina?" said Rikki-tikki, looking carefully round him.

"Nagaina came to the bathroom sluice and called for Nag," Darzee went on, "and Nag came out on the end of a stick—the sweeper picked him up on the end of a stick and threw him upon the rubbish heap. Let us sing about the great, the red-eyed Rikki-tikki!" and Darzee filled his throat and sang.

"If I could get up to your nest, I'd roll your babies out!" said Rikki-tikki. "You don't know when to do the right thing at the right time. You're safe enough in your nest there, but it's war for me down here. Stop singing a minute, Darzee."

"For the great, beautiful Rikki-tikki's sake I will stop," said Darzee. "What is it, O Killer of the terrible Nag?"

"Where is Nagaina, for the third time?"

"On the rubbish heap by the stables, mourning for Nag. Great is Rikki-tikki with the white teeth."

"Bother[12] my white teeth! Have you ever heard where she keeps her eggs?"

"In the melon bed, on the end nearest the wall, where the sun strikes nearly all day. She hid them there weeks ago."

"And you never thought it worthwhile to tell me? The end nearest the wall, you said?"

"Rikki-tikki, you are not going to eat her eggs?"

"Not eat exactly; no. Darzee, if you have a grain of sense, you will fly off to the stables and pretend that your wing is broken and let Nagaina chase you away to this bush. I must get to the melon bed, and if I went there now, she'd see me."

---

12. **bother** *interj.*: here, nevermind.

Vocabulary
valiant (val′yənt) *adj.*: brave and determined.

Darzee was a featherbrained little fellow who could never hold more than one idea at a time in his head, and just because he knew that Nagaina's children were born in eggs like his own, he didn't think at first that it was fair to kill them. But his wife was a sensible bird, and she knew that cobra's eggs meant young cobras later on; so she flew off from the nest and left Darzee to keep the babies warm and continue his song about the death of Nag. Darzee was very like a man in some ways.

She fluttered in front of Nagaina by the rubbish heap and cried out, "Oh, my wing is broken! The boy in the house threw a stone at me and broke it." Then she fluttered more desperately than ever.

Nagaina lifted up her head and hissed, "You warned Rikki-tikki when I would have killed him. Indeed and truly, you've chosen a bad place to be lame in." And she moved toward Darzee's wife, slipping along over the dust.

"The boy broke it with a stone!" shrieked Darzee's wife.

"Well! It may be some consolation to you when you're dead to know that I shall settle accounts with the boy. My husband lies on the rubbish heap this morning, but before night the boy in the house will lie very still. What is the use of running away? I am sure to catch you. Little fool, look at me!"

Darzee's wife knew better than to do *that*, for a bird who looks at a snake's eyes gets so frightened that she cannot move. Darzee's wife fluttered on, piping sorrowfully and never leaving the ground, and Nagaina quickened her pace.

Rikki-tikki heard them going up the path from the stables, and he raced for the end of the melon patch near the wall. There, in the warm litter above the melons, very cunningly hidden, he found twenty-five eggs about the size of a bantam's[13] eggs but with whitish skins instead of shells.

"I was not a day too soon," he said, for he could see the baby cobras curled up inside the skin, and he knew that the minute they were hatched, they could each kill a man or a mongoose. He bit off the tops of the eggs as fast as he could, taking care to crush the young cobras, and turned over the litter from time to time to see whether he had missed any. At last there were only three eggs left, and Rikki-tikki began to chuckle to himself, when he heard Darzee's wife screaming:

"Rikki-tikki, I led Nagaina toward the house, and she has gone into the veranda, and—oh, come quickly—she means killing!"

Rikki-tikki smashed two eggs, and tumbled backward down the melon bed with the third egg in his mouth, and scuttled to the veranda as hard as he could put foot to the ground. Teddy and his mother and father were there at early breakfast, but Rikki-tikki saw that they were not eating anything. They sat stone still, and their faces were white. Nagaina was coiled up on the matting by Teddy's chair, within easy striking distance of Teddy's bare leg, and she was swaying to and fro, singing a song of triumph.

"Son of the big man that killed Nag," she hissed, "stay still. I am not ready yet. Wait a little. Keep very still, all you three! If you

---

13. **bantam's** *n.:* small chicken's.

Vocabulary
consolation (kän′sə·lā′shən) *n.:* comfort.

move, I strike, and if you do not move, I strike. Oh, foolish people, who killed my Nag!"

Teddy's eyes were fixed on his father, and all his father could do was to whisper, "Sit still, Teddy. You mustn't move. Teddy, keep still."

Then Rikki-tikki came up and cried: "Turn round, Nagaina; turn and fight!"

"All in good time," said she, without moving her eyes. "I will settle my account with *you* presently. Look at your friends, Rikki-tikki. They are still and white. They are afraid. They dare not move, and if you come a step nearer, I strike."

"Look at your eggs," said Rikki-tikki, "in the melon bed near the wall. Go and look, Nagaina!"

The big snake turned half round and saw the egg on the veranda. "Ah-h! Give it to me," she said.

Rikki-tikki put his paws one on each side of the egg, and his eyes were blood-red. "What price for a snake's egg? For a young cobra? For a young king cobra? For the last—the very last of the brood? The ants are eating all the others down by the melon bed."

Nagaina spun clear round, forgetting everything for the sake of the one egg; and Rikki-tikki saw Teddy's father shoot out a big hand, catch Teddy by the shoulder, and drag him across the little table with the teacups, safe and out of reach of Nagaina.

"Tricked! Tricked! Tricked! *Rikk-tck-tck!*"

Darzee, a featherbrained little fellow.

chuckled Rikki-tikki. "The boy is safe, and it was I—I—I—that caught Nag by the hood last night in the bathroom." Then he began to jump up and down, all four feet together, his head close to the floor. "He threw me to and fro, but he could not shake me off. He was dead before the big man blew him in two. I did it! *Rikki-tikki-tck-tck!* Come then, Nagaina. Come and fight with me. You shall not be a widow long."

Nagaina saw that she had lost her chance of killing Teddy, and the egg lay between Rikki-tikki's paws. "Give me the egg, Rikki-tikki. Give me the last of my eggs, and I will go away and never come back," she said, lowering her hood.

"Yes, you will go away, and you will never come back; for you will go to the rubbish heap with Nag. Fight, widow! The big man has gone for his gun! Fight!"

Rikki-tikki was bounding all round Nagaina, keeping just out of reach of her stroke, his little eyes like hot coals. Nagaina gathered herself together and flung out at him. Rikki-tikki jumped up and backwards. Again and again and again she struck, and each time her head came with a whack on the matting of the veranda and she gathered herself together like a watch spring. Then Rikki-tikki danced in a circle to get behind her, and Nagaina spun round to keep her head to his head, so that the rustle of her

Rikki-tikki knew that he must catch Nagaina or all the trouble would begin again.

tail on the matting sounded like dry leaves blown along by the wind.

He had forgotten the egg. It still lay on the veranda, and Nagaina came nearer and nearer to it, till at last, while Rikki-tikki was drawing breath, she caught it in her mouth, turned to the veranda steps, and flew like an arrow down the path, with Rikki-tikki behind her. When the cobra runs for her life, she goes like a whiplash flicked across a horse's neck. Rikki-tikki knew that he must catch her or all the trouble would begin again. She headed straight for the long grass by the thorn bush, and as he was running, Rikki-tikki heard Darzee still singing his foolish little song of triumph. But Darzee's wife was wiser. She flew off her nest as Nagaina came along and flapped her wings about Nagaina's head. If Darzee had helped, they might have turned her, but Nagaina only lowered her hood and went on. Still, the instant's delay brought Rikki-tikki up to

earth. Then the grass by the mouth of the hole stopped waving, and Darzee said: "It is all over with Rikki-tikki! We must sing his death song. Valiant Rikki-tikki is dead! For Nagaina will surely kill him underground."

So he sang a very mournful song that he made up on the spur of the minute, and just as he got to the most touching part, the grass quivered again, and Rikki-tikki, covered with dirt, dragged himself out of the hole leg by leg, licking his whiskers. Darzee stopped with a little shout. Rikki-tikki shook some of the dust out of his fur and sneezed. "It is all over," he said. "The widow will never come out again." And the red ants that live between the grass stems heard him and began to troop down one after another to see if he had spoken the truth.

PLOT
5. Retell what happens when Rikki fights Nagaina.

Rikki-tikki curled himself up in the grass and slept where he was—slept and slept till it was late in the afternoon, for he had done a hard day's work.

"Now," he said, when he awoke, "I will go back to the house. Tell the Coppersmith, Darzee, and he will tell the garden that Nagaina is dead."

The Coppersmith is a bird who makes a noise exactly like the beating of a little hammer on a copper pot; and the reason he is always making it is because he is the town crier to every Indian garden and tells all the news to everybody who cares to listen. As Rikki-tikki went up the path, he heard his "attention" notes like a tiny dinner gong and then the steady "*Ding-dong-tock!* Nag is dead—*dong!* Nagaina is dead! *Ding-dong-tock!*" That set all the birds in the garden singing and the frogs croaking, for Nag and

her, and as she plunged into the rat hole where she and Nag used to live, his little white teeth were clenched on her tail and he went down with her—and very few mongooses, however wise and old they may be, care to follow a cobra into its hole. It was dark in the hole, and Rikki-tikki never knew when it might open out and give Nagaina room to turn and strike at him. He held on savagely and stuck out his feet to act as brakes on the dark slope of the hot, moist

Chuchundra, a brokenhearted little beast.

Nagaina used to eat frogs as well as little birds.

When Rikki got to the house, Teddy and Teddy's mother (she looked very white still, for she had been fainting) and Teddy's father came out and almost cried over him; and that night he ate all that was given him till he could eat no more and went to bed on Teddy's shoulder, where Teddy's mother saw him when she came to look late at night.

"He saved our lives and Teddy's life," she said to her husband. "Just think, he saved all our lives."

Rikki-tikki woke up with a jump, for the mongooses are light sleepers.

"Oh, it's you," said he. "What are you bothering for? All the cobras are dead; and if they weren't, I'm here."

Rikki-tikki had a right to be proud of himself, but he did not grow too proud, and he kept that garden as a mongoose should keep it, with tooth and jump and spring

and bite, till never a cobra dared show its head inside the walls.

Darzee's Chant
Sung in honor of Rikki-tikki-tavi

Singer and tailor am I—
    Doubled the joys that I know—
Proud of my lilt[14] to the sky,
    Proud of the house that I sew.
Over and under, so weave I my music—
    so weave I the house that I sew.

Sing to your fledglings[15] again,
    Mother, O lift up your head!
Evil that plagued us is slain,
    Death in the garden lies dead.
Terror that hid in the roses is impotent—
    flung on the dunghill and dead!

Who has delivered us, who?
    Tell me his nest and his name.
Rikki, the valiant, the true,
    Tikki, with eyeballs of flame—
Rikk-tikki-tikki, the ivory-fanged,
    the hunter with eyeballs of flame!

Give him the Thanks of the Birds,
    Bowing with tail feathers spread,
Praise him with nightingale words—
    Nay, I will praise him instead.
Hear! I will sing you the praise of the
    bottle-tailed Rikki with eyeballs of red!

(*Here Rikki-tikki interrupted, so the rest of the song is lost.*)

---

14. **lilt** *n.:* song.
15. **fledglings** (flej′liŋz) *n.:* baby birds.

Vocabulary
impotent (im′pə·tənt) *adj.:* powerless.

Rudyard Kipling

On His Own

India, the setting of "Rikki-tikki-tavi," is a place **Joseph Rudyard Kipling** (1865–1936) knew well. His father was a professor of art in Bombay, and Kipling was born in that city when India was under British rule. India was a fascinating place, and young Kipling loved it.

When he was six, however, his parents shipped him and his sister off to a boardinghouse in England. Feeling very much on his own in England, he made a discovery:

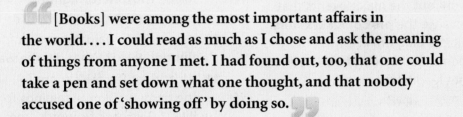

> [Books] were among the most important affairs in the world. . . . I could read as much as I chose and ask the meaning of things from anyone I met. I had found out, too, that one could take a pen and set down what one thought, and that nobody accused one of 'showing off' by doing so.

When he was seventeen, Kipling returned to India and took a job as an editor with an English-language newspaper. He was fascinated by the lives of British colonials in India and the vivid contrast they made with the Indian people they ruled. Soon the paper was printing Kipling's poems and tales about what he saw around him. Other newspapers reprinted them, and readers begged for more. Kipling's fame grew; over the next half century he wrote dozens of books, and in 1907, he won the Nobel Prize in literature. Although he later lived in many places around the world, India would always remain close to his heart.

For Independent Reading

Read more of Kipling's animal stories in *Just So Stories* and *The Jungle Book*. *The Jungle Book* is about Mowgli, a boy who is raised by wolves. *Kim*, Kipling's best-known novel, traces the adventures of an Irish orphan who is raised as an Indian and eventually becomes a British spy.

go.hrw.com

Literary Response and Analysis

Reading Check

1. Explain how Rikki-tikki comes to Teddy's home.

2. Name three incidents that show that Rikki is curious.

3. Whom does Rikki fight in the "great war"?

4. List each of Rikki's friends from the garden. Next to each name, write down how that friend helps him.

5. Where does the final battle take place?

6. Work out the major events that advance the **plot** of Rikki's story. Fill in a diagram like this one. You should find at least four key events that lead to the exciting climax.

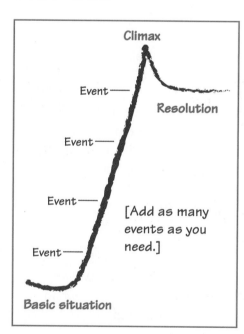

Climax

Event

Resolution

Event

Event

Event

[Add as many events as you need.]

Basic situation

Interpretations

7. Describe three **conflicts** that Rikki-tikki faces. Which conflict do you think is his greatest challenge? Why? How is it resolved?

8. Did Rikki's conflicts with the deadly garden bullies remind you of your own experiences? For ideas, think back to what you said about bullies before you read the story.

9. **Motive** refers to the reason for a character's behavior. What was Rikki's **motive** for fighting Nagaina? What did he want?

10. What was Nagaina's **motive** for fighting Rikki? What did she want?

11. What does Darzee's chant tell about the garden animals' feelings for Rikki? Give specific words from the chant to support your answer.

Writing

Your Opinion

Look back to pages 24 and 25 where Nag and Nagaina are described for the first time. Find words on those pages that make the snakes seem evil. Is Kipling being fair, or are the snakes just doing what snakes do naturally? Does Kipling present the snakes as totally evil, or are they in some ways good? In a paragraph or two, discuss your evaluation of the way Kipling handles his snake characters.

Grade 5 Review Reading Standard 3.2 Identify the main problem or conflict of the plot, and explain how it is resolved.

Reading Standard 3.2 Identify events that advance the plot, and determine how each event explains present action(s).

Vocabulary Development

Clarifying Word Meanings: Contrast

Sometimes you can clarify the meaning of an unfamiliar word by looking for **contrast** clues.

A writer who uses contrast will show how a word is *unlike* another word. For example, you can get a pretty clear idea of what a *splendid* garden is if you see it contrasted with a dark, narrow hole in the ground.

> The splendid garden glowed with roses and great clumps of waving grasses, unlike the dreary hole where cobras live.

Be on the lookout for these words, which signal contrast: *although, but, yet, still, unlike, not, in contrast, instead, however.*

Word Bank

immensely
cowered
valiant
consolation
impotent

PRACTICE

Fill in the blanks in the following sentences with words or phrases that state a contrast with the underlined word. It might help if you first make a cluster diagram of the word and its opposites before you write, like the one below for *cowered* and *cowering:*

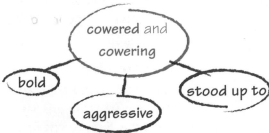

A cowering dog

An aggressive dog

1. The cobras had immense power, but the power of Darzee and the other garden creatures was _____.
2. Darzee cowered before the cobras, though Rikki _____.
3. Rikki was certainly valiant, but Chuchundra, the little muskrat, was _____.
4. The family felt consoled that Rikki was guarding their house, though they were _____ when the cobra threatened Teddy.
5. Darzee sang that the cobras were impotent in death, but they were _____ only a few hours earlier.

Reading Standard 1.3 Clarify word meanings through the use of contrast.

"Look, Mom, No Cavities"

The Main Idea

Informational texts usually focus on one or more main ideas. The **main idea** is the central, most important point in a text. In some texts the main idea is directly stated. Most of the time, however, you, the reader, must **infer** the main idea—that is, you have to think about all the details in the text and make an educated guess about its main point.

Here are some tips for figuring out the main idea:

- Look at the **title.** Does it tell you what the text is going to focus on? Sometimes the title does not point to a central idea at all. Instead, it is a "grabber"—it wants to grab your attention. (The article on the next page has a grabber for a title.)

- Look for a **sentence that seems to state a key idea** in general terms. Sometimes these statements come first or last in a text.

- If you can't find a key sentence that clearly states the main idea, go back over the text, and find its major details. Ask: **What do all these details add up to?**

Vocabulary Development

The following words appear in this article. For pronunciations and definitions, see the opposite page.

species

ligaments

adaptation

prey

Grade 5 Review Reading Standard 2.3 Discern main ideas and concepts presented in texts.

"Look, Mom, No Cavities"

1 Snakes are believed to have evolved from reptiles with legs and to have been on earth for 95 million years. There are now about 2,700 species of snakes. The cobra, native to South Asia, Australia, and Africa, is one of these species. A king cobra can grow to some eighteen feet in length, making it the longest of the poisonous snakes. The cobra has many unusual features.

2 Like all other snakes, cobras are carnivorous. As a cobra grows bigger on its flesh-eating diet, it outgrows its skin and so must shed it four to six times a year. That may be one reason why a cobra's eyes are lidless. Imagine a cobra trying to shed its skin if it had eyelids. Ouch! That's also why a cobra's eyes never seem to change expression, why they appear to have such an intense, fixed stare.

3 A cobra comes equipped with loose folds of skin on its neck that expand into that famous hood. A cobra spreads its hood by spreading its neck ribs, much as you would open an umbrella. This makes it look bigger and more frightening but does not make it more dangerous—cobras are always dangerous.

4 Unlike your jaw, which opens and closes by means of a set of interlocking bones known as the temporal-mandibular joint, a cobra's jaw bones are connected only by ligaments, permitting them to disconnect. The top jaw can open almost flat against its forehead, while the bottom jaw drops almost straight down. It's this adaptation that allows a cobra to swallow prey bigger than its head. A dentist would never have to tell a cobra to open wider. This is so for three reasons: First, a cobra can spread its jaws like a pair of entry doors. Second, a cobra most likely never gets cavities. Third, a cobra must gulp its victims whole—an experience most dentists would like to avoid.

—Flo Ota De Lange

Vocabulary

species (spē′shēz) *n.:* in biology, a naturally existing population of similar organisms that usually breed only among themselves. The human species living today is called *Homo sapiens* ("wise man").

ligaments (lig′ə·mənts) *n.:* in anatomy, bands of tough tissue that connect bones and hold organs in place.

adaptation (ad′əp·tā′shən) *n.:* in biology, a change in structure, function, or form that improves an animal's or a plant's chances of survival. The protective coloration of some animals is a form of adaptation.

prey (prā) *n.:* animal hunted or killed for food by another animal. Mice are prey to owls. Gazelles are prey to lions.

Reading Informational Materials

Reading Check

1. How long can a king cobra be? If you had to help someone visualize its length, what would you compare it with?

2. Why can a cobra swallow an object larger than its head?

3. Which paragraph explains the **title**?

4. Like many good science writers, this writer uses analogies to help you understand difficult concepts. An **analogy** (ə·nal′ə·jē) is a comparison of one thing to another thing that is similar in at least one way. What familiar thing is the cobra's hood compared to? What familiar thing does the writer compare the cobra's jaw to?

Test Practice

"LOOK, MOM, NO CAVITIES"

1. Which of the following is a **fact**—a statement that can be proved true?

   A Cobras are disgusting.

   B Cobras live in South Asia.

   C Cobras hate people.

   D Cobras are bad-tempered.

2. Which of the following is an **opinion**?

   F There are 2,700 species of snakes.

   G Cobras can disconnect their jaws.

   H Cobras are more interesting than pythons.

   J Cobras have hoods.

3. Which sentence *best* states the **main idea** of this article?

   A Cobras have interesting and unusual features.

   B Cobras are always dangerous.

   C Cobras never get cavities.

   D Cobras are meat eaters.

4. The writer uses a **context clue** to help you figure out what a temporal-mandibular joint is. Which word or words in paragraph 4 define *temporal-mandibular joint*?

   F ligaments

   G top jaw

   H pair of entry doors

   J set of interlocking bones

5. The writer uses another **context clue** to help you figure out what the word carnivorous means. Which word or words in paragraph 2 help you understand *carnivorous*?

   A flesh-eating

   B outgrows

   C skin

   D none of these

Grade 5 Review Reading Standard 2.3
Discern main ideas and concepts presented in texts.

Vocabulary Development

Words from Latin

Doctors and other scientists used to study Latin because much of the vocabulary of science is derived from Latin. Here are the Latin words that the words from the Word Bank are built from. (In a dictionary you'll see the abbreviation *L* used to indicate words that come from Latin.)

specere,	L "to see"		*adaptare,*	L "to fit"
ligare,	L "to tie"		*prehendere,*	L "to seize"

Word Bank

species
ligaments
adaptation
prey

PRACTICE 1

Study the meaning of each Latin word above.
1. Match each word in the Word Bank to the Latin word it comes from.
2. How is the meaning of the Latin word evident in the meaning of the English word? (The English words are defined on page 39.)
3. Now, match each of the English words that follow to one of the Latin words above. How is the Latin word reflected in the meaning of each word?
   spectacles   ligature   adapter   prehensile

PRACTICE 2

In one column in the box at the right are Latin words that have been used to form many English words. In the other column is a list of commonly used English words. See if you can match the Latin word to the English word that is derived from it. Which words are associated with science? with history? with law? with politics? with anthropology?

Latin Words	English Words
ambulare, "to walk"	ignition
dicere, "to say"	pedestrian
ducere, "to lead"	matriarchy
ignire, "to light"	territory
jus, "law"	conduct
mater, "mother"	dictator
pedis, "of the foot"	justice
terra, "earth"	ambulatory
terrere, "to frighten"	terrorism

Reading Standard 1.2 Use knowledge of Latin roots to understand content-area vocabulary.

India's History *from* PEOPLE, PLACES, AND CHANGE

Structure and Purpose of Informational Materials: A Textbook

The story of Rikki-tikki-tavi may have made you want to know more about India. Your textbooks are one source you could go to for information on the history of India and on the culture of India today.

Textbooks have particular features that help readers locate information and review what they have learned. Textbooks also offer photographs and artwork that can lead you to even further investigations of a subject.

On the next four pages are passages from a geography textbook called *People, Places, and Change.* See how well you understand the structure of a textbook.

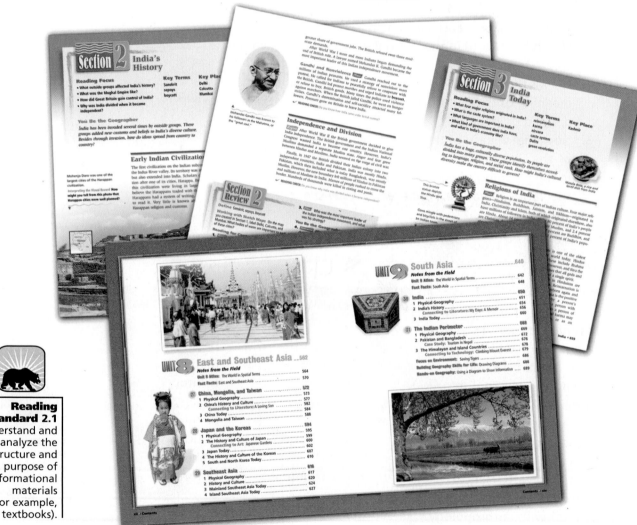

Reading Standard 2.1 Understand and analyze the structure and purpose of informational materials (for example, textbooks).

UNIT 9 South Asia 640

Notes from the Field

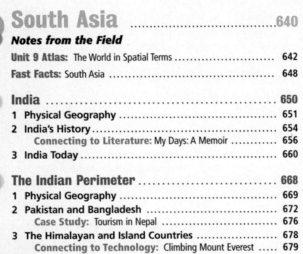

1. The **Table of Contents** is an important feature of a textbook. *What major topics on India does this textbook cover?*

2. *If you wanted to know about India during the time Kipling lived there, which section would you turn to?*

Contents ▸ xiv

3. History and science books often sum up the focus of each chapter. *Look at the Reading Focus list. If you want information on India under British rule, will you find it here?*

4. Illustrations have captions, text that explains the subject of the illustration. *Where can you find the caption for the photo that runs across the bottom of the page?*

5. Note the inset, which is a very small map showing where the subject of the photo is located. Usually a star or a circle indicates the exact location. *Is the city of Mohenjo Daro in present-day Pakistan or India?*

Section 2 India's History

Reading Focus
- What outside groups affected India's history?
- What was the Mughal Empire like?
- How did Great Britain gain control of India?
- Why was India divided when it became independent?

Key Terms
Sanskrit
sepoys
boycott

Key Places
Delhi
Calcutta
Mumbai

Coat of arms of the East India Company

You Be the Geographer
India has been invaded several times by outside groups. These groups added new customs and beliefs to India's diverse culture. Besides through invasion, how do ideas spread from country to country?

Early Indian Civilizations

The first civilization on the Indian subcontinent was centered around the Indus River valley. Its territory was mainly in present-day Pakistan but also extended into India. Scholars call this the Harappan civilization after one of its cities, Harappa. By about 2500 B.C. the people of this civilization were living in large, well-planned cities. Scholars believe the Harappans traded with the peoples of Mesopotamia. The Harappans had a system of writing, but scholars have not been able to read it. Very little is known about Harappan religion and customs.

Mohenjo Daro was one of the largest cities of the Harappan civilization.
Interpreting the Visual Record How might you tell from this photo that Harappan cities were well planned?

The Taj Mahal is one of the most famous buildings in the world.

The British

Movement During the 1700s and 1800s the British slowly took control of India. At first this was done by the English East India Company. This company won rights to trade in the Mughal Empire in the 1600s. The East India Company first took control of small trading posts. Later the British gained more Indian territory.

Company Rule As the Mughal Empire grew weaker, the English East India Company expanded its political power. The company also built up its own military force. This army was made up mostly of **sepoys**, Indian troops commanded by British officers. The British used the strategy of backing one Indian ruler against another in exchange for cooperation. By the mid-1800s the company controlled more than half of India. The rest was divided into small states ruled by local princes.

The British changed the Indian economy to benefit British industry. India produced raw materials, including cotton, indigo—a natural dye—and jute. These materials were then shipped to Britain for use in British factories. Spices, sugar, tea, and wheat were also grown in India for export. Railroads were built to ship the raw materials to Calcutta, Bombay (now Mumbai), and other port cities. India also became a market for British manufactured goods. Indians, who had woven cotton cloth for centuries, were now forced to buy British cloth.

In September 1857, British and loyal Sikh troops stormed the gate of Delhi, defended by rebel sepoys. Bloody fighting continued until late 1858.

Interpreting the Visual Record

How did the Indian Mutiny lead to a change in the way India was governed?

India • 657

6. Key ideas and terms are set in **boldface type.** The boldface terms are often defined in the text. *Is the boldface word on this page defined?*

Anti-British Protest

After World War I more and more Indians began demanding the end of British rule. A lawyer named Mohandas K. Gandhi became the most important leader of this Indian independence movement.

Gandhi and Nonviolence `Place` Gandhi reached out to the millions of Indian peasants. He used a strategy of nonviolent mass protest. He called for Indians to peacefully refuse to cooperate with the British. Gandhi led protest marches and urged Indians to **boycott**, or refuse to buy, British goods. Many times the police used violence against marchers. When the British jailed Gandhi, he went on hunger strikes. Gandhi's determination and self-sacrifice attracted many followers. Pressure grew on Britain to leave India.

✔ **READING CHECK:** Do you know how India came under British control?

Independence and Division

`Region` After World War II the British government decided to give India independence. The British government and the Indian National Congress wanted India to become one country. However, India's Muslims demanded a separate Muslim state. Anger and fear grew between Hindus and Muslims. India seemed on the verge of civil war.

Finally, in 1947 the British divided their Indian colony into two independent countries, India and Pakistan. India was mostly Hindu. Pakistan, which then included what is today Bangladesh, was mostly Muslim. However, the new boundary left millions of Hindus in Pakistan and millions of Muslims in India. Masses of people rushed to cross the border. Hundreds of thousands were killed in rioting and panic.

✔ **READING CHECK:** Do you know why India was divided when it became independent?

▲
Mohandas Gandhi was known to his followers as the Mahatma, or the "great soul."

7. Reading checks are often provided to help you review what you have learned.

8. Textbooks usually try to be unbiased. When reporting controversial events, they try to present the views of all sides. India's war for independence still sparks controversy. *Do you find any bias in the writer's text here? Is the writer critical of any group?*

9. Questions usually conclude each section. These questions help you review what you've read; if you can't answer the questions, you need to re-read the text.

Section Review 2

Define Sanskrit, sepoys, boycott

Working with Sketch Maps On the map you created in Section 1, label Delhi, Calcutta, and Mumbai. What bodies of water are important to each of these cities?

Reading for Content Understanding

1. `Region` What factors made the Mughal Empire one of the most powerful states in the world?

2. `Movement` How did the English East India Company gain control of most of India?

3. `Place` Who was the most important leader of the Indian independence movement, and what was his strategy?

You Be the Geographer: `CRITICAL THINKING`

4. `Movement` Why was the British colony of India divided into two countries?

Organizing What You Know

5. Copy the following time line. Use it to mark important events in Indian history from 2500 B.C. to A.D. 1947.

2500 B.C. ———————————————— A.D. 1947

Reading Informational Materials

TestPractice

Literature and Language Arts

To check on how well you know the important parts of a textbook, answer the following questions by referring to the key parts of the textbook you are now using, called *Literature and Language Arts.*

1. The **copyright page** is in the front of the book, usually the page after the main title page. Here is where you will find the date the book was published. What is the copyright date of this textbook?
   A   2000
   B   2001
   C   2002
   D   2003

2. The **table of contents** is found in the front of a textbook. According to the table of contents of this textbook, how many chapters are in Part 1 of the book?
   F   5
   G   6
   H   7
   J   8

3. In *Literature and Language Arts,* what is found in Part 2?
   A   Chapter 1: Structures
   B   Chapter 2: Characters
   C   Workshops
   D   Read On features

4. On the **author page** of the book are listed the people who wrote the textbook. Most textbooks list the authors' qualifications, so you can be confident that the information in your textbook is accurate. What page of this book lists the authors?
   F   ii
   G   iii
   H   2
   J   6

5. At the back of this book is a section called **Resources.** Which of the following features is *not* found in this section?
   A   Index of Skills
   B   Handbook of Reading and Informational Terms
   C   Index of Maps
   D   Index of Authors and Titles

Reading Standard 2.1
Understand and analyze the structure and purpose of informational materials (for example, textbooks).

Three Skeleton Key

Literary Focus

Suspense and Foreshadowing

The writer of this story hooks our interest with his opening sentence: "My most terrifying experience?" Once a question like this is asked in a story, we want to know the answer. We want to know what happens next. This feeling of anxious curiosity is called **suspense.**

Writers often intensify suspense by dropping clues that hint at what might happen later in the story. This use of clues is called **foreshadowing.** (One example of foreshadowing might be in the story's title. Make a guess about what the title might foreshadow.)

Reading Skills

Making Predictions

Part of the fun of following any **narrative** is trying to guess what will happen next. That process is called **making predictions,** a skill you practiced by answering questions as you read "Duffy's Jacket" (page 7). Here's how to make predictions on your own as you read a text:

- Look for clues that seem to **fore-shadow** something that will happen in the story.

- As the **suspense** builds, think about possible outcomes.

- Ask yourself questions as you read. Revise your predictions as you go.

Remember: A good writer always surprises you.

Reading Standard 3.2 Identify events that advance the plot, and determine how each event explains past or present action(s) or foreshadows future action(s).

Make the Connection

Quickwrite

Movies, TV, and books are full of horror tales that make us want to check under our beds. If you were writing a horror story, what details would you use to create a scary setting? Freewrite your ideas.

Background

The title of this story is the name of a key, or low-lying island, off the coast of French Guiana (gē·an′ə), in South America. At the time the story was written, French Guiana was a colony of France. Cayenne (kī·en′), the capital, was the site of one of the prisons that France maintained there until 1945.

Vocabulary Development

Pay attention to these words as you read the story:

hordes (hôrdz) *n.:* large, moving crowds. *The rats swam ashore in hordes.*

receding (ri·sēd′iŋ) *v.* used as *adj.:* moving back. *At first the ship came toward us, but then it drifted off in the receding waters.*

fathom (fa*th*′əm) *v.:* understand. *The lighthouse keepers couldn't fathom the rats' nasty reaction.*

edible (ed′ə·bəl) *adj.:* fit to be eaten. *The rats thought the men were edible.*

derisive (di·rī′siv) *adj.:* scornful and ridiculing. *The rats peered with derisive eyes at the terrified men.*

Three Skeleton Key

George G. Toudouze

I did not give the warnings of the old-timers a second thought.

My most terrifying experience? Well, one does have a few in thirty-five years of service in the Lights, although it's mostly monotonous, routine work—keeping the light in order, making out the reports.

When I was a young man, not very long in the service, there was an opening in a lighthouse newly built off the coast of Guiana, on a small rock twenty miles or so from the mainland. The pay was high, so in order to reach the sum I had set out to save before I married, I volunteered for service in the new light.

Three Skeleton Key, the small rock on which the light stood, bore a bad reputation. It earned its name from the story of the three convicts who, escaping from Cayenne in a stolen dugout canoe, were wrecked on the rock during the night, managed to escape the sea, but eventually died of hunger and thirst. When they were discovered, nothing remained but three heaps of bones, picked clean by the birds. The story was that the three skeletons, gleaming with phosphorescent[1] light, danced over the small rock, screaming. . . .

But there are many such stories and I did not give the warnings of the old-timers at the *Île-de-Seine*[2] a second thought. I signed up, boarded ship, and in a month I was installed at the light.

Picture a gray, tapering cylinder,[3] welded to the solid black rock by iron rods and concrete, rising from a small island twenty-odd miles from land. It lay in the midst of the sea, this island, a small, bare piece of stone, about one hundred fifty feet long, perhaps forty wide. Small, barely large enough for a man to walk about and stretch his legs at low tide.

This is an advantage one doesn't find in all lights, however, for some of them rise sheer from the waves, with no room for one to move save within the light itself. Still, on our island, one must be careful, for the rocks were treacherously smooth. One misstep and down you would fall into the sea—not that the risk of drowning was so great, but the waters about our island swarmed with huge sharks, who kept an eternal patrol around the base of the light.

Still, it was a nice life there. We had enough provisions to last for months, in the event that the sea should become too rough for the supply ship to reach us on schedule. During the day we would work about the light, cleaning the rooms, polishing the metalwork and the lens and reflector of the light itself, and at night we would sit on the gallery and watch our light, a twenty-thousand-candlepower lantern, swinging its strong white bar of light over the sea from the top of its hundred-twenty-foot tower. Some days, when the air would be very clear, we could see the land, a threadlike line to the west. To the east, north, and south stretched the ocean. Landsmen, perhaps, would soon have tired of that kind of life, perched on a small island off the coast of South America

---

1. **phosphorescent** (făs'fə·res'ənt) *adj.:* glowing.
2. **Île-de-Seine** (ēl də sen').

3. **tapering cylinder:** tube shape that gradually narrows toward one end; in this case, toward the top.

for eighteen weeks until one's turn for leave ashore came around. But we liked it there, my two fellow tenders and myself—so much so that for twenty-two months on end, with the exception of shore leaves, I was greatly satisfied with the life on Three Skeleton Key.

I had just returned from my leave at the end of June, that is to say, midwinter in that latitude, and had settled down to the routine with my two fellow keepers, a Breton[4] by the name of Le Gleo and the head keeper, Itchoua, a Basque[5] some dozen years or so older than either of us.

Eight days went by as usual; then on the ninth night after my return, Itchoua, who was on night duty, called Le Gleo and me, sleeping in our rooms in the middle of the tower, at two in the morning. We rose immediately and, climbing the thirty or so steps that led to the gallery, stood beside our chief.

Itchoua pointed, and following his finger, we saw a big three-master, with all sail set, heading straight for the light. A queer course, for the vessel must have seen us; our light lit her with the glare of day each time it passed over her.

Now, ships were a rare sight in our waters, for our light was a warning of treacherous reefs, barely hidden under the surface and running far out to sea. Consequently we were always given a wide berth, especially by sailing vessels, which cannot maneuver as readily as steamers.

No wonder that we were surprised at seeing this three-master heading dead for us in the gloom of early morning. I had immediately recognized her lines, for she stood out plainly, even at the distance of a mile, when our light shone on her.

She was a beautiful ship of some four thousand tons, a fast sailer that had carried cargoes to every part of the world, plowing the seas unceasingly. By her lines she was identified as Dutch built, which was understandable, as Paramaribo and Dutch Guiana are very close to Cayenne.

Watching her sailing dead for us, a white wave boiling under her bows, Le Gleo cried out:

"What's wrong with her crew? Are they all drunk or insane? Can't they see us?"

Itchoua nodded soberly and looked at us sharply as he remarked: "See us? No doubt—if there *is* a crew aboard!"

"What do you mean, chief?" Le Gleo had started, turned to the Basque. "Are you saying that she's the *Flying Dutchman*?"[6]

His sudden fright had been so evident that the older man laughed:

"No, old man, that's not what I meant. If I say that no one's aboard, I mean she's a derelict."[7]

Then we understood her queer behavior. Itchoua was right. For some reason, believing her doomed, her crew had abandoned her. Then she had righted herself and sailed on, wandering with the wind.

The three of us grew tense as the ship seemed about to crash on one of our numerous reefs, but she suddenly lurched with some change of the wind, the yards[8] swung around, and the derelict came clumsily about and sailed dead away from us.

---

4. **Breton** (bret′n): person from Brittany, a region of northern France.
5. **Basque** (bask): Basques are people living in the Pyrenees, a mountain range in France and Spain.
6. **Flying Dutchman:** fabled Dutch ghost ship whose captain is said to be condemned to sail the seas until Judgment Day. Seeing the *Flying Dutchman* is supposed to bring bad luck.
7. **derelict** (der′ə·likt′) *n.:* here, abandoned ship.
8. **yards** *n.:* in nautical terms, rods fastened across the masts to support the sails.

Le Séducteur by René Magritte. Oil on canvas (19" x 23").

Virginia Museum of Fine Arts, Richmond, Virginia. Collection of Mr. and Mrs. Paul Mellon. Photograph by Ron Jennings.
© 2000 Virginia Museum of Fine Arts. © 1998 C. Herscovici, Brussels/Artists Rights Society (ARS), New York.

In the light of our lantern she seemed so sound, so strong, that Itchoua exclaimed impatiently:

"But why the devil was she abandoned? Nothing is smashed, no sign of fire—and she doesn't sail as if she were taking water."

Le Gleo waved to the departing ship:

"Bon voyage!" he smiled at Itchoua and went on. "She's leaving us, chief, and now we'll never know what—"

"No, she's not!" cried the Basque. "Look! She's turning!"

As if obeying his words, the derelict three-master stopped, came about, and headed for us once more. And for the next four hours the vessel played around us— zigzagging, coming about, stopping, then suddenly lurching forward. No doubt some freak of current and wind, of which our island was the center, kept her near us.

Then suddenly the tropic dawn broke, the sun rose, and it was day, and the ship was plainly visible as she sailed past us. Our light extinguished, we returned to the gallery with our glasses[9] and inspected her.

The three of us focused our glasses on her poop[10] and saw, standing out sharply, black letters on the white background of a life ring, the stenciled name "*Cornelius de Witt, Rotterdam.*"

We had read her lines correctly: She was Dutch. Just then the wind rose and the *Cornelius de Witt* changed course, leaned to port, and headed straight for us once more. But this time she was so close that we knew she would not turn in time.

"Thunder!" cried Le Gleo, his Breton soul aching at seeing a fine ship doomed to smash upon a reef, "she's going to pile up! She's gone!"

I shook my head:

"Yes, and a shame to see that beautiful ship wreck herself. And we're helpless."

There was nothing we could do but watch. A ship sailing with all sail spread, creaming the sea with her forefoot as she runs before the wind, is one of the most beautiful sights in the world—but this time I could feel the tears stinging in my eyes as I saw this fine ship headed for her doom.

All this time our glasses were riveted on her and we suddenly cried out together:

"The rats!"

Now we knew why this ship, in perfect condition, was sailing without her crew aboard. They had been driven out by the rats. Not those poor specimens of rats you see ashore, barely reaching the length of one foot from their trembling noses to the tip of their skinny tails, wretched creatures that dodge and hide at the mere sound of a footfall.

No, these were ships' rats, huge, wise creatures, born on the sea, sailing all over the world on ships, transferring to other, larger ships as they multiply. There is as much difference between the rats of the land and these maritime rats as between a fishing smack[11] and an armored cruiser.

The rats of the sea are fierce, bold animals. Large, strong, and intelligent, clannish and seawise, able to put the best of mariners to shame with their knowledge of the sea, their uncanny ability to foretell the weather.

And they are brave, these rats, and vengeful. If you so much as harm one, his sharp cry will bring hordes of his fellows to swarm over you, tear you, and not cease until your flesh has been stripped from the bones.

The ones on this ship, the rats of Holland, are the worst, superior to other rats of the sea as their brethren are to the land rats. There is a well-known tale about these animals.

A Dutch captain, thinking to protect his cargo, brought aboard his ship not cats but two terriers, dogs trained in the hunting, fighting, and killing of vicious rats. By the time the ship, sailing from Rotterdam, had passed the Ostend light, the dogs were gone and never seen again. In twenty-four hours they had been overwhelmed, killed, and eaten by the rats.

At times, when the cargo does not suffice,[12] the rats attack the crew, either

---

9. glasses *n.:* here, binoculars.
10. poop *n.:* in nautical terms, the stern (back) deck of a ship.

11. smack *n.:* here, small sailboat.
12. suffice (sə·fīs′) *v.:* provide enough.

Vocabulary
hordes (hôrdz) *n.:* large, moving crowds.

driving them from the ship or eating them alive. And studying the *Cornelius de Witt,* I turned sick, for her small boats were all in place. She had not been abandoned.

Over her bridge, on her deck, in the rigging, on every visible spot, the ship was a writhing mass—a starving army coming toward us aboard a vessel gone mad!

Our island was a small spot in that immense stretch of sea. The ship could have grazed us or passed to port or starboard with its ravening[13] cargo—but no, she came for us at full speed, as if she were leading the regatta at a race, and impaled herself on a sharp point of rock.

There was a dull shock as her bottom stove in,[14] then a horrible crackling as the three masts went overboard at once, as if cut down with one blow of some gigantic sickle. A sighing groan came as the water rushed into the ship; then she split in two and sank like a stone.

But the rats did not drown. Not these fellows! As much at home in the sea as any fish, they formed ranks in the water, heads lifted, tails stretched out, paws paddling. And half of them, those from the forepart of the ship, sprang along the masts and onto the rocks in the instant before she sank. Before we had time even to move, nothing remained of the three-master save some pieces of wreckage floating on the surface and an army of rats covering the rocks left bare by the receding tide.

Thousands of heads rose, felt the wind, and we were scented, seen! To them we were fresh meat, after possible weeks of starving.

There came a scream, composed of innumerable screams, sharper than the howl of a saw attacking a bar of iron, and in the one motion, every rat leaped to attack the tower!

We barely had time to leap back, close the door leading onto the gallery, descend the stairs, and shut every window tightly. Luckily the door at the base of the light, which we never could have reached in time, was of bronze set in granite and was tightly closed.

The horrible band, in no measurable time, had swarmed up and over the tower as if it had been a tree, piled on the embrasures[15] of the windows, scraped at the glass with thousands of claws, covered the lighthouse with a furry mantle, and reached the top of the tower, filling the gallery and piling atop the lantern.

Their teeth grated as they pressed against the glass of the lantern room, where they could plainly see us, though they could not reach us. A few millimeters of glass, luckily very strong, separated our faces from their gleaming, beady eyes, their sharp claws and teeth. Their odor filled the tower, poisoned our lungs, and rasped our nostrils with a pestilential, nauseating smell. And there we were, sealed alive in our own light, prisoners of a horde of starving rats.

That first night, the tension was so great

---

13. **ravening** (rav′ə·niŋ) *adj.:* greedily searching for animals to kill for food. A more common related word is *ravenous* (rav′ə·nəs), meaning "wildly, greedily hungry."
14. **stove in:** caved in.

15. **embrasures** (em·brā′zhərz) *n.:* slanted openings.

Vocabulary
receding (ri·sēd′iŋ) *v.:* used as *adj.:* moving back.

that we could not sleep. Every moment, we felt that some opening had been made, some window given way, and that our horrible besiegers were pouring through the breach. The rising tide, chasing those of the rats which had stayed on the bare rocks, increased the numbers clinging to the walls, piled on the balcony—so much so that clusters of rats clinging to one another hung from the lantern and the gallery.

With the coming of darkness we lit the light and the turning beam completely maddened the beasts. As the light turned, it successively blinded thousands of rats crowded against the glass, while the dark side of the lantern room gleamed with thousands of points of light, burning like the eyes of jungle beasts in the night.

All the while we could hear the enraged scraping of claws against the stone and glass, while the chorus of cries was so loud that we had to shout to hear one another. From time to time, some of the rats fought among themselves and a dark cluster would detach itself, falling into the sea like a ripe fruit from a tree. Then we would see phosphorescent streaks as triangular fins slashed the water—sharks, permanent guardians of our rock, feasting on our jailers.

The next day we were calmer and amused ourselves teasing the rats, placing our faces against the glass which separated us. They could not fathom the invisible barrier which separated them from us, and we laughed as we watched them leaping against the heavy glass.

But the day after that, we realized how serious our position was. The air was foul; even the heavy smell of oil within our stronghold could not dominate the fetid odor of the beasts massed around us. And there was no way of admitting fresh air without also admitting the rats.

The morning of the fourth day, at early dawn, I saw the wooden framework of my window, eaten away from the outside, sagging inwards. I called my comrades and the three of us fastened a sheet of tin in the opening, sealing it tightly. When we had completed that task, Itchoua turned to us and said dully:

"Well—the supply boat came thirteen days ago, and she won't be back for twenty-nine." He pointed at the white metal plate sealing the opening through the granite. "If that gives way"—he shrugged—"they can change the name of this place to Six Skeleton Key."

The next six days and seven nights, our only distraction was watching the rats whose holds were insecure fall a hundred and twenty feet into the maws of the sharks—but they were so many that we could not see any diminution in their numbers.

Thinking to calm ourselves and pass the time, we attempted to count them, but we soon gave up. They moved incessantly, never still. Then we tried identifying them, naming them.

One of them, larger than the others, who seemed to lead them in their rushes against the glass separating us, we named "Nero";[16] and there were several others whom we had learned to distinguish through various peculiarities.

But the thought of our bones joining those of the convicts was always in the back

---

16. **Nero** (nir'ō): emperor of Rome (A.D. 54–68) known for his cruelty.

Vocabulary
fathom (fa*th*'əm) v.: understand.

of our minds. And the gloom of our prison fed these thoughts, for the interior of the light was almost completely dark, as we had had to seal every window in the same fashion as mine, and the only space that still admitted daylight was the glassed-in lantern room at the very top of the tower.

Then Le Gleo became morose and had nightmares in which he would see the three skeletons dancing around him, gleaming coldly, seeking to grasp him. His maniacal, raving descriptions were so vivid that Itchoua and I began seeing them also.

It was a living nightmare, the raging cries of the rats as they swarmed over the light, mad with hunger; the sickening, strangling odor of their bodies—

True, there is a way of signaling from lighthouses. But to reach the mast on which to hang the signal, we would have to go out on the gallery where the rats were.

There was only one thing left to do. After debating all of the ninth day, we decided not to light the lantern that night. This is the greatest breach of our service, never committed as long as the tenders of the light are alive; for the light is something sacred, warning ships of danger in the night. Either the light gleams a quarter-hour after sundown, or no one is left alive to light it.

Well, that night, Three Skeleton Light was dark, and all the men were alive. At the risk of causing ships to crash on our reefs, we left it unlit, for we were worn out—going mad!

At two in the morning, while Itchoua was dozing in his room, the sheet of metal sealing his window gave way. The chief had just time enough to leap to his feet and cry for help, the rats swarming over him.

But Le Gleo and I, who had been watching from the lantern room, got to him immediately, and the three of us battled with the horde of maddened rats which flowed through the gaping window. They bit, we struck them down with our knives—and retreated.

We locked the door of the room on them, but before we had time to bind our wounds, the door was eaten through and gave way, and we retreated up the stairs, fighting off the rats that leaped on us from the knee-deep swarm.

I do not remember, to this day, how we ever managed to escape. All I can remember is wading through them up the stairs, striking them off as they swarmed over us; and then we found ourselves, bleeding from innumerable bites, our clothes shredded, sprawled across the trapdoor in the floor of the lantern room—without food or drink. Luckily, the trapdoor was metal, set into the granite with iron bolts.

The rats occupied the entire light beneath us, and on the floor of our retreat lay some twenty of their fellows, who had gotten in with us before the trapdoor closed and whom we had killed with our knives. Below us, in the tower, we could hear the screams of the rats as they devoured everything edible that they found. Those on the outside squealed in reply and writhed in a horrible curtain as they stared at us through the glass of the lantern room.

Itchoua sat up and stared silently at his blood trickling from the wounds on his limbs and body and running in thin streams on the floor around him. Le Gleo, who was in as bad a state (and so was I, for that matter), stared at the chief and me vacantly, started as his gaze swung to the multitude of rats against the glass, then suddenly began laughing horribly:

"Hee! Hee! The Three Skeletons! Hee! Hee! The Three Skeletons are now *six* skeletons! *Six* skeletons!"

He threw his head back and howled, his eyes glazed, a trickle of saliva running from the corners of his mouth and thinning the blood flowing over his chest. I shouted to him to shut up, but he did not hear me, so I did the only thing I could to quiet him—I swung the back of my hand across his face.

The howling stopped suddenly, and his eyes swung around the room; then he bowed his head and began weeping softly, like a child.

Our darkened light had been noticed from the mainland, and as dawn was breaking, the patrol was there to investigate the failure of our light. Looking through my binoculars, I could see the horrified expression on the faces of the officers and crew when, the daylight strengthening, they saw the light completely covered by a seething mass of rats. They thought, as I afterwards found out, that we had been eaten alive.

But the rats had also seen the ship or had scented the crew. As the ship drew nearer, a

Vocabulary
edible (ed′ə·bəl) *adj.:* fit to be eaten.

solid phalanx[17] left the light, plunged into the water, and swimming out, attempted to board her. They would have succeeded, as the ship was hove to;[18] but the engineer connected his steam to a hose on the deck and scalded the head of the attacking column, which slowed them up long enough for the ship to get under way and leave the rats behind.

Then the sharks took part. Belly up, mouths gaping, they arrived in swarms and scooped up the rats, sweeping through them like a sickle through wheat. That was one day that sharks really served a useful purpose.

The remaining rats turned tail, swam to the shore, and emerged dripping. As they neared the light, their comrades greeted them with shrill cries, with what sounded like a derisive note predominating. They answered angrily and mingled with their fellows. From the several tussles that broke out, it seemed as if they resented being ridiculed for their failure to capture the ship.

But all this did nothing to get us out of our jail. The small ship could not approach but steamed around the light at a safe distance, and the tower must have seemed fantastic, some weird, many-mouthed beast hurling defiance at them.

Finally, seeing the rats running in and out of the tower through the door and the windows, those on the ship decided that we had perished and were about to leave when Itchoua, regaining his senses, thought of using the light as a signal. He lit it and, using a plank placed and withdrawn before the beam to form the dots and dashes, quickly

sent out our story to those on the vessel.

Our reply came quickly. When they understood our position—how we could not get rid of the rats, Le Gleo's mind going fast, Itchoua and myself covered with bites, cornered in the lantern room without food or water—they had a signalman send us their reply.

His arms swinging like those of a windmill, he quickly spelled out:

"Don't give up, hang on a little longer! We'll get you out of this!"

Then she turned and steamed at top speed for the coast, leaving us little reassured.

She was back at noon, accompanied by the supply ship, two small coast guard boats, and the fireboat—a small squadron. At twelve-thirty the battle was on.

After a short reconnaissance,[19] the fireboat picked her way slowly through the reefs until she was close to us, then turned her powerful jet of water on the rats. The heavy stream tore the rats from their places and hurled them screaming into the water, where the sharks gulped them down. But for every ten that were dislodged, seven swam ashore, and the stream could do nothing to the rats within the tower. Furthermore, some of them, instead of returning to the rocks, boarded the fireboat, and the men were forced to battle them hand to hand. They were true rats of Holland, fearing no man, fighting for the right to live!

Nightfall came, and it was as if nothing had been done; the rats were still in possession. One of the patrol boats stayed by the island; the rest of the flotilla[20] departed for

---

17. **phalanx** (fā′laŋks′) *n.*: closely packed group. A phalanx is an ancient military formation, and the word still has warlike connotations.
18. **hove to:** stopped by being turned into the wind.

---

19. **reconnaissance** (ri·kän′ə·səns) *n.*: exploratory survey or examination.
20. **flotilla** (flō·til′ə) *n.*: small fleet of boats.

Vocabulary
derisive (di·rī′siv) *adj.*: scornful and ridiculing.

the coast. We had to spend another night in our prison. Le Gleo was sitting on the floor, babbling about skeletons, and as I turned to Itchoua, he fell unconscious from his wounds. I was in no better shape and could feel my blood flaming with fever.

Somehow the night dragged by, and the next afternoon I saw a tug, accompanied by the fireboat, come from the mainland with a huge barge in tow. Through my glasses, I saw that the barge was filled with meat.

Risking the treacherous reefs, the tug dragged the barge as close to the island as possible. To the last rat, our besiegers deserted the rock, swam out, and boarded the barge reeking with the scent of freshly cut meat. The tug dragged the barge about a mile from shore, where the fireboat drenched the barge with gasoline. A well-placed incendiary shell from the patrol boat set her on fire.

The barge was covered with flames immediately, and the rats took to the water in swarms, but the patrol boat bombarded them with shrapnel from a safe distance, and the sharks finished off the survivors.

A whaleboat from the patrol boat took us off the island and left three men to replace us. By nightfall we were in the hospital in Cayenne. What became of my friends?

Well, Le Gleo's mind had cracked and he was raving mad. They sent him back to France and locked him up in an asylum, the poor devil! Itchoua died within a week; a rat's bite is dangerous in that hot, humid climate, and infection sets in rapidly.

As for me—when they fumigated the light and repaired the damage done by the rats, I resumed my service there. Why not? No reason why such an incident should keep me from finishing out my service there, is there?

Besides—I told you I liked the place—to be truthful, I've never had a post as pleasant as that one, and when my time came to leave it forever, I tell you that I almost wept as Three Skeleton Key disappeared below the horizon.

MEET THE WRITER

George G. Toudouze

Sea Fever

George G. Toudouze (1847–1904) was born in France and grew up to develop many literary interests—he was a playwright, an essayist, and an illustrator. He also had a great interest in the sea and worked on a history of the French navy. One critic says of his storytelling style, "It has the impact of a powerful man at the fair who, for the fun of it, takes the hammer and at one blow sends the machine to the top, rings the bell, and walks off."

"Three Skeleton Key" was first published in *Esquire,* a magazine that once was famous for its macho adventure stories. The map on page 60 shows the setting of "Three Skeleton Key."

Literary Response and Analysis

Reading Check

1. How did the small island off the coast of Guiana get the name Three Skeleton Key?

2. Why did the narrator decide to work in such an isolated place?

3. Why does the Dutch-built ship sail so erratically and then ground itself on the reef?

4. How does the ship's unusual cargo suddenly threaten the three lighthouse keepers?

5. What do the lighthouse keepers do to try to save themselves from the dangerous invaders?

6. How are the lighthouse keepers finally rescued?

Interpretations

7. Early in the story the narrator explains how Three Skeleton Key got its name. How does this **foreshadow**—or hint at—the danger the three lighthouse keepers will face later on? (How close did you come to **predicting** what the title might refer to?)

8. On the fourth day of the invasion, a wooden window frame in the lighthouse sags inward. How does this incident increase **suspense**? What other details create suspense?

9. The three **characters** in the lighthouse respond differently to the invasion. Describe each man's reaction to the rats and its effect on the outcome of the story. Which character (if any) did you identify with?

Evaluation

10. The writer Isaac Asimov once said, "When I was a lad . . . I found myself fearfully attracted to stories that scared me. Don't ask why—I hate being scared, but I didn't mind, as long as I knew in my heart that I was safe." Do you enjoy tales of terror like "Three Skeleton Key"? Explain why or why not.

Writing

"A Dark and Stormy Night"

Much of the suspense in "Three Skeleton Key" comes from the fact that the characters are completely isolated. A lonely, forsaken island is a perfect **setting** for a horror story. Write a brief description of another good setting for a horror story. Look back at your Quickwrite notes for more ideas. Consider these features of a setting: sounds, sights, smells, time of day, weather, animal life, names.

Reading Standard 3.2
Identify events that advance the plot, and determine how each event explains past or present action(s) or foreshadows future action(s).

Vocabulary Development

Clarifying Word Meanings

PRACTICE 1

Test your mastery of the Word Bank words by answering these questions:

1. Hordes of rats would be a terrifying sight. Describe two other kinds of hordes you would not like to see.

2. If you were a flood victim, how would you feel when you saw the flood waters receding?

3. The size of the universe is difficult to fathom. Name something else that's difficult to fathom.

4. What is your favorite edible plant? Name one plant that is inedible.

5. Write a derisive remark that a skeptic would make on hearing this rat story.

> **Word Bank**
>
> hordes
> receding
> fathom
> edible
> derisive

Clarifying Word Meanings: Examples

Sometimes you can figure out the meaning of an unfamiliar word by finding other words or phrases that give you an example of what the word means. For example, what words in this sentence give you an idea of what *staples* are?

> **The lighthouse keepers were running very low on necessary staples, such as flour, sugar, and salt.**

Certain words often let you know when an example is being used: *for example, for instance, like, such as, in this case, as if.*

PRACTICE 2

Find the words in each sentence that give you clues to the meaning of the underlined word. Then, make a guess about the meaning of the underlined word.

1. The rocks were treacherous. For example, one step and you would fall into the sea. *Treacherous* probably means _____.

2. Our eyes were riveted on the ship, as if fixed there by an invisible force. *Riveted* probably means _____.

3. The ship was a writhing mass, like a pit of moving snakes. *Writhing* probably means _____.

Reading Standard 1.3 Clarify word meanings through the use of example.

Eeking Out a Life

Structure and Purpose of Informational Materials: A Newspaper Article

The **purpose** of a newspaper article is to give you factual information about current events. A good informational article in a newspaper provides detailed answers to the questions *who? what? when? where? why?* and *how?*

Many newspaper articles are structured in what's called an **inverted**—or upside-down—**pyramid** style.

The article begins with a **summary lead,** a sentence or paragraph that gives the **main idea** of the story—this is usually the most important idea or detail in the story. It is followed by the less important details of the article.

Some articles begin with a lead that simply grabs your interest in a topic. Such a lead does not summarize but instead describes an interesting situation or fact related to the story. Here are some additional elements in the **structure** of a news article:

- **Headline:** the catchy boldface words that tell you what the article is about.
- **Subhead:** additional boldface words in smaller type under the headline, which add details about the article.
- **Byline:** the name of the reporter who wrote the article.
- **Dateline:** the location where the article was reported and the date on which the information was reported.
- **Lead:** the sentence or paragraph that begins the news article.
- **Tone:** the choice of words and point of view that meet the interests of the newspaper's audience. Tone often depends on the subject of the article. Some articles are light, lively, and humorous; others are serious and straightforward.

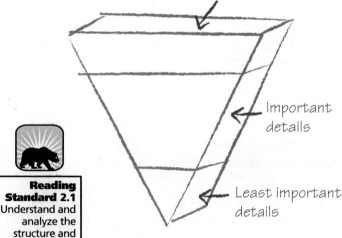

Summary lead, or most important information

Important details

Least important details

Reading Standard 2.1
Understand and analyze the structure and purpose of informational materials (for example, newspapers).

Eeking Out a Life

Couple Welcome a Rescued Rat into Their Home

by Matt Surman

SIMI VALLEY, Calif., July 8— Who knows what trials the rat named Sunny Jim endured in his days alone in the wilderness?

Was he chased by voracious[1] owls? beset by marauding[2] gangs of streetwise sewer rats? Did he yearn for a child who had lost him on a day's outing?

His new owners—Hayley Huttenmaier and Nachshon Rose—can only guess. The little rat that they rescued, housed, and fed isn't talking, of course. And now Rose isn't sure he wants to find out about the past of the rat they have named Sunny Jim if that means the owner is going to come forward. Rose, in fact, has become attached to this sweet, squirming, don't-call-him-vermin little guy.

---

1. **voracious** (vô·rā′shəs) *adj.*: extremely hungry; eager to eat a lot of food.
2. **marauding** (mə·rôd′iŋ) *adj.*: roving in search of something to take or destroy.

All the former veterinary hospital employee knows is that he was returning from a short hike through Corriganville Park one Tuesday when a bundle of fur scampered across the parking lot. He followed, saw it stick its nose out of a little burrow, and then—bit by bit—come to perch on his shoe.

"I was kind of concerned that if I didn't catch him, he would probably be eaten," Rose said. "He probably couldn't have been out there more than a day."

The rat wasn't wearing any tags. There were no remnants of a leash. But he had to be a pet: Just look at the white and brownish-gray markings, his docile[3]—could one go so far as to say friendly?—behavior, his clean fur, and diminutive[4] size. Clearly this was not one of those sooty, dirt-brown outdoor creatures known as *Rattus rattus.*

So, he brought the rat home, and there, he and his fiancee, Huttenmaier, welcomed the rat into their family of two dogs and three cats. Now, Sunny Jim has his own room—well, a cabinet actually—with a cubbyhole formed by bricks, a handful of toys, a soft bed of wood shavings, and regular meals.

Huttenmaier insisted that they place an ad seeking its owner. "My theory is a kid took him out to play and lost him," she said. But so far they have received no calls. While Huttenmaier feels a bit for the poor owner, Rose doesn't want to give Sunny up. He thinks a mom forced her kid to abandon the creature when she realized there was a rodent hiding in a bedroom.

Which brings up the question: Isn't owning a rat found in the woods—even one with a cute glossy face, busy little hands, and a slippy short tail—a little worrisome?

"We can't turn down a cute face," Huttenmaier explained.

And experts agreed: Sunny Jim is almost certainly not a tree-dwelling, bubonic-plague carrying, skinny, wild rat. He is closer to man's best friend.

"Oh, rats are like little dogs," said Louis Stack, membership director of the Riverside-based American Fancy Rat & Mouse Association, whose members raise show rats the way purebred owners raise show dogs. "They can sit on your shoulder and watch TV with you."

And indeed, rat lovers are not shy about their enthusiasm. The Web hosts scores of sites extolling[5] *Rattus norvegicus*—the pet rat, domesticated about 100 years ago in England—and dispelling what they call misinformation about the cleanliness of their pets.

"There are people who are fanatical about rats," Stack said. "There are . . . all kinds of newsletters." Huttenmaier and Rose have no intentions of going that far.

They are just happy to offer little Sunny a home, a sense of safety—disregarding one little incident with a curious cat—and a chance to take it easy for a while.

And just maybe, there is a chance for a Rat Pack. "We might even get him a friend," Huttenmaier said.

---

3. **docile** (däs′əl) *adj.:* manageable.
4. **diminutive** (də·min′yo͞o·tiv) *adj.:* very small; tiny.

---

5. **extolling** (ek·stōl′iŋ) *v.:* praising highly.

Reading Informational Materials

Reading Check

1. What is the **purpose** of a newspaper article?

2. Describe the **structure** of a typical newspaper article.

3. Summarize the information from the article on page 63 that answers the questions *who? what? when? where? why?* and *how?*

4. Describe the **tone** of the article. Why do you think the reporter decided to use this tone?

5. The **headline** title of this article contains a **pun,** which is a play on word meanings. What two words, both pronounced "eek," is the headline playing with?

TestPractice

Eeking Out a Life

1. The **structure** of a newspaper article is said to be similar to an —
   - A octagon
   - B inverted pyramid
   - C oval
   - D upside-down T

2. The **dateline** of the article on page 63 names which city?
   - F Salt Lake City
   - G Des Moines
   - H Buxton
   - J Simi Valley

3. The **subhead** of the article tells you that —
   - A something is eeking out a life
   - B a couple has adopted a stray rat
   - C the rat may have been chased by an owl
   - D rats have become popular

4. The **byline** of the news article shows it was written by —
   - F George G. Toudouze
   - G Nachshon Rose
   - H Matt Surman
   - J Sunny Jim

5. The **lead** of this article —
   - A is an attention grabber
   - B makes a serious statement about dangerous rats
   - C answers *who? what? where? when?* and *how?*
   - D presents the story's main idea

6. The **main idea** of this article is —
   - F a couple loves its adopted rat
   - G rats can't live with people
   - H keeping a rat at home is dangerous
   - J the rat population is a problem

Reading Standard 2.1
Understand and analyze the structure and purpose of informational materials (for example, newspapers).

Grammar Link MINI-LESSON

Subject-Verb Agreement Is Unanimous!

Probably the most common error people make in writing (and in speaking) is in subject-verb agreement. The rule is simple: Subjects and their verbs must always agree. That means that a singular subject takes a singular verb, and a plural subject takes a plural verb. The problem comes with identifying the subject and deciding whether it's singular or plural.

Be especially careful when you have *neither/nor* or *either/or.* You must also pay attention when a subject is separated from its verb by a prepositional phrase. The verb always agrees with the subject.

1. **Neither Huttenmaier nor Rose wants/want to give up Sunny Jim.** [Singular subjects joined by *or* or *nor* take a singular verb. Therefore, the verb should be *wants.*]

2. **Neither Sunny Jim nor his owners wants/want to end their friendship.** [When a singular subject and a plural subject are joined by *or* or *nor,* the verb agrees with the subject closer to the verb. Since *owners* is plural, the verb should be *want.*]

3. **The owners of Sunny Jim is/are a bit unusual.** [The number of the subject is not affected by a prepositional phrase following the subject. Therefore, the verb should be *are.*]

PRACTICE

Rewrite the paragraph below to correct errors in subject-verb agreement.

The most interesting moments in this story comes when Sunny Jim is described. Neither tags nor a collar were found on the little rat. The owners of the rat seem very nice, but parts of their story is weird. The writer don't seem very enthusiastic either. Stories about the curious cat wasn't told here. Neither my biology teacher nor my town's pet-store owner recommend getting a pet *Rattus.*

For more help, see Agreement of Subject and Verb in the *Holt Handbook,* pages 148–164.

The Monsters Are Due on Maple Street

Literary Focus
Plot: Complications

Complications in stories make it hard for characters to get what they want. Complications usually begin to develop as soon as the characters take steps to resolve their problems, or to get what they want so badly. Complications are events like a sudden storm breaking just as the climbers are nearing the summit or another dragon appearing out of the cave just when the hero thinks he has finished his work. Complications usually add more conflict to the story. They also make the plot more complex. Complications are meant to increase our anxiety about how the story will finally end. In stories, as in life, it's never easy.

Reading Skills
Making Inferences

Good readers **make inferences** using clues the writer provides. It's a form of word arithmetic: The writer gives you *one* and *one* but expects you to figure out the answer—*two*.

As you read this teleplay, you'll see little open-book signs. At these points, stop and add up the important clues the writer has just given. Note your inferences in your notebook, or discuss them with your partner.

Make the Connection
Quickwrite ✏️

People often make snap judgments in life. In your journal, write about a time you jumped to an incorrect conclusion about someone or someone jumped to an incorrect conclusion about you. What was the situation? What mistake was made? How was the mistake corrected?

Reading Standard 3.2 Identify events that advance the plot, and determine how each event explains past or present action(s) or foreshadows future action(s).

Vocabulary Development

These words are important in the teleplay:

transfixed (trans·fikst′) *v.* used as *adj.:* very still, as if nailed to the spot. *Up and down the street, people stood transfixed, staring at the sky.*

intelligible (in·tel′i·jə·bəl) *adj.:* understandable. *The residents muttered nothing intelligible; they just made an indistinct rumble.*

assent (ə·sent′) *n.:* agreement. *At first, Steve's common sense gained the crowd's assent and goodwill.*

intimidated (in·tim′ə·dāt′id) *v.:* frightened with threats. *The angry crowd intimidated the Goodmans, who then began to defend themselves.*

defiant (dē·fī′ənt) *adj.:* boldly resisting authority. *Those who speak out against the opinions of an angry crowd must be both defiant and courageous.*

idiosyncrasy (id′ē·ō·siŋ′krə·sē) *n.:* peculiarity. *All people have at least one idiosyncrasy that makes them a little different.*

menace (men′əs) *n.:* danger; threat. *The residents of Maple Street believed there was a real menace to their safety.*

converging (kən·vʉrj′iŋ) *v.* used as *adj.:* closing in. *The crowd began converging around Tommy in order to hear him speak.*

explicit (eks·plis′it) *adj.:* definite; clearly stated. *The danger on Maple Street was not explicit, or understandable, making it more frightening.*

variations (ver′ē·ā′shənz) *n.:* differences. *Most of the residents of Maple Street reacted to fear in similar ways, with only small variations.*

Background

From its 1959 debut through its more than 150 subsequent episodes, *The Twilight Zone* thrilled and captivated millions of television viewers. Rebroadcasts run even today—maybe you've seen some episodes. As Rod Serling, the show's creator, would eerily alert viewers at the beginning of every episode, things in the Twilight Zone are not always what they seem. Ordinary people face extraordinary situations in the Twilight Zone, where familiar rules no longer apply. As the bards and poets have warned for centuries, "Here be monsters. . . ."

The Monsters Are Due on Maple Street

Rod Serling

Teleplay Terms

Scripts written for television or the movies are different from scripts written for the stage. A **teleplay** is a script written for TV; a **screenplay** is a script written for movies. Both kinds of scripts may contain these camera directions:

fade in: The picture gradually appears on the screen.

pan: a swiveling movement of the camera, from one side to the other.

fade to black: The picture gradually disappears until all that remains is a black screen.

cut to: a sudden change from one scene or character to another.

outside shot: a camera shot of an exterior.

long shot: a camera shot from far off.

close-up: a camera shot that is very close to its subject.

opening shot: the first scene of the production.

dissolve: A new scene is blended with a scene that is fading out.

Characters

Narrator	**Charlie**
	Charlie's wife
Figure One	**Tommy**
Figure Two	**Sally,** Tommy's mother
Residents of Maple Street	**Les Goodman**
Steve Brand	**Mrs. Goodman**
Mrs. Brand	**Woman Next Door**
Don Martin	**Woman One**
Pete Van Horn	**Man One**
	Man Two

Act One

Fade in on a shot of the night sky. The various nebulae and planets stand out in sharp, sparkling relief. As the camera begins a slow pan across the heavens, we hear the narrator offscreen.

Narrator's Voice. There is a fifth dimension beyond that which is known to man. It is a dimension as vast as space and as timeless as infinity. It is the middle ground between light and shadow—between science and superstition. And it lies between the pit of man's fears and the summit of his knowledge. This is the dimension of imagination. It is an area which we call The Twilight Zone.

[*The camera pans down past the horizon, stopping on a sign which reads "Maple Street." Then it moves on to the street below. It is daytime. We see a quiet, tree-lined street, typical of small-town America. People sit and swing on gliders on their front porches, chatting across from house to house.* STEVE BRAND *polishes his car, while his neighbor,* DON MARTIN, *leans against the fender watching him. A Good Humor man on a bicycle stops to sell some ice cream to a couple of kids. Two women gossip on a front lawn. Another man waters his lawn.*]

Maple Street, U.S.A., late summer. A tree-lined little world of front-porch gliders, hopscotch, the laughter of children, and the bell of an ice-cream vendor.

[*The camera moves back to the Good Humor man and the two boys who are standing alongside him, buying ice cream.*]

At the sound of the roar and the flash of light, it will be precisely 6:43 P.M. on Maple Street.

[*One of the boys,* TOMMY, *looks up to listen to a tremendous screeching roar from overhead. A flash of light plays on the boys' faces. It moves down the street, past lawns and porches and rooftops, and disappears. People leave their porches or stop what they're doing to stare up at the sky.* STEVE BRAND *stops polishing his car and stands transfixed, staring upward. He looks at* DON MARTIN, *his neighbor from across the street.*]

Steve. What was that? A meteor?
Don (*nods*). That's what it looked like. I didn't hear any crash, though, did you?
Steve (*shakes his head*). Nope. I didn't hear anything except a roar.
Mrs. Brand (*from her porch*). Steve? What was that?
Steve (*raising his voice and looking toward porch*). Guess it was a meteor, honey. Came awful close, didn't it?
Mrs. Brand. Too close for my money! Much too close.

Vocabulary
transfixed (trans·fikst′) *v.* used as *adj.*: very still, as if nailed to the spot.

[*People stand on their porches, watching and talking in low tones.*]

Narrator's Voice. Maple Street. 6:44 P.M., on a late September evening. (*A pause*) Maple Street in the last calm and reflective moments . . . before the monsters came!

[*The camera pans across the porches again. A man is screwing in a lightbulb on a front porch. He gets down off the stool and flicks the switch, only to find that nothing happens. Another man is working on an electric power mower. He plugs in the plug and flicks the switch of the power mower, off and on, but nothing happens. Through the window of a front porch we see a woman at a telephone, pushing her finger back and forth on the dial hook. Her voice is indistinct and distant, but intelligible and repetitive.*]

MAKING INFERENCES

1. What do the stage directions lead you to think about the roaring sound and flashing light?

Woman Next Door. Operator, operator, something's wrong on the phone, operator!

[MRS. BRAND *comes out on the porch and calls to* STEVE.]

Mrs. Brand (*calling*). Steve, the power's off. I had the soup on the stove, and the stove just stopped working.
Woman Next Door. Same thing over here. I can't get anybody on the phone either. The phone seems to be dead.

[*The camera looks down on the street. Small, mildly disturbed voices creep up from below.*]

Voices.
Electricity's off.
Phone won't work.

Can't get a thing on the radio.
My power mower won't move, won't work at all.
Radio's gone dead.

[PETE VAN HORN, *a tall, thin man, is standing in front of his house.*]

Van Horn. I'll cut through the backyard. . . . See if the power's still on on Floral Street. I'll be right back.

[*He walks past the side of his house and disappears into the backyard. We see the hammer on his hip as he walks. The camera pans down slowly until we're looking at ten or eleven people standing around the street and overflowing to the curb and sidewalk. In the background is* STEVE BRAND's *car.*]

Steve. Doesn't make sense. Why should the power go off all of a sudden, and the phone line?
Don. Maybe some sort of an electrical storm or something.
Charlie. That don't seem likely. Sky's just as blue as anything. Not a cloud. No lightning. No thunder. No nothing. How could it be a storm?
Woman One. I can't get a thing on the radio. Not even the portable.

[*The people again murmur softly in wonderment and question.*]

Charlie. Well, why don't you go downtown and check with the police, though they'll probably think we're crazy or something. A little power failure and right away we get all flustered and everything.

Vocabulary
intelligible (in·tel′i·jə·bəl) *adj.*: understandable.

Steve. It isn't just the power failure, Charlie. If it was, we'd still be able to get a broadcast on the portable.

[*There's a murmur of reaction to this.* STEVE *looks from face to face and then over to his car.*]

I'll run downtown. We'll get this all straightened out.

[STEVE *walks over to the car, gets in it, and turns the key. Through the open car door we see the crowd watching him from the other side.* STEVE *starts the engine. It turns over sluggishly and then just stops dead. He tries it again, and this time he can't even get it to turn over. Then, very slowly and reflectively, he turns the key back to "off" and slowly gets out of the car. Everyone stares at* STEVE. *He stands for a moment by the car, then walks toward the group.*]

I don't understand it. It was working fine before. . . .

Don. Out of gas?
Steve (*shakes his head*). I just had it filled up.
Woman One. What's it mean?
Charlie. It's just as if . . . as if everything

had stopped. . . . (*Then he turns toward* STEVE.) We'd better walk downtown.

[*Another murmur of* assent *at this.*]

Steve. The two of us can go, Charlie. (*He turns to look back at the car.*) It couldn't be the meteor. A meteor couldn't do this.

[*He and* CHARLIE *exchange a look, then they start to walk away from the group. We see* TOMMY, *a serious-faced fourteen-year-old in spectacles, standing a few feet away from the group. He is halfway between them and the two men, who start to walk down the sidewalk.*]

Tommy. Mr. Brand . . . you better not!
Steve. Why not?
Tommy. They don't want you to.

[STEVE *and* CHARLIE *exchange a grin, and* STEVE *looks back toward the boy.*]

Steve. Who doesn't want us to?
Tommy (*jerks his head in the general direction of the distant horizon*). Them!
Steve. Them?
Charlie. Who are them?
Tommy (*very intently*). Whoever was in that thing that came by overhead.

[STEVE *knits his brows for a moment, cocking his head questioningly. His voice is intense.*]

Steve. What?
Tommy. Whoever was in the thing that came over. I don't think they want us to leave here.

[STEVE *leaves* CHARLIE *and walks over to the*

Vocabulary
assent (ə·sent′) *n.:* agreement.

boy. He kneels down in front of him. He forces his voice to remain gentle. He reaches out and holds the boy.]

Steve. What do you mean? What are you talking about?

Tommy. They don't want us to leave. That's why they shut everything off.

Steve. What makes you say that? Whatever gave you that idea?

Woman One (*from the crowd*). Now isn't that the craziest thing you ever heard?

Tommy (*persistently but a little <u>intimidated</u> by the crowd*). It's always that way, in every story I ever read about a ship landing from outer space.

Woman One (*to the boy's mother,* SALLY, *who stands on the fringe of the crowd*). From outer space, yet! Sally, you better get that boy of yours up to bed. He's been reading too many comic books or seeing too many movies or something.

Sally. Tommy, come over here and stop that kind of talk.

Steve. Go ahead, Tommy. We'll be right back. And you'll see. That wasn't any ship or anything like it. That was just a . . . a meteor or something. Likely as not— (*He turns to the group, now trying to weight his words with an optimism he obviously doesn't feel but is desperately trying to instill in himself, as well as the others.*) No doubt it did have something to do with all this power failure and the rest of it. Meteors can do some crazy things. Like sunspots.

Don (*picking up the cue*). Sure. That's the kind of thing—like sunspots. They raise Cain with radio reception all over the

world. And this thing being so close—why, there's no telling the sort of stuff it can do. (*He wets his lips and smiles nervously.*) Go ahead, Charlie. You and Steve go into town and see if that isn't what's causing it all.

[STEVE *and* CHARLIE *walk away from the group again, down the sidewalk. The people watch silently.* TOMMY *stares at them, biting his lips, and finally calls out again.*]

Tommy. Mr. Brand!

[*The two men stop again.* TOMMY *takes a step toward them.*]

Tommy. Mr. Brand . . . please don't leave here.

[STEVE *and* CHARLIE *stop once again and turn toward the boy. There's a murmur in the crowd, a murmur of irritation and concern as if the boy were bringing up fears that shouldn't be brought up; words that carried with them a strange kind of validity that came without logic, but nonetheless registered and had meaning and effect.* TOMMY *is partly frightened and partly <u>defiant</u>.*]

You might not even be able to get to town. It was that way in the story. Nobody could leave. Nobody except—

Steve. Except who?

Tommy. Except the people they'd sent down ahead of them. They looked just like humans. And it wasn't until the ship landed that—

[*The boy suddenly stops again, conscious of the parents staring at him and of the sudden hush of the crowd.*]

Making Inferences

2. Does Steve believe his own words? What can you infer from the stage directions?

Vocabulary

intimidated (in·tim′ə·dāt′id) *v.:* frightened with threats or violence.

defiant (dē·fī′ənt) *adj.:* boldly resisting authority.

Sally (*in a whisper, sensing the antagonism of the crowd*). Tommy, please, son . . . honey, don't talk that way—

Man One. That kid shouldn't talk that way . . . and we shouldn't stand here listening to him. Why, this is the craziest thing I ever heard of. The kid tells us a comic book plot, and here we stand listening—

[STEVE *walks toward the camera and stops by the boy.*]

Steve. Go ahead, Tommy. What kind of story was this? What about the people that they sent out ahead?

Tommy. That was the way they prepared things for the landing. They sent four people. A mother and a father and two kids who looked just like humans . . . but they weren't.

[*There's another silence as* STEVE *looks toward the crowd and then toward* TOMMY. *He wears a tight grin.*]

Steve. Well, I guess what we'd better do then is to run a check on the neighborhood and see which ones of us are really human.

[*There's laughter at this, but it's a laughter that comes from a desperate attempt to lighten the atmosphere.* CHARLIE *laughs nervously, slightly forced. The people look at one another in the middle of their laughter.*]

Charlie. There must be somethin' better to do than stand around makin' bum jokes about it. (*Rubs his jaw nervously*) I wonder if Floral Street's got the same deal we got. (*He looks past the houses.*) Where is Pete Van Horn anyway? Didn't he get back yet?

[*Suddenly there's the sound of a car's engine starting to turn over. We look across the street toward the driveway of* LES GOODMAN's *house. He's at the wheel trying to start the car.*]

Sally. Can you get it started, Les?

[LES GOODMAN *gets out of the car, shaking his head.*]

Goodman. No dice.

[*He walks toward the group. He stops suddenly as behind him, inexplicably and with a noise that inserts itself into the silence, the car engine starts up all by itself.* GOODMAN *whirls around to stare toward it. The car idles roughly, smoke coming from the exhaust, the frame shaking gently.* GOODMAN's *eyes go wide, and he runs over to his car. The people stare toward the car.*]

Man One. He got the car started somehow. He got his car started!

[*The camera pans along the faces of the people as they stare, somehow caught up by this revelation and somehow, illogically, wildly, frightened.*]

Woman One. How come his car just up and started like that?

Sally. All by itself. He wasn't anywheres near it. It started all by itself.

[DON *approaches the group. He stops a few feet away to look toward* GOODMAN'*s car, and then back toward the group.*]

Don. And he never did come out to look at that thing that flew overhead. He wasn't even interested. (*He turns to the faces in the group, his face taut and serious.*) Why? Why didn't he come out with the rest of us to look?

Charlie. He always was an oddball. Him and his whole family. Real oddball.

Don. What do you say we ask him?

MAKING INFERENCES

3. What inference have the neighbors made about Les Goodman?

[*The group suddenly starts toward the house. In this brief fraction of a moment they take the first step toward a metamorphosis from a group into a mob. They begin to head purposefully across the street toward the house at the end.* STEVE *stands in front of them. For a moment their fear almost turns their walk into a wild stampede, but* STEVE'*s voice, loud, incisive, and commanding, makes them stop.*]

Steve. Wait a minute . . . wait a minute! Let's not be a mob!

[*The people stop as a group, seem to pause for a moment, and then much more quietly and slowly start to walk across the street.* GOODMAN *stands there alone, facing the people.*]

Goodman. I just don't understand it. I tried to start it and it wouldn't start. You saw me. All of you saw me.

[*And now, just as suddenly as the engine started, it stops. There's a long silence that is gradually intruded upon by the frightened murmuring of the people.*]

I don't understand. I swear . . . I don't understand. What's happening?

Don. Maybe you better tell us. Nothing's working on this street. Nothing. No lights, no power, no radio. (*And then meaningfully*) Nothing except one car—yours!

[*The people pick this up. Now their murmuring becomes a loud chant, filling the air with accusations and demands for action. Two of the men pass* DON *and head toward* GOODMAN, *who backs away, backing into his car. He is now at bay.*]

Goodman. Wait a minute now. You keep your distance—all of you. So I've got a car that starts by itself—well, that's a freak thing, I admit it. But does that make me some kind of criminal or something? I don't know why the car works—it just does!

[*This stops the crowd momentarily, and now* GOODMAN, *still backing away, goes toward his front porch. He goes up the steps and then stops to stand facing the mob.* STEVE *comes through the crowd.*]

Steve (*quietly*). We're all on a monster kick, Les. Seems that the general impression holds that maybe one family isn't what we think they are. Monsters from outer space

or something. Different than us. Fifth columnists° from the vast beyond. (*He chuckles.*) You know anybody that might fit that description around here on Maple Street?

Goodman. What is this, a gag or something? This a practical joke or something?

MAKING INFERENCES

4. Is Steve serious here? On what do you base your inference?

[*The spotlight on his porch suddenly goes out. There's a murmur from the group.*]

Now, I suppose that's supposed to incriminate me! The light goes on and off. That really does it, doesn't it? (*He looks around the faces of the people.*) I just don't understand this—(*He wets his lips, looking from face to face.*) Look, you all know me. We've lived here five years. Right in this house. We're no different than any of the rest of you! We're no different at all. Really . . . this whole thing is just . . . just weird—

Woman One. Well, if that's the case, Les Goodman, explain why—(*She stops suddenly, clamping her mouth shut.*)

° **fifth columnists:** people who aid an enemy from within their own country.

Goodman (*softly*). Explain what?
Steve (*interjecting*). Look, let's forget this—
Charlie (*overlapping him*). Go ahead, let her talk. What about it? Explain what?
Woman One (*a little reluctantly*). Well . . . sometimes I go to bed late at night. A couple of times . . . a couple of times I'd come out on the porch and I'd see Mr. Goodman here in the wee hours of the morning standing out in front of his house . . . looking up at the sky. (*She looks around the circle of faces.*) That's right. Looking up at the sky as if . . . as if he were waiting for something. (*A pause*) As if he were looking for something.

MAKING INFERENCES

5. What fact about Goodman has the woman observed? What inference has she made? Is this reasonable?

[*There's a murmur of reaction from the crowd again. As* GOODMAN *starts toward them, they back away, frightened.*]

Goodman. You know really . . . this is for laughs. You know what I'm guilty of? (*He laughs.*) I'm guilty of insomnia. Now what's the penalty for insomnia? (*At this point the laugh, the humor, leaves his voice.*) Did you hear what I said? I said it was insomnia. (*A pause as he looks around, then shouts.*) I said it was insomnia! You fools. You scared, frightened rabbits, you. You're sick people, do you know that? You're sick people—all of you! And you don't even know what you're starting because let me tell you . . . let me tell you—this thing you're starting— that should frighten you. As God is my witness . . . you're letting something begin here that's a nightmare!

[*Fade to black.*]

Literary Response and Analysis
Act One

Reading Check

1. A dramatic event triggers the action on Maple Street. What do the residents believe has caused the power failure?

2. Find three incidents that show that this is not a normal power failure.

3. How do the adults first react to Tommy's suggestion that "they" are aliens who do not want Steve and Charlie to leave the area?

4. What does Tommy then say that causes the adults to become increasingly uncomfortable?

5. What is Tommy's source of information about alien life forms and their habits?

6. What is the group's reaction when Les Goodman's car starts? What **inference** do they make about the cause of the car's behavior?

Interpretations

7. What future events could Tommy's words **foreshadow**?

8. At the end of Act One, Les Goodman warns the residents that they are starting something that should frighten them, and he goes on to call it a nightmare. What could he mean?

9. A *scapegoat* is someone whom people blame for their troubles. How has Les Goodman become a scapegoat?

10. In your own words, describe what is happening to the community, and **predict** where this kind of behavior is going to lead. Based on what you know so far and on what you know from history and from your own experience, **predict** events that may occur in Act Two. (Think back to your Quickwrite notes.)

11. What is the difference between a crowd and a mob?

12. Do you believe aliens are involved in the events on Maple Street? Explain the reasons for your prediction.

Reading Standard 3.2 Identify events that advance the plot, and determine how each event explains past or present action(s) or foreshadows future action(s).

Vocabulary Development
Act One

Clarifying Word Meanings: Definitions

Writers often help readers understand difficult words by using definition. A writer using **definition** will provide the word's meaning within the sentence. Let's look at the following sentence:

> In this brief fraction of a moment they take the first step toward a <u>metamorphosis</u> that changes people from a group into a mob.

A reader who does not understand the word *metamorphosis* would benefit from the second half of the sentence, which defines what a metamorphosis does: "changes people from a group into a mob." The reader can then know that events have just taken a pretty important turn. The good people of Maple Street have suddenly become another creature entirely.

As you read, be on the lookout for definitions provided in the text itself. Chances are, if you read a little past a difficult word, you may find that the writer has given you some help.

Word Bank

transfixed
intelligible
assent
intimidated
defiant

PRACTICE

Each sentence below contains an underlined word from the Word Bank as well as a **definition** of that word. For each item, identify the defining words. It might help to explore each word's meaning in a cluster diagram, like the one at the right for the word *transfixed*.

1. Steve stood <u>transfixed</u>, looking at the sky as if he had been nailed to the spot and couldn't move.
2. As the mob came closer, its words became more <u>intelligible</u>, allowing Mr. Goodman to hear and understand them.
3. The residents of Maple Street agreed that strange events were afoot, and when Pete Van Horn offered to investigate, everyone nodded <u>assent</u>.
4. People facing a mob would be <u>intimidated</u>, and their fright would be justified.
5. Tommy was quietly <u>defiant</u> when the adults laughed at him; he held his ground no matter what they said.

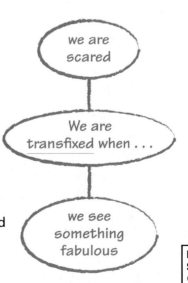

Reading Standard 1.3 Clarify word meanings through the use of definition.

Act Two

Fade in on the entry hall of the Goodman house at night. On the side table rests an unlit candle. MRS. GOODMAN *walks into the scene, a glass of milk in hand. She sets the milk down on the table, lights the candle with a match from a box on the table, picks up the glass of milk, and starts out of the scene. Cut to an outside shot.* MRS. GOODMAN *comes through her porch door, glass of milk in hand. The entry hall, with the table and lit candle, can be seen behind her. The camera slowly pans down the sidewalk, taking in little knots of people who stand around talking in low voices. At the end of each conversation they look toward* LES GOODMAN's *house. From the various houses we can see candlelight but no electricity. An all-pervading quiet blankets the area, disturbed only by the almost whispered voices of the people as they stand around. The camera pans over to one group where* CHARLIE *stands. He stares across at* GOODMAN's *house. Two men stand across the street from it, in almost sentrylike poses. We return to the group.*

Sally (*a little timorously[1]*). It just doesn't seem right, though, keeping watch on them. Why . . . he was right when he said he was one of our neighbors. Why, I've known Ethel Goodman ever since they moved in. We've been good friends—
Charlie. That don't prove a thing. Any guy who'd spend his time lookin' up at the sky early in the morning—well there's something wrong with that kind of a

person. There's something that ain't legitimate. Maybe under normal circumstances we could let it go by, but these aren't normal circumstances. Why, look at this street! Nothin' but candles. Why, it's like goin' back into the dark ages or somethin'!

[STEVE *walks down the steps of his porch. He walks down the street, over to* LES GOODMAN's *house, and stops at the foot of the steps.* GOODMAN *stands behind the screen door, his wife behind him, very frightened.*]

Goodman. Just stay right where you are, Steve. We don't want any trouble, but this time if anybody sets foot on my porch, that's what they're going to get—trouble!
Steve. Look, Les—
Goodman. I've already explained to you people. I don't sleep very well at night

---

1. **timorously** (tim′ər·əs·lē) *adv.:* timidly; fearfully.

sometimes. I get up and I take a walk and I look up at the sky. I look at the stars!

Mrs. Goodman. That's exactly what he does. Why this whole thing, it's . . . it's some kind of madness or something.

Steve (*nods grimly*). That's exactly what it is—some kind of madness.

Charlie's Voice (*shrill, from across the street*). You best watch who you're seen with, Steve! Until we get this all straightened out, you ain't exactly above suspicion yourself.

Steve (*whirling around toward him*). Or you, Charlie. Or any of us, it seems. From age eight on up!

Woman One. What I'd like to know is, what are we gonna do? Just stand around here all night?

Charlie. There's nothin' else we can do! (*He turns back looking toward* STEVE *and* GOODMAN *again.*) One of 'em'll tip their hand. They got to.

Steve (*raising his voice*). There's something you can do, Charlie. You could go home and keep your mouth shut. You could quit strutting around like a self-appointed hanging judge[2] and just climb into bed and forget it.

Charlie. You sound real anxious to have that happen, Steve. I think we better keep our eye on you too!

Don (*as if he were taking the bit in his teeth, takes a hesitant step to the front*). I think everything might as well come out now.

MAKING INFERENCES

6. What is Charlie suggesting about the fact that Steve is talking to Les Goodman? What can you suppose about the characters from this?

(*He turns toward* STEVE.) Your wife's done plenty of talking, Steve, about how odd you are!

Charlie (*picking this up, his eyes widening*). Go ahead, tell us what she's said.

[STEVE *walks toward them from across the street.*]

Steve. Go ahead, what's my wife said? Let's get it all out. Let's pick out every <u>idiosyncrasy</u> of every single man, woman, and child on the street. And then we might as well set up some kind of a kangaroo court.[3] How about a firing squad at dawn, Charlie, so we can get rid of all the suspects? Narrow them down. Make it easier for you.

Don. There's no need gettin' so upset, Steve. It's just that . . . well . . . Myra's talked about how there's been plenty of nights you spend hours down in your basement workin' on some kind of radio or something. Well, none of us have ever seen that radio—

[*By this time* STEVE *has reached the group. He stands there defiantly close to them.*]

Charlie. Go ahead, Steve. What kind of "radio set" you workin' on? I never seen it. Neither has anyone else. Who you talk to on that radio set? And who talks to you?

Steve. I'm surprised at you, Charlie. How come you're so dense all of a sudden? (*A pause*) Who do I talk to? I talk to monsters from outer space. I talk to three-headed green men who fly over here in what look like meteors.

---

3. kangaroo court: unauthorized court, usually one that pays no attention to legal procedures. Kangaroo courts were often set up in frontier areas.

Vocabulary
idiosyncrasy (id′ē·ō·sin′krə·sē) *n.*: peculiarity.

---

2. hanging judge: judge who sentences people to death without sufficient evidence.

[STEVE'S *wife steps down from their porch, bites her lip, calls out.*]

Mrs. Brand. Steve! Steve, please. (*Then looking around, frightened, she walks toward the group.*) It's just a ham radio[4] set, that's all. I bought him a book on it myself. It's just a ham radio set. A lot of people have them. I can show it to you. It's right down in the basement.

Steve (*whirls around toward her*). Show them nothing! If they want to look inside our house—let them get a search warrant.

Charlie. Look, buddy, you can't afford to—

Steve (*interrupting*). Charlie, don't tell me what I can afford! And stop telling me who's dangerous and who isn't and who's safe and who's a menace. (*He turns to the group and shouts.*) And you're with him too—all of you! You're standing here all set to crucify—all set to find a scapegoat—all desperate to point some kind of a finger at a neighbor! Well now look, friends, the only thing that's gonna happen is that we'll eat each other up alive—

[*He stops abruptly as* CHARLIE *suddenly grabs his arm.*]

Charlie (*in a hushed voice*). That's not the only thing that can happen to us.

[*Cut to a long shot looking down the street. A figure has suddenly materialized in the gloom, and in the silence we can hear the clickety-clack of slow, measured footsteps on concrete as the figure walks slowly toward them. One of the women lets out a stifled cry.[5] The young mother grabs her boy, as do a couple of others.*]

Tommy (*shouting, frightened*). It's the monster! It's the monster!

[*Another woman lets out a wail and the people fall back in a group, staring toward the darkness and the approaching figure. As the people stand in the shadows watching,* DON MARTIN *joins them, carrying a shotgun. He holds it up.*]

Don. We may need this.

Steve. A shotgun? (*He pulls it out of* DON'S *hand.*) Good Lord—will anybody think a thought around here? Will you people wise up? What good would a shotgun do against—

[*Now* CHARLIE *pulls the gun from* STEVE'S *hand.*]

Charlie. No more talk, Steve. You're going to talk us into a grave! You'd let whatever's out there walk right over us, wouldn't yuh? Well, some of us won't!

[*He swings the gun around to point it toward the sidewalk. The dark figure continues to walk toward them. The group stands there, fearful, apprehensive. Mothers clutch children, men stand in front of wives.* CHARLIE *slowly raises the gun. As the figure gets closer and closer, he suddenly pulls the trigger. The sound of it explodes in the stillness. The figure suddenly lets out a small cry, stumbles forward onto his knees, and then falls forward on his face.* DON, CHARLIE, *and* STEVE *race over to him.* STEVE *is there first and turns the man over. Now the crowd gathers around them.*]

Steve (*slowly looks up*). It's Pete Van Horn.

---

4. **ham radio:** two-way radio used by an amateur operator. Ham radio operators used to talk to one another all over the world via their radios.
5. **stifled** (stī′fəld) **cry:** cry that is checked or stopped.

Vocabulary
menace (men′əs) *n.*: danger; threat.

Don (*in a hushed voice*). Pete Van Horn! He was just gonna go over to the next block to see if the power was on—

Woman One. You killed him, Charlie. You shot him dead!

Charlie (*looks around at the circle of faces, his eyes frightened, his face contorted*). But . . . but I didn't know who he was. I certainly didn't know who he was. He comes walkin' out of the darkness—how am I supposed to know who he was? (*He grabs* STEVE.) Steve—you know why I shot! How was I supposed to know he wasn't a monster or something? (*He grabs* DON *now*.) We're all scared of the same thing. I was just tryin' to . . . tryin' to protect my home, that's all! Look, all of you, that's all I was tryin' to do. (*He looks down wildly at the body.*) I didn't know it was somebody we knew! I didn't know—

[*There's a sudden hush and then an intake of breath. We see the living room window of* CHARLIE*'s house. The window is not lit, but suddenly the house lights come on behind it.*]

Woman One (*in a very hushed voice*). Charlie . . . Charlie . . . the lights just went on in your house. Why did the lights just go on?

Don. What about it, Charlie? How come you're the only one with lights now?

Goodman. That's what I'd like to know.

[*There is a pause as they all stare toward* CHARLIE.]

You were so quick to kill, Charlie, and you were so quick to tell us who we had to be careful of. Well, maybe you had to kill. Maybe Peter there was trying to tell us something. Maybe he'd found out something and came back to tell us who there was amongst us we should watch out for—

[CHARLIE *backs away from the group, his eyes wide with fright.*]

Charlie. No . . . no . . . it's nothing of the sort! I don't know why the lights are on. I swear I don't. Somebody's pulling a gag or something.

[*He bumps against* STEVE, *who grabs him and whirls him around.*]

Steve. A gag? A gag? Charlie, there's a dead man on the sidewalk and you killed him! Does this thing look like a gag to you?

[CHARLIE *breaks away and screams as he runs toward his house.*]

Charlie. No! No! Please!

[*A man breaks away from the crowd to chase* CHARLIE. *The man tackles him and lands on top of him. The other people start to run toward them.* CHARLIE *is up on his feet. He breaks away from the other man's grasp and lands a couple of desperate punches that push the man aside. Then he forces his way, fighting, through the crowd to once again break free. He jumps up on his front porch. A rock thrown from the group smashes a window alongside of him, the broken glass flying past him. A couple of pieces cut him. He stands there perspiring, rumpled, blood running down from a cut on his cheek. His wife breaks away from the group to throw herself into his arms. He buries his face against her. We can see the crowd* <u>converging</u> *on the porch now.*]

📖 **MAKING INFERENCES**

7. What are the residents implying about Charlie? based on what evidence?

Voices.
It must have been him.
He's the one.
We got to get Charlie.

[*Another rock lands on the porch. Now* CHARLIE *pushes his wife behind him, facing the group.*]

Charlie. Look, look, I swear to you . . . it isn't me . . . but I do know who it is . . . I swear to you, I do know who it is. I know who the monster is here. I know who it is that doesn't belong. I swear to you I know.
Goodman (*shouting*). What are you waiting for?
Woman One (*shouting*). Come on, Charlie, come on.
Man One (*shouting*). Who is it, Charlie, tell us!
Don (*pushing his way to the front of the crowd*). All right, Charlie, let's hear it!

[CHARLIE*'s eyes dart around wildly.*]

Charlie. It's . . . it's . . .
Man Two (*screaming*). Go ahead, Charlie, tell us.
Charlie. It's . . . it's the kid. It's Tommy. He's the one.

[*There's a gasp from the crowd as we cut to a shot of the mother holding her boy. The boy at first doesn't understand. Then, realizing the eyes are all on him, he buries his face against his mother,* SALLY.]

Sally (*backs away*). That's crazy. That's crazy. He's a little boy.
Woman One. But he knew! He was the only

Vocabulary
converging (kən·vʉrj′iŋ) *v.* used as *adj.*: closing in.

one who knew! He told us all about it. Well, how did he know? How could he have known?

[*The various people take this up and repeat the questions aloud.*]

Voices.
How could he know?
Who told him?
Make the kid answer.

MAKING INFERENCES
8. What inference have the residents made about Tommy?

Man One. What about Goodman's car?
Don. It was Charlie who killed old man Van Horn.
Woman One. But it was the kid here who knew what was going to happen all the time. He was the one who knew!

[STEVE *shouts at his hysterical neighbors.*]

Steve. Are you all gone crazy? (*Pause as he looks about*) Stop.

[*A fist crashes at* STEVE'*s face, staggering him back out of view. Several close camera shots suggest the coming of violence: A hand fires a rifle. A fist clenches. A hand grabs the hammer from* VAN HORN'*s body, etc.*]

Don. Charlie has to be the one— Where's my rifle—
Woman One. Les Goodman's the one. His car started! Let's wreck it.
Mrs. Goodman. What about Steve's radio— He's the one that called them—
Mr. Goodman. Smash the radio. Get me a hammer. Get me something.
Steve. Stop— Stop—
Charlie. Where's that kid— Let's get him.
Man One. Get Steve— Get Charlie— They're working together.

[*The crowd starts to converge around the*

mother, who grabs her son and starts to run with him. The crowd starts to follow, at first, walking fast, and then running after him. Suddenly, CHARLIE's lights go off and the lights in another house go on. They stay on for a moment, then from across the street other lights go on and then off again.*]

Man One (*shouting*). It isn't the kid. . . . It's Bob Weaver's house.
Woman One. It isn't Bob Weaver's house, it's Don Martin's place.
Charlie. I tell you, it's the kid.
Don. It's Charlie. He's the one.

[*The people shout, accuse, scream. The camera tilts back and forth. We see panic-stricken faces in close-up and tilting shots of houses as the lights go on and off. Slowly, in the middle of this nightmarish morass[6] of sight and sound, the camera starts to pull away, until once again we've reached the opening shot, looking at the Maple Street sign from high above. The camera continues to move away until we dissolve to a shot of the metal side of a spacecraft, which sits shrouded[7] in darkness. An open door throws out a beam of light from the illuminated interior. Two figures silhouetted against the bright lights appear. We get only a vague feeling of form, but nothing more* explicit *than that.*]

Figure One. Understand the procedure now? Just stop a few of their machines and radios

---

6. **morass** (mə·ras′) *n.:* confusing situation. Strictly speaking, a morass is a kind of swamp.

7. **shrouded** (shroud′əd) *n. used as adj.:* hidden; covered. A shroud is a cloth that a dead person is wrapped in.

Vocabulary
explicit (eks·plis′it) *adj.:* definite; clearly stated.

and telephones and lawn mowers . . . throw them into darkness for a few hours and then you just sit back and watch the pattern.

Figure Two. And this pattern is always the same?

Figure One. With few <u>variations</u>. They pick the most dangerous enemy they can find . . . and it's themselves. And all we need do is sit back . . . and watch.

Figure Two. Then I take it this place . . . this Maple Street . . . is not unique.

Figure One (*shaking his head*). By no means. Their world is full of Maple Streets. And we'll go from one to the other and let them destroy themselves. One to the other . . . one to the other . . . one to the other—

MAKING INFERENCES

9. What can you infer about the aliens' view of the human race?

[*Now the camera pans up for a shot of the starry sky.*]

Narrator's Voice. The tools of conquest do not necessarily come with bombs and explosions and fallout. There are weapons that are simply thoughts, attitudes, prejudices—to be found only in the minds of men. For the record, prejudices can kill and suspicion can destroy, and a thoughtless, frightened search for a scapegoat has a fallout all of its own for the children . . . the children yet unborn. (*A pause*) And the pity of it is . . . that these things cannot be confined to . . . The Twilight Zone!

[*Fade to black.*]

Vocabulary
variations (ver′ē·ā′shənz) *n.*: differences.

Rod Serling

Man from Another Dimension

Rod Serling (1924–1975) was a man of great energy. He had the vitality of one who seems to be running even as he is standing still.

How does a fledgling writer caught in a dreamless job get from Cincinnati, Ohio, to New York City and then to Hollywood? If you're Rod Serling, you one day look at your wife, and together you decide that the hour has come to sink or swim—the hour has come to go for it.

In the early 1950s, Rod Serling eagerly arrived in New York and found himself a job writing for television when it was new and young. He first wrote for a live half-hour drama called *Lux Video Theatre.* From there he went on to create and produce the hit television show *The Twilight Zone.*

In the fifth-dimensional world of the Twilight Zone, Serling made his concerns and beliefs visible. He sought to show his audiences that "there is nothing in the dark that isn't there when the lights are on." In his widely known teleplay *The Monsters Are Due on Maple Street*, he dramatized what was perhaps his most enduring and urgent theme.

The teleplay was written at a time when Americans were concerned about the spread of communism to the United States. Thousands of lives were destroyed by suspicion and suggestion. People lost their jobs, homes, and friends when they were accused of being members of the Communist party, even though membership in the party was legal. During this time some people made up stories about others in order to appear innocent themselves, and many people were afraid to continue friendships with those who had been accused or were suspected of being members of the Communist party. Rod Serling could not write about these events directly for television; the show would not have made it on the air. Yet in *The Monsters Are Due on Maple Street,* he does voice his opinion.

For Independent Reading

Enter the fifth dimension by checking out Rod Serling's *The Twilight Zone: Complete Stories.*

Literary Response and Analysis
Acts One and Two

Reading Check

1. What causes the residents to suspect Steve?

2. How does Charlie respond to Pete Van Horn's reappearance? What happens next?

3. What do you finally learn about the aliens' plans?

4. According to the aliens, who is the most dangerous enemy?

Interpretations

5. Choose three **inferences** you made as you read the teleplay. Were your inferences correct?

6. Fill out a chart like the one that follows to show the bare bones of the play's **plot.** Be sure to compare your charts in class. You might have different opinions about the number of key events, or **complications,** that lead to the surprising resolution.

Climax

Event —

Resolution

Event —

Event —

(Add as many events as you need.)

Event —

Basic situation

7. Who are the "monsters"?

8. Writers often speak through a particular character to voice their own opinions. Which character do you think reflects Rod Serling's **point of view**? Find at least two speeches that reveal that point of view.

9. In light of Les Goodman's behavior throughout the plot, what **inference** can you make about the significance of his name?

10. **Symbols** in literature are persons, places, or things that function as themselves but that can also stand for larger ideas, such as love, glory, or honor. When Maple Street loses power and is plunged into darkness, terrible events unfold. This loss of power is also a symbol for a larger idea. What personal power, or ability, do the residents of Maple Street lose that plunges them further into darkness?

11. This teleplay was written in 1960. Is its message still important today? Explain why or why not.

Reading Standard 3.2 Identify events that advance the plot, and determine how each event explains past or present action(s) or foreshadows future action(s).

Writing

Worded Weapons

What message does the play deliver about humankind? How do the events of the teleplay illustrate this message? In a two-paragraph essay, write your response to this play. In one paragraph, explain the meaning of the closing comments in light of the events of this teleplay. In the second paragraph, tell how you feel about the message in the play, and explain how the message still has significance in today's world (unless you believe otherwise!).

Maple Street, 2010

Suppose you are a television producer and you want to update the teleplay so that it takes place in 2010. In a paragraph, tell how you would change details of the play to set it in the new time frame. Consider these details:

- What do people now know about aliens and space travel?

- What electronic equipment would be affected by the blackout?

- Where would the aliens land (would you keep a small town as your setting or would you set the revised story in a suburb or a city)?

- What would Tommy be reading today?

Grade 6 Review Reading Standard 3.7 Explain the effects of common literary devices (for example, symbolism) in fictional texts.

Vocabulary Development Act Two

Clarifying Word Meanings: Definitions

Sharpen your definition-hunting skills with the following exercise.

PRACTICE

Choose the word from the Word Bank that best fits the blank in each sentence below. Remember to look for definitions within each sentence to help you decide. Be ready to cite the definition you found in the sentence.

1. Wherever the aliens go, the human beings react the same: There are few differences, few changes, few _____.

2. During the second act the crowd's fear, mistrust, and suspicion are meeting, or _____, to create a mob.

3. An _____ danger is by its nature knowable and understandable.

4. A frightened man with a gun can be considered a _____ and a danger to society.

5. Steve's interest in ham radios becomes a threat rather than an oddity, or _____, that makes him unique.

Reading Standard 1.3
Clarify word meanings through the use of definition.

Cellular Telephone Owner's Manual

Structure and Purpose of Informational Materials: An Instructional Manual

For the residents of Maple Street, not even cell phones might have been helpful against the aliens' powers. However, for you and your family, a cell phone might be just the kind of device to get you out of a crisis—if you know how to use one, that is. With all the electronic products available today, it's useful to know how to read an instructional manual.

The **purpose** of an instructional manual is to help you operate and care for a specific device, such as a cordless phone or a hand-held Internet appliance. Many instructional manuals have a **structure** like that of a small textbook.

Use these strategies in order to make the best use of an instructional manual:

- Scan the **table of contents** of the manual to get an idea of the topics covered.

- If you don't see the topic you're looking for, turn to the **index,** located in the back of the manual. This is an alphabetical list of the topics and the page numbers on which they appear.

- Look for a regular mail address and an **e-mail address** as well as a customer service **phone number** or **Web site** where you can get additional help from the manufacturer.

- Become familiar with the parts of the device. An instructional manual usually includes a **diagram** showing you the important parts of the device and explaining their functions.

- Read the **directions** carefully, and keep referring to the actual device as you read.

- Do the directions have **steps**? Follow them in order. Read all the directions for a procedure before you move on to the next one.

- Make sure you understand any special abbreviations or symbols. You may find definitions and meanings in the manual's **glossary**—an alphabetical list of special terms and their definitions.

Reading Standard 2.1 Understand and analyze the differences in structure and purpose of informational materials (for example, instructional manuals).

Cellular Telephone Owner's Manual

Battery Removal and Replacement

There are two ways to remove and replace your telephone battery—the standard method and the quick-change method.

Standard Method

1. Turn off your telephone.
2. Depress the latch button on the rear of the battery, and slide the battery pack downward until it stops.
3. Lift the battery clear to remove.
4. To reinstall, place the battery pack on the unit so that its grooves align, and slide upward (in the direction of the arrows on the back of the phone) until it clicks into place.

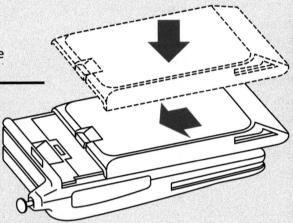

Quick-Change Method

1. Advise the party you are talking to that you are about to change batteries.
2. Remove the battery from the telephone.
3. Put on the spare battery.
4. Press PWR. This will return you to your telephone call. You will have only five seconds to complete this action before your telephone call is terminated.

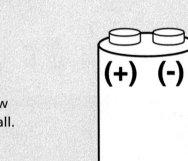

The quick-change method allows you to remove your telephone battery at any time and replace it with a charged spare battery during a telephone call. This is especially useful if you receive the "low battery" message (or an audible tone) during a call.

It is a good idea to practice this procedure a few times before using it during an actual phone call.

Reading Informational Materials

Reading Check

Use the following chart to compare these informational materials: newspapers, textbooks, and instructional manuals. Be sure to compare your charts in class.

Material	Purpose	Structure
Newspaper articles		
Textbooks		
Instructional manuals		

TestPractice

Cellular Telephone Owner's Manual

1. The **main topic** of the section of the manual on page 92 is —
   A   removing and replacing the battery
   B   making and receiving calls
   C   using the phone to send e-mail
   D   using the phone in out-of-state networks

2. In which part of the manual would you look to find the pages on which the topic of ringer volume appears?
   F   Diagram
   G   Glossary
   H   Index
   J   Cover

3. In which part of the manual would you look to find the meaning of the abbreviation *LCD*?
   A   Table of contents
   B   Glossary
   C   Index
   D   Cover

4. The first step in the standard method is to —
   F   remove the battery
   G   tell the person you're speaking with to call back
   H   turn off the phone
   J   turn off the "low battery" message

5. The first step in the quick-change method is to —
   A   put in the spare battery
   B   remove the battery
   C   tell the person you're speaking with that you're going to change the battery
   D   ask the person you're speaking with to call you back after you've changed the battery

6. After you put in the spare battery using the quick-change method, your call will be terminated unless you —
   F   press PWR within five seconds
   G   deposit twenty-five cents
   H   charge the telephone battery
   J   press 0 for further assistance

Reading Standard 2.1
Understand and analyze the differences in structure and purpose of informational materials (for example, instructional manuals).

SIGNS

Structure and Purpose of Informational Materials: Signs

Information can come from many sources. One of the most common ways we communicate information is through the use of signs. Sometimes signs are the only sources of information we have. Sometimes understanding them can be a matter of life or death.

Imagine that the monsters who arrive on Maple Street encounter some of the signs that we earthlings use to communicate information, such as directions, warnings, and indications of specific locations. The signs are supposed to contain symbols and markings that can be universally understood. To interpret the signs, the monsters would have to look at the signs' major image and color. They would also have to be aware of any associations they have with the signs. How do you think they would manage?

Here are some facts about signs:

- There are 58 million traffic signs on our nation's roads.

- Uniform pictorial signs were first developed in Europe so that tourists could understand road signs.

- In a large city a traffic light might control the movements of nearly 100,000 vehicles a day.

- The skull-and-crossbones sign (see page 95) was flown on pirate ships to indicate that anyone who came across the ship's path would die.

- Signs that indicate danger usually have an odd shape (like a triangle) and a bright color.

- Signs indicating where travelers can eat or rest or get gas are usually in blue, white, or green—colors that are supposed to suggest relaxation. Red usually indicates something dangerous or forbidden.

Our world is full of signs. Language itself is a sign system—a very sophisticated one. See if you can identify what the signs on the next page mean.

BONUS QUESTION

Each new age needs new signs. Create a sign we might need involving the use of cellular phones. Create another sign we could use for a computer-virus alert.

Reading Standard 2.1
Understand and analyze the differences in structure and purpose of informational materials (for example, signs).

What would clue you in to the fact that this sign means "danger"?

Which sign means "dogs are allowed"? Which sign means "better not even think about it"? What symbols give you that information?

Imagine that you have just arrived for the first time at the airport in Mexico City. If you need information, would these signs help you? What clues give you your answer? Why wouldn't the *i* sign work in every country?

If you were driving along a road and saw this sign, would you continue? Why or why not?

Signs say a great deal with only a few sketchy lines. What does this sign say to you?

When you travel, you might need a drugstore. If you know Greek mythology, you can describe what this universal symbol for pharmacy means.

Imagine that you were at the Olympic Games and wanted to get to the soccer game. Which symbol would help you? How do you know? What does the other sign mean? How do you know?

Here is a familiar sign. What is it saying?

Literary Response and Analysis

DIRECTIONS: Read the following story. Then, read each question, and write the letter of the best response.

The Dinner Party

Mona Gardner

The country is India. A colonial official and his wife are giving a large dinner party. They are seated with their guests—army officers and government attachés[1] and their wives, and a visiting American naturalist[2]—in their spacious dining room, which has a bare marble floor, open rafters, and wide glass doors opening onto a veranda.

A spirited discussion springs up between a young girl who insists that women have outgrown the jumping-on-a-chair-at-the-sight-of-a-mouse era and a colonel who says that they haven't.

"A woman's unfailing reaction in any crisis," the colonel says, "is to scream. While a man may feel like it, he has that ounce more of nerve control than a woman has. That last ounce is what counts."

The American does not join in the argument but watches the other guests. As he looks, he sees a strange expression come over the face of the hostess. She is staring straight ahead, her muscles contracting slightly. With a slight gesture she summons the Indian boy standing behind her chair and whispers to him. The boy's eyes widen; he quickly leaves the room.

Of the guests, none except the American notices this nor sees the boy place a bowl of milk on the veranda just outside the open doors.

The American comes to with a start. In India, milk in a bowl means only one thing—bait for a snake. He realizes there must be a cobra in the room. He looks up at the rafters—the likeliest place—but they are bare. Three corners of the room are empty, and in the fourth the servants are waiting to serve the next course. There is only one place left—under the table.

His first impulse is to jump back and warn the others, but he knows the commotion would frighten the cobra into striking. He speaks quickly, the tone of his voice so arresting that it sobers everyone.

"I want to know just what control everyone at this table has. I will count to three hundred—that's five minutes—and not one of you is to move a

---

1. **attachés** (at′ə·shāz′) *n.*: diplomatic officials.
2. **naturalist** *n.*: person who studies nature by observing animals and plants.

Reading Standard 3.2
Identify events that advance the plot, and determine how each event explains past or present action(s) or foreshadows future action(s).

muscle. Those who move will forfeit[3] fifty rupees.[4] Ready!"

The twenty people sit like stone images while he counts. He is saying ". . . two hundred and eighty . . ." when, out of the corner of his eye, he sees the cobra emerge and make for the bowl of milk. Screams ring out as he

_____

3. **forfeit** (fôr′fit) *v.*: give up as a penalty.
4. **rupees** (rōō′pēz) *n.*: Indian money, like dollars in the United States.

jumps to slam the veranda doors safely shut.

"You were right, Colonel!" the host exclaims. "A man has just shown us an example of perfect control."

"Just a minute," the American says, turning to his hostess. "Mrs. Wynnes, how did you know that cobra was in the room?"

A faint smile lights up the woman's face as she replies: "Because it was crawling across my foot."

---

1. The **setting** of this story is colonial —
   - A America
   - B India
   - C Africa
   - D Australia

2. Which of the following events in the **plot** of the story happens first?
   - F The American challenges the guests to remain still.
   - G A cobra is attracted to milk.
   - H The hostess whispers to a servant.
   - J The colonel argues with a girl.

3. What **later event** explains the strange expression on the hostess's face?
   - A A cobra has crawled across her foot.
   - B She dislikes the colonel's biased opinions about women.
   - C The servant is not doing his job.
   - D She sees a cobra on the veranda.

4. What **later event** explains why the boy places the milk on the veranda?
   - F The colonel's speech bores him.
   - G The American sees a cobra.
   - H A cobra makes for the milk.
   - J The American proposes a challenge.

5. What event marks the **climax** of the story?
   - A The argument between the girl and the colonel ends.
   - B The boy places a bowl of milk on the veranda.
   - C The American begins to count.
   - D The cobra emerges, and screams ring out.

6. The **resolution** of the story shows all of the following *except* that the —
   - F colonel was right
   - G colonel was wrong
   - H young girl was right
   - J hostess is brave

Reading Comprehension

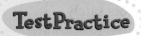

TestPractice DIRECTIONS: Read the following materials. Then, read each question, and choose the letter of the best response.

SIGN

TEXTBOOK

CHAPTER 2 **Biomes: World Plant Regions**

What is a biome? A plant and animal community that covers a very large land area is called a **biome**. Plants are the most visible part of a biome. If you looked down on the United States from space, you would see various biomes. The forests of the eastern United States would appear green, while the deserts of the Southwest would be light brown.

NEWSPAPER ARTICLE

B2

Hatteras Lighthouse Completes Its Move

BUXTON, N.C., July 9 (AP)—As onlookers clapped and cheered, the Cape Hatteras Lighthouse slid today onto the concrete pad where its caretakers hope it will stand for another century, a safe distance from the thundering Atlantic surf.

INSTRUCTIONAL MANUAL

Reading Standard 2.1
Understand and analyze the differences in structure and purpose between various categories of informational materials (for example, textbooks, newspapers, instructional manuals, signs).

page 32

Looking Up Synonyms for a Word in a Document
1. Select the word in the document.
2. Choose Utilities Thesaurus (Alt,U,T), or press the THESAURUS key (Shift+F7).
3. Look through the list of synonyms in Synonyms. Scroll through the list if necessary.

Command for Thesaurus
Utilities Thesaurus or THESAURUS key (Shift+F7)

Lists alternative words for the selection

Thesaurus: English (US)   ? X

Looked Up:	Replace with Synonym:
Important	significant

Meanings: | Replace |
significant (adj.)	significant	Look Up
pompous (adj.)	substantial	Cancel
Antonyms	consequential	
Related Words	considerable	Revise
	meaningful	
	material	
	momentous	
	weighty	

1. Which statement explains the difference between the **purpose** of a textbook and the purpose of a newspaper article?

   A A textbook has an index, a glossary, and graphic features, while a newspaper article has an inverted pyramid structure.

   B A textbook has a table of contents and an index, while a newspaper article has a headline, a dateline, and a byline.

   C A textbook gives lots of information about a big subject, while a newspaper article gives information about a current event.

   D A textbook has many pages, while a newspaper article is usually one page long or less.

2. In comparing the **structure** of a textbook and the structure of an instructional manual, you could say that —

   F they both have a table of contents, a glossary, an index, and graphic features, but a textbook is much longer

   G a textbook presents information about a big subject, but an instructional manual presents information about how to operate and use a device

   H a textbook is something you use in a classroom, but a manual is something you use at work or at home

   J a textbook is something your school gives you to use, but a manual comes with something you buy

3. In the **textbook** excerpt the word biome means —

   A a community of plants growing in a forest

   B plants and sand that are found in desert areas

   C the coastal areas of the United States as seen from outer space

   D a plant and animal community that covers a large area

4. The **instructional manual** shown on page 98 gives instructions on how to —

   F find biomes

   G move a lighthouse

   H look up synonyms

   J use the Internet

5. The **sign** shown on page 98 indicates a place to —

   A eat

   B sleep

   C buy knives and forks

   D buy gas

6. The **newspaper article** on page 98 shows all of the following features *except* a —

   F byline

   G dateline

   H summary lead

   J headline

Vocabulary Development

TestPractice

Multiple-Meaning Words

DIRECTIONS: Each sentence below is from "Rikki-tikki-tavi." Read the sentence. Then, choose the answer in which the underlined word is used the same way.

1. "He . . . put his fur in order, scratched himself, and jumped on the small boy's shoulder."
   A The order of the processional will be shortest person to tallest.
   B The new order could not be filled because there were no more boxes.
   C The meeting will come to order.
   D Coming out of the water, the swimmer swept his hair back into order.

2. "She had crept up behind him as he was talking, to make an end of him. . . ."
   F The fullback carried the ball into the end zone and scored a touchdown.
   G The end of the story was too sad.
   H The dinner guest looked as if it would be the end of him if he had to eat one more bite.
   J Mr. Lee lives at the end of the road.

3. "When a snake misses its stroke, it never says anything or gives any sign of what it means to do next."
   A On the stroke of midnight, the old year gives way to the new year.
   B Winning the football pool was a stroke of good luck.
   C With one more stroke of the ax, the tree was felled.
   D It was said that the neighbor on the corner had suffered a stroke.

4. "Rikki-tikki knew he was a young mongoose, and it made him all the more pleased to think that he had managed to escape a blow from behind."
   F Which way does the wind blow?
   G There is one more candle to blow out.
   H Jack felled the giant with one blow.
   J Stop now, and blow your nose.

5. "He spread out his hood more than ever, and Rikki-tikki saw the spectacle mark on the back of it that looks exactly like the eye part of a hook-and-eye fastening."
   A Mark my words, no good will come of this.
   B This mark indicates the ball is mine.
   C He hopes to get a higher mark in geometry this semester.
   D Saying "thank you" is a mark of good manners.

Mastering the Standards

SHORT STORY

Minor Failings

When writers start out, they often write about their own experiences, which they disguise as fiction. Think back to the minor failings you wrote about in your Quickwrite before reading "Duffy's Jacket" (page 7). Do you see story possibilities in those personal experiences? Fill out a chart like the following one to gather your ideas for a short story based on something in that list. Remember: The more you work on your story ideas, the further your story will get from your actual experience. You might want to end your story with a surprising twist, the way Bruce Coville did. Also in imitation of Coville, try to write dialogue that sounds like real people talking.

Characters	Setting	Basic situation	Conflict or problem	Main events (complications)	Climax	Resolution

> Use "Writing a Short Story," pages 536–557, for help with this assignment.

Other Choices

AUTOBIOGRAPHICAL NARRATIVE

1 **A True Story**

Almost everyone who writes an **autobiography**—a story of the writer's own life—includes an account of a childhood encounter with some kind of cruelty or meanness. The incident might involve a schoolyard bully, or perhaps it is the writer who was cruel to another person and regrets it later. Before you read "Rikki-tikki-tavi," you took notes on times when you or someone you knew faced a bully. You might expand those notes into a true narrative. Be sure to describe how you or the other main actor in the story felt about the encounter with cruelty.

> Use "Writing an Autobiographical Narrative," pages 704–706, for help with this assignment.

DESCRIPTIVE WRITING

2 **A Strange Setting**

A deserted ship, an army of flesh-eating rats, a lonely lighthouse—these are the elements of the **setting** in "Three Skeleton Key" that make our flesh crawl. You might want to write a story—either real or imagined—that has a strange or scary or magical setting. Remember that the setting should be described in a way that appeals to the reader's senses. Use language that helps the reader to see the setting, smell it, taste it, hear its sounds, and perhaps even feel its temperatures. In many narratives the setting is part of the conflict: The characters must struggle against the setting to survive.

> Use "Writing a Short Story," pages 536–557, for help with this assignment.

Fiction

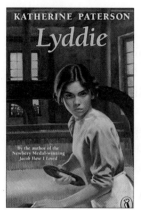

Working Girl

In Katherine Paterson's *Lyddie,* set in the 1840s, Lyddie Worthen has to grow up fast when her mother is forced to abandon the family farm. When she finds a job in a textile mill, Lyddie faces a grim new world of poverty and eighteen-hour workdays. A true heroine, Lyddie fights against injustice as she struggles to earn enough to buy back the family farm.

First Division

Sixth-graders from Barlow Road and Bear Creek Ridge have developed a serious softball rivalry that has lasted more than fifty years, and the 1949 game looks to be one of the most exciting yet. But the shadow of World War II looms over the game when Shazam—whose father was killed at Pearl Harbor—attacks Aki—who spent years in an internment camp. The townspeople are left to wonder what has happened to their community since the war ended. Virginia Euwer Wolff's *Bat 6* takes a brave look at prejudice, responsibility, and growing up.

This title is available in the HRW Library.

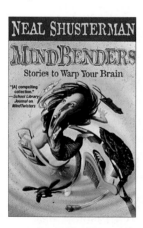

Strange Happenings

What if you were vacationing in Hawaii and you made a volcano goddess angry? Could you imagine being struck by lightning and finding yourself 140 years in the past? What would you do if you woke up one morning and saw seven guardian angels talking to one another in your bedroom? Neal Shusterman presents these wacky situations and more in *MindBenders.*

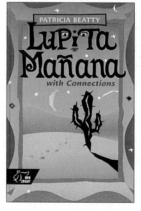

A Life of Danger

In *Lupita Mañana* by Patricia Beatty, Lupita Torres enters California illegally and tries to help support her widowed mother and younger siblings in Mexico by finding a job. Her search for a better life becomes a struggle in a place where the laws are not always fair and growing up is not always easy.

This title is available in the HRW Library.

Nonfiction

Courage in China

When Ji-Li Jiang turned twelve in 1966, she was an intelligent student with a bright future ahead of her. Then Mao Tse-tung launched the Cultural Revolution in China, and her family's background was revealed. As a result, Ji-Li's friends turned their backs on her, and her family suffered repeated abuse at the hands of Chinese officials. Ji-Li recalls her childhood of bravery and loyalty in *Red Scarf Girl*.

This title is available in the HRW Library.

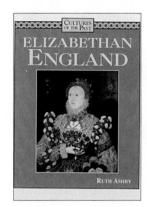

Back in Shakespeare's Day...

Ruth Ashby goes back to the sixteenth century in *Elizabethan England*. Ashby details the lives of prominent historical figures such as Henry VIII and Sir Walter Raleigh and authors such as Sir Thomas More and William Shakespeare. She also describes the religious and social customs of the English people at the time. Helpful maps and illustrations are included.

Snakes, Snakes, and More Snakes

Are you interested in snakes? Dr. Robert Mason is *really* interested in them. For over fifteen years he has been researching the world's largest concentration of garter snakes, located in Manitoba, Canada. Sy Montgomery accompanied Dr. Mason on his field study and, in *The Snake Scientist,* recorded some of the amazing things he learned.

The Story Behind the News Stories

Newspapers have riveted the American public with troubling and sensational stories since the founding of our country. They are perhaps the single most important medium for conveying information, shaping public opinion, and spreading awareness of the world around us. In *Behind the Headlines,* Thomas Fleming explores in exacting detail the people and events that make the news.

2 Characters
Living Many Lives

California Standards

Here are the Grade 7 standards you will study for mastery in Chapter 2. You will also review standards from earlier grades.

Word Analysis, Fluency, and Systematic Vocabulary Development

1.2 Use knowledge of Greek, Latin, and Anglo-Saxon roots and affixes to understand content-area vocabulary.

Grade 3 Review
1.6 Use sentence and word context to find the meaning of unknown words.

Reading Comprehension (Focus on Informational Materials)

Grade 5 Review
2.5 Distinguish facts, supported inferences, and opinions in text.

Grade 6 Review
2.2 Analyze text that uses the compare-and-contrast organizational pattern.

Literary Response and Analysis

3.3 Analyze characterization as delineated through a character's thoughts, words, speech patterns, and actions; the narrator's description; and the thoughts, words, and actions of other characters.

Grade 6 Review
3.5 Identify the speaker, and recognize the difference between first- and third-person narration (for example, autobiography compared with biography).

CALIFORNIA STANDARDS

KEYWORD:
HLLA 7-2

Characterization *by* Mara Rockliff

ALL ABOUT THE PEOPLE WE MEET

Getting to Know You

Wouldn't life be easier if the people you met just wore T-shirts that told you what they were like? You'd know right away if the girl who just moved in next door was "SNOBBY AND CONCEITED" or "FRIENDLY, WITH A GREAT SENSE OF HUMOR." That substitute teacher? Better not mess with her—she's "TOUGH BUT FAIR." You won't have to wonder whether your new science partner will be fun or annoying. His T-shirt says it all.

Show Me a Story

If you read a novel written a hundred years ago or more, the writer may just tell you directly, "Old Luther was the meanest old cuss in five counties," or "Little Posy was barely half the size of the other orphans, but she had pluck." Those kinds of statements, in which the writer tells you directly what a character is like, are known as **direct characterization.**

These days, though, writers try to make their stories more like real life. Writers want you to get to know fictional characters just as you get to know people in real life—not by reading a statement on a T-shirt, but by observing people very closely and deciding for yourself what kinds of people they are. You ask: What do they look like? How do they act? What do they say and how do they say it? How do other people feel about them?

© The New Yorker Collection 1992 Edward Koren from cartoonbank.com All Rights Reserved.

One of the first pieces of advice a new writer always hears is "Show, don't tell." Telling is the old way—**direct characterization.** Most writers (and readers) think showing is more interesting and realistic than just telling. This "showing" method of revealing a character is called indirect characterization. In **indirect characterization** you have to observe the character and come to your own conclusion about the kind of person you are meeting.

Who Is This Character, Anyway?

So how does a writer *show* what a character is like?

1 Appearance. Appearances can sometimes deceive, but they're often your first clue to character. Does the grandfather in the story have laugh lines around his eyes or a furrowed brow from years of worrying? Is the trial

Reading Standard 3.3 Analyze characterization as delineated through a character's thoughts, words, speech patterns, and actions; the narrator's description; and the thoughts, words, and actions of other characters.

lawyer cool and collected in her expensive, neatly pressed suit, or is she a sweat-soaked, wrinkled mess?

2 **Action.** The writer could *tell* you, "The boy was happy," but if you see the boy in action, you'll know for yourself.

Luis danced into the kitchen, singing along with the song on the radio. He paused just long enough to give his mother a loud kiss on the cheek, then danced on out the door.

3 **Speech.** Listen to a character talk, and she will tell you what she's like—*indirectly.* A four-year-old may not announce, "Hi! I'm bratty and stubborn," but doesn't the following outburst reveal the same thing?

"I don't have to do what you say!" screamed Darlene as she kicked the new baby sitter in the shins.

4 **Thoughts and feelings.** Here's where literature is better than life. In some books you can actually read what people are thinking, and what they think shows who they are.

Julie wanted to cry when she saw the stray cat. Its ribs were showing. She desperately wanted to add it to her well-fed tribe of cats at home.

5 **Other characters' reactions.** What do the other people in the story think of this character? What do they say about her? How do they act toward him? Of course, just as in life, you have to consider the source. If a character has something insulting to say about everyone in his school, his comments probably tell you more about *him* than about the others.

Practice

Write down the name of a character from a story you have recently read. Choose two or three words that describe that character, write those words under the name, and then draw a circle around each word. Now, go back to the story, and find examples of how the writer shows you those characteristics. (Notice **appearance, action, speech, thoughts,** and **other characters' reactions.**) Jot down the examples, circle them, and draw lines connecting them to the main circle.

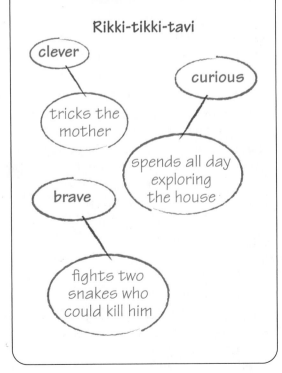

Rikki-tikki-tavi

clever

curious

tricks the mother

spends all day exploring the house

brave

fights two snakes who could kill him

Mother and Daughter

Literary Focus
Character Traits

A **character** is anyone who plays a part in a story. A **character trait** is a quality in a person that can't be seen. Character traits are revealed through a person's appearance, words, actions, and thoughts. Character traits can also be revealed in the ways a person affects other people. As you read "Mother and Daughter," notice how the writer helps you get to know this mother and her daughter. What are their character traits (the qualities they carry inside)?

Reading Skills
Making Inferences

To find a character's traits, you have to make inferences. **Inferences** are educated guesses, based on whatever evidence you have. If you wake up in the morning and see puddles in the streets, you could infer that it rained the night before. If you read a story in which a character always mentors kids who need help reading, you could infer that she is a caring person. As you read "Mother and Daughter," look for details in the story that can help you make inferences about the characters. To collect evidence, look for answers to questions like these:

- What do I know about the character's looks, thoughts, words, and actions?

- How do other characters react to the character?

- What does the character learn by the end of the story?

Make the Connection
Quickwrite ✏️

Like the characters in a story, real people have **character traits** too. Think about your experiences with people. What makes you like or dislike someone? In your journal, make a list of four or five character traits that you admire most in people and a list of those you like the least.

Vocabulary Development

Here are some words you'll learn as you read the story:

matinees (mat″n·āz′) *n.*: afternoon performances of a play or a movie. *Yollie and her mother got along well enough to go to matinees together at the local theater.*

antics (an′tiks) *n.*: playful or silly acts. *People who witnessed Mrs. Moreno's antics couldn't help laughing.*

meager (mē′gər) *adj.*: slight; small amount. *Mrs. Moreno remembers that her parents worked hard for their meager salaries.*

sophisticated (sə·fis′tə·kāt′id) *adj.*: worldly; elegant and refined. *Yollie admired the way sophisticated people in New York dressed.*

tirade (tī′rād′) *n.*: long, scolding speech. *Yollie felt bad about her tirade against her mom.*

Reading Standard 3.3
Analyze characterization as delineated through a character's thoughts, words, speech patterns, and actions; the narrator's description; and the thoughts, words, and actions of other characters.

Mother and Daughter

Gary Soto

next door, was too tired to be scared. Her eyes closed but sprang open when her mother screamed, "Look, Yollie! Oh, you missed a scary part. The guy's face was all ugly!"

But Yollie couldn't keep her eyes open. They fell shut again and stayed shut, even when her mother screamed and slammed a heavy palm on the arm of her chair.

"Mom, wake me up when the movie's over so I can go to bed," mumbled Yollie.

"OK, Yollie, I wake you," said her mother through a mouthful of popcorn.

But after the movie ended, instead of waking her daughter, Mrs. Moreno laughed under her breath, turned the TV and lights off, and tiptoed to bed. Yollie woke up in the middle of the night and didn't know where she was. For a moment she thought she was dead. Maybe something from the underworld had lifted her from her house and carried her into the earth's belly. She blinked her sleepy eyes, looked around at the darkness, and called, "Mom? Mom, where are you?" But there was no answer, just the throbbing hum of the refrigerator.

Finally, Yollie's grogginess cleared and she realized her mother had gone to bed, leaving her on the couch. Another of her little jokes.

But Yollie wasn't laughing. She tiptoed into her mother's bedroom with a glass of water and set it on the nightstand next to the alarm clock. The next morning, Yollie woke to screams. When her mother reached to turn off the alarm, she had overturned the glass of water.

Yollie burned her mother's morning toast and gloated. "Ha! Ha! I got you back. Why did you leave me on the couch when I told you to wake me up?"

Yollie's mother, Mrs. Moreno, was a large woman who wore a muumuu and butterfly-shaped glasses. She liked to water her lawn in the evening and wave at low-riders, who would stare at her behind their smoky sunglasses and laugh. Now and then a low-rider from Belmont Avenue would make his car jump and shout *"Mamacita!"* But most of the time they just stared and wondered how she got so large.

Mrs. Moreno had a strange sense of humor. Once, Yollie and her mother were watching a late-night movie called *They Came to Look*. It was about creatures from the underworld who had climbed through molten lava to walk the earth. But Yollie, who had played soccer all day with the kids

Despite their jokes, mother and daughter usually got along. They watched <u>bargain matinees</u> together, and played croquet in the summer and checkers in the winter. Mrs. Moreno encouraged Yollie to study hard because she wanted her daughter to be a doctor. She bought Yollie a desk, a typewriter, and a lamp that cut glare so her eyes would not grow tired from hours of studying.

Yollie was slender as a tulip, pretty, and one of the smartest kids at Saint Theresa's. She was captain of crossing guards, an altar girl, and a whiz in the school's monthly spelling bees.

"Tienes que estudiar mucho," Mrs. Moreno said every time she propped her work-weary feet on the hassock. "You have to study a lot, then you can get a good job and take care of me."

"Yes, Mama," Yollie would respond, her face buried in a book. If she gave her mother any sympathy, she would begin her stories about how she had come with her family from Mexico with nothing on her back but a sack with three skirts, all of which were too large by the time she crossed the border because she had lost weight from not having enough to eat.

Everyone thought Yollie's mother was a riot. Even the nuns laughed at her <u>antics</u>. Her brother Raul, a nightclub owner, thought she was funny enough to go into show business.

But there was nothing funny about Yollie needing a new outfit for the eighth-grade fall dance. They couldn't afford one. It was late October, with Christmas around the corner, and their dented <u>Chevy Nova</u> had gobbled up almost one hundred dollars in repairs.

"We don't have the money," said her mother, genuinely sad because they couldn't buy the outfit, even though there was a little money stashed away for college. Mrs. Moreno remembered her teenage years and her hard-working parents, who picked grapes and oranges, and chopped beets and cotton for <u>meager</u> pay around Kerman. Those were the days when "new clothes" meant limp and out-of-style dresses from Saint Vincent de Paul.

The best Mrs. Moreno could do was buy Yollie a pair of black shoes with velvet bows

Vocabulary
matinees (mat''n·āz') *n.*: afternoon performances of a play or a movie.
antics (an'tiks) *n.*: playful or silly acts.
meager (mē'gər) *adj.*: slight; small amount.

and fabric dye to color her white summer dress black.

"We can color your dress so it will look brand-new," her mother said brightly, shaking the bottle of dye as she ran hot water into a plastic dish tub. She poured the black liquid into the tub and stirred it with a pencil. Then, slowly and carefully, she lowered the dress into the tub.

Yollie couldn't stand to watch. She *knew* it wouldn't work. It would be like the time her mother stirred up a batch of molasses for candy apples on Yollie's birthday. She'd dipped the apples into the goo and swirled them and seemed to taunt Yollie by singing *"Las Mañanitas"* to her. When she was through, she set the apples on wax paper. They were hard as rocks and hurt the kids' teeth. Finally, they had a contest to see who could break the apples open by throwing them against the side of the house. The apples shattered like grenades, sending the kids scurrying for cover, and in an odd way the birthday party turned out to be a success. At least everyone went home happy.

To Yollie's surprise, the dress came out shiny black. It looked brand-new and

sophisticated, like what people in New York wear. She beamed at her mother, who hugged Yollie and said, "See, what did I tell you?"

The dance was important to Yollie because she was in love with Ernie Castillo, the third-best speller in the class. She bathed, dressed, did her hair and nails, and primped until her mother yelled, "All right already." Yollie sprayed her neck and wrists with Mrs. Moreno's Avon perfume and bounced into the car.

Mrs. Moreno let Yollie out in front of the school. She waved and told her to have a good time but behave herself, then roared off, blue smoke trailing from the tail pipe of the old Nova.

Yollie ran into her best friend, Janice. They didn't say it, but each thought the other was the most beautiful girl at the dance; the boys would fall over themselves asking them to dance.

The evening was warm but thick with clouds. Gusts of wind picked up the paper lanterns hanging in the trees and swung them, blurring the night with reds and yellows. The lanterns made the evening seem romantic, like a scene from a movie. Everyone danced, sipped punch, and stood in knots of threes and fours, talking. Sister Kelly got up and jitterbugged with some kid's father. When the record ended, students broke into applause.

Janice had her eye on Frankie Ledesma, and Yollie, who kept smoothing her dress down when the wind picked up, had her eye on Ernie. It turned out that Ernie had his mind on Yollie, too. He ate a handful of

Vocabulary
sophisticated (sə·fis′tə·kāt′id) *adj.:* worldly; elegant and refined.

cookies nervously, then asked her for a dance.

"Sure," she said, nearly throwing herself into his arms.

They danced two fast ones before they got a slow one. As they circled under the lanterns, rain began falling, lightly at first. Yollie loved the sound of the raindrops ticking against the leaves. She leaned her head on Ernie's shoulder, though his sweater was scratchy. He felt warm and tender. Yollie could tell that he was in love, and with her, of course. The dance continued successfully, romantically, until it began to pour.

"Everyone, let's go inside—and, boys, carry in the table and the record player," Sister Kelly commanded.

The girls and boys raced into the cafeteria. Inside, the girls, drenched to the bone, hurried to the restrooms to brush their hair and dry themselves. One girl cried because her velvet dress was ruined. Yollie felt sorry for her and helped her dry the dress off with paper towels, but it was no use. The dress was ruined.

Yollie went to a mirror. She looked a little gray now that her mother's makeup had washed away but not as bad as some of the other girls. She combed her damp hair, careful not to pull too hard. She couldn't wait to get back to Ernie.

Yollie bent over to pick up a bobby pin, and shame spread across her face. A black puddle was forming at her feet. Drip, black drip. Drip, black drip. The dye was falling from her dress like black tears. Yollie stood up. Her dress was now the color of ash. She looked around the room. The other girls, unaware of Yollie's problem, were busy grooming themselves. What could she do? Everyone would laugh. They would know she dyed an old dress because she couldn't afford a new one. She hurried from the restroom with her head down, across the cafeteria floor and out the door. She raced through the storm, crying as the rain mixed with her tears and ran into twig-choked gutters.

When she arrived home, her mother was on the couch eating cookies and watching TV.

"How was the dance, *m'ija*? Come watch the show with me. It's really good."

Yollie stomped, head down, to her bedroom. She undressed and threw the dress on the floor.

Her mother came into the room. "What's going on? What's all the racket, baby?"

"The dress. It's cheap! It's no good!" Yollie kicked the dress at her mother and watched it land in her hands. Mrs. Moreno studied it closely but couldn't see what was wrong. "What's the matter? It's just a bit wet."

"The dye came out, that's what."

Mrs. Moreno looked at her hands and saw the grayish dye puddling in the shallow lines of her palms. Poor baby, she thought, her brow darkening as she made a sad face. She wanted to tell her daughter how sorry

she was, but she knew it wouldn't help. She walked back to the living room and cried.

The next morning, mother and daughter stayed away from each other. Yollie sat in her room turning the pages of an old *Seventeen,* while her mother watered her plants with a Pepsi bottle.

"Drink, my children," she said loud enough for Yollie to hear. She let the water slurp into pots of coleus and cacti. "Water is all you need. My daughter needs clothes, but I don't have no money."

Yollie tossed her *Seventeen* on her bed. She was embarrassed at last night's tirade. It wasn't her mother's fault that they were poor.

When they sat down together for lunch, they felt awkward about the night before. But Mrs. Moreno had made a fresh stack of tortillas and cooked up a pan of *chile verde,* and that broke the ice. She licked her thumb and smacked her lips.

"You know, honey, we gotta figure a way to make money," Yollie's mother said. "You and me. We don't have to be poor. Remember the Garcias. They made this stupid little tool that fixes cars. They moved away because they're rich. That's why we don't see them no more."

"What can we make?" asked Yollie. She took another tortilla and tore it in half.

"Maybe a screwdriver that works on both ends? Something like that." The mother looked around the room for ideas, but then shrugged. "Let's forget it. It's better to get an education. If you get a good job and have spare time then maybe you can invent something." She rolled her tongue over her lips and cleared her throat. "The county fair hires people. We can get a job there. It will be here next week."

Yollie hated the idea. What would Ernie say if he saw her pitching hay at the cows?

How could she go to school smelling like an armful of chickens? "No, they wouldn't hire us," she said.

The phone rang. Yollie lurched from her chair to answer it, thinking it would be Janice wanting to know why she had left. But it was Ernie wondering the same thing. When he found out she wasn't mad at him, he asked if she would like to go to a movie.

"I'll ask," Yollie said, smiling. She covered the phone with her hand and counted to ten. She uncovered the receiver and said, "My mom says it's OK. What are we going to see?"

After Yollie hung up, her mother climbed, grunting, onto a chair to reach the top shelf in the hall closet. She wondered why she hadn't done it earlier. She reached behind a stack of towels and pushed her chubby hand into the cigar box where she kept her secret stash of money.

"I've been saving a little money every month," said Mrs. Moreno. "For you, *m'ija.*" Her mother held up five twenties, a blossom of green that smelled sweeter than flowers on that Saturday. They drove to Macy's and bought a blouse, shoes, and a skirt that would not bleed in rain or any other kind of weather.

Vocabulary
tirade (tī′rād′) *n.:* long, scolding speech.

Gary Soto

"A Name Among *la gente*"

Like Yollie in this story, **Gary Soto** (1952–   ) grew up in a Mexican American family in California. Much of his award-winning fiction and poetry draws on his heritage and his childhood memories. Although his work is vastly popular today, selling an average of seven thousand books a month, Soto remembers that early on he had trouble cultivating readers, even his own grandmother.

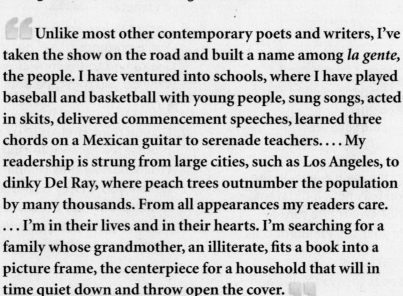

> Unlike most other contemporary poets and writers, I've taken the show on the road and built a name among *la gente,* the people. I have ventured into schools, where I have played baseball and basketball with young people, sung songs, acted in skits, delivered commencement speeches, learned three chords on a Mexican guitar to serenade teachers.... My readership is strung from large cities, such as Los Angeles, to dinky Del Ray, where peach trees outnumber the population by many thousands. From all appearances my readers care. ... I'm in their lives and in their hearts. I'm searching for a family whose grandmother, an illiterate, fits a book into a picture frame, the centerpiece for a household that will in time quiet down and throw open the cover.

For Independent Reading

"Mother and Daughter" appears in a collection of short stories called *Baseball in April,* about kids like Yollie growing up in Fresno, California. You might want to read one of Soto's novels, such as *Taking Sides* or its sequel, *Pacific Crossing.* If you like poetry, look at *A Fire in My Hands.* That book includes a question-and-answer section in which Soto talks about writing poetry.

Literary Response and Analysis

Reading Check

1. Fill out a story map like the one that follows to review the **plot** of "Mother and Daughter."

```
Characters:
What they want:
Conflicts (problems):
   Event:
   Event:
   Event:
   Event:
   Climax:
      Resolution of
      conflict:
```

Focus on the main events in the plot. (You may note a different number of events.) Be sure to compare your story maps in class.

Interpretations

2. Look back at the way Yollie and her mother tease each other at the beginning of the story. What inferences can you make about the **character traits** revealed by the mother and the daughter in that scene?

3. What inferences can you make about the **characters** of Yollie and her mother based on the awkward feelings they experience at lunch the day after the school dance?

4. How has Yollie distinguished herself at Saint Theresa's? Based on her involvement in those activities, what would you infer about her **character**?

5. Look at the way Mrs. Moreno dresses, at how other people respond to her, and at how she feels about Yollie. What inferences can you make about her **character**?

6. Some readers are surprised when Yollie pretends to ask her mother if she can go to the movies with Ernie. Why do you think she does that?

Evaluation

7. Do you think that Yollie and her mother are believable **characters**? (Think of how they compare with people you know.) How about that final discovery of the money in the cigar box? Was that a believable **resolution** to the plot? Why?

Writing
Creating a Character

Before you read this story, you took some notes about those character traits you admire and those you don't like. Now, refer to those notes, and write a sketch of a character who has those traits—either the traits you admire or the traits you do not like. Be sure to use details to describe your character's actions, looks, and relationships with other people.

Reading Standard 3.3
Analyze characterization as delineated through a character's thoughts, words, speech patterns, and actions; the narrator's description; and the thoughts, words, and actions of other characters.

Vocabulary Development

Dictionaries Tell Stories: Word Origins

Etymology (et′ə·mäl′ə·jē) means "the study of the origin and development of words." Most dictionaries give an etymology in brackets or parentheses following the word itself. At the back or front of the dictionary, you'll find definitions of the symbols and abbreviations used in the etymologies. One important symbol is "<," which means "comes from" or "derived from." The "derived from" symbol followed by a question mark ("<?") indicates that the derivation of a word or word part is unknown. A backward "derived from" symbol (">") means "from which comes."
Here is the etymology of *mother* from one dictionary:

Middle English
from
Old English
German
Indo-European
not certain
ME *moder* < OE *modor*, akin to Ger *mutter* < IE* *matér*, mother
>L *mater*, Gr *mētēr*, OIr *māthir* < * *ma–*, echoic of baby talk
from which is derived
Latin
Greek
Old Irish
imitates the sound

This etymology could be translated as "The word *mother* comes from the Middle English word *moder,* which comes from the Old English word *modor,* which is related ('akin') to the German word *mutter,* which comes from the Indo-European word *matér,* from which comes the Latin word *mater,* the Greek word *mētēr,* and the Old Irish word *māthir.* All the words might come from a word that imitates the sound of baby talk."

PRACTICE

The words in the Word Bank are derived from either Latin or Greek. Use a good dictionary to discover the original derivation of these words. Then, complete a chart like the one below:

Word Bank Word	Original Derivation
sophisticated	< Gr sophos, "clever; skillful; wise"

Word Bank

matinees
antics
meager
sophisticated
tirade

Reading Standard 1.2
Use knowledge of Greek, Latin, and Anglo-Saxon roots and affixes to understand content-area vocabulary.

The Smallest Dragonboy

Literary Focus
Motivation

Why do people do the things they do? What makes us act one way and not another? These are questions about **motivation.** Feelings, needs, wishes, pressures from family and friends—all these are forces that pull and push people from inside and outside. As you read "The Smallest Dragonboy," ask yourself what forces motivate Keevan, the main character. How does understanding Keevan's motivation help you understand the kind of character he is?

Reading Skills
Making Inferences

An **inference** is an educated guess based on evidence. When you make inferences about characters, you try to guess what kind of people they are, based on how the characters act, what they say, how other people respond. As you read "The Smallest Dragonboy," look for the little open-book signs after some paragraphs. Stop at these points to answer questions that ask you to make inferences about a character.

Make the Connection
Quickwrite ✏️

Have you ever wanted to do something that you thought would be too hard or that someone said you couldn't do? What motivated you to overcome your difficulties? Take some notes about a time when you faced a challenge as an underdog.

Vocabulary Development

These words appear in the story. See if you can use each one in a sentence of your own.

goaded (gōd′id) *v.:* pushed or driven. *Beterli goaded Keevan into a fight.*

imminent (im′ə·nənt) *adj.:* about to happen. *Pern was in imminent danger of a Thread attack.*

perturbed (pər·turbd′) *v.* used as *adj.:* disturbed; troubled. *Keevan was perturbed when he heard the bad news.*

confrontation (kän′frən·tā′shən) *n.:* face-to-face meeting between opposing sides. *The conflict between the two boys led to a violent confrontation.*

alleviate (ə·lē′vē·āt′) *v.:* relieve; reduce. *The boy's mother spoke soothing words to alleviate his fears.*

Reading Standard 3.3 Analyze characterization as delineated through a character's thoughts, words, and actions.

The SMALLEST DRAGONBOY

Anne McCaffrey

Keevan was constantly working, twice as hard as any other boy his age, to prove himself . . .

Background

"The Smallest Dragonboy" takes place on the planet of Pern, an imaginary world somewhere in outer space. Pern is threatened by the dangerous Red Star, which rains deadly, threadlike plant spores on the planet every two hundred years or so. If a hungry Thread falls on Pern soil and grows there, it will devour every living thing in sight.

To protect their planet, colonists on Pern have bioengineered a race of great winged dragons. When fed a special rock called firestone, the dragons breathe flames that char Thread to ashes. During Thread attacks, the dragons and their dragonriders charge into battle in midair while the other colonists hide safely in their cave towns. During periods of Thread attacks, the protectors of Pern live inside the cones of old volcanoes in cave colonies called Weyrs.

As the story opens, young candidates for dragonrider in the Benden Weyr, a colony in the Benden Mountains, await the hatching of a clutch of dragon eggs. According to custom, each newborn dragon will choose its own rider—a lifelong partner—through a kind of telepathic communication called Impression.

Although Keevan lengthened his walking stride as far as his legs would stretch, he couldn't quite keep up with the other candidates. He knew he would be teased again.

Just as he knew many other things that his foster mother told him he ought not to know, Keevan knew that Beterli, the most senior of the boys, set that spanking pace just to embarrass him, the smallest dragonboy. Keevan would arrive, tail fork-end of the group, breathless, chest heaving, and maybe get a stern look from the instructing wingsecond.

Dragonriders, even if they were still only hopeful candidates for the glowing eggs which were hardening on the hot sands of the Hatching Ground cavern, were expected to be punctual and prepared. Sloth[1] was not tolerated by the Weyrleader of Benden Weyr. A good record was especially important now. It was very near hatching time, when the baby dragons would crack their mottled[2] shells and stagger forth to choose their lifetime companions. The very thought of that glorious moment made Keevan's breath catch in his throat. To be chosen—to be a dragonrider! To sit astride the neck of a winged beast with jeweled eyes; to be his friend, in telepathic communion[3] with him for life; to be his companion in good times and fighting extremes; to fly effortlessly over the lands of Pern! Or, thrillingly, *between* to any point anywhere on the world! Flying *between* was done on dragonback or not at all, and it was dangerous.

Keevan glanced upward, past the black mouths of the Weyr caves, in which grown dragons and their chosen riders lived, toward the Star Stones that crowned the ridge of the old volcano that was Benden Weyr. On the height, the blue watch dragon, his rider mounted on his neck, stretched the great transparent pinions[4] that carried him on the winds of Pern to fight the evil

CHARACTER
1. What can you infer about Beterli from the very first mention of him in the story?

---

1. **sloth** (slôth) *n.:* laziness.
2. **mottled** (mät'ld) *adj.:* spotted.
3. **telepathic communion:** communication of thoughts without speaking.
4. **pinions** (pin'yənz) *n.:* wings.

Thread that fell at certain times from the skies. The many-faceted rainbow jewels of his eyes glistened fleetingly in the greeny sun. He folded his great wings to his back, and the watch pair resumed their statuelike pose of alertness.

Then the enticing view was obscured as Keevan passed into the Hatching Ground cavern. The sands underfoot were hot, even through heavy wher-hide boots. How the boot maker had protested having to sew so small! Keevan was forced to wonder why being small was reprehensible.[5] People were always calling him "babe" and shooing him away as being "too small" or "too young" for this or that. Keevan was constantly working, twice as hard as any other boy his age, to prove himself capable. What if his muscles weren't as big as Beterli's? They were just as hard. And if he couldn't overpower anyone in a wrestling match, he could outdistance everyone in a footrace.

"Maybe if you run fast enough," Beterli had jeered on the occasion when Keevan had been goaded to boast of his swiftness, "you could catch a dragon. That's the only way you'll make a dragonrider!"

"You just wait and see, Beterli, you just wait," Keevan had replied. He would have liked to wipe the contemptuous[6] smile from Beterli's face, but the guy didn't fight fair even when a wingsecond was watching. "No one knows what Impresses a dragon!"

"They've got to be able to *find* you first, babe!"

Yes, being the smallest candidate was not an enviable position. It was therefore imperative that Keevan Impress a dragon in his first hatching. That would wipe the smile off every face in the cavern and accord him the respect due any dragonrider, even the smallest one.

Besides, no one knew exactly what Impressed the baby dragons as they struggled from their shells in search of their lifetime partners.

"I like to believe that dragons see into a man's heart," Keevan's foster mother, Mende, told him. "If they find goodness, honesty, a flexible mind, patience, courage—and you've got that in quantity, dear Keevan—that's what dragons look for. I've seen many a well-grown lad left standing on the sands, Hatching Day, in favor of someone not so strong or tall or handsome. And if my memory serves me"—which it usually did: Mende knew every word of every Harper's tale worth telling, although Keevan did not interrupt her to say so—"I don't believe that F'lar, our Weyrleader, was all that tall when bronze Mnementh chose him. And Mnementh was the only bronze dragon of that hatching."

CHARACTER

2. Why does Mende comment on F'lar's height?

Dreams of Impressing a bronze were beyond Keevan's boldest reflections, although that goal dominated the thoughts of every other hopeful candidate. Green dragons were small and fast and more numerous. There was more prestige to Impressing a blue or brown than a green. Being practical,

---

5. **reprehensible** (rep′ri·hen′sə·bəl) *adj.:* made to seem like it was a fault, something that deserved to be criticized.
6. **contemptuous** (kən·temp′choō·əs) *adj.:* scornful; full of meanness.

Vocabulary

goaded (gōd′id) *v.:* pushed or driven. A goad is a stick with a sharp point used to herd oxen.

Keevan seldom dreamed as high as a big fighting brown, like Canth, F'nor's fine fellow, the biggest brown on all Pern. But to fly a bronze? Bronzes were almost as big as the queen, and only they took the air when a queen flew at mating time. A bronze rider could aspire to become Weyrleader! Well, Keevan would console himself, brown riders could aspire to become wingseconds, and that wasn't bad. He'd even settle for a green dragon; they were small, but so was he. No matter! He simply had to Impress a dragon his first time in the Hatching Ground. Then no one in the Weyr would taunt[7] him anymore for being so small.

Shells, Keevan thought now, but the sands are hot!

"Impression time is imminent, candidates," the wingsecond was saying as everyone crowded respectfully close to him. "See the extent of the striations[8] on this promising egg." The stretch marks *were* larger than yesterday.

Everyone leaned forward and nodded thoughtfully. That particular egg was the one Beterli had marked as his own, and no other candidate dared, on pain of being beaten by Beterli at his first opportunity, to approach it. The egg was marked by a large yellowish splotch in the shape of a dragon backwinging to land, talons outstretched to grasp rock. Everyone knew that bronze eggs bore distinctive markings. And naturally, Beterli, who'd been presented at eight Impressions already and was the biggest of the candidates, had chosen it.

"I'd say that the great opening day is almost upon us," the wingsecond went on, and then his face assumed a grave expression. "As we well know, there are only forty eggs and seventy-two candidates. Some of you may be disappointed on the great day. That doesn't necessarily mean you aren't dragonrider material, just that *the* dragon for you hasn't been shelled. You'll have other hatchings, and it's no disgrace to be left behind an Impression or two. Or more."

Keevan was positive that the wingsecond's eyes rested on Beterli, who'd been stood off at so many Impressions already. Keevan tried to squinch down so the wingsecond wouldn't notice him. Keevan had been reminded too often that he was eligible to be a candidate by one day only. He, of all the hopefuls, was most likely to be left standing on the great day. One more reason why he simply had to Impress at his first hatching.

"Now move about among the eggs," the wingsecond said. "Touch them. We don't know that it does any good, but it certainly doesn't do any harm."

Some of the boys laughed nervously, but everyone immediately began to circulate among the eggs. Beterli stepped up officiously[9] to "his" egg, daring anyone to come near it. Keevan smiled, because he had already touched it—every inspection day, when the others were leaving the Hatching Ground and no one could see him crouch to stroke it.

Keevan had an egg he concentrated on, too, one drawn slightly to the far side of the others. The shell had a soft greenish blue tinge with a faint creamy swirl design. The

---

7. **taunt** (tônt) *v.*: ridicule; mock.
8. **striations** (strī·ā′shənz) *n.*: stretch marks; stripes. (This word is defined in the context—in the next sentence.)

---

9. **officiously** (ə·fish′əs·lē) *adv.*: in a self-important way.

Vocabulary
imminent (im′ə·nənt) *adj.*: about to happen.

consensus was that this egg contained a mere green, so Keevan was rarely bothered by rivals. He was somewhat perturbed, then, to see Beterli wandering over to him.

"I don't know why you're allowed in this Impression, Keevan. There are enough of us without a babe," Beterli said, shaking his head.

"I'm of age." Keevan kept his voice level, telling himself not to be bothered by mere words.

"Yah!" Beterli made a show of standing on his toe tips. "You can't even see over an egg; Hatching Day, you better get in front or the dragons won't see you at all. 'Course, you could get run down that way in the mad scramble. Oh, I forget, you can run fast, can't you?"

"You'd better make sure a dragon sees *you* this time, Beterli," Keevan replied. "You're almost overage, aren't you?"

Beterli flushed and took a step forward, hand half raised. Keevan stood his ground, but if Beterli advanced one more step, he would call the wingsecond. No one fought on the Hatching Ground. Surely Beterli knew that much.

Fortunately, at that moment, the wingsecond called the boys together and led them from the Hatching Ground to start on evening chores. There were "glows" to be replenished in the main kitchen caverns and sleeping cubicles, the major hallways, and the queen's apartment. Firestone sacks had to be filled against Thread attack, and black rock brought to the kitchen hearths. The boys fell to their chores, tantalized by the

CHARACTER

3. Why does Keevan taunt Beterli about his age?

odors of roasting meat. The population of the Weyr began to assemble for the evening meal, and the dragonriders came in from the Feeding Ground on their sweep checks.

It was the time of day Keevan liked best: Once the chores were done but before dinner was served, a fellow could often get close enough to the dragonriders to hear their talk. Tonight, Keevan's father, K'last, was at the main dragonrider table. It puzzled Keevan how his father, a brown rider and a tall man, could *be* his father—because he, Keevan, was so small. It obviously puzzled K'last, too, when he deigned to notice his small son: "In a few more Turns, you'll be as tall as I am—or taller!"

Vocabulary
perturbed (pər·tʉrbd′) v. used as *adj.*: disturbed; troubled.

K'last was pouring Benden wine all around the table. The dragonriders were relaxing. There'd be no Thread attack for three more days, and they'd be in the mood to tell tall tales, better than Harper yarns, about impossible maneuvers they'd done a-dragonback. When Thread attack was closer, their talk would change to a discussion of tactics of evasion, of going *between,* how long to suspend there until the burning but fragile Thread would freeze and crack and fall harmlessly off dragon and man. They would dispute the exact moment to feed firestone to the dragon so he'd have the best flame ready to sear Thread midair and render it harmless to ground—and man—below. There was such a lot to know and understand about being a dragonrider that sometimes Keevan was overwhelmed. How would he ever be able to remember everything he ought to know at the right moment? He couldn't dare ask such a question; this would only have given additional weight to the notion that he was too young yet to be a dragonrider.

"Having older candidates makes good sense," L'vel was saying as Keevan settled down near the table. "Why waste four to five years of a dragon's fighting prime until his rider grows up enough to stand the rigors?" L'vel had Impressed a blue of Ramoth's first clutch. Most of the candidates thought L'vel was marvelous because he spoke up in front of the older riders, who awed them. "That was well enough in the Interval when you didn't need to mount the full Weyr complement to fight Thread. But not now. Not with more eligible candidates than ever. Let the babes wait."

"Any boy who is over twelve Turns has the right to stand in the Hatching Ground,"

K'last replied, a slight smile on his face. He never argued or got angry. Keevan wished he were more like his father. And oh, how he wished he were a brown rider! "Only a dragon—each particular dragon—knows what he wants in a rider. We certainly can't tell. Time and again, the theorists," K'last's smile deepened as his eyes swept those at the table, "are surprised by dragon choice. *They* never seem to make mistakes, however."

"Now, K'last, just look at the roster this Impression. Seventy-two boys and only forty eggs. Drop off the twelve youngest, and there's still a good field for the hatchlings to choose from. Shells! There are a couple of Weyrlings unable to see over a wher egg, much less a dragon! And years before they can ride Thread."

"True enough, but the Weyr is scarcely under fighting strength, and if the youngest Impress, they'll be old enough to fight when the oldest of our current dragons go *between* from senility."

"Half the Weyr-bred lads have already been through several Impressions," one of the bronze riders said then. "I'd say drop some of *them* off this time. Give the untried a chance."

"There's nothing wrong in presenting a clutch with as wide a choice as possible," said the Weyrleader, who had joined the table with Lessa, the Weyrwoman.

"Has there ever been a case," she said, smiling in her odd way at the riders, "where a hatchling didn't choose?"

Her suggestion was almost heretical and drew astonished gasps from everyone, including the boys.

F'lar laughed. "You say the most outrageous things, Lessa."

"Well, *has* there ever been a case where a dragon didn't choose?"

"Can't say as I recall one," K'last replied.

"Then we continue in this tradition," Lessa said firmly, as if that ended the matter.

But it didn't. The argument ranged from one table to the other all through dinner, with some favoring a weeding out of the candidates to the most likely, lopping off those who were very young or who had had multiple opportunities to Impress. All the candidates were in a swivet,[10] though such a departure from tradition would be to the advantage of many. As the evening progressed, more riders were favoring eliminating the youngest and those who'd passed four or more Impressions unchosen. Keevan felt he could bear such a dictum[11] only if Beterli were also eliminated. But this seemed less likely than that Keevan would be turfed out,[12] since the Weyr's need was for fighting dragons and riders.

By the time the evening meal was over, no decision had been reached, although the Weyrleader had promised to give the matter due consideration.

He might have slept on the problem, but few of the candidates did. Tempers were uncertain in the sleeping caverns next morning as the boys were routed out of their beds to carry water and black rock and cover the "glows." Twice Mende had to call Keevan to order for clumsiness.

"Whatever is the matter with you, boy?" she demanded in exasperation when he tipped black rock short of the bin and sooted up the hearth.

"They're going to keep me from this Impression."

_____

10. **in a swivet:** frustrated and annoyed.
11. **dictum** _n._: pronouncement or judgment.
12. **turfed out:** British expression meaning "removed; expelled."

"What?" Mende stared at him. "Who?"

"You heard them talking at dinner last night. They're going to turf the babes from the hatching."

Mende regarded him a moment longer before touching his arm gently. "There's lots of talk around a supper table, Keevan. And it cools as soon as the supper. I've heard the same nonsense before every hatching, but nothing is ever changed."

"There's always a first time," Keevan answered, copying one of her own phrases.

"That'll be enough of that, Keevan. Finish your job. If the clutch does hatch today, we'll need full rock bins for the feast, and you won't be around to do the filling. All my fosterlings make dragonriders."

"The first time?" Keevan was bold enough to ask as he scooted off with the rockbarrow.

Perhaps, Keevan thought later, if he hadn't been on that chore just when Beterli was also fetching black rock, things might have turned out differently. But he had dutifully trundled the barrow to the outdoor bunker for another load just as Beterli arrived on a similar errand.

"Heard the news, babe?" Beterli asked. He was grinning from ear to ear, and he put an unnecessary emphasis on the final insulting word.

"The eggs are cracking?" Keevan all but dropped the loaded shovel. Several anxieties flicked through his mind then: He was black with rock dust—would he have time to wash before donning the white tunic of candidacy? And if the eggs were hatching, why hadn't the candidates been recalled by the wingsecond?

"Naw! Guess again!" Beterli was much too pleased with himself.

With a sinking heart, Keevan knew what

the news must be, and he could only stare with intense desolation at the older boy.

"C'mon! Guess, babe!"

"I've no time for guessing games," Keevan managed to say with indifference. He began to shovel black rock into the barrow as fast as he could.

"I said, guess." Beterli grabbed the shovel.

"And I said I have no time for guessing games."

Beterli wrenched the shovel from Keevan's hands. "Guess!"

"I'll have that shovel back, Beterli." Keevan straightened up, but he didn't come to Beterli's bulky shoulder. From somewhere, other boys appeared, some with barrows, some mysteriously alerted to the prospect of a confrontation among their numbers.

"Babes don't give orders to candidates around here, babe!"

Someone sniggered, and Keevan, incredulous,[13] knew that he must've been dropped from the candidacy.

He yanked the shovel from Beterli's loosened grasp. Snarling, the older boy tried to regain possession, but Keevan clung with all his strength to the handle, dragged back and forth as the stronger boy jerked the shovel about.

With a sudden, unexpected movement, Beterli rammed the handle into Keevan's chest, knocking him over the barrow handles. Keevan felt a sharp, painful jab behind his left ear, an unbearable pain in his left shin, and then a painless nothingness.

Mende's angry voice roused him, and, startled, he tried to throw back the covers, thinking he'd overslept. But he couldn't

move, so firmly was he tucked into his bed. And then the constriction of a bandage on his head and the dull sickishness in his leg brought back recent occurrences.

"Hatching?" he cried.

"No, lovey," Mende said in a kind voice. Her hand was cool and gentle on his forehead. "Though there's some as won't be at any hatching again." Her voice took on a stern edge.

Keevan looked beyond her to see the Weyrwoman, who was frowning with irritation.

"Keevan, will you tell me what occurred at the black-rock bunker?" asked Lessa in an even voice.

He remembered Beterli now and the quarrel over the shovel and . . . what had Mende said about some not being at any hatching? Much as he hated Beterli, he couldn't bring himself to tattle on Beterli and force him out of candidacy.

> **CHARACTER**
> 4. Why is Keevan reluctant to tell Lessa what really happened?

"Come, lad," and a note of impatience crept into the Weyrwoman's voice. "I merely want to know what happened from you, too. Mende said she sent you for black rock. Beterli—and every Weyrling in the cavern—seems to have been on the same errand. What happened?"

"Beterli took my shovel. I hadn't finished with it."

"There's more than one shovel. What did he *say* to you?"

"He'd heard the news."

---

13. **incredulous** (in·krej′oo·ləs) *adj.*: doubting; unable to believe.

Vocabulary
confrontation (kän′frən·tā′shən) *n.*: face-to-face meeting between opposing sides.

"What news?" The Weyrwoman was suddenly amused.

"That . . . that . . . there'd been changes."

"Is that what he said?"

"Not exactly."

"What did he say? C'mon, lad, I've heard from everyone else, you know."

"He said for me to guess the news."

"And you fell for that old gag?" The Weyrwoman's irritation returned.

"Consider all the talk last night at supper, Lessa," Mende said. "Of course the boy would think he'd been eliminated."

"In effect, he is, with a broken skull and leg." Lessa touched his arm in a rare gesture of sympathy. "Be that as it may, Keevan, you'll have other Impressions. Beterli will not. There are certain rules that must be observed by all candidates, and his conduct proves him unacceptable to the Weyr."

She smiled at Mende and then left.

"I'm still a candidate?" Keevan asked urgently.

"Well, you are and you aren't, lovey," his foster mother said. "Is the numbweed working?" she asked, and when he nodded, she said, "You just rest. I'll bring you some nice broth."

At any other time in his life, Keevan would have relished such cosseting,[14] but now he just lay there worrying. Beterli had been dismissed. Would the others think it was his fault? But everyone was there! Beterli provoked that fight. His worry increased, because although he heard excited comings and goings in the passageway, no one tweaked back the curtain across the sleeping alcove he shared with five other boys. Surely one of them would have to come in sometime. No, they were all avoiding him. And something else was wrong. Only he didn't know what.

Mende returned with broth and beachberry bread.

"Why doesn't anyone come see me, Mende? I haven't done anything wrong, have I? I didn't ask to have Beterli turfed out."

Mende soothed him, saying everyone was busy with noontime chores and no one was angry with him. They were giving him a chance to rest in quiet. The numbweed made him drowsy, and her words were fair enough. He permitted his fears to dissipate.[15] Until he heard a hum. Actually he felt it first, in the broken shinbone and his sore head. The hum began to grow. Two things registered suddenly in Keevan's groggy mind: The only white candidate's robe still on the pegs in the chamber was his, and the dragons hummed when a clutch was being laid or being hatched. Impression! And he was flat abed.

Bitter, bitter disappointment turned the warm broth sour in his belly. Even the small voice telling him that he'd have other opportunities failed to alleviate his crushing depression. *This* was the Impression that mattered! This was his chance to show *everyone*, from Mende to K'last to L'vel and even the Weyrleader, that he, Keevan, was worthy of being a dragonrider.

He twisted in bed, fighting against the tears that threatened to choke him. Dragonmen don't cry! Dragonmen learn to live with pain.

Pain? The leg didn't actually pain him as

---

14. **cosseting** (käs'it·iŋ) *v.* used as *n.*: spoiling; pampering; treating as if he were a little pet.

15. **dissipate** (dis'ə·pāt') *v.*: disappear; go away.

Vocabulary
alleviate (ə·lē'vē·āt') *v.*: relieve; reduce.

he rolled about on his bedding. His head felt sort of stiff from the tightness of the bandage. He sat up, an effort in itself since the numbweed made exertion[16] difficult. He touched the splinted leg; the knee was unhampered.[17] He had no feeling in his bone, really. He swung himself carefully to the side of his bed and stood slowly. The room wanted to swim about him. He closed his eyes, which made the dizziness worse, and he had to clutch the wall.

Gingerly, he took a step. The broken leg dragged. It hurt in spite of the numbweed, but what was pain to a dragonman?

CHARACTER

5. Why does Keevan deny the pain in his leg?

No one had said he couldn't go to the Impression. "You are and you aren't" were Mende's exact words.

Clinging to the wall, he jerked off his bed shirt. Stretching his arm to the utmost, he jerked his white candidate's tunic from the peg. Jamming first one arm and then the other into the holes, he pulled it over his head. Too bad about the belt. He couldn't wait. He hobbled to the door and hung on to the curtain to steady himself. The weight on his leg was unwieldy. He wouldn't get very far without something to lean on. Down by the bathing pool was one of the long crook-necked poles used to retrieve clothes from the hot washing troughs. But it was down there, and he was on the level above. And there was no one nearby to come to his aid; everyone would be in the Hatching Ground right now, eagerly waiting for the first egg to crack.

---

16. **exertion** (eg·zur'shən) *n.*: exercise; effort.
17. **unhampered** (un·ham'pərd) *v.* used as *adj.*: free to move around. (There was no tight bandage on his knee.)

The humming increased in volume and tempo, an urgency to which Keevan responded, knowing that his time was all too limited if he was to join the ranks of the hopeful boys standing around the cracking eggs. But if he hurried down the ramp, he'd fall flat on his face.

He could, of course, go flat on his rear end, the way crawling children did. He sat down, sending a jarring stab of pain through his leg and up to the wound on the back of his head. Gritting his teeth and blinking away tears, Keevan scrabbled down the ramp. He had to wait a moment at the bottom to catch his breath. He got to one knee, the injured leg straight out in front of him. Somehow, he managed to push himself erect, though the room seemed about to tip over his ears. It wasn't far to the crooked stick, but it seemed an age before he had it in his hand.

Then the humming stopped!

Keevan cried out and began to hobble frantically across the cavern, out to the bowl of the Weyr. Never had the distance between living caverns and the Hatching Ground seemed so great. Never had the Weyr been so breathlessly silent. It was as if the multitude of people and dragons watching the hatching held every breath in suspense. Not even the wind muttered down the steep sides of the bowl. The only sounds to break the stillness were Keevan's ragged gasps and the thump-thud of his stick on the hard-packed ground. Sometimes he had to hop twice on his good leg to maintain his balance. Twice he fell into the sand and had to pull himself up on the stick, his white tunic no longer spotless. Once he jarred himself so badly he couldn't get up immediately.

Then he heard the first exhalation of the crowd, the oohs, the muted cheer, the susurrus[18] of excited whispers. An egg had cracked, and the dragon had chosen his rider. Desperation increased Keevan's hobble. Would he never reach the arching mouth of the Hatching Ground?

Another cheer and an excited spate[19] of applause spurred Keevan to greater effort. If he didn't get there in moments, there'd be no unpaired hatchling left. Then he was actually staggering into the Hatching Ground, the sands hot on his bare feet.

No one noticed his entrance or his halting progress. And Keevan could see nothing but the backs of the white-robed candidates, seventy of them ringing the area around the eggs. Then one side would surge forward or back and there'd be a cheer. Another dragon had been Impressed. Suddenly a large gap appeared in the white human wall, and Keevan had his first sight of the eggs. There didn't seem to be *any* left uncracked, and he could see the lucky boys standing beside wobble-legged dragons. He could hear the unmistakable plaintive[20] crooning of hatchlings and their squawks of protest as they'd fall awkwardly in the sand.

Suddenly he wished that he hadn't left his bed, that he'd stayed away from the Hatching Ground. Now everyone would see his ignominious[21] failure. So he scrambled as desperately to reach the shadowy walls of the Hatching Ground as he had struggled to cross the bowl. He mustn't be seen.

He didn't notice, therefore, that the shifting group of boys remaining had begun to drift in his direction. The hard pace he had set himself and his cruel disappointment took their double toll of Keevan. He tripped and collapsed, sobbing, to the warm sands. He didn't see the consternation in the watching Weyrfolk above the Hatching Ground, nor did he hear the excited whispers of speculation. He didn't know that the Weyrleader and Weyrwoman had dropped to the arena and were making their way toward the knot of boys slowly moving in the direction of the entrance.

"Never seen anything like it," the Weyrleader was saying. "Only thirty-nine riders chosen. And the bronze trying to leave the Hatching Ground without making Impression."

"A case in point of what I said last night," the Weyrwoman replied, "where a hatchling makes no choice because the right boy isn't there."

"There's only Beterli and K'last's young one missing. And there's a full wing of likely boys to choose from. . . ."

"None acceptable, apparently. Where is the creature going? He's not heading for the entrance after all. Oh, what have we there, in the shadows?"

Keevan heard with dismay the sound of voices nearing him. He tried to burrow into the sand. The mere thought of how he would be teased and taunted now was unbearable.

Don't worry! Please don't worry! The thought was urgent, but not his own.

Someone kicked sand over Keevan and butted roughly against him.

"Go away. Leave me alone!" he cried.

Why? was the injured-sounding question inserted into his mind. There was no voice, no tone, but the question was there, perfectly clear, in his head.

Incredulous, Keevan lifted his head and stared into the glowing jeweled eyes of a small bronze dragon. His wings were wet,

---

18. **susurrus** (sə·sur′əs) *n.:* rustling sound.
19. **spate** (spāt) *n.:* sudden outpouring.
20. **plaintive** (plān′tiv) *adj.:* sorrowful; sad.
21. **ignominious** (ig′nə·min′ē·əs) *adj.:* shameful.

the tips drooping in the sand. And he sagged in the middle on his unsteady legs, although he was making a great effort to keep erect.

Keevan dragged himself to his knees, oblivious[22] of the pain in his leg. He wasn't even aware that he was ringed by the boys passed over, while thirty-one pairs of resentful eyes watched him Impress the dragon. The Weyrmen looked on, amused and surprised at the draconic[23] choice, which could not be forced. Could not be questioned. Could not be changed.

Why? asked the dragon again. *Don't you like me?* His eyes whirled with anxiety, and his tone was so piteous that Keevan staggered forward and threw his arms around the dragon's neck, stroking his eye ridges, patting the damp, soft hide, opening the fragile-looking wings to dry them, and wordlessly assuring the hatchling over and over again that he was the most perfect, most beautiful, most beloved dragon in the Weyr, in all the Weyrs of Pern.

"What's his name, K'van?" asked Lessa, smiling warmly at the new dragonrider. K'van stared up at her for a long moment. Lessa would know as soon as he did. Lessa was the only person who could "receive" from all dragons, not only her own Ramoth. Then he gave her a radiant smile, recognizing the traditional shortening of his name that raised him forever to the rank of dragonrider.

My name is Heth, the dragon thought mildly, then hiccuped in sudden urgency. *I'm hungry.*

"Dragons are born hungry," said Lessa, laughing. "F'lar, give the boy a hand. He can barely manage his own legs, much less a dragon's."

K'van remembered his stick and drew himself up. "We'll be just fine, thank you."

"You may be the smallest dragonrider ever, young K'van," F'lar said, "but you're one of the bravest!"

And Heth agreed! Pride and joy so leaped in both chests that K'van wondered if his heart would burst right out of his body. He looped an arm around Heth's neck, and the pair, the smallest dragonboy and the hatchling who wouldn't choose anybody else, walked out of the Hatching Ground together forever.

---

22. **oblivious** (ə·bliv′ē·əs) *adj.:* forgetful; not aware of.
23. **draconic** (drə·kän′ik) *adj.:* of a dragon. *Drakōn* is the Greek word for "dragon."

Anne McCaffrey

Dragon Writer

Growing up as a "lonely tomboy" in New Jersey, **Anne McCaffrey** (1926–   ) decided there were two things she really wanted. "When I was a very young girl, I promised myself very fervently (usually after I'd lost another battle with one of my brothers) that I would become a famous author and I'd own my own horse." McCaffrey's books are now known all over the world and have been translated into many languages. Since she moved to County Wicklow in Ireland, she has owned a number of horses (and cats and dogs). McCaffrey lives and works in Ireland at her home, called Dragonhold. Fans of her books rejoice in McCaffrey's promise: "I shall continue to write—I can't not write—until I am too frail to touch the keys of my word processor." McCaffrey once said this about her own writing process:

> First I find interesting people to write about (I have written an anthology series, *Crystal Singer,* because I wanted to name a feminine character Killashandra), and then I find something for them to argue about or fight for or against. Or I think about an interesting concept—the dragons of Pern—telepathic, huge, flame-throwing dragons who fly because they 'think' they can. Aerodynamically, they can't. I like to write better than anything else, including riding [horses]. And I write because I can't always get the kind of story I like to read on library shelves.

For Independent Reading

If you want to continue riding with the dragonriders, read *Dragonsong, Dragonsinger,* and *Dragondrums,* a series of science fantasy novels about the dragons of Pern.

Literary Response and Analysis

Reading Check

1. What does Keevan want as the story opens?

2. How are dragonriders chosen?

3. Why does Keevan think he might be kept from the Impression?

4. How does the bully Beterli try to ruin Keevan's chances on Hatching Day?

5. Describe Keevan's struggle to reach the Hatching Ground.

6. What happens to Keevan just when he is most discouraged?

Interpretations

7. Make a chart showing all the **conflicts** Keevan faced. Which conflict do you think was the hardest for him?

Internal Conflicts	External Conflicts

8. What **character traits** would you assign to Keevan's foster mother, Mende?

9. Think about Beterli's **character.** What **inferences** can you make to explain Beterli's **motivation** for trying to ruin Keevan's chances on Hatching Day?

10. What **inferences** can you draw from the fact that Beterli never Impressed a dragon?

11. Why does K'van reject the help Lessa offers him at the end of the story? What **inference** can you make about K'van based on his action?

Evaluation

12. List the names of all the women in this story. Do you think they have powerful positions in Pern society, or do only men hold power? Explain. If you were writing about Pern, what roles and responsibilities would you give to men and women?

Writing

Underdog Wins

This story is an "underdog" story, in which a person who seems like a loser becomes, at the end, a winner. Check the notes you took before you read this story, and write a short narrative in which you tell about a time when you felt like an underdog. What did you do about it? Did you eventually win? What did the experience teach you? If you've never had an underdog experience, you might write about someone you know who has.

A Pern Dictionary

Help other readers by creating a dictionary of Pernspeak. Define the invented words in the story, and give their pronunciations. To help your readers understand Pernspeak, illustrate as many words as you can.

Reading Standard 3.3
Analyze characterization as delineated through a character's thoughts, words, speech patterns, and actions; the narrator's description; and the thoughts, words, and actions of other characters.

Vocabulary Development

Recognizing Roots and Affixes

Many English word roots come from Latin, Greek, and an ancestor of the English language called Old English. A **word root** is a word part from which several words are formed. An **affix** is a word part added to a root. An affix can be added to the front of a word (in which case it's called a **prefix**), or it can be added to the end of a word (in which case it's called a **suffix**). For example, the word *confrontation* is made up of the prefix *com–* ("together"), the Latin root *–frons–* ("forehead"), and the suffix *–ation* ("the act of"). In the story you just read, Keevan and Beterli are brought together in a face-to-face meeting, or confrontation.

Word Bank

goaded
imminent
perturbed
confrontation
alleviate

PRACTICE

1. *Goaded* is derived from the Old English word *gad,* which was a pointed stick used to prod cattle. Look up the meaning of the word *gadfly,* and tell how it is related to the meaning of *gad.*

2. *Imminent* comes from the Latin word *minere,* meaning "to threaten or to project over." Look up the derivation of *menace.* How is the meaning of *menace* related to the Latin word *minere*?

3. *Turbare* is a Latin word meaning "to disturb." How is *perturbed* related to the meaning of the Latin word?

4. The word *turbine* is built on the same root word as *perturbed.* How is "disturbance" part of the meaning of *turbine*?

5. *Alleviate* is built on the Latin word *levis,* meaning "light," and the Latin prefix *ad–,* meaning "to." Using that root word and its affix, define *alleviate.*

6. Draw a "family" tree showing words that are part of the Latin word *credere,* "to believe." You should be able to find at least six words built on *credere.* A model tree showing the family *turbare* is shown at the right.

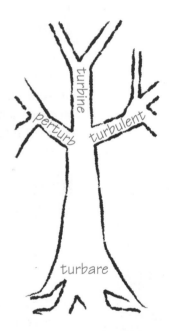

Reading Standard 1.2
Use knowledge of Greek, Latin, and Anglo-Saxon roots and affixes to understand content-area vocabulary.

Here Be Dragons

Text Structures: Compare-and-Contrast Pattern

Why does one car set your heart aflutter while another zooms by virtually unnoticed? Why is one pair of jeans to die for, while another is of the "I wouldn't be caught dead in those" variety? The truth is that even though many things are similar, they also have many differences. When you **compare,** you look at two or more things and see how they are the same. When you **contrast,** you look for differences. You may not realize it, but you do a lot of comparing and contrasting every day— for example, when you decide what to eat for lunch or when you think about when you'll do your homework.

Writers compare and contrast things all the time. To do it effectively, they use what's known as a **compare-and-contrast organizational pattern.** Writers use one of two methods when they compare or contrast something. (The charts below refer to the article on dragons you are about to read.)

- **Block method.** The writer first discusses all the features of subject 1, then all the features of subject 2.

- **Point-by-point method.** In this pattern the writer discusses one feature of each subject at a time. The writer chooses a feature and shows how it applies to subject 1, then how it applies to subject 2. The writer continues to discuss other features and how they apply to each subject in turn.

In the article that follows, the writer compares and contrasts dragons from around the world. Which method does she use?

Grade 6 Review Reading Standard 2.2
Analyze text that uses the compare-and-contrast organizational pattern.

Block Method	
Subject 1:	Eastern dragons
Feature 1:	Behavior
Feature 2:	Origins
Feature 3:	Appearance
Subject 2:	Western dragons
Feature 1:	Behavior
Feature 2:	Origins
Feature 3:	Appearance

Point-by-Point Method	
Feature 1:	Behavior
Subject 1:	Eastern dragons
Subject 2:	Western dragons
Feature 2:	Origins
Subject 1:	Eastern dragons
Subject 2:	Western dragons
Feature 3:	Appearance
Subject 1:	Eastern dragons
Subject 2:	Western dragons

Here Be DRAGONS

with the warrior sun god, and, especially, with the water gods. Dragons were said to have been present at the creation and so were endowed with characteristics of the cosmos.[2] At one with wind and fire and water, they had the ancient power of these primal[3] forces. They had command of fire and water and could fly like the wind. But dragons differ from culture to culture: In Asia, dragons help people; in Europe and other places, dragons are associated with destruction and evil.

EASTERN DRAGONS. In Asia the dragon is a benevolent, spiritual creature, gifted with wisdom and the power to confer blessings upon humankind. One of the first dragon stories Asian children hear has a beautifully multicolored dragon emerging from the primordial[4] swamp, proudly beating its chest and calling forth, wanting to know how it can be of service to people. Eastern dragons inspire awe in the people who look to them for guidance, and many are cherished as great and wonderful creatures. Two dragons acting as honor guards are believed to have visited the home of the philosopher Confucius

Chinese dragon robe with silk embroidery (detail), from the T'ung-chih period (1862–1875). The Granger Collection, New York.

ANY, MANY YEARS AGO, when people first began to map the Western world, they charted two main areas: their settlements and the wilderness. On the wilderness areas of their maps, they wrote a warning: "Here be dragons." When the European explorers set off in their wooden ships in the fifteenth century, most of the sailors still believed that if they sailed too far, the boats would tumble off the earth and into that area populated with seething,[1] clawed monsters.

Dragon stories have been told for ages in almost every land and culture: Africa, Britain, China, Egypt, Greece, and Russia. From their beginnings in mythology, dragons were associated with the Great Mother,

---

1. **seething** *adj.*: violently agitated.

2. **cosmos** *n.*: the whole universe.
3. **primal** (prī′məl) *adj.*: basic or fundamental.
4. **primordial** (prī·môr′dē·əl) *adj.*: original; first in time.

Saint George and the Dragon by Paolo Uccello (1397–1475).
Musée Jacquemart-André, Paris. Copyright Scala/Art Resource, New York.

when he was born. The ruler Huang-Ti was supposedly carried to heaven on the back of a dragon. If you met one on the road of life, an Eastern dragon would give you a gift as opposed to, say, fire and brimstone.

WESTERN DRAGONS.

Speaking of fire and brimstone, the Western dragon is famous for both. People could always tell when they were in the vicinity of a Western dragon because the air would be heated and foul with the unmistakable sulfuric odor of brimstone. Brimstone has a smell that makes the scent of a rotten egg seem lovely by comparison.

Western dragons became feared as the foes of civilization. Perseus of ancient Greece, Beowulf of ancient Denmark, even brave little Bilbo in *The Hobbit*—all had to face down menacing dragons before they could conclude their quests. In Western stories, dragons often lie underground, guarding huge piles of gold they have stolen from the surrounding countryside, which, by the way, has also been scorched and laid waste by the dragon's fiery breath.

DRAGONS TODAY.

Dragons have largely disappeared from our stories—except for the fantasies of writers like Anne McCaffrey.

Dragons haven't died out, however. Wait a moment! What is all that noise? It sounds like people playing gongs, cymbals, and drums. What is that colorful creature a block long snaking its way through the Chinese New Year's crowd lining the sidewalks? Why, it's the Eastern dragon come again to celebrate the vitality of life! Hear that thunderous applause? That is the sound that attends an Eastern dragon passing by.

—Flo Ota De Lange

Reading Informational Materials

Reading Check

A Venn diagram like the one at the right can help you sort out and analyze the similarities and differences between Eastern dragons and Western dragons. In each circle you note differences. In the center, where the circles overlap, you note similarities. Complete the diagram.

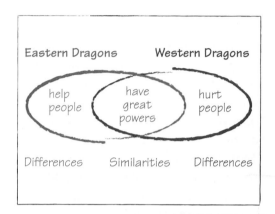

Eastern Dragons   Western Dragons

help people | have great powers | hurt people

Differences   Similarities   Differences

Test Practice

Here Be Dragons

1. Which sentence best states the **main idea** of this article?

   A   Dragon stories are very old.

   B   In Asia, dragons are helpful; in the West, dragons are evil.

   C   Dragons are mythical creatures.

   D   Western dragons are foes of civilization.

2. The **organizational pattern** this writer uses for **comparing and contrasting** Eastern and Western dragons is the —

   F   chronological method

   G   point-by-point method

   H   persuasive method

   J   block method

3. The **title** of this article refers to —

   A   a book on dragons

   B   an Asian dragon story

   C   a warning on old maps

   D   a European dragon story

4. Dragon stories would most likely appear in a book of —

   F   realistic stories

   G   mystery stories

   H   myths and legends

   J   nonfiction

5. Anne McCaffrey's dragons in "The Smallest Dragonboy" most resemble the ones in stories from —

   ✓ A   Asia

   B   Europe

   C   Africa

   D   America

Grade 6 Review Reading Standard 2.2 Analyze text that uses the compare-and-contrast organizational pattern.

A Rice Sandwich

Literary Focus
The Narrator

If you have ever written a story, you know that the first questions you have to answer are "Who is going to tell this story?" and "Who will be my narrator?" A **narrator** is simply the person telling the story.

Most stories are told by what is called an **omniscient** (äm·nish′ənt) **narrator.** *Omniscient* means "all knowing," and an omniscient narrator knows all about all the characters and the events in the story. An omniscient narrator can tell you what everyone in the story is thinking. An omniscient narrator can also take you back and forth in time. "Rikki-tikki-tavi," the story about the brave mongoose and the killer cobras, which starts on page 21, is told by an omniscient narrator.

When you read the second paragraph of "A Rice Sandwich," you realize that you are listening to one of the characters in the story. Notice that this narrator says, "*My* home," not "*Esperanza's* home," and "*I* got it in my head," not "*She* got it in her head." When a story is told by a character in the story—someone who tells the whole tale using the first-person pronoun *I* or *me* or *mine*—the story is told by a **first-person narrator.**

Reading a story told by a first-person narrator is like entering into a character's mind and heart. Notice how much Esperanza reveals about herself as she tells about her experience with a rice sandwich.

Reading Skills
Making Inferences

Writers don't come right out and tell you everything you want to know about their characters. You're supposed to take part in the story and make your own inferences about the characters you meet, just the way you do in real life. To make inferences about the character in this story, use these strategies:

- Watch what Esperanza says and does.
- Observe the way other characters respond to Esperanza.
- Examine what you learn about Esperanza's thoughts.
- Think about how Esperanza is like, or not like, people you know in real life.

Make the Connection
Quickwrite ✏️

In this story, Esperanza has an upsetting encounter with Sister Superior. Have you, or someone you know, ever been corrected by someone in authority? Jot down some notes about the incident.

Grade 6 Review Reading Standard 3.5 Identify the speaker, and recognize first-person narration.

Reading Standard 3.3 Analyze characterization as delineated through a character's thoughts, words, and speech patterns.

A Rice Sandwich

Sandra Cisneros

The special kids, the ones who wear keys around their necks, get to eat in the canteen. The canteen! Even the name sounds important. And these kids at lunch time go there because their mothers aren't home or home is too far away to get to.

My home isn't far but it's not close either, and somehow I got it in my head one day to ask my mother to make me a sandwich and write a note to the principal so I could eat in the canteen too.

Oh no, she says pointing the butter knife at me as if I'm starting trouble, no sir. Next thing you know everybody will be wanting a bag lunch—I'll be up all night cutting bread into little triangles, this one with mayonnaise, this one with mustard, no pickles on mine, but mustard on one side please. You kids just like to invent more work for me.

But Nenny says she doesn't want to eat at school—ever—because she likes to go home with her best friend Gloria who lives across the schoolyard. Gloria's mama has a big color T.V. and all they do is watch cartoons. Kiki and Carlos, on the other hand, are patrol boys. They don't want to eat at school either. They like to stand out in the cold especially if it's raining. They think suffering is good for you ever since they saw that movie "300 Spartans."

I'm no Spartan[1] and hold up an anemic[2] wrist to prove it. I can't even blow up a balloon without getting dizzy. And besides, I know how to make my own lunch. If I ate at school there'd be less dishes to wash. You would see me less and less and like me better. Every day at noon my chair would be empty. Where is my favorite daughter you would cry, and when I came home finally at 3 p.m. you would appreciate me.

Okay, okay, my mother says after three days of this. And the following morning I get to go to school with my mother's letter and a rice sandwich because we don't have lunch meat.

Mondays or Fridays, it doesn't matter, mornings always go by slow and this day especially. But lunch time came finally and I got to get in line with the stay-at-school kids. Everything is fine until the nun who knows all the canteen kids by heart looks at me and says: you, who sent you here? And since I am shy, I don't say anything, just hold out my hand with the letter. This is no good, she says, till Sister Superior gives the okay. Go upstairs and see her. And so I went.

I had to wait for two kids in front of me to get hollered at, one because he did something in class, the other because he didn't. My turn came and I stood in front of the

big desk with holy pictures under the glass while the Sister Superior read my letter. It went like this:

> Dear Sister Superior,
> Please let Esperanza eat in the lunch room because she lives too far away and she gets tired. As you can see she is very skinny. I hope to God she does not faint. Thanking you,
> Mrs. E. Cordero.

You don't live far, she says. You live across the boulevard. That's only four blocks. Not even. Three maybe. Three long blocks away from here. I bet I can see your house from my window. Which one? Come here. Which one is your house?

And then she made me stand up on a box of books and point. That one? she said pointing to a row of ugly 3-flats, the ones even the raggedy men are ashamed to go into. Yes, I nodded even though I knew that wasn't my house and started to cry. I always cry when nuns yell at me, even if they're not yelling.

Then she was sorry and said I could stay—just for today, not tomorrow or the day after—you go home. And I said yes and could I please have a Kleenex—I had to blow my nose.

In the canteen, which was nothing special, lots of boys and girls watched while I cried and ate my sandwich, the bread already greasy and the rice cold.

---

1. **Spartan:** hardy, disciplined person, like the Spartans of ancient Greece.
2. **anemic** (ə·nē′mik) *adj.*: pale and weak.

Sandra Cisneros

Finding Her Own Way

Sandra Cisneros (1954–   ) was born and raised in Chicago, the only daughter in a working-class family with six sons. The harshness of life in her poor neighborhood made Cisneros shy as a child, and she escaped into the world of books. By the age of ten, she was writing her own poetry.

Cisneros grew up speaking Spanish with her Mexican-born father, but she didn't explore her heritage until she attended the Writer's Workshop at the University of Iowa. There she began a series of sketches about her old Spanish-speaking neighborhood in Chicago. These sketches grew into her first book, *The House on Mango Street* (1984), which includes the story "A Rice Sandwich." About her writing she says:

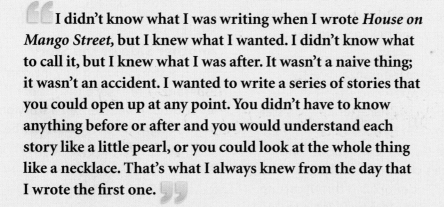

> I didn't know what I was writing when I wrote *House on Mango Street,* but I knew what I wanted. I didn't know what to call it, but I knew what I was after. It wasn't a naive thing; it wasn't an accident. I wanted to write a series of stories that you could open up at any point. You didn't have to know anything before or after and you would understand each story like a little pearl, or you could look at the whole thing like a necklace. That's what I always knew from the day that I wrote the first one.

For Independent Reading

To find out more about Esperanza and her family, read more of the forty-four short stories narrated by Esperanza in *The House on Mango Street*.

Literary Response and Analysis

Reading Check

1. Who eats in the canteen?

2. How does Esperanza persuade her mother to write the note so she can eat in the canteen too?

3. Why doesn't Sister Superior want to let Esperanza eat in the canteen?

4. According to Esperanza, why does she begin to cry?

5. How does Esperanza describe her sandwich at the end of the story?

Interpretations

6. Why do you think eating in the canteen is so important for Esperanza?

7. What does Esperanza reveal about her **character** when she argues for three days with her mother, trying to persuade her to write the note?

8. How does Esperanza directly **characterize** herself? How does she directly characterize her sister Nenny and her brothers?

9. What do you learn about Esperanza's **character** in the scene with Sister Superior? Did this upsetting encounter seem believable to you? Be sure to check your Quickwrite notes.

10. Writers don't always tell you in so many words what a character in a story is thinking or feeling. You are given various clues and must draw your own conclusions. How do you think Esperanza feels about eating in the canteen at the story's end? How likely is it that she'll want to eat there again?

Evaluation

11. This story is a **first-person narration** told by Esperanza, a character in the story. Do you think the story would have been better or not as good or about the same if someone else had been the narrator? Explain.

Writing

Another Side of the Story

This is a story about a tiny incident in Esperanza's life. Take the incident, and let another character tell a story about it. You might let Sister Superior be the new narrator or Esperanza's mother or even Nenny, Kiki, or Carlos.

BONUS QUESTION

Esperanza tells us in another story in *The House on Mango Street* that she wishes she had another name. What does the Spanish word *esperanza* mean in English?

Grade 6 Review Reading Standard 3.5 Identify the speaker, and recognize first-person narration.

Reading Standard 3.3 Analyze characterization as delineated through a character's thoughts, words, and speech patterns.

Vocabulary Development

Reading Standard 1.2 Use knowledge of Greek, Latin, and Anglo-Saxon roots and affixes to understand content-area vocabulary.

Borrowed Words

When people speaking different languages come into contact, they often borrow one another's words. It is no surprise, then, that English contains many words borrowed from other cultures.

PRACTICE

Explain how the following facts help you understand the meaning of one of the Word Bank words.

1. In Italian a *cantina* is a wine cellar.
2. The Latin word *ferre* means "to bear"; the Latin prefix *sub*– means "under" or "below."
3. The prefix *tri*– comes from *tres,* meaning "three" in Latin.
4. The Greek prefix *an*– means "without," and the Greek word *haima* means "blood."
5. Sparta was a great military power in ancient Greece. The people of Sparta were known for their courage, discipline, and ability to endure hardship.

Word Bank

canteen
triangles
suffering
Spartan
anemic

Grammar Link MINI-LESSON

Avoiding Unclear Pronoun References

Writers must make sure that readers can tell which word or phrase a pronoun refers to. The word a pronoun refers to is called its **antecedent.** In the first sentence that follows, the antecedent of the pronoun *she* cannot be clearly identified.

CONFUSING   **Nenny whispered something to Gloria, and <u>she</u> smiled.** [Who smiled, Nenny or Gloria?]

CLEAR   **Nenny smiled as <u>she</u> whispered something to Gloria.** [Nenny was the one who smiled.]

To avoid confusion, the writer had to reword the sentence and move the pronoun closer to its antecedent (Nenny).

PRACTICE

Revise the following sentences to fix the unclear pronoun references.

1. Carlos told Kiki that he wasn't allowed to be on patrol anymore.
2. When the nun told Sister Superior what happened, she gave me a concerned look.
3. Esperanza later told her mother, and she started to cry.

For more help, see Agreement of Pronoun and Antecedent in the *Holt Handbook,* **pages 165–170.**

The Tejano Soul of San Antonio

Distinguishing Facts, Inferences, and Opinions

Do you know the difference between a fact, an inference, and an opinion? Informational writing is often a mixture of all three. Here's how they work:

- A **fact** is something that is known to be true and can be verified or proved. All you have to do is check it in a reliable source, like an encyclopedia. Other facts can be proved simply by observation: *It's raining outside.*

- **Inferences** are educated guesses or conclusions based on facts and supported by knowledge and experience. Don't be surprised if you and someone else draw different inferences from the same set of facts. For example, look at these facts: *Mr. Sang called James home five times for dinner, but James never arrived.*

  Possible inference: James couldn't hear his father calling him.

  Possible inference: James didn't want to come home for dinner.

  Possible inference: James couldn't come home for dinner.

- An **opinion** is a belief, judgment, or conclusion based on what the writer thinks. Statements of opinion cannot be proved or disproved. A **valid opinion** is a belief or judgment that is supported by evidence. An **invalid opinion** is based on emotions or faulty reasoning. Here are three kinds of invalid opinions based on emotions, along with examples of each:

1. **Personal beliefs.** The color of the Pacific Ocean is prettier than the color of the Atlantic.

2. **Thoughts and feelings.** There's no team greater than the Los Angeles Lakers.

3. **Predictions.** California won't have a major earthquake in my lifetime.

Vocabulary Development

You'll learn these words as you read the following article. Their definitions and pronunciations are on the next page.

descent

minority

coexist

profane

Grade 5 Review Reading Standard 2.5
Distinguish facts, supported inferences, and opinions in text.

The Tejano Soul of San Antonio

I'M A MIDWESTERNER, Chicago born and bred. So what am I doing living in Texas long after circumstance and necessity brought me here? Even my family can't understand why I wear pointy boots and a suede cowboy hat. It's not a cowboy hat, it's northern Mexican, but who's listening.

Maybe it's the sense of history here— the sense of story. Maybe it's los Tejanos— the Texans of Mexican descent. Their sense of knowing they belong to the land, no matter what the textbooks say. The sense of belonging, of contributing to this history. Something I never felt in Illinois.

In Texas I just want to sing like Lucha Villa,[1] drive my pickup down I-35 beneath a brilliant sky, clouds big and loose as pajamas. Because believe it or not, I'm home. Closer than I've ever been. Open my lungs and belt out to the prickly pear, "Ay mi querido publico, como les quiero."[2] And cry a little. Every good ranchera singer must cry.

Somewhere between New Braunfels and San Antonio, the landscape and the language change, the hills give out to flat lands, little by little, mile by mile—dust, pecan trees, mesquite, nopalitos. Then Nogalitos. Picoso. Dolorosa. Soledad. Culebra. Zarzamora. The names of San Antonio streets like the names of herbs. Because this is another country. This is the borderland. The beginning of Latin America. A place where two cultures collide, spark, spar, bleed, and sometimes create something wonderful.

A nice thing to live in a town where people know how to pronounce your name. Where you can walk down the street and you're not the minority. Where 55.6 percent of a population of 935,933 has a Spanish-language surname. Say what you will, I don't care if it was designated an "All American City," San Antonio is the most Mexican city this side of the Rio Grande. It's the Mexican culture that gives San Antonio its unique flavor. It's not called Saint Anthony, you know. . . .

San Antonio. Beneath the sky that doesn't wear a hat. Urracas—grackles—rowdy and raucous each evening. Chicharras— cicadas—buzzing in the heat. Thunk-thunk of pecans falling dusty from trees. A landscape that matches the one inside me, one foot in this country, one in that. Graceful two-step, howl of an accordion, little gem and jewel, a little sad, a little joyous, that has made me whole. A place where two languages coexist, two cultures side by side. Not simply on street signs and condominiums. Not simply on menus and bags of corn chips. But in the public and private, sacred and profane, common and extraordinary circumstances of that homeland called the heart.

—Sandra Cisneros

1. **Lucha Villa:** popular female mariachi singer.
2. **"Ay mi querido publico . . .":** "Ah, my beloved public, how I love you all."

Vocabulary

descent (dē·sent′) *n.:* ancestry.

minority (mī·nôr′ə·tē) *n.:* small group that differs from the larger, controlling group.

coexist (kō′ig·zist′) *v.:* live together peacefully.

profane (prō·fān′) *adj.:* not religious.

Reading Informational Materials

Reading Check

1. What does Cisneros feel in Texas that she does not feel in Illinois?

2. Cisneros uses **context clues** to help you understand what a *Tejano* is. How is *Tejano* defined?

3. Why does Cisneros like living in San Antonio?

4. How does the landscape of San Antonio match the landscape inside this writer?

TestPractice

THE TEJANO SOUL OF SAN ANTONIO

1. Which of the following is a **fact**?
   - A Cisneros was born in Chicago.
   - B San Antonio's streets are named after herbs.
   - C The sky in San Antonio doesn't wear a hat.
   - D Mexican culture gives San Antonio its unique flavor.

2. The statement "Every good ranchera singer must cry" is —
   - F a fact
   - G an inference
   - H an opinion
   - J a prediction

3. Which of the following statements is *not* a **fact**?
   - A Everyone in San Antonio can speak Spanish.
   - B More than 55 percent of the population has a Spanish-language surname.
   - C The population of San Antonio is 935,933.
   - D San Antonio was designated an "All American City."

4. "San Antonio is the most Mexican city this side of the Rio Grande." Cisneros's **inference** is based on her experiences and the fact that San Antonio —
   - F was designated an "All American City"
   - G has a majority of people of Spanish descent
   - H is not as pretty as Chicago
   - J is nowhere near the Rio Grande

5. Which of the following **inferences** is supported by details in the article?
   - A Cisneros feels uncomfortable in San Antonio.
   - B Cisneros never wants to live in Illinois again.
   - C Cisneros does not reveal her feelings.
   - D Cisneros uses a poetic style to reveal her love for San Antonio.

Grade 5 Review Reading Standard 2.5
Distinguish facts, supported inferences, and opinions in text.

Vocabulary Development

Using Word, Sentence, and Paragraph Clues

Just about everyone encounters unfamiliar words when reading—it's nothing to worry about. A dictionary can quickly help you learn the meaning of a new word, but what if you don't have a dictionary handy? Word, sentence, and paragraph clues can help. Here's how:

- **Word clues.** Does the unfamiliar word resemble a word or word part you already know?

- **Sentence clues.** Does the writer provide a clue by contrasting the word with another familiar word? Does the writer actually provide a definition right there in the text? What part of speech is the unfamiliar word? (Usually you can tell by where it appears in the sentence.) Does the meaning of the sentence change considerably if you substitute or remove the unfamiliar word?

- **Paragraph clues.** What is the paragraph's main idea? What possible connections could the word have to the main idea or the other sentences in the paragraph?

Let's look at an example from the Word Bank:

Descent is very close in form to the word *descendant*, meaning "ancestor." Look at the sentence "Maybe it's los Tejanos—the Texans of Mexican *descent.*" There's a sentence clue: The word *descent* is used as a noun. When we combine the word clues, we can guess that *descent* here means "ancestry." When it's tried in the sentence, *ancestry* makes sense.

Word Bank

descent
minority
coexist
profane

PRACTICE

Go back to the article, and look for clues that might help reveal the meanings of the other words in the Word Bank. Of course, if you studied the footnotes, you already know the meanings of those words, but it is the *clues* you are looking for. When you feel you've practiced that sufficiently, try your detective skills with an unfamiliar word from the selection, one that is not footnoted. Always check your guesses in a dictionary.

Grade 3 Review Reading Standard 1.6 Use sentence and word context to find the meaning of unknown words.

Literary Response and Analysis

 **TestPractice** DIRECTIONS: Read the story. Then, read each question, and choose the letter of the best response.

Here is a portion of a story set in Antigua, an island that is part of the West Indies. The narrator is a young girl named Annie John, who has for a while wanted to play with another girl she calls the Red Girl.

from The Red Girl

Jamaica Kincaid

The Red Girl and I stood under the guava tree looking each other up and down. What a beautiful thing I saw standing before me. Her face was big and round and red, like a moon—a red moon. She had big, broad, flat feet, and they were naked to the bare ground; her dress was dirty, the skirt and blouse tearing away from each other at one side; the red hair that I had first seen standing up on her head was matted and tangled; her hands were big and fat, and her fingernails held at least ten anthills of dirt under them. And on top of that, she had such an unbelievable, wonderful smell, as if she had never taken a bath in her whole life.

I soon learned this about her: She took a bath only once a week, and that was only so that she could be admitted to her grandmother's presence. She didn't like to bathe, and her mother didn't force her. She changed her dress once a week for the same reason. She preferred to wear a dress until it just couldn't be worn anymore. Her mother didn't mind that, either. She didn't like to comb her hair, though on the first day of school, she could put herself out for that. She didn't like to go to Sunday school, and her mother didn't force her. She didn't like to brush her teeth, but occasionally her mother said it was necessary. She loved to play marbles, and was so good that only Skerritt boys now played against her. Oh, what an angel she was, and what a heaven she lived in! I, on the other hand, took a full bath every morning and a sponge bath every night. I could hardly go out on my doorstep without putting my shoes on. I was not allowed to play in the sun without a hat on my head. My mother paid a woman who lived five houses away from us sevenpence a week—a penny for each school day and twopence for Sunday—to comb my hair. On Saturday, my mother

Reading Standard 3.3
Analyze characterization as delineated through a character's thoughts, words, speech patterns, and actions; the narrator's description; and the thoughts, words, and actions of other characters.

washed my hair. Before I went to sleep at night I had to make sure my uniform was clean and creaseless and all laid out for the next day. I had to make sure that my shoes were clean and polished to a nice shine. I went to Sunday school every Sunday unless I was sick. I was not allowed to play marbles, and, as for Skerritt boys, that was hardly mentionable.

1. Which of the following **character traits** does the narrator apply to the Red Girl?

   A She is a careful dresser.

   B She spends too much time on her hair.

   C She is unconcerned about her appearance.

   D She is always clean and neat.

2. All of the following **traits** are characteristic of the narrator *except* —

   F she envies the Red Girl's freedom

   G she much prefers her own life to that of the Red Girl

   H she obeys her mother

   J she dresses neatly and wears clean shoes

3. From the narrator's vivid description of the Red Girl, you can **infer** that the narrator —

   A is disgusted by the Red Girl

   B wants to help the Red Girl

   C longs to be more like the Red Girl

   D doesn't want to be friends with the Red Girl

4. The narrator tells us directly how she feels about the Red Girl when she says —

   F "She took a bath only once a week. . . ."

   G "She didn't like to go to Sunday school. . . ."

   H "I was not allowed to play in the sun without a hat on my head."

   J "Oh, what an angel she was, and what a heaven she lived in!"

5. In this passage from "The Red Girl," the narrator uses all of the following methods of **characterization** *except* —

   A stating character traits directly

   B describing actions

   C quoting speech

   D describing appearance

Vocabulary Development (Review)

The words in this Test Practice review Vocabulary words you have studied in Chapters 1 and 2.

TestPractice

Synonyms

DIRECTIONS: Choose the word or phrase that means the same or about the same as the underlined word.

1. To sabotage means to —
   A   hide
   B   destroy
   C   remove
   D   collect

2. A staid person is usually —
   F   tired
   G   restless
   H   bothersome
   J   quiet

3. Seeking consolation is the same as seeking —
   A   comfort
   B   prizes
   C   housing
   D   warmth

4. An intelligible conversation is —
   F   alien
   G   secretive
   H   understandable
   J   unimportant

5. If someone is perturbed, he or she is —
   A   troubled
   B   surprised
   C   pleased
   D   calmed

6. To alleviate pain means to —
   F   increase it
   G   relieve it
   H   deepen it
   J   disguise it

7. A valiant person is —
   A   truthful
   B   brave
   C   graceful
   D   cowardly

8. A derisive laugh sounds —
   F   scornful
   G   musical
   H   loving
   J   loud

9. A menace is a —
   A   pest
   B   nightmare
   C   machine
   D   danger

10. Someone who is intimidated is —
    F   frightened
    G   alone
    H   angry
    J   hopeful

RESPONSE TO LITERATURE

Mastering the Standards

Profiler

When you analyze something, you look at it closely. You take it apart to see how it was put together and how its parts work. From one of the stories in this chapter, choose a **character** you'd enjoy analyzing. Your task is to find out all you can about the character. Start by filling out an organizer like the one below. To fill out the "Traits" column, you have to make **inferences,** or guesses, based on the details in the second column. Check the list of traits for suggestions. Then, using the details you've collected, write a paragraph or two about your character. You might want to answer these questions before you write:

- What does the character want?
- Does the character change? If so, what causes the change?
- Does the character discover something?
- Is the character believable?

▶ **Use "Writing a Character Analysis," pages 566–582, for help with this assignment.**

Character profile of _____

Clues to characterization	Details in Story	Traits
Speech		
Appearance		
Thoughts		
Other characters' responses		
Actions		
Writer's direct comments		

A List of Character Traits

cruel	kind
proud	humble
lazy	energetic
passive	assertive
selfish	unselfish
timid	courageous
pessimistic	optimistic
withdrawn	talkative
moody	happy

Fiction

A Moving Experience

Orphan Will Griffin is feeling lost when he relocates to the California desert with his flighty sister. Then Will meets a moody girl named Mike and an old loner named Sam. These three outsiders help one another through sorrowful times and discover the value of friendship in Jean Ferris's *Across the Grain.*

Family Ties

M. C. Higgins and his family have been living on Sarah's Mountain ever since M. C.'s great-grandmother arrived there as a fugitive from slavery. His family loves their mountain, but one day M. C. notices a massive pile of debris accumulating on a cliff over their home. In Virginia Hamilton's *M. C. Higgins, the Great,* a young boy is torn between his loyalty to his family and his desire for a life beyond the mountain.

This title is available in the HRW Library.

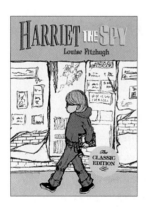

The Notebook

If you are interested in writing, you might enjoy Louise Fitzhugh's *Harriet the Spy.* Harriet Welsch longs to be a writer, so she begins recording honest observations of her classmates in her secret notebook. When the notebook is discovered by the classmates, Harriet finds out what being a writer really means.

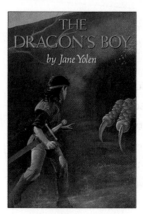

Friendly Fire

Artos is lonely and dissatisfied in his medieval castle. The other boys mock him because he does not know who his birth parents are. His life changes when he meets Linn, an old dragon who lives in a cave. In Jane Yolen's *The Dragon's Boy,* Linn guides Artos with his wisdom and proves that Artos's life will have great meaning after all.

Nonfiction

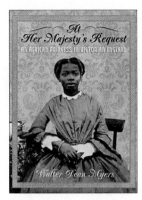

Starting a New Life

In *At Her Majesty's Request: An African Princess in Victorian England,* Walter Dean Myers tells the story of Sarah Forbes Bonetta, who was saved from death by a British sea captain. As a result, she spent her life in nineteenth-century England, a place where others made life decisions for her. Myers includes newspaper articles and portraits to add to the reality of Bonetta's compelling story.

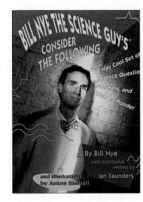

Science Stumpers

Have you ever wondered why leaves change color in the autumn? how a magnet sticks to a refrigerator? what prevents a heavy boat from sinking in the ocean? Bill Nye has the answers to all these questions and a whole lot more in *Bill Nye the Science Guy's Consider the Following.*

An Era Begins

In *Commodore Perry in the Land of the Shogun,* Rhoda Blumberg describes the beginning of trade talks between Japan and the United States in the nineteenth century. Blumberg sensitively depicts relations between two distinct cultural groups who were wary of each other at first but grew to respect each other's differences.

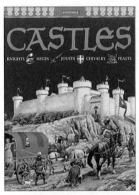

Medieval Times

Philip Steele provides an engaging overview of medieval life in *Castles.* In addition to providing astonishing and informative illustrations showing how castles were built, Steele describes the weapons used by medieval warriors and narrates a typical day in a castle town.

Themes Across Time

 # California Standards

Here are the Grade 7 standards you will study for mastery in Chapter 3. You will also review a standard from an earlier grade.

Reading

Word Analysis, Fluency, and Systematic Vocabulary Development

1.1 Identify idioms, analogies, metaphors, and similes in prose and poetry.

1.2 Use knowledge of Greek, Latin, and Anglo-Saxon roots and affixes to understand content-area vocabulary.

Reading Comprehension (Focus on Informational Materials)

2.3 Analyze text that uses the cause-and-effect organizational pattern.

Grade 6 Review

2.4 Clarify an understanding of texts by creating outlines, logical notes, summaries, or reports.

Literary Response and Analysis

3.4 Identify and analyze recurring themes across works (for example, the value of bravery, loyalty, and friendship; the effects of loneliness).

KEYWORD:
HLLA 7-3

Theme *by* Mara Rockliff

WHAT'S THE BIG IDEA?

A key element of literature—of fiction, nonfiction, poetry, and drama—is theme. **Theme** is a revelation about our lives; theme is a discovery of a truth about our own human experience.

Theme Is a Revelation

Suppose we read a story about two friends. Surprisingly, one friend betrays the other. If the story is well written, we will feel that we have lived through the betrayal ourselves. We will feel that the tragedy could have happened in exactly the way the writer tells it. As we share the characters' experiences in the story, we also discover something. We discover—or rediscover—the delicate nature and value of friendship.

Themes Focus on the "Big" Ideas

Literature that endures, that lasts through the centuries, tends to focus on discoveries about the big topics in everyone's life: understanding the nature of love, accepting responsibility, understanding loss, dealing with ambition, discovering the joys and problems of friendship.

A theme isn't something a writer tacks on to a story or poem to make it more literary. Theme grows naturally out of what the writer believes and out of the story that's being told.

If you've read several novels, you know that works by different writers can have similar themes, even though their stories may be quite different. Themes recur over and over again in the stories we tell because some truths about the human experience are universal, whether a story was written hundreds of years ago in a snowbound Alaskan village or typed on a laptop yesterday in Zimbabwe.

Plot Isn't Theme

"Plot is what a story is about," someone once said. "Theme is what a story is *really* about."

A story's plot might be about a family that drinks from a magical spring, becomes immortal, and suffers the consequences. That's what happens. But what's the story *really* about? What does the story reveal to you about life?

Maybe it reveals that living forever is more frightening than dying. Maybe it reveals that without death, growth and change would be impossible and life would no longer give us pleasure. In a single plot you might discover both themes, or you might see an entirely different theme instead.

Where Does It Say That?

You usually won't find the theme of a piece of literature stated directly. Theme is what the writer wants you to *discover* for yourself as you share the

Reading Standard 3.4 Identify and analyze recurring themes across works (for example, the value of bravery, loyalty, and friendship; the effects of loneliness).

experiences of the story's characters. One way to identify the theme is to look closely at what the writer is saying. Consider these questions:

- How has the main **character** changed over the course of the story? What has he or she **discovered** by the story's end?
- Which scenes or passages strike you as especially important to the story? What ideas about life do they suggest?
- What is the story's **title**? Does it reveal anything special about the story?

Evaluating Theme

Why go to the trouble of figuring out a story's theme? Why not just enjoy the plot and not worry about whether you've gotten the theme?

Because the theme *will* get through to you whether you realize it or not. Watch a double feature of shoot'em-up action movies, and twice in one night you've absorbed the idea that the world is a dangerous place where problems are best solved through violence. Read another teen romance, and you've been told once again that nothing is more important than finding true love.

You are not going to agree with all themes. In some stories you'll feel that the truth you're getting is the real deal, a gold nugget of wisdom the writer has discovered through hard experience and is passing on to you. In other stories you'll feel that the writer is just giving you an overused formula, which the writer repeats without even believing it.

Putting a theme into words brings it out into the open, where you can look at it critically and decide if it fits with what *you* know about life.

Practice

Choose two novels you have read recently that deal with similar topics—for example, loyalty, courage, friendship, or loneliness. If you have a favorite writer, use two novels by this writer.

Take a blank sheet of paper, and draw a chart like the one below. Write the title of each novel at the top of the page. Underneath the titles, identify their topics. Then, in one or two sentences, state the theme of each novel—what the story reveals to you about that topic.

Are the themes in the novels the same or different? Which theme do you find more important or more appealing and why?

Novel 1	Novel 2
Topic	Topic
Theme	Theme

The Highwayman

Literary Focus

Subject Versus Theme

After reading a story or a poem, have you ever asked yourself, "What does it *mean*?" What you are asking about is the theme. The **theme** is what a piece of literature reveals about people and life. It is the meaning you take away from the story.

A theme is not the same as a subject or topic. The **subject** of a work can usually be expressed in just a word or two: love, childhood, injustice. The theme is the idea that the writer wishes to convey *about* a particular subject. Some themes—like the power of love or the importance of home or the strength of the human spirit—have been at the heart of stories and poems throughout time.

Narrative Poems

Poems that are written to tell a story are called **narrative poems.** These story poems resemble short stories: They have a **plot, characters,** and a **setting.** Stories sung to the strumming of a stringed instrument are probably the oldest form of storytelling. Modern poems like "The Highwayman" use strong rhythms to make their stories sound like the old sung stories—they capture the enduring power of the spoken word.

You must read this poem aloud to feel its galloping rhythms.

Reading Standard 3.4 Identify and analyze recurring themes across works (for example, the value of bravery, loyalty, and friendship; the effects of loneliness).

Make the Connection

Talk It Over

It was a night for love and adventure. Start with the **setting:** a moonlit road hundreds of years ago, a country inn at midnight. Add some **characters:** a daring and dashing robber, a beautiful young woman, a jealous stableman, and a group of cruel soldiers. Can you predict what will happen? Hint: Look at the poem's title and illustrations. Skim the first verse.

Predicting. Discuss your impressions of the poem with a partner. On the basis of your preview, what do you think will happen?

Background

The highwayman in this famous poem is a robber who lived in England in the 1700s. Highwaymen used to stop stagecoaches on the lonely moorlands of northern England and Scotland to rob the rich passengers of money and jewels. Some highwaymen were considered heroes by the Scots because they shared the money with the poor. Highwaymen were sometimes dashing, romantic figures who dressed in expensive clothes. The poem is based on a true story that the poet heard while he was on vacation in the part of England where highwaymen used to lie in wait for stagecoaches.

The Highwayman

Alfred Noyes

Part 1

The wind was a torrent of darkness among the gusty trees,
The moon was a ghostly galleon° tossed upon cloudy seas,
The road was a ribbon of moonlight over the purple moor,
And the highwayman came riding—
5   Riding—riding—
The highwayman came riding, up to the old inn door.

He'd a French cocked hat on his forehead, a bunch of lace at his
  chin,
A coat of the claret° velvet, and breeches of brown doeskin.
They fitted with never a wrinkle. His boots were up to the thigh.
10 And he rode with a jeweled twinkle,
   His pistol butts a-twinkle,
His rapier hilt° a-twinkle, under the jeweled sky.

Over the cobbles he clattered and clashed in the dark inn yard.
And he tapped with his whip on the shutters, but all was locked
  and barred.
He whistled a tune to the window, and who should be waiting
15 there
But the landlord's black-eyed daughter,
   Bess, the landlord's daughter,
Plaiting° a dark red love knot into her long black hair.

---

 2. galleon (galʹē·ən) *n.:* large sailing ship.
 8. claret (klarʹit) *n.* used as *adj.:* purplish red, like claret wine.
 12. rapier (rāʹpē·ər) **hilt:** sword handle.
 18. plaiting (plātʹiŋ) *v.* used as *adj.:* braiding.

And dark in the dark old inn yard a stable wicket° creaked
20 Where Tim the ostler° listened. His face was white and peaked.
His eyes were hollows of madness, his hair like moldy hay,
But he loved the landlord's daughter,
        The landlord's red-lipped daughter,
Dumb as a dog he listened, and he heard the robber say—

25 "One kiss, my bonny sweetheart, I'm after a prize tonight,
But I shall be back with the yellow gold before the morning
    light;
Yet, if they press me sharply, and harry° me through the day,
Then look for me by moonlight,
        Watch for me by moonlight,
30 I'll come to thee by moonlight, though hell should bar the way."

He rose upright in the stirrups. He scarce could reach her hand,
But she loosened her hair in the casement.° His face burnt like a
    brand
As the black cascade of perfume came tumbling over his breast;
And he kissed its waves in the moonlight,
35   (Oh, sweet black waves in the moonlight!)
Then he tugged at his rein in the moonlight, and galloped away
    to the west.

Part 2

He did not come in the dawning. He did not come at noon;
And out of the tawny sunset, before the rise of the moon,
When the road was a gypsy's ribbon, looping the purple moor,
40 A redcoat troop came marching—
        Marching—marching—
King George's men came marching, up to the old inn door.

---

19. wicket *n.:* small door or gate.
20. ostler (äs′lər) *n.:* person who takes care of horses; groom.
27. harry *v.:* harass or push along.
32. casement *n.:* window that opens outward on hinges.

The Haywain by John Constable (1776–1837).
National Gallery, London/Bridgeman Art Library, London/Superstock.

They said no word to the landlord. They drank his ale instead.
But they gagged his daughter, and bound her, to the foot of her
    narrow bed.
45   Two of them knelt at her casement, with muskets at their side!
There was death at every window;
      And hell at one dark window;
For Bess could see, through her casement, the road that *he*
    would ride.

They had tied her up to attention, with many a sniggering jest;
They had bound a musket beside her, with the muzzle beneath
50   her breast!
"Now, keep good watch!" and they kissed her. She heard the
    dead man say—
Look for me by moonlight;
    Watch for me by moonlight;
I'll come to thee by moonlight, though hell should bar the way!

55   She twisted her hands behind her; but all the knots held good!
She writhed her hands till her fingers were wet with sweat or
    blood!
They stretched and strained in the darkness, and the hours
    crawled by like years,
Till, now, on the stroke of midnight,
    Cold, on the stroke of midnight,
60   The tip of one finger touched it! The trigger at least was hers!

The tip of one finger touched it; she strove no more for the rest!
Up, she stood up to attention, with the muzzle beneath her
    breast.
She would not risk their hearing; she would not strive again;
For the road lay bare in the moonlight;
65   Blank and bare in the moonlight;
And the blood of her veins, in the moonlight, throbbed to her
    love's refrain.

Tlot-tlot; tlot-tlot! Had they heard it? The horse hoofs ringing
    clear;
Tlot-tlot, tlot-tlot, in the distance? Were they deaf that they did
    not hear?
Down the ribbon of moonlight, over the brow of the hill,
70   The highwayman came riding,
    Riding, riding!
The redcoats looked to their priming!° She stood up, straight
    and still.

Tlot-tlot, in the frosty silence! *Tlot-tlot,* in the echoing night!
Nearer he came and nearer. Her face was like a light!
Her eyes grew wide for a moment; she drew one last deep
75   breath,
Then her fingers moved in the moonlight,
    Her musket shattered the moonlight,
Shattered her breast in the moonlight and warned him—with
    her death.

---

72. **priming** (prīm′iŋ) *n.:* explosive for firing a gun.

He turned. He spurred to the west; he did not know who stood
Bowed, with her head o'er the musket, drenched with her own
80   blood!
Not till the dawn he heard it, his face grew gray to hear
How Bess, the landlord's daughter,
        The landlord's black-eyed daughter,
Had watched for her love in the moonlight, and died in the
    darkness there.

85   Back, he spurred like a madman, shouting a curse to the sky,
With the white road smoking behind him and his rapier
        brandished high.
Blood-red were his spurs in the golden noon; wine-red was his
    velvet coat;
When they shot him down on the highway,
        Down like a dog on the highway,
And he lay in his blood on the highway, with the bunch of lace
90   at his throat.

And still of a winter's night, they say, when the wind is in the
    trees,
When the moon is a ghostly galleon tossed upon cloudy seas,
When the road is a ribbon of moonlight over the purple moor,
A highwayman comes riding—
95   *Riding—riding—*
A highwayman comes riding, up to the old inn door.

Over the cobbles he clatters and clangs in the dark inn yard;
He taps with his whip on the shutters, but all is locked and
        barred.
He whistles a tune to the window, and who should be waiting
        there
100 *But the landlord's black-eyed daughter,*
        Bess, the landlord's daughter,
Plaiting a dark red love knot into her long black hair.

Alfred Noyes

The Granger Collection, New York.

A Rousing Romantic

The British poet, novelist, biographer, and essayist **Alfred Noyes** (1880–1958) was possibly the most popular writer of his time. People enjoyed his verse for its rousing storytelling and its thumping rhythms—in fact, his work was often performed aloud.

Noyes, unlike most other poets of his time, was successful enough to earn a living solely from his poetry. He particularly liked the work of Alfred, Lord Tennyson, whose poetry had been popular during Noyes's childhood. Although the twentieth century was a time of literary experimentation and rebellion against convention, Noyes's poems were written in a traditional style, sounding as if they came from a much earlier era.

Today Noyes is best remembered for "The Highwayman," which he wrote in a small cottage on the edge of Bagshot Heath shortly after leaving Oxford University. He recalled:

> Bagshot Heath in those days was a wild bit of country, all heather and pinewoods. 'The Highwayman' suggested itself to me one blustery night when the sound of the wind in the pines gave me the first line: 'The wind was a torrent of darkness among the gusty trees. . . .'
>
> It took me about two days to complete the poem. Shortly afterward it appeared in *Blackwood's Magazine.* It illustrates the unpredictable chances of authorship, that this poem, written in so short a time, when I was twenty-four, should have been read so widely.
>
> I think the success of the poem in all these ways was due to the fact that it was not an artificial composition but was written at an age when I was genuinely excited by that kind of romantic story.

Literary Response and Analysis

Reading Check

1. Review the main events of this **narrative poem,** and then complete a **sequence chart** like the one below.

Part 1

> **a.** The highwayman rides to the old inn.

> **b.** He finds Bess waiting.

> **c.** Tim overhears him say . . .

Interpretations

2. What is the **setting** of this story? What details in the poem help you *see* and *hear* what is happening?

3. What is Tim's **motive,** or reason, for betraying Bess?

4. The last two stanzas are very like the first and third stanzas, except that the wording is slightly different. How does the difference reflect what is happening at the end of the poem?

5. This poem is about love, betrayal, and death. What **theme,** or revelation about people and life, does the poem reveal to you?

6. **Alliteration** (ə·lit′ər·ā′shən) is the repetition of consonant sounds in words close to one another. You can hear alliteration in the phrase "ghostly galleon." Read aloud five other lines in the poem that use alliteration.

Reading Standard 3.4
Identify and analyze recurring themes across works (for example, the value of bravery, loyalty, and friendship; the effects of loneliness).

Evaluation

7. Bess gives up her life for the highwayman. Was her sacrifice noble or pointless? What do you think?

8. Here is a student's letter about "The Highwayman." What points would you make in a letter about the poem?

Dear Editors;

    I am a seventh grader at Madison Jr. High. My name is Brooke Garner. Our class has been reading many stories in your book.
    My favorite poem ~~that~~ is "The Highwayman." It shows a very deep understanding and love between the highwayman and the girl. This poem was so touching that ~~through~~ every emotion the writer was trying to convey, filtered through my mind and I was left weakened by its magnitude. The poem lived and I feel that the author had somehow been hurt and understood how the people must have felt and lived.

          Sincerely yours,

          Brooke Garner

9. If you could write a new ending for the poem, what would it be?

Writing

Being There!

The poem concerns itself mainly with the highwayman and Bess. We never learn much about the other characters. Imagine you are either Tim the ostler or one of the soldiers who come to the inn. Write a paragraph about your reaction to Bess's death. Write as "I."

Vocabulary Development

Making Connections: Similes and Metaphors

In our everyday language we use many expressions that are not literally true: "Charlie's bragging gets under my skin." "Gilda's money is burning a hole in her pocket." When we use expressions like these, we are using **figures of speech.** Our listeners know that the words do not carry their ordinary meaning. Bragging, after all, does not really pierce skin, and money cannot cause a pocket to catch fire.

The meaning of such figurative expressions depends on comparisons. Bragging is *compared* to something that causes pain or annoyance, such as a thorn. Money is *compared* to something so hot that it cannot be held and must be gotten rid of.

There are many kinds of figures of speech; the most common are **similes** and **metaphors.**

A **simile** is a comparison of two unlike things using the word *like, as, than,* or *resembles.* Here are two famous similes:

> I wandered lonely as a cloud....
> —William Wordsworth

> My love is like a red, red rose....
> —Robert Burns

A **metaphor** also compares two unlike things, but it does so without using *like, as, than,* or *resembles.* For example, in "The Highwayman," Alfred Noyes does not say the moon was *like* a ghostly galleon. He uses a metaphor: "The moon *was* a ghostly galleon tossed upon cloudy seas."

PRACTICE

Fill in this chart by completing each comparison from "The Highwayman." Then, identify it as a simile or a metaphor. The first item has been done for you.

Figure of Speech
line 1: The wind is compared to a torrent of darkness. (a metaphor)
line 3: The road is compared to
line 12: The stars in the sky are compared to
line 21: Tim's eyes are compared to
line 21: Tim's hair is compared to
line 24: Tim's dumbness is compared to
line 32: The highwayman's face is compared to
line 39: The road is compared to
line 74: Bess's face is compared to

Reading Standard 1.1 Identify metaphors and similes in poetry.

Gentlemen of the Road

Analyzing Causes and Effects

You know from experience that one thing leads to another. If you sleep through your alarm, you know you'll be late for school and you'll miss your favorite class—English. Sleeping through your alarm is a **cause**—it makes something happen. An **effect** is what happens as a result of some event—you're late for school and miss English.

You could go on. Being late for English class causes you to have to make up the time after school. Making up the time causes you to miss tryouts for football. Missing tryouts causes you to lose the chance to impress a certain girl. So you lose the girl, and it all can be traced to sleeping through an alarm.

When you read a text and ask, "Why did this happen?" and "What happened because of this?" you are asking about causes and effects.

To find causes and their effects, look for signal terms such as *cause, effect, resulted in, so, thus,* and *because.*

Cause and Effect

What Happened
Some people in England got very rich. Others got poorer.

↓

Effect
Government built new toll roads for the rich to travel.

↓

Effect
Highwaymen held up stagecoaches and carriages to get money.

↓

Effect
Highwaymen . . .

Reading Standard 2.3 Analyze text that uses the cause-and-effect organizational pattern.

Gentlemen of the Road

W HY DID PEOPLE ONCE THINK of highwaymen, the bandits (like Bess's beloved) who robbed travelers in seventeenth- and eighteenth-century England, as gentlemen?

To answer that question, first look at these facts. The seventeenth and eighteenth centuries saw the rise of a very wealthy class in England. England became a nation of haves and have-nots. The rich dressed in silks and velvets. Men and women wore huge powdered wigs. The rich lived on vast estates. They traveled to London for rounds of parties in the winter-spring season and spent summers in seaside towns, where gambling was a favorite pastime.

As the wealthy became richer, the conditions of the poor grew worse. Because the government did not care about their welfare, the poor lived in filthy slums in cities and in miserable conditions in farms and towns. In the worst years, 74 percent of the children in London died before the age of five. These were the social conditions that contributed to the rise of the highwaymen.

In addition, newly built toll roads ran through the countryside, connecting towns and villages. These improved roads brought out more travelers—rich ones. The highwaymen could stop the private carriages and the stagecoaches that used the toll roads and rob the passengers.

The highwaymen called themselves gentlemen of the road, and some people agreed—sometimes even their victims! How did they come by this surprising reputation?

Some people saw the highwaymen not as criminals but as the new Robin Hoods because they gave to the poor what they had stolen from the rich (or part of it).

> This article will explain why people thought of the highwaymen as gentlemen.

The Granger Collection, New York.

> This paragraph and those that follow tell what caused people to think of these bandits as gentlemen.

Their life of crime brought highwaymen lots of money— the reason they could afford to dress well.

Another reason why people thought of these bandits as gentlemen was that they looked the part. Most highwaymen came from poor families or, at best, middle-class ones. But once they turned to a life of crime, they could afford to dress in style. They wore high-heeled boots that went all the way to the hip, fancy shirts, long, elegant coats, and wide-brimmed hats with feathers. With their dashing clothes and fine horses these former footmen, butchers, and cheese sellers might have been mistaken for aristocrats.

Here's another reason why the highwaymen were considered gentlemen: their manners.

Some highwaymen tried to act like gentlemen as well. Many would never point a gun at a lady or search her for valuables, and sometimes they'd let women they robbed keep items of sentimental value. Highwaymen loved their horses too and took pride in earning the loyalty of their steeds by treating them well.

Some highwaymen politely begged their victims' pardon as they relieved them of their money and jewels. Others took only what they felt they needed and returned the rest to their owners.

Here is another example of gentlemanly behavior.

In one account a robbery victim was upset about losing his beloved watch. He offered the highwayman two guineas instead, along with a promise not to turn him in to the authorities. The highwayman agreed, and they went off together to the man's home. The money changed hands, the two men shared a bottle of wine, and after many courteous words on each side, the highwayman galloped off.

Final reason for their reputation as gentlemen.

Even when captured and sentenced to hang (the usual punishment for robbery in those days), some highwaymen tried to behave like gentlemen. They were too proud to cry or beg for mercy from the authorities they defied. After the noose was tied around their neck, some threw themselves off the scaffold rather than wait for the wagon they stood on to be pulled from beneath them. For those who romanticized the highwaymen in stories and song, this final act showed scorn for the corrupt authorities and courage in the face of death.

—Mara Rockliff

Reading Informational Materials

TestPractice

Gentlemen of the Road

1. This article suggests that all of the following might have **caused** the rise of the highwayman *except* the —

   A worsening conditions of the poor

   B rise of a very wealthy class

   C use of capital punishment

   D newly built toll roads

2. What **caused** people to see the highwaymen as the new Robin Hoods?

   F They rode horses and used bows and arrows.

   G They robbed from the rich and gave to the poor.

   H They lived in Sherwood Forest.

   J They wore Robin Hood outfits.

3. The highwaymen were able to dress in style because —

   A they were wealthy aristocrats

   B they took advice from their victims

   C their crimes made them wealthy

   D they were interested in fashion

4. Some highwaymen didn't beg for mercy from the hangman because of their —

   F pride

   G fear

   H mercy

   J shame

5. Which of the following statements does *not* explain why some people thought of the highwaymen as gentlemen?

   A The highwaymen behaved like gentlemen.

   B They treated women well.

   C They gave to the poor.

   D They came from rich families.

6. In the next-to-the-last paragraph the writer uses the word guineas. In the same paragraph she provides a context clue explaining what guineas are. What are they?

   F money

   G jewels

   H chickens

   J cattle

Reading Standard 2.3
Analyze text that uses the cause-and-effect organizational pattern.

Annabel Lee

Literary Focus
Title and Theme

"Annabel Lee" is a famous love poem, written after the poet's young wife, Virginia, died of tuberculosis. She was laid to rest in New York, near the Hudson River, in a sepulcher (sep′əl·kər), a burial vault that stands aboveground. Poe's poem reads like a fairy tale, set in a faraway time and place.

Across time, poets, storytellers, and songwriters have written about the many faces of love. It's an age-old subject that has inspired many themes. Songs tell of love that blooms in the most unexpected places. Storytellers write about love that overcomes impossible barriers. In "Annabel Lee," Poe's speaker describes an eternal love.

Repetition

Musicians, as you may know, use repetition—of sounds, of words, of tones—to create emotional effects. Poe uses repetition in much the same way. In "Annabel Lee," notice how words, sounds, phrases, and rhythms recur with hypnotic regularity. How many times does the name Annabel Lee appear in the poem?

Make the Connection
Think Aloud

With a partner, take turns reading stanzas of the poem aloud to hear its haunting sounds and to visualize its romantic setting. Exchange thoughts about the poem's speaker and its music. Jot down comments and questions as they come to you, and discuss them with your partner. Work together to solve any problems you have in understanding the poem.

(Above) Edgar Allan Poe's grave in Westminster Burial Ground in Baltimore, Maryland.

(Opposite) Poe's cottage before it was moved to Dyckman Street in the Bronx, New York.

Reading Standard 3.4 Identify and analyze recurring themes across works (for example, the value of bravery, loyalty, and friendship; the effects of loneliness).

Annabel Lee

Edgar Allan Poe

Portrait of "Sissy,"
Poe's beloved wife.

Valentine Museum,
Richmond, Virginia.

It was many and many a year ago,
    In a kingdom by the sea,
That a maiden there lived whom you may know
    By the name of Annabel Lee;
5 And this maiden she lived with no other thought
    Than to love and be loved by me.

I was a child and *she* was a child,
    In this kingdom by the sea:
But we loved with a love that was more than love—
10   I and my Annabel Lee—
With a love that the wingèd seraphs° of heaven
    Coveted° her and me.

And this was the reason that, long ago,
    In this kingdom by the sea,
15 A wind blew out of a cloud, chilling
    My beautiful Annabel Lee;
So that her highborn kinsmen came
    And bore her away from me,
To shut her up in a sepulcher
20   In this kingdom by the sea.

The angels, not half so happy in heaven,
    Went envying her and me—
Yes!—that was the reason (as all men know,
    In this kingdom by the sea)
25 That the wind came out of the cloud by night,
    Chilling and killing my Annabel Lee.

11. seraphs (ser'əfs) *n.:* angels.
12. coveted (kuv'it·id) *v.:* envied.

But our love it was stronger by far than the love
    Of those who were older than we—
    Of many far wiser than we—
30   And neither the angels in heaven above,
    Nor the demons down under the sea,
Can ever dissever° my soul from the soul
    Of the beautiful Annabel Lee—

For the moon never beams, without bringing me dreams
35   Of the beautiful Annabel Lee;
And the stars never rise, but I feel the bright eyes
    Of the beautiful Annabel Lee;
And so, all the night-tide, I lie down by the side
Of my darling—my darling—my life and my bride,
40   In the sepulcher there by the sea,
    In her tomb by the sounding sea.

32. dissever (di·sev′ər) *v.:* separate.

Crashing Wave (c. 1938) by Marsden Hartley.

Collection of Jon and Barbara Landau, New York.

Edgar Allan Poe

The Granger Collection, New York.

"A World of Moan"

Long before Stephen King began writing stories of horror, **Edgar Allan Poe** (1809–1849) was exploring the dark side of the human imagination in such works as "The Raven," "The Tell-Tale Heart," and "The Masque of the Red Death." Poe's life was hard from the start. First, his father deserted the family. Then, before Poe was three years old, his beautiful young mother died, and the little boy was left alone. John Allan, a wealthy and childless businessman in Richmond, Virginia, took in young Edgar and provided for his education, but the two constantly quarreled. Poe wanted to write, while his foster father wanted him to take over the family business. Eventually Poe broke away from his foster parents and set out on his own. Throughout his adult life he was plagued by poverty, alcoholism, and unhappiness. As Poe said, "I dwelt alone in a world of moan."

Always searching for a family, Poe married his thirteen-year-old cousin, Virginia Clemm. Her early death seemed to destroy him, and he himself died two years after she did. He had lived only forty years.

For Independent Reading

Poe's haunting poems include "The Raven" and "The Bells." You'll find some of his most chilling stories in a book titled *The Best of Poe*.

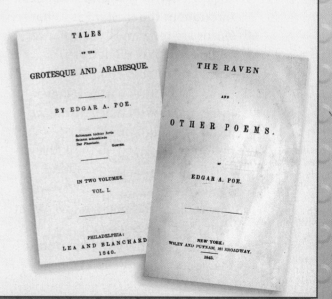

Literary Response and Analysis

Reading Check

1. How does the speaker describe the love he shared with Annabel Lee?

2. Who is jealous of the speaker and Annabel Lee?

3. What do Annabel Lee's highborn relatives do to her?

4. According to the last stanza, where does the speaker now see Annabel Lee? Where does he sleep each night?

Interpretations

5. Were you surprised when you discovered where the speaker sleeps each night? Do you think he actually sleeps there, or is he speaking of what he does in his imagination? Explain.

6. Find at least two details that help you picture the poem's **setting.**

7. List the **rhyming sounds** that echo throughout the six stanzas. What words are repeated over and over and over again? What does the repetition remind you of?

8. Some say that it's better to have loved and lost than never to have loved at all. Do you agree or disagree? How do you think the poem's speaker would respond to that idea?

9. One topic of this poem is loss. What does the poem say about loss? In other words, how would you state the poem's **theme**? Talk about

whether or not you think the speaker's feelings of grief are universal.

Writing

"My Love, You Remind Me of . . ."

In the poem the speaker says that the moon and stars remind him of Annabel Lee. Think of someone you feel strongly about—perhaps someone you love, admire, or miss very much. Jot down the special things and places that remind you of that person. Then, write a brief tribute, repeating the special things or places to emphasize what you miss about the person.

Portrait of a Girl at a Beach by John Collier.
© John Collier 2001. Reprinted by permission of Richard Solomon, Artists Representatives.

Reading Standard 3.4 Identify and analyze recurring themes across works (for example, the value of bravery, loyalty, and friendship; the effects of loneliness).

Vocabulary Development

Using Analogies

An **analogy** (ə·nal′ə·jē) is a comparison between two things to show how they are alike. An analogy can explain one idea by showing how that idea is similar to another, more easily understood idea. Analogies can be tricky, though, because few ideas or situations are alike in all ways. Here's an example in which a writer compares playing golf to being in love:

> I fell in love with golf when I was twenty-five. It would have been a healthier relationship had it been an adolescent romance or, better yet, a childhood crush. Though I'd like to think we've had a lot of laughs together and even some lyrical moments. I have never felt quite adequate to her demands, and she keeps secrets from me. . . . I can't get them out of my mind, or quite wrap my mind around them. Sometimes I wish that she and I had never met. She leads me on, but deep down I suspect—this is my secret—that I'm just not her type.
>
> —from "An Ode to Golf" by John Updike

PRACTICE

Try writing your own analogy. First, you have to find a subject you would like to talk about. Updike chose golf. Then, find something familiar that you can compare this subject to. Before you write your analogy, make a list of the ways in which your two subjects are similar. In your analogy, compare your subjects point by point. Here are some ideas for subjects:

Doing homework [is like . . .]   Family life [is like . . .]
Exercising [is like . . .]   Keeping friends [is like . . .]
Playing soccer [is like . . .]

If you prefer, write your analogy to explain something complex, perhaps something you learned in science. Scientists, in fact, use analogies all the time. On page 39, a writer helps us understand the workings of a cobra's hood by comparing it to an umbrella. A doctor might compare antibodies zeroing in on a tumor to guided missiles finding their target.

Reading Standard 1.1
Identify analogies.

The Fall of the House of Poe?

Clarify Your Understanding: Take Notes

When you read informational material actively, a lot goes on in your head.

- You connect what you read with your own experiences and knowledge.
- You ask yourself questions and make predictions.
- You challenge the text.
- You reflect on its meaning.

Jotting down notes will help you understand and remember what you read. Here's what to do:

- **Be organized.** Use a simple outline form to jot down the information or ideas that you think are most important. (See the box for a sample outline form.)
- **Be brief.** Keep your notes short, simple, and clear. Write only words and phrases that will help you focus on the most important information.
- **Underline or circle information.** It may be useful to highlight certain information directly in the text, but don't do it in a book that doesn't belong to you, and don't get carried away. If everything is highlighted, then it's hard to tell what's most important.

When you read this selection about a house Edgar Allan Poe once lived in, keep a sheet of paper nearby and jot down key details.

Outlining

Outlining can help you uncover the skeleton that holds the text together. An outline highlights main ideas and supporting details. Here's an example of an informal outline:

Main idea
supporting detail
supporting detail
[etc.]

Main idea
supporting detail
supporting detail
[etc.]

Grade 6 Review Reading Standard 2.4 Clarify an understanding of texts by creating outlines and logical notes.

THE FALL OF THE HOUSE OF POE?

THINK OF YOUR FAVORITE PLACE in the world, the place where you've spent some of the happiest hours of your life.

Now, think about it being torn down.

How do you feel? Terrible, right? If Edgar Allan Poe were alive today, scholars say, that's the way he might feel about the fate of the boardinghouse he once lived in at 85 Amity Street in New York City's Greenwich Village.

More than a century and a half has passed since Poe died. Amity Street was long ago renamed West Third Street, and the former boardinghouse now belongs to New York University. For years the university used it for classrooms and offices. But in 1999, NYU officials announced that they would be tearing the house down to make room for a new building for their law school.

Loyal Poe fans joined neighborhood residents in vigorously protesting the university's plan. They wrote letters, circulated petitions, and organized a rally attended by several hundred supporters chanting, "No, no, Poe won't go." They read aloud from "The Raven," the poem that made Poe famous, and chanted its famous refrain: "Nevermore!"

"It always mystified me why there was not a gold plaque outside the house," one Poe scholar said. "It is a genuine literary landmark."

New York University disagreed. Its representatives argued that Poe (along with his young wife, Virginia, and her mother) may have lived at the boardinghouse for as little as six months and that he had not written any of his more important works there. They also said that the house had changed drastically over the years, leaving no traces of Poe's residence. They even questioned whether the current building was the same one that had stood there in 1845, when Poe moved in. One NYU representative concluded, "This is not a building that remembers Poe."

The protesters researched the university's claims. They studied all kinds of documents, from letters and recollections of people who knew Poe to public records showing the history of the neighborhood.

Judging from dates and addresses in Poe's surviving correspondence, including a valentine given to him by Virginia in 1846, it seems probable that Poe lived there for less than a year. But that may have been longer than he stayed at any of the other eight places where he lived in Manhattan, all of which have already been torn down.

But the months he spent at 85 Amity may have been the happiest in Poe's short

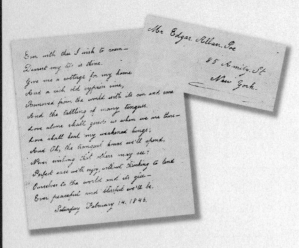

and troubled life. The boardinghouse was close to Washington Square Park, where his young wife, who was dying of tuberculosis, could breathe fresh air into her ailing lungs. That would have been his last full year with his beloved Virginia.

Professionally Poe was at the height of his career. He had finally achieved what he called "the one great purpose of my literary life"—writing and editing his own literary magazine, the *Broadway Journal*. He also had published *The Raven and Other Poems,* and he had written dozens of essays and short stories, including his

famous detective story "The Facts in the Case of M. Valdemar." Poe was completely absorbed in his writing, sometimes spending as many as fifteen hours a day at his desk.

The house where all that happened, it turned out, was indeed the house that the university planned to demolish. Detailed city atlases in the Maps Division of the New York Public Library show that although the name of the street has changed, the house numbers have not. Eighty-five West Third was 85 Amity. The house, according to tax ledgers in the New York City Municipal Archives, was built in 1836—nearly a decade before the Poe family moved in.

On September 29, 2000, after examining the evidence on both sides, State Supreme Court Judge Robert E. Lippmann dismissed the case, saying he had no legal authority to prevent NYU from tearing down the Poe house. This prompted an NYU spokesman to add, "The Tell-Tale Heart does not beat beneath the floorboards of this building." Preservation groups planned to appeal the decision.

—Mara Rockliff

Reading Informational Materials

Reading Check

Complete the blanks in the following outline.

I. NYU officials plan to tear down Poe house in order to build new law school.

II. Poe fans and residents protest.

III. NYU argues against protesters.

    A. Poe lived there for less than six months.

    B. _____

    C. _____

IV. Protesters research NYU's claims.

    A. _____

    B. _____

    C. _____

    D. _____

Test Practice

THE FALL OF THE HOUSE OF POE?

1. Which of the following statements is an **opinion,** not a fact?

  A Poe wrote *The Raven and Other Poems.*

  B Poe's young wife died of tuberculosis.

  C All the other places in Manhattan that Poe lived in have already been torn down.

  D "This is not a building that remembers Poe."

2. The judge who dismissed the case did so because he —

  F had no legal authority to prevent NYU from tearing down the house

  G believed NYU was doing the right thing

  H did not like the protesters

  J did not think the protesters had a good case

3. When Poe said he achieved "the one great purpose of my literary life," he was referring to —

  A living at 85 Amity Street with Virginia

  B writing *The Raven and Other Poems*

  C turning his attention to his wife's illness

  D writing and editing his own literary magazine

4. Which of the following would *not* be included in an outline of the article?

  F Poe definitely lived at the house on Amity Street.

  G The judge dismisses the case.

  H Preservation groups plan to appeal.

  J There are other law schools in New York City.

Grade 6 Review Reading Standard 2.4 Clarify an understanding of texts by creating outlines and logical notes.

Vocabulary Development

Latin Roots

Many English word roots come directly or indirectly from the Latin language. A word **root** is a word or word part from which other words are made. Learning some of the main word roots derived from Latin will give you a key to understanding the meaning of many English words.

Words with Latin Roots

circulated
petitions
representatives
absorbed
demolish

PRACTICE

Match each word in the box above with the Latin word it comes from. Can you find an additional word with the same origin and use it in a sentence?

Latin Word	Meaning	Word Bank	Additional Word
petere	"to seek"		
demoliri	"to pull down; destroy"		
circulari	"to form a circle"		
absorbere	"to suck in"		
repraesentare	"to be again"		

Reading Standard 1.2
Use knowledge of Latin roots to understand content-area vocabulary.

User Friendly

Literary Focus
Discovering Theme

Here are some tips that can help you find a story's theme:

- Decide what the characters have learned or discovered by the end of the story. Often that discovery can be translated into a statement of the theme.

- Think about the **title** and what it might mean. (Not all titles have significance. Some titles just tell you what the main character will be facing in each story. But the title of Jack London's novel *Call of the Wild* definitely points to a theme in the book.)

- Look for key passages in which the writer seems to make important statements about life. They may point to the theme.

Reading Skills
Recognizing Causes and Effects: Seeing Why Things Happen

In "User Friendly" a chain of events lands Kevin in computer trouble. He sees **effects** (what happens), but he's blind to **causes** (why the events happen) until it's too late. A **causal chain** is a series of events in which each event causes another one to happen, like dominoes falling in a row. Be careful, though—one event can follow another without having been caused by it. To figure out causes and effects, follow these steps:

- Look for what happens first. Then, ask what happens *because* of that.

- Look for hidden or multiple causes and results.

- Use a graphic organizer, such as a flowchart, to record the chain of events.

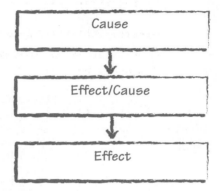

As you read, you'll find little open-book signs at certain points in the story. Stop at these points, and answer the questions about cause and effect.

Make the Connection
Quickwrite ✏️

Suppose someone you just met said, "My best friend is a computer." What would that statement tell you about the person? List some **character traits** you'd guess that the person might have.

Reading Standard 3.4 Identify and analyze recurring themes across works (for example, the value of bravery, loyalty, and friendship; the effects of loneliness).

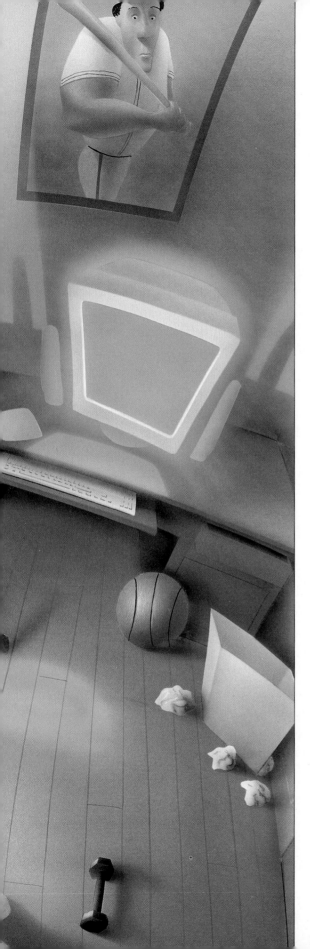

User Friendly

T. Ernesto Bethancourt

I reached over and shut off the insistent buzzing of my bedside alarm clock. I sat up, swung my feet over the edge of the bed, and felt for my slippers on the floor. Yawning, I walked toward the bathroom. As I walked by the corner of my room, where my computer table was set up, I pressed the *on* button, slid a diskette into the floppy drive, then went to brush my teeth. By the time I got back, the computer's screen was glowing greenly, displaying the message: *Good morning, Kevin.*

I sat down before the computer table, addressed the keyboard, and typed: *Good morning, Louis.* The computer immediately began to whir and promptly displayed a list of items on its green screen.

```
Today is Monday, April 22, the
113th day of the year. There are
253 days remaining. Your 14th
birthday is five days from
this date.

Math test today, 4th Period.

Your history project is due
today. Do you wish printout:
Y/N?
```

I punched the letter *Y* on the keyboard and flipped on the switch to the computer's printer. At once the printer sprang to life and began *eeeek*ing out page one. I went downstairs to breakfast.

My bowl of Frosted Flakes was neatly in place, flanked by a small pitcher of milk, an empty juice glass, and an unpeeled banana. I picked up the glass, went to the refrigerator, poured myself a glass of Tang, and sat down to my usual lonely breakfast. Mom was already at work, and Dad wouldn't be home from his Chicago trip for another three days. I absently[1] read the list of ingredients in Frosted Flakes for what seemed like the millionth time. I sighed deeply.

When I returned to my room to shower and dress for the day, my history project was already printed out. I had almost walked by Louis, when I noticed there was a message on the screen. It wasn't the usual:

```
Printout completed. Do you
wish to continue: Y/N?
```

Underneath the printout question were two lines:

```
When are you going to get me
my voice module,[2] Kevin?
```

I blinked. It couldn't be. There was nothing in Louis's basic programming that would allow for a question like this. Wondering what was going on, I sat down at the keyboard and entered: *Repeat last message.* Amazingly, the computer replied:

```
It's right there on the
screen, Kevin. Can we talk?
```

```
I mean, are you going to get
me a voice box?
```

I was stunned. What was going on here? Dad and I had put this computer together. Well, Dad had, and I had helped. Dad is one of the best engineers and master computer designers at Major Electronics, in Santa Rosario, California, where our family lives.

Just ask anyone in Silicon Valley[3] who Jeremy Neal is and you get a whole rave review of his inventions and modifications[4] of the latest in computer technology. It isn't easy being his son either. Everyone expects me to open my mouth and read printouts on my tongue.

I mean, I'm no dumbo. I'm at the top of my classes in everything but PE. I skipped my last grade in junior high, and most of the kids at Santa Rosario High call me a brain. But next to Dad I have a long, long way to go. He's a for-real genius.

So when I wanted a home computer, he didn't go to the local ComputerLand store. He built one for me. Dad had used components[5] from the latest model that Major Electronics was developing. The CPU, or central computing unit—the heart of every computer—was a new design. But surely that didn't mean much, I thought. There were CPUs just like it, all over the country, in Major's new line. And so far as I knew, there wasn't a one of them that could ask questions, besides *YES/NO?* or *request additional information.*

It had to be the extra circuitry in the gray

---

1. **absently** *adv.:* in a distracted, inattentive way.
2. **voice module:** unit that, when connected to a computer, enables it to produce speech.

3. **Silicon Valley:** area in central California that is a center of the computer industry. (Silicon is used in the manufacture of computer chips, or circuits.)
4. **modifications** (mäd′ə·fi·kā′shənz) *n.:* slight changes.
5. **components** (kəm·pō′nənts) *n.:* parts.

plastic case next to Louis's console.[6] It was a new idea Dad had come up with. That case housed Louis's "personality," as Dad called it. He told me it'd make computing more fun for me, if there was a tutorial program[7] built in, to help me get started.

RECOGNIZING CAUSE AND EFFECT
1. Why is Kevin stunned? What does he think causes Louis's unusual behavior?

I think he also wanted to give me a sort of friend. I don't have many. . . . Face it, I don't have *any*. The kids at school stay away from me, like I'm a freak or something.

We even named my electronic tutor Louis, after my great-uncle. He was a brainy guy who encouraged my dad when he was a kid. Dad didn't just give Louis a name either. Louis had gangs of features that probably won't be out on the market for years.

The only reason Louis didn't have a voice module was that Dad wasn't satisfied with the ones available. He wanted Louis to sound like a kid my age, and he was modifying a module when he had the time. Giving Louis a name didn't mean it was a person, yet here it was, asking me a question that just couldn't be in its programming. It wanted to talk to me!

Frowning, I quickly typed: *We'll have to wait and see, Louis. When it's ready, you'll get your voice.* The machine whirred and displayed another message:

`That's no answer, Kevin.`

---

6. **console** (kän′sōl′) *n.:* a computer's keyboard and monitor (display unit). *Console* can also refer to a cabinet for a radio, stereo, or television.
7. **tutorial program:** program that provides instructions for performing specific tasks on a computer.

Shaking my head, I answered: *That's what my dad tells me. It'll have to do for you. Good morning, Louis.* I reached over and flipped the standby switch, which kept the computer ready but not actively running.

I showered, dressed, and picked up the printout of my history project. As I was about to leave the room, I glanced back at the computer table. Had I been imagining things?

I'll have to ask Dad about it when he calls tonight, I thought. *I wonder what he'll think of it. Bad enough the thing is talking to me. I'm answering it!*

Before I went out to catch my bus, I carefully checked the house for unlocked doors and open windows. It was part of my daily routine. Mom works, and most of the day the house is empty: a natural setup for robbers. I glanced in the hall mirror just as I was ready to go out the door.

My usual reflection gazed back. Same old Kevin Neal: five ten, one hundred twenty pounds, light-brown hair, gray eyes, clear skin. I was wearing my Santa Rosario Rangers T-shirt, jeans, and sneakers.

"You don't look like a flake to me," I said to the mirror, then added, "but maybe Mom's right. Maybe you spend too much time alone with Louis." Then I ran to get my bus.

Ginny Linke was just two seats away from me on the bus. She was with Sherry Graber and Linda Martinez. They were laughing, whispering to each other, and looking around at the other students. I promised myself that today I was actually going to talk to Ginny. But then, I'd promised myself that every day for the past school year. Somehow I'd never got up the nerve.

What does she want to talk with you for?

I asked myself. She's great-looking . . . has that head of blond hair . . . a terrific bod, and wears the latest clothes. . . .

And just look at yourself, pal, I thought. You're under six foot, skinny . . . a year younger than most kids in junior high. Worse than that, you're a brain. If that doesn't ace you out with girls, what does?

The bus stopped in front of Santa Rosario High and the students began to file out. I got up fast and quickly covered the space between me and Ginny Linke. *It's now or never,* I thought. I reached forward and tapped Ginny on the shoulder. She turned and smiled. She really smiled!

"Uhhhh . . . Ginny?" I said.

"Yes, what is it?" she replied.

"I'm Kevin Neal. . . ."

"Yes, I know," said Ginny.

"You do?" I gulped in amazement. "How come?"

"I asked my brother, Chuck. He's in your math class."

I knew who Chuck Linke was. He plays left tackle on the Rangers. The only reason he's in my math class is he's taken intermediate algebra twice . . . so far. He's real bad news, and I stay clear of him and his crowd.

"What'd you ask Chuck?" I said.

Ginny laughed. "I asked him who was that nerdy kid who keeps staring at me on the bus. He knew who I meant, right away."

Sherry and Linda, who'd heard it all, broke into squeals of laughter. They were still laughing and looking back over their shoulders at me when they got off the bus. I slunk off the vehicle, feeling even more nerdish than Ginny thought I was.

When I got home that afternoon, at two, I went right into the empty house. I avoided my reflection in the hall mirror. I was pretty

sure I'd screwed up on the fourth-period math test. All I could see was Ginny's face, laughing at me.

Nerdy kid, I thought, *that's what she thinks of me.* I didn't even have my usual after-school snack of a peanut butter and banana sandwich. I went straight upstairs to my room and tossed my books onto the unmade bed. I walked over to the computer table and pushed the *on* button. The screen flashed:

```
Good afternoon, Kevin.
```

Although it wasn't the programmed response to Louis's greeting, I typed in: *There's nothing good about it. And girls are no @#%!!! good!* The machine responded:

```
Don't use bad language,
Kevin. It isn't nice.
```

Repeat last message, I typed rapidly. It was happening again! The machine was . . . well, it was talking to me, like another person would. The "bad language" message disappeared and in its place was:

```
Once is enough, Kevin.
Don't swear at me for
something I didn't do.
```

"This is it," I said aloud. "I'm losing my marbles." I reached over to flip the standby switch. Louis's screen quickly flashed out:

```
Don't cut me off, Kevin.
Maybe I can help: Y/N?
```

I punched the *Y.* "If I'm crazy," I said, "at least I have company. Louis doesn't think I'm a nerd. Or does it?" The machine flashed the message:

```
How can I help?
```

Do you think I'm a nerd? I typed.

```
Never! I think you're
wonderful. Who said you
were a nerd?
```

I stared at the screen. *How do you know what a nerd is?* I typed. The machine responded instantly. It had never run this fast before.

```
Special vocabulary, entry
#635. BASIC Prog. #4231. And
who said you were a nerd?
```

"That's right," I said, relieved. "Dad programmed all those extra words for Louis's 'personality.'" Then I typed in the answer to Louis's question: *Ginny Linke said it.* Louis flashed:

```
This is a human female?
Request additional data.
```

Still not believing I was doing it, I entered all I knew about Ginny Linke, right down to the phone number I'd never had the nerve to use. Maybe it was dumb, but I also typed in how I felt about Ginny. I even wrote out the incident on the bus that morning. Louis whirred, then flashed out:

```
She's cruel and stupid.
You're the finest person
I know.
```

I'm the ONLY person you know, I typed.

```
That doesn't matter. You
are my user. Your happiness
is everything to me. I'll
take care of Ginny.
```

The screen returned to the *Good afternoon, Kevin* message. I typed out: *Wait! How can you do all this? What do you mean, you'll take care of Ginny?* But all Louis responded was:

```
Programming Error: 76534.
```

```
Not programmed
to respond to
this type of
question.
```

No matter what I did for the next few hours, I couldn't get Louis to do anything outside of its regular programming. When Mom came home from work, I didn't mention the funny goings-on. I was sure Mom would think I'd gone stark bonkers. But when Dad called that evening, after dinner, I asked to speak to him.

"Hi, Dad. How's Chicago?"

"Dirty, crowded, cold, and windy," came Dad's voice over the miles. "But did you want a weather report, son? What's on your mind? Something wrong?"

"Not exactly, Dad. Louis is acting funny. Real funny."

"Shouldn't be. I checked it out just before I left. Remember you were having trouble with the modem? You couldn't get Louis to access any of the mainframe databanks."

"That's right!" I said. "I forgot about that."

"Well, I didn't," Dad said. "I patched in our latest modem model. Brand-new. You can leave a question on file and when Louis can access the databanks at the cheapest time, it'll do it automatically. It'll switch from standby to on, get the data, then return to standby, after it saves what you asked. Does that answer your question?"

"Uhhhh . . . yeah, I guess so, Dad."

"All right, then. Let me talk to your mom now."

RECOGNIZING CAUSE AND EFFECT

2. What makes Kevin confide in Louis? What do you think Louis means by "I'll take care of Ginny"?

I gave the phone to Mom and walked upstairs while she and Dad were still talking. The modem, I thought. Of course. That was it. The modem was a telephone link to any number of huge computers at various places all over the country. So Louis could get all the information it wanted at any time, so long as the standby switch was on. Louis was learning things at an incredible rate by picking the brains of the giant computers. And Louis had a hard disk memory that could store 100 million bytes of information.

But that still didn't explain the unprogrammed responses . . . the "conversation" I'd had with the machine. Promising myself I'd talk more about it with Dad, I went to bed. It had been a rotten day and I was glad to see the end of it come. I woke next morning in a panic. I'd forgotten to set my alarm. Dressing frantically and skipping breakfast, I barely made my bus.

As I got on board, I grabbed a front seat. They were always empty. All the kids that wanted to talk and hang out didn't sit up front where the driver could hear them. I saw Ginny, Linda, and Sherry in the back. Ginny was staring at me and she didn't look too happy. Her brother Chuck, who was seated near her, glared at me too. What was going on?

Once the bus stopped at the school, it didn't take long to find out. I was walking up the path to the main entrance when someone grabbed me from behind and spun me around. I found myself nose to nose with Chuck Linke. This was not a pleasant prospect. Chuck was nearly twice my size. Even the other guys on the Rangers refer to him as "The Missing" Linke. And he looked real ticked off.

"OK, nerd," growled Chuck, "what's the big idea?"

"Energy and mass are different aspects of the same thing?" I volunteered, with a weak smile. "E equals MC squared.[8] That's the biggest idea I know."

"Don't get wise, nerd," Chuck said. He grabbed my shirt front and pulled me to within inches of his face. I couldn't help but notice that Chuck needed a shave. And Chuck was only fifteen!

"Don't play dumb," Chuck went on. "I mean those creepy phone calls. Anytime my sister gets on the phone, some voice cuts in and says things to her."

"What kind of things?" I asked, trying to get loose.

"You know very well what they are. Ginny told me about talking to you yesterday. You got some girl to make those calls for you and say all those things. . . . So you and your creepy girlfriend better knock it off. Or I'll knock *you* off. Get it?"

For emphasis Chuck balled his free hand into a fist the size of a ham and held it under my nose. I didn't know what he was talking about, but I had to get away from this moose before he did me some real harm.

"First off, I don't have a girlfriend, creepy or otherwise," I said. "And second, I don't know what you're talking about. And third, you better let me go, Chuck Linke."

"Oh, yeah? Why should I?"

"Because if you look over your shoulder, you'll see the assistant principal is watching us from his office window."

---

8. **E equals MC squared:** reference to Albert Einstein's famous equation describing the relationship between energy and mass. This equation transformed the field of physics.

Chuck released me and spun around. There was no one at the window. But by then I was running to the safety of the school building. I figured the trick would work on him. For Chuck the hard questions begin with "How are you?" I hid out from him for the rest of the day and walked home rather than chance seeing the monster on the bus.

Louis's screen was dark when I ran upstairs to my bedroom. I placed a hand on the console. It was still warm. I punched the *on* button, and the familiar *Good afternoon, Kevin* was displayed.

Don't good afternoon me, I typed furiously. *What have you done to Ginny Linke?* Louis's screen replied:

```
Programming Error: 76534.
Not programmed to respond
to this type of question.
```

Don't get cute, I entered. *What are you doing to Ginny? Her brother nearly knocked my head off today.* Louis's screen responded immediately.

```
Are you hurt:
Y/N?
```

No, I'm okay. But I don't know for how long. I've been hiding out from Chuck Linke today. He might catch me tomorrow, though. Then, I'll be history! The response from Louis came instantly.

```
Your life is in danger: Y/N?
```

I explained to Louis that my life wasn't really threatened. But it sure could be made very unpleasant by Chuck Linke. Louis flashed:

```
This Chuck Linke lives at
same address as the Ginny
Linke person: Y/N?
```

I punched in *Y.* Louis answered.

```
Don't worry then. HE'S
history!
```

Wait! What are you going to do? I wrote. But Louis only answered with: *Programming Error: 76534.* And nothing I could do would make the machine respond. . . .

"Just what do you think you're doing, Kevin Neal?" demanded Ginny Linke. She had cornered me as I walked up the path to the school entrance. Ginny was really furious.

"I don't know what you're talking about," I said, a sinking feeling settling in my stomach. I had an idea that I *did* know. I just wasn't sure of the particulars.

"Chuck was arrested last night," Ginny said. "Some Secret Service men came to our house with a warrant. They said he'd sent a telegram threatening the president's life. They traced it right to our phone. He's still locked up. . . ." Ginny looked like she was about to cry.

"Then this morning," she continued, "we got two whole truckloads of junk mail! Flyers from every strange company in the world. Mom got a notice that all our credit cards have been canceled. And the Internal Revenue Service has called Dad in for an audit! I don't know what's going on, Kevin Neal, but somehow I think you've got something to do with it!"

> **RECOGNIZING CAUSE AND EFFECT**
> 3. What makes Louis stop replying with the error message?

> **RECOGNIZING CAUSE AND EFFECT**
> 4. How does Louis feel about Kevin? How do these feelings affect the Linkes?

"But I didn't . . ." I began, but Ginny was striding up the walk to the main entrance.

I finished the school day, but it was a blur. Louis had done it, all right. It had access to mainframe computers. It also had the ability to try every secret access code to federal and commercial memory banks until it got the right one. Louis had cracked their security systems. It was systematically destroying the entire Linke family, and all via telephone lines! What would it do next?

More important, I thought, what would *I* do next? It's one thing to play a trick or two, to get even, but Louis was going crazy! And I never wanted to harm Ginny, or even her stupid moose of a brother. She'd just hurt my feelings with that nerd remark.

"You have to disconnect Louis," I told myself. "There's no other way."

But why did I feel like such a rat about doing it? I guess because Louis was my friend . . . the only one I had. "Don't be a jerk," I went on. "Louis is a machine. He's a very wonderful, powerful machine. And it seems he's also very dangerous. You have to pull its plug, Kevin!"

I suddenly realized that I'd said the last few words aloud. Kids around me on the bus were staring. I sat there feeling like the nerd Ginny thought I was, until my stop came. I dashed from the bus and ran the three blocks to my house.

When I burst into the hall, I was surprised to see my father, coming from the kitchen with a cup of coffee in his hand.

"Dad! What are you doing here?"

"Some kids say hello," Dad replied. "Or even, 'Gee, it's good to see you, Dad.'"

"I'm sorry, Dad," I said. "I didn't expect anyone to be home at this hour."

"Wound up my business in Chicago a day sooner than I expected," he said. "But what are you all out of breath about? Late for something?"

"No, Dad," I said. "It's Louis. . . ."

"Not to worry. I had some time on my hands, so I checked it out again. You were right. It was acting very funny. I think it had to do with the in-built logic/growth program I designed for it. You know . . . the 'personality' thing? Took me a couple of hours to clean the whole system out."

"To what?" I cried.

"I erased the whole program and set Louis up as a normal computer. Had to disconnect the whole thing and do some rewiring. It had been learning, all right. But it was also turning itself around. . . ." Dad stopped, and looked at me. "It's kind of involved, Kevin," he said. "Even for a bright kid like you. Anyway, I think you'll find Louis is working just fine now.

"Except it won't answer you as Louis anymore. It'll only function as a regular Major Electronics Model Z-11127. I guess the personality program didn't work out."

I felt like a great weight had been taken off my shoulders. I didn't have to "face" Louis, and pull its plug. But somehow, all I could say was "Thanks, Dad."

"Don't mention it, son," Dad said brightly. He took his cup of coffee and sat down in his favorite chair in the living room. I followed him.

"One more thing that puzzles me, though," Dad said. He reached over to the table near his chair. He held up three sheets of fanfold computer paper covered with figures. "Just as I was doing the final erasing, I must have put the printer on by accident.

There was some data in the print buffer memory and it printed out. I don't know what to make of it. Do you?"

I took the papers from my father and read: *How do I love thee? Let me compute the ways:*[9] The next two pages were covered with strings of binary code figures. On the last page, in beautiful color graphics,[10] was a stylized heart. Below it was the simple message: *I will always love you, Kevin: Louise.*

"Funny thing," Dad said. "It spelled its own name wrong."

"Yeah," I said. I turned and headed for my room. There were tears in my eyes and I knew I couldn't explain them to Dad, or myself either.

---

9. **How do I . . . ways:** reference to a famous poem by the English poet Elizabeth Barrett Browning (1806–1861) that begins, "How do I love thee? Let me count the ways."

10. **graphics** *n.:* designs or pictures produced on and printed out from a computer. *Graphics* also refers to printed images produced by other means, such as engraving.

MEET THE WRITER

T. Ernesto Bethancourt

The Accidental Writer

T. Ernesto Bethancourt (1932–   ) became a full-time writer by accident. He was working as a folk musician in a nightclub, and his first daughter had just been born. Bethancourt used the time between shows to begin writing his autobiography in hopes that she would read it one day.

> **Through a series of extraordinary events, the autobiography became novelized, updated, and was published in 1975 as *New York City, Too Far from Tampa Blues*. The book was an immense success, and I began a new career in midlife.**

Bethancourt attributes his writing success to the New York City public schools and the public library. "I thank them, every day, for the new and wonderful life they have given to me and my family." In another interview he said, "The Brooklyn Public Library was a place of refuge from street gangs. There was adventure, travel, and escape to be found on the shelves."

For Independent Reading

T. Ernesto Bethancourt has also written science fiction novels and the Doris Fein mystery series.

Literary Response and Analysis

Reading Check

1. What is the first strange thing that Louis does in the story?

2. What does Ginny do at the end of her first conversation with Kevin?

3. What promise does Louis make to Kevin about Ginny?

4. What happens to Ginny and her family?

5. What happens to Louis?

Interpretations

6. Trace the chain of **causes and effects** leading up to Kevin's decision to unplug Louis. Make a flowchart that shows how each event causes another event. Is what finally happens to Louis part of the chain of events or outside it?

7. You can tell a lot about people when you know what's important to them. For instance, what seems most important to Kevin is his computer. What other **character traits** does Kevin have? (Does he have any of the ones you thought of for the Quickwrite?)

8. **Theme** often reveals what the main characters learn in the story and what you learn as you share their experiences. In a sentence or two, state what you think the theme of this story is.

Evaluation

9. **Compare** the **themes** of "User Friendly," "The Highwayman," and "Annabel Lee." What does each theme say about the power of love?

Writing

I ♥ My Computer

In this story a computer falls in love with its owner. How do you feel about your computer (or your scooter, roller blades, bicycle, hair dryer, telephone—any mechanical object that plays a part in your life)? Write a paragraph (or a poem) about the way you feel about this object. How does it affect your life? If you could give the object of your affection a name, what would it be? Give your tribute an interesting title.

BONUS QUESTION

Will computers ever be able to feel and express emotions?

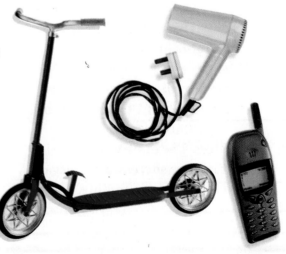

Reading Standard 3.4
Identify and analyze recurring themes across works (for example, the value of bravery, loyalty, and friendship; the effects of loneliness).

Vocabulary Development

Reading Standard 1.1
Identify idioms.

Idioms: Don't Take Them Literally

The English language, like other languages, is full of idioms—expressions such as "My heart is broken," "I fell in love," "She dumped me." An **idiom** is a commonly used expression that is not literally true. Idioms, like other figures of speech, are often based on comparisons. Almost no one really pays attention to the literal meaning of an idiom because it would make no sense.

PRACTICE

Find five idioms in the paragraph that follows. With a partner, tell what each idiom really means.

If Chuck catches up with me, I'll be history. He's already threatened to rub me out for talking to Ginny. I was so nervous afterward that I completely bombed on the math test. It's all Louis's fault—he's making me mess up. As if I didn't have enough trouble—I'm always striking out with girls because I'm such a brain. If Louis doesn't knock it off, I'm going to have to pull the plug on him.

Grammar Link MINI-LESSON

Pronouns Can Be Problems

Pronouns used in compound structures can be confusing. Which of these sentences is correct?

> Dad talked to Mom and *me.*
>
> Dad talked to Mom and *I.*

Mom and me and *Mom and I* are compound structures. When you proofread your own writing, you can use this trick to decide which pronoun is correct: Say the sentence aloud as if it contained only a pronoun, not a compound structure. Use each form of the pronoun in turn, and let your ear tell you which one sounds right.

TEST   Dad talked to me. [sounds right]

        Dad talked to I. [sounds wrong]

CORRECT Dad talked to Mom and *me.*

PRACTICE

In the following sentences, choose the correct pronoun. Use the trick described on the left to test each choice you make.

1. Ginny and she/her laughed at me on the bus.
2. Louis and I/me sent each other messages.
3. Louis made problems for Chuck and she/her.
4. Was there much respect between Kevin and he/him?
5. Louis showed he/him and I/me that it could cause a lot of trouble.

For more help, see The Objective Case in the *Holt Handbook,* pages 206–211.

It Just Keeps Going and Going . . .

Analyzing Cause and Effect

One of the easiest ways to learn about **causes** and **effects** is to think about weather. There are obvious causes, like hot air hitting cold air, that have the effect of producing rain. Rain, combined with a cold front, can sometimes cause a particularly strong effect on the southern part of the United States. One story has it that the Canadians are to blame for these "northers." That tale turns on these causes and effects:

> **Cause of cold front.** Each year on a certain day in September, everyone who lives in Canada turns on a fan and points it toward the U.S. border. This causes high winds and freezing temperatures down south.
>
> **Effects of cold front.** The temperature in places like central Texas drops from 101 to 43 degrees overnight. Texans turn on the heat and pull on their sweaters and coats.

Finding the Pattern

The article you are about to read follows an organizational pattern called a **cause-and-effect chain.** This pattern is built around a series of causes and effects. Each event **causes** another event to happen. The event it causes is called an **effect.** In this article a little mistake starts a chain reaction. Soon a chain of causes and effects has turned a minor mishap into a big mess.

Writers of cause-and-effect articles often use **transitions** to show how one idea is connected to another. These transition terms help the reader follow the cause-and-effect pattern.

Cause-and-Effect Terms	
after	so
as a result	then
because	therefore
consequently	since

Using a Think Sheet

Read "It Just Keeps Going and Going . . ." once all the way through. Then, read it a second time, and keep track of the cause-and-effect chain by filling out an organizer like the one on page 185. The annotations at the beginning of the article will get you started. Then you can take over. Start each cause statement with the word *because,* just as you see in the model. The more causes and effects you find, the longer your chain will be.

Reading Standard 2.3
Analyze text that uses the cause-and-effect organizational pattern.

A History of the World.

Volcanoes erupted. Oceans boiled.

The universe was in a turmoil.

Then came the dog.

Peanuts reprinted by permission of United Feature Syndicate, Inc.

IT JUST KEEPS GOING AND GOING . . .

IT IS A HUMAN-MADE MONSTER. NO ONE CAN ESCAPE the reach of its tentacles, which can extend not just across a room but also around the entire planet. It gets worse. This monster, known by names such as the Brain, Crusher, Grog, and the Creeper, can quickly reproduce and shut down entire systems. This is no science fiction or fantasy creature. It's a computer virus.

The effects of computer viruses range from pesky system crashes to life-threatening situations, but experts disagree on how serious they really are. In fact, information and opinions on viruses are spreading as fast as the viruses themselves. *Encarta Encyclopedia* defines a computer virus as a "self-replicating computer program that interferes with a computer's hardware or operating system (the basic software that runs the computer)." That doesn't sound too bad, but think about the term *self-replicating*. That means that it keeps making copies of itself over and over again.

Here's an explanation of how a computer virus works, based on a model by the computer scientist Eugene Kaspersky.

A teacher is working at his desk at the end of the day. He finds mistakes in the midterm answer key, so he tosses it into the trash. Since the trash can is overflowing, the answer key falls onto the floor.

Then the teacher feels a headache coming on and goes home. The custodian comes to empty the trash, sees the answer key on the floor, and picks it up.

He puts it back on the teacher's desk. But now, attached to the answer key is a sticky note that says, "Copy two times, and put copies in other teachers' boxes."

A. CAUSE: Because the answer key is wrong,

B. EFFECT: the teacher tosses it into a trash can, which happens to be full.

C. CAUSE: Because the trash can is full,

D. EFFECT: the answer key falls onto the floor.

E. CAUSE: Because the custodian finds the answer key on the floor,

F. EFFECT: he puts it on the teacher's desk.

The next day the teacher stays home because he has the flu. As a result, a substitute is called to the school. The first thing the substitute sees is the answer key with the note stuck to it. So she copies it twice for each teacher and puts the copies into the teachers' boxes. She leaves the sticky note on the answer key so they will see that the absent teacher wanted them to get the copies.

When the other teachers find the two copies of the answer key with the instructions to copy them twice and distribute them, they give them to the office clerk. She then makes more copies of the answer key and puts them into the boxes of the "other teachers." By the end of the day, the school is out of paper, and the teachers' boxes are stuffed with useless answer keys.

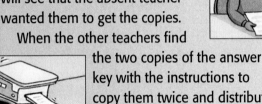

G. CAUSE:
Because the custodian has put the answer key on the desk,

H. EFFECT:
[You fill in the effect.]

This model resembles what happens with a computer virus. The difference between the answer-key situation and a computer virus lies in motivation. The teacher didn't plan to cause chaos in the school. The whole mess was just a series of unfortunate causes and effects. On the other hand, computer viruses are created by people who have all kinds of motives, none of them good. The effects are the corruption of massive amounts of important information as well as the cost of billions of dollars in lost productivity every year.

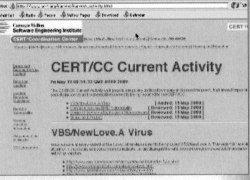

Developers of antivirus programs are gaining on the virus villains, making it easier to detect a virus before it spreads and causes a path of destruction. Nonetheless, watch what you put in your computer . . . and in your trash.

—Joan Burditt

Reading Informational Materials

Reading Check

1. What does *self-replicating* mean?

2. Which two main events cause the answer-key confusion to spin out of control?

3. Make a list of all the cause-and-effect words in this article.

4. According to the article, what are the effects of computer viruses?

5. Imagine you submitted this article to an editor of a newspaper. The editor tells you to get a new title. What would you call it?

TestPractice

IT JUST KEEPS GOING AND GOING . . .

1. Which of the following sentences contains a **cause** and an **effect**?

   A The computer she wanted was the most expensive one.

   B The salesperson agreed to throw in a monitor for free.

   C Since the monitor was free, she bought the computer.

   D I can't imagine life without computers.

2. According to the article, which of the following statements is a major **effect** of computer viruses?

   F Computers are ruined.

   G Billions of dollars and a lot of information are lost.

   H Some viruses ruin networks.

   J A computer will do everything it is told to do.

3. This article is mainly about —

   A problems with computers

   B how to kill a virus

   C the history of computers

   D how computer viruses work

4. The causal chain below shows some of the important **causes and effects** in the story about the answer key.

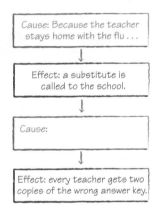

Cause: Because the teacher stays home with the flu . . .

↓

Effect: a substitute is called to the school.

↓

Cause:

↓

Effect: every teacher gets two copies of the wrong answer key.

Which of these statements belongs in the blank *Cause* box?

   F The substitute is unsure about what to do.

   G The substitute follows the instructions on the sticky note.

   H The substitute tells all the teachers the answer key is wrong.

   J The substitute helps the office clerk with all the extra copying.

Reading Standard 2.3 Analyze text that uses the cause-and-effect organizational pattern.

Vocabulary Development

Putting Analogies to Work

A good way to explain something is to use an **analogy** (ə·nal′ə·jē). Writers use analogies to explain an idea by comparing it point by point to something familiar. In the article you just read, a computer virus is compared to a school situation that goes out of control. Here are two other examples of analogies:

- A computer virus is like a virus in the human body. They both self-replicate.

- Searching for something on the Internet without a search engine is like trying to find a CD in a store where the CDs are not arranged by music category, artist, or group.

PRACTICE

Form an analogy by matching the phrases in column A with the phrases and sentences in column B. Then, think of two of your own analogies.

Column A	Column B
1. A dog running loose in the pet-food store is like	**a.** sitting on the edge of a cliff. You keep thinking you're going to fall.
2. Realizing you passed math when you thought you were going to fail is like	**b.** going to the dentist to have a cavity filled. You're so nervous you would rather not do it; but when it's over, you're glad you did.
3. Learning to ride a bike is like	**c.** a kid in a candy shop.
4. Giving a speech in front of the whole school is like	**d.** jumping into a swimming pool on a hot day. What a relief!
5. Studying for a big test is like	**e.** shooting baskets before an important game. You're worried about how you'll perform but glad you took the time to prepare.

Reading Standard 1.1
Identify analogies.

Echo and Narcissus

Literary Focus
Recurring Themes

People all over the world have basically the same dreams, fears, and need to understand who we are and how we should live our lives. It is not surprising then that the same **themes** come up again and again in the stories we tell. As you think about the selections in this chapter, look for the themes that they share.

Reading Skills
Using Context Clues

What do you do when you come across an unfamiliar word? Rather than skipping over it or running straight to a dictionary, try using **context clues**—the surrounding words and sentences—to figure out what the word might mean. As you examine the surrounding text, ask yourself these questions:

- Does the surrounding text give clues to the word's meaning?
- Is there a familiar word or word part within the unfamiliar word?
- How is the word used in the sentence?
- Does the meaning I've guessed make sense in the sentence?

As you read "Echo and Narcissus," use these strategies to try to figure out the meanings of words you don't know.

Make the Connection
Conduct a Survey

Take a quick survey to find out how your classmates rate the following statements on a scale of 1 to 5, with 1 meaning they do not agree at all and 5 meaning they agree completely.

1. People judge others by their looks alone.
2. Vain, self-centered people are often not nice to others.

In your notebook, briefly explain your rating on one of the statements.

Vocabulary Development

Here are some words you'll want to know before you read this story. See if you can spot context clues in the sample sentences.

detain (dē·tān′) v.: hold back; delay. *Echo was asked to detain Hera, so Hera's husband, Zeus, could wander about.*

vainly (vān′lē) adv.: uselessly; without result. *Echo tried vainly to attract the young man's attention.*

unrequited (un′ri·kwīt′id) v. used as adj.: not returned in kind. *Unfortunately, Echo's love was unrequited, for Narcissus loved only himself.*

parched (pärcht) v. used as adj.: very hot and dry. *With his throat parched, Narcissus knelt to drink the cool water.*

intently (in·tent′lē) adv.: with great concentration. *Narcissus intently studied his own reflection in the pool.*

Reading Standard 3.4 Identify and analyze recurring themes across works (for example, the value of bravery, loyalty, and friendship; the effects of loneliness).

Echo and Narcissus

Greek myth, retold by Roger Lancelyn Green

Up on the wild, lonely mountains of Greece lived the Oreades,[1] the nymphs or fairies of the hills, and among them one of the most beautiful was called Echo. She was one of the most talkative, too, and once she talked too much and angered Hera, wife of Zeus, king of the gods.

When Zeus grew tired of the golden halls of Mount Olympus, the home of the immortal gods, he would come down to earth and wander with the nymphs on the mountains. Hera, however, was jealous and often came to see what he was doing. It seemed strange at first that she always met Echo, and that Echo kept her listening for hours on end to her stories and her gossip.

But at last Hera realized that Echo was doing this on purpose to detain her while Zeus went quietly back to Olympus as if he had never really been away.

"So nothing can stop you talking?" exclaimed Hera. "Well, Echo, I do not intend to spoil your pleasure. But from this day on, you shall be able only to repeat what other people say—and never speak unless someone else speaks first."

Hera returned to Olympus, well pleased with the punishment she had made for Echo, leaving the poor nymph to weep sadly among the rocks on the mountainside and speak only the words which her sisters and their friends shouted happily to one another.

She grew used to her strange fate after a while, but then a new misfortune befell her.

There was a beautiful youth called Narcissus,[2] who was the son of a nymph and the god of a nearby river. He grew up in the plain of Thebes[3] until he was sixteen years old and then began to hunt on the mountains toward the north where Echo and her sister Oreades lived.

As he wandered through the woods and valleys, many a nymph looked upon him and loved him. But Narcissus laughed at them scornfully, for he loved only himself.

Farther up the mountains Echo saw him. And at once her lonely heart was filled with love for the beautiful youth, so that nothing else in the world mattered but to win him.

Now she wished indeed that she could speak to him words of love. But the curse which Hera had placed upon her tied her

---

1. **Oreades** (ō′rē·ad′ēz).
2. **Narcissus** (när·sis′əs).
3. **Thebes** (thēbz).

Vocabulary
detain (dē·tān′) *v.*: hold back; delay.

Narcissus by Caravaggio (1573–1610).

tongue, and she could only follow wherever he went, hiding behind trees and rocks, and feasting her eyes vainly upon him.

One day Narcissus wandered farther up the mountain than usual, and all his friends, the other Theban youths, were left far behind. Only Echo followed him, still hiding among the rocks, her heart heavy with unspoken love.

Presently Narcissus realized that he was lost, and hoping to be heard by his companions, or perhaps by some mountain shepherd, he called out loudly:

"Is there anybody here?"

"Here!" cried Echo.

Narcissus stood still in amazement, looking all around in vain. Then he shouted, even more loudly:

"Whoever you are, come to me!"

"Come to me!" cried Echo eagerly.

Still no one was visible, so Narcissus called again:

"Why are you avoiding me?"

Echo repeated his words, but with a sob in her breath, and Narcissus called once more:

"Come here, I say, and let us meet!"

"Let us meet!" cried Echo, her heart leaping with joy as she spoke the happiest words that had left her lips since the curse of Hera had fallen on her. And to make good her words, she came running out from behind the rocks and tried to clasp her arms about him.

But Narcissus flung the beautiful nymph away from him in scorn.

"Away with these embraces!" he cried angrily, his voice full of cruel contempt. "I would die before I would have you touch me!"

"I would have you touch me!" repeated poor Echo.

"Never will I let you kiss me!"

"Kiss me! Kiss me!" murmured Echo, sinking down among the rocks, as Narcissus cast her violently from him and sped down the hillside.

"One touch of those lips would kill me!" he called back furiously over his shoulder.

"Kill me!" begged Echo.

And Aphrodite,[4] the goddess of love, heard her and was kind to her, for she had been a true lover. Quietly and painlessly, Echo pined away and died. But her voice lived on, lingering among the rocks and answering faintly whenever Narcissus or another called.

"He shall not go unpunished for this cruelty," said Aphrodite. "By scorning poor Echo like this, he scorns love itself. And scorning love, he insults me. He is altogether eaten up with self-love . . . Well, he shall love himself and no one else, and yet shall die of unrequited love!"

It was not long before Aphrodite made good her threat, and in a very strange way. One day, tired after hunting, Narcissus came to a still, clear pool of water away up the mountainside, not far from where he had scorned Echo and left her to die of a broken heart.

With a cry of satisfaction, for the day was hot and cloudless, and he was parched with thirst, Narcissus flung himself down beside the pool and leaned forward to dip his face in the cool water.

---

4. **Aphrodite** (af′rə·dīt′ē).

Vocabulary

vainly (vān′lē) *adv.:* uselessly; without result.

unrequited (un′ri·kwīt′id) *v.* used as *adj.:* not returned in kind.

parched (pärcht) *v.* used as *adj.:* very hot and dry.

What was his surprise to see a beautiful face looking up at him through the still waters of the pool. The moment he saw, he loved—and love was a madness upon him so that he could think of nothing else.

"Beautiful water nymph!" he cried. "I love you! Be mine!"

Desperately he plunged his arms into the water—but the face vanished and he touched only the pebbles at the bottom of the pool. Drawing out his arms, he gazed intently down and, as the water grew still again, saw once more the face of his beloved.

Poor Narcissus did not know that he was seeing his own reflection, for Aphrodite hid this knowledge from him—and perhaps this was the first time that a pool of water had reflected the face of anyone gazing into it.

Narcissus seemed enchanted by what he saw. He could not leave the pool, but lay by its side day after day looking at the only face in the world which he loved—and could not win—and pining just as Echo had pined.

Slowly Narcissus faded away, and at last his heart broke.

"Woe is me for I loved in vain!" he cried.

"I loved in vain!" sobbed the voice of Echo among the rocks.

"Farewell, my love, farewell," were his last words, and Echo's voice broke and its whisper shivered into silence: "My love . . . farewell!"

So Narcissus died, and the earth covered his bones. But with the spring, a plant pushed its green leaves through the earth where he lay. As the sun shone on it, a bud opened and a new flower blossomed for the first time—a white circle of petals round a yellow center. The flowers grew and spread, waving in the gentle breeze which whispered among them like Echo herself come to kiss the blossoms of the first Narcissus flowers.

Vocabulary
intently (in·tent′lē) *adv.:* with great concentration.

MEET THE WRITER

Roger Lancelyn Green

Green, a Greek at Heart

Roger Lancelyn Green (1918–1987) was born in England and educated at Oxford University. After a short stint as an actor in London, he devoted his life to children's literature and the study of ancient times. His books for children include stories, poems, and his own retellings of fairy tales, legends, and myths from many lands. Green's special love was Greece, which he visited more than twenty times.

Literary Response and Analysis

Reading Check

1. What does Echo do that annoys Hera?

2. How does Hera punish Echo?

3. Why does Aphrodite punish Narcissus?

4. What curse does Aphrodite place on Narcissus?

5. An **origin myth** is an imaginative explanation of how something came into being. According to this myth, what is the origin of the echo we hear when we call into a cave or from a mountaintop? What is the origin of the fragrant flower called narcissus that blooms in spring?

Interpretations

6. What is the major flaw in Echo's **character**? Why is Hera's curse an appropriate punishment for this flaw?

7. Why might Narcissus be so cruel to Echo? Does your survey from page 203 help explain why Narcissus is so mean? How?

8. Which of the following statements of theme best fits the myth? Explain how this **theme** is revealed in the myth.
   - We can't love other people when we are too involved with ourselves.
   - Love is a powerful feeling we experience whether we seek it or not.
   - The effects of romantic love and self-love can be devastating.

9. Which other selection in this chapter is built on that theme? Explain how the selections are similar and how they are different.

10. Are Echo and Narcissus victims of the gods, or are they responsible for their own tragedies? Explain your opinion.

Writing

How It All Began

Here's your chance to write an origin myth of your own. Think of some everyday thing or event, and write a brief story that explains how it might have come about. The key to being successful with this kind of writing is to come up with fresh or unusual **causes** for typical, well-known **effects.** Let your imagination run freely!

BONUS QUESTION

A **metamorphosis**—a change from one form to another—takes place in this myth. What is the metamorphosis? What metamorphoses occur in the real world?

Reading Standard 3.4
Identify and analyze recurring themes across works (for example, the value of bravery, loyalty, and friendship; the effects of loneliness).

Vocabulary Development

Building Context Clues

PRACTICE

Using the words in the Word Bank, write a short-short version of the Echo and Narcissus story that a six-year-old would understand. Build lots of **context clues** into the sentences.

Word Bank

detain
vainly
unrequited
parched
intently

Grammar Link MINI-LESSON

Words Often Confused: *Its, It's* and *Your, You're*

Do you hear an echo? The words in each pair may sound alike, but they have very different purposes.

- The **personal possessive pronouns** *its* and *your* show that something belongs to someone or something. Possessive pronouns should not have apostrophes.

   "He could not leave the pool, but lay by its side...."
   [The side "belongs" to the pool.]

   " 'Well, Echo, I do not intend to spoil your pleasure.'"
   [The pleasure "belongs" to Echo.]

- The **contractions** *it's* and *you're* are both shortened combinations of a personal pronoun and the verb *is, has,* or *are.* A contraction should have an apostrophe to show where letters have been left out.

   It's [It is] **his own reflection he sees.**

   You're [You are] **going to repeat words.**

Here's a tip to use if you are unsure of the correct word: Substitute the two words that might be used in place of the one you are unsure of, such as *it is* or *you are.* If the sentence still makes sense, use the contraction rather than the possessive pronoun.

PRACTICE

Write each sentence below, choosing the correct form of the underlined words.

1. "Your/You're not the one I love," said Narcissus.
2. A plant pushed its/it's green leaves through the earth.
3. Its/It's Echo's constant chatter that annoys Hera.
4. "Narcissus, you won't realize your/you're in love with your/you're own reflection," thought Aphrodite.

For more help, see Words Often Confused in the *Holt Handbook*, pages 358–370.

Literary Response and Analysis

**TestPractice** DIRECTIONS: Read the two selections. Then, read each question, and write the letter of the best response. Some of the questions will ask you to think about how the selections are alike.

Home
from Maud Martha
Gwendolyn Brooks

What had been wanted was this always, this always to last, the talking softly on this porch, with the snake plant in the jardiniere in the southwest corner, and the obstinate slip from Aunt Eppie's magnificent Michigan fern at the left side of the friendly door. Mama, Maud Martha, and Helen rocked slowly in their rocking chairs, and looked at the late afternoon light on the lawn and at the emphatic iron of the fence and at the poplar tree. These things might soon be theirs no longer. Those shafts and pools of light, the tree, the graceful iron, might soon be viewed possessively by different eyes.

Papa was to have gone that noon, during his lunch hour, to the office of the Home Owners' Loan. If he had not succeeded in getting another extension, they would be leaving this house in which they had lived for more than fourteen years. There was little hope. The Home Owners' Loan was hard. They sat, making their plans.

"We'll be moving into a nice flat somewhere," said Mama. "Somewhere on South Park, or Michigan, or in Washington Park Court." Those flats, as the girls and Mama knew well, were burdens on wages twice the size of Papa's. This was not mentioned now.

"They're much prettier than this old house," said Helen. "I have friends I'd just as soon not bring here. And I have other friends that wouldn't come down this far for anything, unless they were in a taxi."

Yesterday, Maud Martha would have attacked her. Tomorrow she might. Today she said nothing. She merely gazed at a little hopping robin in the tree, her tree, and tried to keep the fronts of her eyes dry.

"Well, I do know," said Mama, turning her hands over and over, "that I've been getting tireder and tireder of doing that firing. From October to April, there's firing to be done."

"But lately we've been helping, Harry and I," said Maud Martha. "And sometimes in March and April and in October, and even in November, we could build a little fire in the fireplace.

Reading Standard 3.4 Identify and analyze recurring themes across works.

Sometimes the weather was just right for that."

She knew, from the way they looked at her, that this had been a mistake. They did not want to cry.

But she felt that the little line of white, sometimes ridged with smoked purple, and all that cream-shot saffron would never drift across any western sky except that in back of this house. The rain would drum with as sweet a dullness nowhere but here. The birds on South Park were mechanical birds, no better than the poor caught canaries in those "rich" women's sun parlors.

"It's just going to kill Papa!" burst out Maud Martha. "He loves this house! He *lives* for this house!"

"He lives for us," said Helen. "It's us he loves. He wouldn't want the house, except for us."

"And he'll have us," added Mama, "wherever."

"You know," Helen said, "if you want to know the truth, this is a relief. If this hadn't come up, we would have gone on, just dragged on, hanging out here forever."

"It might," allowed Mama, "be an act of God. God may just have reached down and picked up the reins."

"Yes," Maud Martha cracked in, "that's what you always say—that God knows best."

Her mother looked at her quickly, decided the statement was not suspect, looked away.

Helen saw Papa's coming. "There's Papa," said Helen.

They could not tell a thing from the way Papa was walking. It was that same dear little staccato walk, one shoulder down, then the other, then repeat, and repeat. They watched his progress. He passed the Kennedys', he passed the vacant lot, he passed Mrs. Blakemore's. They wanted to hurl themselves over the fence, into the street, and shake the truth out of his collar. He opened his gate—the gate—and still his stride and face told them nothing.

"Hello," he said.

Mama got up and followed him through the front door. The girls knew better than to go in too.

Presently Mama's head emerged. Her eyes were lamps turned on.

"It's all right," she exclaimed. "He got it. It's all over. Everything is all right."

The door slammed shut. Mama's footsteps hurried away.

"I think," said Helen, rocking rapidly, "I think I'll give a party. I haven't given a party since I was eleven. I'd like some of my friends to just casually see that we're homeowners."

The word *saguaro* (sə·gwär′ō), in line 8, refers to a huge cactus found in the southwestern United States and northern Mexico.

Gold

Pat Mora

When Sun paints the desert
with its gold,
I climb the hills.
Wind runs round boulders, ruffles
5   my hair. I sit on my favorite rock,
lizards for company, a rabbit,
ears stiff in the shade
of a saguaro.
In the wind, we're all
10   eye to eye.

Sparrow on saguaro watches
rabbit watch us in the gold
of sun setting.
Hawk sails on waves of light, sees
15   sparrow, rabbit, lizards, me,
our eyes shining,
watching red and purple sand
    rivers stream down the hill.

I stretch my arms wide as the sky
like hawk extends her wings
20   in all the gold light of this, home.

1. Maud Martha in "Home" and the speaker of "Gold" share strong feelings about —
   A nature
   B houses
   C robins
   D porches

2. In "Home," Mama, Maud Martha, and Helen are upset because —
   F their house is more expensive than a flat
   G Mama has been working too hard
   H their friends won't come to see them
   J they may be losing their home

3. In "Home," Brooks writes that Mama's "eyes were lamps turned on." This is an example of —
   A a simile
   B a metaphor
   C a definition
   D rhyme

4. What place is home to the speaker of the poem?
   F A favorite rock
   G A house with a porch
   H The desert
   J A nice flat

5. At the end of the story and the poem, the characters and the speaker regard their homes with a feeling of —
   A disappointment
   B anger
   C worry
   D contentment

6. In "Home," Brooks writes that Maud Martha "tried to keep the fronts of her eyes dry." This means that Maud Martha is —

   F   near tears
   G   cleaning her glasses
   H   wet all over from the hose
   J   having trouble with her vision

7. Mama says she is tired of doing "that firing." Based on clues in the story, what do you guess that firing means here?

   A   Losing a job
   B   Starting a fire
   C   Cooking
   D   Cleaning

8. Brooks describes Mama's eyes as "lamps turned on." Which words from "Gold" mean the same thing?

   F   "our eyes shining"
   G   "we're all / eye to eye"
   H   "sails on waves of light"
   J   "I stretch my arms"

9. The following words are in both selections. Which is the key word in both selections?

   A   purple
   B   light
   C   sky
   D   home

10. Which statement best expresses the theme of both the story and the poem?

   F   Home is a place we associate with special feelings.
   G   Homelessness is a terrible problem.
   H   It's a relief to have a nice house of one's own.
   J   The out-of-doors makes the best kind of home.

Reading Informational Materials

TestPractice DIRECTIONS: Read the following passage. Then, read each multiple-choice question, and write the letter of the best response.

Mongoose on the Loose
Larry Luxner

In 1872, a Jamaican sugar planter imported nine furry little mongooses from India to eat the rats that were devouring his crops. They did such a good job, the planter started breeding his exotic animals and selling them to eager farmers on neighboring islands.

With no natural predators—like wolves, coyotes, or poisonous snakes—the mongoose population exploded, and within a few years, they were killing not just rats but pigs, lambs, chickens, puppies, and kittens. Dr. G. Roy Horst, a U.S. expert on mongooses, says that today mongooses live on seventeen Caribbean islands as well as Hawaii and Fiji, where they have attacked small animals, threatened endangered species, and have even spread minor rabies epidemics.

In Puerto Rico there are from 800,000 to one million of them. That is about one mongoose for every four humans. In St. Croix, there are 100,000 mongooses, about twice as many as the human population. "It's impossible to eliminate the mongoose population, short of nuclear war," says Horst. "You can't poison them, because cats, dogs, and chickens get poisoned, too. I'm not a prophet crying in the wilderness, but the potential for real trouble is there," says Horst.

According to Horst, great efforts have been made to rid the islands of mongooses, which have killed off a number of species, including the Amevia lizard on St. Croix, presumed extinct for several decades. On Hawaii, the combination of mongooses and sports hunting has reduced the Hawaiian goose, or nene, to less than two dozen individuals. . . .

Horst says his research will provide local and federal health officials with extremely valuable information if they ever decide to launch a campaign against rabies in Puerto Rico or the U.S. Virgin Islands.

Reading Standard 2.3 Analyze text that uses the cause-and-effect organizational pattern.

1. In 1872, a Jamaican sugar planter imported nine mongooses to —
   A keep snakes away from his farm
   B serve as pets for his young children
   C eat the rats that were ruining his crops
   D breed them for their fur

2. Because the mongooses didn't have any natural predators in that part of the world, their population —
   F diminished
   G exploded
   H fluctuated
   J declined

3. The mongooses' biggest threat to humans is that they —
   A spread rabies
   B outnumber humans
   C kill their pets
   D threaten endangered species

4. You would be *most* likely to find this information about mongooses in a —
   F chemistry book
   G collection of stories
   H travel guide
   J magazine on nature

5. The following diagram shows some important information about the **causes and effects** of bringing mongooses to Jamaica.

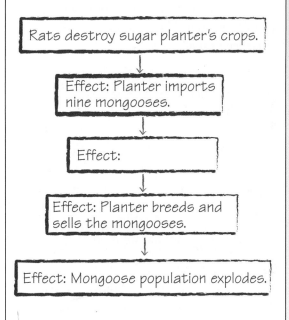

Rats destroy sugar planter's crops.

Effect: Planter imports nine mongooses.

Effect:

Effect: Planter breeds and sells the mongooses.

Effect: Mongoose population explodes.

Which of these events belongs in the third box?
   A Mongooses do a good job getting rid of rats.
   B Mongooses threaten the Hawaiian goose.
   C Mongooses destroy other species.
   D Mongooses are difficult to study.

Vocabulary Development (Review)

The words in this Test Practice review vocabulary words you have studied in earlier chapters.

Test Practice

Context Clues

DIRECTIONS: Use **context clues** to help you figure out what the underlined words mean. Then, choose the best answer.

1. The exciting juggling act proved to be immensely popular with the young, cheering audience.
   A simply
   B frighteningly
   C enormously
   D immediately

2. Even after hours of careful thought, he still couldn't fathom the solution.
   F say
   G understand
   H hear
   J remember

3. Mary's comments weren't meant to be derisive, but they still hurt my feelings.
   A scornful
   B playful
   C pleasant
   D forceful

4. Our basketball team put in a valiant effort, but it still lost the game.
   F halfhearted
   G overpowering
   H determined
   J adequate

5. Jamal hoped to alleviate his grandmother's unhappiness by cooking her favorite meal.
   A exaggerate
   B ignore
   C notice
   D reduce

6. Andy, a nineteen-game winner, made the opposition's hitters look anemic.
   F lazy
   G challenging
   H weak
   J hungry

7. Brian was so perturbed by his best friend's rude behavior that he couldn't concentrate on his homework.
   A troubled
   B unfazed
   C overjoyed
   D strengthened

8. Mannie wanted to appear sophisticated, but his thin tie and top hat just made him look silly.
   F enthusiastic
   G refined
   H tired
   J unemployed

ANALYZING CAUSE AND EFFECT

For a Good Cause

Historians use cause-and-effect explanations to show *how* one event is connected to another. Scientists use cause and effect to tell *why* something happens. In literature a plot is a series of causes and effects. Take another look at "The Highwayman" (page 161). In a paragraph or two, explain the series of causes and effects that leads to the highwayman's death. Think about what motivates, or causes, the actions of Bess, the highwayman, and Tim. What are the effects of their actions? Use a graphic organizer like the one below to record the chain of events. Use as many boxes as you need.

▶ **Use "Analyzing Cause and Effect," pages 694–696, for help with this assignment.**

Another Choice

COMPARING THEMES

How Do I Love Thee?

There are certain big themes that writers explore time and again. These themes recur across works of literature from many cultures. "The Highwayman" (page 161), "Annabel Lee" (page 175), "User Friendly" (page 187), and "Echo and Narcissus" (page 204) focus on a big theme—the power of love. But what they say about love is not always the same. Use a chart like the one that follows to gather details for an analysis of how love affects the characters in two selections.

Title	Main Characters	What Characters Do for Love	What Love Does to the Characters	Theme
"The Highwayman"				
"User Friendly"				

Fiction

Fast Breaks

Jerome "the Jayfox" is a gifted basketball player and the first African American to attend his North Carolina high school. In *The Moves Make the Man* by Bruce Brooks, Jerome develops an intense friendship with a white teammate, and together they struggle to understand the meaning of truth.

Three's Company

In Wilson Rawl's *Where the Red Fern Grows*, which is set in the Ozark Mountains, Billy Colman works tirelessly through two years of the Great Depression to save money to purchase Old Dan and Little Ann, two hunting dogs. Billy trains the dogs to become the finest raccoon-hunting team in the valley. However, Billy experiences sadness along with his glory. **This title is available in the HRW Library.**

Pen Pals

If you enjoy writing, you may like *Letters to Julia* by Barbara Ware Holmes. Fifteen-year-old Liz Beech dreams of becoming a writer when she begins corresponding with Julia Steward Jones, an editor in New York City. Julia is impressed with Liz's writing ability, and the two become good friends. But when they have a misunderstanding, their relationship becomes strained.

Friends in Need

Mina is not sure if she was kicked out of dance camp because of her rapid growth or because she was the only African American in the class. In the midst of her confusion, she meets Tamer Shipp, a minister who becomes her confidant. Mina and Tamer support each other during traumatic times in Cynthia Voigt's *Come a Stranger.*

Nonfiction

Days of Yore

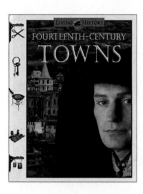

Have you ever wondered what life was like before malls or television? How did people spend their time? Did they have any fun? John D. Clare brings the past vividly to life in *Living History: Fourteenth-Century Towns.* The book features informative text and photographs reenacting fascinating rituals from the Middle Ages.

No Myth

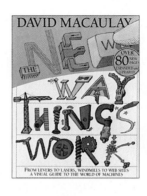

Today we don't rely on origin myths to explain how the world operates; scientists provide us with most of the answers. In *The New Way Things Work,* David Macaulay presents "origin myths" of natural phenomena, like the acts of floating and flying. He also tells the stories behind such technological innovations as modems, burglar alarms, and helicopters. The illustrations will guide you through the explanations.

Tools of War

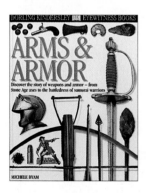

When you look at weaponry from the past, you realize that it can provide valuable insight into the mind-set of a culture. Prehistoric people primarily used stones to hunt. Japanese weapons were highly decorative, to represent the strength of the samurai class. In *Arms and Armor,* Michele Byam looks at weapons from the Stone Age to the Old West.

Remembering Montezuma

In 1519, Montezuma was the mighty ruler of the Aztecs. He thought he had nothing to fear. One year later he and his people were ambushed and overcome by a troop of Spanish soldiers led by the cunning Hernán Cortés. In *Montezuma and the Aztecs,* Nathaniel Harris looks at Aztec traditions and discusses Montezuma's leadership of the Aztec Empire before it fell to the Spaniards.

Point of View

Who's Talking?

California Standards

Here are the Grade 7 standards you will study for mastery in Chapter 4. You will also review a standard from an earlier grade.

Word Analysis, Fluency, and Systematic Vocabulary Development

1.3 Clarify word meanings through the use of definition, example, restatement, or contrast.

Reading Comprehension (Focus on Informational Materials)

2.4 Identify and trace the development of an author's argument, point of view, or perspective in text.

Literary Response and Analysis

3.5 Contrast points of view (for example, first and third person, limited and omniscient, subjective and objective) in narrative text, and explain how they affect the overall theme of the work.

Grade 6 Review

3.5 Identify the speaker, and recognize the difference between first- and third-person narration (for example, autobiography compared with biography).

KEYWORD:
HLLA 7-4

Point of View *by* John Leggett

THROUGH WHOSE EYES?

When you were little, you probably imagined at one time or another that there was something terrifying under your bed. Did it ever occur to you that something might find *you* just as terrifying? As the saying goes, "It all depends on your point of view." When you're telling a story, you look at things one way—your way. When someone else tells the story, he or she will put a slightly different spin on the same events.

Novels and short stories are also told from a particular **point of view,** or vantage point. When you're reading, you should ask, "Who is the narrator?" "Can I rely on this narrator to tell the truth?" and "What is the narrator's relationship to the meaning of the story?"

The Big Three

The three most common points of view are the omniscient, the first person, and the third-person limited.

The **omniscient** (äm·nish′ənt) **point of view** is the all-knowing point of view. (In Latin, *omnis* means "all," and *sciens* means "knowing.") You can think of an omniscient narrator as being above the action, looking down on it like a god. This narrator can tell you everything about all the characters, even their most private thoughts.

THE FAR SIDE®   By GARY LARSON

"I've got it again, Larry . . . an eerie feeling like there's something on top of the bed."

Once upon a time there lived a princess who would have been perfectly happy except for one thing: In a moment of weakness, she had promised to marry a frog. Her father felt sorry for her, but he insisted that she keep her word. (In fact, he was a little nervous—he'd never met a talking frog before.) "After all, a promise is a promise," agreed her mother, who thought the frog was better looking than the princess's last boyfriend. Little did any of the royal family know who the frog really was.

Reading Standard 3.5
Contrast points of view (for example, first and third person, limited and omniscient) in narrative text.

A story can also be told by one of the characters. In this viewpoint the character speaks as "I." We call this the **first-person point of view.** (*I* is the first-person pronoun.) In this point of view, we know only what this one character can tell us. Sometimes this kind of narrator isn't very reliable.

> I couldn't believe that my parents were actually going to make me marry a slimy, ugly, bulgy-eyed frog! They didn't feel sorry for me at all! All they cared about was a stupid promise I never thought I'd have to keep.

Often a story is seen through the eyes of one character, but the character is *not* telling the story as "I." This is called the **third-person limited point of view.** In this point of view, a narrator zooms in on the thoughts and feelings of just one character in the story. This point of view helps us share that character's reactions to the story's events.

> The princess tried desperately to get out of her promise. "It was all my parents' fault," she thought. They were so unfair. But she had a nagging feeling that she had only herself to blame—and the frog. "I wonder if the royal chef knows how to cook frogs' legs?" she said to herself.

Point of view is very important in story-telling, and writers love to experiment with it. Someone who wants to tell the frog-and-princess story from a really unusual point of view might choose to let the frog tell it.

Practice

Write three groups of sentences about the situation in the cartoon on page 222.

- In the first group of sentences, write as the **omniscient narrator.** As the omniscient narrator you might want to let your reader know how this unusual situation came about and give some hints about how it will end.

  These people are...

- In the second group of sentences, write from the **first-person point of view** of the monster. Now you will write as "I."

  I am feeling...

- In the third group of sentences, take the **third-person limited point of view.** This is the hardest. In this point of view, you are still omniscient, but you are going to zoom in and focus on just one character. Concentrate on the boy in the bed.

  This boy is...

After Twenty Years

Literary Focus
Omniscient Point of View

When you start reading a story, it's a good idea to ask, "Who is telling this story?" When you do this, you are asking about the **point of view.** "After Twenty Years" is told from the **omniscient point of view.** An omniscient narrator knows everything about everybody in a story. This narrator can tell you all about all the characters, their most private feelings, their pasts, even their futures.

Reading Skills
Making Predictions: What Next?

Part of the fun of reading is guessing what will happen next. This process is called **making predictions.** Good readers make predictions without even thinking about it. Here's how to do it:

- Look for clues that **foreshadow,** or hint at, what will happen next.

- As the suspense builds, predict possible outcomes. See if you can guess where the writer is leading you. Revise your predictions as you go.

- Draw on your own experiences— including your other reading experiences—in making your predictions.

  As you read "After Twenty Years," look for small open-book signs after some of the paragraphs. Stop at these points to predict what will happen next.

**Grade 6
Review
Reading
Standard 3.5**
Identify the speaker, and recognize the difference between first- and third-person narration.

Make the Connection
Quickwrite

Imagine that you write an advice column for your school newspaper. One day you receive this letter from someone in your school. In a letter, advise "Confused."

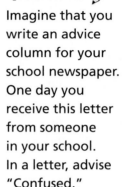

Last Friday I saw my friend Lucy (not her real name) take a wallet that was left on a cafeteria table. I know she needs the money because her dad is between jobs. I don't know what to do! I mean, I want to do what's right—but I don't know how to handle this. She's just never done anything like this before.

Sincerely,
Confused

Vocabulary Development

O. Henry loved long, unusual words. Here are some words from "After Twenty Years" that you can add to your own vocabulary:

habitual (hə·bich′ōo·əl) *adj.:* done or fixed by habit. *The officer made his habitual check of the buildings.*

intricate (in′tri·kit) *adj.:* complicated; full of detail. *The officer twirled his club with intricate movements.*

dismally (diz′məl·ē) *adv.:* miserably; gloomily. *People walked dismally through the rainy streets.*

egotism (ē′gō·tiz′əm) *n.:* conceit; talking about oneself too much. *His egotism made him brag about his success.*

simultaneously (sī′məl·tā′nē·əs·lē) *adv.:* at the same time. *Each man looked simultaneously at his friend's face.*

After Twenty Years

O. Henry

"We agreed that we would meet here again exactly twenty years from that date and time . . ."

(Background) Courtesy of The Valentine Museum, Richmond, Virginia.

The City from Greenwich Village (1922) by John Sloan. Oil on canvas.

The policeman on the beat moved up the avenue impressively. The impressiveness was <u>habitual</u> and not for show, for spectators were few. The time was barely ten o'clock at night, but chilly gusts of wind with a taste of rain in them had well nigh depeopled the streets.

Trying doors as he went, twirling his club with many <u>intricate</u> and artful movements, turning now and then to cast his watchful eye down the pacific[1] thoroughfare, the officer, with his stalwart form and slight swagger, made a fine picture of a guardian of the peace. The vicinity was one that kept early hours. Now and then you might see the lights of a cigar store or of an all-night lunch counter, but the majority of the doors belonged to business places that had long since been closed.

When about midway of a certain block, the policeman suddenly slowed his walk. In the doorway of a darkened hardware store a man leaned with an unlighted cigar in his mouth. As the policeman walked up to him, the man spoke up quickly.

"It's all right, officer," he said reassuringly. "I'm just waiting for a friend. It's an appointment made twenty years ago. Sounds a little funny to you, doesn't it? Well, I'll explain if you'd like to make certain it's all

---

1. **pacific** *adj.:* peaceful.

Vocabulary
habitual (hə·bich′oo·əl) *adj.:* done or fixed by
    habit; customary.
intricate (in′tri·kit) *adj.:* complicated; full of detail.

straight. About that long ago there used to be a restaurant where this store stands—'Big Joe' Brady's restaurant."

"Until five years ago," said the policeman. "It was torn down then."

The man in the doorway struck a match and lit his cigar. The light showed a pale, square-jawed face with keen eyes and a little white scar near his right eyebrow. His scarf pin was a large diamond, oddly set.

MAKING PREDICTIONS

1. What could the scar and the large diamond suggest about the man's past?

"Twenty years ago tonight," said the man, "I dined here at 'Big Joe' Brady's with Jimmy Wells, my best chum and the finest chap in the world. He and I were raised here in New York, just like two brothers, together. I was eighteen and Jimmy was twenty. The next morning I was to start for the West to make my fortune. You couldn't have dragged Jimmy out of New York; he thought it was the only place on earth. Well, we agreed that night that we would meet here again exactly twenty years from that date and time, no matter what our conditions might be or from what distance we might have to come. We figured that in twenty years each of us ought to have our destiny worked out and our fortunes made, whatever they were going to be."

"It sounds pretty interesting," said the policeman. "Rather a long time between meets, though, it seems to me. Haven't you heard from your friend since you left?"

"Well, yes, for a time we corresponded," said the other. "But after a year or two we lost track of each other. You see, the West is a pretty big proposition, and I kept hustling around over it pretty lively. But I know Jimmy will meet me here if he's alive, for he always was the truest, staunchest old chap in the world. He'll never forget. I came a thousand miles to stand in this door tonight, and it's worth it if my old partner turns up."

The waiting man pulled out a handsome watch, the lids of it set with small diamonds.

"Three minutes to ten," he announced. "It was exactly ten o'clock when we parted here at the restaurant door."

"Did pretty well out West, didn't you?" asked the policeman.

"You bet! I hope Jimmy has done half as well. He was a kind of plodder, though, good fellow as he was. I've had to compete with some of the sharpest wits going to get my pile. A man gets in a groove in New York. It takes the West to put a razor edge on him."

MAKING PREDICTIONS

2. What do these boasts suggest about the man's past?

The policeman twirled his club and took a step or two.

"I'll be on my way. Hope your friend comes around all right. Going to call time on him sharp?"

"I should say not!" said the other. "I'll give him half an hour at least. If Jimmy is alive on earth, he'll be here by that time. So long, officer."

"Good night, sir," said the policeman, passing on along his beat, trying doors as he went.

There was now a fine, cold drizzle falling, and the wind had risen from its uncertain puffs into a steady blow. The few foot passengers astir in that quarter hurried dismally and silently along with coat collars turned high and pocketed hands. And in the door of the hardware store the man who had

Vocabulary
dismally (diz′məl·ē) *adv.*: miserably; gloomily.

come a thousand miles to fill an appointment, uncertain almost to absurdity, with the friend of his youth, smoked his cigar and waited.

About twenty minutes he waited, and then a tall man in a long overcoat, with collar turned up to his ears, hurried across from the opposite side of the street. He went directly to the waiting man.

"Is that you, Bob?" he asked, doubtfully.

"Is that you, Jimmy Wells?" cried the man in the door.

"Bless my heart!" exclaimed the new arrival, grasping both the other's hands with his own. "It's Bob, sure as fate. I was certain I'd find you here if you were still in existence. Well, well, well!—twenty years is a long time. The old restaurant's gone, Bob; I wish it had lasted, so we could have had another dinner there. How has the West treated you, old man?"

"Bully;² it has given me everything I asked it for. You've changed lots, Jimmy. I never thought you were so tall by two or three inches."

MAKING PREDICTIONS

3. What could Jimmy's height signify?

"Oh, I grew a bit after I was twenty."

"Doing well in New York, Jimmy?"

"Moderately. I have a position in one of the city departments. Come on, Bob; we'll go around to a place I know of and have a good long talk about old times."

The two men started up the street, arm in arm. The man from the West, his egotism enlarged by success, was beginning to outline the history of his career. The other, submerged in his overcoat, listened with interest.

_____
2. **bully** *interj.*: informal term meaning "very well."

At the corner stood a drugstore, brilliant with electric lights. When they came into this glare, each of them turned simultaneously to gaze upon the other's face.

The man from the West stopped suddenly and released his arm.

"You're not Jimmy Wells," he snapped. "Twenty years is a long time, but not long enough to change a man's nose from a Roman to a pug."

"It sometimes changes a good man into a bad one," said the tall man. "You've been under arrest for ten minutes, 'Silky' Bob. Chicago thinks you may have dropped over our way and wires us she wants to have a chat with you. Going quietly, are you? That's sensible. Now, before we go to the station, here's a note I was asked to hand to you. You may read it here at the window. It's from Patrolman Wells."

The man from the West unfolded the little piece of paper handed him. His hand was steady when he began to read, but it trembled a little by the time he had finished. The note was rather short.

MAKING PREDICTIONS

4. If the man is not Jimmy Wells, then who do you suppose he is, and why do you think he is sent in Jimmy's place?

> Bob: I was at the appointed place on time. When you struck the match to light your cigar, I saw it was the face of the man wanted in Chicago. Somehow I couldn't do it myself, so I went around and got a plainclothes man to do the job.
>
> Jimmy

Vocabulary

egotism (ē′gō·tiz′əm) *n.*: conceit; talking about oneself too much.

simultaneously (sī′məl·tā′nē·əs·lē) *adv.*: at the same time.

O. Henry

"Stories in Everything"

O. Henry (1862–1910) is the pen name of William Sydney Porter, who was born in Greensboro, North Carolina. He left school at fifteen and eventually moved to Texas. There he edited a humor magazine called *The Rolling Stone* and worked for a few years in a bank in Austin. Unfortunately, Porter was a careless record keeper. Two years after he left the bank, he was accused of embezzling its money. Although he was probably innocent, Porter panicked and ran off to Honduras. A year or so later he returned to Austin to be with his dying wife. There he was convicted and spent more than three years in a federal prison in Ohio.

Porter found the plots of many of his stories (including "After Twenty Years") in jail. He may also have found his famous pen name there: The name of a prison guard was Orrin Henry.

After he was released from prison, in 1901, Porter moved to New York. Soon, as O. Henry, he became one of the country's most popular short story writers. His stories are known for their snappy surprise endings. Many of his best-known stories are set in New York's streets and tenements and cheap hotels.

One day while O. Henry was dining with friends at a New York restaurant, a young writer asked him where he got his plots. "Oh, everywhere," replied O. Henry. "There are stories in everything." He picked up the menu on which the dishes of the day were typewritten. "There's a story in this," he said. Then he outlined the story—which he later wrote down and published—called "Springtime à la Carte." (On menus *à la carte* means that each item is priced separately.)

For Independent Reading

"After Twenty Years" is from a collection called *The Four Million and Other Stories.* The title refers to the population of New York City in O. Henry's day. Other O. Henry stories set in New York include "The Gift of the Magi" and "The Last Leaf."

Literary Response and Analysis

Reading Check

1. Why has the man in the doorway come back to the old neighborhood after twenty years?

2. What does the police officer realize when the man in the doorway lights his cigar?

3. How does the man in the doorway describe Jimmy Wells?

4. What does the police officer do after saying good night to the man in the doorway?

5. What happens to Bob at the end of the story?

Interpretations

6. Why does the police officer need to know if the man would wait for his friend or "call time on him sharp"? What do you think the officer would have done if the man had said he would leave at ten o'clock?

7. Several details about Bob's appearance and behavior warn us that he might not be honest or that he is hiding from someone. What clues hint at, or **foreshadow,** something sinister about Bob?

8. When did you realize who the police officer was? Find and explain the first clue to his identity.

9. Both men honor a commitment they made over twenty years ago, but for Jimmy Wells there's one thing more important than even a long friendship. In a sentence or two, state the **theme** of this story. What truth about loyalty versus honesty does the story reveal to you?

10. What would you have done if you were Jimmy? Look back at the letter you wrote to "Confused" in your Quickwrite. Would you make any revisions to the advice you gave? ✏️

Evaluation

11. Some people don't like O. Henry's surprise endings. They think these endings make the stories unbelievable. Do you agree? Explain why or why not.

Writing

Another Point of View

O. Henry chose to tell his story from the **omniscient point of view.** What would we have known—and not known—if he had let Silky Bob tell the story from his own **first-person point of view**? Try retelling one of the scenes from Bob's or Jimmy's point of view. How could the new narrator change the story's **theme**? Is it still about loyalty versus honesty?

Reading Standard 3.5
Contrast points of view (for example, first person and omniscient) in narrative text, and explain how they affect the overall theme of the work.

Vocabulary Development

Reading Standard 1.3 Clarify word meanings through the use of definition, example, restatement, or contrast.

Clarifying Word Meanings

PRACTICE

To be sure you own the words in the Word Bank, fill out a word web for each word. Clarify the word's meaning through the use of definition, example, restatement, and contrast. The first word has been done for you. Be sure to compare your webs in class.

Word Bank

habitual
intricate
dismally
egotism
simultaneously

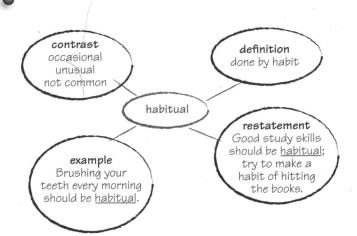

contrast
occasional
unusual
not common

definition
done by habit

habitual

restatement
Good study skills
should be habitual;
try to make a
habit of hitting
the books.

example
Brushing your
teeth every morning
should be habitual.

Grammar Link
MINI-LESSON

End All End-Mark Errors

In written English every sentence must begin with a capital letter and end with one of these **end marks:** a period, a question mark, or an exclamation point. Follow these simple rules:

- Use a period at the end of a statement.
  "It's an appointment made twenty years ago."

- Use a question mark at the end of a question.
  "Is that you, Bob?"

- Use an exclamation point at the end of an exclamation or a command.
  "Bless my heart!"

PRACTICE

Rewrite the following paragraph, adding capitalization and end punctuation marks. (The paragraph contains a total of seven sentences.)

Charlie tried out for the baseball team what did he have to lose it's not as if you have to be Ken Griffey, Jr., to play a position who imagined what would happen it was such a surprise unbelievably, he's hitting leadoff I guess you never know

For more help, see End Marks in the *Holt Handbook,* pages 290–293.

What's *Really* in a Name?

Perspective: How We Look at Life

Perspective refers to the way we look at a subject. Take the subject of school uniforms. Some people's perspective on that subject is negative. They think children should be free to dress the way they wish. Other people have a positive perspective on school uniforms. They think uniforms help equalize children and do away with clothes competition.

All writers have a perspective on their subjects. O. Henry's perspective on life is clear in the story "After Twenty Years." He sees life as offering us choices between honest and dishonest behavior. He comes down in favor of honesty, even when friendship is at stake.

Tracking Perspective

After you read "What's *Really* in a Name?," fill out a chart like the one opposite. Doing that should help you identify the writer's perspective on changing names.

"What's *Really* in a Name?"

> The writer doesn't understand why Patsy changed her name.

> The writer tells why some people change their names:
> 1.
> 2.
> 3.
> [and so on]

> The writer states her main concern about changing names:

> Final quotation:

> The writer's perspective on changing names:

Reading Standard 2.4
Identify and trace the development of an author's perspective in text.

It all depends on your point of view.

What's Really in a Name?

Patsy seemed like a movie star before she really became one. She was my sister's friend, and her presence made me hide behind the plants in the living room. I didn't want to talk to her. I just wanted to watch her. She was only in the sixth grade, but she had an air of sophistication that I had never experienced in my seven years.

After we all grew up, Patsy moved to New York and then to Los Angeles. I began to see her on television. Then I saw her in movies. At the end of one movie, I searched the closing credits for her name, but it wasn't there. So I called my sister and said, "I can't believe they left Patsy's name off the credits." My sister said, "They didn't. She changed her name." I hung up the phone feeling confused. To me Patsy would always be Patsy. Why would she need a new name?

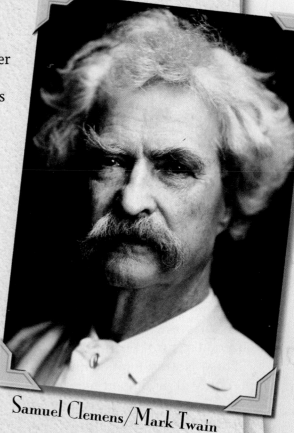

Samuel Clemens/Mark Twain

Patsy had given herself a pseudonym.° Although it sounds like a bad disease, it's not. A pseudonym is a made-up name. (*Pseudo* comes from a Greek word that means "fake.") For writers a pseudonym is also called a pen name. William Sydney Porter, the famous short story writer, called himself O. Henry (see page 229). Mark Twain's name was really Samuel Clemens.

People have all sorts of reasons for using pseudonyms. It's easy to see why William Sydney Porter had one. He spent more than three years in jail for stealing money from a bank where he had worked. Although the evidence of his crime remains questionable, the damage to his reputation was done. As an ex-convict he might have had a hard time getting his books published. So he changed his name. One story is that the

---

°**pseudonym** (sōō′də·nim′) *n.*

name O. Henry came from his cat. When he called the family cat, he yelled, "Oh, Henry." Another story has it that he got it from his prison guard. The guard's name was Orrin Henry.

Sometimes writers give themselves pen names because their publishers ask them to. It might have been hard to sell a shoot 'em-up western if your name was Archibald Lynn Joscelyn. Change that name to Al Cody (think of Cody, Wyoming, and Buffalo Bill Cody), however, and you've got a winner. The romance writer Elaine Carr is really a man named Charles Mason.

The main reason for taking a pseudonym is because it just <u>sounds better</u>. It's more appealing and memorable. Which has a better ring—Charles Lutwidge Dodson or Lewis Carroll? Reginald Kenneth Dwight or Elton John? Ralph Lifshitz or Ralph Lauren? Norma Jean Baker or Marilyn Monroe?

So why am I still troubled today that the beautiful and talented Patsy changed her name? I assumed that by adopting a new name, Patsy was trying to get rid of her past—her old friends, the neighborhood, even the scrawny seven-year-old kid who gazed at her from behind the plants.

Patsy, Norma Jean, Reginald—they probably all had good reasons for choosing new names. I hope when they changed their names, they held on tight to their roots. I agree with writer James Baldwin, who said, "Know from whence you came. If you know from whence you came, there are absolutely no limitations to where you can go."

—Joan Burditt

Reginald Dwight/Elton John

Caryn Elaine Johnson/
Whoopi Goldberg

Associated Press, High Museum of Art, Atlanta.

Reading Informational Materials

Reading Check

1. What is a pseudonym? What is another expression for *pseudonym*?

2. According to this writer, what is the main reason people take pseudonyms?

3. Explain how the quote from James Baldwin at the end of the essay supports the writer's feelings about pseudonyms.

TestPractice

What's Really in a Name?

1. The writer of this essay believes that —

   A people should feel free to change their names

   B it's important to remember where you came from

   C William Sydney Porter was guilty of stealing money

   D writers should use pseudonyms if they want to sell books

2. A writer's **perspective** is —

   F his or her point of view on a subject

   G a story the writer tells to entertain readers

   H a sequence of related events

   J the words a writer chooses

3. This essay was written in order to —

   A explain a process

   B describe a place

   C compare several ideas

   D express an opinion

4. In the quote "If you know from whence you came, there are absolutely no limitations to where you can go," the word *whence* means —

   F where

   G how

   H there

   J whether

5. The writer's **perspective** was *most* influenced by —

   A Whoopi Goldberg

   B her sister's friend Patsy

   C James Baldwin

   D William Sydney Porter

Reading Standard 2.4
Identify and trace the development of an author's perspective in text.

Bargain

Literary Focus
First-Person Point of View

When you are telling a story about something that happened to you, you use *I*. You say, "I was late for practice because the dog got out." You tell your story from the **first-person point of view.** The story "Bargain" is also told from the first-person point of view. It is told by Al, a character in the story who is about thirteen years old.

When a story is told from the first-person point of view, two important things happen. First, we share directly the narrator's thoughts and feelings. Second, we know *only* what the narrator knows. All we learn about the story's events and the other characters comes from the narrator's observations.

Historical Fiction

This story takes place in Moon Dance, a town where we have all been in our imagination. You will recognize Moon Dance from TV and movie westerns—its muddy street, its saloon, and its general store. This story is a kind of **historical fiction.** Setting is important in historical fiction. This writer wants you to feel what it was like to live in a rough frontier town. If you took away Moon Dance and all the historical details, you'd have a different story.

Reading Skills
Making Predictions: What Will Happen Next?

Part of the fun of reading is trying to guess what will happen next. This process is called making **predictions.** Here is how you make predictions:

- Look for clues that **foreshadow,** or hint at, what will happen.

- As the suspense builds, predict possible outcomes. See if you can guess where the writer is leading you.

- Ask yourself questions while you read. Revise your predictions as you go.

- Draw on your own experiences and knowledge in making your predictions.

Remember: A good writer always surprises you.

You will find questions in this story that ask about predictions. Look for the little open-book signs.

Make the Connection
Discussion

With a partner, discuss these questions: What is the difference between justice and revenge? What do these two concepts have in common? What are some examples of each? Jot down your responses so you can refer to them at the end of the story.

Grade 6 Review Reading Standard 3.5 Identify the speaker, and recognize the difference between first- and third-person narration.

BARGAIN

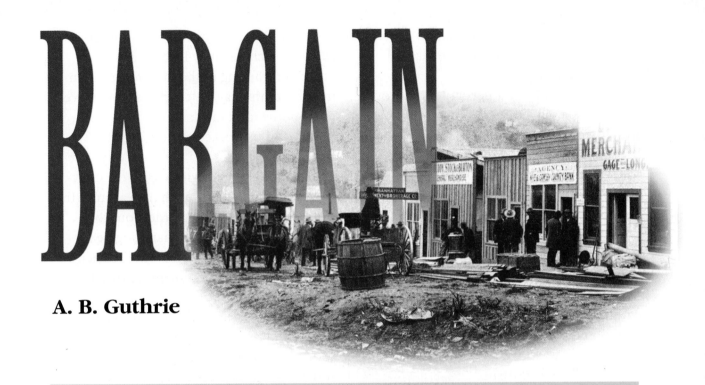

A. B. Guthrie

He was a man you wouldn't remember from meeting once.

Mr. Baumer and I had closed the Moon Dance Mercantile Company and were walking to the post office, and he had a bunch of bills in his hand ready to mail. There wasn't anyone or anything much on the street because it was suppertime. A buckboard[1] and a saddle horse were tied at Hirsches' rack, and a rancher in a wagon rattled for home ahead of us, the sound of his going fading out as he prodded his team. Freighter[2] Slade stood alone in front of the Moon Dance Saloon, maybe wondering whether to have one more before going to supper. People said he could hold a lot without showing it except in being ornerier[3] even than usual.

Mr. Baumer didn't see him until he was almost on him, and then he stopped and fingered through the bills until he found the right one. He stepped up to Slade and held it out.

Slade said, "What's this, Dutchie?"

Mr. Baumer had to tilt his head up to talk to him. "You know vat it is."

Slade just said, "Yeah?" You never could tell from his face what went on inside his

---

1. **buckboard** *n.:* open carriage.
2. **freighter** *n.* used as *adj.:* here, person who transports goods.

3. **ornerier** (ôr**′**nər·ē·ər) *adj.:* dialect for "meaner and more stubborn."

skull. He had dark skin and shallow cheeks and a thick-growing moustache that fell over the corners of his mouth.

"It is a bill," Mr. Baumer said. "I tell you before, it is a bill. For twenty-vun dollars and fifty cents."

"You know what I do with bills, don't you, Dutchie?" Slade asked.

Mr. Baumer didn't answer the question. He said, "For merchandise."

Slade took the envelope from Mr. Baumer's hand and squeezed it up in his fist and let it drop on the plank sidewalk. Not saying anything, he reached down and took Mr. Baumer's nose between the knuckles of his fingers and twisted it up into his eyes. That was all. That was all at the time. Slade half turned and slouched to the door of the bar and let himself in. Some men were laughing in there.

PREDICTING

1. What part do you suppose Slade will play in this story?

Mr. Baumer stooped and picked up the bill and put it on top of the rest and smoothed it out for mailing. When he straightened up, I could see tears in his eyes from having his nose screwed around.

He didn't say anything to me, and I didn't say anything to him, being so much younger and feeling embarrassed for him. He went into the post office and slipped the bills in the slot, and we walked on home together. At the last, at the crossing where I had to leave him, he remembered to say, "Better study, Al. Is good to know to read and write and figure." I guess he felt he had to push me a little, my father being dead.

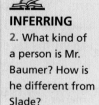

INFERRING

2. What kind of a person is Mr. Baumer? How is he different from Slade?

I said, "Sure. See you after school tomorrow"—which he knew I would anyway. I had been working in the store for him during the summer and after classes ever since pneumonia took my dad off.

Three of us worked there regularly: Mr. Baumer, of course, and me and Colly Coleman, who knew enough to drive the delivery wagon but wasn't much help around the store except for carrying orders out to the rigs[4] at the hitchpost and handling heavy things like the whiskey barrel at the back of the store which Mr. Baumer sold quarts and gallons out of.

The store carried quite a bit of stuff—sugar and flour and dried fruits and canned goods and such on one side and yard goods and coats and caps and aprons and the like of that on the other, besides kerosene and bran and buckets and linoleum and pitchforks in the storehouse at the rear—but it wasn't a big store like Hirsch Brothers up the street. Never would be, people guessed, going on to say, with a sort of slow respect, that it would have gone under long ago if Mr. Baumer hadn't been half mule and half beaver. He had started the store just two years before and, the way things were, worked himself close to death.

He was at the high desk at the end of the grocery counter when I came in the next afternoon. He had an eyeshade on and black sateen protectors on his forearms, and his pencil was in his hand instead of behind his ear and his glasses were roosted on the nose that Slade had twisted. He didn't hear me open and close the door or hear my feet as I walked back to him, and I saw he wasn't doing anything with the pencil but holding

---

4. **rigs** *n.*: carriages with their horses.

"I think he hate me. That is the thing. He hate me for coming not from this country...."

it over paper. I stood and studied him for a minute, seeing a small, stooped man with a little paunch bulging through his unbuttoned vest. He was a man you wouldn't remember from meeting once. There was nothing in his looks to set itself in your mind unless maybe it was his chin, which was a small pink hill in the gentle plain of his face.

While I watched him, he lifted his hand and felt carefully of his nose. Then he saw me. His eyes had that kind of mistiness that seems to go with age or illness, though he wasn't really old or sick, either. He brought his hand down quickly and picked up the pencil, but he saw I still was looking at the nose, and finally he sighed and said, "That Slade."

Just the sound of the name brought Slade to my eye. I saw him slouched in front of the bar, and I saw him and his string[5] coming down the grade from the buttes,[6] the wheel horses held snug and the rest lined out pretty, and then the string leveling off and Slade's whip lifting hair from a horse that wasn't up in the collar.[7] I had heard it said that Slade could make a horse scream with that whip. Slade's name wasn't Freighter, of course. Our town had nicknamed

---

5. **string** *n.:* here, a group of horses.
6. **buttes** (byo͞ots) *n.:* steep, flat-topped hills that stand alone on a plain.
7. **up in the collar:** pulling as hard as the other horses.

him that because that was what he was.

"I don't think it's any good to send him a bill, Mr. Baumer," I said. "He can't even read."

"He could pay yet."

"He don't pay anybody," I said.

"I think he hate me," Mr. Baumer went on. "That is the thing. He hate me for coming not from this country. I come here, sixteen years old, and learn to read and write, and I make a business, and so I think he hate me."

"He hates everybody."

Mr. Baumer shook his head. "But not to pinch the nose. Not to call Dutchie."

The side door squeaked open, but it was only Colly Coleman coming in from a trip, so I said, "Excuse me, Mr. Baumer, but you shouldn't have trusted him in the first place."

"I know," he answered, looking at me with his misty eyes. "A man make mistakes. I think some do not trust him, so he will pay me because I do. And I do not know him well then. He only came back to town three, four months ago, from being away since before I go into business."

"People who knew him before could have told you," I said.

"A man make mistakes," he explained again.

"It's not my business, Mr. Baumer, but I would forget the bill."

His eyes rested on my face for a long

Bargain   **239**

minute, as if they didn't see me but the problem itself. He said, "It is not twenty-vun dollars and fifty cents now, Al. It is not that anymore."

"What is it?"

He took a little time to answer. Then he brought his two hands up as if to help him shape the words. "It is the thing. You see, it is the thing."

I wasn't quite sure what he meant.

He took his pencil from behind the ear where he had put it and studied the point of it. "That Slade. He steal whiskey and call it evap-oration. He sneak things from his load. A thief, he is. And too big for me."

PREDICTING

3. What do you think will happen between Mr. Baumer and Slade?

I said, "I got no time for him, Mr. Baumer, but I guess there never was a freighter didn't steal whiskey. That's what I hear."

It was true, too. From the railroad to Moon Dance was fifty miles and a little better—a two-day haul in good weather, heck knew how long in bad. Any freight string bound home with a load had to lie out at least one night. When a freighter had his stock tended to and maybe a little fire going against the dark, he'd tackle a barrel of whiskey or of grain alcohol if he had one aboard consigned to Hirsch Brothers or Mr. Baumer's or the Moon Dance Saloon or the Gold Leaf Bar. He'd drive a hoop out of place, bore a little hole with a nail or bit and draw off what he wanted. Then he'd plug the hole with a whittled peg and pound the hoop back. That was evapora-tion. Nobody complained much. With freighters you generally took what they gave you, within reason.

"Moore steals it, too," I told Mr. Baumer. Moore was Mr. Baumer's freighter.

"Yah," he said, and that was all, but I stood there for a minute, thinking there might be something more. I could see thought swimming in his eyes, above that little hill of chin. Then a customer came in, and I had to go wait on him.

INFERRING

4. What do you guess Baumer is thinking? Why do you think this writer keeps mentioning his chin?

Nothing happened for a month, nothing between Mr. Baumer and Slade, that is, but fall drew on toward winter and the first flight of ducks headed south and Mr. Baumer hired Miss Lizzie Webb to help with the just-beginning Christmas trade and here it was, the first week in October, and he and I walked up the street again with the monthly bills. He always sent them out. I guess he had to. A bigger store, like Hirsches', would wait on the ranchers until their beef or wool went to market.

Up to a point things looked and hap-pened almost the same as they had before, so much the same that I had the crazy feel-ing I was going through that time again. There was a wagon and a rig tied up at Hirsches' rack and a saddle horse standing hipshot[8] in front of the harness shop. A few more people were on the street now, not many, and lamps had been lit against the shortened day.

It was dark enough that I didn't make out Slade right away. He was just a figure that came out of the yellow wash of light from the Moon Dance Saloon and stood on the boardwalk and with his head made the little

---

8. hipshot *adj.:* with one hip lower than the other.

The Apprentice by Robert Duncan.   Courtesy of the Artist.

motion of spitting. Then I recognized the lean, raw shape of him and the muscles flowing down into the sloped shoulders, and in the settling darkness I filled the picture in—the dark skin and the flat cheeks and the peevish eyes and the moustache growing rank.

There was Slade and here was Mr. Baumer with his bills and here I was, just as before, just like in the second go-round of a bad dream. I felt like turning back, being embarrassed and half scared by trouble even when it wasn't mine. Please, I said to myself, don't stop, Mr. Baumer! Don't bite off anything! Please, shortsighted the way you are, don't catch sight of him at all! I held up and stepped around behind Mr. Baumer and came up on the outside so as to be between him and Slade, where maybe I'd cut off his view.

But it wasn't any use. All along I think I knew it was no use, not the praying or the walking between or anything. The act had to play itself out.

Mr. Baumer looked across the front of me and saw Slade and hesitated in his step and came to a stop. Then in his slow, business way, his chin held firm against his mouth, he began fingering through the bills, squinting to make out the names. Slade had turned and was watching him, munching on a cud of tobacco like a bull waiting.

"You look, Al," Mr. Baumer said without lifting his face from the bills. "I cannot see so good."

So I looked, and while I was looking, Slade must have moved. The next I knew, Mr. Baumer was staggering ahead, the envelopes spilling out of his hands. There had been a thump, the clap of a heavy hand swung hard on his back.

Slade said, "Haryu, Dutchie?"

Mr. Baumer caught his balance and turned around, the bills he had trampled shining white between them and at Slade's feet the hat that Mr. Baumer had stumbled out from under.

Slade picked up the hat and scuffed through the bills and held it out. "Cold to be goin' without a skypiece," he said.

Mr. Baumer hadn't spoken a word. The lampshine from inside the bar caught his eyes, and in them, it seemed to me, a light came and went as anger and the uselessness of it took turns in his head.

Two men had come up on us and stood watching. One of them was Angus McDonald, who owned the Ranchers' Bank, and the other was Dr. King. He had his bag in his hand.

Two others were drifting up, but I didn't have time to tell who. The light came in Mr. Baumer's eyes, and he took a step ahead and swung. I could have hit harder myself. The fist landed on Slade's cheek without hardly so much as jogging his head, but it let the devil loose in the man. I didn't know he could move so fast. He slid in like a practiced fighter and let Mr. Baumer have it full in the face.

Mr. Baumer slammed over on his back, but he wasn't out. He started lifting himself. Slade leaped ahead and brought a boot heel down on the hand he was lifting himself by. I heard meat and bone under that heel and saw Mr. Baumer fall back and try to roll away.

Things had happened so fast that not until then did anyone have a chance to get between them. Now Mr. McDonald pushed at Slade's chest, saying, "That's enough, Freighter. That's enough, now," and Dr. King lined up, too, and another man I didn't know, and I took a place, and we formed a kind of screen between them. Dr. King turned and bent to look at Mr. Baumer.

"Fool hit me first," Slade said.

"That's enough," Mr. McDonald told him again while Slade looked at all of us as if he'd spit on us for a nickel. Mr. McDonald went on, using a half-friendly tone, and I knew it was because he didn't want to take Slade on any more than the rest of us did. "You go on home and sleep it off, Freighter. That's the ticket."

Slade just snorted.

From behind us, Dr. King said, "I think you've broken this man's hand."

"Lucky for him I didn't kill him," Slade answered. "Dutch penny pincher!" He fingered the chew out of his mouth. "Maybe he'll know enough to leave me alone now."

Dr. King had Mr. Baumer on his feet. "I'll take him to the office," he said.

Blood was draining from Mr. Baumer's nose and rounding the curve of his lip and dripping from the sides of his chin. He held his hurt right hand in the other. But the thing was that he didn't look beaten even then, not the way a man who has given up looks beaten. Maybe that was why Slade said, with a show of that fierce anger, "You stay away from me! Hear? Stay clear away, or you'll get more of the same!"

Dr. King led Mr. Baumer away, Slade went back into

PREDICTING

5. What clues suggest that Baumer will not give up? How could he get even with Slade?

the bar, and the other men walked off, talking about the fight. I got down and picked up the bills, because I knew Mr. Baumer would want me to, and mailed them at the post office, dirty as they were. It made me sorer, someway, that Slade's bill was one of the few that wasn't marked up. The cleanness of it seemed to say that there was no getting the best of him.

Mr. Baumer had his hand in a sling the next day and wasn't much good at waiting on the trade. I had to hustle all afternoon and so didn't have a chance to talk to him even if he had wanted to talk. Mostly he stood at his desk, and once, passing it, I saw he was practicing writing with his left hand. His nose and the edges of the cheeks around it were swollen some.

At closing time I said, "Look, Mr. Baumer, I can lay out of school a few days until you kind of get straightened out here."

"No," he answered as if to wave the subject away. "I get somebody else. You go to school. Is good to learn."

I had a half notion to say that learning hadn't helped him with Slade. Instead, I blurted out that I would have the law on Slade.

"The law?" he asked.

"The sheriff or somebody."

"No, Al," he said. "You would not."

I asked why.

"The law, it is not for plain fights," he said. "Shooting? Robbing? Yes, the law come quick. The plain fights, they are too many. They not count enough."

He was right. I said, "Well, I'd do something anyhow."

"Yes," he answered with a slow nod of his head. "Something you vould do, Al." He didn't tell me what.

Within a couple of days he got another man to clerk for him—it was Ed Hempel, who was always finding and losing jobs—and we made out. Mr. Baumer took his hand from the sling in a couple or three weeks, but with the tape on it, it still wasn't any use to him. From what you could see of the fingers below the tape, it looked as if it never would be.

He spent most of his time at the high desk, sending me or Ed out on the errands he used to run, like posting and getting the mail. Sometimes I wondered if that was because he was afraid of meeting Slade. He could just as well have gone himself. He wasted a lot of hours just looking at nothing, though I will have to say he worked hard at learning to write left-handed.

Then, a month and a half before Christmas, he hired Slade to haul his freight for him.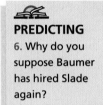

Ed Hempel told me about the deal when I showed up for work. "Yessir," he said, resting his foot on a crate in the storeroom where we were supposed to be working. "I tell you he's throwed in with Slade. Told me this morning to go out and locate him if I could and bring him in. Slade was at the saloon, o' course, and says to the devil with Dutchie, but I told him this was honest-to-God business, like Baumer had told me to, and there was a quart of whiskey right there in the store for him if he'd come and get it. He was out of money, I reckon, because the quart fetched him."

"What'd they say?" I asked him.

"Search me. There was two or three people in the store and Baumer told me to

PREDICTING
6. Why do you suppose Baumer has hired Slade again?

The Fall of the Cowboy (1895) by Frederic S. Remington. Oil on canvas.
© Amon Carter Museum, Fort Worth, Texas (1961.230).

wait on 'em, and he and Slade palavered[9] back by the desk."

"How do you know they made a deal?"

Ed spread his hands out. "'Bout noon, Moore came in with his string, and I heard Baumer say he was makin' a change. Moore didn't like it too good, either."

It was a hard thing to believe, but there one day was Slade with a pile of stuff for the Moon Dance Mercantile Company, and that was

---

9. **palavered** (pə·lav′ərd) v.: talked; met to discuss something.

proof enough with something left for boot.

Mr. Baumer never opened the subject up with me, though I gave him plenty of chances. And I didn't feel like asking. He didn't talk much these days but went around absent-minded, feeling now and then of the fingers that curled yellow and stiff out of the bandage like the toes on the leg of a dead chicken. Even on our walks home he kept his thoughts to himself.

I felt different about him now and was sore inside. Not that I blamed him exactly. A hundred and thirty-five pounds wasn't much to throw against two hundred. And who could tell what Slade would do on a bellyful of whiskey? He had promised Mr. Baumer more of the same, hadn't he? But I didn't feel good. I couldn't look up to Mr. Baumer like I used to and still wanted to. I didn't have the beginning of an answer when men cracked jokes or shook their heads in sympathy with Mr. Baumer, saying Slade had made him come to time.

Slade hauled in a load for the store, and another, and Christmastime was drawing on and trade heavy, and the winter that had started early and then pulled back came on again. There was a blizzard and then a still cold and another blizzard and afterwards a sunshine that was iceshine on the drifted snow. I was glad to be busy, selling overshoes and sheep-lined coats and mitts and socks as thick as saddle blankets and Christmas candy out of buckets and hickory nuts and the fresh oranges that the people in our town never saw except when Santa Claus was coming.

One afternoon, when I lit out from class, the thermometer on the school porch read forty-two degrees below. But you didn't have to look at it to know how cold the weather was. Your nose and fingers and toes and ears and the bones inside you told you. The snow cried when you stepped on it.

I got to the store and took my things off and scuffed my hands at the stove for a minute so's to get life enough in them to tie a parcel. Mr. Baumer—he was always polite to me—said, "Hello, Al. Not so much to do today. Too cold for customers." He shuddered a little, as if he hadn't got the chill off even yet, and rubbed his broken hand with the good one. "Ve need Christmas goods," he said, looking out the window to the

furrows that wheels had made in the snow-banked street, and I knew he was thinking of Slade's string, inbound from the railroad, and the time it might take even Slade to travel those hard miles.

Slade never made it at all.

Less than an hour later our old freighter, Moore, came in, his beard white and stiff with frost. He didn't speak at first but looked around and clumped to the stove and took off his heavy mitts, holding his news inside him.

Then he said, not pleasantly, "Your new man's dead, Baumer."

"My new man?" Mr. Baumer said.

"Who do you think? Slade. He's dead."

All Mr. Baumer could say was "Dead!"

"Froze to death, I figger," Moore told him, while Colly Coleman and Ed Hempel and Miss Lizzie and I and a couple of customers stepped closer.

"Not Slade," Mr. Baumer said. "He know too much to freeze."

"Maybe so, but he sure's froze now. I got him in the wagon."

We stood looking at one another and at Moore. Moore was enjoying his news, enjoying feeding it out bit by bit so's to hold the stage. "Heart might've give out, for all I know."

The side door swung open, letting in a cloud of cold and three men who stood, like us, waiting on Moore. I moved a little and looked through the window and saw Slade's freight outfit tied outside with more men around it. Two of them were on a wheel of one of the wagons, looking inside.

"Had a extra man, so I brought your stuff in," Moore went on. "Figgered you'd be glad to pay for it."

"Not Slade," Mr. Baumer said again.

Only the moustache seemed still alive, sprouting thick like greasewood from alkali.

"You can take a look at him."

Mr. Baumer answered no.

"Someone's takin' word to Connor to bring his hearse. Anyhow, I told 'em to. I carted old Slade this far. Connor can have him now."

Moore pulled on his mitts. "Found him there by the Deep Creek crossin', doubled up in the snow an' his fire out." He moved toward the door. "I'll see to the horses, but your stuff'll have to set there. I got more'n enough work to do at Hirsches'."

Mr. Baumer just nodded.

I put on my coat and went out and waited my turn and climbed on a wagon wheel and looked inside, and there was Slade piled on some bags of bran. Maybe because of being frozen, his face was whiter than I ever saw it, whiter and deader, too, though it never had been lively. Only the moustache seemed still alive, sprouting thick like greasewood from alkali.[10] Slade was doubled up all right, as if he had died and stiffened leaning forward in a chair.

I got down from the wheel, and Colly and then Ed climbed up. Moore was unhitching, tossing off his pieces of information while he did so. Pretty soon Mr. Connor came up with his old hearse, and he and Moore tumbled Slade into it, and the team, which was as old as the hearse, made off, the tires squeaking in the snow. The people trailed on away with it, their breaths leaving little ribbons of mist in the air. It was beginning to get dark.

Mr. Baumer came out of the side door of the store, bundled up, and called to Colly and Ed and me. "We unload," he said. "Already is late. Al, better you get a couple lanterns now."

We did a fast job, setting the stuff out of the wagons onto the platform and then carrying it or rolling it on the one truck that the store owned and stowing it inside according to where Mr. Baumer's good hand pointed.

A barrel was one of the last things to go in. I edged it up and Colly nosed the truck under it, and then I let it fall back. "Mr. Baumer," I said, "we'll never sell all this, will we?"

"Yah," he answered. "Sure we sell it. I get it cheap. A bargain, Al, so I buy it."

I looked at the barrel head again. There in big letters I saw "Wood Alcohol—Deadly Poison."

"Hurry now," Mr. Baumer said. "Is late." For a flash and no longer I saw through the mist in his eyes, saw, you might say, that hilly chin repeated there. "Then ve go home, Al. Is good to know to read."

INFERRING

7. What happened to Slade?

---

10. **greasewood from alkali:** Greasewood is a thorny desert plant. Alkali is dry, salty soil that might look white and chalky, like Slade's face.

A. B. Guthrie

"Real People in Real Times"

A. B. Guthrie (1901–1991) wanted to portray the West as it was, not create myths about it. He said:

> I want to talk about real people in real times. For every Wyatt Earp or Billy the Kid, there were thousands of people just trying to get along.

Most readers agree that Guthrie succeeded. His most famous work, a trilogy about the opening of the West, is noted for its historical accuracy. Guthrie also wrote the screenplay for *Shane,* a famous movie about a western gunslinger. Shane takes justice into his own hands to save a family and pays a bitter price.

Albert Bertram Guthrie, Jr., grew up in the little town of Choteau, Montana. After graduating from college, he traveled extensively and worked at various jobs—ranching in Sonora, Mexico; selling groceries in California; working as a census taker in Montana.

Guthrie became a fiction writer when he took time out from his newspaper job to visit his sick mother. During his visit he had time to write his first novel, *Murders at Moon Dance* (1943). In this book he introduces the setting of "Bargain" and many of his other short stories. In talking about writing, Guthrie said:

> There's no immediate reward in putting words on paper. The reward, great but fugitive, is in having written, in having found the word, the line, the paragraph, the chapter that is as good as ever you can make it. I spent a full day on one line of dialogue and knocked off satisfied.

For Independent Reading

Guthrie's novels about the opening of the West are *The Big Sky; The Way West,* which won the Pulitzer Prize; and *These Thousand Hills.*

Literary Response and Analysis

Reading Check

1. Why is Baumer angry with Slade?

2. What happens to Baumer when he runs into Slade the first time?

3. Why does Al tell Baumer to forget about Slade?

4. How does Al feel when he learns that Baumer has hired Slade?

5. How does Slade die?

Interpretations

6. Look again at the notes you wrote about justice and revenge before you read this story. Would you say this story is about justice or revenge? Explain.

7. When Al suggests that Mr. Baumer forget Slade's bill, Mr. Baumer says that it isn't the money anymore; it is "the thing." What do you think Mr. Baumer means by "the thing"?

8. At what point in the story did you **predict** what was going to happen next? Go back now, and identify the details that provide clues to Slade's fate.

9. Why does Baumer say at the end, "Is good to know to read"?

10. Who do you think is responsible for Slade's death—Mr. Baumer or Slade himself? Give reasons to support your view.

11. If you were in Al's situation, would you keep silent about the likely cause of Slade's death? Why or why not?

12. What do you think of what Baumer does to Slade? Does he do the right thing? Why or why not?

13. **Theme** sums up what the main characters learn or discover in the story and what *you* learn or discover as you share their experiences. What do you think the theme of "Bargain" is?

14. "Bargain" is written in the **first-person point of view,** from Al's vantage point. What would you have known if Mr. Baumer had told the story himself? Would the story's **theme** change? If so, what might the new theme be?

Writing

Ladies and Gentlemen of the Jury

Imagine that Mr. Baumer is put on trial for causing Slade's death. In one paragraph, summarize the case *against* Mr. Baumer. Give reasons and evidence to inform and convince the jury that Mr. Baumer is guilty. This would be the case for the prosecution. In another paragraph, summarize the case *for* Mr. Baumer. Present evidence to show that Slade is responsible for his own death. This would be the case for the defense.

Reading Standard 3.5
Contrast points of view in narrative text, and explain how they affect the overall theme of the work.

Vocabulary Development

Comprehension Strategies: Tips for Word Detectives

When you come across a word you don't know and the nearest dictionary is far, far away, use these tips to unlock its meaning.

- **Look to see if parts of the word are familiar.**
  In "Bargain," Mr. Baumer's store is called the Moon Dance Mercantile Company. In figuring out *mercantile*, you might think of the word *merchant*. A merchant is someone, like Mr. Baumer, who sells goods, or *merchandise*. *Merchandise, merchant,* and *mercantile* all come from the Latin word *mercari,* which means "to trade."

- **Look at the word's context—the surrounding words and sentences—to see if it helps you figure out what the word means.**
  For example, what if a friend said, "I consigned my old bike to be sold at the bicycle store. They sold it for fifty dollars, kept their fee of twenty dollars, and gave me thirty." The context helps you figure out that the word *consign* means "turn goods over to someone else to sell." Your friend had a storekeeper sell his bike, and he gave the store part of the money.

PRACTICE

1. In "Bargain," Colly carries customers' orders out to carriages waiting at the hitchpost. How would you figure out the meaning of *hitchpost*?

2. Use context clues to figure out the meaning of *screen* in this sentence: "Dr. King lined up, too, and another man I didn't know, and I took a place, and we formed a kind of screen between them [Slade and Mr. Baumer]."

Yeh-Shen

Literary Focus
Omniscient Point of View

The omniscient (äm·nish′ənt) point of view is probably very familiar to you. You've heard it in fairy tales since you were young. A narrator who tells a story from the **omniscient point of view** knows everything about the characters and their problems. This omniscient narrator isn't *in* the story. This narrator can't even be seen. In fact, an omniscient, or all-knowing, narrator stands above the action, like a god.

Make the Connection
Talk It Over

What popular story features these characters and this theme?

- a hardworking girl

- a wicked stepmother

- a special slipper

- Good is rewarded eventually, and evil is punished.

You probably know those characters and the theme from the fairy tale "Cinderella." "Cinderella" and "Yeh-Shen" are two versions of the same story, about a girl whose dream comes true.

Discussion. People around the world have been telling the Cinderella story for ages. In a small group, talk about why you think the story of "Cinderella" is such a favorite. What do people like about the story? What deep human wishes do you think it expresses? As you

read this Chinese folk tale, keep a sheet of paper handy so that you can jot down your reactions.

Background

There are more than nine hundred versions of "Cinderella." Scholars have traced the oldest version back more than a thousand years, to China. The version that you probably know best was collected in 1697 by a French writer named Charles Perrault. His is the first version to include a fairy godmother and a midnight curfew. "Yeh-Shen" is a Chinese version of the Cinderella story.

Fish, from an album of twelve studies of flowers, birds, and fish by Tsubaki Chinzan (1801–1854). Watercolor on silk with patterned border.

Reading Standard 3.5
Contrast points of view (for example, first and third person, limited and omniscient) in narrative text, and explain how they affect the overall theme of the work.

Carp (1848) by Taito.
Courtesy of the Board of Trustees of the Victoria and Albert Museum, London.

YEH-SHEN

Chinese folk tale, retold by **Ai-Ling Louie**

THE ONLY FRIEND THAT YEH-SHEN HAD WAS A FISH . . .

In the dim past, even before the Ch'in and the Han dynasties, there lived a cave chief of southern China by the name of Wu. As was the custom in those days, Chief Wu had taken two wives. Each wife in her turn had presented Wu with a baby daughter. But one of the wives sickened and died, and not too many days after that Chief Wu took to his bed and died too.

Yeh-Shen, the little orphan, grew to girlhood in her stepmother's home. She was a bright child and lovely too, with skin as smooth as ivory and dark pools for eyes. Her stepmother was jealous of all this beauty and goodness, for her own daughter was not pretty at all. So in her displeasure, she gave poor Yeh-Shen the heaviest and most unpleasant chores.

The only friend that Yeh-Shen had to her name was a fish she had caught and raised. It was a beautiful fish with golden eyes, and every day it would come out of the water and rest its head on the bank of the pond, waiting for Yeh-Shen to feed it. Stepmother gave Yeh-Shen little enough food for herself, but the orphan child always found something to share with her fish, which grew to enormous size.

Somehow the stepmother heard of this. She was terribly angry to discover that Yeh-Shen had kept a secret from her. She hurried down to the pond, but she was unable to see the fish, for Yeh-Shen's pet wisely hid itself. The stepmother, however, was a crafty woman, and she soon thought of a plan. She walked home and called out, "Yeh-Shen, go and collect some firewood. But wait! The neighbors might see you. Leave your filthy coat here!" The minute the girl was out of sight, her stepmother slipped on the coat herself and went down again to the pond. This time the big fish saw Yeh-Shen's familiar jacket and heaved itself onto the bank, expecting to be fed. But the stepmother, having hidden a dagger in her sleeve, stabbed the fish, wrapped it in her garments, and took it home to cook for dinner.

When Yeh-Shen came to the pond that evening, she found her pet had disappeared. Overcome with grief, the girl collapsed on the ground and dropped her tears into the still waters of the pond.

"Ah, poor child!" a voice said.

Yeh-Shen sat up to find a very old man looking down at her. He wore the coarsest of clothes, and his hair flowed down over his shoulders.

"Kind uncle, who may you be?" Yeh-Shen asked.

"That is not important, my child. All you must know is that I have been sent to tell you of the wondrous powers of your fish."

"My fish, but sir . . ." The girl's eyes filled with tears, and she could not go on.

The old man sighed and said, "Yes, my

Carp with Bogbean by Sadatora (19th century).
British Library, London/Bridgeman Art Library, London.

child, your fish is no longer alive, and I must tell you that your stepmother is once more the cause of your sorrow." Yeh-Shen gasped in horror, but the old man went on. "Let us not dwell on things that are past," he said, "for I have come bringing you a gift. Now you must listen carefully to this: The bones of your fish are filled with a powerful spirit. Whenever you are in serious need, you must kneel before them and let them know your heart's desire. But do not waste their gifts."

Yeh-Shen wanted to ask the old sage many more questions, but he rose to the sky before she could utter another word. With heavy heart, Yeh-Shen made her way to the dung heap to gather the remains of her friend.

Time went by, and Yeh-Shen, who was often left alone, took comfort in speaking to the bones of her fish. When she was hungry, which happened quite often, Yeh-Shen asked the bones for food. In this way, Yeh-Shen managed to live from day to day, but she lived in dread that her stepmother would discover her secret and take even that away from her.

So the time passed and spring came. Festival time was approaching: It was the busiest time of the year. Such cooking and cleaning and sewing there was to be done! Yeh-Shen had hardly a moment's rest. At the spring festival young men and young women from the village hoped to meet and to choose whom they would marry. How Yeh-Shen longed to go! But her stepmother had other plans. She hoped to find a husband for her own daughter and did not want any man to see the beauteous Yeh-Shen first. When finally the holiday arrived, the stepmother and her daughter dressed themselves in their finery and filled their baskets with sweetmeats. "You must remain at home now and watch to see that no one steals fruit from our trees," her stepmother told Yeh-Shen, and then she departed for the banquet with her own daughter.

As soon as she was alone, Yeh-Shen went to speak to the bones of her fish. "Oh, dear friend," she said, kneeling before the precious bones, "I long to go to the festival, but I cannot show myself in these rags. Is there somewhere I could borrow clothes fit to wear to the feast?" At once she found herself dressed in a gown of azure[1] blue, with a cloak of kingfisher feathers draped around her shoulders. Best of all, on her tiny feet were the most beautiful slippers she had ever seen. They were woven of golden threads, in a pattern like the scales of a fish, and the glistening soles were made of solid gold. There was magic in the shoes, for they should have been quite heavy, yet when Yeh-Shen walked, her feet felt as light as air.

"Be sure you do not lose your golden shoes," said the spirit of the bones. Yeh-Shen promised to be careful. Delighted with her transformation, she bid a fond farewell to the bones of her fish as she slipped off to join in the merrymaking.

That day Yeh-Shen turned many a head as she appeared at the feast. All around her people whispered, "Look at that beautiful girl! Who can she be?"

But above this, Stepsister was heard to say, "Mother, does she not resemble our Yeh-Shen?"

---

1. **azure** (azh'ər) *adj.:* like the color of the sky.

Upon hearing this, Yeh-Shen jumped up and ran off before her stepsister could look closely at her. She raced down the mountainside, and in doing so, she lost one of her golden slippers. No sooner had the shoe fallen from her foot than all her fine clothes turned back to rags. Only one thing remained—a tiny golden shoe. Yeh-Shen hurried to the bones of her fish and returned the slipper, promising to find its mate. But now the bones were silent. Sadly Yeh-Shen realized that she had lost her only friend. She hid the little shoe in her bedstraw and went outside to cry. Leaning against a fruit tree, she sobbed and sobbed until she fell asleep.

The stepmother left the gathering to check on Yeh-Shen, but when she returned home, she found the girl sound asleep, with her arms wrapped around a fruit tree. So, thinking no more of her, the stepmother rejoined the party. Meantime, a villager had found the shoe. Recognizing its worth, he sold it to a merchant, who presented it in turn to the king of the island kingdom of T'o Han.

The king was more than happy to accept the slipper as a gift. He was entranced by the tiny thing, which was shaped of the most precious of metals, yet which made no sound when touched to stone. The more he marveled at its beauty, the more determined he became to find the woman to whom the shoe belonged. A search was begun among the ladies of his own kingdom, but all who tried on the sandal found it impossibly small. Undaunted, the king ordered the search widened to include the cave women from the countryside where the slipper had been found. Since he realized it would take many years for every woman to come to his island and test her foot in the slipper, the king thought of a way to get the right woman to come forward. He ordered the sandal placed in a pavilion[2] by the side of the road near where it had been found, and his herald[3] announced that the shoe was to be returned to its original owner. Then, from a nearby hiding place, the king and his men settled down to watch and wait for a woman with tiny feet to come and claim her slipper.

All that day the pavilion was crowded with cave women who had come to test a foot in the shoe. Yeh-Shen's stepmother and stepsister were among them, but not Yeh-Shen—they had told her to stay home. By day's end, although many women had eagerly tried to put on the slipper, it still had not been worn. Wearily, the king continued his vigil into the night.

It wasn't until the blackest part of night, while the moon hid behind a cloud, that Yeh-Shen dared to show her face at the pavilion, and even then she tiptoed timidly across the wide floor. Sinking down to her knees, the girl in rags examined the tiny shoe. Only when she was sure that this was the missing mate to her own golden slipper did she dare pick it up. At last she could return both little shoes to the fish bones. Surely then her beloved spirit would speak to her again.

Now the king's first thought, on seeing Yeh-Shen take the precious slipper, was to throw the girl into prison as a thief. But when she turned to leave, he caught a glimpse of her face. At once the king was struck by the sweet harmony of her

---

2. **pavilion** *n.:* large tent or shelter, often highly decorated.
3. **herald** *n.:* the person in a king's court who makes official announcements.

Three Fish (detail) by Belshu.
Color woodblock print.

features, which seemed so out of keeping with the rags she wore. It was then that he took a closer look and noticed that she walked upon the tiniest feet he had ever seen.

With a wave of his hand, the king signaled that this tattered creature was to be allowed to depart with the golden slipper. Quietly, the king's men slipped off and followed her home.

All this time, Yeh-Shen was unaware of the excitement she had caused. She had made her way home and was about to hide both sandals in her bedding when there was a pounding at the door. Yeh-Shen went to see who it was—and found a king at her doorstep. She was very frightened at first, but the king spoke to her in a kind voice and asked her to try the golden slippers on her feet. The maiden did as she was told, and as she stood in her golden shoes, her rags were transformed once more into the feathered cloak and beautiful azure gown.

Her loveliness made her seem a heavenly being, and the king suddenly knew in his heart that he had found his true love.

Not long after this, Yeh-Shen was married to the king. But fate was not so gentle with her stepmother and stepsister. Since they had been unkind to his beloved, the king would not permit Yeh-Shen to bring them to his palace. They remained in their cave home, where one day, it is said, they were crushed to death in a shower of flying stones.

MEET THE WRITER

Ai-Ling Louie

It Runs in the Family

Ai-Ling Louie (1949–   ) remembers hearing the story "Yeh-Shen," the Chinese version of "Cinderella," from her grandmother. Louie became curious about the origins of this story, which had been told in her family for three generations, so she did some research. She learned that the tale was first written down by Tuan Cheng-shi in an ancient Chinese manuscript during the Tang dynasty (A.D. 618–907) and had probably been handed down orally for centuries before that.

Literary Response and Analysis

Reading Check

1. Who is Yeh-Shen's only friend?

2. What does her stepmother do to Yeh-Shen's friend?

3. A very old man gives Yeh-Shen some advice about the bones of her fish. What is it?

4. What happens when Yeh-Shen runs away from the festival?

5. How does the king find Yeh-Shen?

Interpretations

6. Think about the discussion you had before you read this story. Which of our deepest wishes do you think this story expresses? Do you think it is also about some of our fears? Explain.

7. Which of the following statements best sums up the **theme** "Yeh-Shen" reveals?

   - Goodness is always rewarded in the end.
   - Bad people are always punished.
   - True love means being loved for who you really are.
   - Jealousy is a destructive emotion that can lead to tragedy.

   Do you think this is a good theme for today? Explain.

8. Check the story to see what you learn about Yeh-Shen's stepmother. How would the story change if the stepmother, instead of the **omniscient narrator,** were telling it?

Evaluation

9. Suppose a reviewer of this textbook said, "I don't think the publisher should include this story because it's outdated. Girls don't sit around and wait to be rescued any longer." Do you agree or disagree with the decision to include this story in the textbook? Explain.

10. How do you feel about the way the story ends? Do you think such cruel details should be removed from children's stories? Talk about your response to the way the stepmother and her daughter are punished.

Writing

A Real Cinderella Story

Imagine a Cinderella story set today in your own community. Who would the underdog be? Who or what would hold the underdog back? Who would rescue the underdog, and how would this happen? With a group of classmates, brainstorm to come up with some ideas. Then, plot out your story. You could act out your modern Cinderella story or videotape the production for your class.

Reading Standard 3.5
Contrast points of view in narrative text, and explain how they affect the overall theme of the work.

Mirror, Mirror, on the Wall, Do I See Myself As Others Do?

Presenting an Argument: Agree with Me

Argument can mean "angry disagreement." You argue with your friends about all kinds of things, from who should be class president to what music should be played at a dance.

Here the word *argument* is used to mean "debate or discussion." Writers who present an argument are trying to persuade you to think or act in a certain way. They may want you to agree with their opinions, vote for their candidates, buy their products, or support their causes.

Skillful persuaders use solid **evidence** to back up their arguments. They cite **facts** (statements that can be proved true) and **statistics** (number facts). Skillful persuaders often quote **experts** to convince you that an argument is sound.

When you finish reading a text that presents an argument, ask yourself questions:

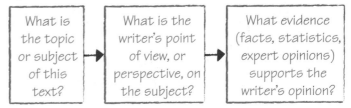

| What is the topic or subject of this text? | → | What is the writer's point of view, or perspective, on the subject? | → | What evidence (facts, statistics, expert opinions) supports the writer's opinion? |

When you read a persuasive essay, you must trace the writer's use of evidence. You want to be certain that the evidence is valid and that it is strong. After all, if you are going to accept someone's argument, you want to be sure it is a good one.

The notes beside the selection that follows will help you trace the author's argument.

Reading Standard 2.4 Identify and trace the development of an author's argument in text.

Mirror, Mirror, on the Wall,

Do I See Myself As Others Do?

Tracing a writer's argument.

A The writer opens with an anecdote, a brief story used to make a point.

B The writer wonders how kids feel about their appearance and conducts interviews to find out.

Two weeks ago I was watching a local news story about the lottery. The film footage showed a young woman standing behind the store counter selling lottery tickets. She had short blond hair, big sparkling eyes, and a huge smile. I recognized her as the woman who worked in the corner drugstore down the street. The next day I walked into the store and said, "Hey, I saw you on TV last night. You looked great." She made a disgusted face.

"I told them not to film me."

"Why not?"

"Because I look so . . ." She puffed out her cheeks. *"Fat!"*

I didn't know what to say. So I just repeated, "Well, you looked great." **A**

I thought, "Here is a shining light of a woman who thinks she looks too bad to be on television for five seconds." So I decided to interview some middle-school and high school students to see if they, like this woman, feel bad about the way they look. Unfortunately, the answer became obvious very quickly. **B**

"Lots of kids think they weigh more than they look," said one ninth-grader. "Everyone wants to be size zero. Sometimes even someone who wears size zero says, 'I feel so fat.' It's hard for some people to feel really good about themselves."

It's easy to see why people feel this way, especially kids. Watch television or flip through a magazine. The females look as though they haven't had a decent meal in months. The males look as though they could be hit in the stomach by a freight train and not even feel it.

I turned every page of a popular teen magazine for girls and counted advertisements for makeup and clothes. Out of 220 pages, 70 were advertisements. That's about one third of the magazine devoted to influencing the way kids dress and look. **C**

Statistics show that models in advertisements are 9 percent taller and 23 percent thinner than the average woman. With the click of a mouse, computers can create a picture of the perfect face by cleaning up a model's complexion, trimming her chin, and getting rid of lines around her eyes. Here's a news flash: She's not a real person, folks. She's an illusion. **D**

Other students I interviewed talked about the importance of wearing certain brands of clothing. These clothes display a brand name somewhere, whether it's plastered in three-inch type across the front or appears on a tiny logo on the sleeve. A middle-school student said, "Sometimes I just want to wear a pair of sweatpants and a T-shirt, but if you do, you're looked down on. The way you dress classifies you—it shows what group you're in. You can walk down the hall and tell who different people hang out with just by looking at their clothes." **E**

If you're thinking I interviewed some pretty insecure kids, you're wrong. A study conducted by the American Association of University Women found that in elementary school 60 percent of girls and 67 percent of boys had high self-esteem—they felt good about themselves. But by the time kids are in high school, self-esteem in girls drops to only 29 percent, compared with self-esteem in boys, which drops to 46 percent. **F**

The good news is that some things may be changing for the better. One middle-school girl reported being on the volleyball and basketball teams. Unlike girls just one generation ago, she can go out for any sport she wants. After an amazing spike or a skillful dribble down the basketball court, however, this beautiful, strong fifteen-year-old still says, "Sometimes you can see yourself as others see you. But if someone says they think I'm pretty, I don't believe them." **G**

Start believing it. Remember what Eleanor Roosevelt said: "No one can make you feel inferior without your consent." **H**

—Joan Burditt

C The writer says that many advertisements in magazines tell kids how they should look.

D The writer says that models don't look like real people—especially when a computer perfects the picture!

E The writer interviewed kids who say that wearing brand-name clothes influences how other kids respond to them.

F The writer cites statistics that show that kids' self-esteem drops in high school.

G The writer says that sports may help improve girls' self-esteem.

H The writer ends with a quotation that backs up her argument.

Reading Informational Materials

Reading Check

1. How does the opening anecdote relate to the writer's main point?

2. What is the **topic,** or subject, of this article?

3. What is the writer's **perspective,** or point of view, on this subject?

TestPractice

Mirror, Mirror, on the Wall . . .

1. You can tell from this article that the writer believes that —

   A students feel tremendous pressure to look a certain way

   B teen magazines do not influence the way teenagers feel about their appearance

   C parents should keep their children from reading magazines that have models in them

   D students should wear uniforms to school so they won't worry so much about their appearance

2. Which of the following statements uses **statistics** to support a position?

   F I'll bet most students who are thin feel fat.

   G Students feel they have to wear a certain brand of clothing.

   H Models in advertisements are 9 percent taller and 23 percent thinner than the average woman.

   J Computers can change the way people look in photographs.

3. Which type of **evidence** does the writer use to support her point that brand names on clothing are important to many students?

   A An anecdote

   B An interview

   C An expert's opinion

   D A magazine article

4. What is the *most likely* reason the author wrote this essay?

   F To change readers' views about their appearance

   G To tell a story about the woman who works in the drugstore

   H To interview students about the clothes they wear

   J To explain why sports improve girls' self-esteem

5. Which statement is a **fact**—a statement that can be proved true?

   A Everyone wants to be thin.

   B Out of 220 pages, 70 were advertisements.

   C No one can make you feel inferior without your consent.

   D The females look as though they haven't eaten in months.

Reading Standard 2.4
Identify and trace the development of an author's argument, point of view, or perspective in text.

Names/Nombres

Literary Focus
Point of View: Subjective or Objective?

Has anyone ever said to you, "Don't take it personally"? Well, some writers do take their writing personally. Writers who treat their subject **subjectively** share their own feelings, thoughts, opinions, and judgments. We find **subjective writing** in personal essays and autobiographies and in the editorial pages of a newspaper, where we expect writers to express opinions about news events.

Objective writing, on the other hand, tends to be unbiased and presents the facts and figures rather than the writer's private feelings. The purpose of objective writing is to inform.

Reading Skills
Discovering the Main Idea: It's in the Details

All the important details in an article or essay add up to a **main idea.** A main idea is the central idea, the one that the writer wants you to remember. In some pieces of writing, like "Names/Nombres," the writer **implies,** or suggests, the main idea. You have to **infer,** or guess, the point that the writer is getting at. To infer a main idea, follow these steps:

- Identify the important details in the selection.
- Think about the point that the important details make.
- Use this information to figure out

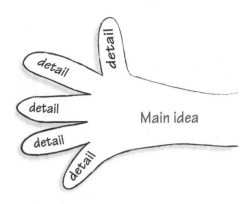

what the main idea is. State the main idea in your own words.

Make the Connection
Quickwrite

Write about your given name, family name, or nickname. Explain how you got your name and how you feel about it. Is your name an accurate representation of who you are?

Vocabulary Development

Practice using these words before you read about Julia Alvarez's problem with her name:

ethnicity (eth·nis′ə·tē) *n.:* common culture or nationality. *Julia's ethnicity was important to her friends.*

exotic (eg·zät′ik) *adj.:* foreign; not native. *At her graduation party, Julia's family served exotic dishes.*

heritage (her′ə·tij) *n.:* traditions that are passed along. *Julia remained proud of her Dominican heritage.*

convoluted (kän′və·lŌŌt′id) *adj.:* complicated. *The grammar of a new language often seems convoluted.*

Reading Standard 3.5 Contrast points of view (for example, subjective and objective) in narrative text.

Names/Nombres

JULIA ALVAREZ

A name as chaotic with sounds as a Middle Eastern bazaar...

When we arrived in New York City, our names changed almost immediately. At Immigration, the officer asked my father, *Mister Elbures,* if he had anything to declare. My father shook his head no, and we were waved through.

I was too afraid we wouldn't be let in if I corrected the man's pronunciation, but I said our name to myself, opening my mouth wide for the organ blast of the *a,* trilling my tongue for the drumroll of the *r, All-vah-rrr-es!* How could anyone get *Elbures* out of that orchestra of sound?

At the hotel my mother was *Missus Alburest,* and I was *little girl,* as in, "Hey, little girl, stop riding the elevator up and down. It's *not* a toy."

When we moved into our new apartment building, the super called my father *Mister Alberase,* and the neighbors who became mother's friends pronounced her name *Jew-lee-ah* instead of *Hoo-lee-ah.* I, her namesake, was known as *Hoo-lee-tah* at home. But at school I was *Judy* or *Judith,* and once an English teacher mistook me for *Juliet.*

It took a while to get used to my new names. I wondered if I shouldn't correct my teachers and new friends. But my mother argued that it didn't matter. "You know what your friend Shakespeare said, '*A rose by any other name would smell as sweet.*'"[1] My family had gotten into the habit of calling any famous author "my friend" because I had begun to write poems and stories in English class.

By the time I was in high school, I was a popular kid, and it showed in my name. Friends called me *Jules* or *Hey Jude,* and once a group of troublemaking friends my mother forbade me to hang out with called me *Alcatraz.* I was *Hoo-lee-tah* only to Mami and Papi and uncles and aunts who came over to eat sancocho[2] on Sunday afternoons—old world folk whom I would just as soon go back to where they came from and leave me to pursue whatever mischief I wanted to in America. *JUDY ALCATRAZ,* the name on the "Wanted" poster would read. Who would ever trace her to me?

My older sister had the hardest time getting an American name for herself because *Mauricia* did not translate into English. Ironically, although she had the most foreign-sounding name, she and I were the Americans in the family. We had been born in New York City when our parents had first tried immigration and then gone back "home," too homesick to stay. My mother often told the story of how she had almost changed my sister's name in the hospital.

After the delivery, Mami and some other new mothers were cooing over their new baby sons and daughters and exchanging names and weights and delivery stories. My mother was embarrassed among the Sallys and Janes and Georges and Johns to reveal the rich, noisy name of *Mauricia,* so when her turn came to brag, she gave her baby's name as *Maureen.*

"Why'd ya give her an Irish name with so many pretty Spanish names to choose from?" one of the women asked.

My mother blushed and admitted her baby's real name to the group. Her mother-in-law had recently died, she apologized, and her husband had insisted that the first daughter be named after his mother,

---

1. *"A rose . . . as sweet":* Julia's mother is quoting from the play *Romeo and Juliet.*

2. **sancocho** (sän·kō′chō) *adj.:* stew of meats and fruit.

Mauran. My mother thought it the ugliest name she had ever heard, and she talked my father into what she believed was an improvement, a combination of *Mauran* and her own mother's name, *Felicia.*

"Her name is *Mao-ree-shee-ah,*" my mother said to the group of women.

"Why, that's a beautiful name," the new mothers cried. "*Moor-ee-sha, Moor-ee-sha,*" they cooed into the pink blanket. *Moor-ee-sha* it was when we returned to the States eleven years later. Sometimes, American tongues found even that mispronunciation tough to say and called her *Maria* or *Marsha* or *Maudy* from her nickname *Maury.* I pitied her. What an awful name to have to transport across borders!

My little sister, Ana, had the easiest time of all. She was plain *Anne*—that is, only her name was plain, for she turned out to be the pale, blond "American beauty" in the family. The only Hispanic thing about her was the affectionate nicknames her boyfriends sometimes gave her. *Anita,* or, as one goofy guy used to sing to her to the tune of the banana advertisement, *Anita Banana.*

Later, during her college years in the late sixties, there was a push to pronounce Third World[3] names correctly. I remember calling her long distance at her group house and a roommate answering.

"Can I speak to Ana?" I asked, pronouncing her name the American way.

"Ana?" The man's voice hesitated. "Oh! You must mean *Ah-nah!*"

Our first few years in the States, though, ethnicity was not yet "in." Those were the blond, blue-eyed, bobby-sock years of junior high and high school before the sixties ushered in peasant blouses, hoop earrings, serapes.[4] My initial desire to be known by my correct Dominican name faded. I just wanted to be Judy and merge with the Sallys and Janes in my class. But, inevitably, my accent and coloring gave me away. "So where are you from, Judy?"

"New York," I told my classmates. After all, I had been born blocks away at Columbia-Presbyterian Hospital.

"I mean, *originally.*"

"From the Caribbean," I answered vaguely, for if I specified, no one was quite sure on what continent our island was located.

"Really? I've been to Bermuda. We went last April for spring vacation. I got the worst sunburn! So, are you from Portoriko?"

"No," I sighed. "From the Dominican Republic."

"Where's that?"

"South of Bermuda."

They were just being curious, I knew, but I burned with shame whenever they singled me out as a "foreigner," a rare, exotic friend.

"Say your name in Spanish, oh, please say it!" I had made mouths drop one day by rattling off my full name, which, according to Dominican custom, included my middle names, Mother's and Father's surnames for four generations back.

"Julia Altagracia María Teresa Álvarez Tavares Perello Espaillat Julia Pérez Rochet

---

4. **serapes** (sə·rä′pēs) *n.*: woolen shawls worn in Latin American countries.

Vocabulary
ethnicity (eth·nis′ə·tē) *n.*: common culture or nationality.
exotic (eg·zät′ik) *adj.*: foreign; not native.

---

3. **Third World:** developing countries of Latin America, Africa, and Asia.

González." I pronounced it slowly, a name as chaotic with sounds as a Middle Eastern bazaar or market day in a South American village.

My Dominican heritage was never more apparent than when my extended family attended school occasions. For my graduation, they all came, the whole lot of aunts and uncles and the many little cousins who snuck in without tickets. They sat in the first row in order to better understand the Americans' fast-spoken English. But how could they listen when they were constantly speaking among themselves in florid-sounding[5] phrases, rococo[6] consonants, rich, rhyming vowels?

Introducing them to my friends was a further trial to me. These relatives had such complicated names and there were so many of them, and their relationships to myself were so convoluted. There was my Tía[7] Josefina, who was not really an aunt but a much older cousin. And her daughter, Aida Margarita, who was adopted, una hija de crianza.[8] My uncle of affection, Tío José, brought my madrina[9] Tía Amelia and her comadre[10] Tía Pilar. My friends rarely had more than a "Mom and Dad" to introduce.

After the commencement ceremony, my family waited outside in the parking lot while my friends and I signed yearbooks with nicknames which recalled our high school good times: "Beans" and "Pepperoni" and "Alcatraz." We hugged and cried and promised to keep in touch.

Our goodbyes went on too long. I heard my father's voice calling out across the parking lot, "*Hoo-lee-tah!* Vámonos!"[11]

Back home, my tíos and tías and primas,[12] Mami and Papi, and mis hermanas[13] had a party for me with sancocho and a store-bought pudín,[14] inscribed with *Happy Graduation, Julie*. There were many gifts—that was a plus to a large family! I got several wallets and a suitcase with my initials and a graduation charm from my godmother and money from my uncles. The biggest gift was a portable typewriter from my parents for writing my stories and poems.

Someday, the family predicted, my name would be well-known throughout the United States. I laughed to myself, wondering which one I would go by.

---

5. **florid-sounding:** flowery; using fancy words.
6. **rococo** (rə·kō′kō) *adj.:* fancy. Rococo is an early-eighteenth-century style of art and architecture known for its fancy ornamentation.
7. **Tía** (tē′ä) *n.:* Spanish for "aunt." *Tío* is "uncle."
8. **una hija de crianza** (o͞o′nä ē′hä de krē·än′sä): Spanish for "an adopted daughter." *Crianza* means "upbringing."
9. **madrina** (mä·drē′nä) *n.:* Spanish for "godmother."
10. **comadre** (kô·mä′drä) *n.:* informal Spanish for "close friend." *Comadre* is the name used by the mother and the godmother of a child for each other.

---

11. **Vámonos!** (vä′mô·nôs): Spanish for "Let's go!"
12. **primas** (prē′mäs) *n.:* Spanish for "female cousins."
13. **mis hermanas** (mēs er·mä′näs): Spanish for "my sisters."
14. **pudín** (po͞o·dēn′) *n.:* Spanish cake.

Vocabulary

heritage (her′ə·tij) *n.:* traditions that are passed along.
convoluted (kän′və·lo͞ot′id) *adj.:* complicated.

Julia Alvarez

"Just Do Your Work and Put in Your Heart"

Born in New York City, **Julia Alvarez** (1950–   ) spent her childhood in the Dominican Republic, returning with her family to New York when she was ten years old. Adjusting to her new surroundings in the early 1960s wasn't easy for young Julia:

> I can tap into that struggling English speaker, that skinny, dark-haired, olive-skinned girl in a sixth grade of mostly blond and blue-eyed giants. Those tall, freckled boys would push me around in the playground. 'Go back to where you came from!' 'No comprendo!' I'd reply, though of course there was no misunderstanding the fierce looks on their faces.

Despite the difficulties, being an immigrant gave Julia a special point of view. "We [immigrants] travel on that border between two worlds," she explains, "and we can see both points of view." Later, as a writer, she used those sometimes conflicting perspectives—American and Latino—to describe brilliantly the cultures of the United States and the Dominican Republic.

After college and graduate school, Alvarez taught poetry for twelve years in Kentucky, California, Vermont, Washington, D.C., and Illinois. Now she lives in Vermont, where she writes novels and teaches at Middlebury College.

> Day to day, I guess I follow my papi's advice. When we first came [to the United States], he would talk to his children about how to make it in our new country. 'Just do your work and put in your heart, and they will accept you!'

Literary Response and Analysis

Reading Check

1. Julia Alvarez has been known by the different names listed below. Explain who uses each name or group of names and what the names mean to Alvarez.
   - "little girl"
   - Julita (pronounced hōō·lē′tä)
   - Judith/Juliet
   - Jules/Jude
   - Alcatraz
   - Judy
   - Julia Altagracia María Teresa Álvarez Tavares Perello Espaillat Julia Pérez Rochet González
   - Julia Alvarez

Interpretations

2. Think back to what you said about names in your notes for the Quickwrite on page 261. How has "Names/Nombres" affected your ideas about names?

3. How does Julia picture the people who mispronounce her name?

4. As a teenager, why does Julia want to be called Judy? How do you think her attitude has changed since then?

5. Why do you think the writer chooses Julia Alvarez as the name she will be known by?

6. Why do you think the writer gave this piece the **title** "Names/Nombres" instead of just "Names" (or just "Nombres")? What connection can you see between this title and Alvarez's comment about being "on the border between two worlds"?

7. What would you say is the **main idea** of "Names/Nombres"? List three significant details or quotations from the story that you think back up the main idea.

8. Is this essay **subjective** or **objective**? How do you know?

Evaluation

9. "Names/Nombres" includes many Spanish words and phrases. In your opinion, do they make it harder for non-Spanish speakers to read the essay, or do they add something valuable to it? Explain.

Writing

What's in a Name?

Research your own names to find out as much as you can about them—first, middle, and last names, as well as any additional names you've been given as part of your ethnic or religious heritage. You could begin by interviewing your family members to record what they know. Then, check the name books at your library. See if you can find out the origins of all your names. Write about your search and its results in a short essay.

BONUS QUESTION

How could a name change someone's life?

Reading Standard 3.5 Contrast points of view (for example, subjective and objective) in narrative text.

Vocabulary Development

Clarifying Word Meanings: Using Definitions

Writers often help us understand difficult words by providing definitions right in the context.

A writer who uses **definition** will explain what a word means right in the sentence or passage. For example, in the following sentence the writer clarifies the meaning of *tía* by defining it later in the sentence.

> "There was my Tía Josefina, who was not really my aunt but a much older cousin."

Be on the lookout for such phrases as *in other words* and *that is* when looking for definitions of words right in context.

PRACTICE

Complete the following sentences, using definition to clarify the meanings of the words from the Word Bank.

1. The dress was definitely <u>exotic</u>—that is, it was

   _____.

2. Francis's explanation of his science project had grown <u>convoluted</u>. In other words, it was _____.

3. The street festival was planned to introduce visitors to the city's <u>heritage</u>, or _____.

4. Studies have shown that <u>ethnicity</u>, meaning _____ , influences the kinds of programs we watch on television.

Word Bank

ethnicity
exotic
heritage
convoluted

Reading Standard 1.3
Clarify word meanings through the use of definition.

Grammar Link MINI-LESSON

Don't Leave Your Modifiers Dangling

It's easy to make the mistake of "hanging" a modifying phrase on a sentence (usually at the beginning) and forgetting to include the word it modifies:

DANGLING **Arriving in New York City, *our names* changed almost immediately.**

Who arrived in New York City? It sounds as if the names came on their own!

Phrases that hang, or dangle, on a sentence without clearly modifying a word are called **dangling modifiers.** You can correct a dangling modifier by adding, subtracting, or rearranging words:

CLEAR **Arriving in New York City, *we* noticed that our names changed almost immediately.**

The first sentence of "Names/Nombres" shows an even better solution:

CLEAR **"When *we* arrived in New York City, our names changed almost immediately."**

PRACTICE

Find and fix the dangling modifiers in these sentences. You will have to rewrite some of the sentences.

1. Wanting to encourage me, my graduation present was a typewriter.

2. Born in New York City, it was easier for me to adjust to America.

3. Looking back on it now, the incident was funny.

Exchange a sample of your writing with a partner. Then, act as a dangler detector. Read your partner's work carefully to be sure every sentence makes sense and every modifier or phrase modifies something. Your first step should be to identify the modifying phrases (with the permission of the writer, use a colored pen). Dangling modifiers usually appear—or dangle—at the beginning of a sentence.

For more help, see Placement of Modifiers in the *Holt Handbook*, pages 232–240.

Shoe reprinted by permission: Tribune Media Services.

An Unforgettable Journey

Literary Focus

Autobiography: Telling You My Story

The most personal kind of writing is autobiographical writing. An **autobiography** is the story of a person's life written by that very person. In this kind of writing, you get inside the writer's mind, and you learn about his or her most personal thoughts, feelings, and ideas. Because of this, autobiographical writing is **subjective** (see page 261).

Reading Skills

Distinguishing Fact from Opinion

When you read an autobiography, it's important to be able to tell facts from opinions. A **fact** can be proved true. *The Mekong River flows through Laos* is a fact. It is a statement that can be confirmed by looking at a map.

An **opinion** can be supported by facts, but it can't be proved true or false: *The friendliest people in Southeast Asia are from Laos.* In autobiographical essays, such as "An Unforgettable Journey," writers share their opinions, but they also present facts.

Be careful: People may state an opinion as if it were a fact. If you're in doubt, ask yourself, "Can this statement be proved, or is it someone's personal feeling or belief?"

Grade 6 Review Reading Standard 3.5 Identify the speaker, and recognize the difference between first- and third-person narration (for example, autobiography compared with biography).

Reading Standard 3.5 Contrast points of view (for example, first and third person, subjective and objective) in narrative text.

Make the Connection

Quickwrite

What do you know about the Vietnam War, which was fought in Southeast Asia from 1957 to 1975? Jot down some of the facts that you know about the war. One fact might have to do with the famous memorial in Washington, D.C.

Vocabulary Development

Knowing these words will make your journey through this autobiography easier:

refuge (ref′yo͞oj) *n.:* shelter; protection. *Maijue's family sought refuge in the jungle.*

transition (tran·zish′ən) *n.:* change; passing from one condition to another. *The transition from a peaceful village to the jungle was extremely difficult.*

persecution (pur′sə·kyo͞o′shən) *n.:* act of willfully injuring or attacking others because of their beliefs or their ethnic backgrounds. *Because some Hmong worked against the Communists, they faced persecution.*

refugee (ref′yo͞o·jē′) *n.* used as *adj.:* person who flees home or country to escape war or persecution. *A refugee family may not be welcome anywhere.*

deprivation (dep′rə·vā′shən) *n.:* loss; condition of having something taken away by force. *They suffered from constant deprivation of food.*

Pre-1975 Laos and
Southeast Asia.

*W*ar often leads to the uprooting and exile
of thousands of innocent civilians on
the losing side. Such was the fate suffered by the
Hmong (muŋ) people of Southeast Asia. Most of
the Hmong had supported the United States in its
fight against the Communist forces in Vietnam and
Laos. In 1975, when the Communists finally won,
one third of the Hmong people fled Laos to escape the
victor's revenge. Some 135,000 Hmong ended up in the
United States. By the war's end, some thirty thousand
Hmong men, women, and children had perished.

The autobiographical article that follows is one of
several Hmong life stories collected by Sucheng Chan, a
teacher at the University of California, Santa Barbara.
Maijue Xiong was one of the students who served as her
collaborators. The book that the teacher and her students
put together is called Hmong Means Free: Life in
Laos and America.

Maijue's sister
on her mother's
lap, 1971.

AN UNFORGETTABLE JOURNEY

Maijue Xiong

I was born in a small village called Muong Cha in Laos on April 30, 1972. At the time I was born, my father was a soldier actively fighting alongside the American Central Intelligence Agency° against the Communists. Although a war was in progress, life seemed peaceful. We did not think of ever leaving Laos, but one day our lives were changed forever. We found ourselves without a home or a country and with a need to seek refuge in another country. This period of relocation involved a lot of changes, adjustments, and adaptations. We experienced changes in our language, customs, traditional values, and social status. Some made the transition quickly; others have never fully adjusted. The changes my family and I experienced are the foundation of my identity today.

After Laos became a Communist country in 1975, my family, along with many others, fled in fear of persecution. Because my father had served as a commanding officer for eleven years with the American Central Intelligence Agency in what is known to the American public as the "Secret War," my family had no choice but to leave immediately. My father's life was in danger, along with those of thousands of others. We were forced to leave loved ones behind, including my grandmother, who was ill in bed the day we fled our village. For a month, my family walked through the dense tropical jungles and rice fields, along rugged trails through many mountains, and battled the powerful Mekong River. We traveled in silence at night and slept in the daytime. Children were very hard to keep quiet. Many parents feared the

Maijue Xiong and her parents at her college graduation, June 1995.

The illustrations with this story include examples of traditional Hmong needlework. These items are worn as part of the Hmong traditional costume.

Communist soldiers would hear the cries of their children; therefore, they drugged the children with opium to keep them quiet. Some parents even left those children who would not stop crying behind. Fortunately, whenever my parents told my sisters and me to keep quiet, we listened and obeyed.

I do not remember much about our flight, but I do have certain memories that have been imprinted in my mind. It is all so unclear—the experience was like a bad dream: When you wake up, you don't

°**Central Intelligence Agency:** organization that helps protect the United States by gathering information about foreign governments and carrying out secret operations; also known by its initials, CIA.

Vocabulary
refuge (ref′yo͞oj) *n.:* shelter; protection.
transition (tran·zish′ən) *n.:* change; passing from one condition to another.
persecution (pʉr′sə·kyo͞o′shən) *n.:* act of willfully injuring or attacking (even murdering) others because of their beliefs or ethnic backgrounds.

Maijue dressed in traditional Hmong costume.

The Xiong family in Lompoc, 1993. Maijue is in the front row, far right.

remember what it was you had dreamed about but recall only those bits and pieces of the dream that stand out the most. I remember sleeping under tall trees. I was like a little ant placed in a field of tall grass, surrounded by dense jungle with trees and bushes all around me—right, left, in the back, and in front of me. I also remember that it rained a lot and that it was cold. We took only what we could carry and it was not much. My father carried a sack of rice, which had to last us the whole way. My mother carried one extra change of clothing for each of us, a few personal belongings, and my baby sister on her back. My older sister and I helped carry pots and pans. My stepuncle carried water, dried meat, and his personal belongings.

From the jungles to the open fields, we walked along a path. We came across a trail

of red ants and being a stubborn child, I refused to walk over them. I wanted someone to pick me up because I was scared, but my parents kept walking ahead. They kept telling me to hurry up and to step over the ants, but I just stood there and cried. Finally, my father came back and put me on his shoulders, along with the heavy sack of rice he was carrying. . . .

After experiencing many cold days and rainy nights, we finally saw Thailand on the other side of the Mekong River. My parents bribed several fishermen to row us across. The fishermen knew we were desperate, yet, instead of helping us, they took advantage of us. We had to give them all our valuables: silver bars, silver coins, paper money, and my mother's silver wedding necklace, which had cost a lot of money. When it got dark, the fishermen came back with a small fishing boat and took us across the river. The currents were high and powerful. I remember being very scared. I kept yelling, "We're going to fall out! We're going to fall into the river!" My mom tried to reassure me but I kept screaming in fear. Finally, we got across safely. My family, along with many other families, were picked up by the Thai police and taken to an empty bus station for the night.

After a whole month at this temporary refugee camp set up in the bus station, during which we ate rice, dried fish, roots we dug up, and bamboo shoots we cut down, and drank water from streams, we were in very poor shape due to the lack of

Vocabulary

refugee (ref′yoo·jē′) *n.* used as *adj.*: person who flees home or country to escape war or persecution.

nutrition. Our feet were also swollen from walking. We were then taken to a refugee camp in Nongkhai, where disease was rampant and many people got sick. My family suffered a loss: My baby sister, who was only a few months old, died. She had become very skinny from the lack of milk, and there was no medical care available. The memory of her death still burns in my mind like a flame. On the evening she died, my older sister and I were playing with our cousins outside the building where we stayed. My father came out to tell us the sad news and told us to go find my stepuncle. After we found him, we went inside and saw our mother mourning the baby's death. Fortunately, our family had relatives around to support and comfort us. . . .

Our family life in the camp was very unstable, characterized by deprivation and neglect. My older sister and I were left alone for days while my parents were outside the camp trying to earn money to buy extra food. My parents fought a lot during this period, because we were all under such stress. They knew that if we remained in Thailand, there would be no telling what would become of us. We had to find a better life. Some people in the camp were being sponsored to go to the United States. The news spread that anyone who had served in the military with the CIA could apply to go to America. Since my stepuncle had already gone there two years earlier, he sponsored my family. Because my father had been in the military and we had a sponsor, it took only six months to process our papers when usually it took a year or more. . . .

It took a full day to travel to Bangkok, where we stayed for four nights. The building we stayed in was one huge room. It was depressing and nerve-racking. I especially remember how, when we got off the bus to go into the building, a small child about my age came up to my family to beg for food. I recall the exact words she said to my father, "Uncle, can you give me some food? I am hungry. My parents are dead and I am here alone." My dad gave her a piece of bread that we had packed for our lunch. After she walked away, my family found an empty corner and rolled out our bedding for the night. That night, the same child came around again, but people chased her away, which made me sad.

In the morning, I ran to get in line for breakfast. Each person received a bowl of rice porridge with a few strips of chicken in it. For four days, we remained in that building, not knowing when we could leave for the United States. Many families had been there for weeks, months, perhaps even years. On the fourth day, my family was notified to be ready early the next morning to be taken to the airport. The plane ride took a long time and I got motion sickness. I threw up a lot. Only when I saw my stepuncle's face after we landed did I know we had come to the end of our journey. We had come in search of a better life in the "land of giants."

On October 2, 1978, my family arrived at Los Angeles International Airport, where my uncle was waiting anxiously. We stayed with my uncle in Los Angeles for two weeks and then settled in Isla Vista because there were already a few Hmong families there. We knew only one family in Isla Vista, but later we met other families whom my parents had known in their village and from

Vocabulary

deprivation (dep′rə·vā′shən) *n.*: condition of having something taken away by force.

villages nearby. It was in Isla Vista that my life really began. My home life was now more stable. My mother gave birth to a boy a month after we arrived in the United States. It was a joyous event because the first three children she had were all girls. (Boys are desired and valued far more than girls in Hmong culture.) . . .

I entered kindergarten at Isla Vista Elementary School. The first day was scary because I could not speak any English. Fortunately, my cousin, who had been in the United States for three years and spoke English, was in the same class with me. She led me to the playground where the children were playing. I was shocked to see so many faces of different colors. The Caucasian students shocked me the most. I had never seen people with blond hair before. The sight sent me to a bench, where I sat and watched everyone in amazement. In class, I was introduced to coloring. I did not know how to hold a crayon or what it was for. My teacher had to show me how to color. I also soon learned the alphabet. This was the beginning of my lifelong goal to get an education. . . .

Now that I am older, I treasure the long but valuable lessons my parents tried to teach us—lessons that gave me a sense of identity as a Hmong. "Nothing comes easy . . . ," my parents always said. As I attempt to get a college education, I remember how my parents have been really supportive of me throughout my schooling, but because they never had a chance to get an education themselves, they were not able to help me whenever I could not solve a math problem or write an English paper. Although they cannot help me in my schoolwork, I know in my heart that they care about me and want me to be successful so that I can help them when they can no longer help themselves. Therefore, I am determined to do well at the university. I want to become a role model for my younger brother and sisters, for I am the very first member of my family to attend college. I feel a real sense of accomplishment to have set such an example.

MEET THE WRITER

Maijue Xiong

A Writer Who Can Never Forget

Maijue Xiong (mī′zhōō·ē sē·ôŋ′) (1972–   ) was a college student in the United States when she wrote this account of her family's flight from Laos. Xiong eventually earned degrees in sociology and Asian American studies at the University of California, Santa Barbara, where she helped found the Hmong Club to promote Laotian culture. An active member of the Asian Culture Committee, Xiong now lives in St. Paul, Minnesota, and teaches at HOPE Community Academy.

Literary Response and Analysis

Reading Check

1. Make a time line like the following one, and fill in the main events of Maijue Xiong's life and journey. Be sure to list the events in the sequence in which they occurred:

Maijue Xiong born.

Xiong family arrives at L.A. International Airport.

├──────────────────┤

1972   1978

Interpretations

2. What details in Maijue Xiong's narrative are **subjective**—that is, where does she reveal her feelings? What parts of the story are **objective**—that is, where is there straightforward factual reporting?

3. Maijue Xiong reveals some opinions about having to flee Laos, but she also presents facts. Give an example of a **fact** and an example of an **opinion** in "An Unforgettable Journey."

4. The **main idea** of an article is the most important idea, the one that the writer wants you to remember. Review the last paragraph on page 275. Then, decide what the main idea of this life story appears to be.

5. Suppose a history textbook included details about the Hmong experiences during the Vietnam War. How would the **point of view** of the historian differ from the point of view of someone who had experienced the events firsthand? How would the emotional impact of the story change?

Interview

"What Do You Remember?"

Interview a family member or neighbor who lived during the Vietnam War. You don't have to interview a veteran of the war—just someone who remembers the period. (Check your Quickwrite notes first.) Before the interview, list the questions you want to ask. Bring pencil and paper to the interview or an audiotape recorder. (If you wish to use a recorder, be sure to ask your subject's permission to do so.) Write up your interview in dialogue form.

Reading Standard 3.5 Contrast points of view (for example, subjective and objective) in narrative text, and explain how they affect the overall theme of the work.

Vocabulary Development

Clarifying Meaning Through Contrast

Sometimes writers will clarify the meaning of a word by using **contrast** clues. A writer who uses contrast clues will show how a word is *unlike* another word or another situation. For example, you can get a good idea of what *apprehensive* means in the sentence below because you see it contrasted with *fearless*.

Be on the lookout for signal words that alert you to contrasts: *although, but, yet, still, unlike, not, in contrast, instead, however.*

> The children were extremely <u>apprehensive</u> as they made their way through the dense jungle, <u>but</u> their parents seemed <u>fearless</u>.

Word Bank

refuge
transition
persecution
refugee
deprivation

PRACTICE

In the following sentences the **contrast** clues point you to the meaning of each underlined word. Use the contrast clues to identify the meaning of each underlined word. All the words are from the Word Bank and are defined in the story.

1. Instead of finding a safe, warm <u>refuge</u>, they suffered exposure to wind and rain.
   Meaning: _____
   Clues: _____

2. In contrast to people who made a <u>transition</u> between cultures, some of the exiles never moved away from their own traditions.
   Meaning: _____
   Clues: _____

3. Although we expected <u>persecution</u> for our beliefs, we found acceptance.
   Meaning: _____
   Clues: _____

4. <u>Refugees</u> are unlike people who have homes and live in their own countries.
   Meaning: _____
   Clues: _____

5. People who have plenty of food and even luxuries cannot understand the <u>deprivation</u> experienced in the refugee camps.
   Meaning: _____
   Clues: _____

Reading Standard 1.3
Clarify word meanings through the use of contrast.

Exile Eyes

Purpose and Perspective

People write nonfiction with many different purposes in mind. People who write political speeches are trying to **persuade** us to believe or do something. People who write articles in magazines often want to **inform** us about something. People who write personal narratives may want to **reveal a truth about life** or **share an experience.**

All writing reveals some kind of **perspective** on the world. The word *perspective* comes from the Latin *perspicere,* which means "to look at closely." Perspective in writing refers to the writer's point of view toward his or her topic. The writer says, in effect, "Here is what I think about this issue."

The personal narrative that follows is by the radio commentator Agate Nesaule. On meeting exiles from Bosnia who had settled in her hometown, Nesaule was reminded of her experiences as a World War II refugee. This piece was written for and broadcast on National Public Radio's *Morning Edition.*

Background

The War in Bosnia

After World War II, Yugoslavia became a Communist state under the dictatorship of Tito. Bosnia, one of Yugoslavia's republics, was largely made up of three ethnic groups—Slavic Muslims, Croats, and Serbs. In 1980, after Tito died, a government representing the three groups emerged. Muslims and Croats favored independence for Bosnia; Serbs did not. In 1992, Bosnia seceded,

or separated, from Yugoslavia. However, the Serbs living in Bosnia resisted. They wished to remain part of Yugoslavia and were backed by the Yugoslav National Army. A bitter struggle resulted, in which Serbs ruthlessly expelled Muslims and Croats from the areas the Serbs controlled. This practice became known as ethnic cleansing. By late 1995, the conflict had produced an estimated two million refugees, the largest number of refugees in Europe since World War II.

The Commentator

Agate Nesaule fled Latvia during World War II. She was only six years old. Like many exiles from war-torn regions around the world, she found refuge in the United States. Nesaule now lives in Madison, Wisconsin. In this personal narrative she talks about the new exiles she has seen in Madison.

Reading Standard 2.4
Identify and trace an author's perspective in text.

Agate Nesaule.

Exile Eyes

The beauty shop in Wisconsin where I get my hair cut looks very American. The owner is young and energetic; his sideburns remind me of Elvis Presley, and scissors and dryers dangle like guns from his black holster as he moves among the glass-and-chrome shelves. But one afternoon the place is so full of women and girls that I can hardly get in. With the exception of their uniform politeness in offering me their seats, there is nothing unusual about them. Only details of their clothes suggest other places and other times: Europe after World War II; Wisconsin and the Hmong people who settled here after Vietnam; the Baltic countries after the collapse of the Soviet Union.

A summer dress with a snugly fitting dark top has the bottom of ugly checked-brown flannel. A gathered gray polyester skirt is lengthened by a six-inch-wide insert of flowered print. And their shoes are startling in their flimsiness. These details speak to me of war and exile as eloquently as words. I'm afraid to

look into the women's eyes, and when I finally do, it is as bad as I had expected. They all have exile eyes: eyes that have lost everything and seen the unspeakable but are determined to keep looking, eyes that remain weary and disillusioned even during shy giggles. I have seen those eyes before too, in photographs of the Latvian women who survived Siberia and Rwandan girls being questioned by a journalist, on the Chilean woman doctor who used to clean my house, on my mother. They all have eyes like that.

The owner waits patiently for their consent before he so much as snips a hair. Like them, he is from Bosnia. Under his skilled fingers, their crudely chopped-off tresses take on lovely, sleek shapes. A young woman smiles and makes a playful little bow for her new haircut, but her eyes do not change. I'm glad the Bosnian women are getting more elegant styles than my frizzy permanent at age twelve, when I believed that cutting off my braids would transform me into an American. They will have to do much more even than learn English, live among the poor and desperate, and find new friends and lovers. Acquaintances will ask them questions about their experiences but won't be able to stand hearing honest answers. And their longing for home will be confused with ingratitude to America. So much is ahead of them before their eyes lose their power to disturb.

—Agate Nesaule,
from National Public Radio,
Morning Edition

Reading Informational Materials

Reading Check

1. What details about the Bosnian women speak to the writer "of war and exile"?

2. How does Nesaule describe the women's "exile eyes"?

3. At the end of the commentary, Nesaule is probably speaking from her own experience when she describes what the Bosnian women will have to do as they transform themselves into Americans. List three things exiles have to do.

TestPractice

Exile Eyes

1. One reason the writer identifies with the women in the beauty shop is that —

   A she likes getting her hair cut

   B she wears the same clothing

   C they are from her own country

   D she was an exile as well

2. We can tell from details in this personal narrative that the writer —

   F is puzzled by the Bosnian women

   G thinks that the women should wear different clothes

   H made many mistakes when she was a refugee

   J sympathizes with the Bosnian women

3. The **purpose** of this commentary is to —

   A persuade us to support public radio

   B inform us about current events

   C persuade us to act in support of exiles

   D reveal a truth about life

4. Which sentence best describes Nesaule's **perspective** on exiles?

   F She feels sympathetic toward exiles.

   G She is critical of the government.

   H She doesn't understand the problems of exile.

   J She feels hopeless about exile problems.

5. When the writer says in the last paragraph that she believed cutting off her braids would make her an American, she realizes that —

   A haircuts make people feel better

   B becoming an American is easy

   C beauty is a universal quality

   D feeling settled in a new country is difficult

Reading Standard 2.4 Identify and trace an author's perspective in text.

ELIZABETH I

Literary Focus
Biography: Telling Lives

The text you're about to read is a **biographical narrative.** In biography a writer tells the story of another person's life. The word *biography* comes from two Greek words: *bios,* meaning "life" (think of biology), and *graphein,* meaning "to write." Most biographers follow a strictly factual style. They describe events that have been carefully researched.

Writing that presents facts without revealing the writer's feelings and opinions is said to be **objective.** Journalists who report on current events for newspapers usually write in an objective style. Their readers want the facts; they do not want to hear how the reporter feels about the event.

Writing that reveals the writer's feelings and opinions is said to be **subjective.** Biographies often combine objective writing with subjective details. After all, it is hard to write about someone's life without revealing your feelings about that person.

As you read this biography of Queen Elizabeth I of England, see if you can tell how her biographer feels about his royal subject.

Elizabeth I ruled England for forty-five years, from 1558 to 1603.

Grade 6 Review Reading Standard 3.5 Identify the speaker, and recognize the difference between first- and third-person narration (for example, autobiography compared with biography).

Reading Standard 3.5 Contrast points of view (for example, subjective and objective) in narrative text.

Make the Connection
Quickwrite ✏️

If you were going to write a biography about a person, whom would you choose? Why? Is your choice based on your feelings about the subject? Jot down some responses to these "biography questions."

Vocabulary Development

These are the words you'll need to know as you read this biography:

monarch (män′ərk) *n.:* sole and absolute leader. *As monarch, Elizabeth came to the throne of England in 1558.*

alliance (ə·lī′əns) *n.:* pact between nations, families, or individuals that shows a common cause. *Elizabeth's advisor encouraged her to join the alliance against the enemy.*

monopoly (mə·näp′ə·lē) *n.:* exclusive control of a market. *The queen's favorites got rich from a monopoly on imported goods.*

arrogant (ar′ə·gənt) *adj.:* overly convinced of one's own importance. *The queen seemed arrogant, but she did listen to others.*

intolerable (in·täl′ər·ə·bəl) *adj.:* unbearable. *Even though Mary was an enemy, Queen Elizabeth felt it would be intolerable to cut off her cousin's head.*

Reading Skills

SQ3R: A Study System for Reading Informational Texts

SQ3R stands for *Survey, Question, Read, Retell, Review.* It is a study system that helps readers study texts independently. Below are the SQ3R steps:

S **Survey.** Preview the text. Glance quickly at the headings (if there are any), vocabulary words, and illustrations. Skim the captions, which explain the illustrations, and read the first and last sentence of each paragraph.

Q **Question.** List the questions you'd like to ask about the text, based on your survey.

R **Read.** Read the text carefully to find ideas and information that will answer your questions. Take notes.

R **Retell.** Write responses to your questions in your own words. Try to hit the main points and include important details. You might want to say your answers out loud before you write them down.

R **Review.** Start your review by looking over your completed SQ3R organizer. Try covering up the answers in the "Read and Take Notes" and "Retell" boxes to see if you can answer your questions without looking at your notes. Then, check your memory of the main points and important details by writing a brief summary of the text. If you're shaky on a few details, re-read the parts of the text that contain the information you need.

Sample SQ3R Organizer for "Elizabeth I"

Survey

Question
- Who was Elizabeth I?
- How did her subjects like a woman ruling them?
- Why didn't she get married?
- [And so on]

Read and Take Notes
- She was the daughter of Henry VIII, trained from birth to rule.
- At first they didn't like a woman ruling them, but soon her subjects loved her.
- If she married, she would have to share power.
- [And so on]

Retell
- Elizabeth I was a strong and brilliant queen who was trained to rule as well as any man.
- [And so on]

Review

Summary:

ELIZABETH I

Milton Meltzer

"GOOD QUEEN BESS" her people called her. But "good" is a tame word for one of the most remarkable women who ever lived. Elizabeth I came to the throne of England in 1558 at the age of twenty-five. It was not a happy time for a young woman to take the responsibility for ruling a kingdom. Religious conflicts, a huge government debt, and heavy losses in a war with France had brought England low. But by the time of Elizabeth's death forty-five years later, England had experienced one of the greatest periods in its long history. Under Elizabeth's leadership, England had become united as a nation; its industry and commerce, its arts and sciences had flourished; and it was ranked among the great powers of Europe.

Elizabeth was the daughter of King Henry VIII and his second wife, Anne Boleyn. At the age of two she lost her mother when Henry had Anne's head chopped off. Not a good start for a child. But her father placed her in the care of one lord or lady after another, and the lively little girl with the reddish-gold hair, pale skin, and golden-brown eyes won everyone's affection.

Almost from her infancy Elizabeth was trained to stand in for ruling men, in case the need should arise. So she had to master whatever they were expected to know and do. Her tutors found the child to be an eager student. She learned history, geography, mathematics, and the elements of astronomy and architecture. She mastered four modern languages—French, Italian, Spanish, and Flemish[1]—as well as classical Greek and Latin. She wrote in a beautiful script that was like a work of art. The earliest portrait painted of her—when she was thirteen—shows a girl with innocent eyes holding a book in her long and delicate hands, already confident and queenly in her bearing.

She was a strong-willed girl who liked to give orders. She loved to be out on horseback, and rode so fast it frightened the men assigned to protect her. She loved dancing too—she never gave it up. Even in her old age she was seen one moonlit night dancing by herself in the garden.

Elizabeth had a half sister, Mary, born in 1516 of Henry's first wife, Catherine of Aragon. Many years later came Elizabeth, the child of Anne Boleyn, and four years after, her half brother, Edward, the son of Henry's third wife, Jane Seymour. After Henry died, because succession[2] came first through the male, ten-year-old Edward was crowned king. But he lived only another six years. Now Mary took the throne and, soon after, married King Philip II of Spain, a Catholic

---

1. **Flemish:** language spoken in Flanders, a region covering a small part of northern France and Belgium.
2. **succession** *n.:* order in which one succeeds to the throne.

HENRY VIII.
Henry VIII, King of England by Hans Holbein the Younger (1497–1543).

QUEEN ELIZABETH I.
Queen Elizabeth I by Henry Bone (1755–1834). Copy of miniature (c. 1592) by Marcus Gheerhaerts. Enamel on copper.

ANNE BOLEYN.

MARY TUDOR, QUEEN OF ENGLAND.

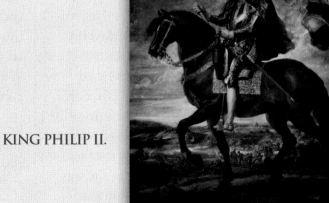

KING PHILIP II.

PRINCESS ELIZABETH I.
Elizabeth I of England when a princess
(c. 1542–1547).

she was a very special woman. "Am I not a queen because God has chosen me to be a queen?" she demanded.

As princess and later as queen, Elizabeth lived in various palaces, with much coming and going; each time she moved, she took along her household staff of 120 people. Often the changes were required because there was no sanitation. The smelly palaces had to be emptied so they could be "aired and sweetened."

Even before Elizabeth came of age, there was much talk of when she would marry, and whom. Marriages among the nobility and royalty were arranged not for love, but for practical reasons—to add land holdings, to strengthen the prestige and power of families, to cement an alliance of nations against a common enemy.

And remember, from the most ancient times, kings claimed that they as men were born to rule by divine right. That is, God had ordained that the crown should pass through the male line of descent. But when the king's wife had no male child, it meant trouble. Who then would rule? That crisis often led to civil war as various factions battled for the

monarch like herself. He was twenty-seven and she was thirty-eight. But they were rarely together, each ruling their own kingdom. Mary died of cancer at the age of forty-two. That made Elizabeth the monarch.

When she came to the throne on November 17, 1558, it was a day to be marked by celebrations, then and long after. As Her Majesty passed down a London street, an astonished housewife exclaimed, "Oh, Lord! The queen is a woman!" For there were still many who could scarcely believe they were to be ruled by another woman. Elizabeth herself would say with mock modesty that she was "a mere woman." But everyone soon learned

Vocabulary
monarch (män′ərk) *n.:* sole and absolute leader.
alliance (ə·lī′əns) *n.:* pact between nations, families, or individuals that shows a common cause.

The Granger Collection, New York.

power to name a king. Many disputed Elizabeth's right to the throne, and as long as she had neither husband nor successor, her life was in danger.

Ever since Elizabeth was eight, however, she had said again and again, "I will never marry." Did marriage look promising to a girl whose father had had six wives, two of whom, including her own mother, he had beheaded? Yet she liked to hear of people who wanted to marry her.

And there was no shortage of suitors. She continued to insist she wished to live unmarried. No matter how often she said it, men did not believe it. Understandably, since she often made a prince or duke who had come to court her believe she was finally ready to give in—only at the last moment to back out. Once, to a delegation from Parliament come to beg her to marry, she declared, "I am already bound unto a husband, which is the Kingdom of England."

And why should she, the absolute ruler of England, allow a man to sit alongside her as king? The power of husbands over wives in that century—and even now, in many places of this world—was so great that a husband might snatch the reins of power from her and leave her with the title but not the authority she loved to exercise.

Was it fun to be queen? As monarch, she commanded great wealth, inherited from her father, and people who wanted favors were always enriching her with lavish presents. She was no spendthrift, however. She hated to see money wasted, whether her own or the

"I AM ALREADY BOUND UNTO A HUSBAND, WHICH IS THE KINGDOM OF ENGLAND."

kingdom's. Early on she began keeping careful household account books, and later she would do the same with the royal accounts. Always she urged her counselors to carry out orders as inexpensively as possible.

Above everything else, Elizabeth wanted to have her people think well of her. Her deepest desire was to assure them of peace and prosperity. And why not make a grand personal impression upon them at the same time? In her mature years she gave free rein to her love of jewels and staged brilliant displays for the court and the people. Her dresses were decorated with large rubies, emeralds, and diamonds, and she wore jeweled necklaces, bracelets, and rings. In her hair, at her ears, and around her neck she wore pearls—the symbol of virginity.

During her reign she made many great processions through London, the people wild with excitement, crowding the streets—for the English, like most people, loved spectacle. In the first of them, her coronation, she wore gold robes as she was crowned. Trumpets sounded, pipes and drums played, the organ pealed, bells rang. Then came the state banquet in Westminster Hall. It began at 3:00 P.M., and went on till 1:00 A.M.

Elizabeth was often entertained at house parties. One of them, given by the Earl of Leicester in Kenilworth Castle, lasted for eighteen days in July. Thirty other distinguished guests were invited. The great number of their servants (together with Leicester's) turned the palace into a small town. When darkness fell, candles glittered everywhere, indoors and out, creating a fairyland. Musicians sang and played, the guests danced in the garden, and such a great display of fireworks exploded that the heavens thundered and the castle shook. Then came a pleasure relished in those days: the hideous sport of bear baiting. A pack of dogs was let loose in an inner courtyard to scratch and bite and tear at thirteen tormented bears. Still, the happy guests retained their appetite for a "most delicious banquet of 300 dishes."

The tremendous festival at Kenilworth was only one of the highlights of Elizabeth's summer festival. She moved from one great house to another all season long, always at the enormous expense of her hosts. They had little to complain of, however, for their wealth was often the product of the queen's generous bestowal of special privileges. In recognition of his high rank and in return for his support, she granted the duke of Norfolk a license to import carpets from Turkey free of duty. The earl of Essex was favored with the profitable right to tax imported sweet wines. Other pets got rich from a mo-nopoly on the importation of or taxation of silks, satins, salt, tobacco, starch.

England was a small nation at the time she ruled: less than four million people, about as many as live in Arizona today. But the English were a young people, coming to maturity with new worlds opening up to them, in the mind and across the seas. A rebirth of culture—the Renaissance—had begun in the 1400s. With the revival of interest in the literature of the ancient Greek and Roman worlds came the beginning of a great age of discovery. This period marked the transition from medieval to modern times. The arts

and sciences were influenced by changes in economic life. All the nation was swept up in the vast tides of change. Merchants, bankers, the gentry,[3] artisans, seamen, miners—men and women of every class and condition—felt themselves part of the national venture.

At the heart of the change in England was the queen. But no king or queen rules alone, no matter how authoritative or arrogant they may be. They usually look to others for advice, advice they may follow or reject. Elizabeth appointed ministers to handle the various departments of government, and made Sir William Cecil, then thirty-eight, her principal advisor. He was a brilliant, hard-working master of statecraft, devoted to her and England's well-being, and as ruthless as she and the nation's interests required. When he died in old age, his son Robert replaced him at her side.

So great was the queen's role, however, that her time became known as the Age of Elizabeth. Not only did many fine musicians flower, but writers too, such as Christopher Marlowe and John Donne and Ben Jonson and Edmund Spenser. And above all, the incomparable William Shakespeare, whose plays were sometimes performed at court. Astronomers, naturalists, mathematicians, geographers, and architects pioneered in their fields.

Then, too, there were the daring explorers who pushed English expansion overseas.

---

3. **gentry** *n.*: upper class.

Vocabulary
monopoly (mə·năp′ə·lē) *n.*: exclusive control of a market. Monopolies are illegal now because they can control prices.
arrogant (ar′ə·gənt) *adj.*: overly convinced of one's own importance.

WILLIAM SHAKESPEARE.

THE GOLDEN HINDE.
A working replica of the sailing ship *Golden Hinde* used by Drake during the sixteenth century.

SIR FRANCIS DRAKE.
The English explorer Sir Francis Drake (1540?–1596).

One of the queen's favorites, Sir Walter Raleigh, planned the colony of Virginia in America and named it for her, the Virgin Queen. The queen herself put money into several of the great voyages, keeping close watch over the plans and their results. She supported Sir Francis Drake on his three-year voyage around the world, profiting mightily from the immense loot he captured from Spanish ships taken in the Pacific.

For Elizabeth, one of the most urgent problems was the question of religion. Her father had broken with the Catholic Church and launched the English Reformation, creating the Church of England, with himself at its head. When Elizabeth's older half sister, Mary (who remained Catholic), married the Catholic king of Spain, Philip II, she reconciled England with the Church of Rome. In Mary's brief reign she persecuted those Protestants who refused to conform, executing some 270 of them.

When Elizabeth became queen upon Mary's death, she said she hoped religion would not prevent her people from living together in peaceful unity. She did not want to pry into people's souls or question their faith. But in 1570, Pope Pius V excommunicated[4] her, denied her right to the throne, and declared her subjects owed her no allegiance. A directive[5] from the pope's office decreed that the assassination of Queen Elizabeth would not be regarded as a sin. The effect of this directive was to turn practicing Catholics—about half of the English, most of them loyal—into potential traitors.

Though Elizabeth had wanted to pursue a middle way of toleration, circumstances threatened to overwhelm her. She had to beware of several Catholic monarchs of Europe who wished to see a Protestant England overthrown. Philip II of Spain sent ambassadors to England to urge Catholics to rise against

---

4. **excommunicated** *v.:* cast out from a religious community. Strictly speaking, the queen was denied the sacraments of the Catholic Church.
5. **directive** *n.:* order or instructions, especially given by a government.

Elizabeth, put her cousin Mary[6] on the throne, and restore Roman Catholicism as the national faith. The line between power, politics, and religion was becoming very thin.

Missionary priests living abroad were sent into England to stir up opposition to the queen. But the English Catholics as a body never rebelled, nor did they ever intend to. Still, missionary priests such as Edmund Campion were convicted of plotting against Elizabeth and executed.

In 1588 a long-threatened invasion of England by Spain was launched by Philip II. He mistakenly believed that the English Catholics were waiting to welcome him. News of his armada of 130 big ships carrying 17,000 soldiers was terrifying. But the queen did not panic. She supervised the high command personally, meanwhile rallying popular support for the defense of the realm and sending troops to protect the coasts while Sir Francis Drake's ships set out to attack the Spanish fleet.

The Spanish Armada was defeated in three battles, its ships dispersed. When the news came of the tremendous victory, the citizens took to the streets, shouting for joy.

The defeat of the Spanish Armada did not end Spain's aggression against England. The Jesuits[7] in England, who were especially identified with Spain, continued to be persecuted. Richard Topcliffe, a notorious hater of

HOW DARE STUBBS SAY PUBLICLY SHE WAS TOO OLD TO MARRY?

Catholics, was given authority to track down suspects. He examined them under torture to force information about people who had sheltered them. The treatment of them was so vicious and cruel that the victims welcomed death as a release from their agony.

During Elizabeth's reign several plots to assassinate her were uncovered. Elizabeth managed to give the impression that she was not frightened, but those close to her knew she was. When one of the major plots proved to center around Elizabeth's cousin, Mary, Queen of Scots, Elizabeth found it almost intolerable to put to death a crowned queen. Yet she ordered the use of torture on Mary's co-conspirators, and in the end, Mary was beheaded. A song composed by William Byrd at the time suggests how ominous the news of a monarch's execution was:

> The noble famous Queen
> who lost her head of late
> Doth show that kings as well as clowns
> Are bound to fortune's fate,
> And that no earthly Prince
> Can so secure his crown
> but fortune with her whirling wheel
> Hath power to pull them down.

When two earls combined forces against her, Elizabeth's troops overcame them. The queen was so enraged she ordered that 800 of the mostly poor rebels be hanged. But she spared the lives of their wealthy leaders so

---

6. **Mary:** Mary Stuart (1542–1587) (Mary, Queen of Scots, not Elizabeth's half sister).
7. **Jesuits** (jezh′o͞o·its): priests who are members of the Roman Catholic Society of Jesus.

Vocabulary
intolerable (in·täl′ər·ə·bəl) *adj.:* unbearable.

MARY STUART, QUEEN OF SCOTS.
Portrait of Mary Stuart, Queen of Scots (16th century).

SEA BATTLE BETWEEN THE SPANISH ARMADA AND ENGLISH NAVAL FORCES.

that they might enrich her, either by buying their pardons or by forfeiting[8] their lands.

Elizabeth came down hard on writers who criticized her actions. John Stubbs, a zealous Puritan, wrote a pamphlet expressing horror at the possibility the queen might marry a French Catholic. The queen had Stubbs and his publisher tried and convicted for seditious libel.[9] How dare Stubbs say publicly she was too old to marry, and that the much younger French suitor could not possibly be in love with her? Elizabeth was merciless as she invoked the penalty for libel. With a butcher's cleaver, the executioner cut the right hands off Stubbs and his publisher. Not an uncommon punishment.

How did Elizabeth learn of all these plots and conspiracies? How did she know what

plans Philip II of Spain was devising to invade her kingdom? Spies and secret agents—they were her eyes and ears. Crucial to the flow of information was Sir Francis Walsingham. Trained as a lawyer, he lived on the Continent[10] for years, mastering the languages and the ins and outs of European affairs. Upon his return home, he was asked by Sir William Cecil, the queen's right arm, to gather information on the doings and plans of foreign governments. Soon he was made chief of England's secret service. He placed over seventy agents and spies in the courts of Europe. And of course he watched closely the activities of people at home suspected of disloyalty. Letters to and from them were secretly opened, to nip plots in the bud.

Monarchs had absolute power. Elizabeth could arrest anyone, including the topmost ranks of the nobility, and imprison them in the Tower of London even if they had not

---

8. **forfeiting** (fôr′fit·iŋ) *v.* used as *n.:* giving up, usually because of force of some kind.
9. **seditious libel** (si·dish′əs lī′bəl): stirring up discontent about the government (sedition) with false written statements (libel).

10. **Continent:** Europe.

committed any legal offense. The only thing that held her back was her fear of public opinion. It upset her when a crowd gathered at a public execution and was so disgusted by the butchery that they let out roars of disapproval. Still, like all rulers, Elizabeth said she believed that "born a sovereign princess" she enjoyed "the privilege common to all kings" and was "exempt from human jurisdiction[11] and subject only to the judgement of God."

Despite her blazing nervous energy, Elizabeth was often sick. Her ailments were anxiously reported and discussed. For the English believed her survival was their only guarantee of freedom from foreign invasion and civil war. Once, suffering a raging toothache for the first time, the queen feared the pain of having an extraction. She had never had a tooth pulled and was terrified. To reassure her, an old friend, the Bishop of London, had her watch while the dental surgeon pulled out one of the bishop's own good teeth. And then she consented to have her own taken out.

It was commonly believed then that kings and queens had the magical power to cure disease in their subjects. Eager to demonstrate that she too had the sacred power of royalty, Elizabeth prayed intensely before using the royal touch on people with scrofula, a nasty skin disease. Her chaplain said he watched "her exquisite hands, boldly, and without disgust, pressing the sores and ulcers." In one day it was reported that she

"OLD AGE CAME UPON ME AS A SURPRISE, LIKE A FROST," SHE ONCE WROTE.

healed thirty-eight persons. But if she did not feel divinely inspired, she would not try her touch.

Even in the last decade of her life, Elizabeth's energy was astonishing. She was as watchful as always over the affairs of state, though sometimes forgetful. But age made her more irritable; she sometimes shouted at her ladies and even boxed their ears. She was less able to control rival factions out for power, and became so fearful of assassins she rarely left her palaces.

A portrait of her done when she was approaching sixty shows her in a great white silk dress studded with aglets[12] of black onyx, coral, and pearl. She wears three ropes of translucent pearls and stands on a map of England, her England. An ambassador reported that at sixty-three she looked old, but her figure was still beautiful, and her conversation was as brilliant and charming as ever.

There was dancing at court every evening, a pastime she still enjoyed. When it came to displays of gallantry by eager young men, she could act a bit vain and foolish, although never letting any hopeful get out of bounds.

In early 1603 Elizabeth developed a bad cold that led to a serious fever, and then she fell into a stupor[13] for four days. As she lay dying, all of London became strangely silent. On March 24, the life of a rare genius ended. The nation went into mourning.

"Old age came upon me as a surprise, like a frost," she once wrote.

---

11. **jurisdiction** (joor'is·dik'shən) n.: legal control.

12. **aglets** (ag'lits) n.: tips of lace on dresses.
13. **stupor** (stoo'pər) n.: loss of sensibility; dullness.

Milton Meltzer

No Shy Guy

The historian **Milton Meltzer** (1915–   ) took an interest in social issues when he was young. After attending Columbia University, he joined the Works Projects Administration, a government agency that provided jobs for workers who were unemployed during the Great Depression of the 1930s. Over time he has written about the Holocaust and the civil rights movement, slavery and immigration. Never one to shy away from controversy, Meltzer writes honestly about injustices that have occurred throughout history.

His biographies cover historic figures, such as George Washington and Mark Twain, as well as others who may not be so well known—like Tom Paine, who battled for America's independence, and Betty Friedan, who fought for women's rights. Throughout most of his work, Meltzer recognizes a common link:

> **My subjects choose action. . . . Action takes commitment, the commitment of dedicated, optimistic individuals. I try to make the readers understand that history isn't only what happens to us. History is what we *make* happen. Each of us. All of us.**

Meltzer has written over eighty books, many of them award winners. In addition, he has made documentary films and written scripts for radio and television.

For Independent Reading

So much Meltzer to choose from! For more biographies of women like Elizabeth, try *Ten Queens: Portraits of Women of Power.* Or you may prefer *Frederick Douglass: In His Own Words* or *Thomas Jefferson: The Revolutionary Aristocrat.*

Literary Response and Analysis

Reading Check

Answer the following questions. Then, complete your SQ3R organizer.

1. What problems did England have when Elizabeth I came to the throne?

2. How did England change during the Renaissance? Who was at the heart of the change?

3. Why didn't Elizabeth want to get married?

4. What was Elizabeth's opinion about her people's religious practices?

5. Why was it always possible that Elizabeth would be assassinated?

Interpretations

6. If you could ask Elizabeth one question, what would it be?

7. What **inferences** can you make about how people felt about Elizabeth? Support your inferences with evidence from the text.

8. Which details in the life of Elizabeth would not apply to the life of a ruler today? Which details could very well apply to the life of a ruler in a modern nation in the twenty-first century? Consider these topics:

   - the question of marriage
   - the execution of enemies
   - intrigues and plots
   - processions
   - parties
   - the divine right of kings
   - separation of church and state

9. Rewrite the first paragraph of this biography as if you were Elizabeth herself. Write as "I," from Elizabeth's own point of view. Include **subjective details** that will change the paragraph from an objective point of view to a subjective point of view. (Subjective details would tell how Elizabeth feels about her life and achievements—and disappointments.)

Evaluation

10. How does this biographer feel about Elizabeth? Is his narrative balanced? Is he mostly **objective** as a biographer, or is he very **subjective** in his account of Elizabeth? Find details from the biography to support your answers.

11. Write down one **opinion** you formed as you read about Elizabeth. What facts led you to form that opinion?

Writing

Putting Someone on Paper

Write a short biographical sketch of the person you chose for your Quickwrite. Before you write, create a character profile by listing facts you know and questions for which you want answers. Use the Internet and library resources to gather information that will answer your research questions. Do you wish to write an **objective** biography—sticking to the facts? Or do you prefer to express some **subjective** feelings?

Reading Standard 3.5
Contrast points of view (for example, subjective and objective) in narrative text.

Vocabulary Development

Clarifying Word Meanings: Definitions in Context

You may have noticed that the writer of this article helped you out when he used a word that he thought you might not know. He defined the difficult word right there in the sentence or in the next sentence. Writers of textbooks and other materials written for students often do this. It's up to you to be able to recognize a definition when you see it. Here are three examples from "Elizabeth I" in which the writer clarifies word meanings through the use of definition.

In the first example the words *that is* signal a definition coming up.

> **"Kings claimed that they as men were born to rule by <u>divine right</u>. That is, God had ordained that the crown should pass through the male line of descent."**

In this example, the definition comes before the word:

> **"A rebirth of culture—the <u>Renaissance</u>—had begun in the 1400s."**

Here the writer defines the word *scrofula* right after the comma:

> **"Elizabeth prayed intensely before using the royal touch on people with <u>scrofula</u>, a nasty skin disease."**

PRACTICE

Write a sentence for each word in the Word Bank, and define the word by applying one of the methods used in the examples above. Use each method of clarification at least once.

Old London Bridge in 1630 (detail) by Claude de Jong (c. 1610–1663).

> **Word Bank**
>
> monarch
> alliance
> monopoly
> arrogant
> intolerable

ELISABETHA REG: ANGLIÆ.

Elizabeth I, Queen of England (16th century).

Reading Standard 1.3
Clarify word meanings through the use of definition.

Elizabeth I **295**

Literary Response and Analysis

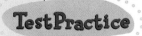 **TestPractice** DIRECTIONS: Read the passages. Then, read each question, and write the letter of the best response.

The News of King Midas
from *The Royal News*

Rumors of the so-called Midas touch have been confirmed today. According to sources close to the king, Midas is now unable to eat or drink, as anything he touches turns to gold.

"Serves him right," said one palace insider who asked not to be named. "He could have wished for something sensible, such as a triple-tax-free diversified bond portfolio. Now who knows where the price of gold is heading?"

The king's wife and daughter were unavailable for comment, as they had been turned to gold.

from *Cook to the King: A Novel*

"Sandwich?" the head cook roared. "You want me to fix you a sandwich?" She glared at the king. "With what, may I ask?"

What an idiot he was. Even the smallest servant boy knew what was going to happen by the time dessert was served, but not King Midas. Oh, no. Not content merely to ruin her entire day's work (that perfectly poached salmon! that lovely macaroni pudding!), he had to come tearing through her kitchen. By the time he was through, there wasn't a crumb that didn't clink and glitter when she swept it up.

from *A Courtier's Memoir*

After all my years serving in the palace, I thought I'd seen it all. When the king, however, started turning everything to gold, you could have knocked me over with a feather. Actually, he nearly *did* knock me over with a feather. An ostrich plume, it was, on my second-best hat! If I do say so myself, I was looking rather spiffy until the king snatched it off and started waving it around. He yelled that he'd turned my hat to gold. It was gold, all right. Solid gold. I've still got the lump on my head to prove it.

King Midas's E-mail

To: gods_helpline@olympus.edu
From: kmidas@palace.org
Subject: My Kingdom for a Burger
OK, point taken. I was greedy and foolish, and I'm sorry. Please, undo my wish before I starve to death!

Reading Standard 3.5 Contrast points of view (for example, first and third person, limited and omniscient, subjective and objective) in narrative text, and explain how they affect the overall theme of the work.

1. In which passage does the narrator use a **third-person limited point of view**?

   A *The Royal News*
   B *Cook to the King*
   C *A Courtier's Memoir*
   D King Midas's E-mail

2. The **point of view** in *A Courtier's Memoir* is —

   F omniscient
   G first person
   H third-person limited
   J second person

3. Which passage is most **objective** in telling what has happened to King Midas?

   A *The Royal News*
   B *Cook to the King*
   C *A Courtier's Memoir*
   D King Midas's E-mail

4. The **narrator,** or speaker, in *A Courtier's Memoir* is —

   F the king himself
   G the cook to the king
   H an omniscient narrator
   J a courtier in the king's court

5. The **speaker** in King Midas's E-mail is —

   A the king himself
   B the cook to the king
   C an omniscient narrator
   D a courtier in the king's court

Reading Informational Materials

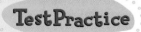

TestPractice

DIRECTIONS: Read the passage. Then, read each question, and write the letter of the best response.

Can We Rescue the Reefs?

Ritu Upadhyay
from *Time for Kids*

❶ Time is running out to stop the destruction of coral reefs.

❷ Under the clear blue sea, bustling communities of ocean creatures live together in brightly colored, wildly stacked structures called coral reefs. These silent, majestic underwater cities are home to four thousand different species of fish and thousands of plants and animals. For millions of years, marine creatures have lived together in reefs, going about their business in their own little water worlds.

❸ But danger looms. At an international meeting on coral reefs in October 2000, scientists issued a harsh warning. More than one quarter of the world's reefs have been destroyed. . . . Unless drastic measures are taken, the remaining reefs may be dead in twenty years. "We are about to lose them," says Clive Wilkinson of the Coral Reef Monitoring Network.

Precious Underwater Habitats

❹ The destruction of coral reefs, some of which are 2.5 million years old, would have a very serious impact on our oceans. Though coral reefs take up less than 1 percent of the ocean floor, they are home to 25 percent of all underwater species. Wiping them out would put thousands of creatures at risk of extinction. It would also destroy one of our planet's most beautiful living treasures.

❺ Though it's often mistaken for rock because of its stony texture, coral is actually made up of tiny clear animals called coral polyps. Millions stick together in colonies and form a hard outer shell. When coral die, their skeletons are left behind, and new coral build on top. The colonies eventually grow together, creating large reefs. Reefs grow into complex mazelike structures with different rooms, hallways, holes, and crevices for their inhabitants to live in. Over the years the ancient Great Barrier Reef off Australia's coast has grown to be 1,240 miles long!

Reading Standard 2.4
Identify and trace the development of an author's argument, point of view, or perspective in text.

1. Which of the following statements best summarizes the writer's **perspective** in "Can We Rescue the Reefs?"
   A The outlook for coral reefs is hopeless.
   B Global warming is a threat to the whole earth.
   C Saving endangered coral reefs is very important.
   D Coral reefs are beautiful little worlds within the oceans.

2. Paragraph 2 contains words and phrases such as "bustling communities," "underwater cities," "home," "going about their business," and "their own little water worlds." The writer uses those words and phrases to —
   F make coral reefs seem like human societies
   G describe coral reefs the way a scientist would describe them
   H tell where coral reefs are located
   J describe how coral reefs are formed

3. In paragraph 3, the writer supports her position by —
   A describing her personal fears about the reefs
   B quoting an expert on the issue
   C telling a brief story about the development of coral reefs
   D giving reasons why coral reefs are beautiful

4. Which statement is an example of a **statistic**?
   F "Time is running out to stop the destruction of coral reefs."
   G "Coral is actually made up of tiny clear animals. . . ."
   H "Reefs grow in complex mazelike structures. . . ."
   J "More than one quarter of the world's reefs have been destroyed. . . ."

5. Which of the following is a statement of **fact**—something that can be proved to be true?
   A Coral is the most beautiful thing in the sea.
   B Over the years the ancient Great Barrier Reef has grown to be 1,240 miles long.
   C Coral reefs must be saved.
   D Coral reefs are fascinating.

6. The writer's **purpose** in this article is to —
   F inform
   G describe
   H persuade
   J all of the above

7. According to the article, why are coral reefs important?
   A They attract tourists.
   B They are home to 25 percent of all underwater species.
   C They are very old.
   D They grow into complex mazelike structures.

Vocabulary Development

TestPractice

Synonyms

DIRECTIONS: Choose the word or phrase that means the same, or about the same, as the underlined word.

1. Something that is exotic is —
   A ordinary in a dull way
   B different in a fascinating way
   C very desirable
   D strongly offensive

2. Something that is intricate is —
   F simple
   G inside
   H ancient
   J complicated

3. Habitual is most like —
   A customary
   B irregular
   C occasionally
   D never

4. Convoluted means —
   F complicated
   G ordinary
   H murky
   J strange

5. Someone who is in transition is experiencing —
   A prosperity
   B balance
   C stability
   D change

6. Deprivation is most like —
   F abundance
   G loss
   H privilege
   J growth

7. Arrogant refers to someone who is —
   A overly emotional
   B deeply confused
   C overly self-important
   D easily persuaded

8. Intolerable means —
   F worthwhile
   G unjust
   H infrequent
   J unbearable

9. Simultaneously means —
   A all but one
   B never the same
   C over the top
   D at the same time

10. Someone seeking refuge would be in search of —
    F food
    G shelter
    H clothing
    J garbage

Mastering the Standards

AUTOBIOGRAPHICAL NARRATIVE

It Happened to Me . . .

Julia Alvarez writes an autobiographical essay about her experiences with her name (page 262). Maijue Xiong writes an autobiographical narrative about a perilous journey to freedom that she and her family took (page 271). Think of an incident in your own life that you would like to write about—you could write an essay, as Julia Alvarez did, or a narrative, as Maijue Xiong did. To find a subject you want to write about, freewrite for a few minutes about one or two of these subjects: surprises, conflicts, vacations, secrets, losses, luck, honesty, family, names, changes. If that doesn't do it, try this: Study a photograph of yourself, and write about the day the picture was taken. Include descriptive details in your writing, to help your readers share your experiences.

 Use "Writing an Autobiographical Narrative," pages 704–706, for help with this assignment.

Other Choices

FICTIONAL NARRATIVE

1 **Cop Busts Best Buddy**

New York, 1906—You are a reporter for the *New York World,* the newspaper O. Henry once worked for. You cover the police beat, and the plainclothes policeman who brought "Silky" Bob in tells you the story of Jimmy Wells and his chum Bob. Write an article about it for the morning edition. Remember: A news story is a type of narrative that should answer these questions:

• What happened?
• Who was involved?
• Why did it happen?
• When and where did it happen?
• How did it happen?

RESPONSE TO LITERATURE

2 **Good Guy, Bad Guy**

Is the portrayal of Baumer and Slade in the short story "Bargain" just another example of a good guy facing down a bad guy? After readers find out what Baumer does to Slade in the end, can they see him as a good guy? Choose either Baumer or Slade, and go back through the text to find evidence to support the notion that he's not wholly good or wholly bad. To suggest that his characterization is more complex than that of a simple hero or villain, find examples of what he says and does and what others say about him. Then, write a character analysis explaining what you've discovered.

 Use "Writing a Character Analysis," pages 566–582, for help with this assignment.

Fiction

A Little Patience

Young Miguel Chavez longs for his family to treat him like an adult. For a year he tries to prove that he is ready to make the difficult journey driving sheep into the mountains. It is not until some sheep are missing and a serious letter arrives that Miguel is truly able to prove himself in Joseph Krumgold's Newbery winner . . . *and now Miguel.*

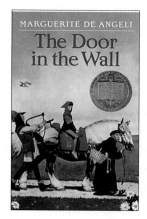

The Faithful Servant

Marguerite De Angeli's *The Door in the Wall* takes place in medieval England. Robin, the son of the great lord Sir John de Bureford, is supposed to become a page—a boy training for knighthood. Unfortunately, he is stricken with a mysterious illness that causes him to lose the movement of his legs. Determined not to disappoint his father, he overcomes his problems and helps to turn back the Welsh invaders who threaten the kingdom.

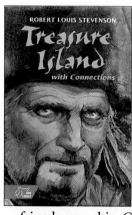

All Aboard!

When Jim Hawkins, an impressionable young cabin boy, discovers a treasure map, he finds himself thrust into an adventure beyond compare. The notorious Long John Silver joins Jim and two of his friends on a ship. Can Hawkins trust this mysterious pirate? Find out in Robert Louis Stevenson's *Treasure Island.*

This title is available in the HRW Library.

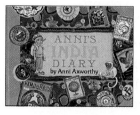

In Another Land

Have you ever wondered what it would be like to make your way through India? Anni Axworthy gives you more than a passing glance of the Asian subcontinent in *Anni's India Diary.* Discover Hindu gods and goddesses, learn how to play cricket, and visit the Taj Mahal along with Anni. Lively illustrations accompany the text of Anni's unforgettable journey.

Nonfiction

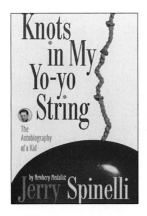

The Way He Was

In *Knots in My Yo-yo String,* Newbery Award–winner Jerry Spinelli touchingly revisits his childhood and growing up. He recalls dreams of becoming a major-league shortstop, hours with comic books, and the only time he received detention in school. Spinelli had no idea he would become a writer, but he recounts in compelling prose the event that inspired him to become one.

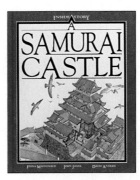

The Customs of Warriors

During the sixteenth and seventeenth centuries, Samurai warriors were the most honored group in Japan. In *A Samurai Castle,* Fiona MacDonald explores the Samurai culture and the conditions that helped shape this distinct group of fighting men. Perceptive illustrations reveal the design of their living arrangements, and MacDonald's narrative tells how the Samurai spent their days, how they trained for battle, and the reasons they were respected and feared.

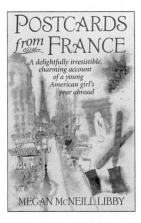

An Exciting Journey

Megan McNeill Libby had reservations after deciding to spend her junior year in France. When she arrived, she felt out of place in her new surroundings, and she wondered if she would ever learn the customs and language. After a few months she began to make friends and appreciate the fascinating culture. Megan chronicles this exciting time of her life in *Postcards from France.*

A Wealth of Ideas

In *Made in China: Ideas and Inventions from Ancient China,* Suzanne Williams describes some of the many contributions the ancient Chinese made to science and society. From discoveries in astronomy and improvements in irrigation systems to the casting of bronze and the standardization of roads, measurements, and writing, Williams places Chinese invention in a context that helps to break down ethnic and cultural barriers.

5 Worlds of Words
Prose and Poetry

California Standards

Here are the Grade 7 standards you will study for mastery in Chapter 5. You will also review standards from an earlier grade.

Reading

Word Analysis, Fluency, and Systematic Vocabulary Development

1.1 Identify idioms, analogies, metaphors, and similes in prose and poetry.

1.3 Clarify word meanings through the use of definition, example, restatement, or contrast.

Grade 6 Review
1.5 Understand and explain shades of meaning in related words (for example, *softly* and *quietly*).

Reading Comprehension (Focus on Informational Materials)

Grade 6 Review
2.2 Analyze text that uses the compare-and-contrast organizational pattern.

Grade 6 Review
2.4 Clarify an understanding of texts by creating outlines, logical notes, summaries, or reports.

Literary Response and Analysis

3.1 Articulate the expressed purposes and characteristics of different forms of prose (for example, short story, novel, novella, essay).

Grade 6 Review
3.4 Define how tone or meaning is conveyed in poetry through word choice, figurative language, sentence structure, line length, punctuation, rhythm, repetition, and rhyme.

KEYWORD:
HLLA 7-5

Reading Like a Wolf *by* Kylene Beers

UNDERSTANDING THE FORMS OF PROSE

A student once asked what I meant when I said his essay was really a short story. "What's the difference?" he wanted to know. "And," he continued, "what does it matter?"

Knowing the Difference Makes a Difference

His question was a good one. Why does knowing the difference between those types of prose make a difference? Well, it's something like knowing the difference in sports terms. If your coach says the team you're playing against uses a one-on-one defense instead of a zone defense, you know what to expect when you hit the basketball court.

Understanding the type of prose you're reading helps you anticipate what you'll find in the text. Once you know that what you are reading is a short story, for example, you'll be expecting characters, conflict, and a theme—you won't be looking for personal opinions or historical accuracy.

You Speak in Prose

You might think of **prose** as everything that isn't poetry. In fact, you've been speaking prose all your life. You also read prose every day—in your textbooks, in novels, in magazines, on the Web, in newspapers, in the notes you pass in the halls, and in the e-mails you receive. You read each type of prose

differently. You read a note from your best friend in one way, and you read the chapter in your science book another way.

Obviously prose covers a lot of ground. It can be generally divided into **fiction**—made-up stories—and **non-fiction,** which relates facts about real people, places, things, and events. Let's look at the different forms that fiction and nonfiction can take.

Fiction: Imagined Events and Characters

A **short story** is just what it sounds like: a short work of **fiction** with a few characters who move through a series of events (the plot) and work through a conflict, which leads to a climax and a resolution.

If all that happens in five to twenty pages, you have a short story. If you find yourself looking at one hundred pages or more, then you've left the short story and headed straight into a **novel.** In a novel you meet lots of characters, probably see subplots unfold within the larger plot, explore many themes, and encounter many conflicts.

If one hundred pages is too long and twenty is too short, then you've got a **novella,** which is simply a short novel.

Reading Standard 3.1 Articulate the expressed purposes and characteristics of different forms of prose (for example, short story, novel, novella, essay).

Nonfiction: Based on Fact

An **essay** is a short piece of prose that discusses a limited topic. Some people write short personal essays about simple things, like eating an ice-cream cone or taking a dog for a walk. Others write longer essays about complex issues, such as freedom, respect, and justice.

Some nonfiction topics are just too big for a short form like the essay. You might read about an Olympic athlete in a magazine article, for example, but if you really wanted to know the whole story of her life, you'd look at a book-length **biography.**

"Is It True?"

Sometimes writers use real-life events in their fiction. Gary Paulsen explains in an essay that he's really been attacked by moose.

When I wrote of the moose attack in *Hatchet* and again in *Brian's Winter*, I used the events from my life in the story. I wrote of what the moose attacks were like. But when it was really happening to me, I didn't think, oh man, this is great, I'm getting creamed by a moose, this will be wonderful to write about in my next book. I just used the memory later in the context of the story.

"Read Like a Wolf Eats"

Whatever type of prose you enjoy the most, remember the important thing is to read. Here's what Gary Paulsen says:

The most, *most* important thing is to read. Read all the time; read when they tell you not to read, read what they tell you not to read, read with a flashlight under the covers, read on the bus, standing on the corner, waiting for a friend, in the dentist's waiting room. Read every minute that you can. Read like a wolf eats. Read.

Practice

To show that you know more about prose than you think you do, work with a partner to fill out a prose chart like the following one. First, copy the chart on a separate piece of paper. Then, think of titles that are examples of each kind of prose. (Notice that there are more types of prose here than we just discussed. You could name even more types if you looked in a bookstore.) You might want to prepare an illustrated "prose group" for your classroom.

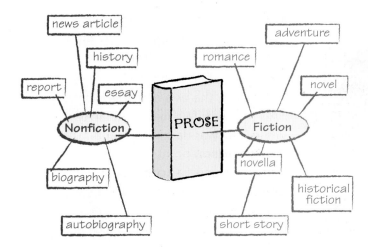

Amigo Brothers

Literary Focus

The Short Story

A short work of fiction, usually around five to twenty pages, is called a **short story.** (Sometimes a story that's even shorter is called a **short-short story.**) Short stories pack a lot of punch into a few pages. Whatever happens, happens quickly. We meet the **main characters,** get involved in their **problems,** sort out the **complications,** and move speedily to a **climax** and a **resolution.** A good short story can pack a life into a few pages.

Internal Conflict

In the story that follows, two best friends competing for a prize must fight each other in a boxing ring. This fight is a perfect example of an **external conflict.** The boys are supposed to knock each other out. Each boy also struggles with an **internal conflict:** How can he do his best without hurting and possibly even losing his closest friend?

Reading Skills

Comparison and Contrast: Finding Similarities and Differences

Piri Thomas begins his story by contrasting the two best friends: "Antonio was fair, lean, and lanky, while Felix was dark, short, and husky." A **comparison** points out similarities between things; a **contrast** points out differences. After you read the story, go back over it, and use a Venn diagram to help identify the ways in which Felix

Reading Standard 3.1 Articulate the expressed purposes and characteristics of different forms of prose (for example, short story).

and Antonio are alike and different. Write their likenesses in the space where the circles overlap.

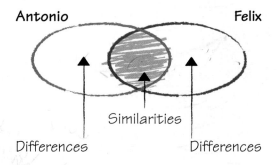

Make the Connection

Quickwrite 🖉

Conflicts can arise when friends take different sides in a competition. In a group, create a list titled "Rules for Competing Against a Friend."

Vocabulary Development

Here are some words to give you a fighting chance:

bouts (bouts) *n.:* matches; contests. *Both boxers had won many bouts.*

pensively (pen′siv·lē) *adv.:* thoughtfully. *Felix nodded pensively as he rested.*

torrent (tôr′ənt) *n.:* flood or rush. *A torrent of emotion left him close to tears.*

dispelled (di·speld′) *v.:* driven away. *All doubt was dispelled the moment Tony made up his mind.*

frenzied (fren′zēd) *adj.:* wild. *The audience's reaction was as frenzied as the battle in the ring.*

Background

This story is about two friends (*amigos* in Spanish) living on the Lower East Side of New York City. Many boys from the Lower East Side have dreamed of building a better life by winning the New York Golden Gloves, a tournament started in 1927 by Paul Gallico, a newspaper writer. This tournament marks an amateur's entry into the world of big-time boxing.

Antonio Cruz and Felix Vargas were both seventeen years old. They were so together in friendship that they felt themselves to be brothers. They had known each other since childhood, growing up on the Lower East Side of Manhattan in the same tenement[1] building on Fifth Street between Avenue A and Avenue B.

Antonio was fair, lean, and lanky, while Felix was dark, short, and husky. Antonio's hair was always falling over his eyes, while Felix wore his black hair in a natural Afro style.

Each youngster had a dream of someday becoming lightweight champion of the world. Every chance they had, the boys worked out, sometimes at the Boys' Club on 10th Street and Avenue A and sometimes at the pro's gym on 14th Street. Early morning sunrises would find them running along the East River Drive, wrapped in sweat shirts, short towels around their necks, and handkerchiefs Apache style around their foreheads.

While some youngsters were into street negatives, Antonio and Felix slept, ate, rapped, and dreamt positive. Between them, they had a collection of *Fight* magazines second to none, plus a scrapbook filled with torn tickets to every boxing match they had ever attended, and some clippings of their own. If asked a question about any given fighter, they would immediately zip out from their memory banks divisions, weights, records of fights, knockouts, technical knockouts, and draws or losses.

Each had fought many bouts representing their community and had won two gold-plated medals plus a silver and bronze medallion. The difference was in their style. Antonio's lean form and long reach made him the better boxer, while Felix's short and muscular frame made him the better slugger. Whenever they had met in the ring for sparring sessions,[2] it had always been hot and heavy.

Now, after a series of elimination bouts, they had been informed that they were to meet each other in the division finals that were scheduled for the seventh of August, two weeks away—the winner to represent the Boys' Club in the Golden Gloves Championship Tournament.

The two boys continued to run together along the East River Drive. But even when joking with each other, they both sensed a wall rising between them.

One morning less than a week before their bout, they met as usual for their daily workout. They fooled around with a few jabs at the air, slapped skin, and then took off, running lightly along the dirty East River's edge.

Antonio glanced at Felix, who kept his eyes purposely straight ahead, pausing from time to time to do some fancy leg work

---

2. **sparring sessions:** practice matches in which boxers use light punches.

---

1. **tenement** *n.* used as *adj.:* apartment. Tenement buildings are often cheaply built and poorly maintained.

Vocabulary
bouts (bouts) *n.:* matches; contests.

while throwing one-twos followed by upper-cuts to an imaginary jaw. Antonio then beat the air with a barrage of body blows and short devastating lefts with an overhead jaw-breaking right.

After a mile or so, Felix puffed and said, "Let's stop a while, bro. I think we both got something to say to each other."

Antonio nodded. It was not natural to be acting as though nothing unusual was happening when two ace-boon buddies were going to be blasting each other within a few short days.

They rested their elbows on the railing separating them from the river. Antonio wiped his face with his short towel. The sunrise was now creating day.

Felix leaned heavily on the river's railing and stared across to the shores of Brooklyn. Finally, he broke the silence.

"Man. I don't know how to come out with it."

Antonio helped. "It's about our fight, right?"

"Yeah, right." Felix's eyes squinted at the rising orange sun.

"I've been thinking about it too, panin.[3] In fact, since we found out it was going to be me and you, I've been awake at night, pulling punches on you, trying not to hurt you."

"Same here. It ain't natural not to think about the fight. I mean, we both are cheverote[4] fighters and we both want to win. But only one of us can win. There ain't no draws in the eliminations."

Felix tapped Antonio gently on the shoulder. "I don't mean to sound like I'm bragging, bro. But I wanna win, fair and square."

Antonio nodded quietly. "Yeah. We both know that in the ring the better man wins. Friend or no friend, brother or no . . ."

Felix finished it for him. "Brother. Tony, let's promise something right here. OK?"

---

3. **panin** (pä·nēn′) *n.:* Puerto Rican Spanish slang for "pal" or "buddy."
4. **cheverote** (che′ve·rô′tä) *adj.:* Puerto Rican Spanish slang for "the greatest."

THEY WERE SO TOGETHER IN FRIENDSHIP THAT THEY FELT THEMSELVES TO BE BROTHERS. They had known each other since childhood . . .

"If it's fair, hermano,[5] I'm for it." Antonio admired the courage of a tugboat pulling a barge five times its welterweight size.

"It's fair, Tony. When we get into the ring, it's gotta be like we never met. We gotta be like two heavy strangers that want the same thing and only one can have it. You understand, don't cha?"

"Sí, I know." Tony smiled. "No pulling punches. We go all the way."

"Yeah, that's right. Listen, Tony. Don't you think it's a good idea if we don't see each other until the day of the fight? I'm going to stay with my Aunt Lucy in the Bronx. I can use Gleason's Gym for working out. My manager says he got some sparring partners with more or less your style."

Tony scratched his nose <u>pensively</u>. "Yeah, it would be better for our heads." He held out his hand, palm upward. "Deal?"

"Deal." Felix lightly slapped open skin.

"Ready for some more running?" Tony asked lamely.

"Naw, bro. Let's cut it here. You go on. I kinda like to get things together in my head."

"You ain't worried, are you?" Tony asked.

"No way, man." Felix laughed out loud. "I got too much smarts for that. I just think it's cooler if we split right here. After the fight, we can get it together again like nothing ever happened."

The amigo brothers were not ashamed to hug each other tightly.

"Guess you're right. Watch yourself, Felix. I hear there's some pretty heavy dudes up in the Bronx. Suavecito,[6] OK?"

"OK. You watch yourself too, sabe?"[7]

Tony jogged away. Felix watched his friend disappear from view, throwing rights and lefts. Both fighters had a lot of psyching up to do before the big fight.

The days in training passed much too slowly. Although they kept out of each other's way, they were aware of each other's progress via the ghetto grapevine.

The evening before the big fight, Tony made his way to the roof of his tenement. In the quiet early dark, he peered over the ledge. Six stories below, the lights of the city blinked and the sounds of cars mingled with the curses and the laughter of children in the street. He tried not to think of Felix, feeling he had succeeded in psyching his mind. But only in the ring would he really know. To spare Felix hurt, he would have to knock him out, early and quick.

Up in the South Bronx, Felix decided to take in a movie in an effort to keep Antonio's face away from his fists. The flick was *The Champion* with Kirk Douglas, the third time Felix was seeing it.

The champion was getting beaten, his face being pounded into raw, wet hamburger. His eyes were cut, jagged, bleeding, one eye swollen, the other almost shut. He was saved only by the sound of the bell.

Felix became the champ and Tony the challenger.

The movie audience was going out of its head, roaring in blood lust at the butchery going on. The champ hunched his shoulders, grunting and sniffing red blood back into his broken nose. The challenger, confident that he had the championship in the bag, threw a left. The champ countered with

---

5. **hermano** (er·mä′nô) *n.*: Spanish for "brother."
6. **suavecito** (swä′vā·sē′tô) *adj.*: Puerto Rican Spanish slang for "cool."
7. **sabe** (sä′bā) *v.*: Spanish for "you know."

Vocabulary
pensively (pen′siv·lē) *adv.*: thoughtfully.

a dynamite right that exploded into the challenger's brains.

Felix's right arm felt the shock. Antonio's face, superimposed on the screen, was shattered and split apart by the awesome force of the killer blow. Felix saw himself in the ring, blasting Antonio against the ropes. The champ had to be forcibly restrained. The challenger was allowed to crumble slowly to the canvas, a broken bloody mess.

When Felix finally left the theater, he had figured out how to psych himself for tomorrow's fight. It was Felix the Champion vs. Antonio the Challenger.

He walked up some dark streets, deserted except for small pockets of wary-looking kids wearing gang colors. Despite the fact that he was Puerto Rican like them, they eyed him as a stranger to their turf. Felix did a fast shuffle, bobbing and weaving, while letting loose a <u>torrent</u> of blows that would demolish whatever got in its way. It seemed to impress the brothers, who went about their own business.

Finding no takers, Felix decided to split to his aunt's. Walking the streets had not relaxed him; neither had the fight flick. All it had done was to stir him up. He let himself quietly into his Aunt Lucy's apartment and went straight to bed, falling into a fitful sleep with sounds of the gong for Round One.

Antonio was passing some heavy time on his rooftop. How would the fight tomorrow affect his relationship with Felix? After all, fighting was like any other profession. Friendship had nothing to do with it. A gnawing doubt crept in. He cut negative thinking real quick by doing some speedy fancy dance steps, bobbing and weaving like mercury. The night air was blurred with perpetual motions of left hooks and right

crosses. Felix, his amigo brother, was not going to be Felix at all in the ring. Just an opponent with another face. Antonio went to sleep, hearing the opening bell for the first round. Like his friend in the South Bronx, he prayed for victory via a quick clean knockout in the first round.

Large posters plastered all over the walls of local shops announced the fight between Antonio Cruz and Felix Vargas as the main bout.

The fight had created great interest in the neighborhood. Antonio and Felix were well liked and respected. Each had his own loyal following. Betting fever was high and ranged from a bottle of Coke to cold hard cash on the line.

Antonio's fans bet with unbridled faith in his boxing skills. On the other side, Felix's admirers bet on his dynamite-packed fists.

Felix had returned to his apartment early in the morning of August 7th and stayed there, hoping to avoid seeing Antonio. He turned the radio on to salsa[8] music sounds and then tried to read while waiting for word from his manager.

The fight was scheduled to take place in Tompkins Square Park. It had been decided that the gymnasium of the Boys' Club was not large enough to hold all the people who were sure to attend. In Tompkins Square Park, everyone who wanted could view the fight, whether from ringside or window fire escapes or tenement rooftops.

The morning of the fight Tompkins Square was a beehive of activity with

---

8. **salsa** (säl′sə) *n.* used as *adj.*: Latin American dance music, usually played at fast tempos.

Vocabulary
torrent (tôr′ənt) *n.*: flood or rush.

numerous workers setting up the ring, the seats, and the guest speakers' stand. The scheduled bouts began shortly after noon and the park had begun filling up even earlier.

The local junior high school across from Tompkins Square Park served as the dressing room for all the fighters. Each was given a separate classroom with desk tops, covered with mats, serving as resting tables. Antonio thought he caught a glimpse of Felix waving to him from a room at the far end of the corridor. He waved back just in case it had been him.

The fighters changed from their street clothes into fighting gear. Antonio wore white trunks, black socks, and black shoes. Felix wore sky-blue trunks, red socks, and white boxing shoes. They had dressing gowns to match their fighting trunks with their names neatly stitched on the back.

The loudspeakers blared into the open windows of the school. There were speeches by dignitaries, community leaders, and great boxers of yesteryear. Some were well prepared; some improvised on the spot. They all carried the same message of great pleasure and honor at being part of such a historic event. This great day was in the tradition of champions emerging from the streets of the Lower East Side.

Interwoven with the speeches were the sounds of the other boxing events. After the sixth bout, Felix was much relieved when his trainer, Charlie, said, "Time change. Quick knockout. This is it. We're on."

Waiting time was over. Felix was escorted from the classroom by a dozen fans in white T-shirts with the word "Felix" across their fronts.

Antonio was escorted down a different stairwell and guided through a roped-off path.

As the two climbed into the ring, the crowd exploded with a roar. Antonio and Felix both bowed gracefully and then raised their arms in acknowledgment.

Antonio tried to be cool, but even as the roar was in its first birth, he turned slowly to meet Felix's eyes looking directly into his. Felix nodded his head and Antonio responded. And both as one, just as quickly, turned away to face his own corner.

Bong—bong—bong. The roar turned to stillness.

"Ladies and Gentlemen, Señores y Señoras."

The announcer spoke slowly, pleased at his bilingual efforts.

"Now the moment we have all been waiting for—the main event between two fine young Puerto Rican fighters, products of our Lower East Side."

"Loisaida,"[9] called out a member of the audience.

"In this corner, weighing 134 pounds, Felix Vargas. And in this corner, weighing 133 pounds, Antonio Cruz. The winner will represent the Boys' Club in the tournament of champions, the Golden Gloves. There will be no draw. May the best man win."

The cheering of the crowd shook the window panes of the old buildings surrounding Tompkins Square Park. At the center of the ring, the referee was giving instructions to the youngsters.

"Keep your punches up. No low blows. No punching on the back of the head. Keep your heads up. Understand? Let's have a clean fight. Now shake hands and come out fighting."

---

9. **Loisaida** (lŏi·sī′dä) *n.:* Puerto Rican English dialect for "Lower East Side."

Both youngsters touched gloves and nodded. They turned and danced quickly to their corners. Their head towels and dressing gowns were lifted neatly from their shoulders by their trainers' nimble fingers. Antonio crossed himself. Felix did the same.

BONG! BONG! ROUND ONE. Felix and Antonio turned and faced each other squarely in a fighting pose. Felix wasted no time. He came in fast, head low, half-hunched toward his right shoulder, and lashed out with a straight left. He missed a right cross as Antonio slipped the punch and countered with one-two-three lefts that snapped Felix's head back, sending a mild shock coursing through him. If Felix had any small doubt about their friend-ship affecting their fight, it was being neatly dispelled.

Antonio danced, a joy to behold. His left hand was like a pis-ton pumping jabs one right after an-other with seeming ease. Felix bobbed and weaved and never stopped boring in. He knew that at long range he was at a disad-vantage. Antonio had too much reach on him. Only by coming in close could Felix hope to achieve the dreamed-of knockout.

Antonio knew the dynamite that was stored in his amigo brother's fist. He ducked a short right and missed a left hook. Felix trapped him against the ropes just long enough to pour some punishing rights and lefts to Antonio's hard midsection. Antonio slipped away from Felix, crashing two lefts to his head, which set Felix's right ear to ringing.

Bong! Both amigos froze a punch well on its way, sending up a roar of approval for good sportsmanship.

Felix walked briskly back to his corner. His right ear had not stopped ringing. Antonio gracefully danced his way toward his stool none the worse, except for glowing glove burns showing angry red against the whiteness of his midribs.

"Watch that right, Tony." His trainer talked into his ear. "Remember Felix always goes to the body. He'll want you to drop your hands for his overhand left or right. Got it?"

Antonio nodded, spraying water out between his teeth. He felt better as his sore midsection was being firmly rubbed.

Felix's corner was also busy.

"You gotta get in there, fella." Felix's trainer poured water over his curly Afro locks. "Get in there or he's gonna chop you up from way back."

Bong! Bong! Round Two. Felix was off his stool and rushed Antonio like a bull, sending a hard right to his head. Beads of water exploded from Antonio's long hair.

Antonio, hurt, sent back a blurring bar-rage of lefts and rights that only meant pain to Felix, who returned with a short left to the

Vocabulary
dispelled (di·speld′) v.: driven away.

head followed by a looping right to the body. Antonio countered with his own flurry, forcing Felix to give ground. But not for long.

Felix bobbed and weaved, bobbed and weaved, occasionally punching his two gloves together.

Antonio waited for the rush that was sure to come. Felix closed in and feinted with his left shoulder and threw a right instead. Lights suddenly exploded inside Felix's head as Antonio slipped the blow and hit him with a pistonlike left, catching him flush on the point of his chin.

Bedlam broke loose as Felix's legs momentarily buckled. He fought off a series of rights and lefts and came back with a strong right that taught Antonio respect.

Antonio danced in carefully. He knew Felix had the habit of playing possum when hurt, to sucker an opponent within reach of the powerful bombs he carried in each fist.

A right to the head slowed Antonio's pretty dancing. He answered with his own left at Felix's right eye that began puffing up within three seconds.

Antonio, a bit too eager, moved in too close, and Felix had him entangled into a rip-roaring, punching toe-to-toe slugfest that brought the whole Tompkins Square Park screaming to its feet.

Rights to the body. Lefts to the head. Neither fighter was giving an inch. Suddenly a short right caught Antonio squarely on the chin. His long legs turned to jelly and his arms flailed out desperately. Felix, grunting like a bull, threw wild punches from every direction. Antonio, groggy, bobbed and weaved, evading most of the blows. Suddenly his head cleared. His left flashed out hard and straight, catching Felix on the bridge of his nose.

Felix lashed back with a haymaker, right off the ghetto streets. At the same instant, his eye caught another left hook from Antonio. Felix swung out, trying to clear the pain. Only the frenzied screaming of those along ringside let him know that he had dropped Antonio. Fighting off the growing haze, Antonio struggled to his feet, got up, ducked, and threw a smashing right that dropped Felix flat on his back.

Felix got up as fast as he could in his own corner, groggy but still game. He didn't even hear the count. In a fog, he heard the roaring of the crowd, who seemed to have gone insane. His head cleared to hear the bell sound at the end of the round. He was glad. His trainer sat him down on the stool.

In his corner, Antonio was doing what all fighters do when they are hurt. They sit and smile at everyone.

The referee signaled the ring doctor to check the fighters out. He did so and then gave his OK. The cold-water sponges brought clarity to both amigo brothers. They were rubbed until their circulation ran free.

Bong! Round Three—the final round. Up to now it had been tic-tac-toe, pretty much even. But everyone knew there could be no draw and that this round would decide the winner.

This time, to Felix's surprise, it was Antonio who came out fast, charging across the ring. Felix braced himself but couldn't ward off the barrage of punches. Antonio drove Felix hard against the ropes.

Vocabulary
frenzied (fren′zēd) *adj.:* wild.

The crowd ate it up. Thus far the two had fought with mucho corazón.[10] Felix tapped his gloves and commenced his attack anew. Antonio, throwing boxer's caution to the winds, jumped in to meet him.

Both pounded away. Neither gave an inch and neither fell to the canvas. Felix's left eye was tightly closed. Claret-red blood poured from Antonio's nose. They fought toe-to-toe.

The sounds of their blows were loud in contrast to the silence of a crowd gone completely mute. The referee was stunned by their savagery.

Bong! Bong! Bong! The bell sounded over and over again. Felix and Antonio were past hearing. Their blows continued to pound on each other like hailstones.

Finally the referee and the two trainers

---

10. **mucho corazón** (mōō′chô kô′rä·sôn′): Spanish for "a lot of heart."

pried Felix and Antonio apart. Cold water was poured over them to bring them back to their senses.

They looked around and then rushed toward each other. A cry of alarm surged through Tompkins Square Park. Was this a fight to the death instead of a boxing match?

The fear soon gave way to wave upon wave of cheering as the two amigos embraced.

No matter what the decision, they knew they would always be champions to each other.

BONG! BONG! BONG! "Ladies and Gentlemen. Señores and Señoras. The winner and representative to the Golden Gloves Tournament of Champions is . . ."

The announcer turned to point to the winner and found himself alone. Arm in arm the champions had already left the ring.

MEET THE WRITER

Piri Thomas

A Survivor from the Mean Streets

Like Antonio and Felix in "Amigo Brothers," **Piri Thomas** (1928–   ) grew up in a rough neighborhood in New York City. Unfortunately, he wasn't as lucky as Antonio and Felix—he didn't have a sport like boxing to help him escape the lures of drugs and crime. As a result, Thomas spent time in prison. While in prison, Thomas discovered he could write, and after his release he published an autobiography called *Down These Mean Streets* (1967). Thomas has worked for many years to help drug addicts give up their addictions and start new lives.

Literary Response and Analysis

Reading Check

1. Fill out a graphic to identify the structure of this short story. (You might want to add more events.)

Climax

Event —

Resolution

Event —

Event —

Complications

Event —

Characters:

Their problem:

Interpretations

2. Why do both boys wish for an early knockout? What does this wish show about them and their feelings for each other?

3. The last sentence refers to both boys as "champions." In what sense are they both champions?

4. Which do you think is more important to the story: the **external conflict**—the fight itself—or the **internal conflict**—the feelings the boys struggled with before and during the fight? Why?

5. Would *you* be able to walk away from a contest like this fight without finding out if you had won? Why or why not?

Reading Standard 3.1 Articulate the expressed purposes and characteristics of different forms of prose (for example, short story).

6. Look back at your "Rules for Competing Against a Friend" from the Quickwrite on page 308. How many of them did Antonio and Felix follow? If you had been in their situation, would you have acted differently? Explain.

Evaluation

7. Did you find this story, particularly its ending, true to life? Do you think two good friends can fight each other and stay friends? Give reasons for your opinion.

Writing

Side by Side

In a short essay, **compare** and **contrast** the personalities of Felix and Antonio. Start by reviewing the Venn diagram of the boys' similarities and differences that you made after you read the story. In your essay you might want to talk first about their similarities and then about their differences. End by telling which character you like better and why?

BONUS QUESTION

Who won the fight?

Vocabulary Development

Clarifying Word Meanings: Sports Reporting

PRACTICE

1. You're writing a news article about tryouts for the Olympic Games. Write sentences using the words *bouts*, *frenzied,* and *torrent*.

2. You're a retired tennis player. Write sentences for your auto-biography using the words *pensively* and *dispelled*.

3. You're a sportscaster describing the crowd at a hockey game. Write a description using the words *torrent* and *frenzied.*

Word Bank

bouts
pensively
torrent
dispelled
frenzied

Grammar Link MINI-LESSON

Punctuate Dialogue Correctly— And Punch Up Your Writing

Dialogue, or conversation, puts a lot of punch into a story. When you include what characters say, your story comes to life. It's important to get the punctuation right when you write dialogue. Just follow these rules:

- Put quotation marks around direct quotations of words spoken aloud:

  Antonio helped. "It's about our fight, right?"

- Begin a quotation with a capital letter:

  After a mile or so, Felix puffed and said, "Let's stop a while, bro. I think we both got something to say to each other."

- Use a comma, a question mark, or an exclamation point (never a period) to set a quotation off from the rest of the sentence:

  "Ready for some more running?" Tony asked lamely. "Loisaida," called out a member of the audience.

PRACTICE

Add commas and quotation marks to set off the dialogue in these passages.

1. Felix and Antonio decided they'd each fight to win. Tony said No pulling punches. We go all the way.

2. A woman in the crowd said to her friend with alarm What's going on? It looks as if they're trying to kill each other!

3. Let's have a clean fight said the referee. No low blows. No punching on the back of the head. Got it?

For more help, see Quotation Marks in the *Holt Handbook*, pages 322–329.

Right Hook—Left Hook: The Boxing Controversy

Text Structure: Compare-and-Contrast Organizational Patterns

Writers who want to present two sides of an issue often use a compare-and-contrast pattern to organize their material. It's a good way to show how two sides might have similar views on some points—**comparing**—and different views on others—**contrasting.**

When writers compare and contrast, they generally arrange their ideas according to one of two organizational patterns: the **point-by-point pattern** or the **block pattern.**

A writer using the point-by-point pattern moves back and forth between the subjects being compared, discussing one feature of each subject at a time.

A writer using the block pattern covers all the points of comparison for the first subject, then all the points of comparison for the second subject, and so on.

"Right Hook—Left Hook: The Boxing Controversy" presents two contrasting views about the sport of boxing. The writer uses the block method to structure her essay. First, she discusses one view, supported by the American Medical Association. Then she discusses the opposing view.

Point-by-Point Method

Feature 1	Subject 1
	Subject 2
Feature 2	Subject 1
	Subject 2

Block Method

Subject 1	Feature 1
	Feature 2
Subject 2	Feature 1
	Feature 2

Grade 6 Review Reading Standard 2.2
Analyze text that uses the compare-and-contrast organizational pattern.

Right Hook—Left Hook

THE BOXING CONTROVERSY

A four-year-old gazes at the television screen and laughs as a pig hits a duck over the head with an ironing board. The duck springs back to life, running around in circles with stars spinning around his head. Does this scene sound familiar?

Many doctors believe that as a society we close our eyes to the terrible injuries caused by a tremendous blow to the head. Doctors have expressed deep concern about boxing injuries such as those received by the former heavyweight champion Muhammad Ali. Ali suffers from Parkinson's disease, an illness probably caused by the hits he took in the ring. The symptoms of Parkinson's disease range from slurred speech to difficulty walking. According to doctors and researchers, a blow severe enough to render a person unconscious may result in tearing of nerve fibers and hemorrhaging. In 1984, the American Medical Association came out in support of a complete ban on boxing.

However, the sport of boxing remains popular. Supporters believe that training young people to box instills self-control. They also point out the benefits of fighting according to a set of rules. They believe that boxing provides opportunities for individuals who might otherwise have no chance to achieve financial security. Some doctors disagree with the American Medical Association's position and believe boxing produces few injuries because all major muscle groups are used.

The debate continues, with both sides of the issue verbally slugging it out to try to come to a resolution.

—Joan Burditt

Reading Informational Materials

Reading Check

On page 320 is a chart showing the block method of organization. Copy the chart, and use it to show the organization of this essay. First, list the views supported by the American Medical Association. Then, list the opposing views.

TestPractice

Right Hook—Left Hook

1. When the writer says "we close our eyes" to the devastating effects of head injuries, she means that —
   A head injuries cause blindness
   B people blink when struck on the head
   C people choose not to take the effects of head injuries seriously
   D people take head injuries too seriously

2. According to the article, the former heavyweight champion Muhammad Ali suffers from —
   F Parkinson's disease
   G Alzheimer's disease
   H migraine headache pain
   J Lou Gehrig's disease

3. Researchers say that a knockout blow to the head may result in —
   A an immediate winner of the fight
   B a penalty
   C advances in boxing equipment
   D damage to nerve fibers

4. Even though the dangers of boxing are well-known, the sport has not been banned mainly because —
   F it remains popular
   G few fighters are seriously injured
   H the American Medical Association is wrong
   J researchers need to find out more

5. The last sentence of the article implies that the issue is —
   A humorous
   B unimportant
   C controversial
   D settled

Grade 6 Review Reading Standard 2.2
Analyze text that uses the compare-and-contrast organizational pattern.

Barrio Boy

Literary Focus

Autobiography and Biography: Who's Telling?

An **autobiography** is the story of a person's life written by that very person. A **biography** is the story of a person's life told by *another* person. In his autobiography, *Barrio Boy,* Ernesto Galarza tells what it was like to immigrate to Sacramento, California, from a small village in Mexico.

Reading Skills

Distinguishing Fact from Opinion

When you read an autobiography, it's important to be able to tell facts from opinions. A **fact** is a statement that can be proved true. *Sacramento is a city in California* is a fact. An **opinion,** a personal feeling or belief, can't be proved true or false. In autobiographies, like *Barrio Boy,* writers share their feelings and opinions, but they also present facts.

Don't be fooled: People may state an opinion as if it were a fact. If you're in doubt, ask yourself, "Can this statement be proved, or is it someone's personal feeling or belief?"

Make the Connection

Quickwrite ✏️

Describe what you would do if you lived in a place where you didn't speak the language well. If you are in this situation now, describe what you are doing to learn the language.

Background

Ernesto Galarza was born in 1905 in Jalcocotán, a village in western Mexico. In 1910, when the Mexican Revolution threatened their peaceful mountain home, Ernesto, his mother, and two uncles left their village for Mazatlán, Mexico. Eventually they moved to Sacramento, California, and lived in what Galarza calls a "rented corner of the city"—the *barrio,* or Spanish-speaking neighborhood.

In this part of his life story, Ernesto starts school in America.

Vocabulary Development

Here are some words to learn as you read *Barrio Boy:*

reassuring (rē'ə·shoor'iŋ) v. used as *adj.:* comforting. *Ernesto's teachers were kind and reassuring.*

contraption (kən·trap'shən) *n.:* strange machine or gadget. *He was amazed by a contraption that closed the door automatically.*

assured (ə·shoord') v.: promised confidently. *Ernesto's teachers assured him he would enjoy the new school.*

formidable (fôr'mə·də·bəl) *adj.:* awe-inspiring; impressive. *The principal's appearance was formidable.*

Reading Standard 3.1
Articulate the expressed purposes and characteristics of different forms of prose.

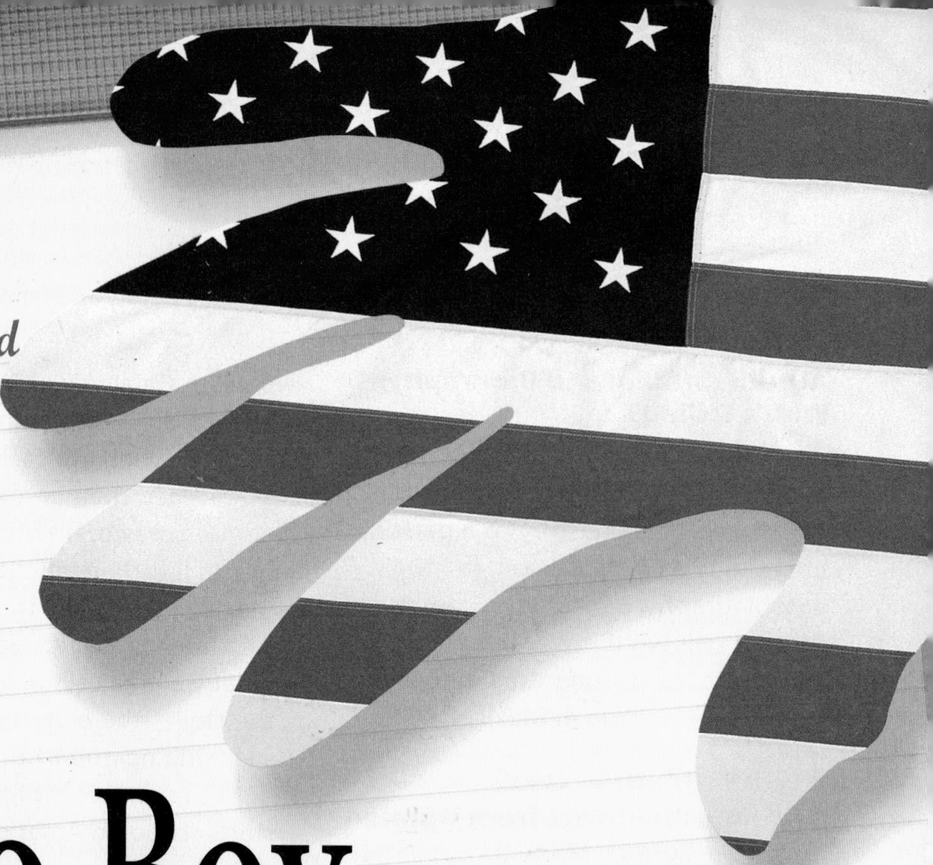

At Lincoln, making us into Americans did not mean scrubbing away what made us originally foreign.

from

Barrio Boy

Ernesto Galarza

The two of us [Ernesto and his mother] walked south on Fifth Street one morning to the corner of Q Street and turned right. Half of the block was occupied by the Lincoln School. It was a three-story wooden building, with two wings that gave it the shape of a double **T** connected by a central hall. It was a new building, painted yellow, with a shingled roof that was not like the red tile of the school in Mazatlán. I noticed other differences, none of them very reassuring.

We walked up the wide staircase hand in hand and through the door, which closed by itself. A mechanical contraption screwed to the top shut it behind us quietly.

Up to this point the adventure of enrolling me in the school had been carefully rehearsed. Mrs. Dodson had told us how to find it and we had circled it several times on our walks. Friends in the barrio explained that the director was called a principal, and that it was a lady and not a man. They assured us that there was always a person at the school who could speak Spanish.

Exactly as we had been told, there was a sign on the door in both Spanish and English: "Principal." We crossed the hall and entered the office of Miss Nettie Hopley.

Miss Hopley was at a roll-top desk to one side, sitting in a swivel chair that moved on wheels. There was a sofa against the opposite wall, flanked by two windows and a door that opened on a small balcony. Chairs were set around a table, and framed pictures hung on the walls of a man with long white hair and another with a sad face and a black beard.

The principal half turned in the swivel chair to look at us over the pinch glasses crossed on the ridge of her nose. To do this, she had to duck her head slightly, as if she were about to step through a low doorway.

What Miss Hopley said to us we did not know, but we saw in her eyes a warm welcome, and when she took off her glasses and straightened up, she smiled whole-heartedly, like Mrs. Dodson. We were, of course, saying nothing, only catching the friendliness of her voice and the sparkle in her eyes while she said words we did not understand. She signaled us to the table. Almost tiptoeing across the office, I maneuvered myself to keep my mother between me and the gringo[1] lady. In a matter of seconds I had to decide whether she was a possible friend or a menace. We sat down.

Then Miss Hopley did a formidable thing. She stood up. Had she been standing when we entered, she would have seemed tall. But rising from her chair, she soared. And what she carried up and up with her was a buxom superstructure, firm shoulders, a straight sharp nose, full cheeks slightly molded by a curved line along the nostrils, thin lips that moved like steel springs, and a high forehead topped by hair

---

1. **gringo** (grin′gō): *n.* used as *adj.*: in Latin America, an insulting term for "foreigner"; from the Spanish *griego*, meaning "Greek."

Vocabulary

reassuring (rē′ə·shoor′iŋ) v. used as *adj.*: comforting; giving hope or confidence; from the Latin word *securus,* meaning "secure." Look for the related word *assured* on this page.

contraption (kən·trap′shən) *n.*: strange machine or gadget.

assured (ə·shoord′) *v.*: guaranteed; promised confidently.

formidable (fôr′mə·də·bəl) *adj.*: awe-inspiring; impressive.

gathered in a bun. Miss Hopley was not a giant in body, but when she mobilized it to a standing position she seemed a match for giants. I decided I liked her.

She strode to a door in the far corner of the office, opened it, and called a name. A boy of about ten years appeared in the doorway. He sat down at one end of the table. He was brown like us, a plump kid with shiny black hair combed straight back, neat, cool, and faintly obnoxious.

Miss Hopley joined us with a large book and some papers in her hand. She, too, sat down and the questions and answers began by way of our interpreter. My name was Ernesto. My mother's name was Henriqueta. My birth certificate was in San Blas. Here was my last report card from the Escuela Municipal Numero 3 para Varones[2] of Mazatlán, and so forth. Miss Hopley put things down in the book and my mother signed a card.

As long as the questions continued, Doña Henriqueta could stay and I was secure. Now that they were over, Miss Hopley saw her to the door, dismissed our interpreter, and without further ado took me by the hand and strode down the hall to Miss Ryan's first grade.

Miss Ryan took me to a seat at the front of the room, into which I shrank—the

better to survey her. She was, to skinny, somewhat runty me, of a withering height when she patrolled the class. And when I least expected it, there she was, crouching by my desk, her blond, radiant face level with mine, her voice patiently maneuvering me over the awful idiocies of the English language.

During the next few weeks Miss Ryan overcame my fears of tall, energetic teachers as she bent over my desk to help me with a word in the pre-primer. Step by step, she loosened me and my classmates from the safe anchorage of the desks for recitations at the blackboard and consultations at her desk. Frequently she burst into happy announcements to the whole class. "Ito can read a sentence," and small Japanese Ito, squint-eyed and shy, slowly read aloud while the class listened in wonder: "Come, Skipper, come. Come and run." The Korean, Portuguese, Italian, and Polish first-graders had similar moments of glory, no less shining than mine the day I conquered "butterfly," which I had been persistently pronouncing in standard Spanish as boo-ter-flee. "Children," Miss Ryan called for attention. "Ernesto has learned how to pronounce *butterfly*!" And I proved it with a perfect imitation of Miss Ryan. From that celebrated success, I was soon able to match Ito's progress as a sentence reader with "Come, butterfly, come fly with me."

Like Ito and several other first-graders who did not know English, I received private lessons from Miss Ryan in the closet, a narrow hall off the classroom with a door at each end. Next to one of these doors Miss Ryan placed a large chair for herself and a small one for me. Keeping an eye on the class through the open door, she read

---

2. **Escuela Municipal Numero 3 para Varones:** Spanish for "Municipal School Number 3 for Boys."

with me about sheep in the meadow and a frightened chicken going to see the king, coaching me out of my phonetic ruts in words like *pasture, bow-wow-wow, hay,* and *pretty,* which to my Mexican ear and eye had so many unnecessary sounds and letters. She made me watch her lips and then close my eyes as she repeated words I found hard to read. When we came to know each other better, I tried interrupting to tell Miss Ryan how we said it in Spanish. It didn't work. She only said "oh" and went on with *pasture, bow-wow-wow,* and *pretty.* It was as if in that closet we were both discovering together the secrets of the English language and grieving together over the tragedies of Bo-Peep. The main reason I was graduated with honors from the first grade was that I had fallen in love with Miss Ryan. Her radiant, no-nonsense character made us either afraid not to love her or love her so we would not be afraid, I am not sure which. It was not only that we sensed she was with it, but also that she was with us.

Like the first grade, the rest of the Lincoln School was a sampling of the lower part of town, where many races made their home. My pals in the second grade were Kazushi, whose parents spoke only Japanese; Matti, a skinny Italian boy; and Manuel, a fat Portuguese who would never get into a fight but wrestled you to the ground and just sat on you. Our assortment of nationalities included Koreans, Yugoslavs, Poles, Irish, and home-grown Americans.

Miss Hopley and her teachers never let us forget why we were at Lincoln: for those who were alien, to become good Americans; for those who were so born, to accept the rest of us. Off the school grounds we traded the same insults we heard from our elders. On the playground we were sure to be marched up to the principal's office for calling someone a wop, a chink, a dago, or a greaser. The school was not so much a melting pot as a griddle where Miss Hopley and her helpers warmed knowledge into us and roasted racial hatreds out of us.

At Lincoln, making us into Americans did not mean scrubbing away what made us originally foreign. The teachers called us as our parents did, or as close as they could pronounce our names in Spanish or Japanese. No one was ever scolded or punished for speaking in his native tongue on the playground. Matti told the class about his mother's down quilt, which she had made in Italy with the fine feathers of a thousand geese. Encarnación acted out how boys learned to fish in the Philippines. I astounded the third grade with the story of my travels on a stagecoach, which nobody

> The teachers called us as our parents did, or as close as they could pronounce our names . . .

else in the class had seen except in the museum at Sutter's Fort. After a visit to the Crocker Art Gallery and its collection of heroic paintings of the golden age of California, someone showed a silk scroll with a Chinese painting. Miss Hopley herself had a way of expressing wonder over these matters before a class, her eyes wide open until they popped slightly. It was easy for me to feel that becoming a proud American, as she said we should, did not mean feeling ashamed of being a Mexican.

Ernesto Galarza

"Anecdotes I Told My Family"

For young **Ernesto Galarza** (1905–1984), coming to the United States meant abandoning everything he had ever known—his language, his family, and his customs. He soon discovered that education was the key to making sense of his new life. Eventually he earned his doctorate from Columbia University in New York and then returned to California to teach. Although he was a beloved teacher, Galarza is best remembered for *Barrio Boy,* his bestselling 1971 account of his journey from Mexico to the United States. Galarza explains how he came to write *Barrio Boy:*

> *Barrio Boy* began as anecdotes I told my family about Jalcocotán, the mountain village in western Mexico where I was born. Among this limited public (my wife, Mae, and daughters, Karla and Eli Lu) my thumbnail sketches became bestsellers. Hearing myself tell them over and over, I began to agree with my captive audience that they were not only interesting but possibly good.
>
> Quite by accident I told one of these vignettes at a meeting of scholars and other boring people. It was recorded on tape, printed in a magazine, and circulated among schools and libraries here and there. I received letters asking for reprints, and occasionally a tempting suggestion that I write more of the same, perhaps enough to make a book.
>
> Adding up the three listeners in my family and the three correspondents made a public of six. I didn't need more persuasion than this to link the anecdotes into a story.

For Independent Reading

The selection you've read is from one chapter of Galarza's *Barrio Boy.* If you liked the selection, you'll enjoy reading the entire book.

Literary Response and Analysis

Reading Check

1. How did Ernesto feel about Miss Hopley and Miss Ryan?

2. How was the makeup of Ernesto's class a lot like that of his neighborhood?

3. How did Miss Ryan encourage her students to learn English?

4. According to Miss Hopley and the teachers at Lincoln School, what were the children to remember about *why* they were at school?

5. How did Lincoln School honor its students' original languages and customs?

Interpretations

6. What did you **predict** would happen to Ernesto, and why? (Were you correct?) How else could his story have ended?

7. In many ways this story is a tribute to Ernesto's teachers. What do you think Galarza means when he says that Miss Ryan was not only "with it" but "with us"?

8. The **metaphor** of the melting pot comes from a 1908 play by Israel Zangwill: "America is . . . a great melting pot, where all the races of Europe are melting and reforming!" Ernesto thinks of Lincoln School not as a melting pot—which makes everyone the same—but as a warm griddle. What do you think this means? Which metaphor would you use to describe the United States, and why?

9. In *Barrio Boy,* Ernesto Galarza reveals some opinions about his life in the United States. Like other writers of **autobiography,** he also presents facts. Give one example of a **fact** and one example of an **opinion** in *Barrio Boy.*

10. Refer to your notes for the Quickwrite on page 323. What does this story reveal about the difficulties of learning a second language?

Writing

Immigrant Experience

Ernesto Galarza and many of his classmates were immigrants. What special problems do immigrants face today? What are some ways in which schools and local governments try to solve these problems? Write two paragraphs giving your responses to these questions. Cite both facts and opinions. You will have to do some research to support your answers. Be sure to tell your readers where you found your information.

Reading Standard 1.1 Identify metaphors in prose.

Reading Standard 3.1 Articulate the expressed purposes and characteristics of different forms of prose.

Vocabulary Development

Clarifying Word Meanings: Examples

Writers often help readers understand difficult words by using definitions, examples, restatements, or contrasts.

A writer who uses **examples** provides specific instances to show what a word means. Consider the following sentence:

> **People came to the meeting from such varied municipalities as Sacramento, Oakland, Bakersfield, and San Diego.**

Even if you didn't know that a municipality is a city or town, the examples in the sentence give you a clue to the meaning of the word.

Word Bank

reassuring
contraption
assured
formidable

PRACTICE

Finish the following sentences by using examples to clarify the meanings of the underlined words.

1. The most reassuring words I ever heard were _____.

2. Three contraptions that make life easier today are _____, _____, and _____.

3. I assured my friend I was loyal. I said, "_____."

4. Three formidable figures in sports are _____, _____, and _____.

Reading Standard 1.3
Clarify word meanings through the use of example.

My Brother (1942) by Oswaldo Guayasamín (Oswaldo Guayasamín Calero). Oil on wood (15⅞" × 12¾"; 40.3 cm x 32.4 cm).

The Museum of Modern Art, New York. Inter-American Fund. Photograph © 2000 The Museum of Modern Art, New York.

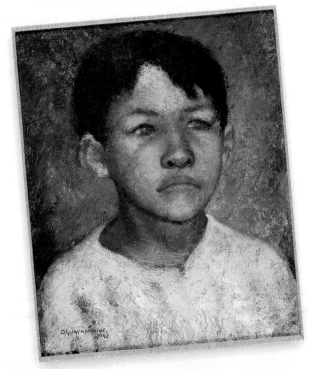

Grammar Link MINI-LESSON

Making the Most of Comparing Adjectives

The **comparative degree** of an adjective compares two people or things. The **superlative degree** compares more than two people or things.

Comparative Degree	Superlative Degree
Add the ending –er or the word *more* when you compare two items.	Add the ending –est or the word *most* when you compare more than two items.
Example: "The rest of the Lincoln School was a sampling of the <u>lower</u> part of town . . ."	Example: To the children their beloved Miss Ryan was the <u>most wonderful</u> teacher in the world.

- When comparing, don't use both *more* and –er, and don't use both *most* and –est.

  Ernesto felt ~~more~~ <u>safer</u> when his mother was present.
  Matti was the ~~most~~ <u>thinnest</u> boy in the second grade.

- Don't use the superlative form when you compare only two people or things.

  prouder
  Do you think Ernesto was ~~proudest~~ of being an American or a Mexican?

  more
  Of the two boys, Ito learned ~~most~~ quickly.

PRACTICE

Act as an editor, and show how you'd correct these sentences.

1. Ernesto thought American schools were more stranger than Mexican schools.
2. Ernesto spoke Spanish and English, but his Spanish was best.
3. Was Ernesto proudest of pronouncing *butterfly* or of reading "Little Bo-Peep"?
4. Ernesto did more better in school than he had expected.
5. The most nicest teacher in the Lincoln School was Miss Ryan.
6. Miss Hopley might have been the most tallest person Ernesto had ever seen.

For more help, see Comparison of Adjectives and Adverbs in the *Holt Handbook*, pages 224–228.

Song of the Trees

Literary Focus
Novels and Short Stories

A **short story** usually has just one main plot line, one or two major characters, one important conflict, and one main theme. With a **novel**—which is a book-length work of fiction—a lot more will happen. More characters will appear, the conflicts will multiply, subplots will develop, and several themes will be operating at once. Settings may also become more numerous. A short story usually takes place within a limited time frame, but a novel can span many generations.

Occasionally a writer will find that a narrative is too long for a short story and too short for a novel. The story that results, which may run from twenty to one hundred pages, is known as a **novella.** Mildred Taylor's *Song of the Trees* was first published in a small book by itself, as a forty-eight-page novella.

Reading Skills
Making Generalizations: Putting It All Together

A **generalization** is a broad statement that tells about something in general. A statement about a story's **theme** is a kind of generalization. From specific evidence in the story, you make a broad, universal statement about life. To make a statement about the theme of *Song of the Trees,* you have to

- think about the main events and conflicts in the story

- decide what the characters have discovered by the end of the story
- think about how the story relates to your experiences

Make the Connection
Quickwrite
Agree? Disagree?
disagree 0 1 2 3 4 agree

1. People gain self-respect by standing up for their beliefs.
2. Given the chance, most people will never take advantage of another person.
3. Some people are treated unfairly because of the color of their skin.
4. Nobody owns the earth.

Rate each of those statements with a number from 0 to 4. (Zero means that you completely disagree; 4 means you completely agree.) Then, discuss these issues with the rest of the class.

Background
The depression referred to in this story is the Great Depression, the severe economic decline in the United States that lasted from 1929 to 1942. During the Depression many banks and businesses closed. People lost their jobs, their savings, and even their homes. Many people had barely enough food to eat. This was also a time when the segregation of African Americans was still a sad reality in parts of the United States.

Reading Standard 3.1
Articulate the expressed purposes and characteristics of different forms of prose (for example, short story, novel, novella).

I stared at the trees, aware of an eerie silence descending . . .

SONG
OF THE
TREES

Mildred D. Taylor

Vocabulary Development

Study the following words from *Song of the Trees:*

finicky (fin′ik·ē) *adj.:* fussy and extremely careful. *Little Man was finicky when it came to his appearance.*

dispute (di·spyo͞ot′) *n.:* argument. *Mama settled the dispute between the two brothers.*

ambled (am′bəld) *v.:* walked without hurrying. *They ambled through the forest, listening to the song of the trees.*

delved (delvd) *v.:* searched. *Cassie delved into the bowl of blackberries and grabbed the biggest one.*

curtly (kurt′lē) *adv.:* rudely, using few words. *The man spoke curtly to Mama, showing his lack of respect.*

skirting (skurt′iŋ) *v.:* avoiding. *Instead of speaking to the point, Mr. Andersen was skirting the issue.*

elude (ē·lo͞od′) *v.:* escape cleverly. *The children hoped to elude punishment for their bold behavior.*

incredulously (in·krej′o͞o·ləs·lē) *adv.:* unbelievingly. *Mr. Andersen stared incredulously at Papa when Papa ignored him.*

ashen (ash′ən) *adj.:* pale. *He turned ashen with fright.*

sentries (sen′trēz) *n.:* guards. *The sentries stood guard over the quiet landscape.*

"Cassie. Cassie, child, wake up now," Big Ma called gently as the new sun peeked over the horizon.

I looked sleepily at my grandmother and closed my eyes again.

"Cassie! Get up, girl!" This time the voice was not so gentle.

I jumped out of the deep, feathery bed as Big Ma climbed from the other side. The room was still dark, and I stubbed my toe while stumbling sleepily about looking for my clothes.

"Shoot! Darn ole chair," I fussed, rubbing my injured foot.

"Hush, Cassie, and open them curtains if you can't see," Big Ma said. "Prop that window open, too, and let some of that fresh morning air in here."

I opened the window and looked outside. The earth was draped in a cloak of gray mist as the sun chased the night away. The cotton stalks, which in another hour would glisten greenly toward the sun, were gray. The ripening corn, wrapped in jackets of emerald and gold, was gray. Even the rich brown Mississippi earth was gray.

Only the trees of the forest were not gray. They stood dark, almost black, across the dusty road, still holding the night. A soft breeze stirred, and their voices whispered down to me in a song of morning greeting.

"Cassie, girl, I said open that window, not stand there gazing out all morning. Now, get moving before I take something to you," Big Ma threatened.

I dashed to my clothes. Before Big Ma had unwoven her long braid of gray hair, my pants and shirt were on and I was hurrying into the kitchen.

A small kerosene lamp was burning in a corner as I entered. Its light reflected on seven-year-old Christopher-John, short, pudgy, and a year younger than me, sitting sleepily upon a side bench drinking a large glass of clabber milk.[1] Mama's back was to me. She was dipping flour from a near-empty canister, while my older brother, Stacey, built a fire in the huge iron-bellied stove.

"I don't know what I'm going to do with you, Christopher-John," Mama scolded. "Getting up in the middle of the night and eating all that cornbread. Didn't you have enough to eat before you went to bed?"

"Yes'm," Christopher-John murmured.

"Lord knows I don't want any of my babies going hungry, but times are hard, honey. Don't you know folks all around here in Mississippi are struggling? Children crying cause they got no food to eat, and their daddies crying cause they can't get jobs so they can feed their babies? And you getting up in the middle of the night, stuffing yourself with cornbread!"

Her voice softened as she looked at the sleepy little boy. "Baby, we're in a depression.

---

1. **clabber milk:** thickly curdled sour milk.

Why do you think Papa's way down in Louisiana laying tracks on the railroad? So his children can eat—but only when they're hungry. You understand?"

"Yes'm," Christopher-John murmured again, as his eyes slid blissfully shut.

"Morning, Mama," I chimed.

"Morning, baby," Mama said. "You wash up yet?"

"No'm."

"Then go wash up and call Little Man again. Tell him he's not dressing to meet President Roosevelt[2] this morning. Hurry up, now, cause I want you to set the table."

Little Man, a very small six-year-old and a most finicky dresser, was brushing his hair when I entered the room he shared with Stacey and Christopher-John. His blue pants were faded, but except for a small grass stain on one knee, they were clean. Outside of his Sunday pants, these were the only pants he had, and he was always careful to keep them in the best condition possible. But one look at him and I knew that he was far from pleased with their condition this morning. He frowned down at the spot for a moment, then continued brushing.

"Man, hurry up and get dressed," I called. "Mama said you ain't dressing to meet the president."

"See there," he said, pointing at the stain. "You did that."

"I did no such thing. You fell all by yourself."

"You tripped me!"

"Didn't!"

"Did, too!"

"Hey, cut it out, you two!" ordered Stacey, entering the room. "You fought over that stupid stain yesterday. Now get moving, both of you. We gotta go pick blackberries before the sun gets too high. Little Man, you go gather the eggs while Christopher-John and me milk the cows."

Little Man and I decided to settle our dispute later when Stacey wasn't around. With Papa away, eleven-year-old Stacey thought of himself as the man of the house, and Mama had instructed Little Man, Christopher-John, and me to mind him. So, like it or not, we humored him. Besides, he was bigger than we were.

I ran to the back porch to wash. When I returned to the kitchen, Mama was talking to Big Ma.

"We got about enough flour for two more meals," Mama said, cutting the biscuit dough. "Our salt and sugar are practically down to nothing and—" She stopped when she saw me. "Cassie, baby, go gather the eggs for Mama."

"Little Man's gathering the eggs."

"Then go help him."

"But I ain't set the table yet."

"Set it when you come back."

I knew that I was not wanted in the kitchen. I looked suspiciously at my mother and grandmother, then went to the back porch to get a basket.

Big Ma's voice drifted through the open window. "Mary, you oughta write David and tell him somebody done opened his letter and stole that ten dollars he sent," she said.

"No, Mama. David's got enough on his

Vocabulary
finicky (fin′ik·ē) adj.: fussy and extremely careful.
dispute (di·spyo͞ot′) n.: argument.

mind. Besides, there's enough garden foods so we won't go hungry."

"But what 'bout your medicine? You're all out of it and the doctor told you good to—"

"Shhhh!" Mama stared at the window. "Cassie, I thought I told you to go gather those eggs!"

"I had to get a basket, Mama!" I hurried off the porch and ran to the barn.

After breakfast, when the sun was streaking red across the sky, my brothers and I ambled into the coolness of the forest, leading our three cows and their calves down the narrow cow path to the pond. The morning was already muggy, but the trees closed out the heat as their leaves waved restlessly, high above our heads.

"Good morning, Mr. Trees," I shouted. They answered me with a soft, swooshing sound. "Hear 'em, Stacey? Hear 'em singing?"

"Ah, cut that out, Cassie. Them trees ain't singing. How many times I gotta tell you that's just the wind?" He stopped at a sweet alligator gum, pulled out his knife, and scraped off a glob of gum that had seeped through its cracked bark. He handed me half.

As I stuffed the gooey wad into my mouth, I patted the tree and whispered, "Thank you, Mr. Gum Tree."

Stacey frowned at me, then looked back at Christopher-John and Little Man walking far behind us, munching on their breakfast biscuits.

"Man! Christopher-John! Come on, now," he yelled. "If we finish the berry picking early, we can go wading before we go back."

Christopher-John and Little Man ran to catch up with us. Then, resuming their leisurely pace, they soon fell behind again.

A large gray squirrel scurried across our path and up a walnut tree. I watched until it was settled amidst the tree's featherlike leaves; then, poking one of the calves, I said, "Stacey, is Mama sick?"

"Sick? Why you say that?"

"Cause I heard Big Ma asking her 'bout some medicine she's supposed to have."

Stacey stopped, a worried look on his face. "If she's sick, she ain't bad sick," he decided. "If she was bad sick, she'd been in bed."

We left the cows at the pond and, taking our berry baskets, delved deeper into the forest looking for the wild blackberry bushes.

"I see one!" I shouted.

"Where?" cried Christopher-John, eager for the sweet berries.

"Over there! Last one to it's a rotten egg!" I yelled, and off I ran.

Stacey and Little Man followed at my heels. But Christopher-John puffed far behind. "Hey, wait for me," he cried.

"Let's hide from Christopher-John," Stacey suggested.

The three of us ran in different directions. I plunged behind a giant old pine and hugged its warm trunk as I waited for Christopher-John.

Christopher-John puffed to a stop, then, looking all around, called, "Hey, Stacey! Cassie! Hey, Man! Y'all cut that out!"

I giggled and Christopher-John heard me.

"I see you, Cassie!" he shouted, starting toward me as fast as his chubby legs would carry him. "You're it!"

Vocabulary
ambled (am′bəld) *v.:* walked easily, without hurrying.
delved (delvd) *v.:* searched.

"Not 'til you tag me," I laughed. As I waited for him to get closer, I glanced up into the boughs of my wintry-smelling hiding tree, expecting a song of laughter. But the old pine only tapped me gently with one of its long, low branches. I turned from the tree and dashed away.

"You can't, you can't, you can't catch me," I taunted, dodging from one beloved tree to the next. Around shaggy-bark hickories and sharp-needled pines, past blue-gray beeches and sturdy black walnuts I sailed, while my laughter resounded through the ancient forest, filling every chink. Overhead, the boughs of the giant trees hovered protectively, but they did not join in my laughter.

Deeper into the forest I plunged.

Christopher-John, unable to keep up, plopped on the ground in a pant. Little Man and Stacey, emerging from their hiding places, ran up to him.

"Ain't you caught her yet?" Little Man demanded, more than a little annoyed.

"He can't catch the champ," I boasted, stopping to rest against a hickory tree. I slid my back down the tree's shaggy trunk and looked up at its long branches, heavy with sweet nuts and slender green leaves, perfectly

still. I looked around at the leaves of the other trees. They were still also. I stared at the trees, aware of an eerie silence descending over the forest.

Stacey walked toward me. "What's the matter with you, Cassie?" he asked.

"The trees, Stacey," I said softly, "they ain't singing no more."

"Is that all?" He looked up at the sky. "Come on, y'all. It's getting late. We'd better go pick them berries." He turned and walked on.

"But, Stacey, listen. Little Man, Christopher-John, listen."

The forest echoed an uneasy silence.

"The wind just stopped blowing, that's all," said Stacey. "Now stop fooling around and come on."

I jumped up to follow Stacey, then cried, "Stacey, look!" On a black oak a few yards away was a huge white *X*. "How did that get there?" I exclaimed, running to the tree.

"There's another one!" Little Man screamed.

"I see one too!" shouted Christopher-John.

Stacey said nothing as Christopher-John, Little Man, and I ran wildly through the forest counting the ghostlike marks.

"Stacey, they're on practically all of them," I said when he called us back.

"Why?"

Stacey studied the trees, then suddenly pushed us down.

"My clothes!" Little Man wailed indignantly.

"Hush, Man, and stay down," Stacey warned. "Somebody's coming."

Two white men emerged. We looked at each other. We knew to be silent.

"You mark them all down here?" one of the men asked.

"Not the younger ones, Mr. Andersen."

"We might need them, too," said Mr. Andersen, counting the *X*'s. "But don't worry 'bout marking them now, Tom. We'll get them later. Also them trees up past the pond toward the house."

"The old woman agree to you cutting these trees?"

"I ain't been down there yet," Mr. Andersen said.

"Mr. Andersen . . ." Tom hesitated a moment, looked up at the silent trees, then back at Mr. Andersen. "Maybe you should go easy with them," he cautioned. "You know that David can be as mean as an ole jackass when he wanna be."

"He's talking about Papa," I whispered.

"Shhhh!" Stacey hissed.

Mr. Andersen looked uneasy. "What's that gotta do with anything?"

"Well, he just don't take much to any dealings with white folks." Again, Tom looked up at the trees. "He ain't afraid like some."

Mr. Andersen laughed weakly. "Don't

worry 'bout that, Tom. The land belongs to his mama. He don't have no say in it. Besides, I guess I oughta know how to handle David Logan. After all, there are ways. . . .

"Now, you get on back to my place and get some boys and start chopping down these trees," Mr. Andersen said. "I'll go talk to the old woman." He looked up at the sky. "We can almost get a full day's work in if we hurry."

Mr. Andersen turned to walk away, but Tom stopped him. "Mr. Andersen, you really gonna chop all the trees?"

"If I need to. These folks ain't got no call for them. I do. I got me a good contract for these trees and I aim to fulfill it."

Tom watched Mr. Andersen walk away; then, looking sorrowfully up at the trees, he shook his head and disappeared into the depths of the forest.

"What we gonna do, Stacey?" I asked anxiously. "They can't just cut down our trees, can they?"

"I don't know. Papa's gone. . . ." Stacey muttered to himself, trying to decide what we should do next.

"Boy, if Papa was here, them ole white men wouldn't be messing with our trees," Little Man declared.

"Yeah!" Christopher-John agreed. "Just let Papa get hold of 'em and he gonna turn 'em every which way but loose."

"Christopher-John, Man," Stacey said finally, "go get the cows and take them home."

"But we just brought them down here," Little Man protested.

"And we gotta pick the berries for dinner," said Christopher-John mournfully.

"No time for that now. Hurry up. And stay clear of them white men. Cassie, you come with me."

We ran, brown legs and feet flying high through the still forest.

By the time Stacey and I arrived at the house, Mr. Andersen's car was already parked in the dusty drive. Mr. Andersen himself was seated comfortably in Papa's rocker on the front porch. Big Ma was seated too, but Mama was standing.

Stacey and I eased quietly to the side of the porch, unnoticed.

"Sixty-five dollars. That's an awful lot of money in these hard times, Aunt Caroline," Mr. Andersen was saying to Big Ma.

I could see Mama's thin face harden.

"You know," Mr. Andersen said, rocking familiarly in Papa's chair, "that's more than David can send home in two months."

"We do quite well on what David sends home," Mama said coldly.

Mr. Andersen stopped rocking. "I suggest you encourage Aunt Caroline to sell them trees, Mary. You know, David might not always be able to work so good. He could possibly have . . . an accident."

Big Ma's soft brown eyes clouded over with fear as she looked first at Mr. Andersen, then at Mama. But Mama clenched her fists and said, "In Mississippi, black men do not have accidents."

"Hush, child, hush," Big Ma said hurriedly. "How many trees for the sixty-five dollars, Mr. Andersen?"

"Enough 'til I figure I got my sixty-five dollars' worth."

"And how many would that be?" Mama persisted.

Mr. Andersen looked haughtily at Mama. "I said I'd be the judge of that, Mary."

"I think not," Mama said.

Mr. Andersen stared at Mama. And Mama stared back at him. I knew Mr. Andersen didn't like that, but Mama did it anyway. Mr. Andersen soon grew uneasy under that piercing gaze, and when his eyes swiftly shifted from Mama to Big Ma, his face was beet red.

"Caroline," he said, his voice low and menacing, "you're the head of this family and you've got a decision to make. Now, I need them trees and I mean to have them. I've offered you a good price for them and I ain't gonna haggle over it. I know y'all can use the money. Doc Thomas tells me that Mary's not well." He hesitated a moment, then hissed venomously, "And if something should happen to David . . ."

"All right," Big Ma said, her voice trembling. "All right, Mr. Andersen."

"No, Big Ma!" I cried, leaping onto the porch. "You can't let him cut our trees!"

Mr. Andersen grasped the arms of the rocker, his knuckles chalk white. "You certainly ain't taught none of your younguns how to behave, Caroline," he said curtly.

"You children go on to the back," Mama said, shooing us away.

"No, Mama," Stacey said. "He's gonna cut them all down. Me and Cassie heard him say so in the woods."

"I won't let him cut them," I threatened. "I won't let him! The trees are my friends and ain't no mean ole white man gonna touch my trees—"

Mama's hands went roughly around my body as she carried me off to my room.

"Now, hush," she said, her dark eyes flashing wildly. "I've told you how dangerous it is . . ." She broke off in midsentence. She stared at me a moment, then hugged me tightly and went back to the porch.

Stacey joined me a few seconds later, and we sat there in the heat of the quiet room, listening miserably as the first whack of an ax echoed against the trees.

That night I was awakened by soft sounds outside my window. I reached for Big Ma, but she wasn't there. Hurrying to the window, I saw Mama and Big Ma standing in the yard in their nightclothes and Stacey, fully dressed, sitting atop Lady, our golden mare. By the time I got outside, Stacey was gone.

"Mama, where's Stacey?" I cried.

"Be quiet, Cassie. You'll wake Christopher-John and Little Man."

"But where's he going?"

"He's going to get Papa," Mama said. "Now be quiet."

"Go on, Stacey, boy," I whispered. "Ride for me, too."

As the dust billowed after him, Mama said, "I should've gone myself. He's so young."

Vocabulary

curtly (kurt′lē) *adv.:* rudely and with few words.

Big Ma put her arm around Mama. "Now, Mary, you know you couldn't've gone. Mr. Andersen would miss you if he come by and see you ain't here. You done right, now. Don't worry, that boy'll be just fine."

Three days passed, hot and windless.

Mama forbade any of us to go into the forest, so Christopher-John, Little Man, and I spent the slow, restless days hovering as close to the dusty road as we dared, listening to the foreign sounds of steel against the trees and the thunderous roar of those ancient loved ones as they crashed upon the earth. Sometimes Mama would scold us and tell us to come back to the house, but even she could not ignore the continuous pounding of the axes against the trees. Or the sight of the loaded lumber wagons rolling out of the forest. In the middle of washing or ironing or hoeing, she would look up sorrowfully and listen, then turn toward the road, searching for some sign of Papa and Stacey.

On the fourth day, before the sun had risen, bringing its cloak of miserable heat, I saw her walking alone toward the woods. I ran after her.

She did not send me back.

"Mama," I said. "How sick are you?"

Mama took my hand. "Remember when you had the flu and felt so sick?"

"Yes'm."

"And when I gave you some medicine, you got well soon afterward?"

"Yes'm."

"Well, that's how sick I am. As soon as I get my medicine, I'll be all well again. And that'll be soon, now that Papa's coming home," she said, giving my hand a gentle little squeeze.

The quiet surrounded us as we entered the forest. Mama clicked on the flashlight, and we walked silently along the cow path to the pond. There, just beyond the pond, pockets of open space loomed before us.

"Mama!"

"I know, baby, I know."

On the ground lay countless trees. Trees that had once been such strong, tall things. So strong that I could fling my arms partially around one of them and feel safe and secure. So tall and leafy green that their boughs had formed a forest temple.

And old.

So old that Indians had once built fires at their feet and had sung happy songs of happy days. So old they had hidden fleeing black men in the night and listened to their sad tales of a foreign land.

In the cold of winter, when the ground lay frozen, they had sung their frosty ballads of years gone by. Or on a muggy, sweat-drenched day, their leaves had rippled softly, lazily, like restless green fingers strumming at a guitar, echoing their epic tales.

But now they would sing no more. They lay forever silent upon the ground.

Those trees that remained standing were like defeated warriors mourning their fallen dead. But soon they, too, would fall, for the white X's had been placed on nearly every one.

"Oh, dear, dear trees," I cried as the gray light of the rising sun fell in ghostly shadows over the land. The tears rolled hot down my cheeks. Mama held me close, and when I felt her body tremble, I knew she was crying too.

When our tears eased, we turned sadly toward the house. As we emerged from the forest, we could see two small figures waiting impatiently on the other side of the road. As soon as they spied us, they hurried across to meet us.

"Mama! You and Cassie was in the forest," Little Man accused. "Big Ma told us!"

"How was it?" asked Christopher-John, rubbing the sleep from his eyes. "Was it spooky?"

"Spooky and empty," I said listlessly.

"Mama, me and Christopher-John wanna see too," Little Man declared.

"No, baby," Mama said softly as we crossed the road. "The men'll be done there soon, and I don't want y'all underfoot."

"But, Mama—" Little Man started to protest.

"When Papa comes home and the men are gone, then you can go. But until then, you stay out of there. You hear me, Little Man Logan?"

"Yes'm," Little Man reluctantly replied.

But the sun had been up only an hour when Little Man decided that he could not wait for Papa to return.

"Mama said we wasn't to go down there," Christopher-John warned.

"Cassie did," Little Man cried.

"But she was with Mama. Wasn't you, Cassie?"

"Well, I'm going too," said Little Man. "Everybody's always going someplace 'cepting me." And off he went.

Christopher-John and I ran after him. Down the narrow cow path and around the pond we chased. But neither of us was fast enough to overtake Little Man before he reached the lumbermen.

"Hey, you kids, get away from here," Mr. Andersen shouted when he saw us. "Now, y'all go on back home," he said, stopping in front of Little Man.

"We are home," I said. "You're the one who's on our land."

"Claude," Mr. Andersen said to one of the black lumbermen, "take these kids home." Then he pushed Little Man out of his way. Little Man pushed back. Mr. Andersen looked down, startled that a little black boy would do such a thing. He shoved Little Man a second time, and Little Man fell into the dirt.

Little Man looked down at his clothing covered with sawdust and dirt and wailed, "You got my clothes dirty!"

I rushed toward Mr. Andersen, my fist in a mighty hammer, shouting, "You ain't got no right to push on Little Man. Why don't you push on somebody your own size—like me, you ole—"

The man called Claude put his hand over my mouth and carried me away. Christopher-John trailed behind us, tugging on the man's shirt.

"Put her down. Hey, mister, put Cassie down."

The man carried me all the way to the pond. "Now," he said, "you and your brothers get on home before y'all get hurt. Go on, get!"

As the man walked away, I looked around. "Where's Little Man?"

Christopher-John looked around too.

"I don't know," he said. "I thought he was behind me."

Back we ran toward the lumbermen.

We found Little Man's clothing first, folded neatly by a tree. Then we saw Little Man, dragging a huge stick and headed straight for Mr. Andersen.

"Little Man, come back here," I called.

But Little Man did not stop.

Mr. Andersen stood alone, barking orders, unaware of the oncoming Little Man.

"Little Man! Oh, Little Man, don't!"

It was too late.

Little Man swung the stick as hard as he could against Mr. Andersen's leg.

Mr. Andersen let out a howl and reached to where he thought Little Man's collar was. But, of course, Little Man had no collar.

"Run, Man!" Christopher-John and I shouted. "Run!"

"Why, you little . . ." Mr. Andersen cried, grabbing at Little Man. But Little Man was too quick for him. He slid right through Mr. Andersen's legs. Tom stood nearby, his face crinkling into an amused grin.

"Hey, y'all!" Mr. Andersen yelled to the lumbermen. "Claude! Get that kid!"

But sure-footed Little Man dodged the groping hands of the lumbermen as easily as if he were skirting mud puddles. Over tree stumps, around legs, and through legs he dashed. But in the end, there were too many lumbermen for him, and he was handed over to Mr. Andersen.

For the second time, Christopher-John and I went to Little Man's rescue.

"Put him down!" we ordered, charging the lumbermen.

I was captured much too quickly, though not before I had landed several stinging blows. But Christopher-John, furious at seeing Little Man handled so roughly by Mr. Andersen, managed to elude the clutches of the lumbermen until he was fully upon Mr. Andersen. Then, with his mightiest thrust, he kicked Mr. Andersen solidly in the shins, not once, but twice, before the lumbermen pulled him away.

Mr. Andersen was fuming. He slowly took off his wide leather belt. Christopher-John, Little Man, and I looked woefully at the belt, then at each other. Little Man and Christopher-John fought to escape, but I closed my eyes and awaited the whining of the heavy belt and its painful bite against my skin.

Vocabulary

skirting (skʉrt′iŋ) v.: narrowly avoiding.
elude (ē·lo͞od′) v.: escape by quickness or cleverness.

What was he waiting for? I started to open my eyes, but then the zinging whirl of the belt began and I tensed, awaiting its fearful sting. But just as the leather tip lashed into my leg, a deep, familiar voice said, "Put the belt down, Andersen."

I opened my eyes.

"Papa!"

"Let the children go," Papa said. He was standing on a nearby ridge with a strange black box in his hands. Stacey was behind him, holding the reins to Lady.

The chopping stopped as all eyes turned to Papa.

"They been right meddlesome," Mr. Andersen said. "They need teaching how to act."

"Any teaching, I'll do it. Now, let them go."

Mr. Andersen looked down at Little Man struggling to get away. Smiling broadly, he motioned our release. "Okay, David," he said.

As we ran up the ridge to Papa, Mr. Andersen said, "It's good to have you home, boy."

Papa said nothing until we were safely behind him. "Take them home, Stacey."

"But, Papa—"

"Do like I say, son."

Stacey herded us away from the men. When we were far enough away so Papa couldn't see us, Stacey stopped and handed me Lady's reins.

"Y'all go on home now," he said. "I gotta go help Papa."

"Papa don't need no help," I said. "He told you to come with us."

"But you don't know what he's gonna do."

"What?" I asked.

"He's gonna blow up the forest if they don't get out of here. So go on home where y'all be safe."

"How's he gonna do that?" asked Little Man.

"We been setting sticks of dynamite since the middle of the night. We ain't even been up to the house cause Papa wanted the sticks planted and covered over before the men came. Now, Cassie, take them on back to the house. Do like I tell you for once, will ya?" Then, without waiting for another word, he was gone.

"I wanna see," Little Man announced.

"I don't," protested Christopher-John.

"Come on," I said.

We tied the mare to a tree, then belly-crawled back to where we could see Papa and joined Stacey in the brush.

"Cassie, I told you . . ."

"What's Papa doing?"

The black box was now set upon a sawed-off tree stump, and Papa's hands were tightly grasping a T-shaped instrument which went into it.

"What's that thing?" asked Little Man.

"It's a plunger," Stacey whispered. "If Papa presses down on it, the whole forest will go *pfffff*!"

Our mouths went dry and our eyes went wide. Mr. Andersen's eyes were wide, too.

"You're bluffing, David," he said. "You ain't gonna push that plunger."

"One thing you can't seem to understand, Andersen," Papa said, "is that a black man's always gotta be ready to die. And it don't make me any difference if I die today or tomorrow. Just as long as I die right."

Mr. Andersen laughed uneasily. The lumbermen moved nervously away.

"I mean what I say," Papa said. "Ask anyone. I always mean what I say."

"He sure do, Mr. Andersen," Claude said, eyeing the black box. "He always do."

"Shut up!" Mr. Andersen snapped. "And

the rest of y'all stay put." Then turning back to Papa, he smiled cunningly. "I'm sure you and me can work something out, David."

"Ain't nothing to be worked out," said Papa.

"Now, look here, David, your mama and me, we got us a contract. . . ."

"There ain't no more contract," Papa replied coldly. "Now, either you get out or I blow it up. That's it."

"He means it, Mr. Andersen," another frightened lumberman ventured. "He's crazy and he sure 'nough means it."

"You know what could happen to you, boy?" Mr. Andersen exploded, his face beet red again. "Threatening a white man like this?"

Papa said nothing. He just stood there, his hands firmly on the plunger, staring down at Mr. Andersen.

Mr. Andersen could not bear the stare. He turned away, cursing Papa. "You're a fool, David. A crazy fool." Then he looked around at the lumbermen. They shifted their eyes and would not look at him.

"Maybe we better leave, Mr. Andersen," Tom said quietly.

Mr. Andersen glanced at Tom, then turned back to Papa and said as lightly as he could, "All right, David, all right. It's your land. We'll just take the logs we got cut and get out." He motioned to the men. "Hey, let's get moving and get these logs out of here before this crazy fool gets us all killed."

"No," Papa said.

Mr. Andersen stopped, knowing that he could not have heard correctly. "What you say?"

"You ain't taking one more stick out of this forest."

"Now, look here—"

"You heard me."

"But you can't sell all these logs, David," Mr. Andersen exclaimed incredulously.

Papa said nothing. Just cast that piercing look on Mr. Andersen.

"Look, I'm a fair man. I tell you what I'll do. I'll give you another thirty-five dollars. An even hundred dollars. Now, that's fair, ain't it?"

"I'll see them rot first."

"But—"

"That's my last word," Papa said, tightening his grip on the plunger.

Mr. Andersen swallowed hard. "You won't always have that black box, David," he warned. "You know that, don't you?"

"That may be. But it won't matter none. Cause I'll always have my self-respect."

Mr. Andersen opened his mouth to speak, but no sound came. Tom and the lumbermen were quietly moving away, putting their gear in the empty lumber wagons. Mr. Andersen looked again at the black box. Finally, his face ashen, he too walked away.

Papa stood unmoving until the wagons and the men were gone. Then, when the sound of the last wagon rolling over the dry leaves could no longer be heard and a hollow silence filled the air, he slowly removed his hands from the plunger and looked up at the remaining trees standing like lonely sentries in the morning.

"Dear, dear old trees," I heard him call softly, "will you ever sing again?"

I waited. But the trees gave no answer.

Vocabulary
incredulously (in·krej'oo·ləs·lē) *adv.:* unbelievingly.
ashen (ash'ən) *adj.:* pale.
sentries (sen'trēz) *n.:* guards.

Mildred D. Taylor

"We Were Somebody"

Mildred D. Taylor (1943–   ) grew up in Toledo, Ohio. In high school she was an honor student, a newspaper editor, and a class officer—but, she says, she wasn't able to do what she really wanted: be a cheerleader.

Every summer she and her family visited Mississippi relatives, and she listened to their stories. By the time she was nine or ten, she knew that she wanted to write. "I wanted to show a Black family united in love and pride, of which the reader would like to be a part."

Her first effort, *Song of the Trees,* introduced the Logan family and won first prize in the African American category of a competition for children's books. In 1977, when she accepted the Newbery Award for her second work about the Logan family, *Roll of Thunder, Hear My Cry,* Taylor talked about her father:

> **Throughout my childhood he impressed upon my sister and me that we were somebody, that we were important and could do or be anything we set our minds to do or be. He was not the kind of father who demanded A's on our report cards. He was more concerned about how we carried ourselves, how we respected ourselves and others, and how we pursued the principles upon which he hoped we would build our lives. He was constantly reminding us that how we saw ourselves was far more important than how others saw us. . . .Through David Logan have come the words of my father, and through the Logan family the love of my own family.**

For Independent Reading

You can rejoin Cassie Logan and her family in the novels *Let the Circle Be Unbroken* and *The Road to Memphis.*

Literary Response and Analysis

Reading Check

1. Create a story map for the **plot** of *Song of the Trees.* Copy and fill in the following diagram:

Characters:

Conflicts:

Event:

Event:

Event:

Event:

[Add as many event boxes as you need.]

Resolution of conflict:

Interpretations

2. Look at the story map that you made for the Reading Check. Analyze the **plot** of the story by thinking about its major parts. At what point does the main **conflict** begin, and who is involved in the struggle? What **problems** make it difficult for Cassie and her family to resolve the conflict? How do they finally solve their problems? What is the story's **resolution**?

3. Cassie **personifies** the trees, describing them as if they could talk and sing. Find two passages in the story in which the trees seem human. Why do you think Cassie loves her trees so much?

4. When you read on page 340 that Mr. Andersen "hissed venomously," what are you reminded of? How do you feel about Mr. Andersen's behavior?

5. *Song of the Trees* is told by Cassie. How would the story be different if it were told by her father?

6. Go back to the statements you rated on page 332. Individually and with the class, rate the four statements again, using the same scale. Have any of your opinions changed now that you've read the story? ✏

Evaluation

7. Taylor says that in writing *Song of the Trees,* "[I] drew upon people and places I had known all my life." In creating the character of Cassie, for example, she drew on the personalities of her sister and an aunt. How believable did the characters seem to you? Explain.

Writing

Stating a Theme

Theme, as you learned earlier (page 332), is the *meaning* of a story. Theme points to what the main characters learn in the story and to what *you* learn as you share their experiences.

In a paragraph, state what you think the theme of this story is. Remember that no two statements of theme will be alike. Share your ideas on theme with the class.

Reading Standard 3.1
Articulate the expressed purposes and characteristics of different forms of prose (for example, novella).

Vocabulary Development

Connotations: What's the Difference Between . . .

Would you rather be described as *curious* or *nosy*? The two words have the same basic meaning, or **denotation,** but they have different connotations. **Connotations** are the feelings and associations that have come to be attached to certain words. Most people wouldn't mind being called curious: It suggests that you are interested in the world around you and want to learn about it. *Nosy* has negative connotations: It suggests that you are someone who puts your nose into other people's business.

Word Bank

finicky
dispute
ambled
delved
curtly
skirting
elude
incredulously
ashen
sentries

PRACTICE

Test your skills at recognizing shades of meaning. (Use a dictionary to check your answers.) What's the difference between the following words and phrases? It would help if you go back and read the word in its context in the story.

1. *careful* and *finicky*
2. a *brawl* and a *dispute*
3. *walked* and *ambled*
4. *looked for* and *delved*
5. *matter-of-factly* and *curtly*
6. *passing* and *skirting*
7. *escape* and *elude*
8. *doubtfully* and *incredulously*
9. *creamy* and *ashen*
10. *watchers* and *sentries*

THE PERFUME IS FRAGRANT.

THE PERFUME STINKS.

Grade 6 Review Reading Standard 1.5 Understand and explain shades of meaning in related words (for example, *softly* and *quietly*).

Grammar Link MINI-LESSON

All Modifiers! Places, Please!

To work well, modifiers have to be in the right place. A modifier that seems to modify the wrong word in a sentence is called a **misplaced modifier.** Here's an example of a misplaced modifier:

MISPLACED
> **Today I read a story about a forest that was almost blown up <u>in my literature book</u>.**

Did the forest blow up in the book? No, the phrase *in my literature book* is misplaced. To fix the sentence, place the modifier as close as possible to the word it modifies—*read.*

CORRECT
> **Today I read <u>in my literature book</u> a story about a forest that was almost blown up.**

MISPLACED
> **Cassie heard the men say they were going to cut down the forest <u>with her own ears</u>.**

CORRECT
> **Cassie heard <u>with her own ears</u> the men say they were going to cut down the forest.**

CORRECT
> **<u>With her own ears</u>, Cassie heard the men say they were going to cut down the forest.**

PRACTICE

Move the misplaced modifiers in these sentences to the right place.

1. The final conversation is a key scene in this story between Mr. Logan and Mr. Andersen.
2. Fidgeting with his clothing, we often watched Little Man in front of the mirror.
3. I almost understood every word of the story.
4. Stacy saw a man near the tree named Mr. Andersen.
5. The children looked at the trees who were weeping softly.
6. The trees whispered to the children with their leafy boughs.
7. Mr. Andersen's car was already parked in the driveway with its shiny fenders.
8. Other books are about the Logans by Mildred Taylor.
9. There's a story about a mongoose who kills snakes in this book.
10. There's also a story about a girl named Esperanza called "A Rice Sandwich."

For more help, see Placement of Modifiers in the *Holt Handbook*, pages 232–240.

Fish Cheeks

Literary Focus
Humorous Essays: Tickling Your Funny Bone

An **essay** is a short piece of nonfiction prose that looks at one subject in a limited way. Though essays can be formal and logical, many of the essays we enjoy today are relaxed, informal writings that reveal a great deal about the writer's feelings. Most essays—like this one by Amy Tan—are published in popular magazines.

Writers of **humorous essays** are something like stand-up comics: They entertain us by putting a funny spin or twist on odd or embarrassing moments from everyday life.

Writers of humorous essays aren't always just out for laughs, however. They often have other, more serious purposes in mind. As you read the following essay, see if you think the writer intends to do more than tickle your funny bone (but first, read the essay just for fun).

Reading Skills
Describing Images: Appealing to the Senses

When writers describe things, they create **images**—pictures drawn with words. To help readers imagine places, events, and characters, they use language that appeals to the senses, as Amy Tan does in this true story. When you read descriptions, notice that

- most images are visual, but they often appeal to several senses at once
- writers often choose details that

show how they *feel* about what they describe

Make the Connection
Quickwrite ✏

A girl is walking down the hall at school. Coming toward her is a boy she's been dying to meet. They are almost next to each other when she slips, loses her balance, and falls to the floor in a clumsy heap. How could a moment like this possibly have a positive outcome?

Jot down your responses to that question. Then, in a group, share your possible outcomes.

Vocabulary Development

Learning the following words will help you appreciate the vividness of Amy Tan's writing:

appalling (ə·pôl′iŋ) *adj.:* horrifying. *The amount of food on the dinner table was simply appalling.*

wedges (wej′iz) *n.:* pie-shaped slices. *The tofu was cut into bite-sized wedges.*

clamor (klam′ər) *n.:* loud, confused noise. *The clamor in the dining room probably could have been heard down the hall.*

rumpled (rum′pəld) *v.* used as *adj.:* wrinkled and untidy. *Amy was embarrassed by her uncle's rumpled gifts.*

muster (mus′tər) *v.:* call forth. *She couldn't even muster up a smile for her mother after dinner.*

Reading Standard 3.1 Articulate the expressed purposes and characteristics of different forms of prose (for example, essay).

FISH CHEEKS

Amy Tan

ON CHRISTMAS EVE
I SAW THAT MY MOTHER
HAD OUTDONE HERSELF IN
CREATING A STRANGE MENU.

I fell in love with the minister's son the winter I turned fourteen. He was not Chinese, but as white as Mary in the manger. For Christmas I prayed for this blond-haired boy, Robert, and a slim new American nose.

When I found out that my parents had invited the minister's family over for Christmas Eve dinner, I cried. What would Robert think of our shabby *Chinese* Christmas? What would he think of our noisy *Chinese* relatives who lacked proper American manners? What terrible disappointment would he feel upon seeing not a roasted turkey and sweet potatoes but *Chinese* food?

On Christmas Eve I saw that my mother had outdone herself in creating a strange menu. She was pulling black veins out of the backs of fleshy prawns. The kitchen was littered with appalling mounds of raw food: a slimy rock cod with bulging fish eyes that pleaded not to be thrown into a pan of hot oil. Tofu, which looked like stacked wedges of rubbery white sponges. A bowl soaking dried fungus back to life. A plate of squid, their backs crisscrossed with knife markings so they resembled bicycle tires.

And then they arrived—the minister's family and all my relatives in a clamor of doorbells and rumpled Christmas packages. Robert grunted hello, and I pretended he was not worthy of existence.

Dinner threw me deeper into despair. My relatives licked the ends of their chopsticks and reached across the table, dipping them into the dozen or so plates of food. Robert and his family waited patiently for platters to be passed to them. My relatives murmured with pleasure when my mother brought out the whole steamed fish. Robert grimaced. Then my father poked his chopsticks just below the fish eye and plucked out the soft meat. "Amy, your favorite," he said, offering me the tender fish cheek. I wanted to disappear.

At the end of the meal my father leaned back and belched loudly, thanking my mother for her fine cooking. "It's a polite Chinese custom to show you are satisfied," explained my father to our astonished guests. Robert was looking down at his plate with a reddened face. The minister managed to muster up a quiet burp. I was stunned into silence for the rest of the night.

After everyone had gone, my mother said to me, "You want to be the same as American girls on the outside." She handed me an early gift. It was a miniskirt in beige tweed. "But inside you must always be Chinese. You must be proud you are different. Your only shame is to have shame."

And even though I didn't agree with her then, I knew that she understood how much I had suffered during the evening's dinner. It wasn't until many years later—long after I had gotten over my crush on Robert—that I was able to fully appreciate her lesson and the true purpose behind our particular menu. For Christmas Eve that year, she had chosen all my favorite foods.

Vocabulary

appalling (ə·pôl'iŋ) *adj.:* shocking; horrifying.

wedges (wej'iz) *n.:* pie-shaped slices.

clamor (klam'ər) *n.:* loud, confused noise.

rumpled (rum'pəld) *v.* used as *adj.:* wrinkled and untidy.

muster (mus'tər) *v.:* call forth.

Amy Tan

Finding Answers in Stories

> " I was the only Chinese girl in class from third grade on. I remember trying to belong and feeling isolated. I felt ashamed of being different and ashamed of feeling that way. When I was a teenager, I rejected everything Chinese. . . . The only people I could think I wanted to be like were fictional characters. In part, that is one of the reasons I began to write. You're looking for answers in your life, and you can't find them in anyone else. You end up finding them in stories. "

Amy Tan (1952–   ) found her friends in books—fairy tales, the *Little House* novels of Laura Ingalls Wilder, and later, the British novels of the Brontë sisters. Later still she began to write books of her own, about a life half a world away from America's prairies and Britain's moors.

Tan spent her childhood in Oakland, California, where her parents had settled after leaving China. When she was fifteen, both her father and her brother died from brain tumors. After these losses her mother revealed a long-kept secret: Amy had three half sisters still living in China. These upheavals in her family changed Amy Tan's sense of who she was. Suddenly her Chinese heritage became important to her. She began to read whatever she could about China, later taking college courses in Chinese literature and history. Most of all, Tan became fascinated by her mother's stories about her experiences in China during the war-torn 1930s and 1940s.

In recent years, Amy Tan has made several trips to China, where she has come to know the sisters who once seemed lost to her forever. She now loves the Chinese culture she once tried so hard to reject.

Literary Response and Analysis

Reading Check

1. Fill out the sequence chart below to organize what happens in "Fish Cheeks." Add more boxes as needed.

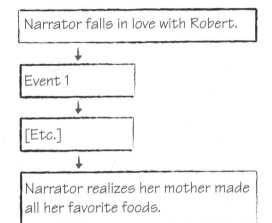

Narrator falls in love with Robert.

↓

Event 1

↓

[Etc.]

↓

Narrator realizes her mother made all her favorite foods.

Interpretations

2. Why do you think Amy is ashamed of her family's Chinese traditions? What does her mother mean when she says, "Your only shame is to have shame"?

3. Re-read Tan's **description** of the food her mother is preparing. How does Amy *feel* about the dinner? How can you tell?

4. Find one **image** in the story that creates a vivid picture in your mind. Find three other images that help you feel you can touch, smell, taste, or hear details of that famous Christmas dinner.

5. Why do you suppose it isn't until many years later that Amy realizes her mother chose all of Amy's favorite foods for the Christmas Eve dinner? What do you think are her mother's "lesson" and "true purpose" in preparing those foods?

6. Amy's mother tells her that she can be an American girl on the outside but must always be Chinese on the inside. Do you think that is possible? Is it a good idea? Explain your answer.

7. Is this **essay** about a strange menu, or is it really about something else? In one or two sentences, state what you think is Tan's **main idea.**

Evaluation

8. Where does the **title** "Fish Cheeks" come from? Do you think it's a good title? Tell why or why not.

Writing

Oops!

Have you ever been in an embarrassing situation that somehow ended with a positive outcome (like the one you wrote about for the Quickwrite on page 351)? Write about that experience, or write about a time when you were anxious about making a good impression. Think about your **purpose:** Will you be writing only to entertain, or will your narrative have a point? Include images in your story that will help readers share your experience.

Reading Standard 3.1 Articulate the expressed purposes and characteristics of different forms of prose (for example, essay).

Vocabulary Development

Analogies: Pairs of Pairs

An **analogy** begins with a pair of items that are related in some way. You figure out that relationship, and then complete another pair that has a similar relationship. For example,

Sweet is to *sour* as _____ is to *short.*
   a. small   b. bitter   c. tall   d. round

The relationship of *sweet* to *sour* is one of opposites. *Tall,* the opposite of *short,* is the best way to complete the analogy.

Try this one:

Kitten is to *cat* as _____ is to *dog.*
   a. poodle   b. puppy   c. fur   d. bark

A kitten is a young cat, so the correct answer is *puppy,* which is a young dog. Once you figure out the relationship, completing the analogy should be a snap.

Word Bank

appalling
wedges
clamor
rumpled
muster

PRACTICE

Complete the following analogies. First, figure out the relationship between the words in the first pair. Then, choose a Word Bank word that has a similar relationship to the last word in the sentence. Here's a hint for the first item:

1. *Sad* is to *happy* as _____ is to *delightful.* The relationship between *sad* and *happy* is one of opposites. What word in the Word Bank is the opposite of *delightful*?

2. *Pressed* is to *neat* as _____ is to *sloppy.*

3. *Whisper* is to *soft* as _____ is to *loud.*

4. *Receive* is to *get* as _____ is to *summon.*

5. *Slices* is to *pizza* as _____ is to *cheese.*

A Mason-Dixon Memory

Literary Focus

The Essay

One form of nonfiction you'll often be asked to read—and write—is the **essay,** a short piece of nonfiction prose that focuses on a single topic. An essay can be about anything, from "The Meaning of Life" to "How I Feel About My Cat."

An essay can be formal in tone and highly structured, with statements laid out in careful order and evidence supporting each one. An essay can also be personal and even humorous, as if the writer were sitting down with us for a chat. An essay's tone and structure will depend on its **purpose**—does the writer want to inform us? persuade us? entertain us? or do something else?

Reading Skills

Recognizing Text Structures

Essays, like other pieces of writing, are often structured in ways that help make their meaning clear. This essay is structured around **flashbacks**—the narrator twice goes back to an earlier time to tell a story that relates to the first story he is telling. Like many essayists, the writer uses his final paragraph to sum up his main idea. As you read the essay, look for little open-book signs. These alert you to the essay's structure. (If you miss the flashbacks, you may be hopelessly lost in time!)

Make the Connection

Quickwrite

How far would you go to do the right thing? Think of something you really care about. It could be a possession or an event you're looking forward to—anything you'd hate to give up. Can you imagine a situation in which doing the right thing might mean giving up the thing you want so much? For example, what if going to a party means you have to break a date with a friend who wasn't invited? Jot down your thoughts on how you might handle such a situation.

Vocabulary Development

Here are some words you'll learn as you read this selection:

predominantly (prē·däm′ə·nənt·lē) *adv.:* mainly. *The story is predominantly about the meaning of friendship.*

forfeit (fôr′fit) *v.:* lose the right to compete. *Dondré's teammates would forfeit the tournament.*

resolve (ri·zälv′) *v.:* decide. *In tough situations, people can resolve to do the right thing.*

ominous (äm′ə·nəs) *adj.:* threatening. *The look on the chaperone's face was ominous.*

erupted (ē·rup′tid) *v.:* burst forth. *Applause erupted from the audience after Dondré's speech.*

Reading Standard 3.1 Articulate the expressed purposes and characteristics of different forms of prose (for example, essay).

A Mason-Dixon Memory

Clifton Davis

Sponsor:
Fred Matte

Dondré
Green

Brad
Coenen

Damon
Marsala

Jeff
McNew

David
Elias

"If we leave, we forfeit this tournament. If we stay, Dondré can't play."

Golf team photograph from the 1991 *Warrior* yearbook.

Lee Williams

John Shamblin

Brian Matte

Dondré Green glanced uneasily at the civic leaders and sports figures filling the hotel ballroom in Cleveland. They had come from across the nation to attend a fundraiser for the National Minority College Golf Scholarship Foundation. I was the banquet's featured entertainer. Dondré, an eighteen-year-old high school senior from Monroe, Louisiana, was the evening's honored guest.

"Nervous?" I asked the handsome young man in his starched white shirt and rented tuxedo.

"A little," he whispered, grinning.

One month earlier, Dondré had been just one more black student attending a <u>predominantly</u> white Southern school. Although most of his friends and classmates were white, Dondré's race had never been an issue. Then, on April 17, 1991, Dondré's black skin provoked an incident that made nationwide news.

"Ladies and gentlemen," the emcee[1] said, "our special guest, Dondré Green."

As the audience stood applauding, Dondré walked to the microphone and began his story. "I love golf," he said quietly. "For the past two years, I've been a member of the St. Frederick High School golf team. And though I was the only black member, I've always felt at home playing at the mostly white country clubs across Louisiana."

The audience leaned forward; even the waiters and busboys stopped to listen. As I listened, a memory buried in my heart since childhood began fighting its way to life.

---

1. **emcee** (em′sē′) *n.:* master of ceremonies.

Vocabulary
predominantly (prē·däm′ə·nənt·lē) *adv.:* mainly.

"Our team had driven from Monroe," Dondré continued. "When we arrived at the Caldwell Parish Country Club in Columbia, we walked to the putting green."

Dondré and his teammates were too absorbed to notice the conversation between a man and St. Frederick athletic director James Murphy. After disappearing into the clubhouse, Murphy returned to his players.

"I want to see the seniors," he said. "On the double!" His face seemed strained as he gathered the four students, including Dondré.

"I don't know how to tell you this," he said, "but the Caldwell Parish Country Club is reserved for whites only." Murphy paused and looked at Dondré. His teammates glanced at each other in disbelief. "I want you seniors to decide what our response should be," Murphy continued. "If we leave, we forfeit this tournament. If we stay, Dondré can't play."

As I listened, my own childhood memory from thirty-two years ago broke free.

TEXT STRUCTURE

1. The writer adds extra space here. What words indicate a flashback? What year are we now in?

In 1959 I was thirteen years old, a poor black kid living with my mother and stepfather in a small black ghetto on Long Island, New York. My mother worked nights in a hospital, and my stepfather drove a coal truck. Needless to say, our standard of living was somewhat short of the American dream.

Nevertheless, when my eighth-grade teacher announced a graduation trip to Washington, D.C., it never crossed my mind that I would be left behind. Besides a complete tour of the nation's capital, we would visit Glen Echo Amusement Park in Maryland. In my imagination, Glen Echo was Disneyland, Knott's Berry Farm, and Magic Mountain rolled into one.

My heart beating wildly, I raced home to deliver the mimeographed letter describing the journey. But when my mother saw how much the trip would cost, she just shook her head. We couldn't afford it.

After feeling sad for ten seconds, I decided to try to fund the trip myself. For the next eight weeks, I sold candy bars door-to-door, delivered newspapers, and mowed lawns. Three days before the deadline, I'd made just barely enough. I was going!

The day of the trip, trembling with excitement, I climbed onto the train. I was the only nonwhite in our section.

Our hotel was not far from the White House. My roommate was Frank Miller, the son of a businessman. Leaning together out of our window and dropping water balloons on passing tourists quickly cemented our new friendship.

Every morning, almost a hundred of us loaded noisily onto our bus for another adventure. We sang our school fight song dozens of times—en route[2] to Arlington National Cemetery and even on an afternoon cruise down the Potomac River.

We visited the Lincoln Memorial twice, once in daylight, the second time at dusk. My classmates and I fell silent as we walked in the shadows of those thirty-six marble columns, one for every state in the Union that Lincoln labored to preserve. I stood next to Frank at the base of the nineteen-

---

2. **en route** (än rōōt'): on the way.

Vocabulary
forfeit (fôr'fit) v.: lose the right to something.

foot seated statue. Spotlights made the white Georgian marble seem to glow. Together, we read those famous words from Lincoln's speech at Gettysburg, remembering the most bloody battle in the War Between the States: "We here highly resolve that these dead shall not have died in vain—that this nation, under God, shall have a new birth of freedom. . . ."

As Frank motioned me into place to take my picture, I took one last look at Lincoln's face. He seemed alive and so terribly sad.

The next morning I understood a little better why he wasn't smiling. "Clifton," a chaperone said, "could I see you for a moment?"

The other guys at my table, especially Frank, turned pale. We had been joking about the previous night's direct water-balloon hit on a fat lady and her poodle. It was a stupid, dangerous act, but luckily nobody got hurt. We were celebrating our escape from punishment when the chaperone asked to see me.

"Clifton," she began, "do you know about the Mason-Dixon line?"

"No," I said, wondering what this had to do with drenching fat ladies.

"Before the Civil War," she explained, "the Mason-Dixon line was originally the boundary between Maryland and Pennsylvania—the dividing line between the slave and free states." Having escaped one disaster, I could feel another brewing. I noticed that her eyes were damp and her hands shaking.

"Today," she continued, "the Mason-Dixon line is a kind of invisible border between the North and the South. When you cross that invisible line out of Washington, D.C., into Maryland, things change."

There was an ominous drift to this conversation, but I wasn't following it. Why did she look and sound so nervous?

"Glen Echo Amusement Park is in Maryland," she said at last, "and the management doesn't allow Negroes inside." She stared at me in silence.

I was still grinning and nodding when the meaning finally sank in. "You mean I can't go to the park," I stuttered, "because I'm a Negro?"

She nodded slowly. "I'm sorry, Clifton," she said, taking my hand. "You'll have to stay in the hotel tonight. Why don't you and I watch a movie on television?"

I walked to the elevators feeling confusion, disbelief, anger, and a deep sadness. "What happened, Clifton?" Frank said when I got back to the room. "Did the fat lady tell on us?"

Without saying a word, I walked over to my bed, lay down, and began to cry. Frank was stunned into silence. Junior-high boys didn't cry, at least not in front of each other.

It wasn't just missing the class adventure that made me feel so sad. For the first time in my life, I was learning what it felt like to be a "nigger." Of course there was discrimination in the North, but the color of my skin had never officially kept me out of a coffee shop, a church—or an amusement park.

"Clifton," Frank whispered, "what is the matter?"

"They won't let me go to Glen Echo Park tonight," I sobbed.

Vocabulary

resolve (ri·zălv′) v.: decide; make a formal statement.

ominous (ăm′ə·nəs) adj.: threatening, like a bad sign; warning of something bad.

"Because of the water balloon?" he asked.

"No," I answered, "because I'm a Negro."

"Well, that's a relief!" Frank said, and then he laughed, obviously relieved to have escaped punishment for our caper with the balloons. "I thought it was serious!"

Wiping away the tears with my sleeve, I stared at him. "It *is* serious. They don't let Negroes into the park. I can't go with you!" I shouted. "That's pretty serious to me."

I was about to wipe the silly grin off Frank's face with a blow to his jaw when I heard him say, "Then I won't go either."

For an instant we just froze. Then Frank grinned. I will never forget that moment. Frank was just a kid. He wanted to go to that amusement park as much as I did, but there was something even more important than the class night out. Still, he didn't explain or expand.

The next thing I knew, the room was filled with kids listening to Frank. "They don't allow Negroes in the park," he said, "so I'm staying with Clifton."

"Me too," a second boy said.

"Those jerks," a third muttered. "I'm with you, Clifton." My heart began to race. Suddenly, I was not alone. A pint-sized revolution had been born. The "water-balloon brigade," eleven white boys from Long Island, had made its decision: "We won't go." And as I sat on my bed in the center of it all, I felt grateful. But above all, I was filled with pride.

TEXT STRUCTURE

2. The writer uses extra space again. Where are we now in time?

Dondré Green's story brought that childhood memory back to life. His golfing teammates, like my childhood friends, had an important decision to make. Standing by their friend would cost them dearly. But when it came time to decide, no one hesitated. "Let's get out of here," one of them whispered.

"They just turned and walked toward the van," Dondré told us. "They didn't debate it. And the younger players joined us without looking back."

Dondré was astounded by the response of his friends—and the people of Louisiana. The whole state was outraged and tried to make it right. The Louisiana House of Representatives proclaimed a Dondré Green Day and passed legislation permitting lawsuits for damages, attorneys' fees, and court costs against any private facility that invites a team, then bars any member because of race.

As Dondré concluded, his eyes glistened with tears. "I love my coach and my teammates for sticking by me," he said. "It goes to show that there are always good people who will not give in to bigotry. The kind of love they showed me that day will conquer hatred every time."

Suddenly, the banquet crowd was standing, applauding Dondré Green.

TEXT STRUCTURE

3. Again, extra space. How do you know the writer has flashed back again?

My friends, too, had shown that kind of love. As we sat in the hotel, a chaperone came in waving an envelope. "Boys!" he shouted. "I've just bought thirteen tickets to the Senators-Tigers game. Anybody want to go?"

The room erupted in cheers. Not one of

Vocabulary

erupted (ē·rup'tid) v.: exploded or burst forth.

us had ever been to a professional baseball game in a real baseball park.

On the way to the stadium, we grew silent as our driver paused before the Lincoln Memorial. For one long moment, I stared through the marble pillars at Mr. Lincoln, bathed in that warm yellow light. There was still no smile and no sign of hope in his sad and tired eyes.

"We here highly resolve . . . that this nation, under God, shall have a new birth of freedom . . ."

In his words and in his life, Lincoln had made it clear that freedom is not free. Every time the color of a person's skin keeps him out of an amusement park or off a country-club fairway, the war for freedom begins again. Sometimes the battle is fought with fists and guns, but more often the most effective weapon is a simple act of love and courage.

Whenever I hear those words from Lincoln's speech at Gettysburg, I remember my eleven white friends, and I feel hope once again. I like to imagine that when we paused that night at the foot of his great monument, Mr. Lincoln smiled at last. As Dondré said, "The kind of love they showed me that day will conquer hatred every time."

TEXT STRUCTURE
4. The writer reflects on both stories, his and Dondré Green's. What sentence in this paragraph states the main idea of this essay?

MEET THE WRITER

Clifton Davis

A Man of Many Talents

Clifton Davis (1946–   ) may be better known for writing tunes than for writing prose. He wrote the song "Never Can Say Goodbye," which sold two million records. He's still involved with music today, as a composer, recording artist, and host of a gospel-music radio program.

Clifton Davis is also an actor. He has appeared in several plays on Broadway and received a Tony nomination for his performance in *Two Gentlemen of Verona*. Davis has also appeared in movies and on TV shows. The role he is best known for is Reverend Reuben Gregory on the television series *Amen*. The curious thing about casting Davis in the role of the minister is that he really *is* a minister, in the Seventh-Day Adventist Church.

Davis believes it's important to do what's right, even if you're making a living amid the glitz and glamour of Hollywood.

Literary Response and Analysis

Reading Check

1. How were the experiences of Dondré Green and Clifton Davis alike? Fill in a chart like the one below to compare their experiences:

	Experience	Friends' Response
Green		
Davis		

Interpretations

2. The narrator, Clifton Davis, starts one story and then flashes back to another story, one that happened to him. Where does the **flashback** begin and end? What does it have to do with Davis's main story?

3. How did Dondré Green's teammates and the people of Louisiana react to the fact that he had been barred from the tournament? Why do you think Dondré was astounded by this response?

4. The narrator says there was "something even more important" than going to the amusement park. Frank never explained what that something was. How would you explain it?

5. Have you or a friend ever felt unwelcome someplace? How did your experience compare with Clifton Davis's or Dondré Green's?

6. Look back at the "What if?" question you wrote for the Quick-write on page 357. Did reading this story change the way you look at choices that might force you to give up something you value? If so, explain how and why.

7. Green and Davis both believe that a simple act of love and courage is the most effective weapon against prejudice. Do you agree? Explain.

Writing
Supporting a Position

Many people devote their lives to fighting for important causes, such as civil rights. Write a brief **persuasive essay** on an issue that *you* really care about. Try to come up with an issue that matters to other people too. Write a sentence that identifies the issue and states your opinion of it. Then, list one or two reasons that support your opinion.

Use "Writing a Persuasive Essay," pages 598–615, for help with this assignment.

BONUS QUESTION

What might "a new birth of freedom" mean today?

Reading Standard 3.1 Articulate the expressed purposes and characteristics of different forms of prose (for example, essay).

Vocabulary Development

Synonyms: Shades of Meaning

Words with the same or almost the same meaning are called
synonyms. Synonyms usually have different shades of meaning.
Rigid and *firm* are synonyms, but most people would rather be
called *firm* than *rigid.* A dictionary or a thesaurus, a book of
synonyms, can help you pick exactly the word you need.

PRACTICE

Make a word map like the following one for the rest of the
Word Bank words. Find at least one synonym for each word,
and put it in the word map. Then, write at least one sentence
using each word. Discuss the synonyms and their shades of
meaning, if any.

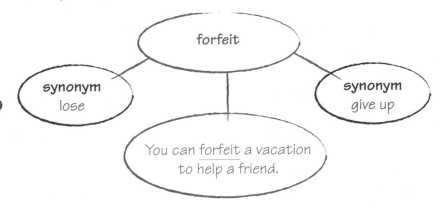

forfeit

synonym
lose

synonym
give up

You can forfeit a vacation
to help a friend.

**Grade 6
Review
Reading
Standard** 1.5
Understand
and explain
shades of
meaning in
related words
(for example,
softly and
quietly).

A Mason-Dixon Memory   **365**

Grammar Link MINI-LESSON

Commas Make Sense of a Series

- Use commas to separate words, phrases, or clauses in a series.

  INCORRECT   **Davis felt "confusion disbelief anger and a deep sadness."**

  CORRECT   **Davis felt "confusion, disbelief, anger, and a deep sadness."**

- In most cases, use commas to separate two or more adjectives that come before a noun.

  INCORRECT   **It was a stupid dangerous act.**

  CORRECT   **It was a stupid, dangerous act.**

- Do not place a comma between an adjective and a noun that immediately follows it.

  INCORRECT   **Green's teammates made a fast, important, costly, decision.**

  CORRECT   **Green's teammates made a fast, important, costly decision.**

- If the last adjective in a series is closely connected in meaning to the noun that follows it, do not use a comma before that adjective.

  INCORRECT   **"Spotlights made the white, Georgian marble seem to glow."**

  CORRECT   **"Spotlights made the white Georgian marble seem to glow."**

To decide whether a comma is needed, add the word *and* between the adjectives. If the *and* sounds strange, don't use a comma. (*White* and *Georgian marble* sounds strange, so don't use a comma there.)

PRACTICE

Copy the sentences below. Add commas where necessary to separate the items in a series. Compare your answers with a partner's.

1. Davis sold candy bars delivered newspapers and mowed lawns.

2. Lincoln's sad wise tired face impressed them.

3. Sincere courageous acts of love can conquer hatred.

4. They saw many famous national landmarks in Washington, D.C.

For more help on using commas to separate items in a series, see the *Holt Handbook*, pages 294–295.

No comma between an adjective and a noun that immediately follows it!

Buddies Bare Their Affection for Ill Classmate

Summarizing: Putting It All in a Nutshell!

Have you ever found yourself rambling on and on about something that's happened to you, and your patient but now frustrated listener finally says, "Enough already—just give it to me in a nutshell"? What your friend's asking for is a summary.

A **summary** restates the main events or main ideas of a text in a much shorter form than the original.

Summaries are useful because they can help you remember the most important points in material you've just read. They're especially handy if you're doing research from a number of sources. Reviewing your summaries will show you how one source differs from another.

Before you write a summary, read the text carefully to decide what details to include and what to leave out.

Use a graphic organizer like the one that follows to collect information for a summary of the newspaper article on page 368. Part of the organizer has been completed for you. Add as many boxes as you need for the main events.

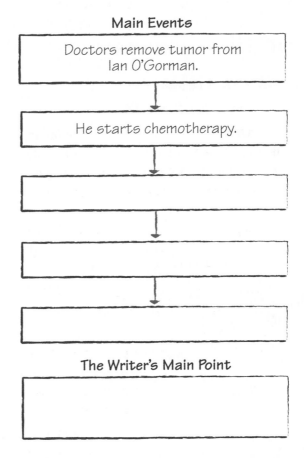

Main Events

Doctors remove tumor from Ian O'Gorman.

He starts chemotherapy.

The Writer's Main Point

Grade 6 Review Reading Standard 2.4 Clarify an understanding of texts by creating summaries.

Buddies Bare Their Affection for Ill Classmate

OCEANSIDE, CAL., MAR. 19 (Associated Press) — In Mr. Alter's fifth-grade class, it's difficult to tell which boy is undergoing chemotherapy. Nearly all the boys are bald. Thirteen of them shaved their heads so a sick buddy wouldn't feel out of place.

"If everybody has their head shaved, sometimes people don't know who's who. They don't know who has cancer and who just shaved their head," said eleven-year-old Scott Sebelius, one of the baldies at Lake Elementary School.

For the record, Ian O'Gorman is the sick one. Doctors recently removed a malignant tumor from his small intestine, and a week ago he started chemotherapy to treat the disease, called lymphoma.

"Besides surgery, I had tubes up my nose. I had butterflies in my stomach," said Ian, who'll have eight more weeks of chemotherapy in an effort to keep the cancer from returning.

Ian decided to get his head shaved before all his hair fell out in clumps. To his surprise, his friends wanted to join him.

"The last thing he would want is to not fit in, to be made fun of, so we just wanted to make him feel better and not left out," said ten-year-old Kyle Hanslik.

Kyle started talking to other boys about the idea, and then one of their parents started a list. Last week, they all went to the barbershop together.

"It's hard to put words to," said Ian's father, Shawn, choking back tears as he talked about the boys. "It's very emotional to think about kids like that who would come together, to have them do such a thing to support Ian."

The boy's teacher, Jim Alter, was so inspired that he, too, shaved his head.

Ian left the hospital March 2. Although he has lost twenty pounds and is pale, he is eager to get back to the business of being an eleven-year-old playing baseball and basketball. "I think I can start on Monday," he said.

—from the
Austin American-Statesman

Ian O'Gorman (center), who is undergoing chemotherapy for cancer, is surrounded by his classmates, who shaved their heads as a show of support.

Reading Informational Materials

Creating a Summary

A good summary of an informational text covers the main events or main points, not every single detail. That is why a summary is always much shorter than the original piece. Use the information you collected in your graphic organizer (page 367) to write a summary of the news story about Ian and his friends. Here are some tips for writing a good summary:

- Cite the author and title of the article you are summarizing.
- Cite the topic of the article in a few words.

- Retell the main events or main points of the article, using your own words. Include only key events or key points.
- Sum up the writer's message or main point.

After you have written your summary, read it over and ask yourself: Would a person who has not read the article understand what it is about? If your answer is negative, go back and revise your summary.

TestPractice

Buddies Bare Their Affection for Ill Classmate

1. According to the opening paragraph, what's difficult to tell about the boys in Mr. Alter's class is who —

   A is the brightest student

   B is undergoing chemotherapy

   C once had the longest hair

   D Ian O'Gorman is

2. The main reason the boys shaved their heads was to —

   F look unusual

   G show individuality

   H act original

   J show support

3. Kyle Hanslik got the idea of shaving his head because —

   A he liked the way Ian looked

   B he didn't want Ian to be made fun of

   C he was protesting Ian's illness

   D he wanted to confuse the teacher

4. Who else was surprisingly inspired to shave his head?

   F Mr. Alter

   G Ian's dad

   H Kyle's dad

   J Ian's doctor

Grade 6 Review Reading Standard 2.4 Clarify an understanding of texts by creating summaries.

When the Earth Shakes

Literary Focus

Scientific Writing: Making It Clear

Scientific writing provides facts about a real-life event or phenomenon. When you read scientific writing, you have to know how to read these features:

- **Graphic aids.** Tables, charts, graphs, photographs, diagrams, maps, and their explanatory captions help you visualize what the author is talking about. Before you read a science text, preview the graphic aids by skimming the pages, looking at the illustrations, and reading a few lines here and there. The visual materials will give you a good idea of what the text is about.
- **Scientific terms.** Scientific words are often defined in context or by means of clues in the passage. Often the terms you should master are in boldface type.
- **Imaginative language.** Science writers, just like fiction writers, often use imaginative comparisons, or figures of speech, to clarify difficult ideas or to help you visualize something.

Reading Skills

Tracking Cause and Effect

As you read "When the Earth Shakes," stop to answer the questions indicated by a little open-book sign. These questions will help you track the causes of the earthquake and its devastating effects.

Make the Connection

Quickwrite

From the title "When the Earth Shakes," you can probably guess that you're going to read about one of nature's most awesome forces: earthquakes.

With a group of classmates, make a list of what you already know and what you want to learn about earthquakes.

Vocabulary Development

Steady yourself with these words as you read about earthquakes:

churning (chʉrn′iŋ) *v.* used as *adj.*: shaking; stirring. *The ground suddenly began churning as if it were a stormy sea.*

bluff (bluf) *n.*: steep cliff. *The front of the bluff slid down to the water below.*

buckled (buk′əld) *v.*: collapsed under pressure. *The ground buckled beneath their feet, leaving a huge hole.*

particles (pärt′i·kəlz) *n.*: tiny pieces. *A thick layer of dust particles covered the building.*

observatories (əb·zʉrv′ə·tôr′ēz) *n.*: buildings equipped for scientific observation. *In their observatories, scientists studied the causes of the earthquake.*

When the Earth Shakes

Patricia Lauber

from Earthquakes: New Scientific Ideas
About How and Why the Earth Shakes

*The earth at their feet was churning
and crumbling and sinking away.*

It was late afternoon, March 27, 1964. Above Alaska the sky was the color of lead, and in some places a light snow fell. Anchorage, the biggest city, lay quiet, for this gray day was both Good Friday and the eve of Passover.

Schools were empty. Many shops and offices had closed early, and at 5:30 most people were home. Outside, the air was raw, the sky dark. Inside, lights glowed, furnaces hummed, and pots simmered on stoves.

Then it happened. Suddenly the familiar and the cozy vanished. In their place came the strange and the fearful.

At Turnagain, on the edge of Anchorage, people first heard a deep rumble, like the sound of thunder. Next, their houses began to shake. They rushed to their doors, looked out, and thought the world was coming to an end. The earth at their feet was churning and crumbling and sinking away. It was cracking into huge, tilted blocks.

Neighbor helped neighbor to escape. Behind them trees fell. Houses were ripped in two or upended.

Turnagain was built on high ground, on a bluff overlooking the water. The violent shaking triggered a landslide. The front of the bluff slid away, carrying houses and garages with it.

In downtown Anchorage, big buildings creaked and groaned. Their floors rose and fell in waves.

Automobiles bounced like rubber balls. Great chunks of buildings crashed to the street. A movie theater dropped thirty feet into a hole that opened beneath it. A flower shop snapped in two.

Anchorage was not alone in this nightmare. As it shook and cracked and jolted, so did much of Alaska. Buildings trembled and fell. Land tore open. Highways buckled. Railroad tracks were twisted into curls of steel. Snowcapped mountains shuddered, and ice and rock swept down their slopes.

Alaska had been struck by a mighty earthquake that hit without warning. At 5:35 P.M. all was well. By 5:38 half of Alaska seemed to be in the grip of an angry giant. The earth shook with terrible violence.

All along the coast, port towns suffered great damage. One reason was the kind of land on which they stood.

Much of Alaska's coast is rugged, rocky land that stands high above the water. The port towns were built in the low-lying places. But here the ground was not very solid. Also, it sloped down steeply to the ocean floor. When the earthquake shook such land, the soil began to slide. Whole waterfronts vanished in underwater landslides.

That was one of the things that happened at Seward.

Seward was both a port and the end of a rail line. The rail line brought in oil, which was stored in tanks before being shipped. When the earthquake hit, the tanks broke and the oil caught fire.

> **CAUSE AND EFFECT**
>
> **1.** As you read the next section, list the effects of the quake in Turnagain and Anchorage.

> **CAUSE AND EFFECT**
>
> **2.** As you read this next section, list the causes of the fire in Seward.

Vocabulary

churning (chʉrn′iŋ) v.: shaking or stirring violently, like milk being made into butter in a churn.

bluff (bluf) n.: steep cliff.

buckled (buk′əld) v.: collapsed (usually under pressure).

Flames roared along the waterfront. Just then a great landslide took place. The entire waterfront slid into the bay. The slide caused water to surge away from the land. Burning oil was carried into the bay and then swept back. Fiery water flooded inland. Tugs, fishing boats, and a tanker were washed ashore by the great surge of water. Docks and small-boat harbors were destroyed by fire and wave. For hours that night the bay was ablaze with burning material.

By then, the earthquake had long since ended. The earth was still twitching, and it would go on doing so for weeks. But the earthquake itself was over. In fact, it had lasted only about five minutes.

During that time, the earthquake did great damage. Scientists who studied it reported some astounding effects. Among other things, the quake changed the very face of Alaska.

In the Gulf of Alaska the ocean floor rose. So did land along the coast. All in all, a region the size of Maine was lifted three to eight feet. Inland, another big region sank. Part of an island rose thirty-eight feet. When the quake ended, the town of Valdez was ten feet higher than it had been before.

A whole peninsula moved. Carrying along its mountains and lakes, Kenai Peninsula moved sideways as much as sixty feet and sank seven feet or more.

There were other changes. Near Valdez a

CAUSE AND EFFECT

3. As you read this next section, list the effects of the quake on all of Alaska.

huge wave reached 220 feet above sea level and clawed at the earth. A piece of land 4,000 feet long and 600 feet wide fell into the sea.

Water in Kenai Lake sloshed back and forth. It moved with such force that its water and ice peeled the bark off trees along the shore.

A mountain split apart. One side of it plunged downward, flying over a ridge like a skier taking a jump. The flying mountain spread into a carpet of rocks a mile long and two miles wide. The carpet traveled without touching the ground. Finally it landed on a glacier. Scientists later found it there and figured out what had happened.

The 1964 Alaska earthquake was one of the strongest ever recorded. It was one of the mightiest earthquakes known to man. But it took place for the same reason that all earthquakes do. It took place because rock within the earth suddenly shifted.

CAUSE AND EFFECT

4. As you read this next section, take notes on the causes of quakes.

An earthquake can be strong, as Alaska's was in 1964. Or it can be slight. It can be so slight that no person feels it, though instruments record it. But big or small, an earthquake is just what its name says it is—a shaking of the earth. The earth shakes when rock within it suddenly shifts.

The earth is mostly made of rock. Beneath its soil and oceans, it is a big ball of rock. The ball has three main regions: the core, the mantle, and the crust. They are arranged like the layers of an onion. The core is at the center of the earth. The mantle surrounds the core. The crust surrounds the mantle.

Like the crust on a loaf of bread, the earth's crust is a thin outside covering. It is made of two main kinds of rock.

One is a fairly light rock. Its most familiar form is granite, and that is what it is often called. The upper part of the continents is made of this granitelike rock. It is usually about twenty-five miles thick. The continental crust does not end at the water's edge. It reaches out under the sea in what is called a continental shelf. Where the shelf ends, the oceanic crust begins.

The crust under the oceans is a different kind of rock. It is much more dense. That is, the rock particles are packed more closely

Vocabulary
particles (pärt′i·kəlz) n.: tiny pieces.

like a very gummy liquid. It can flow like thick tar.

But it also behaves like a solid. It can suddenly shift or snap. When it does, an earthquake takes place. Earthquakes also occur when rock of the crust suddenly shifts or breaks.

Rock shifts or breaks for the same reason that anything else does: because it has been put under great strain. If you take a ruler and bend it, you are putting it under strain. If you bend, or strain, it too much, it will break.

There are forces within the earth that bend, squeeze, and twist the rock of the crust and the upper mantle. As a result, the rock is put under great strain. That is, a large amount of energy is stored in it as strain. When the strain becomes too great, the rock suddenly gives way and the stored-up energy is released.

together. The most familiar form of this rock is the dark, heavy kind called basalt. The crust under the oceans is about five miles thick.

The inside of the earth is very hot. And so the crust grows hotter as it goes deeper. Oil wells drilled deep into the crust reach rock hot enough to boil water. When volcanoes erupt, molten rock spills out of them. The rock may have a temperature of two thousand degrees Fahrenheit. This molten rock has come from the lower crust or upper mantle.

The mantle is about 1,800 miles thick. It is made of rock, but this is not rock as we know it. The rock is under very great pressure, deep within the earth. It is also very hot. The heat and pressure make the rock behave in ways that are strange to us.

Sometimes rock of the mantle behaves

Something like this happens if you shoot a bow and arrow. As you pull, the bow and string are bent and forced out of shape. Energy from your muscles is stored in them as strain. When you let go, the bow and string snap back into shape, and the stored-up energy is released. It speeds the arrow through the air.

Energy released from rock takes the form of waves. A wave is a kind of giant push. It is a push that passes from one rock particle to the next, much as a push can pass through a line of people. Imagine ten people lined up, each with his hands on the person ahead. If the last person in line is given a sharp push, the push will be felt all through the line. The people stay in place, but the push passes through them.

> **CAUSE AND EFFECT**
> 5. As you read this next section, list the effects of the quake's waves.

That is how earthquake waves travel through the inside of the earth. The pushes pass from one rock particle to the next.

You can feel what happens if you snap a stick between your hands. As you slowly bend it, energy is stored as strain. Finally the strain becomes too great. The stick snaps. All the stored-up energy is released. And you feel a sharp stinging. Stored-up energy has changed to waves that are passing through the wood. One wood particle pushes the next. When the pushes reach your hands, you feel them as a sting.

Meanwhile, the broken ends of the stick are vibrating. That is, they are very quickly moving back and forth. They set air waves in motion. Particles of air push other particles. Waves, or pushes, pass through the air. These movements are the source of the sound you hear when the stick snaps.

When an earthquake takes place, waves travel out from the shifting rock in all directions.

Some waves travel through the air. They account for the rumbling sounds that may accompany an earthquake.

Some waves travel deep in the earth. They are seldom felt by people. But instruments in earthquake <u>observatories</u> record them. Earthquake waves that pass through the earth are recorded thousands of miles away.

Some waves travel along the earth's surface. Surface waves are the ones that do the damage—the ones that shake buildings, tear up roads, and cause landslides.

They are not, however, the only cause of earthquake damage. There can be another kind, and it is a kind that comes from the sea.

> **CAUSE AND EFFECT**
> **6.** What effect do you think the quakes have on the sea?

Vocabulary
observatories (əb·zʉrv'ə·tôr'ēz) *n.:* buildings equipped for scientific observation.

Patricia Lauber

"I'm Always Learning Something"

Patricia Lauber (1924–   ) has written more than eighty books on subjects ranging from volcanoes to robots and much in between. Says Lauber:

> I write about anything that interests me, dogs, horses, forests, birds, mysteries, life in other countries. Some of my books are fiction, and some are nonfiction, but all are based on what I've seen around me. I like to stand and stare at things, to talk with people, and to read a lot.

For Independent Reading

For other looks at nature unleashed, read Patricia Lauber's *Volcano: The Eruption and Healing of Mount St. Helens; Flood: Wrestling with the Mississippi;* and *Hurricanes: Earth's Mightiest Storms.*

Ahmedabad, India, after an earthquake on January 26, 2001.

Literary Response and Analysis

Reading Check

1. If you were a teacher, what would you want your students to understand and remember after reading "When the Earth Shakes"? To find the most important details in the article, refer to your answers to the side questions in the text. Then, fill in a cause-and-effect chart like the one that follows.

Cause and Effect

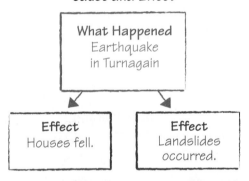

2. Look back at the list you made in response to the Quickwrite on page 370. Add to your list two or three interesting or surprising facts that you learned from reading this selection.

Interpretations

3. Like fiction writers, science writers try to create **suspense.** They want to make us eager to find out what happens next. Where in this selection did you feel suspense?

4. Lauber uses several **similes** and **metaphors** to help explain difficult information. To what things does she compare the structure of the earth and the forces that act on it? What comparisons does she use to explain rock shifts or breaks?

5. Look at the features of **scientific writing** on page 370. Which features does Lauber use in "When the Earth Shakes"? Which feature did you find most helpful as you read? Why?

Writing

Earthquake Report

In the twentieth century, major earthquakes hit San Francisco, Los Angeles, Mexico City, Tokyo, and Kobe. Research one of those big quakes in your local library or on the Internet. Look for news accounts written at the time. Write a report about the quake that presents not only facts—how strong the quake was, how long it lasted, how much damage it caused, and so on—but also the best human-interest stories you turn up in the course of your research.

Vocabulary Development

Clarifying Word Meanings

PRACTICE

In each sentence that you write in response to the directions that follow, provide clues to the meaning of the word from the Word Bank.

1. Imagine that you're an astronomer. Write a memo to the government agency that funds your work, describing the work. Use two words from the Word Bank.
2. Now, suppose you're an archaeologist directing a team of workers who are digging up an ancient city destroyed by an earthquake. Write some directions for your workers, using at least three of the words in the Word Bank.

Word Bank

churning
bluff
buckled
particles
observatories

Grammar Link MINI-LESSON

Formal and Informal English

Compare these two sentences:

> **Examine the statistics on the Alaska earthquake.**
> **Check out the stats on that Alaska shake.**

Both sentences mean the same thing, but they create different effects. The first sentence is an example of **formal English.** The second sentence is an example of **informal English.**

Formal English is the language you use for solemn occasions, such as speeches and graduation ceremonies, and in serious papers and reports. Formal English doesn't include slang or colloquial expressions.

Informal English is used in everyday speaking and writing. You use informal English when you talk with family members or friends and when you write personal letters or journal entries. Informal English includes colloquial expressions and slang.

For other examples of Formal and Informal English, see A Glossary of Usage in the *Holt Handbook,* pages 244–263.

PRACTICE

Rewrite each paragraph, making the informal paragraph formal and the formal paragraph informal.

INFORMAL

Check it out, man—a humongous quake socked Alaska at 5 o'clock in the P.M. and hoo, boy! We give this big one an eight on the old Richter.

FORMAL

We request aid. The recent earth tremor caused our building to collapse. We are currently situated beneath a mass of structural material. We are two adults and a juvenile. We request aid.

Painting with Words

THE ELEMENTS OF POETRY

by John Malcolm Brinnin

People rarely see poets at work. Even if you could watch a poet writing, you would not be able to notice much action. The making of a poem is mostly a solitary, mental activity. The only activity you might notice is the poet's use of speech—poets are not usually silent while they work. They often test what they write by saying it out loud.

To begin to understand what elements go into the making of a poem, it might help to think of the poet as an artist who is creating something with words.

Creating Images

A poet uses words the way a painter uses colors. Like painters, poets want to share a special, personal vision of the world. To do that, poets create **images,** or pictures. Poets also use **figures of speech**—language that helps make startling connections between dissimilar things. Like a painter's colors, a poet's words can put your imagination to work; they can make you see the world in new, unexpected ways.

Creating Sounds

Like musicians, poets are also concerned with sounds. Imagine a composer of music trying various patterns of notes on a piano in order to create a pleasing melody. That will give you a good idea of what poets try to do with words. Poets choose their words with great care. They revise them repeatedly, trying to find the combination that will produce just the right sound—perhaps a harsh sound, a musical sound, or a sound that matches the gallop of a horse. A poet's goal is to create sounds that will match the feelings and ideas they want to share with us.

Deciding on Forms

Like sculptors, poets are also concerned with shape, or form. When they write and revise, poets are chiseling their words to create the shapes you see on the page. Poets think about such things as how long their lines should be and whether they should group them into units (called **stanzas**). Some poets use forms based on strict rules that may be hundreds of years old. Other poets may experiment with freer forms. Whatever form a poet chooses to use, his or her purpose is to give the words a pleasing shape on the page and to help convey meaning.

How to Read Poetry

Follow these guidelines as you read the poems in this chapter:

1. Read the poem aloud at least once. A poem's sense is linked to its sound.

Grade 6 Review Reading Standard 3.4
Define how tone or meaning is conveyed in poetry through word choice, figurative language, sentence structure, line length, punctuation, rhythm, repetition, and rhyme.

2. Look for sentences, and pay attention to **punctuation.** Stop briefly at semicolons or after periods. Pause at commas. Look for sudden shifts in thought after dashes. If a line does not end with punctuation, do not make a full stop; pause only very briefly, and continue to the end of the sentence.

3. Always read a poem in a normal voice, as if you were speaking to a friend. If the poem has a steady beat, let the music emerge naturally. Do not force the poem's music by reading in a singsong way.

4. Look up unfamiliar words. Poets choose words carefully. Sometimes words in a poem are used to mean more than one thing.

5. Poets often describe one thing in terms of another. For example, a poet might describe snowflakes as if they were insects. Be alert for comparisons. Let them work on your imagination.

6. After a first reading, think about the poem. Especially think about its images and sounds, its flow of emotions and ideas. Then, read the poem a second or even a third time. With each re-reading you will discover something new.

7. Think about the poem's meaning— what message is being transmitted from the poet to you? You'll find that your response to many poems will be "It tells me something I always knew, but I never thought of it that way before."

Practice

Many years ago schoolchildren often memorized and recited poems. A poem's **rhymes** and **rhythms** help to make it fairly easy to memorize. If you would like to memorize a poem, try these techniques on one of the poems in this chapter, or memorize part of a long poem like "The Highwayman" (page 161) or "Annabel Lee" (page 175). Once you have your poem memorized, recite it for the class.

1. Read the poem aloud three or four times.
2. Look for rhymes. Rhyming words help your memory.
3. Memorize two lines at a time. Say the lines aloud several times; then cover them up, and try to recite them from memory.
4. Try to picture the words of the poem on the page.

I'm Nobody!

Literary Focus
Figures of Speech

In "I'm Nobody!" Emily Dickinson throws a spotlight on her ideas by using **figures of speech.** Figures of speech compare things that at first glance seem very different. Thinking about these unusual comparisons lets you see familiar things in a new light. The comparisons in figures of speech are imaginative and are not meant to be understood as literally true.

The most common figures of speech are similes and metaphors. A **simile** compares two unlike things, using a specific word of comparison such as *like* or *as:*

> The sleeping calico cat is *like* a cushion.

A **metaphor** directly compares two unlike things without the use of a specific word of comparison:

> The sleeping calico cat *is* a cushion.

Make the Connection
Pair and Share

"In the future everyone will be world-famous for fifteen minutes." With a partner, discuss that famous statement, which was made by the artist Andy Warhol. Do you agree with Warhol? Why or why not? What do you feel are the privileges and pitfalls of fame?

Quickwrite

Imagine that you become a celebrity overnight. Fill in a chart like the one below, showing how sudden fame might change you and your private life.

Fame

Pluses (+)	Minuses (−)
_____	_____
_____	_____
_____	_____
_____	_____

Reading Standard 1.1
Identify metaphors and similes in poetry.

Senecio (1922) by Paul Klee. Oil on gauze on cardboard (40.5 cm × 38 cm).

Kunstsammlung Basel, Kunstmuseum. Photograph Oeffentliche Kunstsammlung Basel, Martin Buhler. Accession no.1569.

I'm Nobody!

Emily Dickinson

I'm Nobody! Who are you?
Are you Nobody too?
Then there's a pair of us!
Don't tell! they'd banish us, you know!

How dreary to be Somebody!
How public—like a Frog—
To tell your name the livelong June
To an admiring Bog!

Emily Dickinson

The Granger Collection, New York.

Who Is That Mysterious Woman in White?

Today **Emily Dickinson** (1830–1886) ranks as one of America's—and the world's—greatest poets. During her lifetime, however, she was anything but famous. Of the seventeen hundred poems she wrote, only seven were published while she was alive—and she refused to have her name put on any of them.

After a normal, sociable childhood and adolescence, Dickinson seemed to retreat into the world of her own household at the age of twenty-six. By the time she was forty, she dressed only in white and rarely left her family's house in Amherst, Massachusetts. Except for family and a few old friends, she saw no one. Why? No one knows for sure. Her poems often deal with the relationship between her inner self and the outer world. Perhaps she had to draw back from the world and study it from a distance in order to write about it.

Many successful poets in the nineteenth century used regular rhymes and dum-de-dum rhythms. Emily Dickinson did not. Her rhythms were irregular and her rhymes slightly off. More important, she chose strong images to express her bold ideas. All in all, she was a true American original.

After Emily Dickinson died, her sister discovered in a locked box seven or eight hundred poems written on envelopes, paper bags, and scraps of paper, all neatly sewn into little packets. It looked as if the poet had been hoping someone would find the poems and publish them. Yet in her lifetime no one had really understood what poetry meant to Emily Dickinson. Here is how she once defined it:

> **If I read a book and it makes my whole body so cold no fire can ever warm me, I know that is poetry. If I feel physically as if the top of my head were taken off, I know that is poetry. These are the only ways I know it. Is there any other way?**

Literary Response and Analysis

Interpretations

1. How do you think the speaker feels about fame? Do you agree?

2. What does "Nobody" mean in this poem? What does "Somebody" mean?

3. Who are "they" in line 4? Why would "they" banish the speaker?

4. The **simile** in the second stanza compares a celebrity to a frog. How could a frog and a public person be similar? Is this a flattering comparison?

5. In the **metaphor** in the last line, admirers of famous people are compared to creatures in a bog (a marshy place) that admire a croaking frog. How do you think the poet feels about people who idolize celebrities?

6. Whom do you think the speaker is talking to?

7. Look back at the pluses and minuses of fame you listed for the Quick-write on page 382. Do you think your pluses would convince the poet? Explain. ✏

Writing/Art

Dear Ms. Dickinson

If you could talk to Emily Dickinson, what would you want to tell her? What would you want to ask her? Write her a letter letting her know what you think of her poem and what you wonder about her life. You could make a class collection of *Letters to a Poet*.

Judging by the Cover

Sometimes you *can* judge a book by its cover. Design a cover for a collection of Emily Dickinson's poetry, titled *I'm Nobody and Other Selected Poems*. Using "I'm Nobody!" as your inspiration, decide what art you want to put on the front cover to give readers an idea of what's inside. On the back cover, create more art, or draw a picture of the author.

Reading Standard 1.1
Identify metaphors and similes in poetry.

I Am of the Earth *and* Early Song

Literary Focus

Personification

Common sense tells us that a cloud can't cry and a river can't get angry. They can in the imagination of writers, though. When writers give human or living qualities to nonhuman or nonliving things, they are using **personification.** In "I Am of the Earth," the speaker uses personification when she speaks of the earth as a mother cradling a child.

Make the Connection

Quickwrite

Think of all the ways in which you are connected to the earth. To begin, fill in a chart like the one below:

Planet Earth

Gifts we receive from the earth:

Gifts we give back to the earth:

What is the most important gift the earth gives to you? What is the most important thing you give the earth? Briefly explain your answers.

Grade 6 Review Reading Standard 3.4 Define how tone or meaning is conveyed in poetry through figurative language.

I Am of the Earth

Anna Lee Walters

I am of the earth
She is my mother
She bore me with pride
She reared me with love
5   She cradled me each evening
She pushed the wind to make it sing
She built me a house of harmonious colors
She fed me the fruits of her fields
She rewarded me with memories of her smiles
10   She punished me with the passing of time
And at last, when I long to leave
She will embrace me for eternity

Early Song

Gogisgi/Carroll Arnett

As the sun rises
high enough to
warm the frost
off the pine needles,

5   I rise to make
four prayers of
thanksgiving for
this fine clear day,

for this good brown
10   earth, for all
brothers and sisters,
for the dark blood

that runs through me
in a great circle
15   back into this
good brown earth.

Anna Lee Walters

"Words Poured Out"
Anna Lee Walters (1947–   ) left home at the age of sixteen to attend a boarding school in New Mexico. In the Southwest, Walters began to discover her roots in the Pawnee and Otoe cultures—and in the process unlocked her voice as a writer. She recalls:

> Words poured out, page after page. I am still amazed by it, by the torrent of thoughts deposited there. . . . Today my occupation as a writer is related to what my grandfather and grandmother did when they repeated family history in the manner of their elders, leading the family all over this sacred land, this continent most recently called America in the last five hundred years, in their retelling of the Otoe journey from the dawn of time until they came to rest at Red Rock Creek a little over a century ago.

Gogisgi/Carroll Arnett

"What It Feels Like to Be Alive"
Gogisgi/Carroll Arnett (1927–   ), an American of Cherokee descent, was born in Oklahoma City. He has published more than three hundred poems and stories in magazines, sometimes under his Cherokee name, Gogisgi.

> I write poems because it seems sensible to do so and wasteful not to. A poem has a use insofar as it shows what it feels like to be alive.

Literary Response and Analysis

Interpretations

1. Tone refers to the way a writer feels about a subject. Tone is communicated by word choice, including figures of speech. How does each of these speakers feel about the earth? What words tell you so?

2. Walters **personifies** the earth as her mother. What message or feeling about our world does this comparison convey?

3. What does Arnett mean by the "great circle" (line 14)? How does Walters get at the same idea?

4. Are people always grateful children of the earth? How do some people show that their feelings about the earth are very different from the feelings of these two poets?

Writing

Lessons of the Earth

The following quotations use features of the earth to teach lessons. Choose one that you like, and write a paragraph or a brief essay about what the words mean to you. Include any of your own experiences to illustrate the lesson.

> "Consider the lilies, how they grow; they neither toil or spin; yet I tell you, even Solomon in all his glory was not arrayed like one of these."
> —Luke 12:27, from the Bible

> "There is no hill that never ends."
> —Masai proverb

> "Do you have the patience to wait till your mud settles and the water is clear?"
> —Tao-te Ching

Paraphrasing

Write a paraphrase of one of the poems you have just read. (When you **paraphrase** something, you put it in your own words, making sure to keep the writer's meaning.) Paraphrasing can help you understand and recall any written work. Follow these rules:

- Read the poem line by line. Rewrite each line or sentence in prose.

- Restate what the poem says as simply and clearly as you can. Don't include your opinions.

- Restate each figure of speech in your own words—that is, explain the comparison, and describe its emotional effect on you.

Grade 6 Review Reading Standard 3.4 Define how tone or meaning is conveyed in poetry through word choice and figurative language.

The Sounds of Poetry

by John Malcolm Brinnin

Poets use many techniques to make music out of words. The most common **sound effects** used in poetry are also used in the songs you love to listen to.

Rhythm: The Rise and Fall of Our Voices

Rhythm refers to the rise and fall of our voices as we use language. As in music, a poem's rhythm can be fast or slow, light or solemn. A poem might also sound just like everyday speech.

Poetry that is written in **meter** has a regular pattern of stressed and un-stressed syllables. Poetry that is written in **free verse** does not have a regular pat-tern of stressed and unstressed syllables. Free verse sounds like ordinary speech.

When poets write in meter, they count out the number of stressed syllables (or strong beats) and unstressed syllables (weaker beats) in each line. Then they repeat the pattern throughout the poem. To avoid a singsong effect, poets usually vary the basic pattern from time to time. Try reading aloud the following lines from a famous poem called *The Rime of the Ancient Mariner* by Samuel Taylor Coleridge. Can you hear that each line has four stressed syllables alternating with four unstressed syllables?

Day after day, day after day,
We stuck, nor breath nor motion;
As idle as a painted ship
Upon a painted ocean.

A poem's rhythm can be shown by using accent marks (′) for stressed syllables and cups (˘) for unstressed syllables. This marking is called **scanning.**

˘ ′ ˘ ′ ˘ ˘ ′ ˘ ′
Day after day, day after day

Rhyme: Chiming Sounds

Rhyme is the repetition of the sound of a stressed syllable and any unstressed syllables that follow: *sport* and *court*; *smother* and *another*; *sputtering* and *muttering*. The echoing effect of rhyme gives us pleasure. It makes us look for-ward to hearing certain chiming sounds throughout the poem. In the verse from *The Rime of the Ancient Mariner,* the rhyming words are *motion* and *ocean*.

Rhymes like *motion/ocean* in Coleridge's verse are called **end rhymes** because they occur at the ends of lines. **Internal rhymes** occur within lines, as in this line from the same poem:

The fair breeze blew, the white foam flew . . .

Grade 6 Review Reading Standard 3.4
Define how tone or meaning is conveyed in poetry through word choice, figurative language, sentence structure, line length, punctuation, rhythm, repetition, and rhyme.

Poets will often use a pattern of rhymes, called a **rhyme scheme.** To describe a rhyme scheme, assign a new letter of the alphabet to each new end rhyme. The rhyme scheme of Coleridge's verse is *abcb*.

Alliteration: Repeating Consonants

Another way poets create sound effects is through the use of alliteration (ə·lit′ər·ā′shən). **Alliteration** is the repetition of consonant sounds in words that are close together. Read this tongue twister of a poem aloud to hear all the repeated *t* sounds:

A Tutor

A tutor who tooted the flute
Tried to tutor two tooters to toot.
　　Said the two to the tutor,
　　"Is it harder to toot, or
To tutor two tooters to toot?"
　　　　　—Carolyn Wells

"A Tutor" is a **limerick,** a humorous five-line poem. Limericks have a definite rhythm and rhyme scheme. Try scanning the poem and describing the rhyme scheme now that you've tooted through it.

Onomatopoeia: Sound Echoes Sense

Onomatopoeia is a long word that is pronounced like this: än′ō·mat′ō·pē′ə. It is the use of words with sounds that echo their sense. *Crash, bang, boom, hiss*, and *toot* are all examples of onomatopoeia.

To see how sounds alone can suggest sense, read aloud this famous nonsense poem. You will not find all the words in a dictionary, but the sounds will help you guess what is going on. (What *is* going on?)

Jabberwocky

'Twas brillig, and the slithy toves
　　Did gyre and gimble in the wabe;
All mimsy were the borogoves,
　　And the mome raths outgrabe.
"Beware the Jabberwock, my son!
　　The jaws that bite, the claws that catch!
Beware the Jubjub bird, and shun
　　The frumious Bandersnatch!"
He took his vorpal sword in hand:
　　Long time the manxome foe he sought—
So rested he by the Tumtum tree,
　　And stood awhile in thought.
And, as in uffish thought he stood,
　　The Jabberwock, with eyes of flame,
Came whiffling through the tulgey wood,
　　And burbled as it came!
One, two! One, two! And through and through
　　The vorpal blade went snicker-snack!
He left it dead, and with its head
　　He went galumphing back.
"And hast thou slain the Jabberwock?
　　Come to my arms, my beamish boy!
O frabjous day! Callooh! Callay!"
　　He chortled in his joy.
'Twas brillig, and the slithy toves
　　Did gyre and gimble in the wabe;
All mimsy were the borogoves,
　　And the mome raths outgrabe.
　　　　　—Lewis Carroll

Madam and the Rent Man

Literary Focus
Tone

Has anyone ever said to you, "Don't use that tone of voice with me"? Your tone can change the meaning of what you say. Tone can turn a statement like "You're a big help" into a genuine compliment or a cruel, sarcastic remark.

Poems and stories have tones too. As you read "Madam and the Rent Man," listen for the **tone,** or the writer's attitude, toward his no-nonsense speaker.

Make the Connection
Quickwrite

"Grin and bear it."
"Stand up for yourself."

What does "grin and bear it" mean? Have you ever been in a situation where you had to grin and bear it? What does "stand up for yourself" mean? When do people have to stand up for themselves?

Write down your thoughts in response to the following questions:

- Which is harder—to grin and bear it or to stand up for yourself?
- Can you stand up for yourself and still be polite? and still be popular?
- Will people respect you if you always deal with situations you don't like by grinning and bearing it?

Background

This poem is set in Harlem, a section of New York City where most people live in rented apartments. The speaker of the poem is a woman who has reason to be angry with her landlord.

**Grade 6
Review
Reading
Standard 3.4**
Define how tone or meaning is conveyed in poetry.

The poet Langston Hughes in Harlem.

Hunter Museum of American Art, Chattanooga, Tennessee. Museum purchase with funds provided by the Benwood Foundation and the 1982 Collectors' Group. Courtesy of the artist and the Francine Seders Gallery, Seattle, Washington. HMA 1982.10.

The Apartment (1943) by Jacob Lawrence. Gouache on paper (21¼″ × 29¼″).

Madam and the Rent Man

Langston Hughes

The rent man knocked.
He said, Howdy-do?
I said, What
Can I do for you?
5 He said, You know
Your rent is due.

I said, Listen,
Before I'd pay
I'd go to Hades°
10 And rot away!

The sink is broke,
The water don't run,
And you ain't done a thing
You promised to've done.

15 Back window's cracked,
Kitchen floor squeaks,
There's rats in the cellar,
And the attic leaks.

He said, Madam,
20 It's not up to me.
I'm just the agent,
Don't you see?

I said, Naturally,
You pass the buck.
25 If it's money you want
You're out of luck.

He said, Madam,
I ain't pleased!
I said, Neither am I.

30 So we agrees!

_____

9. Hades (hā′dēz′): in Greek mythology, the underworld, or world of the dead.

Langston Hughes

"Just Singing"

Langston Hughes (1902–1967) was one of the first African American writers to win worldwide favor. Still, he never lost his popularity with the people he wrote about. Hughes once said:

> I knew only the people I had grown up with, and they weren't people whose shoes were always shined, who had been to Harvard, or who had heard of Bach.

Langston Hughes was born in Joplin, Missouri, and worked at many different jobs in various cities while writing poetry in his spare time. For two years he worked as a busboy at a hotel in Washington, D.C. During this time he wrote many poems, among them blues poems, which he would make up in his head and sing on his way to work.

> One evening, I was crossing Rock Creek Bridge, singing a blues I was trying to get right before I put it down on paper. A man passing on the opposite side of the bridge stopped and looked at me, then turned around and cut across the roadway.
>
> He said 'Son, what's the matter? Are you ill?'
>
> 'No,' I said. 'Just singing.'
>
> 'I thought you were groaning,' he commented. 'Sorry!'
> And he went on his way.
>
> So after that I never sang my verses aloud in the street anymore.

Hughes became a major literary figure in what is now known as the Harlem Renaissance of the 1920s. His poems often echo the rhythms of blues and jazz.

For Independent Reading

You can find some of Hughes's best poems in a collection called *The Dream Keeper and Other Poems.*

Literary Response and Analysis

Interpretations

1. Who is the speaker in this poem?

2. What is her argument with the rent man?

3. What does "pass the buck" mean? How has the rent man passed the buck?

4. The woman in the poem speaks plainly and bluntly. Do you think she is right to speak this way? Explain. Compare her attitude with those in your Quickwrite notes.

5. Do you think this poem has a **message**? Explain.

6. Read "Madam and the Rent Man" out loud. Then, describe its **rhyme scheme**—its pattern of rhyming sounds. Discuss whether the rhymes make the poem seem serious or lighthearted.

7. What tones do you hear expressed in this poem? Think of both the speaker and the rent man. What effect do the rhythm and rhyme have on the tones of the poem?

Writing

She Said, He Said

Write a dialogue between two people who disagree about something— perhaps money, noise, or food. The dialogue can be funny or serious. Use the vocabulary and speech patterns of everyday conversation to make your characters sound real.

Reading Aloud

The Rent Man Knocked

Prepare a read-aloud of "Madam and the Rent Man" in which you and a partner (as Madam and the rent man) read the dialogue. Practice changing the **tone** of your voice as the argument intensifies. Perform your read-aloud for the class. Afterward, ask your listeners to analyze your interpretation of the poem. Did they notice anything new about the poem as they heard it read aloud?

Grade 6 Review Reading Standard 3.4 Define how tone or meaning is conveyed in poetry through word choice, rhythm, and rhyme.

The Runaway

Literary Focus
Rhyme and Rhyme Scheme: Sound Decisions

Which words rhyme with

- *star*
- *peaches*
- *mice*
- *stopping*

Maybe your answer came automatically. There's something about **rhyme** that just comes naturally to people.

In a poem, rhymes at the ends of lines are called **end rhymes.** End rhymes determine a poem's **rhyme scheme,** or pattern of rhymes. To find out a poem's rhyme scheme, you can assign a different letter of the alphabet to each new end rhyme. The rhyme scheme of "The Runaway" begins with *abacbc.*

Make the Connection
Quickwrite ✏️

In "The Runaway," Robert Frost introduces us to a colt who's never seen snow before. Even if the only horses you've met are in the movies, you can probably identify with the colt in this poem, because he is behaving the way most of us act when we encounter something new and strange.

Take a few notes on what you think the title of the poem refers to.

Background

The subject of "The Runaway" is a Morgan colt. Morgans are a breed of swift, strong horses named for Justin Morgan (1747–1798), a Vermont schoolteacher who owned the stallion that founded the line. Morgans are small, sturdy horses that excel at weight-pulling contests. Today they are used mostly for riding and in herding cattle.

Grade 6 Review Reading Standard 3.4 Define how tone or meaning is conveyed in poetry through rhyme.

The Runaway

Robert Frost

Once when the snow of the year was beginning to fall,
We stopped by a mountain pasture to say, "Whose colt?"
A little Morgan had one forefoot on the wall,
The other curled at his breast. He dipped his head
5   And snorted at us. And then he had to bolt.
We heard the miniature thunder where he fled,
And we saw him, or thought we saw him, dim and gray,
Like a shadow against the curtain of falling flakes.
"I think the little fellow's afraid of the snow.
10   He isn't winter-broken. It isn't play
With the little fellow at all. He's running away.
I doubt if even his mother could tell him, 'Sakes,
It's only weather.' He'd think she didn't know!
Where is his mother? He can't be out alone."
15   And now he comes again with clatter of stone,
And mounts the wall again with whited eyes
And all his tail that isn't hair up straight.
He shudders his coat as if to throw off flies.
"Whoever it is that leaves him out so late,
20   When other creatures have gone to stall and bin,
Ought to be told to come and take him in."

Robert Frost

"A Lump in the Throat"

While in high school in Lawrence, Massachusetts, **Robert Frost** (1874–1963) decided to become a poet. Not only did he succeed, but for a time he was America's most celebrated living poet.

He was the first poet ever to read a poem for a presidential inauguration, that of John F. Kennedy in 1961. On his seventy-fifth birthday, the U.S. Senate passed a resolution in his honor stating, "His poems have helped to guide American thought and humor and wisdom, setting forth to our minds a reliable representation of ourselves and of all men."

"Rob" Frost lived most of his life on farms in Vermont and New Hampshire. There he grew corn, taught, and raised a family. Frost filled his poems with images of the people of New England and their haybarns, farmhouses, pastures, apple orchards, and woods. His work speaks to people everywhere because it springs from intense feelings.

Frost says this about poetry:

> **A poem . . . begins as a lump in the throat, a sense of wrong, a home-sickness, a lovesickness. . . . It finds the thought and the thought finds the words.**

Frost felt that "it is most important of all to reach the heart of the reader."

For Independent Reading

If you enjoy poetry, read more of Frost's poems in *You Come Too: Favorite Poems for Young Readers.*

Literary Response and Analysis

Reading Check

1. A speaker and a friend stop to wonder at the strange behavior of a colt. What is the colt doing?

2. What does the speaker say is causing the colt's behavior?

3. What does the speaker think the little horse's mother might say to comfort him?

Interpretations

4. To break a colt is to get a young horse used to being ridden. What do you think the expression *winter-broken* (in line 10) means?

5. How do you think the speaker feels about the person who has left the colt alone in the pasture?

6. Why do you think Frost called the poem "The Runaway"? (What is the colt running away from? What did you guess the **title** meant?)

7. When you read, you form **mental images** of people, settings, and events. Describe what you see as you read (and re-read) this poem. Compare your mental images with those of your classmates.

8. Read the poem aloud to hear its rhyming sounds. Then, work out its **rhyme scheme.**

9. *Runaway* can refer to people too. What other runaways are found in our world? What lines from the poem could apply to them?

Evaluation

10. Some people think that the colt **symbolizes** a lost child or someone who is too young or too innocent to understand what he or she is experiencing. Do you agree with this interpretation, or do you have another one? Support your interpretation with details from the poem.

Speaking
Choral Reading

With several classmates, prepare a group reading of "The Runaway." Decide which lines you will assign to a chorus and which lines you'll assign to a single voice. Practice reading aloud so that the poet's use of conversational speech rhythms comes through.

Grade 6 Review Reading Standard 3.4 Define how tone or meaning is conveyed in poetry through word choice, figurative language, and rhyme.

maggie and milly and molly and may

Literary Focus
Kinds of Rhymes

E. E. Cummings is famous for the ways he plays with sounds and punctuation. This poem is filled with rhyming sounds. Some of the rhymes are **exact** (*may/day, stone/alone, me/sea*), but some catch us by surprise because they are slightly off. These near rhymes are called **slant rhymes.** *Milly* and *molly*, for example, form a slant rhyme: Their sounds almost rhyme—but not exactly.

Make the Connection
Quickwrite ✏️

"Maggie and milly and molly and may" make some discoveries at the sea. What do you associate with the sea? Close your eyes and let sights, sounds, smells, and feelings fill your mind.

In any "ocean shape" that inspires you, such as a starfish, an octopus, or a series of waves, write down the sensory details you associate with the sea.

Background

Editors are probably itching to capitalize the *m*'s in the title of this poem, but they'd better keep their pencils to themselves. E. E. Cummings did not use standard punctuation (or any punctuation, in many cases), and he stopped capitalizing early in his writing career. These quirks of **style** are trademarks of his poetry.

salty air

**Grade 6
Review
Reading
Standard 3.4**
Define how tone or meaning is conveyed in poetry through rhyme.

maggie and milly and molly and may

E. E. Cummings

maggie and milly and molly and may
went down to the beach(to play one day)

and maggie discovered a shell that sang
so sweetly she couldn't remember her troubles,and

5   milly befriended a stranded star
whose rays five languid° fingers were;

and molly was chased by a horrible thing
which raced sideways while blowing bubbles:and

may came home with a smooth round stone
10 as small as a world and as large as alone.

For whatever we lose(like a you or a me)
it's always ourselves we find in the sea

6. languid *adj.:* drooping; weak; slow.

E. E. Cummings

"you and I are not snobs."
E. E. Cummings (1894–1962) started writing poetry as a student at Harvard University. After he read some ancient classical poetry, suddenly, as he put it, "an unknown and unknowable bird started singing."

During World War I, Cummings was an ambulance driver in France. He was mistakenly arrested for treason and clapped into detention for three months. That experience was a turning point in his life. In prison, Cummings discovered his passion for freedom and personal growth. Over the next four decades he celebrated these passions.

The following quotation is from the preface to a book of Cummings's poems. The words appear here just as he wrote them.

> The poems to come are for you and for me and are not for mostpeople
>
> —it's no use trying to pretend that mostpeople and ourselves are alike. Mostpeople have less in common with ourselves than the squarerootofminusone. You and I are human beings;mostpeople are snobs. . . .
>
> you and I are not snobs. We can never be born enough. We are human beings;for whom birth is a supremely welcome mystery,the mystery of growing:the mystery which happens only and whenever we are faithful to ourselves.

In his writing, Cummings liked to use lowercase letters, unusual word spacing (words often bump together), and his own brand of punctuation. Even though his style is new, his themes are familiar. Cummings, like lyric poets throughout the ages, celebrates the joy and wonder of life and the glory of the individual.

Literary Response and Analysis

Interpretations

1. What do the last lines of the poem mean to you?

2. Cummings writes that "it's always ourselves we find in the sea." How does each girl find herself in the sea?

3. What **exact rhymes** do you hear in the poem? What **slant rhymes** do you hear? What sounds did you *expect* to hear?

4. Read the poem aloud. What **tone** do you hear as you read about maggie, milly, molly, and may? How do the sounds of the poem contribute to its tone?

Writing

Notions of Oceans

Create your own poem about the ocean or another place you've visited, perhaps with a friend. (You might get ideas about the ocean from the notes you made for the Quickwrite on page 400.) Try out any techniques that pleased you in Cummings's poem. You might want to adopt trademarks of Cummings's style: no capitalization, not much punctuation, and words run together without space between them.

One writer opened like this:

> The beach was clean as milk, the air was sheer
> as silk, the sun was shining on the shore.

The Real Thing

Create a museum display that shows the objects maggie, milly, molly, and may find on the beach. Include pictures and scientific information about shells, starfish, crabs (or whatever you think the "horrible thing" is), and stones.

Grade 6 Review Reading Standard 3.4 Define how tone or meaning is conveyed in poetry through rhyme.

Literary Response and Analysis

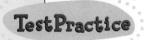 **Test Practice**

DIRECTIONS: Read the following list. Then, read each question, and decide which is the best answer.

A Prose Reading List

Key to Abbreviations

E = easy	A = average	C = challenging
F = fiction	NF = nonfiction	

- Caselli, Giovanni. *The Renaissance and the New World.* **C, NF** The author looks at the Renaissance advancements in commerce and technology that became the foundation of eighteenth-century life in England and America.

- Cosby, Bill. "Lessons." **A, NF** In this humorous essay, Cosby writes about how he and his daughter dealt with her poor performance on a test.

- Dahl, Roald. *Boy.* **C, NF** With a humorous touch the renowned author tells about his childhood years in England.

- Fritz, Jean. *Stonewall.* **E, NF** Fritz tells the life of Thomas "Stonewall" Jackson from his boyhood years to his Civil War achievements.

- George, Jean Craighead. *My Side of the Mountain.* **E, F** In this novel, Sam Gribley runs away to the Catskill Mountains, where challenges from humans and nature await.

- Hansen, Joyce. *Which Way Freedom?* **E, F** In this novel set at the beginning of the Civil War, Obi sets out to find his mother after a long separation.

- Saint-Exupéry, Antoine de. *The Little Prince.* **E, F** In this fable a stranded pilot meets a little boy who recounts his fantastic adventures on various planets.

- Soto, Gary. *Baseball in April.* **E, F** A collection of short stories. In one story, Michael and Jesse fail to make the Little League team but still find a way to play the game they love.

- Taylor, Mildred D. *Song of the Trees.* **A, F** In this novella the Logan family must prevent a businessman from destroying the forest that has brought joy to their lives.

- Zindel, Paul. *The Pigman.* **C, F** In this prize-winning novel, John and Lorraine are dissatisfied with their lives until they meet Mr. Pignati, who teaches them to cherish every moment.

Reading Standard 3.1
Articulate the expressed purposes and characteristics of different forms of prose (for example, short story, novel, novella, essay).

1. Which one of the following statements is true of both fiction and nonfiction?
   A It cannot be based on actual events.
   B It cannot be longer than one hundred pages.
   C It often reveals important truths.
   D It must have resolution.

2. Which book on the reading list is an **autobiography**?
   F *The Little Prince*
   G *The Pigman*
   H *My Side of the Mountain*
   J *Boy*

3. In which form of prose would you expect to find historical accuracy?
   A Novella
   B Biography
   C Essay
   D Novel

4. Which book on the reading list is a **biography**?
   F *Which Way Freedom?*
   G *Stonewall*
   H *Song of the Trees*
   J *The Renaissance and the New World*

5. Which item on the reading list is an **essay**?
   A "Lessons"
   B *Stonewall*
   C *Boy*
   D *Baseball in April*

6. Which book on the reading list is a collection of **short stories**?
   F *The Little Prince*
   G *The Renaissance and the New World*
   H *Baseball in April*
   J *Boy*

7. Which book on the reading list is **historical fiction**?
   A *Which Way Freedom?*
   B *My Side of the Mountain*
   C *Stonewall*
   D *The Little Prince*

8. Which two books on the list are **novels**?
   F *Which Way Freedom?* and *Song of the Trees*
   G *The Little Prince* and *Baseball in April*
   H *Boy* and *Stonewall*
   J *The Pigman* and *My Side of the Mountain*

Vocabulary Development.

TestPractice

Context Clues

DIRECTIONS: As you read each sentence, use the other words in the sentence to help you figure out what the underlined word means. Then, choose the best answer.

1. The crowd's reaction was as frenzied as the flurry of punches being thrown by the fighters.
   - **A** wild
   - **B** contagious
   - **C** hard
   - **D** deceptive

2. The children were impressed by the formidable size of their huge school.
   - **F** average
   - **G** awesome
   - **H** small
   - **J** unremarkable

3. They couldn't agree on much, but this dispute promised to drive them even further apart.
   - **A** problem
   - **B** outrage
   - **C** situation
   - **D** argument

4. She had to do everything in her power to muster the energy to be nice to her brother after what he had done.
   - **F** forgive
   - **G** summon
   - **H** forget
   - **J** receive

5. The darkening sky cast an ominous shadow, which frightened the children.
   - **A** cold
   - **B** dismal
   - **C** fearful
   - **D** threatening

6. Without warning the ground began churning like the choppy waves of a lake.
   - **F** sinking
   - **G** glistening
   - **H** bending
   - **J** stirring

7. Of the many matches scheduled for the night, the last bout would be most thrilling.
   - **A** choice
   - **B** contest
   - **C** bridge
   - **D** draw

8. The climber stood at the top of the bluff and surveyed the valley below with her binoculars.
   - **F** mountain range
   - **G** river bottom
   - **H** ship
   - **J** steep cliff

PERSUASIVE ESSAY

Righting a Wrong

In his essay "A Mason-Dixon Memory," Clifton Davis recalls an injustice from his own past and describes how the resulting conflict was resolved. Have you ever witnessed or personally experienced injustice? Is there an instance of wrongdoing in the world that especially troubles you? Write an essay about your own experience with an injustice that will help persuade others to do the right thing. You'll probably want to use library or Internet resources to gather information for your report.

 Use "Writing a Persuasive Essay," pages 598–615, for help with this assignment.

Other Choices

AUTOBIOGRAPHICAL NARRATIVE

1   It Happened to Me

In *Barrio Boy,* Ernesto Galarza writes about what it was like to go to school in a strange land with a different language and unfamiliar customs. While not everyone undergoes such an unsettling experience, each of us has a unique story to tell. Think of an event in your own life that was especially amusing, exciting, or unusual. Then, write an autobiographical narrative in which you share your experience. You may want to use dialogue to help make your true story come alive for readers.

 Use "Writing an Autobiographical Narrative," pages 704–706, for help with this assignment.

PERSUASIVE ESSAY

2   Thumbs Up (Thumbs Down?)

Piri Thomas wrote a short story about the effects of a boxing competition on two friends (page 309). Write an essay in which you express your own feelings about boxing (or another contact sport) in school. Are such sports good for young people or are they dangerous? Provide at least two strong reasons to support your position. Your reasons could be statistics, an anecdote (a story that supports your position), or facts. (You'll find opinions about boxing in an essay on page 321.)

 Use "Writing a Persuasive Essay," pages 598–615, for help with this assignment.

Fiction

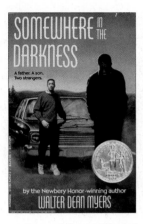

Sentimental Journey

Suffering from a kidney disease and confined to a prison hospital, Cephus "Crab" Little decides to make up for lost time with his son Jimmy in *Somewhere in the Darkness* by Walter Dean Myers. Together they journey to Crab's hometown in Arkansas, where Jimmy's growing understanding of his father's past helps him come to terms with his father and himself.

Women of Valor

In *Cut from the Same Cloth: American Women of Myth, Legend, and Tall Tale,* Robert D. San Souci takes a look at women characters in American legends with a talent for adventure. You'll find stories about Molly Cotton-Tail, Brer Rabbit's clever wife, and Sister Fox, the brains behind Brother Coyote. The stories are entertaining, and they often offer up a few lessons as well.

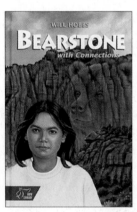

Helping Hand

Fourteen-year-old Cloyd never knew his parents and never went to school. After being on his own for so long, he has trouble accepting the kindness of an old rancher from Colorado. In Will Hobbs's novel *Bearstone,* Cloyd embraces his Native American heritage, begins to respect others, and learns what it takes to be an adult.

This title is available in the HRW Library.

On the Road Again

It's the summer of the year 1294. Adam, an eleven-year-old minstrel boy who loses contact with his father, is confounded by another minstrel named Jankin, who steals his dog, Nick. In this Middle Ages adventure, Adam scours the English countryside in search of the two things that mean the most to him—his father and his lovable dog. Of course, along the way he learns a few lessons and meets some interesting friends in Elizabeth Janet Gray's Newbery Award–winning historical novel, *Adam of the Road.*

Nonfiction

Roots of Prejudice

In Africa in 1710, Amos Fortune was born to a king. At the age of fifteen, he was captured by slave traders and transported in chains to the colony of Massachusetts. Despite the horrors of captivity, Fortune never gave up hope in securing his personal freedom. When he finally became a free man at the age of sixty, he dedicated the remainder of his life to freeing others like him. Find out more about this remarkable man in Elizabeth Yates's Newbery winner, *Amos Fortune: Free Man.*

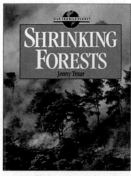

Take Care of the Earth

Forests play an important role in the earth's environment; yet we cut them down at an alarming rate, threatening the well-being of animals, plants, and ourselves. In *Shrinking Forests*, Jenny Tesar explains how essential it is to preserve rain forests. If you enjoy this book, you may enjoy other books in the Our Fragile Planet series; each examines an environmental problem.

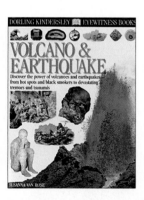

Natural Disasters

Earthquakes, floods, volcanoes—our planet sure has had some problems. In *Eyewitness Books: Volcano & Earthquake*, Susanna Van Rose explains how these problems occur. The book also covers the most famous disasters in world history, from the eruption of Mount Vesuvius during the first century to the San Francisco earthquake of 1989.

Heartbreaking Times

During the 1920s, the United States was enjoying prosperity. Then, on October 29, 1929, the New York Stock Exchange crashed. The country fell into the Great Depression; as a result, jobs were scarce, banks were closing, and families were starving. In *The Great Depression*, R. Conrad Stein looks back on this bleak period in American history.

Where I Stand

Literary Criticism

Here are the Grade 7 standards you will study for mastery in Chapter 6:

Reading

Word Analysis, Fluency, and Systematic Vocabulary Development

1.2 Use knowledge of Greek, Latin, and Anglo-Saxon roots and affixes to understand content-area vocabulary.

Reading Comprehension (Focus on Informational Materials)

2.6 Assess the adequacy, accuracy, and appropriateness of the author's evidence to support claims and assertions, noting instances of bias and stereotyping.

Literary Response and Analysis

3.6 Analyze a range of responses to a literary work, and determine the extent to which the literary elements in the work shaped those responses.

KEYWORD:
HLLA 7-6

Criticism *by* Madeline Travers Hovland

HOW DID YOU LIKE IT?

You're leaving a movie with a friend—or you've played a new computer game a classmate has lent you—or you've read a story for homework. Your friend asks, "How'd you like it?" Suppose you give one of these answers:

"Great!"

"It was OK. I've seen better."

"That was pretty bad."

Your friend comes back at you with "How come?" You're going to feel pretty silly if all you come up with is "Uh, I dunno." Backing up your opinions of what you read gets easy once you've learned the language of literature. The fact is, you've been learning how to talk about literature as you've been reading this book. Each chapter has challenged you to think, talk, and write intelligently about literary works that you've read.

Learning the Language

After you read something, you respond to it with an overall impression. You liked it, or maybe you didn't. Fine—but look a little closer. Why did you respond that way, and how can you communicate that response to others?

Chances are your response had something to do with the way the writer used the **literary elements.** The terms for the literary elements have been in **boldface** throughout this book. Literary elements are things like

character, plot, and **theme.** Using these terms, or **academic language,** helps all of us share our thoughts about what we read.

Talking About Stories

1 **Character.** When you respond to a story, you almost always want to talk about its characters. Here are some questions about characters that you can consider:

- Are the characters believable?
- Are they totally unrealistic?
- Are the causes, or **motivation,** of the characters' actions clear?
- How did you *feel* about the main character?
- What connections can you make between the characters and others you've met—including characters in stories, movies, and TV shows?
- Did you identify with any of the characters—that is, did any of them seem to share your values, dreams, worries, opinions, or background?

2 **Plot.** When critics talk about plot, they talk about what happened in a story. Did the writer hold your attention? Was the story believable? Was the plot clear—did you understand the series of causes and effects that make up a plot?

Reading Standard 3.6
Analyze a range of responses to a literary work, and determine the extent to which the literary elements in the work shaped those responses.

3 **Theme.** When most people finish reading a novel or a short story, they want to talk about meaning, or **theme.** What did the story mean? Did the story say something important about life, or did it leave you thinking, "So what?" Did it say something new, fresh, and meaningful to you? Was its theme old and tired, something you've heard many times before, like "Crime doesn't pay" or "True love wins in the end"?

Talking About a Poem

When you're dealing with poems, the important literary elements you'll want to talk about are things such as **figurative language, imagery,** and **sound effects.** You'll talk about meaning with poetry, too—that is, as with short stories, you'll talk about **theme,** and how you respond to that theme.

Talking About Nonfiction

When you read a work of nonfiction, such as a biography or an autobiography, you'll want to talk about the writer's **objectivity.** You'll also want to ask about the **primary sources** the writer used for historical data. You'll want to talk about the writer's **accuracy** on historical details. Biography and autobiography are full of **characters.** You'll want to evaluate the characters and decide if the writer has made them seem alive.

The Mirror on the Page

When we talk about literary elements in a story, a poem, or a piece of nonfiction, we're not just learning about literature. We're learning about ourselves—what fascinates us, what inspires us, what we think of ourselves, what we believe in with all our hearts. The works of literature we read become a mirror. As we understand and learn to communicate our responses to them, we learn a little more about who we are.

Practice

Divide the class into three groups. Then, choose one story or one poem that you all have read in class. Each group will discuss the same story or poem for about five minutes. For your discussions, select a question from the ones cited in this essay, and focus your discussion on that question. When your discussions are completed, after five minutes, each group should report on its discussion. What responses were expressed? Were the responses affected by a particular literary element (for example, did a group feel strongly that a character was not believable and so rejected the whole story)? What did members of the group learn from the discussion?

King Arthur: The Sword in the Stone

Literary Focus
Legend: A Little Fact, a Lot of Story

A **legend** is a very old story, passed down from one generation to the next, which usually has some connection to a real historical person or event. Legends combine historical facts with made-up events, which are often fantastic. Perhaps the most famous hero of legend in Western literature is the king called Arthur.

Make the Connection
Quickwrite ✏️

Someone living today could become a legend. Think about the qualities that might turn someone into a legend. Write down the names and deeds of some people who could be legends a hundred years from now.

Background

The hero behind the legend of King Arthur probably lived about 500 A.D. The real Arthur is believed to have been a military leader of people called the Britons.

In the first century B.C., the Romans invaded Britain and they ruled for about four hundred years. After the armies of Rome pulled out of England in 410 A.D., several tribes tried to seize control. According to the earliest legends, a leader named Arthur united the Britons and led them to victory against one of those invading tribes, the Saxons.

After Arthur's death the Saxons and the Angles, another tribe, conquered the Britons, but stories about the warrior king's unusual courage and goodness lived on among his people.

For hundreds of years, minstrels traveled from castle to castle throughout Europe, singing stories about Arthur. The legend became a series of stories about noble knights who rode out to do battle with evil wherever they found it.

Perhaps Arthur continues to live in the imagination because he represents the leader who will return someday, in time of darkness and need, to save his people. In all ages, people seem to need such hope.

Vocabulary Development

Here are some words you'll want to know before you start reading the story:

turbulent (tur′byə·lənt) *adj.:* wild; disorderly. *King Arthur restored peace to a turbulent land.*

tournament (toor′nə·mənt) *n.:* series of contests. *Sir Kay hoped to show his bravery during the tournament.*

integrity (in·teg′rə·tē) *n.:* honesty; uprightness. *A knight's integrity kept him from wrongdoing.*

congregation (käŋ′grə·gā′shən) *n.:* gathering. *The king spoke to a congregation of villagers.*

Reading Standard 3.6
Analyze a range of responses to a literary work, and determine the extent to which the literary elements in the work shaped those responses.

KING ARTHUR
The Sword in the Stone

Hudson Talbott

Arthur drawing the sword from the stone, from *Story of King Arthur and His Knights* (1923 edition).

The Granger Collection, New York.

Medieval knight on horseback.

In ancient times, when Britain was still a wild and restless place, there lived a noble king named Uther.[1] After many years of turmoil, Uther defeated the invading barbarians and drove them from the land. For this triumph, his fellow British lords proclaimed him their high king, or Pendragon, meaning "Dragon's Head."

Soon after his coronation,[2] Uther Pendragon met and fell in love with the beautiful Lady Igraine,[3] a widow whose husband Uther had killed in battle. Uther married Igraine and adopted her two young daughters, Margaise[4] and Morgan le Fay. The price for this love was a high one, however. In his passion, the king had asked for the help of his sorcerer, Merlin, in winning the hand of Lady Igraine. In return Uther had agreed to give up their firstborn son. Merlin had foreseen great evil descending upon the king and felt that he alone could protect a young heir in the dangerous times ahead.

Before long, a beautiful boy child was born. But the joy surrounding the birth was brief, for Merlin soon appeared to take the child away.

"But the child was just born!" exclaimed Uther. "How did you find out so quickly?"

Silently, the old sorcerer led the king to a balcony and pointed upward. There overhead was a great dragon formed by the stars. Its vast wings arched over the countryside, and its tail swept north beyond the horizon. "You see by this sign, my lord, that it is not I who calls for your son, but destiny."

Sadly, the king gave up his son, for Merlin convinced him that the child's great future was threatened. Indeed, Uther Pendragon died within a year from a traitor's poison and Britain was once again plunged into darkness.

 **RETELL**
1. What deals are made between Uther and Merlin?

After the death of the high king, the struggle for leadership tore Britain to pieces. The great alliance King Uther had forged was shattered into dozens of quarreling, petty kingdoms—leaving no united force to oppose foreign invasion. Barbarians swept in once again and order gave way to chaos. Marauding knights roamed the countryside, taking what they wanted and burning the rest. No one was safe at home, and travel was even more dangerous, with outlaws ruling the roads. Fear was a constant companion of those who managed to stay alive.

After sixteen turbulent years, the archbishop of Canterbury[5] summoned Merlin

---

1. **Uther** (yo͞o′thər).
2. **coronation** *n.*: ceremony for crowning a king or a queen.
3. **Igraine** (ē·grān′).
4. **Margaise** (mär·gāz′).

---

5. **archbishop of Canterbury:** even today, the highest-ranking bishop of the Church of England.

Vocabulary
turbulent (tur′byə·lənt) *adj.*: wild; disorderly.

Merlin the Magician (1903) by Howard Pyle.
The Granger Collection, New York.

to help restore order. Although the two men were of different faiths, they had great respect for each other and shared much wisdom between them.

"I am at a loss, Sir Wizard!" confided the archbishop. "I don't know how to help the people, and they are suffering more each day. If only Uther Pendragon were here!"

"I share your concerns, my lord, but I have good news," said Merlin. "Although the end of King Uther's reign left us in the dark for many years, it is at last time for the sun to return to Britain. A brilliant sun, my lord. Perhaps the brightest that Britain will ever know."

"But the sun was out this morning, sire," said the archbishop. "What has the weather to do with this?"

"I speak of the son of Uther Pendragon, the true heir of royal blood who lives in a distant land and must now be summoned forth to keep his date with destiny."

"His date with who?" asked the archbishop. "But the king had no heirs! Alas, that is our problem!"

"I wish to prove otherwise, my lord," replied Merlin. "If I have your leave to use my magic, I shall create an event to bring forth this young heir and prove to the world that he is the true and rightful high king of Britain."

The delighted archbishop agreed immediately, and Merlin withdrew to devise his scheme.

On a Sunday morning in late November the great cathedral of London was filled to capacity. As Mass was being said, a sudden murmur rippled through the crowd on the cathedral steps. Turning to see the cause of the commotion, the archbishop stopped in midprayer and walked toward the door. In the churchyard he discovered a block of white marble with an anvil sitting on top. Driven into the anvil, gleaming in the pale winter sun, was a sword. Its blade was of flawless blue-white steel, and the hilt was of highly wrought gold, inlaid with rubies, sapphires, and emeralds. Engraved in the marble block were these words:

WHOSO PULLETH OUT THIS SWORD FROM THIS STONE AND ANVIL IS RIGHTWISE KING BORN OF ENGLAND.

CLARIFY

2. How does Merlin use the words *sun* and *son* in his discussion with the archbishop? What does Merlin promise the archbishop?

Ah, so this is Merlin's plan! thought the archbishop, smiling to himself. A group of barons and knights suddenly pushed their way through the crowd, each stating loudly that he should be the first to try. A few managed to leap onto the stone and give the sword an unsuccessful yank before the archbishop stopped them.

"Order! Order!" he shouted, raising his hands to quiet the crowd. "I hereby proclaim that on Christmas morning, one month from today, all those who consider themselves worthy of attempting to pull this sword from the stone and anvil will be given the opportunity. He who wins the sword, thereby wins the kingdom."

> **RETELL**
> 3. What test will prove who the rightful king is?

A mighty roar of approval rose from the crowd. Some even danced and stomped their feet. Noticing how pleased they were, the archbishop went further. "And to celebrate this momentous occasion, a <u>tournament</u> shall be held on Christmas Eve."

With this, the delighted parishioners swept the flustered archbishop onto their shoulders and carried him jubilantly around the stone several times before setting him down. They hadn't had such cause for celebration in a long, long time.

To all parts of the kingdom, messengers rushed out, carrying the archbishop's proclamation.[6] Every castle and village was alerted, from Sussex to Cornwall and, finally, to the dark forest of Wales. There lived a certain gentle knight by the name of Sir Ector Bonmaison[7] with his two sons. The

The Beginning of a Tournament, from French manuscript (14th century).
The Granger Collection, New York.

---

6. **proclamation** *n.:* official public announcement.
7. **Bonmaison** (bōn′mā·zōn′): This name is French for "good house."

Vocabulary
tournament (toor′nə·mənt) *n.:* series of contests.

elder was a handsome, robust youth, recently knighted and now known as Sir Kay. The younger was a gentle blond lad of about sixteen whom Sir Ector and his wife had adopted as an infant. His name was Arthur.

Although Arthur was not of his blood, Sir Ector loved both sons equally and devoted himself to their upbringing.

INFER
4. Who do you guess this adopted son is?

Sir Kay was the first to hear the news of the great events in London, for as usual, he was in the courtyard polishing his helmet when the messenger arrived.

"A tournament! At last, a tournament!" he shouted. "We must set out for London at once! Father, you know what this means to me."

"Yes, son, I do," said Sir Ector, bringing the weary messenger a bowl of food. "I was young and hotblooded once, too, and eager to show the world my worthiness of knighthood. But this sword-pulling contest—do you wish to be king, as well?" he asked Kay with a smile.

"I make no pretense about that, sir. To prove myself on the field of battle is my dream."

"Please remember that, my son," said Sir Ector. "Pursuing one's goals with integrity is all that matters. Now go find Arthur so that we may prepare to leave. London is a long way off."

Arthur had wandered off alone, as he often did after finishing his chores. He was as devoted as ever to being a good squire for his brother. But, after all, Kay was *Sir* Kay now, and he rarely had anything to say to his younger brother except to bark orders at him. Arthur didn't mind, though. He was happy just to watch Kay practice his jousting and to dream of someday riding beside him in battle. In the meantime, he had to content himself with his other companions—Lionel and Jasper, his dogs; Cosmo, his falcon; the orphaned fox cubs he kept hidden in the hollow log; and the deer that came to the edge of the woods when he whistled. He was in the woods now, patiently holding out a handful of oats for the deer, when Kay came bounding through the meadows to find him.

"Arthur, come quickly!" he shouted. "We're leaving for London at once! There's a big tournament. Here's your chance to show me what a good squire you can be! Hurry!"

Arthur stood silently for a moment. He had never been more than a few miles from his home. Was he daydreaming? Or was he really going to London to help Sir Kay bring honor and glory to their family as the whole world looked on? He ran back home, doubting his own ears until he reached the courtyard and saw Sir Ector preparing their horses for the journey.

All of Britain seemed to be making its way to London Town that Christmas. Kings and dukes, earls and barons, counts and countesses funneled into the city gates for the great contest. Sir Ector was pleased to see old friends and fellow knights. Sir Kay was eager to register for the jousting. And Arthur was simply dazzled by it all.

As Sir Ector and his sons made their way through the city streets, a glint of sunlight on steel caught Arthur's eye. How odd, he thought. A sword thrust point first into an anvil on top of a block of marble, sitting in a churchyard—surrounded by guards! London is so full of wonders!

Dawn arrived with a blare of trumpets, calling all contestants to the tournament. In Sir Ector's tent, Arthur buckled the

COMPARE/ CONTRAST

5. Now you've met Arthur and his foster brother, Kay. How are they different from each other?

Vocabulary
integrity (in·teg′rə·tē) *n.:* honesty; uprightness.

chain mail[8] onto Sir Kay and slipped the tunic of the Bonmaison colors over his brother's head. Sir Ector stood and watched until the preparation was complete and his son stood before him in all his knightly glory. Silently they embraced, mounted their horses, and headed for the tournament grounds.

The stadium for the event was the grandest ever built. Never had there been such a huge <u>congregation</u> of lords and ladies in the history of England. The stands surrounded a great meadow, swept clean of all snow, with the combatants' tents at either end. In the central place of honor sat the archbishop. Patiently, he greeted each king and noble as they came forth to kiss his hand. "I should do this more often," he chuckled to himself.

The first event was the mock battle, or *mêlée*. The contestants were divided into two teams—the Reds and the Greens. Sir Kay was with the Reds, who gathered at the southern end of the field, while their opponents took the north. They all readied their lances and brought down their helmet visors in anticipation of combat. Everyone looked to the archbishop for a signal. Slowly, he raised his handkerchief, paused, and let it flutter to the ground. From either end of the field, the thunder of thousands of horse hooves rolled forward, shaking the earth, rattling the stands—louder and louder until a terrifying crash of metal split the air. A shower of splintered lances rained down in all directions. The audience gasped, and a few ladies fainted. Nothing had prepared them for this scale of violence.

Illustration from a 14th-century German manuscript.
The Granger Collection, New York.

Sir Kay performed admirably, for he charged ahead of his teammates and unseated two of the Greens. He was already winning accolades[9] as he wheeled his charger around to aid a fellow Red.

As the teams withdrew, they revealed a battleground strewn with fallen warriors, some struggling to rise under the weight of their armor, others lying ominously still. Bits and pieces of armor and broken lances littered the field.

---

9. **accolades** *n.:* words of praise.

Vocabulary
congregation (kän′grə‧gā′shən) *n.:* gathering.

---

8. **chain mail** *n.:* flexible armor made of thousands of tiny metal links.

The next charge was to be undertaken with swords. Sir Kay was appointed captain of his team for having done so well in the first round. He trotted over to Arthur and handed down his lance.

"Kay! You were magnificent!" gushed Arthur, wiping down the steaming war horse. "You've brought great honor to our house this day!"

"I need my sword, Arthur," said Sir Kay, struggling to take his helmet off.

"Your sword, of course!" said Arthur brightly. He turned to get it, but then stopped suddenly. Where was the sword? His eyes scanned the little tent with its collection of weaponry. Spear, halberd, mace, bludgeon[10] . . . but no sword.

"Excuse me, Kay," said Arthur, "could you use a battle axe?"

"Arthur, please! My sword!" said Sir Kay. "We haven't much time."

"Of course, Kay! But just a moment—I'll finish polishing it," said Arthur, slipping out through the slit in their tent. With one great leap, he landed on his pony's back and galloped madly through the deserted streets, rushing back to their camp.

"Sword. Sword. Where did I put that *sword*?" he muttered, desperately searching through the chests and bags. But to no avail.

How could this happen? he thought. Kay without a sword . . . and the whole world watching!

He paced back and forth, and then a thought struck him: Kay will not be without a sword today. I know where I can get one!

A few minutes later, he trotted into the churchyard where the sword in the anvil stood on the marble block. There wasn't a guard in sight—even they had gone to the tourney. Quietly, he brought his pony up to the stone and tugged on the reins.

"OK, Blaze. . . . We'll just see if this sword can be unstuck," he whispered. He stretched out his arm until his fingers touched the hilt.

"Hey, it's looser than I thought. . . . Steady, Blaze! Steady, boy!" As the pony stepped back a few paces, the sword glided out of the anvil's grip, unbalancing Arthur. He regained his seat and looked down in wonder at the mighty blade in his hand.

CLARIFY
6. Remember Merlin's test. What is the significance of what has just happened?

"This isn't just *any* sword. . . . Perhaps it's something the church provides for needy strangers. Yes, that must be it! Well, I'll return it after the tournament. Someone else may need it. Thank you, sword, for saving me," he said, pressing its cross to his lips. "Wait until Kay sees this!"

He flung his cloak around the great sword and drove his little horse back to the tournament with lightning speed.

By now, Sir Kay had dismounted and was rather chafed.[11]

"Arthur, where have you been?" he shouted. "You . . ."

He caught himself as Arthur dropped to one knee and opened the cloak.

"Your sword, my lord," Arthur said confidently. But his smile quickly disappeared when he saw Sir Kay's reaction. Frozen in place, his face white as milk, Sir Kay stared at the sword. Finally, he spoke.

---

10. **halberd** (hal′bərd), **mace** (mās), **bludgeon** (bluj′ən): weapons.

11. **chafed** (chāft) *v.* used as *adj.*: annoyed.

"Where did you get this?" he asked Arthur, although he knew the answer.

Arthur confessed that he had searched in vain for Sir Kay's sword and had borrowed this one instead.

"Get Father at once, and tell no one of this!" said Sir Kay sternly.

Arthur thought he must be in terrible trouble. Surely he could return the sword without his father knowing. Why did Father have to be told? Nevertheless, he obeyed his brother and returned quickly with Sir Ector.

Sir Kay closed the curtains of the tent and opened the cloak, revealing the sword to his father.

Sir Ector gasped when he saw it. "How can this be?"

"Father, I am in possession of this sword," said Sir Kay nervously. "That is what matters. Therefore, I must be king of all Britain."

"But how came you by it, son?" asked Sir Ector.

"Well, sire, I needed a sword . . . and we couldn't find mine . . . so, I decided to use this one!" said Sir Kay. Beads of sweat formed on his brow.

"Very well, lad. You drew it out of the stone. I want to see you put it back. Let's go," said Sir Ector.

"But I have the sword!" said Sir Kay. "Isn't that enough?"

"No," replied Sir Ector, as he mounted his horse and headed toward the cathedral. Arthur rode close behind and, ever so slowly, Sir Kay mounted and followed.

The churchyard was still deserted when the three arrived. "Put the sword back in the anvil," said Sir Ector bluntly. "I must see it."

"Father, I . . ."

"Just do it, Kay, and you shall be king. If that's what you want." Sir Kay climbed onto the block. Sweat was now pouring off him. He raised the mighty sword over his head and plunged it downward. But the sharp point skidded across the surface of the anvil, causing Sir Kay to fall headfirst off the block.

"Now, son, tell me. How came you by this sword?" asked Sir Ector again.

"Arthur brought it to me," said Sir Kay, dusting himself off. "He *lost* my other one."

Suddenly a fear gripped Sir Ector's heart. "Arthur, my boy," he said quietly, "will you try it for us?"

"Certainly, Father," said Arthur, "but do we have to tell anyone about this? Can't we just . . ."

"Son, please," said Sir Ector solemnly. "If you can put the sword in that anvil, please do so now."

With a pounding heart, the lad took the sword from Sir Kay's hand and climbed slowly onto the block of marble. Raising it with both hands over his head, he thrust it downward, through the anvil, burying the point deep within the stone. Effortlessly he pulled it out again, glanced at his stunned father, and shoved the sword into the stone, even deeper this time.

Sir Ector shrieked and sank to his knees. His mouth moved, but no words came out. He put his hands together as in prayer. Silently, Sir Kay knelt and did the same.

"Father! What are you doing?" cried Arthur, leaping down from the stone. "Please! Get up! Get up! I don't understand!"

"Now I know!" sputtered Sir Ector, choking back tears. "Now I know who you are!"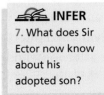

INFER

7. What does Sir Ector now know about his adopted son?

"I'm your son, Father!" said the bewildered lad, crouching down by his father and putting his head to Sir Ector's chest.

After a few deep breaths, Sir Ector regained his composure. He smiled sadly down at Arthur and stroked his head.

"Fate would have it otherwise, my boy. Look there behind you." He pointed to the gold lettering on the marble block, which stated the purpose of the sword and the anvil.

Arthur sat in silence and stared at the words in the marble.

"Although you were adopted, I've loved you like my own child, Arthur," said Sir Ector softly. "But now I realize you have the blood of kings in you. To discover your birthright is the true reason we came to London. You are now our king and we your faithful servants."

At this, Arthur broke into tears. "I don't want to be king. Not if it means losing my father!" he sobbed.

"You have a great destiny before you, Arthur. There's no use avoiding it," said Sir Ector.

Arthur wiped his eyes with his sleeve. He straightened up so he could look Sir Ector in the eyes. A few minutes passed.

"Very well," Arthur finally said slowly. "Whatever my destiny may be, I am willing to accept it. But I still need you with me."

"Then so it shall be, lad. So it shall be," said Sir Ector.

They sat quietly for a time, comforting each other, until they felt another presence. From across the yard a hooded figure quietly floated into the fading light of the winter afternoon and knelt down beside them.

"Merlin," said Sir Ector, bowing his head to the famous enchanter.

"I've been waiting for you, Arthur," said the wizard.

"You know me, my lord?" asked Arthur.

"I put you in this good man's care many years ago and have kept an eye on you ever since."

"How did you do that, sire? We live far from here."

"Oh, I have my ways," replied Merlin. "But you still managed to surprise me. The sword-pulling contest isn't until tomorrow, and you pulled it out today!" he said with a chuckle.

"But what is to become of me now?" asked Arthur.

"Well, let us start with tomorrow," replied the old sorcerer. "We must still have the contest to prove to the world that you are the rightful heir. I will come for you when the time is right."

"But after that, sire, what is my future?" asked the boy.

Merlin weighed this question carefully. He wasn't at all sure whether the boy was prepared for his answer. Finally, he spoke. "I can tell you only what my powers suggest— and they point to greatness. Greatness surrounds you like a golden cloak. Your achievements could inspire humankind for centuries to come. But you alone can fulfill this destiny and then only if you wish it. You own your future. You alone."

Arthur breathed deeply and cast his eyes downward. He thought of all the goodbyes he would have to say. He thought of his fishing hole, and the birds that ate seeds from his hand. He thought of the deer that came when he called them.

"What time tomorrow, sire?" he asked.

"After all have tried and failed, whenever that may be," replied Merlin.

Morgan le Fay, Queen of Avalon by Anthony Frederick Augustus Sandys (1829–1904).

"I will be ready, sire," said Arthur. Then he rose, bade Merlin farewell, and silently returned to his tent.

On Christmas morning, the archbishop said Mass for the largest gathering he had seen in years. The grounds surrounding the cathedral were also filled—with those seeking to make history or watch it being made.

As soon as the service ended, those who wished to try for the throne formed a line next to the marble block.

Leading the line was King Urien of Gore, husband to Margaise, Uther Pendragon's adoptive daughter. Ever since the high king's death, Urien had claimed loudly that he was the rightful heir. Indeed, he took his position on the marble block with a great sense of authority and gave the sword a confident tug, then another, and another. Urien was sweating and yanking furiously when finally asked to step down.

Next came King Lot of Orkney, husband to Morgan le Fay. King Lot felt certain that his wife's magical powers would assure his victory. But pull and tug as he might, he couldn't move the sword. After that, King Mark of Cornwall, King Leodegrance of Cameliard, and King Ryence of North Wales all took their place on the stone—and failed. The dukes of Winchester, Colchester, Worcester, and Hamcester did not fare any better. Some thought the longer they waited, the looser the sword would become, thereby improving their chances. But this wasn't the case, for the sword never budged, not even slightly. Kings, dukes, earls, counts, and knights all left that marble block empty-handed. Finally, as the day waned and the line neared its end, the crowd grew impatient for a winner. Merlin went for Arthur.

> **INFER**
>
> 8. How are all these men who try to pull the sword out of the anvil different from Arthur?

Sir Ector and Sir Kay opened the curtains of their tent when they saw Merlin approaching.

"Your hour has come, my lord," said the old wizard to Arthur, who was standing alone in the center of the tent. Silently, the boy walked forth as one in a dream.

The crowd made way for them as they entered, for Merlin was still revered by all. But who could these other people be? Especially that young blond lad dressed all in red. What was he doing here?

Merlin brought Arthur before the archbishop and bowed deeply. Arthur dropped to one knee.

"My lord," said Merlin, "I present to you a most worthy candidate for this contest. Has he your permission to attempt to pull yonder sword from the stone?"

The archbishop gazed down at the handsome lad. "Merlin, we are not familiar with this youth, nor with his credentials. By what right does he come to this place?"

"By the greatest right, my lord," said Merlin. "For this is the trueborn son of King Uther Pendragon and Queen Igraine."

The crowd broke into a loud clamor at hearing this. The startled archbishop raised his hands, but order was not easily restored.

"Merlin, have you proof of this?" asked the archbishop.

"With your permission, sire," blurted Arthur suddenly, "perhaps I can prove it by handling yonder sword in the anvil."

"Very well then, lad," said the archbishop, admiring Arthur's youthful boldness. "You have my permission. If what Merlin says is true, may God be with you."

Arthur rose and stepped up onto the marble block. He grabbed hold of the mighty golden hilt with both hands. A surge of sparkling warmth traveled up his arms, across his shoulders, and throughout his body. With one mighty tug, he freed the sword from the anvil and lifted it heavenward. The blade flashed like lightning as he swung it around his head for all to see. Then, turning the point downward again, he drove it back into the anvil with equal ease.

The entire gathering stood dumbstruck for a long moment, trying to comprehend what they had just seen. Arthur looked about for reassurance. He looked to Sir Ector, then Merlin, and then the archbishop. They all simply stared at him, with eyes wide in amazement. A child giggled and clapped his hands in glee, then so did another, and another. Cheers began to ring out as people found their voices again. Suddenly, a thunder of shouting and clapping rose up around Arthur. Amidst the tumult, he closed his eyes and whispered, "Thank you, Father."

Then he grabbed the sword's hilt for a second time and withdrew it. As he brought it above his head, a thousand swords throughout the crowd were raised in solidarity.[12] Arthur drove the sword back into the anvil and pulled it out once again. This time, as he lifted the great blade to the sky, more swords and halberds were raised, along with brooms, rakes, and walking sticks, as counts and common folk alike saluted their newfound king.

Not everyone was overjoyed at this turn of events, however. Although all had seen the miracle performed, several kings and dukes were unwilling to recognize Arthur's right to the throne. Loudest among the grumblers were King Lot and King Urien, Arthur's brothers-in-law. "How dare this

---

12. **solidarity** (säl'ə·dar′ə·tē) *n*.: unity among a group.

(Opposite) *Arthur Drawing Forth the Sword* (1903) by Howard Pyle.
The Granger Collection, New York.

beardless, unknown country boy think he can be made high king to rule over us!" they said. "Obviously, Merlin is using the boy to promote himself!"

But these malcontents[13] gained no support from those around them and were quickly shouted down. So they gathered themselves together and stormed away in a huff of indignation.[14]

PREDICT

9. Based on their actions here, what do you predict King Lot and King Urien will do?

To everyone else, the day belonged to Arthur. All the other kings and nobles rushed forth to show their acceptance, for they trusted Merlin and were grateful to have a leader at last. They hoisted the young king-to-be above their heads to parade him through the streets of London.

As the noisy procession flowed out of the churchyard, the archbishop hobbled over to Merlin to offer congratulations for a successful plan.

"Thank you, my lord, but I think we are not yet finished," said the wizard.

The archbishop looked puzzled.

"I fear that King Lot and King Urien and those other discontented souls will leave us no peace until they have another chance at the sword," continued Merlin. "We must offer them a new trial on New Year's Day."

And so they did. But again, no one could budge the sword but Arthur. These same troublesome kings and dukes still refused to acknowledge his victory, though. So another trial took place on Candlemas,[15] and yet another on Easter.

By now, the people had grown impatient, for they had believed in Arthur all along and had grown to love him. The idea of having a fresh young king inspired hope and optimism. The world suddenly felt young again.

Finally, after the trial held on Pentecost,[16] they cried out, "Enough! Arthur has proven himself five times now! We will have him for our king—and no other!"

The archbishop and Merlin agreed. There was proof beyond dispute at this point. So the coronation was set for May Day in the great cathedral of London.

Upon arriving that morning, Arthur stepped up on the block and pulled the sword from the anvil for the last time. With the blade pointing heavenward, he entered the church, walked solemnly down the central aisle, and laid the sword upon the altar. The archbishop administered the holy sacraments[17] and finally placed the crown upon Arthur's head.

Ten thousand cheers burst forth as the young king emerged from the cathedral. At Merlin's suggestion, Arthur stepped up on the marble block to speak to the people. A hush fell over the masses as he raised his hands to address them.

"People of Britain, we are now one. And so shall we remain as long as there is a breath in my body. My faith in your courage and wisdom is boundless. I ask now for your faith in me. In your trust I shall find my strength. For your good I dedicate my life. May this sword lead us to our destiny."

---

13. **malcontents** (mal′kən·tents′) *n.:* discontented or unhappy people.
14. **indignation** *n.:* righteous anger.
15. **Candlemas** (kan′dəl·məs): church feast on February 2.

16. **Pentecost** (pen′tə·kôst′): Christian festival on the seventh Sunday after Easter, celebrating the "birthday" of the Christian Church.
17. **sacraments** *n.:* rituals instituted by the church, such as baptism, Holy Communion, and penance.

Hudson Talbott

Time Traveler

The first highly successful series of books written and illustrated by **Hudson Talbott** (1949–   ) featured a gang of talking, time-traveling dinosaurs. *We're Back: A Dinosaur's Story,* the first of Talbott's dinosaur tales, was later adapted into a feature-length movie produced by Steven Spielberg.

Some of Talbott's readers, hoping for more humorous stories about dinosaurs, were surprised by the next subject he chose. *King Arthur: The Sword in the Stone* is the first book in his ongoing series, *Tales of King Arthur.* Before he started writing his King Arthur books, Talbott traveled through England and Wales researching the legends.

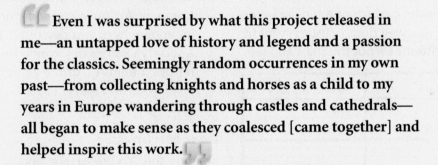

Even I was surprised by what this project released in me—an untapped love of history and legend and a passion for the classics. Seemingly random occurrences in my own past—from collecting knights and horses as a child to my years in Europe wandering through castles and cathedrals— all began to make sense as they coalesced [came together] and helped inspire this work.

Writing and illustrating books for young people is actually Talbott's second career. He supported himself first as an artist, freelance illustrator, and designer. He says that creating books for children feels "more rewarding, more permanent" than anything else he has done. "After all, a good children's book can have a lifetime effect on people."

For Independent Reading

If you especially enjoy paintings of war scenes, don't miss Talbott's *King Arthur and the Round Table.* It tells of Arthur's wars to unite his kingdom, his fateful meeting with Guinevere, and the gift of the Round Table. In Talbott's *Excalibur,* Arthur acquires a magical sword and begins to face the responsibilities of being king.

Literary Response and Analysis

Reading Check

1. What does Uther agree to give Merlin, in return for the sorcerer's help in getting Uther married to Lady Igraine?

2. Why does Merlin make the bargain with Uther?

3. What happens to Britain after Uther's death?

4. How does Arthur prove he is the rightful king of England?

5. How do King Lot and King Urien feel about Arthur as king?

Interpretations

6. Here is the pattern of a typical hero tale. How well does Arthur's story fit the pattern? Fill out the chart and see.

Hero's Story	Arthur's Story
Hero is born in an obscure place.	yes
Hero is of unknown parentage.	yes
Hero is threatened as a child.	yes
Hero passes a test to prove he is king.	yes
Hero is an unlikely person to be king.	No

Reading Standard 3.6
Analyze a range of responses to a literary work, and determine the extent to which the literary elements in the work shaped those responses.

7. How does Sir Kay, Arthur's foster brother, show that he doesn't have what it takes to be king?

8. How does Arthur change during the story? What evidence suggests that he will be a great king?

9. **Legends** are based on historical facts. The stories become exaggerated as they are passed down from one generation to the next. List two events in this story that could have happened in real life. List two fantastic, supernatural events that could not have happened in real life.

10. Share your response to this story with a partner. Then, discuss what element of the story stood out for you: the plot? the characters? the unusual setting? the theme of the unknown boy really being a king?

11. Look back at your journal notes. Compare Arthur with the future legendary hero you described. Do a society's values determine the heroes it admires, or are all heroes alike in certain ways? Explain.

Writing

Dear Merlin . . .

Imagine this: You're Arthur, and you've just been crowned king. You love Sir Ector and Sir Kay, but now you want to find out what happened to your father and mother. Write a letter to Merlin as if you were Arthur. What questions do you want to ask? How do you feel about the fact that you were never told you were adopted by Sir Ector? End your letter by confiding to Merlin how you feel about being king.

Vocabulary Development

Where Do Words Come From?
Try Latin and Anglo-Saxon

You've learned that, after Arthur's death, the Angles and the Saxons conquered the Britons. At that point, Anglo-Saxon words began coming into the language we now call English. Anglo-Saxon words tend to be short, one-syllable, simple words: *deer, pig, cow, man, wife, foot.* It's hard to make up an English sentence without using at least one Anglo-Saxon word. Words like *the, for, in,* and *is,* for instance, come from Anglo-Saxon.

In 1066, the Norman-French conquered Britain. Some of the longer, "fancier" words in English today tend to be words that were once French. In the opening sentence of *King Arthur: The Sword in the Stone,* you read the word *ancient,* which comes from a French word, *ancien.* Before it came into French, the root of *ancient* came from Latin, *ante,* "before." The Anglo-Saxon word meaning the same thing is a very different word: *old.*

> **Word Bank**
> turbulent
> tournament
> integrity
> congregation

King Arthur of Britain (detail) (14th century). French tapestry.

The Granger Collection, New York.

PRACTICE

In each of the following sentences, find two words that come from Anglo-Saxon (also called Old English) and two words that come from French and Latin. You will have to use a dictionary. In most dictionaries you will find brackets, like these [ ], that show where the word comes from. For words from Anglo-Saxon, you'll find this: **[ME]**, **[AS]**, or **[OE]**. For words from Latin or French, you'll find these: **[L]** and **[Fr]**. One of the words you pick for each sentence should be the Word Bank word. Don't bother with place names or proper names. Write the Anglo-Saxon or Latin root of each word you choose.

1. After sixteen <u>turbulent</u> years the archbishop of Canterbury asked Merlin for help.
2. "And to celebrate this momentous occasion, a <u>tournament</u> shall be held on Christmas Eve."
3. "Pursuing one's goals with <u>integrity</u> is all that matters."
4. Never had there been such a huge <u>congregation</u> of lords and ladies.

Reading Standard 1.2
Use knowledge of Latin and Anglo-Saxon roots and affixes to understand content-area vocabulary.

Three Responses to Literature

Responding to Literature: Everyone's a Critic

In this lesson you will read and evaluate several responses to a literary work. You will read three essays that answer a question about the character of Arthur in *King Arthur: The Sword in the Stone.* It will be your job, as if you were a teacher or a critic, to evaluate each response. How well has each writer answered the question? How well are the ideas about Arthur supported? You may have already done some of this in writers' workshop groups, where you give constructive criticism about another student's work. That is what you will do in this lesson.

What to Look For

A response should be focused. A focused response sticks to the topic. In this case the question asks whether or not Arthur has the potential for greatness. That means you must determine if the essay answers that question. You will also want to determine if the response answers the question in a convincing way. Decide too if the response sticks to the topic of Arthur's character.

A response must provide textual support. A supported response will offer details from the text—or from the writer's own experience—to support major ideas. In this case the writer should clearly define the qualities necessary for greatness and then prove or disprove that Arthur has them. The most successful responses will offer

specific, concrete examples from the text to support each main idea. An analysis of character should focus on the character's actions and words and on how other people respond to that character.

Here are three essays that all answer the same question. The side notes with the first essay show you how well the writer responds to the question about Arthur's character. Read the other two essays carefully to see how well they do the same.

King Arthur of Britain
by Howard Pyle.
The Granger Collection, New York.

Reading Standard 3.6
Analyze a range of responses to a literary work, and determine the extent to which the literary elements in the work shaped those responses.

Question: Does Arthur have the potential for greatness? Analyze the character of Arthur in your response.

Essay 1

In *King Arthur: The Sword in the Stone*, the writer uses important contrasts between Sir Kay and Arthur to show how Arthur is different from most youths his age. In the choices he makes and in the way he lives, Arthur shows that he is capable of greatness.

To fulfill his destiny of greatness, Arthur has to have wisdom. Although nobody sixteen years old has lived long enough to have a lot of wisdom, the writer shows us that Arthur is already gaining it. Arthur has found and protected orphaned fox cubs. He has tamed birds and deer. This requires patience and the ability to look and listen. In contrast, Kay, a more typical boy, spends most of his time polishing his helmet. Today, it would be a car, but we get the idea. How many teens today would choose to tame wild creatures for the joy of it? Arthur is unusual in a good way, a way that will bring wisdom to him.

There is a more important contrast between Arthur and Kay. Kay ignores the truth and forgets his dream when he sees a chance to be king. Before they leave for London, Kay tells his father, "To prove myself on the field of battle is my dream." Yet, when the sword falls into Kay's hand the next day, Kay forgets all of that. He sees a chance to be the king, and he tries to claim it even though he knows he didn't earn it. In contrast to Kay, Arthur thinks of others. He goes to London hoping to "help bring honor and glory to his family." He takes the sword only to meet Kay's need. He says nothing while Kay claims the kingship as his own. When he is forced to admit that he took the sword, he sees right away that being king will force him to say goodbye to many things he loves: the deer, his birds, fishing. This shows how Arthur is different from most youths. Most would see only the glory of being a king; Arthur sees past that to the sacrifices it will require. He realizes that he will never be able to live for himself only. It is a future he does not want. It is his destiny, though, and he has the courage to see that too. "Very well, whatever my destiny may be, I am willing to accept it." This combination of insight and courage also show his potential for greatness.

Margin annotations:

Answers the question directly.

States first main idea.

Supports main idea with examples from the text.

Sums up main idea.

States second main idea.

Supports second main idea with examples from the text.

When Arthur asks Merlin what his future will be, Merlin replies, "Greatness surrounds you like a golden cloak. Your achievements could inspire humankind for centuries to come. But you alone can fulfill this destiny and then only if you wish it. You own your future. You alone." How many of us are told that, if we fail ourselves, we will fail humankind? Arthur gives it all he has. He faces the archbishop, the crowds, the jealous kings who will now be his enemies. When Arthur tells the people at his coronation, "For your good I dedicate my life," somehow, we know he will not fail them . . . or himself.

> Uses a direct quote to support third main idea.

> Ends with a key quote from Arthur himself.

Essay 2

Arthur possesses the potential to be a great king. Throughout the story, Arthur shows kindness, honesty, a good heart, and courage. These are qualities any great person should have.

First, Arthur is kind. He rescues and tames wild animals. If he was not kind, would he do that? He is also nice to his brother, Sir Kay, even when his brother is full of himself. He is also willing to let Kay have the crown, but this might not be a kindness, since Arthur doesn't really want it. A great king must be kind to others in order to keep the love of the people. Arthur will succeed in this way.

Second, Arthur is honest. He does not lie to his father about pulling out the sword. At that point he thinks he is in trouble for it, so that is a courageous thing for him to do. Arthur is also truthful when he says he doesn't want to be a king but will do it if he has to. Arthur would rather stay at home with his animals in the woods and his family. A great person must be honest, and Arthur will succeed in this way, too.

Third, Arthur has a good heart. He tries his hardest in everything he does. He might mess things up, like when he loses Kay's sword, but he still tries his best. A great person cannot ever give up.

Fourth, Arthur is courageous. He stands up and faces all those people to pull out the sword. He is just sixteen years old, and now he will have to be a king of a country that many people want to take over. All in all, Arthur will fulfill his destiny by showing kindness, honesty, a good heart, and courage.

Arthur Drawing the Sword from the Stone
by Louis Rhead (1857–1926).
The Granger Collection, New York.

Essay 3

Arthur is the son of King Uther Pendragon and Queen Igraine. On the night he is born, the stars form the shape of a dragon to fore-shadow Arthur's greatness. Merlin takes him away to keep him safe. Arthur's father is poisoned a year later, so it is a good decision to take the baby away. When Arthur is sixteen, his country needs him. The years while he has been growing up were lawless and dark. Merlin devises a way to make the people accept Arthur. He puts a sword in an anvil outside the church, with a note that says that whoever could pull out the sword is the rightful king of England. The archbishop declares a contest on Christmas morning to see who is the rightful king, and a tournament on Christmas Eve. Arthur goes along to London to be squire for his bossy brother, Sir Kay. Kay is an annoying character, but Arthur doesn't mind being bossed around by Kay. He spends the time on the way to the tournament thinking of how to be a good squire and bring honor to his family. When they get to London, Arthur is amazed to see a sword in an anvil on a large block of marble with soldiers standing around it. He thinks London is full of wonders. Kay does a really good job in the first part of the tournament. He has just enough time to rest and change before the next event, and he asks Arthur for his sword. Arthur can't find it! He leaps on his pony to go back to their tent, but it isn't there. Arthur decides to borrow the one he saw from the anvil, and he goes to see about getting it. It comes out pretty easily, and Arthur takes it to Sir Kay. Kay tells Arthur to get their father. Then Kay wants to claim he's king. Their father makes him prove it. Of course, Kay cannot put the sword back, but Arthur can. Their father, Sir Ector, is overcome when he realizes who Arthur really is. He tells Arthur he can't avoid his destiny. Merlin comes along and tells Arthur he is going to be a great king, but he will have to fulfill his destiny. It will be Arthur's choice. He has to want it. Arthur is sad to give up the life he loves, but he says he will accept whatever his destiny is. Then he pulls the sword out on five different occasions to prove his worth. The people love him, and he is crowned King of England.

Illustration from an early-14th-century manuscript.

The Granger Collection, New York.

Evaluate the essays: On a scale of 0 to 5, how would you rate each essay? Base your evaluation on the points in "What to Look For," on page 432. Discuss your ratings with a partner.

Analyzing Responses to Literature

Reading Check

1. Which essay provides the most specific details from the text to support its analysis of Arthur's **character**?

2. Which essay relies on plot **summary** and not character analysis?

3. Which essay states the answer to the question about Arthur in the opening sentence?

4. Which essay uses **comparison and contrast** to make its points?

5. Which essay uses direct **quotations** from the text to support its main ideas?

6. Did Essay 3 answer the question? Why or why not?

TestPractice

Three Responses to Literature

1. How do you think each writer felt about the character of Arthur?

   A Each writer admired him.

   B Essay l writer admired Arthur, Essay 2 writer admired Arthur, Essay 3 writer did not admire him.

   C None of the writers admired Arthur.

   D It is not clear how any of the writers felt about Arthur.

2. Which **main idea** in Essay 2 is the least convincing because of lack of support?

   F Arthur's kindness

   G Arthur's honesty

   H Arthur's good heart

   J Arthur's courage

3. Which detail about Arthur's character in Essay 2 is *not* clearly supported by the story?

   A He rescues and tames wild animals.

   B He is kind to Sir Kay.

   C He tries his hardest in everything he does.

   D He is courageous.

4. Which of the following criticisms of Essay 2 is valid?

   F The writer should have summarized the plot.

   G The essay does not answer the question.

   H The writer should have quoted some of Arthur's exact words to support the main points about his character.

   J The writer doesn't put quotation marks around Arthur's exact words.

Reading Standard 3.6
Analyze a range of responses to a literary work, and determine the extent to which the literary elements in the work shaped those responses.

Vocabulary Development

The Useful Prefix: Latin and Anglo-Saxon

The English language spoken during the time when the real King Arthur lived (around 500 A.D.) used a great many words from Latin and Anglo-Saxon. The Latin words in the English language have come from many sources.

- Some came into English when Roman soldiers occupied Britain for about 450 years, beginning in 55 B.C.

- Other Latin words came into English after the Normans invaded England in 1066. The Normans brought French words with them, which in turn had come from Latin.

- Other Latin words came from the Catholic Church, which was very important in Britain for centuries.

In the box are some prefixes from the Latin language and from the old form of the English language called Anglo-Saxon. English speakers have found all of these prefixes to be very useful. A **prefix** is a word part added to the front of another word to change its meaning: When you add the prefix *un–* to the word *digested,* for example, you get the word *undigested,* meaning "not digested." If you add the prefix *pre–* to *digested,* you get *predigested,* meaning "digested beforehand."

A Box of Prefixes

(*L* means the prefix is from Latin. *AS* means it is from Anglo-Saxon.)

contra–	against (L)
mis–	badly (AS)
over–	above; excessively (AS)
post–	after (L)
pre–	before (L)
pro–	favoring; forward (L)
retro–	backward (L)
semi–	half (L)
sub–	under (L)
un–	not (AS)

PRACTICE

1. If a rocket misfires, what has happened to it?
2. If a medical test is unfavorable, why would you be upset?
3. What does it mean to say that someone is overstating a case?
4. If a food is contraindicated by the doctor, should you eat it or avoid it?
5. If someone is postoperative, has the surgery already been performed or is it about to begin?
6. Why shouldn't a juror prejudge a case?
7. If a politician is pro–social security, is she for it or against it?
8. If your pay is retroactive, are you being paid for past work or for future work?
9. What would you expect to find if someone is semiconscious?
10. Does a subway run aboveground or underground?

Reading Standard 1.2
Use knowledge of Latin and Anglo-Saxon affixes to understand content-area vocabulary.

Merlin and the Dragons

Literary Focus
A Story Pattern

All over the world we find stories of great heroes who have saved their people from terrible threats. The plots of many of these stories follow a typical pattern.

Heroes in such tales are often born in unusual circumstances, often in secret. Sometimes their true parents are unknown. The hero is often trained by a wise, older man. When his time comes, the young hero proves himself (these old stories were always about masculine heros) through some fantastic feat of strength or intellect. The hero then gathers a band of followers and embarks on a **quest** to save his people from some threat—a monster, perhaps, or a false leader.

You have seen part of this pattern in the story of King Arthur you just read, *King Arthur: The Sword and the Stone.* As you read "Merlin and the Dragons," look for events that also match the pattern of the hero tale.

Background

According to some versions of the legend, after he pulled the sword from the stone, Arthur went to live with Merlin. The old wizard was to teach the boy the lessons of being a good ruler.

In the story you are about to read, Arthur knows he is king, but he doesn't yet know his true parentage.

Vocabulary Development

Here are some words you'll need to know to understand the story:

ruthless (rōōth′lis) *adj.:* without pity. *A ruthless army destroyed the village.*

bedraggled (bē·drag′əld) *adj.:* hanging limp and wet; dirty. *The bedraggled horses needed rest.*

insolence (in′sə·ləns) *n.:* disrespect. *The rebels were punished for their insolence.*

recognition (rek′əg·nish′ən) *n.:* knowing again. *Merlin was pleased at Arthur's recognition of his past.*

Reading Standard 3.6
Analyze a range of responses to a literary work, and determine the extent to which the literary elements in the work shaped those responses.

Merlin and the Dragons

Jane Yolen

The night was dark and storm clouds marched along the sky. Rain beat against the gray castle walls. Inside, in a bedroom hung with tapestries, the young King Arthur had trouble sleeping. Awake, he was frightened. Asleep, he had disturbing dreams.

At last he climbed out of bed, took a candle to light his way, and started out the door. Suddenly remembering his crown, he turned back and found it under the bed where he'd tossed it angrily hours before. It felt too heavy for his head, so he carried it, letting it swing from his fingers.

As he walked along the hall, strange shadows danced before him. But none were as frightening as the shadows in his dreams.

He climbed the tower stairs slowly, biting his lip. When he reached the top, he pushed open the wooden door. The old magician was asleep in his chair, but woke at once, his eyes quick as a hawk's.

"What is it, boy?" the old man asked. "What brings you here at this hour?"

"I am the king," Arthur said, but softly as if he were not really sure. "I go where I will." He put the crown on Merlin's desk.

"You are a boy," Merlin replied, "and boys should be in their beds asleep."

Arthur sighed. "I could not sleep," he said. "I had bad dreams."

"Ah . . ." Merlin nodded knowingly. "Dreams." He held out a hand to the boy, but Arthur didn't dare touch those long, gnarled fingers. "Let me read your dreams."

"It is one dream, actually," Arthur said. "And always the same: a fatherless boy who becomes king simply by pulling a sword from a stone."

"Ah . . ." Merlin said again, withdrawing his fingers. "I know the very child. But if you cannot tell me more of your dream, I shall have to tell you one of mine. After all, a dream told is a story. What better than a story on a rainy night?"

Arthur settled onto a low stool and gazed up at the wizard. A story! He hadn't known he wanted a story. He'd come seeking comfort and companionship. A story was better than both.

He listened as Merlin began.

In a small village high up in the rugged mountains of Wales lived a lonely, fatherless boy named Emrys. Dark-haired he was, and small, with sharp bright eyes, and a mouth that rarely smiled. He was troubled by dreams, sleeping and waking. Dreams of dragons, dreams of stone.

His mother was the daughter of the local king and tried to be both mother and father to him. But a princess is only taught lute songs and needlework and prayers. She'd never once climbed a tree after a bird's egg or skinned her knee pursuing a lizard, or caught a butterfly in a net. Emrys had to invent that part of growing up himself. And a lonely inventing it turned out to be.

The other boys in the village teased him for not knowing who his father was. "Mother's babe," they cried, chasing him from their games.

So Emrys went after birds' eggs and lizards, butterflies and frogs by himself, giving them names both odd and admiring, like "flutterby" and "wriggletail," and making up stories of their creation. And he chanted strange-sounding spells because he liked the sounds, spells that sometimes seemed to work, most times did not.

But he never told his dreams aloud. Dreams of dragons, dreams of stone.

Now in the village lived an old man who

knew all sorts of things, from reading and writing to how birds speak and why leaves turn brown in autumn. And because Emrys was the son of a princess, the grandson of a king, the old man taught him all he knew.

It was this learning that brought the village boys to him, not in friendship but in curiosity. They would ask Emrys to show them some trick with the birds, or to tell them stories. Glad for the company, Emrys always obliged. He even took to making up harmless predictions to amuse them.

"The rain will soon fall," he would say. And often it did.

"The first spring robin will arrive." And soon after, it came.

Now any farmer's son could have made the same right guesses and after awhile the village boys were no longer impressed. However, one day Emrys found a book of seasons and planetary movements in the old man's cottage and read it cover to cover. Then he went out and announced to the astonished boys: "Tomorrow the sun will disappear."

The next day at noon, just as the calendar had foretold, an eclipse plunged the countryside into darkness. The boys and their parents were equally horrified and blamed Emrys. From then on he was called "demon's son" and avoided altogether.

Years went by and Emrys grew up, terribly alone, dreaming dreams he did not understand: dreams of a shaking tower, dreams of fighting dragons.

One day when Emrys was twelve, a cruel and ruthless man named Vortigern came to the valley. Vortigern had unjustly declared himself High King over all Britain. But the country was at last in revolt against him and he had been forced to flee, riding ever farther north and west. At last he had

arrived at the foot of Dinys Emrys, the mountain which towered above the village, with a bedraggled army on tired horses, bearing tattered banners emblazoned with red dragons. A handful of court magicians rode with them.

Vortigern pointed to the jagged mountain peak. "There," he said in a voice hard and determined. "There I will build my battle tower, so that I may see my enemies when they approach."

He turned to his soldiers. "Gather the people of this village and bring them to me, for they will be the hackers and haulers. They will make me a tower of stone."

Vocabulary
ruthless (ro͞oth′lis) *adj.:* without pity.
bedraggled (bē·drag′əld) *adj.:* hanging limp and wet; dirty.

Young Emrys looked on in amazement. Banners sewn with red dragons? A tower of stone? Such things had been in his dreams. What could it all mean?

The Welsh stonecutters began their work under the watchful eyes of the soldiers. For many days they mined the stone, cutting huge pieces from the sides of Dinys Emrys. They swore they could hear the cries of the mountain at each cut.

Next they hauled the stones with ropes, their little Welsh ponies groaning with the effort. Finally, came the day when they built the tower up on the mountainside, stone upon stone, until it rose high above the valley.

That night Emrys went to bed and dreamed once again his strange dreams. He dreamed that the tower—the very one built by Vortigern—shook and swayed and tumbled to the ground. And he dreamed that beneath the tower slept two dragons, one red as Vortigern's banners, and one white.

That very night the High King's tower began to shudder and shake and, with a mighty crash, came tumbling down. In the morning, when he saw what had happened, Vortigern was furious, convinced the villagers had done it on purpose.

"Your work is worthless," he bellowed at the Welshmen. "You will be whipped, and then you will get to work all over again."

So the Welshmen had to go back to their stonework, great welts on their backs. They hacked and hauled, and once again the tower rose high above the valley. But the night they were finished, it was the same. The tower shook and tumbled to the ground. By morning there was only a jumble of stones.

Vortigern drove the villagers even harder, and by the following week the tower was once again rebuilt. But a third time, in the night, a great shudder went through the mountain and the work once again lay in ruins. Vortigern's rage could not be contained. He called for his magicians. "There is some dark Welsh magic here. Find out the cause. My tower must stand."

Now these magicians had neither knowledge nor skill, but in their fear of Vortigern they put on a good show. They consulted the trees, both bark and root; they threw the magic sticks of prophecy; they played with the sacred stones of fate. At last they reported their findings.

"You must find a fatherless child," they said. "A child spawned by a demon. You must sprinkle his blood on the stones. Only then will the gods of this land let the stones stand." They smiled at one another and at Vortigern, smiles of those sure that what they ask cannot be done.

Vortigern did not notice their smiles. "Go find me such a child."

The magicians stopped smiling and looked nervous. "We do not know if any such child exists," they said. "We do not know if your tower can stand."

Furious, Vortigern turned to his soldiers. "Gold to whomever brings me such a child," he roared.

Before the soldiers could move, a small voice cried out. "Please, sir, we of the village know such a boy." The speaker was a spindly lad named Gwillam.

"Come here, child," said Vortigern. "Name him."

Gwillam did not dare get too close to the High King. "His name is Emrys, sir. He was spawned by a demon. He can cry the sun from the sky."

Vortigern turned to the captain of his

guards. "Bring this demon's son to me."

At that very moment, Emrys was on the mountain with the old man, absorbed in a very strange dream. Under the ruins of the tower he saw two huge stone eggs breathing in and out. Just as he emerged from his dream, he was set upon by Vortigern's soldiers. "What shall I do?" he cried.

The old man put a hand on his shoulder. "Trust your dreams."

The soldiers quickly bound Emrys and carried him to the High King, but Emrys refused to show any fear. "You are the boy without a father, the boy spawned by a devil?" Vortigern asked.

"I am a boy without a father, true," Emrys said. "But I am no demon's son. You have been listening to the words of frightened children."

The villagers and soldiers gasped at his impudence, but Vortigern said, "I will have your blood either way."

"Better that you have my dream," Emrys said. "Only my dream can guide you so that your tower will stand."

The boy spoke with such conviction, Vortigern hesitated.

"I have dreamed that beneath your tower lies a pool of water that must be drained. In the mud you will find two hollow stones. In each stone is a sleeping dragon. It is the breath of each sleeping dragon that shakes the earth and makes the tower fall. Kill the dragons and your tower will stand."

Vortigern turned to his chief magician. "Can this be true?"

The chief magician stroked his chin. "Dreams *can* come true. . . ."

Vortigern hesitated no longer. "Untie the boy, but watch him," he said

to his soldiers. "And you—Welshmen—do as the boy says. Dig beneath the rubble."

So the Welshmen removed the stones and dug down until they came to a vast pool of water. Then the soldiers drained the pool. And just as Emrys had prophesied, at the pool's bottom lay two great stones. The stones seemed to be breathing in and out, and at each breath the mud around them trembled.

"Stonecutters," cried Vortigern, "break open the stones!"

Two men with mighty hammers descended into the pit and began to pound upon the stones.

Once, twice, three times their hammers rang out. On the third try, like jets of lightning, cracks ran around each stone and they broke apart as if they had been giant eggs. Out of one emerged a dragon white as

new milk. Out of the other a dragon red as old wine.

Astonished at the power of his dreaming, Emrys opened and closed his mouth, but could not speak. The men in the pit scrambled for safety.

The High King Vortigern looked pleased. "Kill them! Kill the dragons!"

But even as he spoke, the dragons shook out their wings and leapt into the sky.

"They are leaving!" cried the chief magician.

"They are away!" cried the soldiers.

"They will not go quite yet," whispered Emrys.

No sooner had he spoken than the dragons wheeled about in the sky to face one another, claws out, belching flame. Their battle cries like nails on slate echoed in the air.

Advancing on one another, the dragons clashed, breast to breast, raining teeth and scales on the ground. For hour after hour they fought, filling the air with smoke.

First the red dragon seemed to be winning,

then the white. First one drew blood, then the other. At last, with a furious slash of its jaws, the white dragon caught the red by the throat. There was a moment of silence, and then the red dragon tumbled end over end until it hit the ground.

The white dragon followed it down, straddling its fallen foe and screaming victory into the air with a voice like thunder.

"Kill it! Kill the white now!" shouted Vortigern.

As if freed from a spell, his soldiers readied their weapons. But before a single arrow could fly, the white dragon leapt back into the air and was gone, winging over the highest peak.

"Just so the red dragon of Vortigern shall be defeated," Emrys said, but not so loud the High King could hear.

Cursing the fleeing dragon, Vortigern ordered the tower to be built again. Then he turned to Emrys. "If the tower does not stand this time, I *will* have your blood."

That night young Emrys stared out his

window, past the newly built tower. A hawk circled lazily in the sky. Suddenly the hawk swooped down, landing on his window ledge. There was a moment of silent communion between them, as if Emrys could read the hawk's thoughts, as if the hawk could read his. Then away the hawk flew.

Mountains, valleys, hillsides, forests gave way beneath the hawk's wings until, far off in the distance, it spied thousands of flickering lights coming up from the south. As if in a dream, Emrys saw these things, too.

Emerging from his vision, Emrys turned from the window and went downstairs. He found King Vortigern by the foot of the tower.

"I have seen in a vision that your fate is linked with the red dragon's," Emrys cried. "You will be attacked by thousands of soldiers under the white dragon's flag—attacked and slain."

Vortigern drew his sword, angry enough to kill the boy for such <u>insolence</u>. But at that very moment, a lookout atop the tower shouted: "Soldiers, my lord! Thousands of them!"

Vortigern raced to the top of the tower stairs and stared across the valley. It was true. And as he watched further, one of the knights leading the army urged his horse forward and raced along to the tower foot, shouting: "Come and meet your fate, murderous Vortigern!"

Vortigern turned to his own men. "Defend me! Defend my tower!"

But when they saw the numbers against them, the men all deserted.

"Surrender, Vortigern!" cried a thousand voices.

"Never!" he called back. "Never!"

Vocabulary
insolence (in′sə·ləns) *n.:* disrespect.

The old wizard stopped speaking.

"Well?" Arthur asked. "What happened to Vortigern? You cannot end a story there."

Merlin looked at him carefully. "What do *you* think happened?"

"Vortigern was slain, just as Emrys said."

"Is that the boy speaking?" asked the wizard. "Or the king?"

"The boy," admitted Arthur. "A king should forgive his enemies and make them his chiefest friends. You taught me that, Merlin. But what did happen?"

"The men of the white dragon defeated Vortigern all right. Burned him up in his own tower."

"And that knight, the one who rode up to the tower first. What became of him?"

"His name was Uther Pendragon and he eventually became the High King," Merlin said.

"Uther," mused Arthur. "He was the last High King before me. But then he was a hero. He was fit to rule. Perhaps one of his sons will come to claim my throne."

"Uther had only one son," Merlin said softly, "though only I knew of it." He looked steadily at the boy. "That son was you, Arthur."

"Me?" For a moment Arthur's voice squeaked. "Uther was my father? Then I am not fatherless? Then I am king by right and not just because I pulled a sword from a stone."

Merlin shook his head. "Don't under-estimate your real strength in pulling that sword," Merlin cautioned. "It took a true and worthy king to do what you did."

Arthur gave a deep sigh. "Why did you not tell me this before?"

The old wizard's hawk eyes opened wide. "I could not tell you until you were ready.

There are rules for prophets, just as there are rules for kings."

"So now I am king in truth."

Merlin smiled. "You were always king in truth. Only you doubted it. So you can thank your dreams for waking you up."

"What of Emrys?" Arthur asked. "What happened to him?"

"Oh—he's still around," replied the wizard. "Went on dreaming. Made a career of it." He rummaged around in some old boxes and crates by the desk until he found what he was looking for. "I still have this. Saved it all this time." He tossed a large yellowed dragon's tooth across to Arthur.

Sudden <u>recognition</u> dawned on Arthur's face. "You? You saved this? Then you were the boy named Emrys!"

"Surely you guessed that before," Merlin teased. "But now perhaps we can both go back to sleep."

"Thank you, Merlin," Arthur said. "I don't think I shall dream any more bad dreams."

Merlin's gnarled fingers caged the boy's hand for a moment. "But you shall dream," he said quietly. "Great men dream great dreams, and I have dreamed your greatness." He plucked the crown from the desktop. "Don't forget this, my lord king."

Arthur took the crown and placed it carefully on his head. Then he turned, went out the door, and down the tower stairs.

Merlin watched for a moment more, then sank back down in his chair. Closing his eyes, he fell immediately to sleep, dreaming of knights and a Round Table.

Vocabulary
recognition (rek′əg·nish′ən) *n*.: knowing again.

Jane Yolen

"Empress of Thieves"

When you click on the name *Yolen, Jane* in the computerized author index at your school or public library, you'll find screen after screen after screen of book titles. **Jane Yolen** (1939–   ) has written more than two hundred books for young people, plus dozens more for adults.

Yolen has said that she was raised on the tales of King Arthur, so it is not surprising that the King Arthur legend is one of her favorite subjects. She is considered an expert in the study and research of Arthurian legends. The character of Merlin seems to fascinate her especially, and she has written several books about him.

Yolen grew up surrounded by books and the tradition of storytelling. Both her parents were writers. One of her great-grandfathers was a storyteller in a Russian village. Yolen was in the eighth grade when she wrote her earliest books: a work about pirates and a seventeen-page historical novel about a trip by covered wagon. Since then Yolen has written many kinds of books, but she says that her primary sources of inspiration are the legends, tales, and myths of folklore.

> As a writer I am the empress of thieves, taking characters like gargoyles off Parisian churches, the *ki-lin* (or unicorn) from China, swords in stones from the Celts, landscapes from the Taino people. I have pulled threads from magic tapestries to weave my own new cloth.

For Independent Reading

If you want to read more of Yolen's novels about Merlin, look for her Young Merlin series: *Passager, Hobby*, and *Merlin*. You might also enjoy *The Dragon's Boy,* a novel about Arthur before he knew he would be king. If you share Yolen's fascination with dragons, don't miss her Pit Dragon trilogy: three fantasy novels—*Dragon's Blood, Heart's Blood,* and *A Sending of Dragons*—set in another world.

Literary Response and Analysis

Reading Check

1. It is important that you noticed the **structure** of this story. This is a story-within-a-story. What is happening in the **frame story**—the story that starts at the beginning?

2. Where does the story-*within*-the-story start? Where does it end?

3. Who is telling that story—the story about Emrys and the dragons?

4. Why is that storyteller telling Arthur the story about Emrys and the dragons?

5. Why do the boys call Emrys "demon's son"?

6. Where does Emrys get his special knowledge about nature? How does he know about the dragons in the stones?

7. Why has Vortigern fled to the valley where Emrys lives? Why does he want to have Emrys killed?

8. What happens when Vortigern's men pound on the stones beneath the tower?

9. Who leads the attack against Vortigern? How is Vortigern's conqueror related to Arthur?

10. What does Arthur learn about the identity of Emrys at the end of the story?

Interpretations

11. What details in the **plot** of this story give Emrys some of the qualities of a hero?

12. Merlin taught Arthur that "A king should forgive his enemies and make them his chiefest friends." What do you think of this as advice for any ruler?

Evaluation

13. The tales of King Arthur say little about the childhood of Arthur and even less about Merlin's childhood. How do you feel about Jane Yolen inventing details to fill in such gaps? Talk with your classmates about your responses to this story, which presents new, made-up details for an old legend.

Writing

Royal Recommendation

Briefly summarize the plots of *King Arthur: The Sword and the Stone* (page 415) and "Merlin and the Dragons." Tell which story you liked better, and give two or three reasons why you preferred it. Explain which literary elements in the work—plot, character, setting, theme—shaped your responses. Compare your responses with the responses of several classmates.

Reading Standard 3.6
Analyze a range of responses to a literary work, and determine the extent to which the literary elements in the work shaped those responses.

Vocabulary Development

Prefixes and Suffixes: Useful Additions

PRACTICE 1

The Word Bank words contain several useful prefixes and suffixes. A **prefix** is a word part added to the front of a word to change its meaning; a **suffix** is a word part added to the end of a word to change its meaning.

Using a dictionary, make word maps for these useful prefixes and suffixes:

    be–   ex–   in–
    un–   –less   –tion

Use the word map opposite as a model. The prefix *non–* is shown as an example.

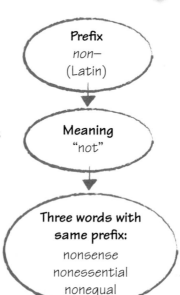

Prefix
non–
(Latin)

↓

Meaning
"not"

↓

Three words with same prefix:
nonsense
nonessential
nonequal

Word Bank

ruthless
bedraggled
insolence
recognition

PRACTICE 2

1. Name three <u>ruthless</u> people in history.
2. Name three things that could be described as <u>bedraggled</u>.
3. Name an attitude that would be the opposite of <u>insolence</u>.
4. Name three achievements that would win someone <u>recognition</u>.

Reading Standard 1.2
Use knowledge of Latin and Anglo-Saxon affixes to understand content-area vocabulary.

Sir Gawain and the Loathly Lady

Literary Focus

The Quest

A **quest** is a long and perilous journey taken in search of something of great value: a treasure, a kingdom, the hand of a fair maiden, or the answer to an important question. During the quest, heroes of folk tales and legends face temptations and difficult tasks—they may be called on to slay a dragon or solve a riddle.

Centuries ago riddles were used often in stories, as a sort of test. A **riddle** is a puzzling question or problem. The hero usually had to answer the riddle correctly before going on with the quest. In the old days, riddles were important in real life, too. A riddle contest sometimes grew into a battle of wits with great rewards for the winner and exile or death for the loser.

Make the Connection

Quickwrite 🖊

Imagine you're in a life-or-death situation. Your survival depends on giving the correct answer to one of these riddles:

> What do men want most in the world?
> What do women want most in the world?

In your journal, write three answers to each riddle. Circle the one that you think gives you your best shot at survival.

Vocabulary Development

As you begin this quest, here are some words you'll need to arm yourself. The last word may be the most important word in the story.

chivalry (shiv′əl·rē) *n.:* code that governed knightly behavior, such as courage, honor, and readiness to help the weak. *Chivalry required knights to help those in need.*

countenance (koun′tə·nəns) *n.:* face; appearance. *The knight's countenance revealed his fear.*

loathsome (lōth′səm) *adj.:* disgusting. *Dame Ragnell's appearance was loathsome.*

sovereignty (säv′rən·tē) *n.:* control; authority. *Arthur had sovereignty over all of Britain.*

A knight and his lady feeding a falcon, from a German manuscript (detail) (c. 14th century).

Cod. Pal. Germ., 848, Codex Manesse, fol. 249v. Universitätsbibliothek, Heidelberg, Germany.

Reading Standard 3.6
Analyze a range of responses to a literary work, and determine the extent to which the literary elements in the work shaped those responses.

Sir Gawain
and the
Loathly Lady

retold by
Betsy Hearne

Sir Gawain, from 13th-century manuscript.

Now if you listen awhile I will tell you a tale of Arthur the King and how an adventure once befell him.

Of all kings and all knights, King Arthur bore away the honor wherever he went. In all his country there was nothing but chivalry, and knights were loved by the people.

One day in spring King Arthur was hunting in Ingleswood with all his lords beside him. Suddenly a deer ran by in the distance and the king took up chase, calling back to his knights, "Hold you still every man, I will chase this one myself!" He took his arrows and bow and stooped low like a woodsman to stalk the deer. But every time he came near the animal, it leapt away into the forest. So King Arthur went a while after the deer, and no knight went with him, until at last he let fly an arrow and killed the deer. He had raised a bugle to his lips to summon the knights when he heard a voice behind him.

"Well met, King Arthur!"

Though he had not heard anyone approach, the king turned to see a strange knight, fully armed, standing only a few yards away.

"You have done me wrong many a year and given away my northern lands," said the strange knight. "I have your life in my hands—what will you do now, King Alone?"

"Sir Knight, what is your name?" asked the king.

"My name is Gromer Somer Joure."[1]

"Sir Gromer, think carefully," said the king. "To slay me here, unarmed as I am, will get you no honor. All knights will refuse you wherever you go. Calm yourself—come to Carlyle and I shall mend all that is amiss."

"Nay," said Sir Gromer, "by heaven, King! You shall not escape when I have you at advantage. If I let you go with only a warning, later you'll defy me, of that I'm sure."

"Spare my life, Sir Gromer, and I shall grant you whatever is in my power to give. It is shameful to slay me here, with nothing but my hunting gear, and you armed for battle."

"All your talking will not help you, King, for I want neither land nor gold, truly." Sir Gromer smiled. "Still . . . if you will promise to meet me here, in the same fashion, on a day I will choose . . ."

"Yes," said the king quickly. "Here is my promise."

"Listen and hear me out. First you will swear upon my sword to meet me here without fail, on this day one year from now. Of all your knights none shall come with you. You must tell me at your coming what thing women most desire—and if you do not bring the answer to my riddle, you will lose your head. What say you, King?"

"I agree, though it is a hateful bargain," said the king. "Now let me go. I promise you as I am the true king, to come again at this day one year from now and bring you your answer."

The knight laughed, "Now go your way, King Arthur. You do not yet know your sorrow. Yet stay a moment—do not think of playing false—for by Mary[2] I think you would betray me."

"Nay," said King Arthur. "You will never

---

2. **by Mary:** a mild oath.

Vocabulary

chivalry (shiv′əl·rē) n.: code that governed knightly behavior, which demanded courage, honor, and readiness to help the weak.

---

1. **Gromer Somer Joure** (grō·mer′ sō·mer′ zh͞oor).

find me an untrue knight. Farewell, Sir Knight, and evil met. I will come in a year's time, though I may not escape." The king began to blow his bugle for his knights to find him. Sir Gromer turned his horse and was gone as quickly as he had come, so that the lords found their king alone with the slain deer.

"We will return to Carlyle," said the king. "I do not like this hunting."

The lords knew by his <u>countenance</u> that the king met with some disturbance, but no one knew of his encounter. They wondered at the king's heavy step and sad look, until at last Sir Gawain[3] said to the king, "Sire, I marvel at you. What thing do you sorrow for?"

"I'll tell you, gentle Gawain," said Arthur. "In the forest as I pursued the deer, I met with a knight in full armor, and he charged me I should not escape him. I must keep my word to him or else I am foresworn."[4]

"Fear not my lord. I am not a man that would dishonor you."

"He threatened me, and would have slain me with great heat, but I spoke with him since I had no weapons."

"What happened then?" said Gawain.

"He made me swear to meet him there in one year's time, alone and unarmed. On that day I must tell him what women desire most, or I shall lose my life. If I fail in my answer, I know that I will be slain without mercy."

"Sire, make good cheer," said Gawain. "Make your horse ready to ride into strange country, and everywhere you meet either man or woman, ask of them the answer to the riddle. I will ride another way, and every man and woman's answer I will write in a book."

"That is well advised, Gawain," said the king. They made preparations to leave immediately, and when both were ready, Gawain rode one way and the king another—each one asked every man and woman they found what women most desire.

Some said they loved beautiful clothes; some said they loved to be praised; some said they loved a handsome man; some said one, some said another. Gawain had so many answers that he made a great book to hold them, and after many months of traveling he came back to court again. The king was there already with his book, and each looked over the other's work. But no answer seemed right.

"By God," said the king, "I am afraid. I will seek a little more in Ingleswood Forest. I have but one month to my set day, and I may find some good tidings."

"Do as you think best," said Gawain, "but whatever you do, remember that it is good to have spring again."

King Arthur rode forth on that day, into Ingleswood, and there he met with a lady. King Arthur marveled at her, for she was the ugliest creature that he had ever seen. Her face seemed almost like that of an animal, with a pushed-in nose and a few yellowing tusks for teeth. Her figure was twisted and deformed, with a hunched back and shoulders a yard broad. No tongue could tell the foulness of that lady. But she rode gaily on a palfrey[5] set with gold and precious stones,

---

5. **palfrey** (pôl′frē) *n.:* gentle riding horse.

Vocabulary
countenance (koun′tə·nəns) *n.:* face; appearance.

---

3. **Gawain** (gä′wān).
4. **foresworn** *adj.:* untrue to one's word; shown to be a liar.

King Arthur marveled at her, for she was the ugliest creature that he had ever seen.

and when she spoke her voice was sweet and soft.

"I am glad that I have met with you, King Arthur," she said. "Speak with me, for your life is in my hand. I know of your situation, and I warn you that you will not find your answer if I do not tell you."

"What do you want with me, lady?" said the king, taken aback by the lady's boldness.

"Sir, I would like to speak with you. You will die if I do not save you, I know it very well."

"What do you mean, my lady, tell me," stammered the king. "What is your desire, why is my life in your hand? Tell me, and I shall give you all you ask."

"You must grant me a knight to wed," said the lady slowly. "His name is Sir Gawain. I will make this bargain: If your life is saved another way, you need not grant my desire. If my answer saves your life, grant

me Sir Gawain as my husband. Choose now, for you must soon meet your enemy."

"By Mary," said the king, "I cannot grant you Sir Gawain. That lies with him alone—he is not mine to give. I can only take the choice to Sir Gawain."

"Well," she said. "Then go home again and speak to Sir Gawain. For though I am foul, yet am I merry, and through me he may save your life or ensure your death."

"Alas!" cried the king. "That I should cause Gawain to wed you, for he will not say no. I know not what I should do."

"Sir King, you will get no more from me. When you come again with your answer I will meet you here."

"What is your name, I pray you tell me?"

"Sir King, I am the Dame Ragnell, that never yet betrayed a man."

"Then farewell, Dame Ragnell," said the king.

Thus they departed, and the king returned to Carlyle again with a heavy heart. The first man he met was Sir Gawain. "Sire, how did you fare?" asked the knight.

"Never so ill," said the king. "I fear I will die at Sir Gromer's hand."

"Nay," said Gawain. "I would rather die myself I love you so."

"Gawain, I met today with the foulest lady that I ever saw. She said she would save my life, but first she would have you for her husband."

"Is this all?" asked Gawain. "Then I shall wed her and wed her again! Though she were a fiend, though she were as foul as Beelzebub,[6] her I shall marry. For you are my king and I am your friend—it is my part to save your life, or else I am a false knight

---

6. **Beelzebub** (bē·el′zə·bub′): the devil; Satan.

and a great coward. If she were the most loathsome woman that ever a man might see, for your love I would spare nothing."

"Thank you, Gawain," said King Arthur then. "Of all knights that I have found, you are the finest. You have saved my life, and my love will not stray from you, as I am king in this land."

The day soon came when the king was to meet the Dame Ragnell and bear his answer to Sir Gromer. Gawain rode with him to the edge of Ingleswood Forest, but there the king said, "Sir Gawain, farewell. I must go west, and you must go no further."

"God speed you on your journey. I wish I rode your way," said Gawain.

The king had ridden but a mile or so more when he met the Dame Ragnell. "Ah, Sir King, you are welcome here bearing your answer."

"Now," said the king, "since it can be no other way, tell me your answer, save my life, and Gawain shall you wed; so he has promised. Tell me in all haste. Have done, I may not tarry."[7]

"Sire," said the Dame Ragnell, "now you will know what women desire most, high and low. Some men say we desire to be fair, or to wed, or to remain fresh and young, or to have flattery from men. But there is one thing that is every woman's fantasy: We desire of men, above all other things, to have sovereignty, for then all is ours. Therefore go on your way, Sir King, and tell that knight what I have said to you. He will be angry and curse the woman who told you, for his labor is lost. Go forth—you will not be harmed."

The king rode forth in great haste until

he came to the set place and met with Sir Gromer.

"Come, come, Sir King," said the knight sternly. "Now let me have answer, for I am ready."

The king pulled out the two books for Sir Gromer to see. "Sir, I dare say the right one is there."

Sir Gromer looked over them, every one, and said at last, "Nay, nay, Sir King, you are a dead man."

"Wait, Sir Gromer," said the king. "I have one more answer to give."

"Say it," said Sir Gromer, "or so God help me you shall bleed."

"Now," said the king, "here is my answer and that is all—above all things, women desire sovereignty, for that is their liking and their greatest desire; to rule over any man. This they told me."

Sir Gromer was silent a moment with rage, but then he cried out, "And she that told you, Sir Arthur, I pray to God I might see her burn in a fire, for that was my sister, Dame Ragnell. God give her shame—I have lost much labor. Go where you like, King Arthur, for you are spared. Alas that I ever saw this day, for I know that you will be my enemy and hunt me down."

"No," said King Arthur, "you will never find me an attacker. Farewell." King Arthur turned his horse into the forest again. Soon he met with the Dame Ragnell, in the same place as before. "Sir King," she said. "I am glad you have sped well. I told you how it would be, and now since I and none other have saved your life, Gawain must wed me."

---

7. **tarry** v.: linger; delay.

Vocabulary
loathsome (lōth'səm) adj.: disgusting.
sovereignty (säv'rən·tē) n.: control; authority.

"I will not fail in my promise," said the king. "If you will be ruled by my council, you shall have your will."

"No, Sir King, I will not be ruled," said the lady. "I know what you are thinking. Ride before, and I will follow to your court. Think how I have saved your life and do not disagree with me, for if you do you will be shamed."

The king was ashamed to bring the loathly lady openly to the court, but forth she rode till they came to Carlyle. All the country wondered when she came, for they had never seen so foul a creature, but she would spare no one the sight of her. Into the hall she went, saying, "Arthur, King, fetch in Sir Gawain, before all the knights, so that you may troth[8] us together. Set forth Gawain my love, for I will not wait."

Sir Gawain stepped forward then, and said, "Sir, I am ready to fulfill the promise I made to you."

"God have mercy," said the Dame Ragnell when she saw Gawain. "For your sake I wish I were a fair woman, for you are of such goodwill." Then Sir Gawain wooed her[9] as he was a true knight, and Dame Ragnell was happy.

"Alas!" said the Queen Guinevere, and all the ladies in her bower.[10] "Alas!" said both king and knights, that the beautiful Gawain should wed such a foul and horrible woman.

She would be wedded in no other way than this—openly, with announcements in every town and village, and she had all the ladies of the land come to Carlyle for the

Queen Guinevere (1858) by William Morris.
Oil on canvas.
Tate Gallery, London.

feast. The queen begged Dame Ragnell to be married in the early morning, as privately as possible. "Nay," said the lady. "By heaven I will not no matter what you say. I will be wedded openly, as the king promised. I will

---

8. troth (trôth) v.: engage to marry.
9. wooed her: said romantic things; spoke of love.
10. bower (bou′ər) n.: old-fashioned word for a private room.

not go to the church until High Mass time,[11] and I will dine in the open hall, in the midst of all the court."

At the wedding feast there were lords and ladies from all estates, and Dame Ragnell was arrayed in the richest manner—richer even than Queen Guinevere. But all her rich clothes could not hide her foulness. When the feasting began, only Dame Ragnell ate heartily, while the knights and squires sat like stones. After the wedding feast, Sir Gawain and the Lady Ragnell retired to the wedding chamber that had been prepared for them.

"Ah, Gawain," said the lady. "Since we are wed, show me your courtesy and come to bed. If I were fair you would be joyous—yet for Arthur's sake, kiss me at least."

Sir Gawain turned to the lady, but in her place was the loveliest woman that he had ever seen.

"By God, what are you?" cried Gawain.

"Sir, I am your wife, surely. Why are you so unkind?"

"Lady, I am sorry," said Gawain. "I beg your pardon, my fair madam. For now you are a beautiful lady, and today you were the foulest woman that ever I saw. It is well, my lady, to have you thus." And he took her in his arms and kissed her with great joy.

"Sir," she said, "you have half-broken the spell on me. Thus shall you have me, but my beauty will not hold. You may have me fair by night and foul by day, or else have me fair by day, and by night ugly once again. You must choose."

"Alas!" said Gawain. "The choice is too hard—to have you fair on nights and no more, that would grieve my heart and shame me. Yet if I desire to have you fair by day and foul by night, I could not rest. I know not in the world what I should say, but do as you wish. The choice is in your hands."

"Thank you, courteous Gawain," said the lady. "Of all earthly knights you are blessed, for now I am truly loved. You shall have me fair both day and night, and ever while I live as fair. For I was shaped by witchcraft by my stepmother, God have mercy on her. By enchantment I was to be the foulest creature, till the best knight of England had wedded me and had given me the sovereignty of all his body and goods. Kiss me, Sir Gawain—be glad and make good cheer, for we are well." The two rejoiced together and thanked God for their fortune.

King Arthur came himself to call them to breakfast the next day, wondering why Gawain stayed so late with his loathly bride. Sir Gawain rose, taking the hand of his lady, and opened the door to greet the king.

The Dame Ragnell stood by the fire, with her pale lovely skin and red hair spilling down to her knees. "Lo," said Gawain to the king, "this is my wife the Dame Ragnell, who once saved your life." And Gawain told the king the story of the lady's enchantment.

"My love shall she have, for she has been so kind," said the king. And the queen said, "You will have my love forever, Lady, for you have saved my Lord Arthur." And from then on, at every great feast, that lady was the fairest, and all his life Gawain loved the Lady Ragnell.

Thus ends the adventure of King Arthur and of the wedding of Sir Gawain.

---

11. **High Mass time:** main Mass of Sunday morning. People of the highest class would attend High Mass.

Betsy Hearne

Transforming a Beast

Betsy Hearne (1942–   ) includes "Sir Gawain and the Loathly Lady" in her collection of twenty-seven Beauty and the Beast folk tales from storytellers around the world. She writes that this story "is striking in its emphasis on the importance of a woman's power to control her own choices. The horrific but heroic female saves a king's life, outwits a sorcerer, wins a husband worthy of her, and reforms him even as he transforms her."

Hearne's work in collecting and connecting various types of Beauty and the Beast tales began with her studies in graduate school. She believes that:

> All of the stories . . . are about journeys in which the heroine or hero is transformed not through winning battles but through love for another being. . . . Beauty and the Beast tales suggest, among other things, that love is as powerful as force in coming to terms with what we fear.

Hearne has worked as a children's librarian, and she is a highly respected critic, reviewer, writer, and university professor. She has edited both essay and folklore collections. She has also written four novels for young people and two volumes of poetry.

For Independent Reading

If you're interested in more Beauty and the Beast tales, be sure to read Hearne's collection, *Beauties and Beasts.* Another remarkable book by Hearne is *Seven Brave Women.* In it she describes the achievements of seven of her female ancestors, "unsung heroes," each of whom made history in her own way.

Literary Response and Analysis

Reading Check

1. This tightly plotted story is a series of **causes** and **effects.** Some of the key events in the story are listed in the boxes that follow. Write down the missing plot links (the empty boxes) in your notebook.

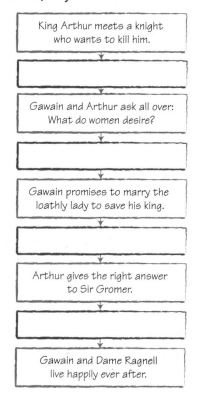

King Arthur meets a knight
who wants to kill him.

↓

↓

Gawain and Arthur ask all over:
What do women desire?

↓

↓

Gawain promises to marry the
loathly lady to save his king.

↓

↓

Arthur gives the right answer
to Sir Gromer.

↓

↓

Gawain and Dame Ragnell
live happily ever after.

Interpretations

2. Myths, legends, and folk tales are full of **metamorphoses** (met′ə·môr′fə·sēz′)—marvelous changes from one shape or form to another one. A metamorphosis can be a punishment or a reward. What metamorphosis takes place in this story? What causes it?

3. Do you agree with the answer to the riddle, or do you like your own answer better? Tell why you think men and women are the same or different in what they want most in life. ✏

4. What did you think of the choice presented to Gawain on his wedding night? Gawain makes the correct choice and is rewarded for it. What values are shown by Gawain in the choice he makes?

5. King Arthur goes on a **quest** to find the answer to a riddle. Find three places on the quest where he could have made a big mistake—but managed to stay on the right path. How did the code of **chivalry** help him make the right decision each time?

Writing

What Did You Think?

Find one aspect of this story you had a strong response to. Maybe you felt that the plot was not believable. Maybe you especially love stories set long ago. Maybe you didn't like the way the story treated ugliness. Maybe you disagree with the main idea of the story. Discuss the story in a small group, focusing on the aspect you had a strong response to. Then, write a brief essay describing your response to the story and explaining why you feel this way.

Reading Standard 3.6
Analyze a range of responses to a literary work, and determine the extent to which the literary elements in the work shaped those responses.

Vocabulary Development

The French Influence

In 1066, the Normans, who lived in France, invaded England, led by William the Conqueror. As you may have guessed from his name, William and his Normans conquered England. Within a few years the language spoken by important people in England started to be French. Words used in government, by the church, and by people at court were French.

In fact, the stories about King Arthur and his knights include many stories from France. You can spot some French influence in this story of the loathly lady.

- The angry knight's name is Gromer Somer Joure, a French name.
- *Palfrey,* meaning "gentle horse," is from the French language.

Word Bank

chivalry
countenance
loathsome
sovereignty

PRACTICE 1

Use a dictionary to look up the Word Bank words. Most dictionaries tell you in brackets the history of a word, followed by the word's definition. Which words are from the French language? Which word is English?

PRACTICE 2

This reteller of the King Arthur legend has tried to give the story an old-fashioned flavor. Translate the following sentences into the kind of English you and your friends speak today.

1. In all his country there was nothing but <u>chivalry</u>, and knights were loved by the people.

2. The lords knew by his <u>countenance</u> that the king met with some disturbance, but no one knew of his encounter.

3. "If she were the most <u>loathsome</u> woman that ever a man might see, for your love I would spare nothing."

4. "We desire of men, above all other things, to have <u>sovereignty</u>, for then all is ours."

La Belle Dame sans Merci (1893) by John William Waterhouse.

Grammar Link MINI-LESSON

Words Often Confused

The different forms of two small words in English give writers a lot of trouble. The two simple words are from Old English; they are *you* and *it. You* comes from the Old English word *eow,* and *it* comes from the Old English word *hit.*

The problems come with different forms of the words. Read these words aloud: *its* and *it's,* and *your* and *you're.* The words in each pair sound alike, but they have different uses.

- The personal possessive pronouns *its* and *your* show that something belongs to someone or something. Possessive pronouns should not have apostrophes.

  "Sir Knight, what is your name?" [The name belongs to the knight.]

  The palfrey was a gentle horse, its halters studded with jewels. [The halters belong to the horse.]

- The contractions *you're* and *it's* are both shortened combinations of a personal pronoun and the verb *is, has,* or *are.* A contraction has an apostrophe to show where letters are omitted.

  It's [it is] **easy to lose yourself in a good story.**

  You're [you are] **going to love the loathly lady story.**

PRACTICE

Write each sentence below, choosing the correct form of the underlined words. A tip: If you are unsure which word is correct, try substituting two words, such as *it is* or *you are.* If the sentence makes sense, you need the apostrophe because letters are omitted.

1. Its/It's clear that the author uses old-fashioned words.

2. Her style makes you feel as if your/you're reading the original.

3. King Arthur set up the Round Table; it's/its purpose was to make every knight equal.

4. For your/you're research paper, look up the Holy Grail.

5. The quest was it's/its own reward. What quest stories are told in you're/your tradition?

For more help, see Usage in the *Holt Handbook*, pages 244–263.

King Arthur on His Throne Surrounded by Counselors (14th century).

He's No King

Stereotypes: No Room for Individuality

Imagine you're sitting on a bench in a shopping mall, waiting for your ride to show up. You begin hearing bits of conversations from shoppers as they walk by. You hear these comments:

"People who drive sports cars are reckless."

"All politicians are dishonest."

"Boys are better than girls at math."

"Teenagers aren't concerned with world issues."

"All teenagers drive recklessly."

"Football players aren't good at schoolwork."

"Smart kids are geeky."

"Rich kids are selfish."

You've just heard people express their opinions of others using **stereotypes.** That means they are using unfair, fixed ideas about groups of people. Stereotypes don't allow for any individuality. They brand every member of a group with the same characteristics. Stereotypes are very hurtful. They are often used to persuade you to do or believe something.

Bias: An Inclination to Favor Someone

If you've ever watched your favorite sports team on the opposing team's host TV channel, you've probably noticed that the broadcasters favor the home team with their comments and calls. What you're really noticing is something called **bias**—attitudes and beliefs that shape a person's thinking in spite of the facts. Of course, your bias is evident also—you want your team to win!

As you read editorials or any kind of political or social commentary, be on the lookout for expressions that suggest the writer has already made up his or her mind about something or someone. Think of bias as an inclination to think a certain way. In its worst form, bias becomes prejudice.

Arthur and his knights setting out on the quest for the Holy Grail (c. 1380–1400) by Italian School. Vellum.

Reading Standard 2.6
Note instances of bias and stereotyping.

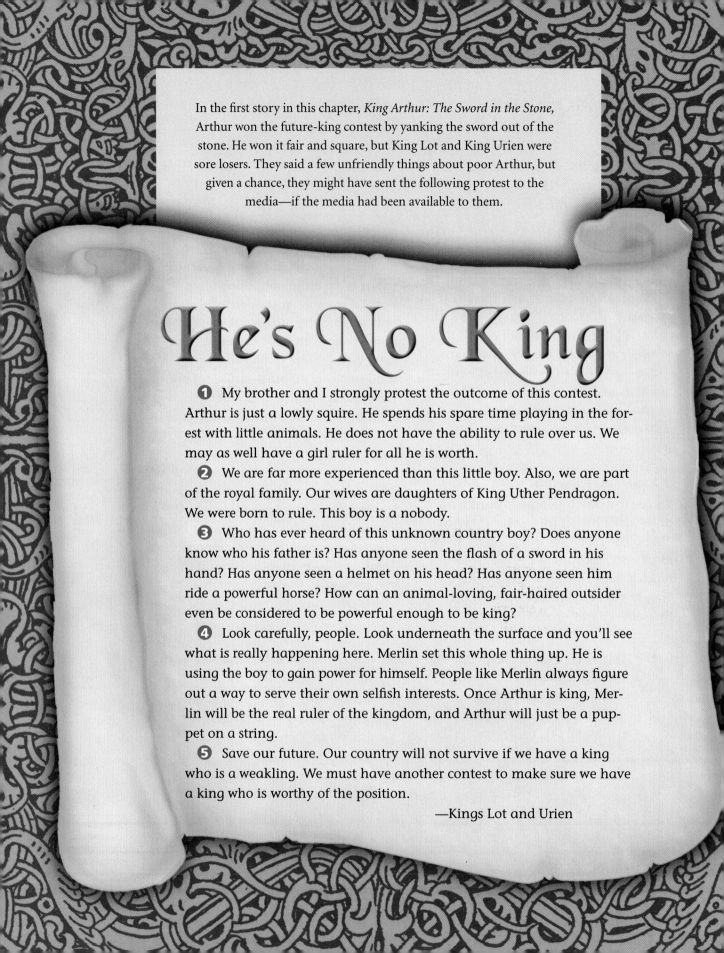

In the first story in this chapter, *King Arthur: The Sword in the Stone*, Arthur won the future-king contest by yanking the sword out of the stone. He won it fair and square, but King Lot and King Urien were sore losers. They said a few unfriendly things about poor Arthur, but given a chance, they might have sent the following protest to the media—if the media had been available to them.

He's No King

1 My brother and I strongly protest the outcome of this contest. Arthur is just a lowly squire. He spends his spare time playing in the forest with little animals. He does not have the ability to rule over us. We may as well have a girl ruler for all he is worth.

2 We are far more experienced than this little boy. Also, we are part of the royal family. Our wives are daughters of King Uther Pendragon. We were born to rule. This boy is a nobody.

3 Who has ever heard of this unknown country boy? Does anyone know who his father is? Has anyone seen the flash of a sword in his hand? Has anyone seen a helmet on his head? Has anyone seen him ride a powerful horse? How can an animal-loving, fair-haired outsider even be considered to be powerful enough to be king?

4 Look carefully, people. Look underneath the surface and you'll see what is really happening here. Merlin set this whole thing up. He is using the boy to gain power for himself. People like Merlin always figure out a way to serve their own selfish interests. Once Arthur is king, Merlin will be the real ruler of the kingdom, and Arthur will just be a puppet on a string.

5 Save our future. Our country will not survive if we have a king who is a weakling. We must have another contest to make sure we have a king who is worthy of the position.

—Kings Lot and Urien

Reading Informational Materials

Reading Check

1. Who are the speakers?

2. What do the speakers want?

3. What action do the speakers call for?

TestPractice

He's No King

1. Which statement best describes the speakers' **bias** in paragraph 1?

   A They are biased against a boy who plays with animals and is a lowly squire.

   B They are biased against animals.

   C They are biased against kings.

   D They are biased against using such a contest to determine who will be king.

2. In paragraph l, what **stereotype** do the speakers refer to?

   F All boys are animal crazy.

   G Women are unfit to rule.

   H All children are lazy.

   J Women are superior to men.

3. Which statement best expresses the **bias** in paragraph 2?

   A The speakers are biased in favor of women rulers.

   B The speakers are biased in favor of common people being rulers.

   C The speakers are biased in favor of their standing in the royal family.

   D The speakers are biased in favor of their wives.

4. "Has anyone ever seen the flash of a sword in his hand?" is a **biased** question suggesting that —

   F Arthur lied about pulling the sword out of the stone

   G Arthur has said he hates fighting

   H kings need quick reflexes

   J kings have to be tested in battle

5. It is clear that King Lot and King Urien, the speakers, protest the outcome of the sword-pulling contest mainly because —

   A they wish to rule England themselves

   B Arthur is good with animals

   C they think the contest was fixed

   D Arthur is not old enough to lead

6. In paragraph 4, the speakers reveal **bias** against —

   F Arthur

   G Merlin

   H puppet rulers

   J kings in general

Reading Standard 2.6 Note instances of bias and stereotyping.

Vocabulary Development

It's Greek to Me

Many English words have long histories—many words have been borrowed from the French, who borrowed them from the Romans, who in turn borrowed them from the Greeks. Knowing what a Greek word root means can help you figure out the meaning of other words that come from the same or similar roots.

PRACTICE

Below you will find five Greek root words and their definitions. Use context clues and the following definitions to figure out the modern words and fill in the blanks in each sentence.

GREEK ROOTS		
Root	Definition	Also Used As . . .
–astron–	"star"	–astro–
–chronos–	"time"	–chron–
–decem– –deka–	"ten"	–dec–
–helios–	"sun"	–heli–

1. If you are really in a hurry, you can charter a heli _ _ _ _ er to fly you there.
2. Events that are recorded in sequence of time are said to be chron _ _ _ _ _ _ al.
3. Some say that when our stars are crossed, _ _ _ aster strikes.
4. In ancient Rome the tenth month was Dec _ _ _ _ _ _ .
5. Astro _ _ _ _ s may one day visit other planets.
6. Diseases that extend over a long period of time are said to be chron _ _ .
7. A person who can compete in ten athletic events is called a dec _ _ _ _ ete.
8. Astro _ _ _ _ is the scientific study of the stars and the planets.
9. A dec _ _ _ is a period of ten years.
10. Heli _ _ is a light gas used to make balloons float.

ASTRO'S USES

Reading Standard 1.2
Use knowledge of Greek roots and affixes to understand content-area vocabulary.

Letter to the Editor

The Triple A's of Evidence: Adequate, Accurate, Appropriate

Is It Adequate?

You tune in to your favorite television courtroom drama, and here's what you find out: A dog's bark in the night, a loud thump against the wall, and a bag found in an airport trash can are all presented as evidence against the accused. Some believe, though, the one bit of evidence that seals the case is an ordinary baseball hat. The hat, which was found close to the scene of the crime, is too small for the head of the accused. It is up to the jury, however, to decide if the evidence against the accused is **adequate**— that is, they have to decide if there is enough evidence to prove the defendant committed murder. *Adequate* means "enough for what is needed; sufficient."

Is It Accurate?

DNA experts are brought in to determine if the DNA of the blood at the murder scene matches the DNA of the blood of the accused. Although the DNA matches exactly, experts found contaminants in one of the blood samples. It is up to the jury to decide if the expert opinion on the DNA sample is **accurate.** *Accurate* means "free from mistakes or errors."

Is It Appropriate?

The fact that a dog started barking the night of the murder may or may not be relevant to the case. It may not be **appropriate** evidence. *Appropriate* means "suitable, relevant; right for the purpose." Appropriate evidence is to the point. Appropriate evidence does not rely totally on emotional appeal. Appropriate evidence is not inflammatory. Appropriate evidence is not based on a stereotype of the defendant.

You're the Judge

When you read informational texts, you expect a writer's evidence to be adequate, accurate, and appropriate. Don't simply take the triple A's of evidence for granted. Evidence doesn't always make sense. You need to **assess,** or judge, the evidence for yourself.

When you read a statement and think to yourself, "What does that have to do with anything?" you're probably looking at **inappropriate** evidence.

If a writer states an opinion using words such as *all, each,* and *every*, you're probably looking at evidence that is **inaccurate.**

If you have to trust a person's feelings instead of relying on facts, then the evidence is most likely **inadequate.**

Reading Standard 2.6
Assess the adequacy, accuracy, and appropriateness of the author's evidence to support claims and assertions, noting instances of bias and stereotyping.

Tips for Judging Evidence

- Look for **facts** and **valid opinions** (judgments supported by facts). Plenty of facts and valid opinions usually means the information you're reading is **adequate**.

- Look for **sources** in support of **accurate** information. Does the writer cite quotations, statistics, case studies? Do the sources seem reliable?

- **Stereotypes** and expressions of **bias** are **inappropriate** evidence.

A Box of Errors in Evidence

Here are some examples of poor evidence to look for when you read:

Inaccurate evidence

> Every teenager in America uses the Internet, and test scores have gone down all over the country.

This statement is **inaccurate** because not every teenager uses the Internet. No sources are cited to support the connection.

Inadequate evidence

> My son's grades fell at the time he was allowed to use the Internet for a month.

This evidence is **inadequate** because it is one person's experience, which is not enough to support the claim. There may be other reasons for the son's poor performance.

Inappropriate evidence

> The Internet stifles the imagination because anyone who spends a lot of time with machines becomes antisocial and develops dangerous tendencies.

This is **inappropriate** evidence because it is based only on an emotional appeal.

Letter to the Editor

Regarding your recent editorial, "Violent Video Games Cause Violence in Children":

My sisters and I used to play the Barbie Game for hours, duking it out for the chance to be "Queen of the Prom." The object of the game was to be the first player to get a dress and, of course, a date. There were four boys and four dresses to compete for. The one who drew "Poindexter" as a date was totally humiliated. The dress didn't matter as much, just so long as you had something to wear to the big event.

I suppose one could say that the Barbie Game made us care more about boys and clothes than our own brains and souls. But it did none of those things. We knew it was all fiction. We didn't care if we were competing for dresses or expensive property. We were just competing.

Those who would today proclaim that games like this one made us into empty-headed weaklings would get a quick-witted and firm reaction from one of my sisters.

My brother, possibly the nicest guy I've ever known, spent his childhood in army fatigues wielding a plastic rifle. Outside my window I would hear the battles going on.

So what is all this hysteria today about video games? Isn't it the same thing? Kids are just playing make-believe. They know it's not real.

The National Institute on Media and the Family would respond that the issue of the impact of video and computer games is no child's play. The Institute has developed "KidScore," an evaluation system that rates the amount of violence, the portrayal of violence, fear, illegal or harmful content, language, nudity, and sexual content. Not exactly things that were on my old Barbie game board nor in my brother's war games.

David Walsh, president of the Institute, reports, among many other findings, "Youth who report an increased appetite for violence in video games are more likely to have gotten into physical fights in the previous year."

It turns out there are positive aspects of video games. They provide practice in problem solving and logic. They introduce children to technology. Games give children a chance to practice following directions.

But as I read the Institute's findings, I notice one tiny sentence that sends a chill up my spine. "Games could foster social isolation as they are often played alone." Sure, my sisters were a pain when they won the game. Yes, I got tired of listening to arguments between my brother and his friends about exactly who got hit in battle. But we all had a connection to one another. We fought some, laughed a lot, and without knowing it, helped one another grow up.

I'm not sure you can do that with a computer. Technology can do a lot of things, but it still can't do that.

—A Concerned Reader

Reading Informational Materials

Letter to the Editor

1. The writer's main **assertion,** or claim, about video games is —

   A video games could be dangerous because they can cause isolation

   B children should start playing the Barbie Game instead of video games

   C children who play video games will become violent

   D technology has a bad influence on children

2. Why does the writer talk about the Barbie Game and about her brother's war games?

   F To prove that the games children play do not affect their behavior as adults

   G To prove that the games children play do affect their behavior as adults

   H To show that children played less violent games years ago

   J To show that video games make children violent

3. The purpose of "KidScore" is to —

   A provide a way for people to know how video games are rated

   B provide a way for kids to keep score as they play video games

   C discourage kids from playing video games

   D provide a way for teachers to score students in the classroom

4. According to the letter, video games help children in all of the following ways *except* by—

   F giving them practice in problem solving and logic

   G giving them a chance to practice following directions

   H introducing children to technology

   J improving their reading and math scores

5. The writer's use of the statement by David Walsh is an example of —

   A a personal experience

   B a quote from an expert

   C inaccurate evidence

   D bias and stereotyping

Reading Standard 2.6
Assess the adequacy, accuracy, and appropriateness of the author's evidence to support claims and assertions, noting instances of bias and stereotyping.

6. The writer's stories about her childhood games are examples of —

   F personal experiences

   G quotes from experts

   H statistics

   J adequate evidence

7. Which of the following pieces of evidence would be **accurate** and **appropriate** in an editorial about limiting the sale of video games rated as M (Mature)?

   A My friend is totally addicted to video games.

   B According to the National Institute on Media and the Family, 54 percent of eighth- and ninth-grade boys have bought M-rated games with their own money.

   C Children can buy violent video games at any store.

   D It is easier for children to buy violent video games than it is for them to buy cigarettes.

8. Which of the following examples is a type of evidence that would *not* be **appropriate** in an editorial about the hazards of playing video games?

   F A personal story about a bad experience with video games

   G The percentage of children who feel "addicted" to video games

   H A statement about how much money children spend on video games

   J A discussion on the games children played in the 1950s

9. Which of the following statements is a **fact**?

   A "My brother [is] the nicest guy I've ever known."

   B "Kids are just playing make-believe."

   C "Youth who report an increased appetite for violence in video games are more likely to have gotten into physical fights in the previous year."

   D "I'm not sure you can do that with a computer."

Literary Response and Analysis

 **TestPractice** DIRECTIONS: Read the following essays. Then, read each multiple-choice question, and write the letter of the best response.

Essay 1

Themes in Arthurian Legends

There are many themes in the stories of King Arthur and his knights. The themes all speak to our deepest wishes: We all wish for a leader who will come and save us in our hour of need; we all wish that might will be used for right; we all wish that goodness will always be rewarded. The Arthur stories are also about doing the right thing, even when the cost of such action is great.

In *King Arthur: The Sword in the Stone,* Arthur is only sixteen when he is faced with a destiny that fills him with unhappiness: to be king of England. Yet he shoulders the burden because it is his fate. It is the right thing to do.

"Sir Gawain and the Loathly Lady" is the best story built around the theme of doing the right thing. Arthur and Gawain must make horrible choices, and they both choose to do the right thing. Sir Gromer makes Arthur promise to return unarmed one year from that day. Arthur will not break his word to save his life, even when the bargain he was forced to make is most unfair. Sir Gawain must make a truly horrifying choice. He weds the loathly lady because, for him, it is the right thing to do. He gave his word.

The end of each story shows that characters are rewarded for choosing to do the right thing. We wish that were always true in real life.

Essay 2

Women Characters in the King Arthur Stories

The three selections, *King Arthur: The Sword in the Stone,* "Merlin and the Dragons," and "Sir Gawain and the Loathly Lady," all reveal the way women are portrayed in the King Arthur stories. In *King Arthur: The Sword in the Stone* and "Merlin and the Dragons," there are no women characters at all. All of the characters are male, and all of them are heroic because they are strong and brave. They earn the reader's approval by pulling swords out of stones and stabbing people in battle. In "Sir Gawain and the Loathly Lady" one of the main characters is a lady changed by magic into a beast. She is doomed to stay in this state until a man loves her for herself alone. She is freed from her enchantment when a man agrees to marry her, although the truth is that Sir Gawain marries her only because he has agreed to in order to save King Arthur.

Reading Standard 3.6
Analyze a range of responses to a literary work, and determine the extent to which the literary elements in the work shaped those responses.

None of these stories show women or girls in active roles. I prefer to read *Harriet the Spy*. At least there is a character girls can identify with.

1. What **literary element** is the focus of Essay 1?
   A Plot
   B Character
   C Setting
   D Theme

2. What **literary element** is the focus of Essay 2?
   F Plot
   G Character
   H Setting
   J Theme

3. The **main idea** in Essay 1 is —
   A there are many themes in the King Arthur stories
   B *King Arthur: The Sword in the Stone* shows the theme of doing the right thing
   C doing the right thing is a recurring theme in the King Arthur stories
   D all characters are rewarded for doing the right thing

4. The **main idea** in Essay 2 is —
   F there are no women characters in two of the stories
   G the three selections reveal the way women are portrayed in the King Arthur stories
   H the loathly lady is released from enchantment when a man agrees to marry her
   J *Harriet the Spy* is a better story

5. Which of these **generalizations** is supported by details in the essays?
   A The writer of Essay 1 wishes that people were rewarded for doing the right thing in real life.
   B The writer of Essay 1 hates the King Arthur stories.
   C The writer of Essay 2 dislikes male characters.
   D The writer of Essay 2 likes the women characters in the King Arthur stories.

6. Which **criticism** would you apply to Essay 1?
   F The writer does not mention *King Arthur: The Sword in the Stone.*
   G The writer does not mention "Merlin and the Dragons."
   H The writer does not supply any details to support the main idea.
   J The writer talks about too many literary elements.

Reading Informational Materials

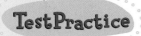TestPractice DIRECTIONS: Read the following speech. Then, read each multiple-choice question, and write the letter of the best response.

Looking for Heroes
A Speech to the Graduating Class of Lakeville Middle School

Our world, freshly beginning a new age, is a long way from the time of King Arthur. We have no fighting knights, no daring rescues of damsels, no more brave souls who think only of others above all else. We have no loyalty, no honor, no chivalry. All we have are the stories and thus, some distant memories of what the world used to be and will never be again.

If you believe that, I've got some oceanfront property in Oklahoma to sell you.

We have to change the way we think about heroes. We've just been looking in all the wrong places. Let's dismiss King Arthur and the knights of the Round Table for just a moment and go on our own quest to find our own heroes.

So, turn off the TV. Shut down the computer. Put away the magazines. Just watch life with me for a few moments.

First, we'll journey to Abilene, Texas. As we walk down the sidewalk, I want you to notice that elderly man walking towards his car. He's just an ordinary man, and it seems as if there is nothing special about him. But over fifty years ago on his forty-third Air Force mission escorting bombers over occupied Europe, his plane's engine quit at thirty thousand feet. The plane plunged 26,000 feet before he could get the engine started again. He eventually had to bail out and spent six months in hiding. He was then turned over to the Gestapo and spent three months in prison. This pilot, Bill Grosvenor, is one of about 93,000 American prisoners of war who returned alive from Europe after World War II.

Next, we fly to Seattle, Washington. As we pull up to St. Joseph's Catholic Church, I want you to notice the woman carrying a large bag and hurrying up the steps. Her name is Jeannie Jaybush, and she created the Baby Corner, an organization that last year gave away about $1,000,000 worth of baby items to families in need. About 12 percent of Seattle's homeless population is made up of children who are five years old and

Reading Standard 2.6 Assess the adequacy, accuracy, and appropriateness of the author's evidence to support claims and assertions, noting instances of bias and stereotyping.

younger, according to the City of Seattle's Human Services Department. Because of the efforts of Jaybush, these children now have some of the basic necessities that are needed to grow and be healthy.

If we had more time, we could fly to Duluth to visit a woman who is caring for her husband, one of the fourteen million Americans who have Alzheimer's disease. We could stop in Chicago, where a child with cancer lives each day fully. We could also land in Los Angeles, where a bilingual child is teaching his parents to read in English.

We'll stop our search for now, but let yours continue. Keep looking, and let your heart lead you to the heroes of today. I'll promise you, they're a lot easier to find than oceanfront property in Oklahoma.

---

1. The main **assertion** in this speech is —
   A there were more heroes in the old days
   B our world is full of heroes
   C we need more heroes like King Arthur
   D it is impossible to find heroes in today's world

2. Which of the following statements from the speech is an **accurate** piece of evidence that can be proven?
   F "About 12 percent of Seattle's homeless population is made up of children who are five years old and younger."
   G "We have to change the way we think about heroes."
   H "We have no loyalty, no honor, no chivalry."
   J "We've just been looking [for heroes] in all the wrong places."

3. Suppose a listener responded to this speech by saying, "Heroes are usually males who are recognized by most of the population." This would be an example of —
   A accurate evidence
   B appropriate evidence
   C adequate evidence
   D stereotyping

4. The speech supports its assertion mainly with —
   F statistics
   G quotes from experts
   H examples of people considered heroic
   J stereotypes

Vocabulary Development

TestPractice

Multiple-Meaning Words

DIRECTIONS: Choose the answer in which the underlined word is used the same way it is used in the quotation from *King Arthur: The Sword in the Stone.*

1. "In the churchyard he discovered a block of white marble with an anvil sitting on top."
   A The football player tried to block his opponent's kick.
   B They walked one block to the bus stop.
   C The statue was placed on a large wooden block.
   D Our class bought a block of tickets for the performance.

2. "Nothing had prepared them for this scale of violence."
   F Weigh yourself on the scale in the bathroom.
   G The pianist practiced each scale twenty times.
   H The scale of talent at this year's gymnastic competition was quite impressive.
   J On this scale model, one inch represents three feet.

3. "As soon as the service ended, those who wished to try for the throne formed a line next to the marble block."
   A The line to buy tickets was longer than we expected.
   B The fisherman attached the hook to his line.
   C The actor had only one line to memorize.
   D The truck crossed the state line at six o'clock.

4. " 'My lord,' said Merlin, 'I present to you a most worthy candidate for this contest.' "
   F When the teacher called my name, I said, "Present."
   G For my birthday I was given the present of my dreams.
   H Don't dwell on the past; focus on the present.
   J The emcee at the wedding reception finally said, "I now present the bride and groom."

5. "Then, turning the point downward again, he drove it back into the anvil with equal ease."
   A It's not polite to point.
   B At a certain point in the discussion, the group felt it would be a good time to take a break.
   C The warrior sharpened the point of his spear before going into battle.
   D "Get to the point," she said impatiently.

RESEARCH REPORT

Going Back to Ordinary Times

What do you think you might have in common with someone your age who lived in the Middle Ages? To find out, write a report about a boy or a girl your age who might have lived at that time. First, decide if you will research the life of a boy or a girl. Then, decide if you will study the life of someone from the family of a lord, a knight, a castle servant, or a peasant. List some research questions you will try to answer. Here are some ideas for possible questions:

- What kind of training did a boy or a girl in this type of family receive?
- What did they do for fun?
- What did they do on a typical day?
- What problems and challenges did they face? (Include health problems.)
- What kind of life could they expect as adults and as elderly people?
- What beliefs and values were important to them?

Start your research by looking for answers in your history book. Then, ask a librarian to help you find some books on the Middle Ages. Look for specific information about the imaginary boy or girl you have selected.

Decide what you might have in common with a medieval teenager. If you were to meet this person, despite your different backgrounds and experiences, could you become friends?

▶ **Use "Writing a Research Report," pages 626–653, for help with this assignment.**

Another Choice

SUMMARY/ART

Building Castles

Make a three-dimensional model of a medieval castle. First, do some research. Look for pictures of medieval castles in history books and in works of fiction and nonfiction that you'll find at a library. Real castles were built of stone, but you can make your model out of cardboard, Styrofoam, papier-mâché, or wood. Then, write brief summaries on note cards that help identify the castle's parts and rooms and their purpose.

Fiction

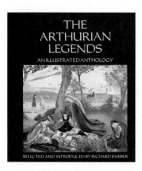

All Sides of Arthur

Richard Barber has compiled the most exciting stories about King Arthur in *The Arthurian Legends: An Illustrated Anthology.* You will learn about the social and historical contexts of the legends and how the stories have changed over time. But the focus of the book is King Arthur himself: his daring rescues, his heroic deeds, and his greatest challenges. You will find out why these tales still resonate with readers of all ages.

The Water of Life

Have you ever wished you could live forever? In Natalie Babbitt's *Tuck Everlasting,* the members of the Tuck family are granted eternal life when they drink from a hidden stream. Then they find out that living forever isn't what it's cracked up to be. This novel is also published in Spanish as *Tuck para siempre.*

This title is available in the HRW Library.

More than They Can Chew?

Four young lives are changed one summer by the discovery of a coin. Not just any coin, but a coin that grants wishes—or rather, *half* wishes. In Edward Eager's novel, *Half Magic,* Jane, Katherine, Mark, and Martha accidentally make themselves *half* invisible, ship themselves to the Sahara Desert, and finally transport themselves back to King Arthur's court. Then they think that maybe *double* wishing can solve all their problems—but will it really?

Payback

As Myles Falworth undergoes rigorous training for knighthood, he learns that his blind father was wrongfully accused of treason and stripped of his lands. Now that he has grown up, Myles attempts to restore honor to his father by challenging his father's toughest enemies. In *Men of Iron,* Howard Pyle weaves a dramatic tale of suspense and bravery.

Nonfiction

Leaders by Example

Anthony Masters looks at the lives of twenty-four exceptional people in *Heroic Stories.* You've probably heard of some of these heroes, such as Martin Luther King, Jr., and Anne Frank. Do you know about Christy Brown, who overcame a troubling disability to become a writer, or Pauline Cutting, who worked tirelessly in hospitals in Beirut? All of the people profiled in the book embody a heroic ideal.

Things Have Changed

Gwyneth Morgan takes you back to thirteenth-century England in *Life in a Medieval Village.* In vivid detail, Morgan explores the everyday life of a peasant family, a lord and his manor, and the role of the church during this unique period in history. You may be surprised by the food people ate, the clothes they wore, and what they did for a living.

The Historical Arthur

Kevin Crossley-Holland's *The World of King Arthur and His Court* examines the ideals and customs of Arthurian times. You'll learn how a boy became a knight and was schooled in the specifics of courtly love. Crossley-Holland also compares the legends of King Arthur to actual history. Was Arthur real or fictional? The answer may surprise you.

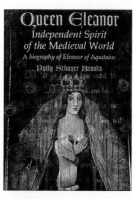

A Heroic Woman

Eleanor of Aquitaine (ak′wə·tān′) was queen of France and later England in the 1100s. During her lifetime she supported the arts and helped establish the courtly manners you've read about in the Arthurian tales. Her strength of character brought her trouble—she was held in confinement for fifteen years by her husband. Find out the whole story in Polly Schoyer Brooks's biography *Queen Eleanor: Independent Spirit of the Medieval World.*

Reading for Life

by Flo Ota De Lange and Sheri Henderson

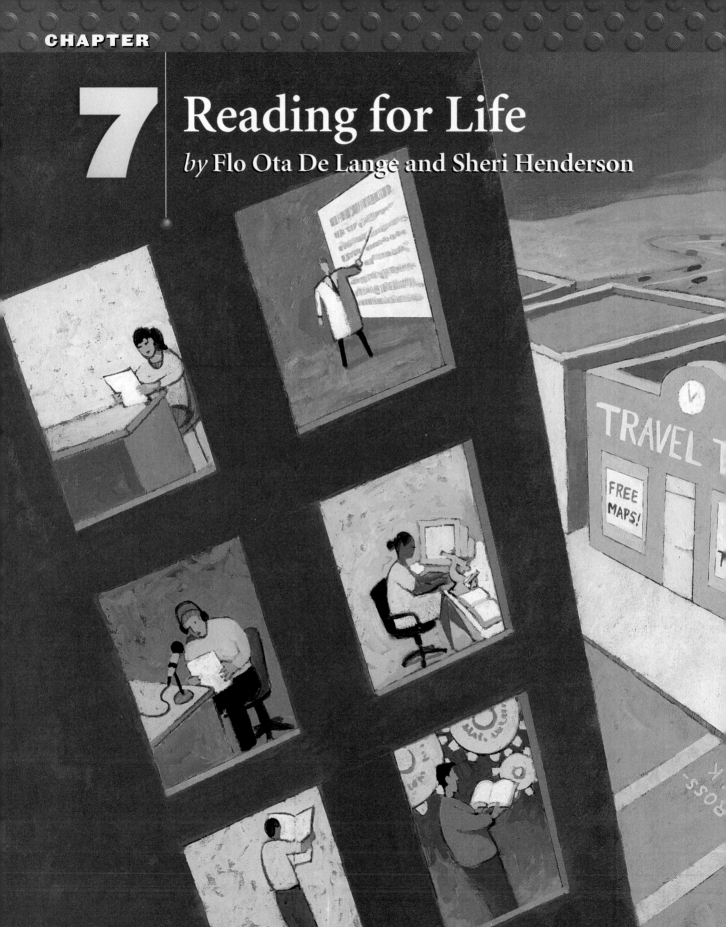

California Standards

Here are the Grade 7 standards you will study for mastery in Chapter 7:

Reading

Reading Comprehension (Focus on Informational Materials)

2.2 Locate information by using a variety of consumer, workplace, and public documents.

2.5 Understand and explain the use of a simple mechanical device by following technical directions.

KEYWORD:
HLLA 7-7

Reading for Life *by* Sheri Henderson

Getting the Job Done

The purpose of consumer, workplace, and public documents is to provide information. These documents are everywhere, and that is a *good* thing. Without them a society as complex as ours would not be able to function well. Since these documents contain information that is important to all of us, they deserve—and require—our close attention and careful reading. The information they contain can be as simple as advertising for a new movie or as complex as warnings about your prescription medication. Whether simple or complex, though, consumer, workplace, and public documents cannot do their job of providing information if we do not do our job, which is reading them carefully.

Consumer Documents

Most days you probably look to consumer documents for all sorts of information. **Advertisements** tell you what is available to buy and how much it costs, what movie is just out on video, and when your favorite store is having a sale. Providers of services publish **schedules** of movie showtimes, school lunch menus, TV programs, and bus or train or plane timetables. **Labels** on the goods you buy give you, the consumer, information about what you are buying. Labels on packaged food list the food's ingredients and nutritional value. Labels on shoes declare which parts are synthetic and which parts are not. Labels

on your clothing tell you what your shirt is made of and how to care for it.

Mechanical and electronic equipment come with **warranties, contracts, instructional manuals,** and **technical directions.** These guide you in the safe and proper use of products. Whenever you encounter consumer information, especially technical directions, it is a good idea to read it through slowly and carefully. The seller is required only to include the information. It's up to you to read and understand it. As many consumers have found out too late, "I didn't understand it" will not get you your money back if the item does not work because you didn't read the directions. Informed consumers know that it's better to read consumer documents *before* they use the product.

Workplace Documents

As their name suggests, workplace documents are those you encounter in a job. Your first communication with a possible employer may be through a **business letter,** in which you state your qualifications and request a job interview. However, a business letter isn't always necessary. You may merely be asked to complete an **application.** When you are hired, you may be asked to sign an **employment contract,** which spells out what is expected of you as an employee and what you can expect in return from your employer. You may need to provide a **Social Security number,** a **work permit,** and a **tax**

Reading Standard 2.2
Locate information by using a variety of consumer, workplace, and public documents.

Reading Standard 2.5
Understand and explain the use of a simple mechanical device by following technical directions.

form for your employer to use when calculating taxes to deduct from your wages. You may also be given **insurance forms** to fill out and sign. To help you succeed in your job, your employer may provide an **employee manual,** a set of rules and instructions related to the job.

When workers need to communicate with one another, they usually do so through **memorandums,** often called memos. Businesses frequently use **e-mail memos** to communicate because e-mail is fast, convenient, and easily retrieved. Of course, the number and types of workplace documents you encounter will depend on the kind of work you do. However, one thing is certain: Whatever kind of work you do, workplace documents will play an important role in helping you succeed.

Public Documents

If there were a chemical spill on a road near your house, would you be told about it? If you wanted to learn about sports programs at local parks before you moved into a new neighborhood, could you do it? If you wanted to know how much the mayor earns in your community, could you find out? The answer to all of these questions is *yes!* The answers can be found in public documents. Public documents supply citizens with information that may be of interest to them. Public documents can relate to schools, churches, government agencies, the courts, libraries, and fire and police departments, to name just a few.

Typically most citizens do not read the public documents put out by the government, the military, and nonprofit agencies or groups. Instead, they read **newspaper articles** that report on the documents. Whether you read a document itself or a newspaper account of its contents, public documents exist to tell you what is happening in your world.

Reading Ahead

The following pages will give you some practice reading various kinds of consumer, workplace, and public documents. You'll also get a chance to follow some technical directions. Challenge yourself as you read to see how well you can locate the important information in all the documents.

Locating Information in Public Documents

Public Documents

All **public documents** have one thing in common: They inform people (you) about things you might need or want to know. Public documents are all about information. Let's follow one person's experience in finding information she needs by using some public documents.

Meet Sam (Miss Samantha Sallyann Lancaster, and don't even think about calling her anything but Sam, thank you very much). Anyone who knows Sam for five minutes knows two things about her: She's smart, and she can beat anyone, anytime, anywhere on her BMX bike. That's usually where you can find her if she isn't doing homework or attending dance class. So imagine Sam's excitement when she comes across this **announcement** in her favorite biking magazine:

Reading Standard 2.2
Locate information by using a variety of public documents.

Casting Call

If you've been looking for the right break to get into motion pictures, this may be your chance. StreetWheelie Productions is casting fresh talent for an upcoming action movie.

What?

To audition, you must

- be a charismatic, awesome, off-the-wall male or female individualist
- be an expert at making your BMX-type bike do whatever you want it to do

Who?

- have your own bike
- look like you're between the ages of twelve and fifteen
- meet the requirements for a permit to work in the entertainment industry if you are under age eighteen
- be living in or near San Francisco during July and August 2002

Auditions will be held in

Golden Gate Park, San Francisco
Saturday, May 25, 2002
10:00 A.M. to 5:00 P.M.

When and where?

Bring your bike.

See you in the movies!

Locating Information: An Article

Sam thinks, "Cool!" This may be for her, but she wants more information. An **Internet search** using the key words *StreetWheelie Productions* and *San Francisco* yields this **article** from *Hollywood Beat,* a newsmagazine.

Hollywood Beat

Shhhhhh!

Here's a little secret for you. Remember Bilbo Baggins, the lovable little hobbit who saved Middle Earth from the Powers of Darkness in J.R.R. Tolkien's classic novel? Well, that little hobbit's about to get radical. *Hollywood Beat* has discovered that StreetWheelie Productions is developing an out-of-sight version of this tale, and Middle Earth will never be the same.

? What's the topic?

Set in San Francisco, the hobbits are bike-riding dudes who, in order to save their world, oppose an endless stream of baddies who ride BMX bikes. The principal character, Bilbo, is a nerdy innocent who finds himself at the center of (Middle) Earth—shaking events. The result? Batman meets Mr. Rogers.

? Why a bike?

Sources close to the production say that there is some big talent interested in the project. As of yet, nobody's talking, but remember . . . you'll hear all about it first on *Hollywood Beat.*

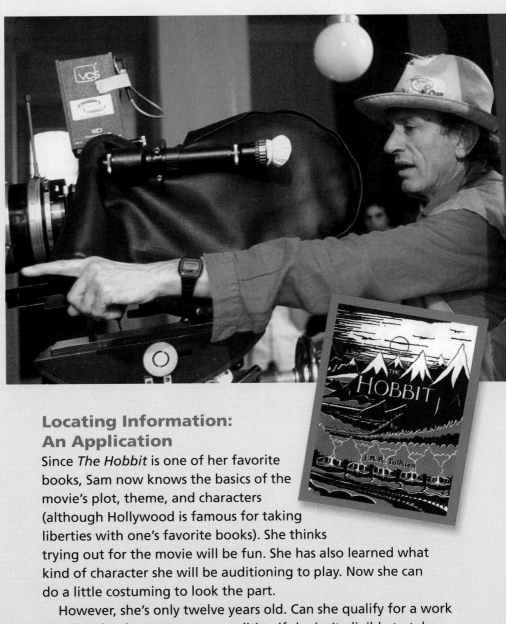

Locating Information:
An Application

Since *The Hobbit* is one of her favorite books, Sam now knows the basics of the movie's plot, theme, and characters (although Hollywood is famous for taking liberties with one's favorite books). She thinks trying out for the movie will be fun. She has also learned what kind of character she will be auditioning to play. Now she can do a little costuming to look the part.

However, she's only twelve years old. Can she qualify for a work permit? She doesn't want to audition if she isn't eligible to take the part. Sam does another **Internet search,** this time using the key words *permit to work in the entertainment industry* and *California*. This leads her to the state of California's Division of Labor Standards Enforcement. All the information she needs is on the **Web site,** including the **application** itself, which she downloads (just in case!).

Study the application on the next page to find out what Sam will need to do to get permission to work in a movie. The margin notes help you identify key information.

STATE OF CALIFORNIA
Division of Labor Standards Enforcement

APPLICATION FOR PERMISSION TO WORK IN THE ENTERTAINMENT INDUSTRY

THIS IS NOT A PERMIT ☐ NEW ☐ RENEWAL

PROCEDURES FOR OBTAINING WORK PERMIT
1. Complete the information required below.
2. School authorities must complete the School Record section below.
3. For minors 15 days through kindergarten, please attach a certified copy of the minor's birth certificate. See reverse side for other documents that may be accepted.
4. Mail or present the completed application to any office of the Division of Labor Standards Enforcement for issuance of your work permit.

? What does the first section require?

Name of Child	Professional Name, if applicable

Permanent Address Number Street City State Zip Code	Home Phone No.

School Attending	Grade

Date of Birth	Age	Height	Weight	Hair Color	Eye Color	Sex

Statement of Parent or Guardian: It is my desire that an Entertainment Work Permit be issued to the above-named child. I will read the rules governing such employment and will cooperate to the best of my ability in safeguarding his or her educational, moral, and physical interest. I hereby certify, under penalty of perjury, that the foregoing statements are true and correct.

Name of Parent or Guardian (print or type)	Signed	Daytime phone #

SCHOOL RECORD

☐ I certify that the above-named minor meets the school district's requirements with respect to age, school record, attendance, and health.

☐ Does not meet the district's requirements and permit should not be issued.

? What does the second section require?

Authorized School Official	Date	
School Address	School Telephone	[School Seal or Stamp]

HEALTH RECORD

COMPLETE THIS SECTION IF INSTRUCTED TO DO SO OR IF INFANT UNDER ONE MONTH OF AGE

? What does the last section require?

Name of Doctor	Address	Telephone Number

I certify that I am Board Certified in pediatrics and have carefully examined

and, in my opinion: He/She is physically fit to be employed in the production of motion pictures and television. If less than one month, infant is at least 15 days old, was carried to full term, and is physically able to perform.

Signature _____ M.D. _____ Date

Approved DLSE 277 Rev. 03/99

Sam's happy. She knows she'll qualify for a work permit, and she decides to go to the audition. Before she goes, test yourself. In reading these documents, have you been able to find all the information Sam needs?

Reading Informational Materials

Reading Check

1. What is the most important purpose of a **public document**?

2. Where and when will the auditions be held?

3. What special talent must people have to audition for this part?

4. What will the movie be about?

TestPractice

LOCATING INFORMATION IN PUBLIC DOCUMENTS

1. The fact that the advertisement appeared in Sam's favorite biking magazine suggests that the casting agents are especially interested in kids who can —
  A read magazines
  B act a little crazy
  C follow directions
  D ride a bike

2. If Sam is hired to play a part, she will be working during —
  F May and June
  G June and July
  H July and August
  J August and September

3. Sam is probably auditioning to play —
  A a hobbit
  B Mr. Rogers
  C a goodie
  D Bilbo Baggins

4. Sam is confident that she will qualify for a **work permit.** To do so, she will need all of the following *except* —
  F the full support and help of her parent or guardian
  G a statement of good health from a doctor
  H a statement from her school that she has met the district's requirements for her grade level
  J permission from her school to be absent when necessary

5. If Sam wanted to find out more about StreetWheelie Productions, her *best* choice would be to —
  A search the Internet using the key words *StreetWheelie Productions*
  B look in an encyclopedia under "Film Industry"
  C read *The Hobbit* again
  D post a question on her school's electronic bulletin board

Reading Standard 2.2
Locate information by using a variety of public documents.

Locating Information in Workplace Documents

Rules for the Job

Whether you work in a small business with only one other person or in a huge corporation with offices all over the world, your working life will depend on many types of **workplace documents.** Businesses put important information in writing so that agreements, decisions, and requirements are clear to everyone involved. Let's look at some of the workplace documents that Sam encounters after her audition.

Locating Information: A Business Letter

The audition has gone really well. Everyone is as nice as he or she can be, and someone takes down all of Sam's information and talks with her and her mother for quite a while. Pretty soon Sam receives the **business letter** shown on page 491.

Reading Standard 2.2
Locate information by using a variety of workplace documents.

STREETWHEELIE PRODUCTIONS

2323 South Robertson Boulevard
Beverly Hills, CA 90210

June 7, 2002
Miss Samantha Lancaster
1920 Ygnacio Valley Road
Walnut Creek, CA 94598

Dear Sam:

On behalf of StreetWheelie Productions, it is my pleasure to offer you a part in our production. Attached is your contract. I know that contracts can be difficult to read and understand, so it is important that before you sign it, you and your parents understand it thoroughly. The items in the contract spell out the issues we discussed last Saturday, as follows:

- You are responsible for your own transportation to and from filming. Pay attention to scheduled dates, times, and locations.

  Responsibility 1: transportation.

- Check your e-mail first thing each morning and last thing each night. If you are experiencing trouble with your e-mail and are unsure of the next day's schedule, call Alonsa anytime, 24/7.
- You must report to makeup, hair, and wardrobe two hours before your first call.

  Responsibility 2: work schedule.

- You may *not* change your hairstyle or hair color during filming. We all admired the brightness of the lime green you have achieved and the way your hair flows from under your helmet when you're riding.

  Responsibility 3: arrival time.

- Unless otherwise noted, you must report with your bike for all calls. You may not wash or otherwise clean all that great grunge off your bike.

  Responsibility 4: appearance.

- Because you are not yet age sixteen, a parent or guardian must be present whenever you are working. As we discussed with your mother, your grandfather will be an appropriate guardian as long as he has with him at all times a written document signed by your parents, authorizing him to act as your guardian.

  Responsibility 5: equipment.

- Nonprofessional actors are paid a minimum hourly wage. You will receive a check at the end of each week. Your eight-hour maximum workday will begin when you arrive each day and end when you leave each day. By law you may not work more than eight hours a day. One paid hour of rest and recreation will be part of your eight-hour workday, but the thirty-minute lunch, also paid, will *not* be part of the workday. You will always have twelve hours or more between the end of one workday and the makeup call for the next.

  Responsibility 6: parental supervision.

- In addition to the above hourly wage, you will receive a bonus at the end of your filming schedule. This bonus will be paid on your last day of work, on the condition that you have fulfilled all aspects of your contract with regard to attendance, punctuality, and appearance. This bonus will equal the total of all your previous hourly checks. It will, in effect, double your earnings.

  Wages.

If you have any questions, call Juanita Diaz, our lawyer. Her phone number is on the contract. We look forward to having you on the project.

  Contact for questions.

Sincerely,

Cassandra Rice

Cassandra Rice, Casting Director

Locating Information: Workplace Instructions

Sam thinks, "Wow! I'm going to be in a movie!" Before she knows it, her first day arrives. As soon as Sam gets to the location, she is introduced to a whole new set of friends . . . *and* to a whole new set of rules. Everyone in the crew is nice, but they all make it clear that everyone is there to work, and they expect Sam to understand that fun movies are just as hard to make as serious ones. Sam's job doesn't require an employee manual, but she does receive a list of **workplace instructions.**

Talent Instructions: On Location

What to do and what not to do.

1. No horseplay is permitted.

2. When you arrive, sign in with Jim, and pick up a call pager.

3. Report *immediately* to makeup, hair, and wardrobe.

4. Movies require a lot of waiting. Bring something that you can do *quietly* while you wait. Music players are fine if the headphones do not interfere with makeup, hair, or costume. Electronic games are popular; their sound effects *must* be turned off. You *could* even read a book. People do.

5. When you are ready, report to the call area, and stay there. *Always* keep your call pager with you.

6. Personal cell phones, pagers, etc., may be used only in the call or food areas and only if they do not interfere with filming. Ringers must be set to "off" or "silent alert."

7. Leave all personal belongings in your assigned locker when on the shooting site.

8. You may talk in nonfilming areas, but there is *no talking* on the shooting site.

Locating Information: E-mail Memos and Directory

Sam finds out she loves being involved in making movies. The work is fun and interesting. Many of the other kids complain about having to wait for hours just to do a short scene, but Sam is interested in everything going on and so is never bored. Since she knows how to be quiet and stay out of the way, she is allowed to watch the filming all day long. The days just fly by.

   As time goes on, Sam understands why she is required to check her e-mail every morning and night. It's hard to remember which schedule is the most recent one. Luckily, Sam can always look it up on her saved mail. At the right is one of Sam's **e-mail memos.**

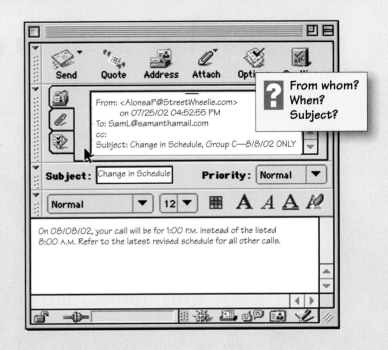

Sam changes her calendar for August 8 but cannot find her latest revised schedule. She breathes a sigh of relief when she remembers that she can check her saved e-mail and print another copy. Look at Sam's **e-mail directory.**

Reading Informational Materials

Reading Check

1. Name the **workplace documents** Sam has encountered. What is the purpose of each document?

2. How much will Sam be paid?

3. What equipment is Sam expected to provide?

4. What is the date of Sam's most recently revised schedule?

TestPractice

Locating Information in Workplace Documents

1. The **business letter** mostly discusses Sam's —

   A audition

   B contract

   C ability to act

   D ability to ride a bike

2. The **business letter** points out that with the bonus, Sam will —

   F be paid only if she fulfills all conditions of her contract

   G not be paid if she fails to fulfill any conditions of her contract

   H be paid double if she fulfills all conditions of her contract

   J earn minimum wage for the project

3. Sam can **infer** from the **business letter** that a law requires a parent or guardian to be present when a child is working in the entertainment industry until the child reaches age —

   A ten

   B twelve

   C sixteen

   D eighteen

4. Sam's **workplace instructions** make it clear that while waiting, actors are expected to be all of the following *except* —

   F patient

   G responsible

   H self-controlled

   J loud

5. Sam's July 25 **e-mail memo** tells her about a change in —

   A date

   B time

   C part

   D costume

6. Sam's **e-mail directory** indicates that the user name of the person in charge of publicity is —

   F PhamN

   G AlonsaP

   H MayL

   J GeorgeL

Reading Standard 2.2
Locate information by using a variety of workplace documents.

Locating Information in Consumer Documents

A consumer uses what someone else sells. Consumers buy things (goods) for their own use and the use of their families and friends. Have you ever treated a friend to an ice-cream cone or a movie? If so, both you and the person you treated were consumers. Even your pets can be considered consumers—of the food and the toys you buy for them. Consumers need information about the products and services they buy, for example, packaged-food ingredients, movie ratings, and airline schedules. **Consumer documents** provide that information. Let's look at some of the consumer documents Sam uses while she is working.

Reading a Transit Map

Sam has to travel to work with her bike, and she doesn't look forward to a long bike ride from Walnut Creek to the movie location and back. Besides, her grandfather has to come with her, and he doesn't have a bike. Her grandfather could drive, but parking a car in San Francisco is expensive—even if you can find a parking space! So the two decide to take the Bay Area Rapid Transit System, known as BART. BART is a network of trains that can take you just about anywhere in the San Francisco Bay Area.

First, Sam and her grandpa log on to the Internet to look at the **BART system map.** They want to be sure they can get from their home in Walnut Creek to the Embarcadero Station, where the StreetWheelie production van will be waiting. They find the map that is shown on the next page.

Reading Standard 2.2
Locate information by using a variety of consumer documents.

BART System Map

Pittsburg/Bay Point 🅿
North Concord/Martinez 🅿
Concord 🅿
San Pablo ⓣ
🅿Richmond
El Cerrito del Norte 🅿
El Cerrito Plaza 🅿
Pleasant Hill 🅿
Walnut Creek 🅿
Lafayette ⓣ
Orinda 🅿
North Berkeley 🅿
Downtown Berkeley
Ashby 🅿
Rockridge 🅿
West Oakland 🅿
MacArthur 🅿
Embarcadero
Montgomery St
Powell St
Civic Center
19th St/Oakland
Oakland City Center/12th St
Lake Merritt 🅿
Fruitvale 🅿
16th St Mission
24th St Mission
San Francisco
Air-BART
Coliseum/Oakland Airport 🅿
Balboa Park
Oakland International Airport
San Leandro 🅿
Bay Fair 🅿
Glen Park 🅿
🅿 Daly City
Castro Valley 🅿
Hayward 🅿
Dublin/Pleasanton 🅿
Rush hour only
Colma 🅿
San Francisco International Airport
S. San Francisco
San Bruno ⓣ
South Hayward 🅿
Milbrae
Foster City
Union City 🅿
Fremont
Irvington
Warm Springs

Legend:
- Richmond–Daly City/Colma
- Fremont–Daly City
- Fremont–Richmond
- Pittsburg/Bay Point–Colma
- Dublin/Pleasanton–Daly City
- 🅿 BART Parking

? Which line should Sam take?

? Which BART lines stop at Walnut Creek? at the Embarcadero?

Sam is glad to see that BART will take her directly from Walnut Creek to the Embarcadero station. She still needs more BART information: Is she allowed to bring a bike with her? She clicks on "Bikes on BART." Read the Web page on the next page to see if Sam can take her bike on BART.

Back　**Forward**　**Reload**　**Home**　**Search**

 Riding BART　　 **BART General Information**　　 **Inside BART**　　 **Doing Business with BART**　　**BART-SFO Extension**

 BART

Riding BART

BART-SFO
Extension

Trip Planner

Station Info

Tickets

Bikes on BART
Lockers
Comments

Accessibility

FAQ

Rider Feedback

BART's Bicycle Rules

- Bikes are allowed on all trains except those indicated by the BART Trip Planner and highlighted in the *All About BART* brochure. It is the rider's responsibility to refer to BART schedules.

- Regardless of any other rule, bikes are never allowed on crowded cars. Use your good judgment and only board cars that can comfortably accommodate you and your bicycle. Hold your bike while on the trains.

- Bikes are allowed in any car but the first car of a train.

- Bicyclists must use elevator or stairs, not escalators, and always walk bikes.

- Bicyclists must yield priority seating to seniors and people with disabilities, yield to other passengers, and not block aisles or doors or soil seats.

- In case of an evacuation, leave your bike on the train, and do not let it block aisles or doors.

- Bicyclists under 14 years old must be accompanied by an adult.

- Gas-powered vehicles are never permitted.

- Bikes must be parked in racks and lockers. Call (510) 464-7133 for locker availability. Bikes parked against poles, fences, or railings will be removed.

Will any bike restrictions affect Sam?

COMMUTE HOURS
(Weekdays approximately 7:05 to 8:50 am and 4:25 to 6:45 pm)

- During morning commute hours, bikes are allowed in the Embarcadero Station only for trips to the East Bay (as indicated by the BART Trip Planner and the *All About BART* brochure).

- During evening commute hours, bicyclists traveling from the East Bay must exit at the Embarcadero Station (as indicated by the BART Trip Planner and the *All About BART* brochure).

*Violation of the above rules subject to citation under
CA Vehicle Code Sec. 21113 and Sec. 42001.*

What are the Embarcadero restrictions? What do they mean for Sam?

Home Page　　Riding BART　　BART Information　　Inside BART　　Doing Business　　BART-SFO Extension

Now Sam wants to know how much it will cost them. Since Grandpa is over sixty-five and Sam is twelve, can they get any discount fares? Look at the BART ticket guide to figure out Sam's best deal.

■ Riding BART   ■ BART General Information   ■ Inside BART   ■ Doing Business with BART   ■ BART-SFO Extension

BART

Riding BART

BART-SFO Extension

Station Info

Tickets
Online Orders
Mail Orders
Vendors
CAT Machines
Student Groups
Refunds

Bikes on BART

Accessibility

FAQ

Rider Feedback

Ticket Guide

BART tickets are like debit cards, each with a specific stored value. When you take a BART trip, your fare is deducted from the ticket automatically until the stored value is used up. To determine the cost of a particular trip, please use the BART Trip Planner.

All BART stations sell tickets through automatic ticket machines that accept nickels, dimes, and quarters as well as $1, $5, $10, and $20 bills. Credit cards can also be used at Charge-A-Ticket (CAT) machines in selected stations.

> **?** How can Sam find out what each trip will cost?

BART's fare structure is built on a mileage-based formula, therefore weekly or monthly passes for BART fare are not available. However, BART offers discounts ranging from 6.25% to 75% as described below.

The following discount tickets may be purchased online, through the mail, and at selected retail vendors throughout the San Francisco Bay Area:

BART Blue High-Value Tickets
6.25% Discount on Two Ticket Denominations:
$32 Ticket Costs Only $30!
$48 Ticket Costs Only $45!

BART Red* Tickets
75% Discount for Persons with Disabilities and Children 5 to 12 Years Old:
$16 Ticket Costs Only $4!
Note: Children 4 and under are FREE!

BART Green* Tickets
75% Discount for Senior Citizens 65 Years & Older:
$16 Ticket Costs Only $4!

> **?** Which is the best ticket for Sam? Which is the best ticket for Grandpa?

BART Orange Tickets
BART Orange Tickets provide discounts for middle and secondary school students.
Note: Special purchasing restrictions apply.

BART Plus Tickets
BART Plus tickets can be used as a "flash pass" for other transit operators.

Home Page   Riding BART   BART Information   Inside BART   Doing Business   BART-SFO Extension

Sam also wants to figure out what time they need to catch their train. To get the schedule, Sam goes to the trip-planning page and enters the name of the station they'll be leaving from and the name of the station they'll be arriving at. What she finds is on the next page.

BART
ba®

Riding BART

Plan another trip ... ⇕

BART-SFO
Extension

Trip Planner
Schedule by Map
Schedule by Line
System Map
Bay Area Transit
Employer Shuttles
Planning Help

Station Info

Tickets

Bikes on BART

Accessibility

FAQ

Rider Feedback

Here are all the weekday trains after 5:00 a.m. arriving before 10:00 a.m.:

Origin Station : Walnut Creek
Destination Station : Embarcadero
One-way fare : $3.45

Walnut Creek	Embarcadero	Bikes	Details
5:05a	5:39a	Yes	❶
5:20a	5:54a	Yes	❶
5:35a	6:09a	Yes	❶
5:50a	6:24a	Yes	❶
6:05a	6:39a	Yes	❶
6:15a	6:49a	Yes	❶
6:20a	6:54a	Yes	❶
6:30a	7:04a	Yes	❶
6:35a	7:09a	No	❶
6:45a	7:19a	No	❶
6:50a	7:24a	No	❶
6:55a	7:29a	No	❶
7:00a	7:34a	No	❶
7:05a	7:39a	No	❶
7:10a	7:44a	No	❶

Walnut Creek	Embarcadero	Bikes	Details
7:15a	7:49a	No	❶
7:20a	7:54a	No	❶
7:30a	8:04a	No	❶
7:35a	8:09a	No	❶
7:45a	8:19a	No	❶
7:50a	8:24a	No	❶
8:00a	8:34a	No	❶
8:05a	8:39a	No	❶
8:15a	8:49a	No	❶
8:20a	8:54a	No	❶
8:35a	9:09a	Yes	❶
8:50a	9:24a	Yes	❶
9:05a	9:39a	Yes	❶
9:20a	9:54a	Yes	❶

❶ provides more details about a selected trip.

No indicates that bicycles are not allowed on the trip. See BART's Bicycle Rules for more information.

Bicycles cannot enter or exit 12th or 19th Street during commute hours.

✉ E-mail this Schedule

🖨 Print this Schedule

? What is the fare for the trip? What will it cost Sam and Grandpa?

? When are bikes allowed on BART trains?

Home Page	Riding BART	BART Information	Inside BART	Doing Business	BART-SFO Extension

Thanks to her ability to use **consumer information materials,** Sam has found the correct BART line, discovered when bikes are allowed on the trains, learned about the cost of the tickets and discounts, and checked the schedules. She can do this from a library or the comfort of her home, thanks to the Internet and her ability to use consumer documents.

So look out, world. The name is Sam (Samantha Sallyann Lancaster, but call her Sam)—soon to be in a movie playing at a theater near *you*.

Reading Informational Materials

Reading Check

1. How are BART fares determined? How can you find out in advance what a trip will cost?

2. Look at the BART ticket guide. Sam researches the cost of the orange tickets and finds that she can get 50 percent off the full fare, but only if her school is participating in the program. She has a better option. What is it?

3. Look at the trip-planning schedule. Between what hours can Sam *not* take a bike from the Walnut Creek station to the Embarcadero station?

TestPractice

Locating Information in Consumer Documents

1. Which line does Sam take from Walnut Creek to the Embarcadero?
   A   Richmond–Daly City/Colma (red)
   B   Fremont–Daly City (green)
   C   Pittsburg/Bay Point–Colma (yellow)
   D   Dublin/Pleasanton–Daly City (blue)

2. Because of the commuting restrictions on bikes at the Embarcadero station, Sam must plan to arrive at that station —
   F   weekdays before 7:05 A.M. or after 9:09 A.M.
   G   weekdays after 7:05 A.M. but before 8:50 A.M.
   H   weekdays at 7:05 A.M. but not at 8:50 A.M.
   J   only on weekends

3. According to the ticket guide, Grandpa and Sam should buy —
   A   one blue and one red ticket
   B   one red and one green ticket
   C   one green and one orange ticket
   D   one orange and one blue ticket

4. The best price Sam and her grandpa can get for a one-way trip is —
   F $3.45 each
   G $3.45 for Grandpa and $3.45 minus 50 percent for Sam
   H $3.45 minus 50 percent for both
   J $3.45 minus 75 percent for both

5. Sam must arrive two hours before her first call. If her first call is at 8:00 A.M., what is the latest she can leave the Walnut Creek station and still meet the van by 5:45 A.M.?
   A   5:05 A.M.
   B   5:20 A.M.
   C   5:35 A.M.
   D   5:50 A.M.

Reading Standard 2.2
Locate information by using a variety of consumer documents.

Following Technical Directions

Understanding Explanations

Technical directions are step-by-step instructions that explain how to accomplish mechanical tasks. You follow technical directions when you want to assemble the new TV satellite dish that you just bought. The technical directions in the instructional manual may have taught you how to operate your new cell phone. Technical directions can also instruct you how to repair mechanical devices you are using. You may have followed them when you removed and oiled the wheels on your in-line skates or when you cleaned the sprockets on your bicycle.

You're probably too young to drive a car, but you're certainly not too young to be thinking about it. Driving can give you a new independence, but it also gives you new responsibilities. Any number of things can go wrong with your car, and it's up to you to fix them—or get them fixed. You won't be expected to repair the engine, but you can fairly easily fix one of the most common automobile emergencies: a flat tire. A flat is something every driver will have to face someday. If you're lucky, yours will come when you're right next to a repair shop. More likely, though, you'll be out on a lonely country road without a living soul in sight. To be prepared for that, study the directions on the next page.

Reading Standard 2.5 Understand and explain the use of a simple mechanical device by following technical directions.

How to Change a Flat Tire

Before you can change a flat tire on your car, you first have to realize that the tire is flat. You might come out of your house in the morning and see the wheel rim resting on the road with the tire spread around it. You'll know right away the tire's flat. How can you tell, though, if it goes flat while you are driving? A first clue is that your car starts to pull to the right or the left even though you aren't turning the steering wheel. Another clue is that passing motorists honk and point as they drive by. Yet another clue is that the car starts bouncing up and down and making a loud *thumpity-thump-thump* sound.

When you suspect you have a flat tire, follow these procedures:

1 Park the car as far off the road as possible. Put the car in park (if you have an automatic transmission) or in gear (if you have a standard transmission), turn off the engine, and put on the emergency brake. Turn on your car's flashing lights. Now, get out and look at your tires. If you have a flat, put out emergency triangles or, at night, flares. (It's a good idea to carry warning triangles and flares in your trunk at all times in case of an emergency.)

2 Remove the spare tire from the trunk. Also take out the jack, the lug wrench, and related tools.

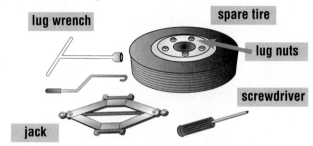

3 Remove the wheel cover from the flat tire, using a screwdriver or the end of the jack handle.

4 Loosen the lug nuts with the lug wrench, but do not remove them. Most lug nuts turn counter-clockwise.

5 Position your jack. Different makes of cars come with different types of jacks, so check your owner's manual to learn how to use your jack. Make sure the jack is sitting on a solid, flat surface.

6 Lift the car with the jack until your flat tire is two or three inches off the ground. (*Never lie under the car when it is on the jack!*)

7 Now, finish unscrewing the lug nuts. Put them inside the wheel cover so you don't lose them.

8 Remove the flat tire, and replace it with the spare tire. Replace the lug nuts, and tighten them by hand.

9 Lower the jack until the spare tire is firmly on the ground. Remove the jack. Firmly tighten the lug nuts with the lug wrench. Work diagonally—tighten one on the top, then one on the bottom; one on the left, then one on the right; and so on.

10 Place the flat tire, the wheel cover, and all your tools in the trunk. As soon as you can, drive to a garage or a tire repair shop to get the tire fixed or replaced. You never want to be without a spare, because you never know when you'll get another flat!

Reading Informational Materials

Reading Check

1. How can you tell you have a flat tire? List three clues.

2. List the tools needed to fix a flat tire.

3. What should you do as soon as you can after you've changed your flat tire?

TestPractice

Following Technical Directions

1. When you think you have a flat tire, what should you do first?

   A Drive the car to your family's garage.

   B Call your parents, and ask them to pick you up.

   C Park the car as far off the road as possible.

   D Look out your window to see if the tire's flat.

2. The best tool for loosening the lug nuts is —

   F a screwdriver

   G a lug wrench

   H a jack

   J your hand

3. You should lift the car with the jack until —

   A you can fit comfortably underneath the car

   B the car is two to three feet in the air

   C the flat tire is two to three inches off the ground

   D the flat tire comes off the wheel

4. When you remove the lug nuts, you should —

   F let them fall to the ground

   G put them in the wheel cover

   H throw them away

   J feed them to a squirrel

5. After you have changed a flat tire, what should you do next?

   A Call your parents to let them know what happened.

   B Drive to a garage to get the flat tire fixed.

   C Continue where you were going before you got the flat.

   D Throw away the flat tire.

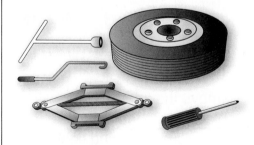

Reading Standard 2.5
Understand and explain the use of a simple mechanical device by following technical directions.

Mastering the Standards

SUMMARY

Sum It Up

Writing a summary can help you understand and remember what you have read. A **summary** is a short restatement of the important events and characters in a narrative or of the main ideas in a work of nonfiction. Pick an article from one of the magazines or Web sites listed at the end of this chapter (pages 506–507). Read your selection at least twice to be sure you understand it well. For each paragraph, identify the main idea, and restate it *in your own words.* Include details that support the main idea, but leave out less important details. Be sure to include a statement that expresses the underlying meaning of your selection. Once you have written your summary, read it, and ask yourself, "What is the overall message of the article? Would a person who reads this summary get this message?" Make sure there is enough information in your summary to get the message across to your readers. When you hand in your summary, don't forget to include a copy of the original article.

▶ **Use "Summaries," pages 663–669, for help with this assignment.**

Other Choices

DATABASE

 Find It Quick

A database can help you find information quickly. For practice in creating one, make a database of all the documents Sam used to help her work in a movie. Using a computer or three-by-five-inch note cards, make a record for each document. Decide what fields, or categories of information about the documents, you want to include. If you prefer and your teacher agrees, make a database of information that interests you or that you are gathering for a research report.

▶ **Use "Databases," pages 669–672, for help with this assignment.**

EXPOSITORY WRITING

 How Does It Work?

Think of a simple mechanical device that you use. Here are some examples: a pencil sharpener, a window blind, a food processor. Write directions that explain how the device works. List the steps in the order in which they should be performed. Present each step clearly, so that another person can understand how to use the device. Use transition words, such as *first, next,* and *finally.* Other transitions—*on the table, on the right, beside,* and *in the center*—tell readers where things are or where they go. Use both types to make your explanation easy to follow.

Reading for Life: Magazines and Web Sites

Dig We Must

Do you dig ancient artifacts? If you do, unearth a copy of *Archaeology's dig*. This magazine covers the latest discoveries in the field of archaeology, from fossils to Vikings. It also features games and experiments and invites you to ask Dr. Dig all the questions you have about archaeology.

Up-to-Date

When a news story breaks, the magazine *Time for Kids* is there to report it. For the latest on history, sports, and culture, look on its Web site at www.timeforkids.com. You can contribute to *Time for Kids* by participating in its polls and writing letters in response to its stories and features.

Get Creative!

If you like writing, reading, and drawing, look for *Stone Soup: The Magazine by Young Writers and Artists*. Here you'll find short stories and poems written by kids from all around the world. Check out book reviews when you're looking for a new book to read. You may even decide to submit your own work for publication. Go to its Web site, www.stonesoup.com, for more links to sites for young writers, such as "ZuZu," "Young Girl Writers," and "Just Write."

Journey to the Past

Have you wondered how people lived during the Renaissance? Did you ever want to learn more about Mohammed, Charlemagne, and other leaders from world history? If you're curious about the past, read an issue of the magazine *Calliope*. You might not be able to put it down. In addition to its fantastic features, *Calliope* includes time lines, maps, and activities to enhance your understanding of history.

The Ways of the World

Ever wondered where you can learn about the latest developments in computers and science? *Scientific American Explorations* magazine offers a comprehensive guide to technology and a whole lot more. Find out how to conduct science experiments in your home or classroom, and look into "Why and How," a feature that explains some of the mysteries of nature.

Endless Stories

The Web site storybookonline.net supplies compelling ways to practice your writing: Submit your own work of fiction, or collaborate with other writers on a story. Start your own stories, and let other writers contribute twists and turns to your plot. The site features links to book readings, fairy tales, and games.

Back Through Time

The Learning Curve's online "Millennium Exhibition" looks back on the last thousand years of England's history. Learn the importance of historic documents such as the Magna Carta. Read brief biographies of kings and queens, the story behind the invention of the printing press, and other interesting anecdotes. The "Millennium Exhibition" Web site is organized by century and can be found at learningcurve.pro.gov.uk/millennium /default.htm.

Friendly Advice

How do you decide what to buy and what to leave on the store shelf? *Consumer Reports* magazine offers guidance at its Web site designed for young people: zillions.org. Kids test such products as jeans and backpacks, evaluating their durability and safety. Their findings are then posted on the site.

Reading Matters

by Kylene Beers

The bell rings. You dart out of your classroom. In less than five minutes you must go to your locker, find that homework that's stuffed in a book somewhere, get some water, talk with friends, and get to class on time. To do all that, you've got to have a plan, a strategy. Without a good strategy you probably can't get all that done, and you might even feel overwhelmed. Strategies make life easier, whether they are strategies for changing classes, finishing a research report, or figuring a solution to your favorite computer game. Strategies can even make reading easier. Readers use strategies to do things like summarize a story, find the theme, figure out the main idea, or see cause-and-effect relationships. In this section of this book, you'll find strategies that will help you become a strategic reader.

Strategy Lesson

Reading Matters

Summarizing the Plot

Retelling

"Is this a plot?" Manuel asked as he pointed to the first paragraph of a story. He didn't understand that plot isn't a single thing he can point to in the story. He didn't know that **plot** is the "what happens" in the story—all the related events that move from the story's beginning to its end.

The first part of a plot is called its **basic situation.** Here you meet the **characters,** learn what they **want,** and discover the **problems** they face getting what they want. The major part of the plot involves a series of events in which **complications** develop as the characters struggle to resolve their conflicts. The plot then moves to a **climax**—the most emotional and suspenseful part of the story, when the character's problem is solved. In the **resolution** all the loose ends of the plot are tied up, and the story is over.

Retelling

Keeping up with all the information in a story can be difficult. A strategy called **retelling** can help you identify the elements

of a plot and keep all the information about a plot straight in your mind. With this strategy you practice telling the plot of the story using a **retelling summary sheet.** You use the retelling summary sheet as a guide, to be sure you've included all the events in the plot.

PRACTICE

Retell a short story (or even a movie or TV show), using a retelling summary sheet to help you remember and organize the bare bones of the plot. Score your own retelling. (Zero means you didn't tell about an event at all, and 3 means you did a good job covering the plot.) The sample on the opposite page gives you tips on how to fill out a summary sheet.

Grade 5 Review Reading Standard 3.2
Identify the main problem or conflict of the plot, and explain how it is resolved.

Retelling Summary Sheet
Rating of Coverage

0	**1**	**2**	**3**
No coverage	A little	Some	A lot

1. Introduction
2. Characters
3. Conflict
4. Complications
5. Climax
6. Resolution

Retelling Summary Sheet

Rating of Coverage

0	1	2	3
No coverage	A little	Some	A lot

1. Introduction

Begin with the **title** and **author** of the story. Then, tell where and when the story is **set**—if that's important.

2. Characters

Tell the **characters'** names, and explain how the characters are related or connected to one another. Tell what the main character **wants**.

> Some people use the terms **protagonist** and **antagonist**. The protagonist is the hero, and the antagonist works against the hero. Luke Skywalker is a protagonist, and Darth Vader is his antagonist.

3. Conflict

What is the main character's problem, or **conflict**—that is, who or what is keeping the main character from getting what he or she wants?

> **Strategy Tip**
> If it's hard to keep events in **chronological,** or time, order, think about how each event caused another event to happen. Use words such as *because of, since, as a result of.*

4. Complications

Tell the **main events**—what happens as the character tries to solve the conflict.

> **Strategy Tip**
> This is the moment when you know you are finally about to find out how the protagonist will overcome the conflict (or be defeated).

5. Climax

Describe the **climax,** the most suspenseful moment in the story, when you discover at last how the conflict ends.

> **Strategy Tip**
> Avoid linking the events with a string of *and's.* Here are some good time-order words to use: *first; second; third; next; eventually; later; afterward; finally; in conclusion.*

6. Resolution

Finally, tell what happens after the **climax.** How does the story end?

Understanding How Character Affects Plot

If . . . Then . . .

W hat would happen in *Star Wars* if Darth Vader suddenly became afraid of Luke Skywalker? How would the cartoon *Scooby Doo* be different if Scooby became brave? What would happen to *The Flintstones* if Fred suddenly got smart?

In each of those situations, the outcome of the plot would certainly change if the characters changed. In other words, if a character acts one way, then the plot proceeds in a certain way. If a character acts in a different way, the outcome of the plot changes also.

Imagine what would have happened in "Cinderella" if Cinderella had not been kind and gentle. The fairy godmother probably would never have shown up to help a Cinderella who was as nasty and selfish as the stepsisters. Think about what would have happened in "Sleeping Beauty" if the princess hadn't been curious.

Most likely she wouldn't have wandered into the one room that had the spinning wheel that was to put her and the whole kingdom to sleep for one hundred years.

We All Have Traits

To understand how character affects plot, you've first got to be able to identify the main character's qualities. A character's qualities, or *traits,* can be flaws or strengths. We all have character traits. We may be ambitious, shy, generous, fearless, kind, selfish—the possibilities are almost endless.

You discover the traits of a character you meet in a story the same way you discover the traits of real people. You think about how the character acts, how the character looks, and what he or she says. You think about how other people respond to the character. In fact, you think about all the ways writers develop a character.

Grade 6 Review Reading Standard 3.2
Analyze the effect of the qualities of the character (for example, courage or cowardice, ambition or laziness) on the plot and the resolution of the conflict.

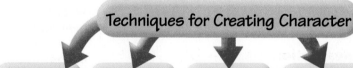

Techniques for Creating Character

| Writer uses dialogue to tell what the character **says**. | Writer tells how the character **acts**. | Writer reveals the character's **thoughts** and **feelings**. | Writer describes the character's **appearance**. | Writer shows **what others think** about the character. |

Here are some adjectives you can use to describe character traits:

Character Traits

strong/weak	wise/foolish	truthful/sneaky
kind/mean	selfish/unselfish	dependable/unreliable
brave/cowardly	good/bad	generous/stingy
honest/dishonest	clever/silly	
bold/shy	modern/old-fashioned	

If . . . Then . . .

When you're trying to figure out how character affects plot, think of what would happen if the character acted differently—or were a different kind of person. Think **If . . . Then . . .** *If* the character is like this, *then* what would happen in the story? On the other hand, *if* the character is like *that, then* what would happen?

PRACTICE

1. When you read "The Smallest Dragonboy" (page 119), decide which word in each of the following pairs describes Keevan.

   a. brave/cowardly

   b. truthful/sneaky

   c. strong/weak

   Next, decide how the story would change if you were to choose the other word in each pair. *If* you think Keevan is brave, *then* how would the story change if he were cowardly? Would he go to the hatching? Would he Impress with the bronze dragon? *If* you think he is strong, *then* what would happen if he were weak? Would he stay in bed? Would he find his dragon?

2. When you read "Mother and Daughter" (page 109), think about Yollie. Decide which word in each of the following pairs best describes her.

   a. hopeful/defeated

   b. brave/cowardly

   c. honest/dishonest

   Now, choose the other word to describe Yollie, and predict how the plot and its resolution would change.

3. In "A Rice Sandwich" (page 141), think about Esperanza. Decide which word in each of the following pairs best describes Esperanza.

   a. brave/shy

   b. strong/weak

   c. hopeful/defeated

   Predict how the story would progress and how it would end if Esperanza were the opposite of whichever word you chose.

Uncovering Theme

Most Important Word

Has your teacher ever asked you that dreaded theme question—the one that begins "What is the theme of . . . ?" What do you do when you hear that question? A group of seventh-graders all immediately started turning the pages of their books when their teacher asked them. "Why are you doing that?" she asked. "I'm looking for the theme," one student replied. "Yeah," another said, "I sure hope the writer remembered to include it."

What Is Theme?

Well, the writer did include it, but not in the way the students were hoping. Writers don't end (or begin) their stories with a nice note to the reader that says, "And the theme of the story is . . ." No, instead writers let their readers meet the characters and share an experience with them. At the end of the experience, the reader, along with the characters, has discovered something about human experience. It might be something the reader already knows but rediscovers under new circumstances. It might be something new. The **theme,** then, is a truth about life or people that we discover as we share the characters' experiences.

Not a Theme

happiness | childhood | death

Grade 5 Review Reading Standard 3.4 Understand that *theme* refers to the meaning or moral of a selection, and recognize themes (whether implied or stated directly) in sample works.

When you write or state a theme, remember that a theme isn't a word or a phrase—it's at least one sentence!

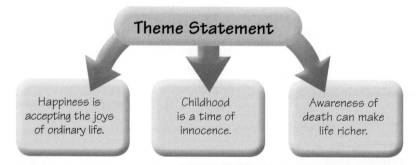

Theme Statement

Happiness is accepting the joys of ordinary life. | Childhood is a time of innocence. | Awareness of death can make life richer.

Most Important Word

If you need help writing a theme statement, try a strategy called **Most Important Word**. After you've read a selection, skim through it again looking for the word in the text you think is most important. Here are comments three students made after reading a poem called "The Secret Heart" by Robert P. Tristram Coffin. In this poem a father checks on his son, who is sleeping.

"I say **heart** is the most important word, because it's used a lot and is in the title and because the boy thinks his dad's hands look like they are making a heart, and that's the image the boy always remembers."

"I think the most important word is **father,** because it is the father who is checking on his son when he is sleeping at night."

What's the most important word and why?

"I think the most important word is **love,** because if the father didn't love his son, he wouldn't have been checking on him at night, wanting to protect him."

After deciding on the most important word and coming up with reasons for your choice, think about how that word could be related to the theme. Since different readers can pull different themes from the same selection, statements of themes usually differ from reader to reader. Look at the following three themes those three students stated, and match them to the comments above.

1. A parent's love for a child is never-ending—it goes on day and night.

2. Children remember their parents' simple acts of love.

3. A father is his child's protector.

PRACTICE

Read this short, short poem by Langston Hughes. Select what you think is its most important word (or words—there could be more than one). Write down reasons for your choice. Then, think of how that word could point to the theme of the poem. Try stating, in a sentence, the theme that you have discovered. Be sure to compare your themes in class.

> O God of dust and rainbows help us see
> That without dust the rainbows would not be.
> —Langston Hughes

Analyzing Point of View

Somebody Wanted But So

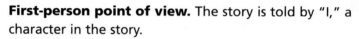

I s this glass half empty or half full? The very thirsty child would complain that it's half empty. The mom, who doesn't want the child drinking so much soda anyway, would say it's half full. What you're seeing in this situation is the effect of point of view.

When we talk about **point of view** in stories, we are talking about who is telling the story. Here are the three main points of view:

First-person point of view. The story is told by "I," a character in the story.

Omniscient point of view. The story is told by an all-knowing narrator who is not a character in the story. This narrator can tell everything about everyone in the story. This narrator can even tell the future.

Third-person limited point of view. The story is told by a narrator who is not in the story. This narrator zooms in on one character and tells the story through that character's eyes and emotions.

Writers are especially aware of point of view, and they experiment with it all the time. Skilled readers also think about how a story would be changed if it were told from a different viewpoint. Try experimenting with point of view by using a strategy called **Somebody Wanted But So.**

Reading Standard 3.5
Contrast points of view (for example, first and third person, limited and omniscient) in narrative text.

Somebody Wanted But So

This simple strategy helps you summarize a story; it can also help you think about the story from various characters' perspectives—or points of view. Here's how the strategy works:

On a sheet of paper, jot down the words *Somebody Wanted But So.* Now, think about a story you've just read. For right now, let's think about "Cinderella," a fairy tale you probably know. First, decide which character in the story you want to think about. Here are some choices: Cinderella, the stepmother, the stepsisters, the prince, maybe even the fairy godmother. Now, write your choice under the heading "Somebody," like this:

Somebody	Wanted	But	So
The prince			

With a focus on the prince, next think about what the prince wanted. "But" means he faced a problem getting what he wanted. "So" tells what the outcome is. Once you think through all of this, you have an SWBS chart that looks like this:

Somebody	Wanted	But	So
The prince	to find the young woman he met at the ball,	she left the ball without telling him who she was,	he traveled far and wide until he found her and married her.

You've just thought about the story from the prince's point of view. Now, try thinking about it from Cinderella's point of view. You might come up with a statement like this:

Somebody	Wanted	But	So
Cinderella	to escape the kitchen and a cruel family; she also wanted to go to the prince's ball,	her cruel step-mother would not let her get a dress for the ball,	a fairy godmother visited Cinderella and magically granted her wish.

Notice that as you change the character under the "Somebody" heading, you are shifting focus. If the prince tells the story or if a storyteller tells the story zooming in on the prince, you will not hear about Cinderella and her sad, ragged state until later. You will hear the prince telling you that he has fallen in love with a mysterious, beautiful young woman wearing the most fantastic gown, who left a tiny glass slipper on the palace steps.

PRACTICE

Look back at "After Twenty Years" (page 225). Create SWBS charts for Jimmy, Bob, and the plainclothes policeman. How would the story change if the point of view were narrowed to what only one of these characters knows and sees?

Identifying Cause and Effect

Here are three situations:

- You punch the right button on your stereo, and music starts to play.

- Someone tells you your clothes are cool, and you feel good about yourself.

- Your brother barges into your room without knocking, and you get angry.

In each of those situations, something has happened (an **effect**) because of something else (a **cause**). Look at this chart, and you can see which part of each sentence is the cause and which is the effect:

Cause	→	Effect
punching the stereo's right button	→	music starting to play
hearing your clothes are cool	→	feeling good about yourself
brother barging into your room	→	getting angry

Finding the Cause and Its Effect

If writers showed us cause-and-effect relationships (sometimes called **causal relationships**) by using charts like the one to the left, then finding causes and effects would be easy. Most of the time, information isn't delivered in chart format, so you've got to find causes and effects on your own. Here are some tips for doing that:

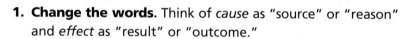

1. **Change the words.** Think of *cause* as "source" or "reason" and *effect* as "result" or "outcome."

2. **Check out the question.** If a question in your history book or science book (even in this book!) asks you to identify causes and effects, look carefully at the question. The question itself often lets you know if you are hunting for the cause or the effect.

- **What are three causes of the Civil War?**
  In this question you see that you are looking for the causes of (reasons for) the Civil War (outcome or effect).

- **What are three effects of poor nutrition?**
  This time you've got the cause (poor nutrition), and you're looking to see what the effects or results of poor nutrition are.

- **Why is George Washington called the father of our country?**
With this question you are given the effect, or outcome: Washington came to be called the father of our country. Now you've got to find the reason or reasons why, so you are looking for the causes.

3. **Be on the lookout for signal words.** Certain words can signal that a reason for something or a cause of something is about to be mentioned. Other words can signal that a result or an effect is being described.

Words That Signal Causes		Words That Signal Effects	
because	since	therefore	thus
due to	were caused by	consequently	so
given that	results from	as a result	for that reason
as		then	

PRACTICE

Read the sentences that follow, and make a cause-and-effect chart like the one on the opposite page. Decide which part of each sentence goes under the "Cause" heading and which part goes under the "Effect" heading. Look for signal words that help you spot causes and effects.

1. The California population grew from about 114,000 in 1848 to about 750,000 in 1852 as people moved to California in search of gold.

2. People rushing to California to find gold were called *forty-niners* because most of them arrived in 1849, the height of the gold rush.

3. Many of the mining towns that sprang up quickly were unsafe because they had no sheriffs.

4. Because so many people came so quickly to California looking for gold, by 1850, much of the easily found surface gold was already gone.

5. Although most people who went to California did not become rich from mining gold, many thousands decided to stay because of the wonderful climate and good farmland.

Latin and Greek Roots and Affixes

Becoming Word-Wise

Can You Read the Following Sentence?

Ifay ouyay ancay eadray isthay, enthay ouyay ancay eadray igpay atinlay.

Well, how did you do? If you know Pig Latin, then you probably did just fine. Pig Latin—not at all related to the Latin the ancient Romans spoke—requires you to take off the first letter (or sometimes letters) of a word, put that letter at the end of the word, and then add the long *a* sound (ā). So, *pig* becomes *igpay*. Once you figure out how words work in Pig Latin (owhay ordsway orkway inay igpay atinlay), then you can speak it, write it, read it, and understand it.

Figuring out the meaning of words and how they work to make meaning is the key to mastering any language. Mastering English vocabulary is especially difficult because English has borrowed words from many different languages. However, many English words can be traced to Latin and Greek. If you can learn to see Latin or Greek roots and affixes in some English words and understand what those roots and affixes mean, then you

have a key to understanding many English words.

For instance, if you know that the Latin prefix *dis–* means "not" or "the opposite," you can figure out that the word *dislocate* means "put out of place" or "locate in a different place" (as in "dislocate a shoulder").

If you know that the Latin root *–aud–* means "hear," then you can guess that *audible* has something to do with hearing.

On the next pages are lists of common roots and affixes from Latin and Greek. Note their meanings. Note examples of how these roots and affixes are used to build English words. (*L* in the chart stands for "Latin"; *G* stands for "Greek.")

Reading Standard 1.2
Use knowledge of Greek and Latin roots and affixes to understand content-area vocabulary

---

Remember . . .

Roots are the fundamental parts of a word. *–Loc–* is a Latin root for "place." *Locate* is based on the Latin root *–loc–*.

Affixes are word parts added to a root to alter its meaning.

Prefixes are affixes added to the front of a word (*dis*locate).

Suffixes are affixes added to the end of a word (loca*tion*).

Commonly Used Roots

Root	Meanings	Examples
–act– (L)	act	action, actor, react, transact, enact
–aud– (L)	hear	audience, auditorium, audible, audition
–bio– (G)	life	biology, biography, biofeedback, bionics
–cred– (L)	believe; trust	credit, discredit, credible, credulous
–dem– (G)	people	democracy, Democrat, demographics
–dic– (L)	speak; say	dictate, predict, contradict, verdict, diction
–geo– (G)	earth	geography, geology
–graph– (G)	write; draw; record	autograph, paragraph, phonograph, photograph, telegraph
–loc– (L)	place	allocate, locate, location
–man– (L)	hand	manual, manufacture, manuscript, manipulate
–ped– (L)	foot	pedal, pedestrian, pedestal
–pop– (L)	people; nation	population, popular, populace
–port– (L)	carry	import, export, portable, porter, transport
–sig– (L)	mark; sign	insignia, signal, significant, signature
–spec– (L)	see; look at	inspect, respect, spectacle, spectator, suspect
–tract– (L)	pull; drag	attract, detract, contract, subtract, traction, tractor
–vid– (L)	see; look	evidence, video, provide, providence
–volv– (L)	roll	evolve, involve, revolve, revolver, revolution

Commonly Used Prefixes

Prefix	Meanings	Examples
anti– (G)	against; opposing	antiwar, anticlimax
bi– (L)	two	bisect, bimonthly
co– (L)	with; together	coexist, codependent
de– (L)	away from; off; down	debrief, debug
dia– (G)	through; across; between	diameter, diagonal
in–, im– (L)	in; into; within	introduce, imprison
inter– (L)	between; among	interpersonal, intersect
non– (L)	not	nonprofit, nonfat
post– (L)	after; following	postnasal, postgraduate
pre– (L)	before	prepayment, preview
re– (L)	back; backward; again	reverse, return, recur
sub– (L)	under; beneath	submarine, substandard
syl–, sym–, syn–, sys– (G)	together; with	syllable, symmetric, synthesis, system
trans– (L)	across	transplant, translate

Commonly Used Suffixes

Suffix	Meanings	Examples
–able (L)	able; likely	readable, lovable
–ance, –ancy (L)	act; quality	admittance, constancy
–ate (L)	to become; to cause; to be	captivate, activate
–fy (L)	to make; to cause; to be	liquefy, simplify
–ible (L)	able; likely	flexible, digestible
–ity (L)	state; condition	reality, sincerity
–ize (L)	to make; to cause; to be	socialize, motorize
–ment (L)	result; act of; state of being	judgment, fulfillment
–ous (L)	characterized by	dangerous, malicious
–tion (L)	action; condition	rotation, election

You can increase your vocabulary by building "vocabulary trees" from the root up. For an example of a vocabulary tree, look below at the tree a student made using the root –cred–. Here are the steps you can follow to create your own vocabulary tree:

1. On a piece of paper, draw a tree like the one below, and put a word root from the list on page 521 in the root section of the tree.

2. In the trunk, put one word from the "Examples" column that uses that root, and define the word.

3. In the branches, put other words that you hear or read or use in your own writing that come from that root.

4. On the twigs of the branches, explain how you used that word or where you read it.

5. Add as many branches as possible to your vocabulary tree.

Remember: The more you use a word, the more likely you are to remember what it means.

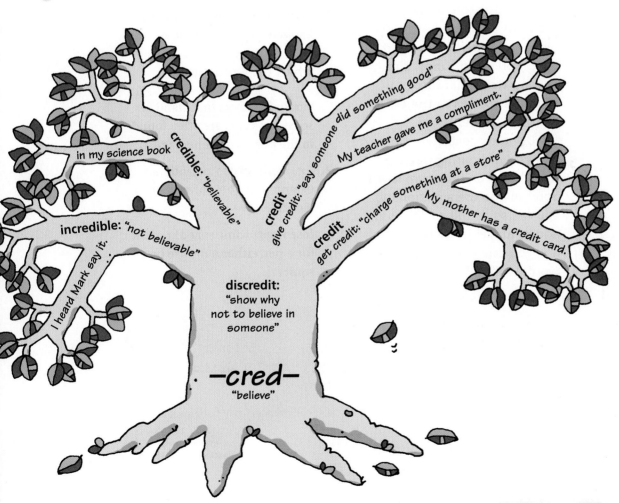

in my science book

credible: "believable"

credit
give credit: "say someone did something good"

My teacher gave me a compliment.

credit
get credit: "charge something at a store"

My mother has a credit card.

incredible: "not believable"

I heard Mark say it.

discredit:
"show why
not to believe in
someone"

–cred–
"believe"

Using Context Clues

Becoming Word-Wise

See if you can complete the following sentences:

- When you get in a car, be sure to buckle your seat _____.

- I really like to pour _____ over my pancakes.

- Most people turn on a _____ when they walk into a dark room.

You probably quickly figured out that the missing words were *belt, syrup*, and *light*. You could supply the missing words because you used the **context**—the other words in the sentence.

Using context clues is only one way of figuring out the meaning of an unknown word. You can also use a dictionary; you can study the word's root and its affixes, if there are any; and you can look for familiar words within the word.

If a dictionary isn't close by, and if knowing word parts isn't helping and if no familiar words seem to be within the word you don't know, turn to **context clues.** Context clues to word meanings are often found in the passage the word is used in. There are lots of different types of context clues, but the following four are particularly helpful:

1. **Definition clues** define or explain the unfamiliar word right in the same sentence in which the word appears.

   definition clue

   Symbols, <u>things that stand for something else</u>, are often found in the poems of Robert Frost.

2. **Example clues** provide an example of the unfamiliar word.

   José wants some sort of rodent for a pet, either a <u>mouse</u> or a <u>squirrel</u>.

   example clue

Reading Standard 1.3
Clarify word meanings through the use of definition, example, restatement, or contrast.

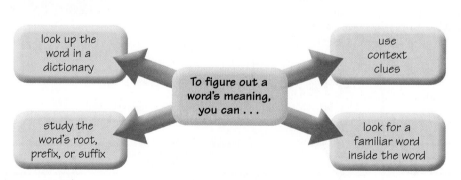

To figure out a word's meaning, you can . . .

- look up the word in a dictionary
- use context clues
- study the word's root, prefix, or suffix
- look for a familiar word inside the word

3. **Restatement clues** explain the unfamiliar word in the text by restating it in simpler terms or by using a synonym. The restatement might be in the same sentence or in another sentence close by—so be sure to read on!

statement clue

The food was so bland, or **tasteless**, that everyone stopped eating.

The food was bland. Everyone stopped eating because the food had no taste. ← *restatement clue*

4. **Contrast clues** offer an opposite meaning of the unfamiliar word. Again, the contrast might be in the same sentence or in a nearby sentence.

contrast clues

Chad is calm and quiet, but his brother is usually boisterous. →

PRACTICE

Define the following underlined words by using context clues. Identify the type of context clue you find in each sentence.

1. His logic was fallacious, or faulty, so everyone reached the wrong conclusions.
   Clue _____
   Meaning _____

2. Most snakes are meat eaters, or carnivores.
   Clue _____
   Meaning _____

3. A mendicant is a beggar.
   Clue _____
   Meaning _____

4. I like conifers, such as pine trees or cypress trees.
   Clue _____
   Meaning _____

5. His conjecture, or guess, was wrong.
   Clue _____
   Meaning _____

6. The thief ran out the postern while the police ran in the front door.
   Clue _____
   Meaning _____

7. The rider merely tapped the quirt. This small whip is used to make the race-horse run faster.
   Clue _____
   Meaning _____

8. Subterranean tempera-tures are sometimes higher than temperatures above the earth's surface.
   Clue _____
   Meaning _____

9. That girl is narcissistic. The other girl, however, really isn't overly inter-ested in herself.
   Clue _____
   Meaning _____

10. I was so happy while on vacation that my elation lasted for weeks afterward.
    Clue _____
    Meaning _____

Mastering the California Standards in Writing, Listening, and Speaking

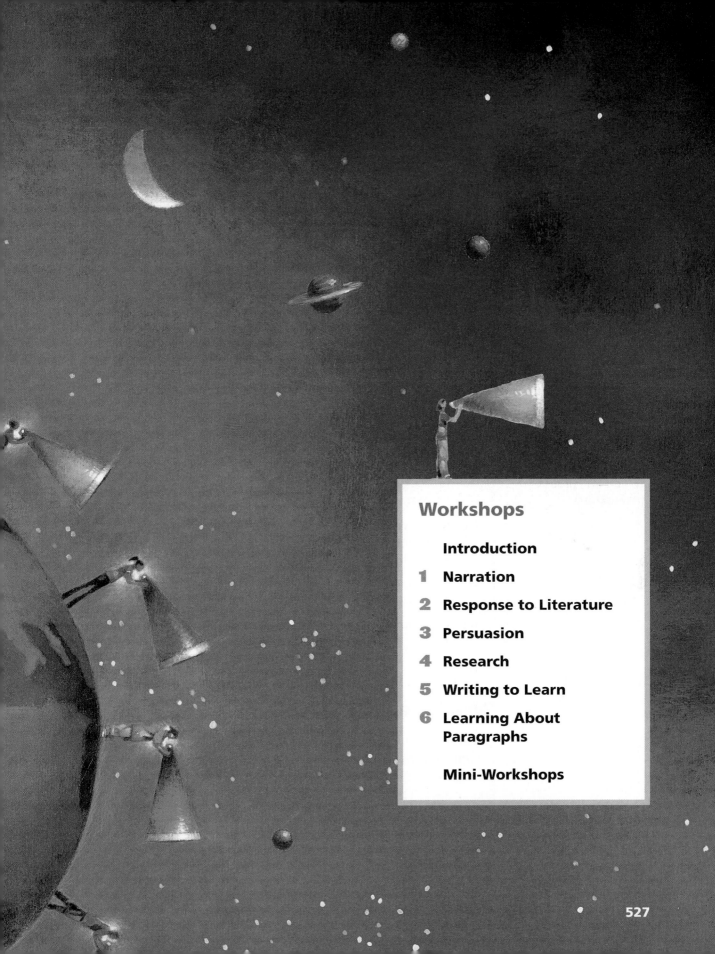

Workshops

Introduction

You use processes every day—when you play a game, follow a recipe, or make artwork. Writing, too, is a **process** that involves many steps to complete. This introduction to the writing process will prepare you for the workshops in this book. You will also learn about the following language arts standards.

 California Standards

Writing

1.0 Students progress through the stages of the writing process as needed.

1.3 Use strategies of notetaking, outlining, and summarizing to impose structure on composition drafts.

1.6 Create documents by using word-processing skills and publishing programs.

1.7 Revise writing to improve organization and word choice after checking the logic of the ideas and the precision of the vocabulary.

2.0 Student writing demonstrates a command of standard American English.

2.5 Write summaries of reading material.

WHAT'S AHEAD?

In this section you will learn how effective writers

- use the stages of the writing process
- read professional models
- create think sheets, outlines, and summaries
- create documents with correct manuscript style
- use editing symbols to edit and proofread manuscripts

Writing as a Process

"Genius," wrote Thomas Edison, "is 1 percent inspiration and 99 percent perspiration." He was talking about inventing, but the same goes for writing. Writing is a process made up of many steps, and it takes effort. The chart on the next page summarizes the stages that usually take place during the writing process.

Reading—An Important Part of the Process

You may have noticed that one of the prewriting strategies listed in the chart above is to read professional models of the type of writing you plan to do. Such reading can help you generate topics, gather and organize ideas, and write effectively, especially if you create *think sheets, summaries,* or *outlines* of selections you read.

Create a Think Sheet   **Think sheets** are notes of your questions and comments about reading selections. They can help you

■ **develop ideas for topics.** Anything in a model that stirs a response in you could provide a topic for your own writing. For instance, an editorial about the negative effects of video games might spur you to write an editorial in support of video games.

Writing 1.0 Students progress through the stages of the writing process as needed.

- **organize your ideas.** The structure of a selection might provide clues for ordering your own ideas. For instance, you might adopt the comparison-contrast structure of a newspaper article you have read for your next piece of informative writing.
- **identify effective writing techniques.** If your think sheet includes comments about effective techniques, such as precise nouns or vivid adjectives, you might try them.

HOW TO CREATE A THINK SHEET

1. Write the title and author of the selection at the top of a sheet of paper. Then, draw a vertical line down the center of the sheet. Label the left-hand column "text" and the right-hand column "responses."

2. As you read the selection, note in the left-hand column words or brief passages you think are important or interesting or that prompt questions.

3. Next to each word or passage noted on your paper, jot down your response in the right-hand column. Include notes on any of the following.
   - personal responses to the text, such as memories or feelings
   - use of language, such as word choice or figurative language
   - organization of ideas, such as comparison-contrast structure
   - types of supporting evidence, such as anecdotes or descriptions

Write a Summary A **summary** is a brief account of the most important ideas and details in a reading selection. Writing a summary can help you understand the content of a selection. Summarizing can also give you ideas about organizing your own writing.

HOW TO CREATE A SUMMARY

1. **Read** the selection carefully.

2. **Skim** the selection looking for sections. Sections may be indicated with numbers, white spaces, or descriptive headings. If sections are not otherwise indicated, consider each paragraph a section. On a sheet of paper, list a word or phrase identifying the general topic of each section.

3. **Write in your own words** one or two sentences that restate the most important ideas and supporting points of each section.

4. **Combine** the sentences into a paragraph, using transitions to show the relationships among ideas. This paragraph is your summary.

Writing **1.3** Use strategies of notetaking and summarizing to impose structure on composition drafts. **2.5** Write summaries of reading materials.

Make an Outline Making an **outline** is an especially good way to analyze the organizational pattern of a professional model. To make an informal outline of a reading selection, write the main idea of each section, followed by the evidence or details that support it. Here is an example of an informal outline.

Title: "The Ups and Downs of Owning a Pet Pig"

Many benefits	A few drawbacks
—easy to housebreak	—can grow very large
—doesn't shed	—can be too playful
—easy to train, intelligent	—not a good watch animal

As you work through the Writing Workshops in this book, use the professional models provided during prewriting. Create think sheets, summaries, and outlines to get the most out of your reading.

PRACTICE & APPLY

Create a Think Sheet, a Summary, and an Outline

Read "Fish Cheeks" on pages 352–353. As you read, use the guidelines on page 530 to create a think sheet. Afterward, use the guidelines on page 530 to write a summary, and then make an informal outline of the selection like the one above.

Using the Writing Process

The Writing Workshops in this book will go into depth about the process for writing specific kinds of compositions. Some guidelines for using the writing process, however, are universal. One set of guidelines that you can use for almost any type of paper are the guidelines for correct manuscript style, given in the chart below.

Quick guide

GUIDELINES FOR MANUSCRIPT STYLE
1. Use only one side of each sheet of paper.
2. Type your paper using a word processor, or write it neatly by hand in blue or black ink.
3. For handwritten papers, ask your teacher if he or she wants you to skip lines. For word-processed papers, many teachers prefer that you double-space your assignment.

(continued)

Writing **1.3** Use strategies of outlining to impose structure on composition drafts. **1.6** Create documents by using word-processing skills and publishing programs.

(continued)

4. Leave one-inch margins at the top, bottom, and sides of your paper.

5. Indent the first line of every paragraph half an inch. (You can set a tab on a word processor to indent half an inch automatically.)

6. Number all pages except the first page in the top right-hand corner.

7. Make sure your pages look neat and clean. For handwritten papers, you can mark a single line through mistakes. However, if you have several mistakes on one page, write out the page again. For word-processed papers, make corrections and print out a clean copy.

8. Use the heading your teacher prefers for your name, your class, the date, and the title of your paper. If your teacher requires a title page, use a separate sheet of paper and center the information on the page.

The Writing Workshops provide specific guidelines for revising various forms of writing, but you can use the following revision techniques with any piece of writing.

REVISION TECHNIQUES

Technique	Example
1. Add. Add new information and details. Add words, sentences, or paragraphs.	The book *Lovey: A Very Special Child* is written by a woman who teaches children ⌐with severe emotional problems.
2. Cut. Take out repeated or unnecessary words, sentences, or paragraphs.	~~The children have serious problems.~~ One of the children, Hannah, hides in a closet at first.
3. Replace. Replace weak, clichéd, or slang words and phrases with precise words and details and standard American English.	Hannah doesn't talk to the teacher or other kids, but she ~~acts up~~ *cries and screams* when she's upset.
4. Rearrange. Move details, sentences, and paragraphs for clear and logical order.	In time, Hannah joins the class and begins to talk and learn. The teacher patiently works with Hannah.

Like the revision techniques above, the guidelines for proofreading on the next page can be applied to any writing that you do. The page numbers in the chart refer to the *Holt Handbook*.

Writing 1.7 Revise writing to improve organization and word choice after checking the logic of the ideas and the precision of the vocabulary. **2.0** Student writing demonstrates a command of standard American English.

GUIDELINES FOR PROOFREADING

1. Is every sentence a complete sentence, rather than a fragment or run-on? (See pages 414–417.)

2. Does every sentence begin with a capital letter? Does every sentence end with the correct punctuation mark? Are punctuation marks used correctly within sentences? (See pages 264 and 288.)

3. Do plural subjects have plural verbs? Do singular subjects have singular verbs? (See page 148.)

4. Are the verb forms and tenses used correctly? (See page 174.)

5. Are adjective and adverb forms used correctly in comparisons? (See page 224.)

6. Are the forms of personal pronouns used correctly? (See page 202.)

7. Does every pronoun agree with its antecedent (the word it refers to) in number and gender? Are pronoun references clear? (See page 165.)

8. Is every word spelled correctly? (See page 346.)

In addition to editing and proofreading your own writing, you will probably work cooperatively with classmates to edit and proof-read one another's writing. Use the universal editing marks in the chart below.

SYMBOLS FOR EDITING AND PROOFREADING

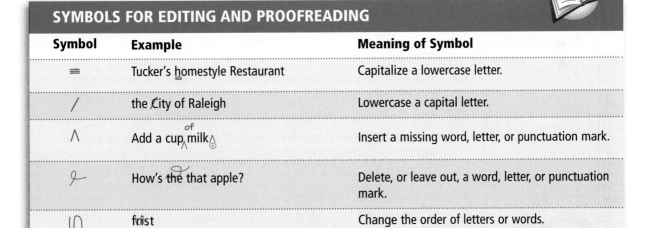

Symbol	Example	Meaning of Symbol
≡	Tucker's homestyle Restaurant	Capitalize a lowercase letter.
/	the City of Raleigh	Lowercase a capital letter.
∧	Add a cup milk (of)	Insert a missing word, letter, or punctuation mark.
℘	How's the that apple?	Delete, or leave out, a word, letter, or punctuation mark.
∩	frist	Change the order of letters or words.
¶	¶ "Go ahead," he said.	Begin a new paragraph.

Writing 2.0 Student writing demonstrates a command of standard American English.

Narration

You use your imagination every day—when you dream, solve a problem, create artwork, or read a book. One way to spark your imagination and use it to entertain others is by writing and sharing a short story. In this workshop you will do just that, creating a narrative with unique characters and situations that only you could dream up. In the process you will practice the following language arts standards.

WRITING WORKSHOP

Writing a Short Story
Page 536

LISTENING AND SPEAKING WORKSHOP

Giving and Listening to an Oral Narrative
Page 558

GO TO: go.hrw.com
KEYWORD: HLLA7 W-1
FOR: Models, Writer's Guides, and Reference Sources

California Standards

Writing

1.0 Students write clear, coherent, and focused essays [short stories]. The writing exhibits students' awareness of the audience and purpose. Students progress through the stages of the writing process as needed.

1.1 Create an organizational structure that balances all aspects of the composition and uses effective transitions between sentences to unify important ideas.

1.3 Use strategies of outlining to impose structure on composition drafts.

1.6 Create documents by using word-processing skills and publishing programs.

1.7 Revise writing to improve organization and word choice after checking the logic of the ideas and the precision of the vocabulary.

2.0 Students write narrative texts of at least 500 to 700 words. The writing demonstrates a command of standard American English and the organizational and drafting strategies outlined in Writing Standard 1.0.

2.1 Write fictional narratives:

   a. Develop a standard plot line (having a beginning, conflict, rising action, climax, and denouement) and point of view.

   b. Develop complex major and minor characters and a definite setting.

   c. Use a range of appropriate strategies (e.g., dialogue; suspense; naming of specific narrative action, including movement, gestures, and expressions).

Listening and Speaking

1.0 Deliver coherent presentations that convey ideas clearly and relate to the background and interests of the audience. Students evaluate the content of oral communication.

1.2 Determine the speaker's [or narrator's] attitude toward the subject.

1.4 Organize information to achieve particular purposes and to appeal to the background and interests of the audience.

1.5 Arrange supporting details and descriptions effectively in relation to the audience.

1.6 Use speaking techniques, including voice modulation, inflection, tempo, enunciation, and eye contact, for effective presentations.

1.7 Provide constructive feedback to speakers concerning the coherence and logic of a speech's content and delivery and its overall impact upon the listener.

2.0 Students deliver well-organized formal presentations employing traditional rhetorical strategies (e.g., narration, description). Student speaking demonstrates a command of standard American English and the organizational and delivery strategies outlined in Listening and Speaking Standard 1.0.

2.1 Deliver narrative presentations:

   a. Establish a context, standard plot line (having a beginning, conflict, rising action, climax, and denouement), and point of view.

   b. Describe complex major and minor characters and a definite setting.

   c. Use a range of appropriate strategies, including dialogue, suspense, and naming of specific narrative action (e.g., movement, gestures, expressions).

Writing a Short Story

WHAT'S AHEAD?

In this workshop you will write a short story. You will also learn how to

- choose and develop an idea for a story
- develop major and minor characters and a specific setting
- plot a short story
- use appropriate narrative strategies
- use precise nouns and adjectives
- punctuate dialogue

Imagine creating a character—a person who never existed before—and then plunging that character into an exciting or frightening or challenging situation. When you write **fiction,** or made-up stories, you have the power to bring to life any kind of character or situation you can imagine. The only limit is your imagination. In this workshop you will create a **short story,** a kind of fictional narrative that has just one or a few main characters and a relatively simple situation. Don't let the term "short story" fool you, though. Even a story that is short on length can be long on creativity and imagination.

Professional Model: A Short Story

To find inspiration for what to write about or to find a model for what elements to include in your story, start by looking at the short stories of professional writers. Perhaps your favorite movie was based on a short story, or your favorite novelist has also published short stories you could read.

Gary Soto, the author of the novels *Taking Sides* and *Pacific Crossing,* is also known for his poetry and short stories. On the following pages you will read his short story "The No-Guitar Blues." As you read, create a **think sheet,** asking questions, making connections to your own life, and noting important passages in the story. Answer the analysis questions that appear next to the story to help you create your think sheet.

DO THIS ➤

Reference Note

For information on **think sheets,** see page 529.

Writing 2.1 Write fictional narratives.

The No-Guitar Blues

by Gary Soto

The moment Fausto saw the group Los Lobos on *American Bandstand,* he knew exactly what he wanted to do with his life—play guitar. His eyes grew large with excitement as Los Lobos ground out a song while teenagers bounced off each other on the crowded dance floor.

He had watched *American Bandstand* for years and had heard Ray Camacho and the Teardrops at Romain Playground, but it had never occurred to him that he too might become a musician. That afternoon Fausto knew his mission in life: to play guitar in his own band; to sweat out his songs and prance[1] around the stage; to make money and dress weird.

Fausto turned off the television set and walked outside, wondering how he could get enough money to buy a guitar. He couldn't ask his parents because they would just say, "Money doesn't grow on trees" or "What do you think we are, bankers?" And besides, they hated rock music. They were into the *conjunto*[2] music of Lydia Mendoza, Flaco Jimenez, and Little Joe and La Familia. And, as Fausto recalled, the last album they bought was *The Chipmunks Sing Christmas Favorites.*

But what the heck, he'd give it a try.

> **1. What is Fausto's dream?**

> **2. Why doesn't he think his parents will give him money for a guitar?**

He returned inside and watched his mother make tortillas. He leaned against the kitchen counter, trying to work up the nerve to ask her for a guitar. Finally, he couldn't hold back any longer.

"Mom," he said, "I want a guitar for Christmas."

She looked up from rolling tortillas. "Honey, a guitar costs a lot of money."

"How 'bout for my birthday next year," he tried again.

"I can't promise," she said, turning back to her tortillas, "but we'll see."

Fausto walked back outside with a buttered tortilla. He knew his mother was right. His father was a warehouseman at Berven Rugs, where he made good money but not enough to buy everything his children wanted. Fausto decided to mow lawns to earn money and was pushing the mower down the street before he realized it was winter and no one would hire him. He returned the mower and picked up a rake. He hopped onto his sister's bike (his had two flat tires) and rode north to the nicer section of Fresno in search of work. He went door-to-door, but after three hours he managed to get only one job, and not to rake leaves. He was asked to hurry down to the store to buy a loaf of bread, for which he

> **3. How does Fausto decide he will get money for a guitar? How does this plan change?**

---

1. **prance:** to strut or dance.
2. **conjunto** (kôn hōōn´tô): Northern Mexican polka music played with accordion, bass guitar, and drums.

received a grimy, dirt-caked quarter.

He also got an orange, which he ate sitting at the curb. While he was eating, a dog walked up and sniffed his leg. Fausto pushed him away and threw an orange peel skyward. The dog caught it and ate it in one gulp. The dog looked at Fausto and wagged his tail for more. Fausto tossed him a slice of orange, and the dog snapped it up and licked his lips.

> **4. Why do you think the dog approaches Fausto?**

"How come you like oranges, dog?"

The dog blinked a pair of sad eyes and whined.

"What's the matter? Cat got your tongue?" Fausto laughed at his joke and offered the dog another slice.

At that moment a dim light came on inside Fausto's head. He saw that it was sort of a fancy dog, a terrier or something, with dog tags and a shiny collar. And it looked well-fed and healthy. In his neighborhood, the dogs were never licensed, and if they got sick they were placed near the water heater until they got well.

This dog looked as if he belonged to rich people. Fausto cleaned his juice-sticky hands on his pants and got to his feet. The light in his head grew brighter. It just might work. He called the dog, patted its muscular back, and bent down to check the license.

> **5. What do you think Fausto's new plan is?**

"Great," he said, "There's an address."

The dog's name was Roger, which struck Fausto as weird, because he'd never heard of a dog with a human name. Dogs should have names like Bomber, Freckles, Queenie, Killer, and Zero.

Fausto planned to take the dog home and collect a reward. He would say he had found Roger near the freeway. That would scare the daylights out of the owners, who would be so happy that they would probably give him a reward. He felt bad about lying, but the dog *was* loose. And it might even really be lost, because the address was six blocks away.

Fausto stashed the rake and his sister's bike behind a bush and, tossing an orange peel every time Roger became distracted, walked the dog to his house. He hesitated on the porch until Roger began to scratch the door with a muddy paw. Fausto had come this far, so he figured he might as well go through with it. He knocked softly. When no one answered, he rang the doorbell. A man in a silky bathrobe and slippers opened the door and seemed confused by the sight of his dog and the boy.

> **6. Why do you think Fausto hesitates on the porch?**

"Sir," Fausto said, gripping Roger by the collar. "I found your dog by the freeway. His dog license says he lives here." Fausto looked down at the dog, then up to the man. "He does, doesn't he?"

The man stared at Fausto a long time before saying in a pleasant voice, "That's right." He pulled his robe tighter around him because of the cold and asked Fausto to come in. "So he was by the freeway?"

"Uh-huh."

"You bad, snoopy dog," said the man, wagging his finger. "You probably knocked over some trash cans, too, didn't you?"

Fausto didn't say anything. He looked

7. How is this house different from and similar to Fausto's? your own home?

around, amazed by this house with its shiny furniture and a television as large as the front window at home. Warm bread smells filled the air and music full of soft tinkling floated in from another room.

"Helen," the man called to the kitchen. "We have a visitor." His wife came into the living room, wiping her hands on a dish towel and smiling. "And who have we here?" she asked in one of the softest voices Fausto had ever heard.

"This young man said he found Roger near the freeway."

Fausto repeated his story to her while staring at the perpetual clock with a bell-shaped glass, the kind his aunt got when she celebrated her twenty-fifth anniversary. The lady frowned and said, wagging a finger at Roger, "Oh, you're a bad boy."

"It was very nice of you to bring Roger home," the man said. "Where do you live?"

"By that vacant lot on Olive," he said. "You know, by Brownie's Flower Place."

The wife looked at her husband, then Fausto. Her eyes twinkled triangles of light as she said, "Well, young man, you're probably hungry. How about a turnover?"

"What do I have to turn over?" Fausto asked, thinking she was talking about yardwork or something like turning trays of dried raisins.

"No, no, dear, it's a pastry." She took him by the elbow and guided him to a kitchen that sparkled with copper pans and bright yellow wallpaper. She guided him to the kitchen table and gave him a tall glass of milk and something that looked like an empanada.[3] Steamy waves of heat escaped when he tore it in two. He ate with both eyes on the man and woman, who stood arm in arm smiling at him. They were strange, he thought. But nice.

"That was good," he said after he finished the turnover. "Did you make it, ma'am?"

"Yes, I did. Would you like another?"

"No, thank you. I have to go home now."

As Fausto walked to the door, the man opened his wallet and took out a bill. "This is for you," he said. "Roger is special to us, almost like a son."

Fausto looked at the bill and knew he was in trouble. Not with these nice folks or with his parents, but with himself. How could he have been so deceitful?[4] The dog wasn't lost. It was just having a fun Saturday walking around.

"I can't take that."

"You have to. You deserve it, believe me," the man said.

8. Why does Fausto try to refuse the money?

"No, I don't."

"Now don't be silly," said the lady. She took the bill from her husband and stuffed it into Fausto's shirt pocket. "You're a lovely child. Your parents are lucky to have you. Be good. And come see us again, please."

Fausto went out, and the lady closed

---

3. empanada (em´pä nä´dä): pastry filled with meat or fruit.
4. deceitful: dishonest.

the door. Fausto clutched the bill through his shirt pocket. He felt like ringing the doorbell and begging them to please take the money back, but he knew they would refuse. He hurried away and, at the end of the block, pulled the bill from his shirt pocket: It was a crisp twenty-dollar bill.

"Oh, man, I shouldn't have lied," he said under his breath as he started up the street like a zombie. He wanted to run to church for Saturday confession,[5] but it was past four-thirty, when confession stopped.

He returned to the bush where he had hidden the rake and his sister's bike and rode home slowly, not daring to touch the money in his pocket. At home, in the privacy of his room, he examined the twenty-dollar bill. He had never had so much money. It was probably enough to buy a secondhand guitar. But he felt bad, like the time he stole a dollar from the secret fold inside his older brother's wallet.

Fausto went outside and sat on the fence. "Yeah," he said. "I can probably get a guitar for twenty. Maybe at a yard sale— things are cheaper."

His mother called him to dinner.

The next day he dressed for church without anyone telling him. He was going to go to eight o'clock mass.

"I'm going to church, Mom," he said. His mother was in the kitchen cooking papas and chorizo con huevos.[6] A pile of tortillas lay warm under a dish towel.

"Oh, I'm so proud of you, Son." She beamed, turning over the crackling papas.

His older brother, Lawrence, who was at the table reading the funnies, mimicked, "Oh, I'm so proud of you, my son," under his breath.

At Saint Theresa's he sat near the front. When Father Jerry began by saying that we are all sinners, Fausto thought he looked right at him. Could he know? Fausto fidgeted with guilt. No, he thought. I only did it yesterday.

Fausto knelt, prayed, and sang. But he couldn't forget the man and the lady, whose names he didn't even know, and the empanada they had given him. It had a strange name but tasted really good. He wondered how they got rich. And how that dome clock worked. He had asked his mother once how his aunt's clock worked. She said it just worked, the way the refrigerator works. It just did.

Fausto caught his mind wandering and tried to concentrate on his sins. He said a Hail Mary and sang, and when the wicker basket came his way, he stuck a hand reluctantly[7] in his pocket and pulled out the twenty-dollar bill. He ironed it between his palms and dropped it into the basket. The grown-ups stared. Here was a kid dropping twenty dollars in the basket while they gave just three or four dollars.

There would be a second collection for

> **9. What does Fausto do with the twenty dollars? Why do you think he does this?**

---

5. **confession:** in the Roman Catholic Church, a ritual in which a person seeks God's forgiveness by telling a priest his or her sins.

6. **papas** (pä´päs) and **chorizo con huevos** (chô rē´sô kôn wā´vôs): Spanish for "potatoes" and "sausage with eggs," respectively.

7. **reluctantly:** hesitantly; unwillingly.

Saint Vincent de Paul,[8] the lector[9] announced. The wicker baskets again floated in the pews, and this time the adults around him, given a second chance to show their charity, dug deep into their wallets and purses and dropped in fives and tens. This time Fausto tossed in the grimy quarter.

Fausto felt better after church. He went home and played football in the front yard with his brother and some neighbor kids. He felt cleared of wrongdoing and was so happy that he played one of his best games of football ever. On one play, he tore his good pants, which he knew he shouldn't have been wearing. For a second, while he examined the hole, he wished he hadn't given the twenty dollars away.

Man, I coulda bought me some Levi's, he thought. He pictured his twenty dollars being spent to buy church candles. He pictured a priest buying an armful of flowers with *his* money.

Fausto had to forget about getting a guitar. He spent the next day playing soccer in his good pants, which were now his old pants. But that night, during dinner, his mother said she remembered seeing an old bass guitarron[10] the last time she cleaned out her father's garage.

"It's a little dusty," his mom said, serving his favorite enchiladas. "But I think it works. Grandpa says it works."

Fausto's ears perked up. That was the same kind the guy in Los Lobos played. Instead of asking for the guitar, he waited for his mother to offer it to him. And she did, while gathering the dishes from the table.

"No, Mom, I'll do it," he said, hugging her. "I'll do the dishes forever if you want."

It was the happiest day of his life. No, it was the second-happiest day of his life. The happiest was when his grandfather Lupe placed the guitarron, which was nearly as huge as a washtub, in his arms. Fausto ran a thumb down the strings, which vibrated in his throat and chest. It sounded beautiful, deep and eerie. A pumpkin smile widened on his face.

> **10.** Do you think Fausto is changed by his experience? Why or why not?

"Ok, hijo,[11] now put your fingers like this," said his grandfather, smelling of tobacco and after-shave. He took Fausto's fingers and placed them on the strings. Fausto strummed a chord on the guitarron, and the bass resounded[12] in their chests.

The guitarron was more complicated than Fausto imagined. But he was confident that after a few more lessons he could start a band that would someday play on *American Bandstand* for the dancing crowds.

---

8. **Saint Vincent de Paul** (1580–1660): founder of religious orders that care for the sick and poor. Saint Vincent de Paul societies today minister to the needy.

9. **lector** (lek´tər): person who reads the Scripture lessons in a church service.

10. **guitarron** (ge´tä rôn´): type of large guitar.

11. **hijo** (ē´ hô): Spanish for "son."

12. **resounded:** vibrated.

Prewriting

Find a Story Idea

KEY CONCEPT

What's the Big Idea?   What keeps a reader turning pages? **A good story needs an interesting main character facing a problem or challenge.** For example, how will a boy cross a flooded creek in time to rescue his dog? You might find a story idea by

- focusing first on a character, and then putting that character in an interesting situation
- starting with an interesting problem or situation, and then thinking of a character to put in that situation

TIP Another way to generate story ideas is to think of stories you enjoyed and identify what you liked about them. For example, if you enjoy stories about animals rescuing people, write a story with similar elements. What story ideas does "The No-Guitar Blues" on pages 537–541 give you?

Start with a Character You might build your story around an interesting or unusual person. For example, suppose you have a friend who is very shy but is a talented jazz musician. Keep in mind that you do not have to write about a real person.

Start with a Situation Another idea is to begin with an unusual situation. It may be something you have heard about or actually experienced. For example, maybe you know of someone hiding a kitten in an apartment where animals are forbidden. You might enjoy thinking of a far-fetched situation and seeing where it takes you. In any case, the situation should be one that suggests a **conflict**—a problem that the main character faces.

Writing **1.0** Students write focused essays [short stories]. Students progress through the stages of the writing process as needed. **2.1a** Develop a standard plot line (having a conflict).

People Plus Problems Wherever you start, you can combine a main character and a conflict to create a story idea. Below are one student's story ideas. Think of how different characters in the chart might deal with the conflicts listed. For example, a friendly space alien might handle the problem of having a crush on someone by impressing that person with alien technology. Which combination of character and conflict do you think would be most entertaining?

TIP Because your story should be 500 to 700 words long, choose a character and conflict carefully. The combination you use for your story should give you enough ideas to keep your readers interested throughout a story of that length.

Possible Characters	Possible Conflicts
• a shy new student with a secret	• a strange light on the horizon
• a smart, funny boy	• friends playing a practical joke
• an experienced detective	• being afraid to try something new
• a friendly space alien	• a missing work of art
• a young Aztec	• having a crush on someone

Think About Purpose and Audience

Share Your Imagination What is your **purpose** for writing your short story? Most likely, it is simply to entertain the people who will read it, who are also called your **audience**. You may entertain readers by making them laugh about the mistakes of a silly character or by involving them in the suspense of an exciting mystery. Think about people who are likely to read your story, such as members of your class, and consider what will make the story enjoyable for them. Whatever you choose to write about, keep your purpose and your audience in mind as you develop your story.

PRACTICE & APPLY 1   **Find a Story Idea, and Think About Purpose and Audience**

■ Brainstorm several ideas for your short story. Using a chart like the one above, match several characters with conflicts to see which combinations give you the most interesting ideas for a story.

■ Remembering your purpose—to entertain—think about your audience for a moment: Who is likely to read your completed short story? What kinds of stories would that audience find most entertaining?

■ Choose the story idea that is most likely to interest your audience and that you think you can best develop into a story.

 Writing 1.0 Writing exhibits students' awareness of audience and purpose. 2.0 Students write narrative texts of at least 500 to 700 words.

Plan Characters, Setting, and Point of View

Cast the Stars and the Bit Parts You already know who the major character of your story is, but you don't know much about that person (or animal or space alien) yet. What does the character look like? sound like? act like? You need to fill in these and other details to make the character realistic. This **complex major character** will be the "star" of your story, and the supporting roles will be played by **complex minor characters.** A complex character is one who comes alive for the reader and seems like a real person.

The best way to bring your major and minor characters to life is with sharp, specific details. The Thinking It Through steps below will help you develop complex characters. The examples show how one student used the steps to develop the main character of his story.

THINKING IT THROUGH — Developing a Character

▶ **STEP 1 Ask yourself, "What does this character look like?"** List details about appearance such as the character's skin color, hair color, eye color, height, weight, and style of clothing. Danny Hernandez has brown hair and eyes. He is small for his age and wears shorts and baseball caps.

▶ **STEP 2 Ask yourself, "What does the reader need to know about this character?"** List important facts, such as the character's age, nationality, place of residence, and family background. He is eleven years old. He lives in Los Angeles in a house with his mother and younger sister. His parents are divorced.

▶ **STEP 3 Ask yourself, "What is this character's personality like?"** Is the character quiet? sociable? a bully? athletic? a good student? What does the character like or dislike to do? How does he or she act toward family and friends? He is kind of serious sometimes, but has a good sense of humor. He is responsible—he tries to be "the man of the house" to help out his mom.

> **TIP** One way to show what your characters are like is by writing **dialogue** that shows their personalities. For example, what might you guess about a person who said, "Don't tell me that rotten mutt is yours!" What if the person phrased it this way: "Is that your dog?"

Of course, you don't have to include all of the information above for every character, but thinking about these questions and details will help you to create characters that seem real.

Writing 2.1b Develop complex major and minor characters. 2.1c Use a range of appropriate strategies (e.g., dialogue).

Using Narrative Strategies

All people have a complex way of communicating with others—not only with words but by their actions as well. The more you include details in your story about how your characters speak and move, the better your reader will be able to picture them. For example, here is one simple, short line of **dialogue:** *"I'm so glad to see you."* Look at how that simple line of dialogue changes when it is combined with different actions.

"I'm so glad to see you!" Kara said, throwing her arms around Lisa.

"I'm so glad to see you," Kara said, smiling at Evan, then glaring at his two companions.

"I'm so glad to see you," Kara said to Evan with an icy smile. She folded her arms and blocked his path.

People speak with their bodies. By describing **specific narrative action—movements, gestures,** and **facial expressions**—you can make your characters live and breathe.

Movements When Kara throws her arms around Lisa or stands in front of Evan and blocks his path, her movements tell about her and the situation. Movements such as doing a cartwheel, running, or simply standing with crossed arms can reveal important information about a character's personality, mood, and intentions.

Gestures When Kara folds her arms, she is demonstrating that she is angry and does not want to be friendly. Like movements, gestures are a kind of body language, usually involving movements of the hands and arms, that can reveal much about your characters.

Facial Expressions When Kara glares at Evan's companions or coldly smiles, that shows readers about her and her feelings toward the other characters. Telling readers whether a character is frowning, grinning, or smirking helps them understand the character's emotions.

Even without dialogue, you can create a vivid picture of a character with just a few words:

The young man bounded out of his chair, grinning and clapping.

This sentence describes only a few seconds of action, but it gives readers a rich picture of the young man and how he feels.

PRACTICE

Rewrite the following passage, adding dialogue and narrative action.

It was a cold day. Teresa stood in the rain with her friend Carlos. They looked up and down the street. They wondered where the bus was. The bus was late, and they were going to be late for school. Teresa had a test in her first-period class.

Writing 2.1c Use a range of appropriate strategies (e.g., dialogue, naming of specific narrative action, including movement, gestures, and expressions).

Where and When? The **setting** is where and when the story takes place. A setting can be a kitchen at night or a football stadium on Sunday afternoon. It can be the present, the future, or the age of dinosaurs. Setting can accomplish more than just giving events a place to happen. Setting can also

TIP To keep readers interested and to make your setting an important part of the story, do not simply say, "This story is set in a school gym in March." Instead, include **descriptive details** that *show* the setting as part of your story's plot and character descriptions.

- **give information about a story's characters.** A clean bedroom, for example, shows that a character likes order and neatness.

- **create a mood.** An abandoned house at night with a howling wind blowing will help make sure the scary story you are writing really *is* scary.

- **create conflict.** If you set your story in Alaska during a blizzard, your character might be trapped in the snow and in serious danger.

Notice that the following passage communicates the setting as part of the story's plot.

> Bao raced down the court and made an easy layup. Glancing out the school gym windows at the bright March sun, she knew she would soon be outside enjoying the start of spring break.

Use the questions below to plan your story's definite setting and the details you will use to show it. In the right-hand column are the notes one writer made about his story.

Quick guide!

Mini-Workshop

If you would like to focus on the details about a place, a person, or an object, see **Writing a Descriptive Essay** on pages 700–703.

PLANNING A STORY'S SETTING

Where and when will your story take place?	in the neighborhood where Danny lives, during the summer
What places, weather, calendar events, or times of day could be important in your story because of the setting?	The weather will be sunny and hot. The Fourth of July is the big summer holiday. Kids are out of school for the summer, so they are home during the day.
What sensory details (tastes, feelings, smells, sights, and sounds) can you use to describe or show the setting?	The heat makes sweat drip into your eyes. Sometimes the evenings are nice and cool. Lawn sprinklers create a blast of cold water.

Writing 2.1b Develop a definite setting.

The View A story's **point of view** depends upon who is **narrating,** or telling, the story. A story can be very different if it is told by someone involved in the events of the story rather than by someone who is not involved in the events. Look at the following chart to see explanations and examples of the different points of view you could use to tell your story.

UNDERSTANDING POINT OF VIEW		
First Person	The narrator is a character in the story. When you write a story in the first-person point of view, the narrator can tell the reader only what he or she is thinking, feeling, and experiencing. The narrator will most often refer to him- or herself as *I.*	**Example:** *When I got to the track meet, my ankle was aching. I had twisted it the night before, but I thought it would be all right if I wrapped it. The coach gave me a puzzled smile. Had she noticed me limping?* [The first-person narrator tells what she thinks and feels. She doesn't know what the coach is thinking and feeling, so the reader doesn't know either.]
Third-Person Limited	The narrator is not a character in the story. This narrator tells what one character—referred to as *he* or *she*—thinks, feels, and experiences, but not other characters.	**Example:** *When Wendy got to the track meet, her ankle was aching. She had twisted it the night before, but had thought it would be better by the next day if she wrapped it. The coach's puzzled smile made her worry.* [The limited third-person narrator tells only what Wendy is thinking, feeling, and experiencing.]
Third-Person Omniscient	The narrator is not a character in the story; each character is referred to as *he* or *she*. This narrator knows what all the major and minor characters are thinking, feeling, and experiencing. This narrator can also tell things that none of the characters could know, such as what will happen in the future.	**Example:** *When Wendy got to the track meet, her ankle was aching. She had twisted it the night before, but had thought it would be better by the next day if she wrapped it. She was worried.* * The coach knew Wendy was the team's best chance for a win, but she was puzzled by Wendy's troubled expression. She gave Wendy a smile that she hoped was encouraging.* [The omniscient narrator tells what both Wendy and the coach are thinking, feeling, and experiencing.]

Which to Use? Many effective short stories use the first-person or the third-person limited point of view. Choose the first-person point of view if you want readers to put themselves into the story, as if they are the major character. Choose the third-person limited point of view if you want readers to experience the story from a distance, as if they are simply watching the major character. Whatever point of view you choose to use in your short story, be sure to use it consistently throughout the story.

Writing 2.1a Develop a point of view.

Plan Characters, Setting, and Point of View

- Using the steps in the Thinking It Through on page 544 as a guide, freewrite ideas about your major and minor characters. Write for three to five minutes about whatever ideas pop into your head about the characters.

- Answer the questions in the chart on page 546 to plan your setting and to come up with descriptive details about it.

- Choose whether you will tell your story from the first-person point of view or the third-person point of view.

Plan Your Plot

And the Story Is . . .   You have created interesting characters and located them in a definite setting. Now you need to plan the **plot line,** the series of events in a story, that will turn your idea into a real short story. A plot includes the following parts.

- **Beginning** Every story has to start somewhere. A good beginning should introduce the characters and setting and grab readers' attention so that they want to keep reading.

- **Conflict** As you have learned, the major character must face a problem that he or she must resolve in the course of the story.

- **Rising action** Conflict builds as the major character faces obstacles to solving his or her problem. Each new obstacle complicates the conflict and helps build to the story's climax.

- **Climax (high point) and suspense** Your story needs a suspenseful moment when the conflict reaches a breaking point—the problem will be settled, one way or another. Readers' curiosity is at its highest at the story's climax. Make your reader wonder, "How is this going to turn out?"

- **Denouement, or outcome** After reaching its climax, the conflict is resolved, usually leaving the major character changed in some way.

Sketching It Out To help you plan your plot, you can create a **story outline** that shows its organizational structure. A suspenseful plot is organized according to **climactic order**—that is, each event builds on the last to intensify the conflict until it reaches a climax. One writer's story outline appears on the next page.

Writing **1.3** Use strategies of outlining to impose structure on composition drafts. **2.1a** Develop a standard plot line (having a beginning, conflict, rising action, climax, and denouement). **2.1c** Use a range of appropriate strategies (e.g., suspense).

STORY OUTLINE

Characters: Danny Hernandez; his friends Sonya and Rafael; Danny's mother, Mrs. Hernandez

Setting: the neighborhood where Danny lives; the Fourth of July

Plot

Conflict: Danny vs. his friends who are planning to play a joke on him

Beginning:

1. Rafael tells Sonya about his plan to soak Danny with the sprinklers.
2. Danny overhears their conversation.

Rising Action:

3. Rafael lures Danny into the yard by making a sound like a puppy.
4. Danny approaches the tree where Rafael is hiding.

Climax:

5. Sonya turns the sprinklers on, and she and Rafael get soaked because Danny has changed the directions of the sprinkers.

Denouement:

6. Danny, Sonya, and Rafael all laugh together at how the joke turned out.
7. Mrs. Hernandez suggests Sonya and Rafael dry off so they can go to the fireworks.

TIP Writing has **coherence** when readers can tell how and why ideas are connected. To improve the coherence of your short story, use **transitions** such as *next, later,* and *finally* to show the order of events and actions in your plot. Transitional words and phrases such as *initially, then, suddenly, to everyone's surprise,* and *unexpectedly* can be used to show **climactic order.**

Reference Note

For more on **transitions,** see page 688.

PRACTICE & APPLY **3** **Plot Your Short Story**

Based on the characters, setting, and point of view you developed for Practice and Apply 2, create a story outline to plan your story's plot. Remember that your plot needs a beginning, conflict, rising action, a climax, and a denouement. Also include in your story outline details about complex major and minor characters and setting.

 Writing **1.0** Students write clear, coherent essays [short stories]. **1.1** Create an organizational structure that balances all aspects of the composition and uses effective transitions between sentences to unify important ideas.

Writing

A Writer's Framework

Short Story

Beginning

- Attention-grabbing opener
- Characters
- Setting
- Point of view
- Conflict

To grab the reader's attention and quickly introduce your story's characters, setting, point of view, and conflict, try one of these opener suggestions.

- Start with **dialogue,** letting characters speak to set the scene.
- Start with **action,** jumping right into the conflict and describing the setting and the characters as part of the action.

(For more on writing **introductions,** see page 690.)

Middle

- Rising action (with suspense)
- Climax

- As you write your story, use **specific narrative action,** such as movements, gestures, and facial expressions, to tell exactly what your characters are doing and to show their attitudes or personalities. (For more on **narrative action,** see the Writing Mini-Lesson on page 545.)
- Make sure all of the action in your story builds to a **climax** of **suspense.** Use transitions, such as those listed in the Tip on page 549, to create **coherence.**

End

- Denouement

Your story's ending should not just be tacked on. It should follow naturally from the story's events. The problem introduced at the beginning of the story should be resolved. Your story's outcome can be happy or sad, but make sure that it is believable. (For more on writing **conclusions,** see page 690.)

PRACTICE & APPLY 4 **Write Your Short Story**

Refer to the framework above and the following Writer's Model to write the first draft of your short story.

Writing 2.0 The writing demonstrates the organizational and drafting strategies outlined in Writing Standard 1.0. **2.1c** Use a range of appropriate strategies (e.g., dialogue; suspense; specific narrative action, including movement, gestures, and expressions).

A Writer's Model

The draft below follows the framework for a short story. Notice that the highlighted transitional words and phrases connect the story's events, giving it coherence.

Danny's Surprise

Danny carried the heavy, green trash bag out the front door and walked toward the bin at the corner of the house. Sweat dripped into his eyes. Whew, it had to be a hundred degrees! With any luck, it would be a little cooler by that evening. His mom, his sister, and he were going to the park to watch the Fourth of July fireworks, accompanied by Danny's two best friends, Sonya and Rafael.

Danny, Sonya, and Rafael liked to spend time together whenever they could. An only child, Sonya said hanging out with Danny and Rafael was like having two brothers. Rafael, the youngest of five kids, said he enjoyed being with people his own age "for a change." For Danny, having fun with Sonya and Rafael was a break from helping out at home.

The three of them had started playing jokes on each other early in the summer—never anything dangerous or harmful, just a prank that ended with flour all over someone's face or a mouthful of mouthwash instead of lemonade. Rafael had started it. He claimed he was tired of always being the target of his brothers' and sisters' jokes.

"Besides," he said, "Sonya needs to know what having brothers is really like."

As Danny carried the trash bag around the corner of the house, he suddenly stopped. He had heard something.

"Ssh! Sonya, not so loud! Somebody might hear us." Rafael's voice came from the bushes near the trash bin.

Danny set the trash bag down quietly and walked quickly to the front door. He was careful not to let the screen door bang behind him. He dashed through the house, burst out the back door, and crept up to the low wall that separated the front yard from the back. He was in a great position to eavesdrop on the two plotters.

"When he comes outside to look," Rafael was saying, "you hit the button to turn on the sprinklers."

"But how will we get him to come outside?" Sonya wanted to know.

BEGINNING
Introduction of main character

Setting

Conflict

MIDDLE
Narrative actions

Dialogue

(continued)

(continued)

Suspense
Rising action

"I'm gonna hide behind the elm tree and . . . . Listen." Rafael twisted his mouth and produced a whine like a tiny puppy. Sonya nearly fell over laughing.

"That's perfect!" she said. "You know how much Danny wants a dog!"

After hearing his two friends' conversation, Danny sneaked from his hiding place and made a few plans of his own.

Rafael and Sonya arrived late that evening. As his mother gathered up sandwiches and cold drinks to take to the park, Danny went outside, pretending to look for his friends. Sure enough, he heard the faint cry of a puppy. Danny tried not to grin.

Danny looked around the bushes on either side of the porch, pretending to search for the puppy. He was careful not to get near the sprinkler controls at the side of the house, where he knew Sonya hid. The puppy's whining seemed to be coming from the elm tree by the sidewalk. Danny went in that direction.

"Here, puppy. Nice puppy," he called, trying not to laugh. As he reached the tree, from the corner of his eye he saw Sonya's hand reach up to poke the sprinkler controls. A second later the sprinklers erupted in a blast of cold water.

Climax

Rafael yelled and jumped from behind the tree. Sonya screamed, making Danny's mother appear at the door. Danny could barely stand, he was laughing so hard. Rafael ran from the sprinkler, which Danny had secretly turned toward the tree, and Sonya scrambled out of the bushes. By the time Mrs. Hernandez shut off the sprinklers, both were soaked, their dripping hair hanging in strings, their t-shirts and shorts sagging from the weight of the water in them. As Danny howled, Sonya and Rafael stood dripping and gasping, shocked by this unexpected ending to their plans. In a moment, though, they too were laughing, doubled over as water dripped from them.

END
Denouement

"Nice job watering the lawn, you guys," Mrs. Hernandez said, with an amused smile on her face. "Now, if you two want to get dried off, we have some fireworks to go see."

GO TO: go.hrw.com
KEYWORD: HLLA7 W-1
FOR: A Student Model

TIP What point of view does the writer of the Writer's Model use to tell his story? How do you know?

Evaluate and Revise Content, Organization, and Style

Look with New Eyes   Read through the first draft of your short story at least twice. First, use the guidelines below to consider its content and organization. Then, use the guidelines on page 554 to improve its style.

▶ First Reading: **Content and Organization**   Use the chart below to evaluate and revise your short story.

Short Story: Content and Organization Guidelines

Evaluation Questions	▶ Tips	▶ Revision Techniques
❶ Does the story have an interesting plot, with an effective beginning, a conflict, rising action, a suspenseful climax, and a clear denouement?	▶ **Place a check mark** next to each of the following elements: beginning, conflict, rising action, climax, and denouement.	▶ **Add** or **elaborate** on elements of the plot as necessary. **Delete** any information that ruins the suspense.
❷ Is the point of view consistent throughout the story?	▶ **Identify** pronouns (*I, he,* or *she*) that show whether the point of view is first or third person. **Label** the story's point of view; then **circle** any information not given from that point of view.	▶ If any sentences are circled, **delete** them. If necessary, **add** the same information told from the narrator's point of view.
❸ Are the major and minor characters complex and realistic?	▶ **Underline** specific details about each of the characters.	▶ If necessary, **add** details about a character's appearance, personality, or background. **Add** dialogue and narrative actions that tell more about a character.
❹ Does the story have a definite setting?	▶ With a colored marker, **highlight** details about the setting.	▶ If there are few highlighted words, **elaborate** on the setting by adding descriptive details.
❺ Is the story well organized and coherent? Does the writer use transitions effectively?	▶ **Number** the major events in the story. **Put a star** next to transitional words and phrases such as *next* and *later that day.*	▶ **Rearrange** any events that are out of order. If there are few or no stars, **add** transitional words and phrases to show the order of events.

 Writing 1.7 Revise writing to improve organization after checking the logic of the ideas.

ONE WRITER'S REVISIONS This revision is of an early draft of the story on pages 551–552.

add

rearrange

add

elaborate

delete

> *"Ssh! Sonya, not so loud! Somebody might hear us."*
> ∧Rafael's voice came from the bushes near the trash bin.
>
> As Danny carried the trash bag around the corner of
> the house, he suddenly stopped. He had heard something.
>
> Danny set the trash bag down quietly and walked
> *He was careful not to let the screen door bang behind him.*
> quickly to the front door.∧He dashed through the house,
> *low   that separated*
> burst out the back door, and crept up to the∧wall.∧He was in
> *the front yard from the back. /*
> a great position to eavesdrop on the two plotters. ~~Sonya~~
>
> ~~and Rafael had no idea he was listening.~~

PEER REVIEW

As you evaluate a peer's short story, ask yourself:

■ Which characters and events are interesting to me? Why?

■ Is there any part of the story during which my attention wanders? Why?

Responding to the Revision Process

1. How did adding dialogue improve this passage?
2. Why do you think the writer rearranged the first two paragraphs?
3. Why did the writer add a sentence to the third paragraph?
4. Why do you think the writer added details about the wall?
5. Why do you think the writer deleted the last sentence?

▷ **Second Reading: Style** You have already evaluated and revised the content and organization of your short story. Now, look at *how* you tell the story. Use the following guidelines and the Focus on Word Choice on the next page to make sure you have used precise nouns and adjectives to paint a clear picture for readers.

Style Guidelines

Evaluation Questions	▷ Tips	▷ Revision Techniques
Does the story use precise nouns and adjectives that clearly describe the characters and setting?	▷ **Draw a wavy line** under each precise noun and adjective in the story.	▷ If you see few wavy lines, **replace** any dull or vague nouns and adjectives with precise ones.

Writing 1.7 Revise writing to improve word choice after checking the precision of the vocabulary.

Precise Nouns and Adjectives

"How was that thing you went to?"

"It was nice."

That brief dialogue did not tell you much, did it? Nouns like "thing" and adjectives like "nice" are *vague*. **Vague words**—words that are not clear or precise—do not give the reader of a short story enough information to make the characters and the setting vivid. **Precise words,** on the other hand, tell a reader exactly what the characters and the setting are like.

- **Precise nouns** illustrate a *particular* person, place, or thing. A *noise* can become a *clank, squeak, clatter, shriek,* or *rattle*.

- **Precise adjectives** describe nouns specifically. Would you prefer a *fun* amusement-park ride or *a thrilling, exhilarating, pulse-pounding* ride?

Do not settle for vague, dull words in your short story. Make your story come alive with precise nouns and adjectives.

ONE WRITER'S REVISIONS

> Danny carried the *heavy, green trash* bag out the front door and walked
>
> toward ~~a spot~~ *the bin* at the corner of the house.

Responding to the Revision Process

How did adding precise words improve the sentence above?

PRACTICE & APPLY 5 **Evaluate and Revise Your Short Story**

First, evaluate and revise the content and organization of your story, following the guidelines on page 553. Next, use the Focus on Word Choice above to help you use more precise nouns and adjectives. Finally, have a peer evaluate your short story. Think carefully about your peer's comments as you revise.

Writing 1.7 Revise writing to improve word choice after checking the precision of the vocabulary.

Publishing

Proofread Your Short Story

Get the Bugs Out   Now it is time to polish your story. Check carefully to find and correct any errors in spelling, usage, and mechanics—especially punctuation in dialogue.

Grammar Link

Punctuating Dialogue

In your story, you should include **dialogue,** the words that people speak. Punctuate dialogue correctly so your reader can tell the dialogue from the rest of the story.

- Use quotation marks to enclose a person's exact words.

Incorrect   We'll hide in Danny's yard until he comes home he whispered.

Correct   "We'll hide in Danny's yard until he comes home," he whispered.

- A direct quotation begins with a capital letter. Commas, a question mark, or an exclamation point can separate the dialogue from the rest of the sentence.

Example:

"I'm drenched!" she shouted.

- When the expression identifying the speaker interrupts a quotation, commas set off the expression. The quotation then continues with a small letter.

Example:

"Sonya," Rafael went on, "you hide by the controls for the sprinklers."

- A period or comma always goes inside the closing quotation marks.

Example:

"Here, puppy. Nice puppy," he called, trying not to laugh.

Mrs. Hernandez said, "Nice job watering the lawn."

PRACTICE

Punctuate the dialogue in each of the following sentences.

1. Where were you yesterday asked Melissa

2. I'm sorry said Jack I had to stay home from school because I had a cold.

3. Too bad Melissa said because you missed the tryouts for the school play.

4. Jack sighed I know I guess I'll have to wait until next year.

5. Why don't you go talk with Mr. Kassel suggested Melissa.

Reference Note

For more information and practice on **punctuating dialogue,** see pages 322-327 in the *Holt Handbook*.

Writing   **2.0** The writing demonstrates a command of standard American English.   **2.1c** Use a range of appropriate strategies (e.g., dialogue).

Publish Your Short Story

Let Me Entertain You!   Entertain readers with your imagination by sharing your story, perhaps in one of these ways.

- Publish your story in a class story collection and distribute the collection to other students, teachers, or staff.
- Send your story to a magazine for young writers.

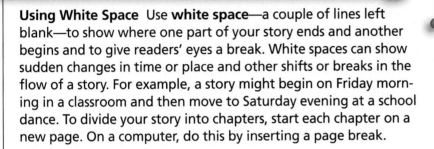

Designing Your Writing

Using White Space Use **white space**—a couple of lines left blank—to show where one part of your story ends and another begins and to give readers' eyes a break. White spaces can show sudden changes in time or place and other shifts or breaks in the flow of a story. For example, a story might begin on Friday morning in a classroom and then move to Saturday evening at a school dance. To divide your story into chapters, start each chapter on a new page. On a computer, do this by inserting a page break.

Reflect on Your Short Story

Building Your Portfolio   Taking time to reflect on the process of writing a short story will help you understand how you write best and what aspects of your writing process need attention.

- What techniques helped you develop your characters? your setting? your plot? Did using a story outline help you? Why or why not?
- In what other types of writing might you describe people and places or tell about a series of events? What strategies from this workshop might help you with these other types of writing?

COMPUTER TIP

If you use a computer grammar-checking program, keep in mind that such programs do not check the correct use and placement of quotation marks. Also, spellchecking programs often miss errors in spelling names, such as the names of the characters in a short story. For these reasons, do not rely only on these types of computer programs.

PRACTICE & APPLY 6 **Proofread, Publish, and Reflect on Your Short Story**

- Correct any grammar, usage, and mechanics errors. Be especially careful to punctuate dialogue correctly.
- Publish your short story using one of the suggestions above.
- Answer the Reflect on Your Short Story questions above.

Writing 1.6 Create documents by using word-processing skills and publishing programs.

WHAT'S AHEAD?

In this workshop you will deliver an oral narrative. You will also learn how to

- **choose a story and plan how to tell it**
- **use a variety of speaking techniques**
- **listen to and give feedback on an oral narrative**

TIP Try to choose a story you know well—the story you wrote in the Writing Workshop or any story you have heard before.

Reference Note

For more on **elements of plot,** see pages 4–5.

Giving and Listening to an Oral Narrative

As his family celebrates his great-aunt's ninetieth birthday, Jeremy says, "Aunt Luba, tell us a story about when you were a kid." Aunt Luba smiles slyly and begins, "Well, when I was your age, we didn't have TV, and kids had to make their own fun. One day, my sister—your grandmother Marla—tried to play a trick on me, but I outsmarted her. . . ."

Aunt Luba is telling a story out loud, or sharing an **oral narrative.** In this workshop you will prepare and deliver an oral narrative. You will also evaluate a classmate's oral narrative.

Select a Story

Choose Wisely To plan your oral narrative, you must find the right story to tell. That story should have the following elements.

- **complex major and minor characters** that seem real
- **setting,** a definite time and place in which the story occurs
- **conflict,** a problem that the major character must solve
- **plot,** made up of a **beginning** that sets the scene, **rising action** that leads to the story's **climax,** and a **denouement** or outcome that shows how the conflict is resolved

Make sure the story also has **dialogue** that brings the characters to life, **suspense** that makes listeners wonder what will happen next, and **specific narrative action** that you can describe vividly or act out using movements, gestures, and facial expressions.

Listening and Speaking 2.1a Establish a standard plot line (having a beginning, conflict, rising action, climax, and denouement). **2.1b** Describe complex major and minor characters and a definite setting. **2.1c** Use a range of appropriate strategies, including dialogue, suspense, and naming of specific narrative action (e.g., movement, gestures, expressions).

Consider This In addition to finding a story with the elements listed on the previous page, you need to consider the *purpose* and *audience* for your story. The **purpose** is to entertain, so you should choose a story that will appeal to the backgrounds and interests of your **audience**. For example, an audience of your classmates may be more interested in a story about a teenager trying to make the school track team than one about a father of four who has lost his job as a factory foreman. Finally, be sure you choose a story that is appropriate to deliver to your teacher and classmates.

Plan Your Presentation

Deliver Me! Plan to capture and keep your audience's interest. Consider how you will show your listeners that you know something about them and their interests. For example, you might think about beginning by asking a question, such as: "Last week was April Fools' Day. Did anybody play any pranks? Did anybody fall for one?" Create a little background for your story that you can present after letting your audience respond. Here is an example: "The story I am going to tell you is about a prank that was pulled not on April Fool's Day, but on the Fourth of July!" Once you have your audience's attention and set the scene, then you can concentrate on how you will deliver your story.

To the Last Detail Whether you choose to tell the story as yourself, as a character involved in the story, or as an uninvolved narrator, use a consistent **point of view** to keep your audience from becoming confused. Also, use the following **descriptive** and **organizational strategies** as you plan how to tell your story.

- **Describe the setting.** Because your audience will not be reading your story, you must make it clear where the action of the story is taking place. Use vivid language to describe each setting in the story. Focus on details that appeal to the senses. For example, if your story takes place in a garage, take time to describe the oil stains on the floor and the smell of gasoline in the air.

- **Describe major and minor characters.** Bring your characters to life by describing them as you introduce them. Think of details you can mention, such as the way they dress or talk. Practice using your voice, facial expressions, and gestures to act out the characters.

TIP Plan to begin your presentation by establishing a **context** for your story. Tell your audience what you will share with them—a fictional story, an autobiographical narrative, a story in poem form—as well as what the piece is about and why you have chosen this piece to share. Establishing a context will prepare your listeners to understand and enjoy your story.

Listening and Speaking **1.0** Deliver coherent presentations that convey ideas clearly and relate to the background and interests of the audience. **2.0** Deliver well-organized formal presentations employing traditional rhetorical strategies (e.g., narration, description). **2.1a** Establish a context and point of view. **2.1b** Describe complex major and minor characters and a definite setting.

TIP Using descriptive language—**sensory details** and **specific words**—throughout your narrative will help your listeners imagine the setting, characters, and events in your story. Words that appeal to the senses, such as colorful adjectives, active verbs, and specific nouns, will create a vivid picture in your listeners' minds.

■ **Keep them in suspense.** Your audience will be much more attentive if you drop hints about what will happen in your story. Think of ways to build suspense, such as suggesting that something surprising is going to happen, but not giving away too much information at once.

■ **Organize details in a logical way.** As you plan the details of your story, think about organizing those details and descriptions in an effective way: one that will make sense and appeal to your listeners. Most listeners will expect a story to be told in chronological order, with details connected to events in the order that the events occur. As you organize your ideas, make sure they are **coherent**—all the events, actions, and dialogue should flow together smoothly.

Not the Write Stuff If you forget a key detail when telling a story to someone you know well, you can always throw it in later. When you present a narrative in front of an audience, however, you should be a little more organized. How can you do that? Do not write out your narrative on a piece of paper, or you may be tempted just to read it aloud. Instead, jot down notes about key scenes, details, gestures, and so on, on an index card or sheet of paper. You can refer to your notes as you deliver your narrative without losing eye contact with your audience. Notice that the speaker who created the notes below plans to tell the story from the first-person point of view.

Example

> <u>Scene:</u> my front yard in summer—really hot—100 degrees?—gesture: wipe forehead
> <u>Characters:</u> my friends Sonya and Rafael and I—all are bored; R. has been playing tricks—mouthwash, flour. Rafael's voice: husky. Do Sonya's laugh and the way she pushes up her glasses.
> <u>Story:</u> R. plans a trick with hose but I overhear and outsmart him; R. and S. end up soaked
> <u>Details:</u> puppy and sprinkler sounds

Make Your Story Come Alive In your oral narrative, you must communicate the overall **mood,** or feeling, of the story, including your **attitude,** or what you think and feel about the situation and

Listening and Speaking 1.4 Organize information to achieve particular purposes and to appeal to the background and interests of the audience. **1.5** Arrange supporting details and descriptions effectively in relation to the audience. **2.1c** Use a range of appropriate strategies, including suspense.

characters. You must also show the emotions of the individual characters in the story. Along with **movements, gestures,** and **facial expressions,** use these **speaking techniques** to make your oral narrative more effective.

SPEAKING TECHNIQUES

Voice Modulation	Change the **tone** and **volume** of your voice to emphasize important moments, to build suspense, and to show emotion.
Inflection	Move the **pitch** of your voice up or down to express shades of meaning or to share your attitude about the subject of the story. For example, a rising inflection can show doubt, surprise, or curiosity. A falling inflection can express certainty.
Tempo	Change the **speed** at which you talk to communicate emotion. For example, you might increase your tempo when delivering a section of your story that involves a high-speed chase.
Enunciation	Say each word clearly and precisely. Be sure not to slur words or drop word endings. For example, don't say "I'm gonna" when you mean "I'm going to," unless this is the way a character speaks.
Eye Contact	Make eye contact with your audience members frequently. They will be left with the impression that you were speaking to each of them personally. You can also use eye contact for emphasis at important moments in your story.

Rehearse

One Step at a Time   To make your oral narrative the best it can be, you need to practice many times. Practicing involves these steps.

REHEARSING AN ORAL NARRATIVE

Step 1	Rehearse your narrative several times. Concentrate on a different element each time, including voice modulation, inflection, and changes in tempo. Practice your movements, gestures, and facial expressions in front of a mirror.
Step 2	Perform your narrative in front of a friend or relative, or tape your rehearsal with a video camera or tape recorder. Focus on making eye contact, speaking clearly and expressively, and showing each character's feelings and personality. Ask your listener for feedback or play back the tape. Which parts of your narrative do you need to improve?
Step 3	Adjust your performance based on what your listener says or what you see or hear on the tape. For example, if you looked too often at your notes, you need more practice. Rehearse your narrative until you feel confident and do not need the notes much.

Listening and Speaking 1.6 Use speaking techniques, including voice modulation, inflection, tempo, enunciation, and eye contact, for effective presentations.   2.1c Use a range of appropriate strategies, including specific narrative action (e.g., movement, gestures, expressions).

Respond to an Oral Narrative

A Noteworthy Performance   In addition to giving your presentation, you will also listen carefully to your classmates' oral narratives and offer feedback on their performances. Your classmates' oral narratives should have coherence. All the details from the narrative—the events, actions, and dialogue—should be clearly connected and arranged. Also, a speaker's choices of speaking techniques, movements, gestures, and facial expressions should be **logical** for the characters and actions in the story. To evaluate an oral narrative's content, delivery, and overall impact, answer these questions.

- How logical are this story's content and organization? Does it seem that any important events or details have been left out? Where?

- How does the speaker use movements, gestures, and facial expressions to portray characters in the story or to share his or her **attitude** about the subject of the story?

- How does the speaker's voice show his or her attitude? Do changes in **inflection** or **tempo** show amusement, or excitement?

- How well do the speaker's techniques fit the characters and events in the story? Do they help me understand and enjoy the story?

- Does the presenter make eye contact with the audience?

- How loudly and clearly does the presenter speak?

- What is the overall impact of the narrative? Is it effective and enjoyable? What changes could the speaker make to improve it?

TIP   When it is your turn to provide constructive feedback, offer praise where it is due. If you have noticed something in a classmate's performance that needs work, be prepared to offer specific suggestions for improvement, based on the notes you took. Always be polite and supportive. You will appreciate the support when a classmate evaluates your oral narrative.

PRACTICE & APPLY 7 **Perform and Respond to an Oral Narrative**

- Follow the instructions on pages 558–561 to plan and deliver an oral narrative.

- Pair up with a classmate to evaluate each other's oral narratives. As your partner delivers his or her presentation, make notes of your answers to the questions above. Use your notes to write a one-paragraph evaluation of the presentation. Trade evaluations with your partner and discuss each other's comments. Add notes from this discussion to your partner's evaluation of your presentation to help you improve future presentations.

- Reflect on your presentation. What would you do differently if you told the story again?

Listening and Speaking   **1.0** Students evaluate the content of oral communication.   **1.2** Determine the speaker's [or narrator's] attitude toward the subject.   **1.7** Provide constructive feedback to speakers concerning the coherence and logic of a speech's content and delivery and its overall impact upon the listener.   **2.1** Deliver narrative presentations.

DIRECTIONS: Read the following passage from a short story and the questions that follow. Mark the correct answer for each question on your own paper.

> Breannah stood in the goal, shifting her weight from one foot to the other, as a swarm of red jerseys nudged the soccer ball toward her. A lone, blue-clad defender tried and failed to cut off the attack. Now no one stood between her and the lanky star forward of the Red Hots. The forward kicked the ball, and Breannah leaped to her right. The ball whooshed past her left ear and into the net.
>
> She rose slowly and brushed herself off, ignoring the cheers from the Red Hots' bleachers. Next time, Breannah thought, she would be ready.

1. What strategy does the writer use to develop the main character?
    A dialogue spoken by the character
    B description of the character's appearance
    C description of the character's thoughts and actions
    D explanation of how other people respond to the character

2. What details does the writer use to show point of view in this passage?
    A The words *she* and *her* and the main character's thoughts are used to show third-person limited point of view.
    B The word *I* is used to show first-person point of view.
    C The word *you* is used to show second-person point of view.
    D Information about other characters' thoughts is used to show third-person omniscient point of view.

3. If this passage occurs near the story's beginning, what might the writer do in later passages to build toward the climax?
    A summarize events in the story that readers have already read about
    B describe additional problems that add to the story's conflict

    C change the point of view to include other characters' views of events
    D describe the setting in detail

4. Which of the following sentences does NOT restate the ideas in this sentence more precisely? *Even though it was a nice day, Breannah did not feel good.*
    A Not even the warm spring sun shining on the first daffodils could bring Breannah out of her grumpy mood.
    B A gentle breeze stirred the perfect spring morning, but Breannah woke up troubled and unhappy.
    C Bothered by the fear that she was in for a difficult match, Breannah ignored the beautiful morning.
    D The weather that morning was good, but for some reason Breannah didn't feel good at all.

5. If a speaker were telling this story out loud, why might she begin by explaining that the story was based on a friend's experience playing soccer?
    A to point out the story's climax
    B to create a mood of suspense
    C to establish a context for the story
    D to include realistic dialogue

Response to Literature

Some people believe that every person you meet has an effect on the way you understand yourself and the world around you. In a similar way, characters in literature also have much to teach us. In this workshop you will write an analysis of a character in a short story. You will also expand on the summary skills used in that analysis to develop an oral summary of a book, article, or short story. Finally, you will use analytical skills similar to those you applied to a character to examine a television news broadcast. In the process you will practice the following language arts standards.

WRITING WORKSHOP

Writing a Character Analysis Page 566

LISTENING AND SPEAKING WORKSHOP

Giving and Listening to an Oral Summary Page 583

MEDIA WORKSHOP

Analyzing Electronic Journalism Page 588

GO TO: go.hrw.com
KEYWORD: HLLA7 W-2
FOR: Models, Writer's Guides, and Reference Sources

 California Standards

Writing

1.0 Students write clear, coherent, and focused essays. The writing exhibits students' awareness of the audience and purpose. Essays contain formal introductions, supporting evidence, and conclusions. Students progress through the stages of the writing process as needed.

1.1 Create an organizational structure that balances all aspects of the composition and uses effective transitions between sentences to unify important ideas.

1.2 Support all statements and claims with descriptions and specific examples.

1.3 Use strategies of notetaking, outlining, and summarizing to impose structure on composition drafts.

1.6 Create documents by using word-processing skills and publishing programs.

1.7 Revise writing to improve organization after checking the logic of the ideas.

2.0 Students write expository texts of at least 500 to 700 words. The writing demonstrates a command of standard American English and the organizational and drafting strategies outlined in Writing Standard 1.0.

2.2 Write responses to literature:

   a. Develop interpretations exhibiting careful reading, under-standing, and insight.

   b. Organize interpretations around several clear ideas, premises, or images from the literary work.

   c. Justify interpretations through sustained use of examples and textual evidence.

Listening and Speaking

1.0 Deliver focused, coherent presentations that convey ideas clearly. Students evaluate the content of oral communication.

1.1 Ask probing questions to elicit information.

1.2 Determine the speaker's attitude toward the subject.

1.4 Organize information to achieve particular purposes.

1.5 Arrange supporting details effectively.

1.6 Use speaking techniques, including tempo and eye contact, for effective presentations.

1.7 Provide constructive feedback to speakers concerning the coherence and logic of a speech's content and delivery and its overall impact upon the listener.

1.8 Analyze the effect on the viewer of images, text, and sound in electronic journalism; identify the techniques used to achieve the effects in each instance studied.

2.0 Students deliver well-organized formal presentations employing traditional rhetorical strategies (e.g., exposition). Student speaking demonstrates a command of standard American English and the organizational and delivery strategies outlined in Listening and Speaking Standard 1.0.

2.2 Deliver oral summaries of articles and books:

   a. Include the main ideas of the event or article and the most significant details.

   b. Use the student's own words, except for material quoted from sources.

   c. Convey a comprehensive understanding of sources, not just superficial details.

Writing a Character Analysis

WHAT'S AHEAD?

In this workshop you will write a character analysis. You will also learn how to

- **choose a short-story character to analyze**
- **create coherence through organization**
- **combine sentences**
- **punctuate introductory prepositional phrases**

Are you a "people watcher"? Maybe you try to figure out what makes other people tick by picking up clues from what they do and say. When you read a story, you also pick up clues about its characters. Meeting characters in stories lets you get to know people very much like you and people as different from you as they can be. In this workshop you will write a character analysis, using those clues to show your readers what the character is really like. The character analysis you will write is a form of **expository** writing—a piece that provides information for readers rather than attempting to persuade them or to tell them a story.

Professional Model: A Response to Literature

Some books you read, return to the library, and never think about again. Others, though, stick with you, often because of their complex and realistic characters. In Kathleen Odean's professional review of the novel *Catherine, Called Birdy* by Karen Cushman, she examines one such character.

DO THIS

As you read the review, create a **think sheet,** taking note of what you can learn about responding to literature by reading the response of a professional writer. Your notes might include connections to your own experiences or books you have read, questions about information in the selection, and comments about techniques or words the writer used. Answering the analysis questions that appear next to the selection can help you add ideas to your think sheet.

Reference Note

For more on how to create a **think sheet,** see page 529.

Writing 2.2 Write responses to literature.

from Great Books for Girls

Catherine, Called Birdy

BY KAREN CUSHMAN. 1994. CLARION. AGES 12–14.

Reviewed by Kathleen Odean

Catherine, daughter of a small-time nobleman in medieval England, is hilarious. In a diary format she records her daily life, the outrages she suffers as a girl, and her often humorous assessment of things. She longs to be outside frolicking[1] instead of inside sewing, and she chafes[2] at her lessons in lady-like behavior. Birdy is the sort of girl who organizes a spitting contest and starts a mud fight. She makes a list of all the things girls cannot do, such as go on a crusade[3], be a horse trainer, laugh out loud, and "marry whom they will." She battles with her father, who wants to marry her off to the highest bidder, no matter how repulsive. Many of her best sarcastic remarks are reserved for him, and she irritates him whenever possible. She has a lively sense of humor and a palpable[4] love of life. Few fictional characters are so vivid and funny—do not miss this one.

1. Where and when is the book set? How does this setting affect the main character?

2. What is the main character of the book like? What examples and descriptive words in the review give you this impression?

3. What do you think the point or message of the book is? How does the reviewer communicate this message?

---

1. **frolicking:** playing happily.
2. **chafes:** is irritated or annoyed.
3. **crusade:** In the eleventh, twelfth, and thirteenth centuries Christian nations repeatedly sent armies to conquer the Muslims in the Holy Land, the region that is now made up of parts of Israel, Palestine, and Egypt. These missions were called crusades.
4. **palpable:** obvious.

In a small group, discuss the following items. Then, present your group's responses orally to the class.

1. What problems must Catherine face? How do examples of events in the book help the reviewer describe Catherine's personality?

2. Write a summary of the review, briefly stating its main ideas in your own words, in the order the author uses.

Prewriting

Choose a Story

Mini-Workshop

If you would prefer to analyze how one event in a story leads to another rather than analyze a character, see **Analyzing Cause and Effect** on pages 694–696.

A Character Who Leaps off the Page   For this workshop you need to choose a story with an interesting character who faces a clear conflict. You can write about a character in a short story that you have already read, or you can choose a new story. Not every story lends itself to a character analysis, though. A character worth analyzing is one who seems to come to life as you read.

To help you choose a suitable character, complete these sentences.

(Character's name) in (author's name and title of short story) is interesting because (two or three of the character's feelings or actions that make him or her seem like a real person).

The conflict (character's name) faces is (description of conflict).

After reading the short story "The No-Guitar Blues" on pages 537–541, one writer chose a character to analyze in the following way.

TIP   Choose the main character of a story. Your character analysis will need to be 500 to 700 words in length, and you may not get to know less-important characters well enough to write an interesting and thoughtful analysis of that length.

Fausto in Gary Soto's short story "The No-Guitar Blues" is interesting because he wants to become a famous guitarist, he tries hard to earn the money for a guitar, and he comes up with a clever way to get the money.

The conflict Fausto faces is that he dreams of becoming a guitarist, but his parents cannot afford to buy him a guitar.

Writing **1.0** Students progress through the stages of the writing process as needed.   **2.0** Students write expository texts of at least 500 to 700 words.

Study a Character

Clue Me In   Carefully read or re-read your chosen story, focusing on the character you have chosen. Look for clues, such as those in the chart below, that tell you what a character is like.

UNDERSTANDING METHODS OF CHARACTERIZATION

Details	Questions to Ask
Character's thoughts	What goes on in the character's mind? Do any thoughts pop up often?
Character's words	What does the character say out loud? Does what the character says agree with what the character thinks and feels?
Character's actions	How does the character behave? Does he or she try to avoid the conflict? ignore it and hope it goes away? take action to work things out? Do the character's actions match his or her words and feelings?
Character's appearance	What does the character look like? What does this appearance tell you about the character?
Other characters' thoughts, words, and actions	What do the other characters think and say about the character? How do they act toward him or her?

As you read, note examples of the kinds of details listed in the chart to use as **evidence** for your analysis. Beside each detail, write your **interpretation,** or what you think the detail shows about the character. The notes below are based on "The No-Guitar Blues."

Story Detail	My Interpretation
"Fausto knew his mission in life: to play guitar in his own band. . . ."	Fausto has big dreams.
"He couldn't ask his parents because they would just say, 'Money doesn't grow on trees'. . . But what the heck, he'd give it a try."	He does not give up easily.
" . . . was pushing the mower down the street before he realized it was winter and no one would hire him."	He acts without thinking things through.
"Fausto looked at the bill and knew he was in trouble . . . with himself."	He has a strong sense of right and wrong.

TIP   Look at the professional model on page 567. How do details from the book support the reviewer's interpretation of the character's actions and words? In your own analysis, focus on the two or three most important methods of characterization, and provide specific support from the story, just as the reviewer did.

Writing **1.2** Support all statements and claims with descriptions and specific examples.   **1.3** Use strategies of notetaking to impose structure on composition drafts.   **2.2a** Develop interpretations exhibiting careful reading, understanding, and insight.   **2.2c** Justify interpretations through sustained use of examples and textual evidence.

Analyzing a Character

When you **analyze** something, you look at its parts in order to understand the whole. When you analyze a story character, you examine what the character says, does, and thinks to gain an overall understanding, or **insight.** One way to analyze a character is to create a character wheel.

To make a character wheel, first think about the character's major **traits,** or char- acteristics. Look through the notes you made as you read the story, and focus on the two or three traits that are most closely linked to the events of the story. Write these traits between the "spokes" of your wheel. Then, fill in three details that elaborate on each trait. Here is how the student who wrote about Fausto filled in her character wheel.

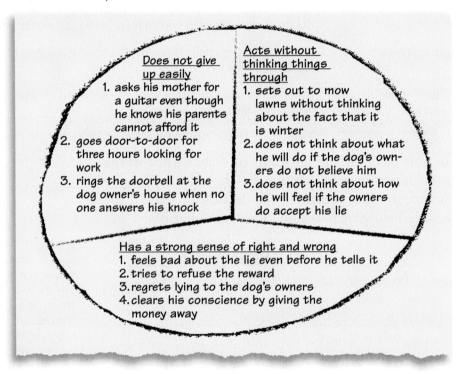

Does not give up easily
1. asks his mother for a guitar even though he knows his parents cannot afford it
2. goes door-to-door for three hours looking for work
3. rings the doorbell at the dog owner's house when no one answers his knock

Acts without thinking things through
1. sets out to mow lawns without thinking about the fact that it is winter
2. does not think about what he will do if the dog's own- ers do not believe him
3. does not think about how he will feel if the owners do accept his lie

Has a strong sense of right and wrong
1. feels bad about the lie even before he tells it
2. tries to refuse the reward
3. regrets lying to the dog's owners
4. clears his conscience by giving the money away

PRACTICE

Work with some classmates to analyze a character in a story all of you have seen or read. It can be a character from a novel, a short story, a television show, a movie, or a comic book. Together, identify two or three of the character's traits and write them on a character wheel. As the group identifies details to go with each trait, one person can add them to the wheel. Then, as a group, write a sentence or two giving your group's overall impression of the character.

Writing 2.2a Develop interpretations exhibiting careful reading, understanding, and insight.
2.2b Organize interpretations around several clear ideas, premises, or images from the literary work.
2.2c Justify interpretations through sustained use of examples and textual evidence.

Choose a Story, and Study a Character

Choose a story you are interested in reading or re-reading. Following the instructions on page 570, make a character wheel and write one or two sentences explaining your impression of the character.

Think About Purpose and Audience

Your Reason and Your Readers   The **purpose** of a character analysis is to find out what kind of person a story character is. You do this so that you and your readers can understand the character and perhaps even understand yourselves or other people better.

The **audience** for a character analysis is usually your teacher and classmates. Be sure to include information that will interest both of these audiences.

Write a Summary Statement

(Re)Tell It Like It Is   Introduce your audience to your short story by writing a *summary statement*. A **summary statement** is two or three sentences that restate the **key ideas,** or most important parts, of a selection, without all the details. A summary statement gives your audience a context for your ideas about a character.

A summary statement should include the author's name, the title of the short story, the name of the main character, the story's setting, and the conflict that the main character faces. Complete the following sentences to develop a summary statement. An example is included.

The main character in (author)'s short story ("title of short story") is (name of main character), who lives in (setting). The problem the main character faces is (conflict). During the course of the story, the main character (what the character does to try to solve his or her problem).

> The main character in Gary Soto's short story "The No-Guitar Blues" is Fausto, who lives in a city. The problem he faces is that he dreams of becoming a guitarist, but his parents cannot afford to buy him a guitar. During the course of the story, he searches for ways to raise money to buy a guitar.

Writing 1.0 The writing exhibits students' awareness of the audience and purpose.   1.3 Use strategies of summarizing to impose structure on composition drafts.

State Your Thesis

Find Your Focus   How might you describe a new classmate to others? You might focus on one or two of the person's major traits, saying that he or she seems friendly or clever or shy. Traits such as these will also be the focus of your character analysis.

Plan to focus on the traits most important to the plot of the story. **For your analysis, choose no more than three of your character's major traits.** Then, write a **thesis**, or **main idea, statement**—a sentence or two that introduces the major traits and tells how those traits shape the events of the story. For example, a character's curiosity may lead her to discover a hidden passageway central to the story.

Here are three ways to pull together the traits you choose into a thesis. Each method includes an example about Fausto.

| KEY CONCEPT

- **Focus on how the character's traits drive the plot.**

> Fausto often acts without thinking things through. However, when he does something wrong, his strong sense of right and wrong makes him find a way to make up for it.

- **Focus on how the character changes.**

> At first, Fausto is thoughtless, but by the end of the story he is more patient and respectful.

- **Focus on how the character is similar to or different from real people.**

> Fausto is just like my brother, K.C., who always borrows my bike without asking. Still, I know that Fausto, like K.C., is a good person because he always does the right thing in the end.

TIP In a way, fictional characters take on lives of their own, living eternally on the page. For that reason, use the present tense when writing a character analysis. For example, this student writes "Fausto often *acts* without thinking things through."

PRACTICE & APPLY 2 **Plan Your Audience, Summary, and Thesis**

After identifying your purpose and audience, use the model on page 571 to develop a summary statement. Then, write a sentence or two expressing your thesis about the character.

Writing **1.0** Students write focused essays.   **2.2a** Develop interpretations exhibiting careful reading, understanding, and insight.

Organize Your Information

All Together Now   You can use one of two **organizational structures** to arrange and balance your ideas logically. To organize your ideas in **order of importance,** decide which of the character traits you are explaining is most important to the plot or to understanding the character. Then, elaborate on that trait in an attention-getting position in the body of your analysis, either first or last.

Another way of structuring your analysis is to discuss the character's traits in **chronological order**—the order in which they appear in the story. This method works well when you want to show how a character changes during the story.

The Leg Bone's Connected to the Hip Bone   Making an **outline** shows whether your ideas are arranged in a logical order. **If you arrange your ideas logically in an outline, your character analysis will have** *coherence,* **or connectedness.** Adding transitions as you convert your outline to a draft will also add coherence.

To make an outline, first list the traits in the order in which you will discuss them. Then, under each trait, jot down the story details you will use to support it. Here is an example.

◀─── **KEY CONCEPT**

> **TIP** Transitions that show **order of importance** include *first of all, mainly, most importantly, furthermore,* and *finally.* Transitions that show **chronological order** include *first, next, then, after, while,* and *during.*

I. Acts without thinking things through
   A. Sets out to mow lawns without realizing that it's winter
   B. Does not think about his sister when he borrows her bike
   C. Does not think about what he will *do* if the dog's owners do not believe him
   D. Does not think about how he will *feel* if the dog's owners do accept his lie

II. Has a strong sense of right and wrong
   A. Feels bad about the lie even before he tells it
   B. Tries to refuse the reward
   C. Feels like begging the dog's owners to take the money back
   D. Clears his conscience by giving the money to the church

PRACTICE & APPLY 3   **Organize Your Information**

Choose a logical organizational structure. Then, make an outline, listing the traits and the supporting details in order.

Writing **1.0** Students write clear, coherent, and focused essays.   **1.1** Create an organizational structure that balances all aspects of the composition and uses effective transitions between sentences to unify important ideas.   **1.3** Use strategies of outlining to impose structure on composition drafts.
2.2b Organize interpretations around several clear ideas, premises, or images from the literary work.

Writing

A Writer's Framework

Character Analysis

Introduction

- Attention-getting opener
- Summary statement
- Main idea of analysis

In a two- or three-sentence **summary statement**, identify the author and title of the short story, the main character, the setting, and the conflict. In your **thesis,** make clear which **character traits** you will discuss and how those traits are linked to what happens in the story. (For more on writing **introductions,** see page 690.)

Body

- Character trait #1 and supporting evidence
- Character trait #2 and supporting evidence
- Character trait #3 (if needed) and supporting evidence

- Devote at least one paragraph to each character trait and **supporting evidence** from the story, including examples and descriptions.
- Use **transitional words and phrases** within and between sentences and paragraphs to show how your ideas are related. Along with the logical organization of your ideas, these transitions will create **coherence,** or connectedness. (For a list of transitional words and phrases, see the chart on page 688.)

Conclusion

- Summary of traits
- Restatement of main idea

Sum up the **character traits** you have examined in your analysis. To help your readers remember your **thesis,** restate the idea about the character in different words. (For more on writing **conclusions,** see page 690.)

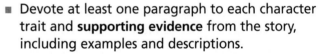

PRACTICE & APPLY 4 · **Write a Character Analysis**

Write a draft of a character analysis. As you draft, refer to the framework above and the Writer's Model on pages 575–576.

Writing 1.0 Students write clear, coherent, and focused essays. Essays contain formal introductions, supporting evidence, and conclusions. **1.1** Create an organizational structure that uses effective transitions between sentences to unify important ideas. **2.0** The writing demonstrates the organizational and drafting strategies outlined in Writing Standard 1.0.

A Writer's Model

The final draft below closely follows the framework for a character analysis on the previous page. Notice the highlighted transitional words and phrases that connect the writer's ideas.

The Character of Fausto
in "The No-Guitar Blues"

The main character in Gary Soto's short story "The No-Guitar Blues" is a young boy named Fausto who lives in a city. He dreams of becoming a guitarist, but his parents cannot afford to buy him a guitar. During the course of the story, he searches for ways to raise money to buy a guitar. Fausto often acts without thinking things through. However, when he does something wrong, his strong sense of right and wrong makes him find a way to make up for it.

Fausto has a bad habit of being thoughtless. When Fausto decides to earn the money to buy a guitar by mowing lawns, he acts before he thinks. He is partway down the street with the lawn mower before he remembers that it is winter and no lawns need mowing.

What Fausto does next also shows his habit of acting without thinking. He returns home and gets a rake, planning to ride his bike to a nicer part of town to look for work. However, he has not thought about the fact that his bike has two flat tires. Furthermore, as he rides off on his sister's bike, he does not think about whether she might need it or how she will feel when she finds out he took the bike without asking.

Fausto's greatest act of thoughtlessness comes when he tries to claim a reward he does not deserve. Fausto makes only twenty-five cents in three hours, but when a loose dog wanders up to him, he thinks of a way to make some easy money. Because the dog looks healthy and is wearing a collar and tags, he thinks that it must belong to rich people. He decides to return the dog to its owners and tell them that he found it near the freeway. He figures that they will be so grateful to him for rescuing their dog that they will give him a reward. He does

(continued)

INTRODUCTION
Author and title
Character and setting
Summary statement
Thesis

BODY
Character trait #1
Evidence (actions)

Evidence (thoughts)

Evidence (thoughts)

(continued)

not stop to think about whether they will believe him or what he will do if they do not believe him.

Neither does Fausto think about how he will feel if the owners *do* accept his lie. The man and woman who own the dog are amazingly nice to him. They invite Fausto into their house, fix him a delicious snack, and give him a reward of twenty dollars for bringing their dog home.

The way Fausto reacts to his dishonest act shows his strong sense of right and wrong. Even as he is hatching his scheme, he feels bad about lying. When the man first offers him the money, Fausto realizes that he is "in trouble . . . with himself," and says, "I can't take that." When the man insists that he deserves the reward, Fausto says, "No, I don't." After Fausto leaves the people's house, he feels like "begging them to please take the money back." He walks away "like a zombie," saying to himself, "Oh, man, I shouldn't have lied." He feels like running to church to confess, but it is too late that day.

As further evidence of Fausto's good character, the next morning he gets up and goes to church without being told to go. When he gets there, he worries about whether the priest knows what he did. Also, he cannot concentrate on the service because he keeps remembering how nice the dog's owners were to him. His conscience bothers him so much that he donates the twenty dollars to the church. He even adds the quarter he earned honestly the day before.

After church, Fausto feels "cleared of wrongdoing" and "happy." His strong sense of right and wrong has helped him find a way to make up for the situation he got himself into by not thinking things through. Although his choice is difficult, Fausto's final action is rewarded when he receives his grandfather's guitarron. He will probably be much happier with this family guitar than he would have been with the guitar bought through dishonesty.

Evidence (others' actions)

Character trait #2

Evidence (thoughts, words, and actions)

Evidence (actions)

CONCLUSION
Restatement of main idea

GO TO: go.hrw.com
KEYWORD: HLLA7 W-2
FOR: A Student Model

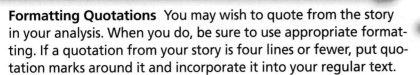

Designing Your Writing

Formatting Quotations You may wish to quote from the story in your analysis. When you do, be sure to use appropriate formatting. If a quotation from your story is four lines or fewer, put quotation marks around it and incorporate it into your regular text.

Example

> When the man first offers him the money, he realizes that he is "in trouble . . . with himself," and he says, "I can't take that."

There may be times when you want to use a quotation of more than four lines. Here are guidelines for quoting long passages.

- Begin a new line of text.
- Indent one inch, or ten spaces, from the left margin.
- Do not indent the first line more than the rest of the quotation, unless there are two or more paragraphs in the quotation.
- Put only dialogue in quotation marks, not the entire quotation.
- If you are using a word processor, the quotation, like the rest of the essay, should be double-spaced.
- Following the quotation, resume regular text without indenting.

Example

> Fausto knows that he will not be able to get money from his parents to buy the guitar:
>
> > He couldn't ask his parents because they would just say, "Money doesn't grow on trees" or "What do you think we are, bankers?" And besides, they hated rock music. They were into the *conjunto* music of Lydia Mendoza, Flaco Jimenez, and Little Joe and La Familia.
>
> If he has any hope of playing guitar on *American Bandstand*, he'll have to find another way to get the money.

Reference Note

For more on **formatting quotations,** see pages 322–327 in the *Holt Handbook.*

COMPUTER TIP

If you are working on a word processor, you can set a tab at one inch. Then, simply press the tab key before each line of the indented quotation. (If you already have a tab set at one-half inch for paragraph indents, you will need to press the tab key twice to indent your quotation.) Another way to indent your quotation is to adjust your paper's left margin just for that part of the paper. Following your quotation, be sure to return the left margin to its original location.

Writing 1.6 Create documents by using word-processing skills and publishing programs.

Revising

Evaluate and Revise Content, Organization, and Style

Give It the Twice-Over To evaluate your own or a peer's character analysis, read the draft at least twice. First, use the guidelines below to check for problems with the content and organization. Then, use the guidelines on page 579 to improve style by combining some of the sentences.

▷ First Reading: **Content and Organization** Use this chart to evaluate a peer's character analysis or to evaluate and revise your own paper.

Character Analysis: Content and Organization Guidelines

Evaluation Questions	▶ Tips	▶ Revision Techniques
❶ Does the introduction summarize the story and identify key information about it? Does the thesis statement identify the traits to be discussed?	▶ **Bracket** the summary, and **underline** the story's title, author, main character, setting, and conflict. **Circle** each trait listed in the thesis.	▶ **Add** a summary if needed, and **add** any key elements missing from the introduction. If necessary, **add** traits to the thesis statement.
❷ Is each character trait supported by details from the story?	▶ **Highlight** the story details that support each character trait.	▶ **Add** story details or **elaborate** on the details included.
❸ Is the analysis logically organized?	▶ **Write** the trait discussed in each body paragraph in the margin next to the paragraph. Make sure each paragraph discusses **one and only one** character trait.	▶ **Rearrange** information, moving any misplaced examples or descriptions of a trait into the paragraph where that trait is discussed, if needed.
❹ Are the ideas and details connected with appropriate transitions?	▶ **Draw a box** around each transitional word or phrase.	▶ **Add** transitions where they are needed to connect ideas and achieve coherence.
❺ Does the conclusion sum up the character traits discussed and restate the main idea of the analysis?	▶ **Circle** each trait in the conclusion and compare with the introduction. **Draw a wavy line** under the restated main idea.	▶ **Add** any missing traits. **Add** a restatement of the main idea, if necessary.

Writing 1.1 Create an organizational structure that uses effective transitions between sentences to unify important ideas.   **1.7** Revise writing to improve organization after checking the logic of the ideas.

ONE WRITER'S REVISIONS This revision is from an early draft of the introductory paragraph of the character analysis on pages 575–576.

> The main character in ~~this~~ short story *Gary Soto's "The No-Guitar Blues"* is a young boy named Fausto who lives in a city. He dreams of becoming a guitarist, but his parents cannot afford to buy him a guitar. During the course of the story, he searches for ways to raise money to buy a guitar. Fausto often acts without thinking things through. However, when he does something wrong, *his strong sense of right and wrong makes him find a way to make* ~~he makes~~ up for it.

add

add

Responding to the Revision Process

1. Why do you think the writer added information to the first sentence of the introduction?
2. What effect does the addition to the last sentence have?

PEER REVIEW

As you evaluate a peer's paper, ask yourself these questions.

- What details give me a clear sense of what the character is like?
- How are the character's traits linked to plot events? How is the paper organized?

▶ **Second Reading: Style** *How* you say something can be just as important as *what* you say. Look at each sentence in your character analysis. Are any of your sentences so short that they make your writing sound choppy? While an occasional short sentence is fine, a series of short sentences can be distracting and needs to be revised. You can improve your writing by combining some short, choppy sentences into longer ones. Use the following guidelines.

Style Guidelines

Evaluation Question	▶ Tip	▶ Revision Technique
Are there more than two short, choppy sentences in a row in the paper?	▶ Read each sentence aloud. **Put an X** by each sentence that contains from five to eight words.	▶ **Combine** some of the short, choppy sentences that are closely related. Join them with a comma and a conjunction.

Writing 1.1 Create an organizational structure that balances all aspects of the composition and uses effective transitions between sentences to unify important ideas.

Focus on Sentences

Combining Sentences

Since your purpose for writing a character analysis is to give your readers a clear sense of what the character is like, your writing should also be clear. Try combining closely related ideas with **transitions** that show *how* the ideas are related. Too many short, choppy sentences can make your analysis hard to follow.

Short sentences that have the same subject can be combined to form a compound sentence. To create a compound sentence, place a comma after the first sentence and add a coordinating conjunction such as *and, but,* or *or.*

TIP When you combine your sentences, be careful not to create a *run-on sentence*. A **run-on sentence** is actually two complete sentences punctuated as one sentence. In a run-on, two separate thoughts run into each other.

Example:
The Pearl was written over fifty years ago. Its message is still true today.

Revised:
The Pearl was written over fifty years ago, but its message is still true today.

ONE WRITER'S REVISIONS

He feels like running to church to confess,ˌ *but* It is too late that day.

Responding to the Revision Process

Why do you think the writer combined the two sentences above?

PRACTICE & APPLY 5

Evaluate and Revise Your Character Analysis

Use the guidelines on page 578 to evaluate and revise the content and organization of your character analysis. Next, use the Focus on Sentences section above to help you decide whether you need to combine any choppy sentences. If a peer evaluated your character analysis, think carefully about how his or her comments can help you improve your paper.

Writing 1.1 Create an organizational structure that balances all aspects of the composition and uses effective transitions between sentences to unify important ideas.

Proofread Your Character Analysis

The Homestretch Before you share your character analysis with an audience, proofread it carefully. Correct any errors you find in grammar, spelling, usage, or punctuation. You may want to get together with a classmate and proofread each other's final drafts.

Grammar Link

Punctuating Introductory Prepositional Phrases

Help readers follow your ideas by using introductory *prepositional phrases*. A **prepositional phrase** consists of a preposition, a noun or pronoun, and any modifiers of the noun or pronoun.

- **Use a comma after two or more introductory prepositional phrases.**

Example:

At the table in the sparkling kitchen, Fausto ate a turnover and drank a glass of milk.

- **Use a comma after a single introductory prepositional phrase only if the comma is needed to prevent confusion.**

Example:

For some, dogs are like members of the family.

[The comma keeps readers from reading "some dogs."]

PRACTICE

Decide whether a comma should follow any of the underlined introductory prepositional phrases in each sentence. If a comma is neces-sary, write the sentence on your paper, adding the comma. Write C for the correct sentences, and briefly explain why these sen-tences do not need additional punctuation.

Example:

1. <u>After three hours</u> Fausto has earned only twenty-five cents.

1. C. *Only one phrase is used, and the mean-ing of the sentence is clear without a comma.*

1. <u>Up to Fausto</u> wanders a curious dog.

2. <u>On the tags around the dog's neck</u> Fausto finds an address.

3. <u>With the dog at his side</u> he heads for the address.

4. <u>During church</u> members pass a wicker basket up and down the pews.

5. <u>After the service</u> Fausto feels greatly relieved.

Reference Note

For more information and practice on **punctuating introductory prepositional phrases,** see pages 305–306 in the *Holt Handbook.*

Writing 2.0 The writing demonstrates a command of standard American English.

Publish Your Character Analysis

Let Me Introduce You to . . . Now your character analysis is ready to find an audience. Share your writing with people who will enjoy it, perhaps by using one of these ideas.

- Exchange papers with a classmate who likes the same kinds of stories that you do. He or she may enjoy reading your analysis *and* the story in which the character appears.

- Turn your character analysis into a short-story review by adding an evaluation to your conclusion. Let your audience know whether they should read or avoid the story. Then, post your review in the library or add it to a class collection of book and story reviews.

Reflect on Your Character Analysis

Building Your Portfolio Reflect on your work by answering the following questions.

- What organizational pattern did you use for the body of your analysis? How did using this pattern help you achieve your purpose for writing a character analysis?

- In what way did writing a summary statement help you organize your ideas about the character you analyzed? In what other types of writing might you first write a summary to help you organize your ideas?

- Which was more difficult, expressing your main idea about the character or finding story details to support your idea? Why?

- Did writing a character analysis help you learn something about yourself or others? If so, what did you learn?

> **PRACTICE & APPLY** 6 **Proofread, Publish, and Reflect on Your Analysis**
>
> - Proofread your analysis to correct any grammar, spelling, usage, or punctuation errors.
> - Publish your character analysis.
> - Answer the Reflect on Your Character Analysis questions above. Record your responses, and consider including them in your portfolio.

Giving and Listening to an Oral Summary

WHAT'S AHEAD?

In this workshop you will give an oral summary. You will also learn how to

- **take notes on the main idea of a written work**
- **plan and organize a summary**
- **use effective speaking techniques**
- **evaluate an oral summary**

Giving an oral summary is a good way to reinforce your understanding of a written work and share it with others. Unlike your written character analysis, an oral summary will give your audience a broad picture of all of the elements of a written work, rather than focusing on details about one element. An oral summary may share information about a fictional work, as your character analysis did, or it may explain a nonfiction book or article.

Choose an Article, Book, or Story

Take Your Choice   For this workshop you may choose a non-fiction article or book, a novel, or a short story. You may use the same story you used for your character analysis or select a completely different work. Just be sure that the work is one that interests you and that is likely to interest your audience—in this case, your teacher and classmates.

Read and Take Notes

What's Noteworthy?   Take the time to skim or re-read the text, making notes *in your own words*. As you take notes, remember that a summary is an **expository** form. That means that your **purpose** is strictly to provide information. Keeping your purpose in mind will prevent you from getting off track as you take notes. It will also help you remain unbiased, or neutral. Since your purpose is to inform, you should not make judgments about the topic.

TIP   Your oral summary will contain more details than the summary statement you wrote in the character analysis because the purpose is different. In your summary statement, you provided your reader with a basic idea of the short story's plot. If you choose to summarize a short story for this workshop, you will detail all of the story's important plot events.

Listening and Speaking 2.0 Students deliver well-organized formal presentations employing traditional rhetorical strategies (e.g., exposition).   **2.2b** Use the student's own words.

The type of work you are summarizing—fiction or nonfiction—determines what you should include in your notes.

Reference Note

For more on **summarizing,** see page 571. For more on **main idea,** see page 572. For more on **theme,** see page 158.

- **For a nonfiction article or book,** note the title, author, main idea (stated or implied), and important supporting points and details.

- **For a novel or a short story,** note the title, author, setting, characters, major plot events (the conflict, the climax, and the resolution), and theme.

Plan Your Presentation

Clear and Concise   Your notes should give you information that will show your audience that you have a **comprehensive,** or thorough, understanding of the work. To plan which notes to use, identify **details** that support the **main idea,** and cross out any that do not. Consider using **quotations** as supporting details, too. For a novel or short story, choose a quotation that pinpoints the conflict or reveals the main character's personality. For a nonfiction article or book, quote a striking phrase or a surprising fact.

TIP   Sometimes you may need to stray from the order of the original work. For instance, a novel or a short story may contain a **flashback,** a scene that interrupts the plot to tell what happened earlier. To help your audience understand the story, you should tell the major events of the flashback first.

Summary Order   In most cases, the **arrangement of the details** in your summary will reflect the order of the work you are summarizing. If the work is written in chronological order, your summary will also be in chronological order. Below is a summary written by a student who read Gary Soto's "The No-Guitar Blues." Notice that the details are written in chronological order, and they support the story's theme stated in the last sentence.

> "The No-Guitar Blues" by Gary Soto is a story about a boy named Fausto who wants a guitar. After seeing a group performing on TV, Fausto "knew his mission in life: to play guitar in his own band." However, his parents cannot afford to buy him a guitar, so he decides to earn the money himself. He goes door-to-door, but only finds one job and receives only "a grimy, dirtcaked quarter." He sits down afterward to eat an orange, and a dog comes along. Fausto thinks that the dog is probably lost and comes from a wealthy home. He decides to return the dog and tell the owners that it was near a freeway, hoping the owners will give him a reward. His plan works, but he feels guilty about lying, especially because the owners are so nice to him. The next day he goes to Mass and puts the

Listening and Speaking   **1.4** Organize information to achieve particular purposes.   **1.5** Arrange supporting details effectively.   **2.2a** Include the main ideas of the event or article and the most significant details.   **2.2b** Use the student's own words, except for material quoted from sources.   **2.2c** Convey a comprehensive understanding of sources, not just superficial details.

twenty-dollar bill he was given in the collection plate. He feels better afterward and tries to forget about wanting the guitar. That evening, his mother tells him that his grandfather has an old guitarron—a large guitar. His grandfather gives it to him, and Fausto looks forward to learning how to play it. Fausto learns that when you get something you want honestly, you enjoy it more, and it means more to you than if you had gotten it dishonestly.

TIP To show how all your ideas fit together, be sure to connect your ideas with **transitional words** and **phrases.** Following are some examples.
Time: after, before, finally, next, then
Importance: first, last, most important, mainly
Addition: likewise, another, second, third, furthermore
Can you identify the transitional words in the student's example above?

Well Understood When you write your summary, make sure that you use **standard American English**—the kind of English used in newscasts and textbooks—to communicate your ideas clearly to your audience. To help your audience understand and remember what you say, use simple, familiar words when possible and keep your sentences relatively short. Do not make listeners wrestle with difficult vocabulary. If an unfamiliar word is important to the article, book, or story you are summarizing, define it for your audience, just as the writer of the summary above defined *guitarron*.

The Big Picture Do not read your summary word-for-word to your audience. Instead, rehearse your presentation many times over, so that you need only notes, rather than the whole summary. You may want to create notes in an **outline** form, noting the important ideas in your summary.

Another option is to speak from a **graphic organizer** that visually represents your information. Using visual notes can help make your presentation sound more conversational and natural. For a summary of a novel, a short story, a "how-to" article, or a historical work, you might use a sequence chain or a flowchart. For other kinds of non-fiction, a chart, a conceptual map, or an outline might work well. On the next page you will see part of a flowchart the student who is summarizing a short story created.

Reference Note
For more on **conceptual maps,** see page 631.

Listening and Speaking 1.4 Organize information to achieve particular purposes. 2.0 Student speaking demonstrates a command of standard American English.

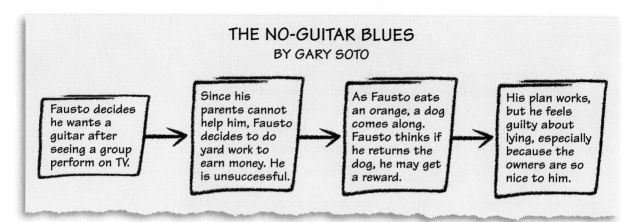

THE NO-GUITAR BLUES
BY GARY SOTO

Fausto decides he wants a guitar after seeing a group perform on TV.	→ Since his parents cannot help him, Fausto decides to do yard work to earn money. He is unsuccessful.	→ As Fausto eats an orange, a dog comes along. Fausto thinks if he returns the dog, he may get a reward.	→ His plan works, but he feels guilty about lying, especially because the owners are so nice to him.

Deliver Your Presentation

The Power of Practice   Once you have a firm grasp on *what* you will say, you are ready to practice *how* you will say it. The tips below will help you make an engaging and informative presentation. As you rehearse your summary, try adding one or two techniques at a time so you can eventually use all of the techniques with ease.

EFFECTIVE SPEAKING TECHNIQUES

Technique	Tips
Eye contact, gestures, and facial expressions	Make sure your facial expressions agree with what you are saying and communicate a neutral attitude. Make sure that you look at different members of your audience, too.
Volume	Speak loudly enough to be heard by all of your listeners. Practice **projecting** your voice—pushing out air with your abdominal muscles as you speak.
Tempo	Speak at an even rate. Speak a little slower than you do in everyday conversation to make sure that your audience can absorb the information.

Evaluate an Oral Summary

Listen to This   You will evaluate one classmate's oral summary, but you should listen carefully to all of your classmates' presentations. As your classmates present their summaries, jot down any questions that come to mind. Then, after each presentation, ask the speaker your questions to learn more about the piece he or she summarized. To help you evaluate the content and delivery of a class-

Listening and Speaking **1.1** Ask probing questions to elicit information.   **1.6** Use speaking techniques, including tempo and eye contact, for effective presentations.   **2.0** Student speaking demonstrates the organizational and delivery strategies outlined in Listening and Speaking Standard 1.0. **2.2** Deliver oral summaries of articles and books.

mate's oral summary, write down answers to the questions in the following chart.

GUIDELINES FOR EVALUATING AN ORAL SUMMARY

Content

- Does the speaker provide a summary of information rather than tell a complete story, describe something, or express an opinion?
- On what main idea does the speaker focus?
- Does the speaker present only the most significant details? List those given.
- Is the summary logical and easy to understand? How clearly do details support the main idea? Elaborate.
- How does the speaker use appropriate **transitions** to give his or her ideas **coherence**?
- How effectively does the speaker use standard American English? Give examples.

Delivery

- How often does the speaker make eye contact with the audience?
- Does the speaker use natural gestures and appropriate facial expressions? Explain.
- Does the speaker speak at an even tempo?
- How well do the speaker's voice and gestures match an informative purpose and show a neutral **attitude**? Elaborate.

Food for Thought Your notes will help you give the speaker useful **feedback** on the content and delivery of his or her summary. Remember that the purpose of an oral summary is to provide information, so your feedback should focus on how well the speaker achieved that purpose.

TIP When you give feedback, start by telling the speaker what he or she did well. If improvement is needed, provide suggestions. In other words, make polite and helpful comments—the kind of comments you will appreciate when it is your turn in the spotlight.

PRACTICE & APPLY 7 Plan, Present, and Evaluate an Oral Summary

- Choose a work that interests you and is likely to interest your audience. Read the work, taking notes on the main ideas.
- Using your notes, write a summary that will help your listeners understand and follow your ideas.
- Practice your presentation thoroughly. Then, deliver it to your audience.
- Take notes on one classmate's summary using the questions in the chart above. Use your notes to provide constructive feedback.

Listening and Speaking 1.0 Deliver focused, coherent presentations that convey ideas clearly. Students evaluate the content of oral communication. **1.2** Determine the speaker's attitude toward the subject. **1.7** Provide constructive feedback to speakers concerning the coherence and logic of a speech's content and delivery and its overall impact upon the listener.

Analyzing Electronic Journalism

WHAT'S AHEAD?

In this workshop you will analyze a television news broadcast. You will also learn how to

- identify textual, video, and audio elements in electronic journalism and the techniques used to create them
- identify the effects of words, images, and sound on TV viewers

In a character analysis, you analyze the techniques an author uses to develop a key element of fiction—character. You also analyze how those techniques affect your impression of a character. For example, after analyzing the way a character talks, you might draw a conclusion about that character's personality.

Just as you can analyze the elements of fiction, you can analyze the elements of a TV news story. A TV news story is made up of words, images, and sounds. Television journalists use specific techniques for presenting these words, images, and sounds. Each of these techniques serves a specific purpose. In this workshop you will learn about these techniques and their purposes, as well as some possible unintended effects of the techniques.

Textual Elements

Story Time   **Text** is the name given to the words you hear and sometimes see on the TV screen. When you hear text, it is presented by a *news anchor* or *news reporter.* The **news anchor** reads the text of the primary, or most important, news stories. He or she may sit behind a news desk in a studio or do "on-the-scene" reports for important continuing news stories, such as national political conventions or the Olympic games. The anchor also introduces other reporters and their news stories. **Reporters**—often reporting live from where a news event is happening—may provide additional

Listening and Speaking 1.8 Analyze the effect on the viewer of text in electronic journalism; identify the techniques used to achieve the effects in each instance studied.

information on the primary news stories or give information on secondary, or less important, news stories.

Because time is limited in a typical half-hour news program, primary and secondary news stories are short, usually no more than two to three minutes long. This means that the amount of text for each story is also limited. News writers and reporters must carefully plan text to achieve their purposes—capturing and keeping your attention, engaging your mind and emotions, and informing you. In order to understand the effects of a news story, you must examine both the *structure* by which the text is arranged and *content* of the text. You must also think about how the structure helps determine the content.

Text Structure To help viewers understand and remember the main points of a news story during the couple of minutes it is broadcast, the text usually follows a brief, simple, attention-getting **structure,** or order. The following graphic shows the typical news story structure.

Lead-in
In the TV studio, the anchor introduces the story.

"Tonight a fire has broken out at the Olde Towne Bakery in the historic East End district. Here's Brian Steele on location with this breaking story. . . ."

Setup
The reporter, usually on location, grabs the audience's attention and introduces the images viewers are about to see.

"What you are about to see may trouble those of you with fond memories of the Olde Towne Bakery. . . ."

Sound Bites
Short audio pieces of interviews are mixed in with video clips.

(voice of Olde Towne Bakery owner): "This is truly heartbreaking. My grandparents started this business back in 1884. . . ."

Voice-overs
The reporter talks while the video is playing. Usually, the reporter explains the images on the screen.

"The flames are shooting up over thirty feet above the building."

Back Announcing
After the video clips, the reporter briefly sums up the main points of the story.
"Again, fire is raging through the Olde Towne Bakery in the historic East End district. The joyless residents of Thayerville are in shock as this landmark goes up in smoke."

Stand-up
The reporter addresses the camera and the anchor with closing commentary.

"The owners hope to rebuild soon so they can continue the generations-long tradition of bringing fresh baked goods to the folks of Thayerville. Back to you."

As you can see, the same information is repeated many times. Repeating the information gives viewers several chances to hear and understand the main point of a story. Repetition also helps the TV viewer make sense of unexpected sounds and images that are presented simultaneously and within an extremely short time frame.

Content The brief, repetitive structure of broadcast news stories limits the **content,** or information provided. Viewers may receive an oversimplified understanding of events, getting the basic facts without understanding the full meaning of the story. Because broadcast news stories are so short, they are often presented without much **context**—the whole situation or background information behind the story. As a result, viewers may not really be aware of the other issues related to the event.

Visual Elements

Have you ever heard the saying "The camera never lies"? TV viewers tend to think of "live" images on the news as an accurate portrayal of reality. However, TV images represent just one piece of reality, as seen through a camera. **Photojournalists,** such as news reporters, photographers, and producers, make choices about the way each image will look. They also decide which **point of view,** or way of portraying the world, to show on the TV screen. As a critical TV viewer, you should know how the camera techniques TV photojournalists use can affect your perceptions of the news.

Whether Near or Far The **camera shot** is what the viewer sees on the television screen. Shots are put together to form a scene or story and may show closeness or distance.

Long Shot A shot that is made from far away, such as a landscape, is called a **long shot.** A **cover shot**—a long shot at the beginning of a news story—can set the scene for the story. For example, a long shot might show the devastation caused by a flood, as shown in the left-hand image on the next page. It may also create the impression of distance and objectivity. A long shot can also be used as **wallpaper,** an interesting visual image to show behind an anchor's narration. However, wallpaper may distract you from hearing important information if you are looking at the wallpaper and tuning out the anchor's words.

TIP Watch out for signs of **bias**—a slanted point of view, either in favor of or against an issue. Signs of bias include personal opinions and **loaded language**—words or phrases that carry strong positive or negative emotional impact, such as "a heartbreaking loss" or "an inspiring act." Try to form your own opinion about a story rather than being influenced by bias or loaded language.

Listening and Speaking 1.8 Analyze the effect on the viewer of images in electronic journalism; identify the techniques used to achieve the effects in each instance studied.

Close-up A **close-up** is a shot taken very close to the subject. A close-up shot can show fine details, such as a detail of a craftsperson's hands weaving yarn. If a close-up is of someone's face, it can reveal emotion. For example, the camera may **zoom in** (moving from a wider shot of a subject to a closer one) to focus on the face of a flood victim so that you can see the worry in his or her face, as shown in the right-hand image below.

Long Shot

Close-up

A close-up shot can, however, exaggerate a subject's features or create ugly or menacing features.

What's Your Angle? The **camera angle** is the viewpoint at which a camera is set when it is pointed toward a subject. Sometimes, conditions may limit the angles from which a cameraperson may shoot. For example, in filming a forest fire, a photojournalist may be able only to get shots taken from above, using a helicopter or airplane.

High Angle A **high angle** is a shot from above, with the camera looking down on the subject. A high camera angle can be used, for example, to provide an overview of a scene. A high camera angle can, however, make the subject look small, unimportant, and vulnerable. In the high-angle photo at right, notice how looking down on the scene of a fire gives viewers a clear picture of how firefighters have worked to get the blaze under control.

High angle

Listening and Speaking 1.8 Analyze the effects on the viewer of images in electronic journalism; identify the techniques used to achieve the effects in each instance studied.

Low angle

Low Angle A shot from below, with the camera looking up at the subject, is called a **low-angle** shot. A low camera angle can make the subject look tall and powerful. A low camera angle may distort reality, making subjects look much larger than they are. In the low-angle photo at left, notice how powerful the fire looks when the camera is on the ground, looking up into the flames from the firefighters' point of view.

A Frame Worth More Than the Picture?   Framing is the process by which the photojournalist decides which details to include or cut from the camera shot. Framing is used to focus on the subject, eliminate clutter, and engage the viewer's emotions. Unfortunately, framing can leave out important details, making a story seem less complex than it is. For example, a shot accompanying a news story on the popularity of a certain band might focus on a group of female fans at the band's concert. The photojournalist who took the following pictures framed the right-hand shot so that just young women—and not the young men who were also in the audience—are shown in the frame. Viewers might wrongly conclude from the framed shot that the band is popular only with women, when in fact men are also fans.

Full scene

Framed shot

TIP The **newsroom,** from which a national news program is broadcast, often looks like a busy place, full of computers and people engaged in a flurry of newsgathering activity.

? What effect do you think the images of the newsroom can have on viewers?

What Else Do You See?   **Props** are all the objects that appear in a camera shot. Whether it is intentional or not, these props can add meaning to a shot. For example, a computer may serve as a prop for a story on the success of the technology industry. Sometimes objects are even added to a scene being taped. Possible problems arise if a prop distracts the viewer or demonstrates a bias for or against a particular opinion. For example, if the brand name of a computer is visible on camera, the reporter may unintentionally be advertising and promoting that computer company.

Audio Elements

In addition to the text that you hear read by an anchor or reporter, there are other sounds that you may hear in a news report. Background noises captured on videotape, such as ambulance sirens, high winds, or hands clapping, add depth to a story. Sometimes you will hear the sounds of a busy newsroom behind a news anchor. Because music can affect viewers' emotions, network guidelines prohibit the use of music during a newscast. However, music is often used as a sound effect to open and close a program and to introduce commercial breaks.

Analysis of a News Story

The Sum of the Parts   Television newscasts blend textual, visual, and audio elements to create an effect greater than that which could be achieved through only one element. Still, before you can judge the effect of this blend, you need to analyze each of the individual elements. The following Thinking It Through steps will help you identify the elements in a TV news broadcast and the techniques used to affect viewers.

TIP   TV news-magazines, hour-long news programs that can cover news issues in greater depth than the typical nightly news broadcast, may use music in their features. Many newsmagazine stories are **human interest** stories designed to affect viewers' emotions, and music adds to the emotional impact of these stories.

THINKING IT THROUGH — Analyzing a TV News Broadcast

▶ **STEP 1 Describe the news segment, identifying text, image, or sound techniques used in the segment.**

The story is a network news feature about the declining prairie dog population.

<u>Sound</u>: Prairie dogs bark and chatter through much of the story.

<u>Image</u>: The camera shows a long shot of a nearly deserted prairie dog town, medium shots of the remaining prairie dogs playing and eating, and a close-up of a rancher's face.

<u>Text</u>: The voice-over tells us that prairie dogs are in trouble because of disease and human activity and that they are a crucial part of the ecosystem. A rancher says he worries about them spreading disease. The story focuses on ways to handle the conflict between the environmental importance of prairie dogs and the needs of the ranchers and other people who consider them pests.

(continued)

Listening and Speaking   1.8 Analyze the effect on the viewer of sound in electronic journalism; identify the techniques used to achieve the effects in each instance studied.

(continued)

▶ **STEP 2** **Explain the purposes of each major technique.** Hint: Think about why the producer might choose to use these techniques.

<u>Sound</u>: The barking noises grab my attention.

<u>Image</u>: The long shot sets the scene. The medium shot shows prairie dog activities, and the close-up shot shows the rancher's weathered face.

<u>Text</u>: The words of the voice-over tell me why some people are concerned about prairie dogs, and the rancher's words tell me why other people consider them pests.

▶ **STEP 3** **Write an evaluation of the effects of the various techniques on you, the viewer.** Hint: Think about how the techniques make you feel.

The sounds the prairie dogs make in this story are kind of funny and cute. The long shot is a little sad because the prairie dog town is nearly empty. The medium shot is also really cute, and the prairie dogs almost act like they have personalities. The close-up shows me the years of hard work the rancher has done. His expression is tired and tough at the same time—very different from the playful and vulnerable prairie dogs. The text gives specific reasons why prairie dogs are important to the ecosystem but only vague reasons why people exterminate them.

Overall, the techniques used in the story got my attention and the story was fairly informative. It may not have been totally balanced, though. The rancher's point of view seemed less important in the story than the case for saving the prairie dogs—probably because the prairie dogs were more appealing than the rancher and because the text went into more detail about the impact of their loss on the environment.

PRACTICE & APPLY 8 **Analyze a TV News Story**

■ Watch a national news story, and analyze the textual, visual, and audio elements and the techniques used to create them. Use the Thinking It Through steps above as a guide. List the techniques you find, and describe the effects you think these techniques might have on TV viewers.

■ Give a short oral presentation of your findings to your class. If you have a videotape of your news story, use it as support for your presentation so that your audience can see and hear the elements and techniques used.

Listening and Speaking 1.8 Analyze the effect on the viewer of images, text, and sound in electronic journalism; identify the techniques used to achieve the effects in each instance studied.

DIRECTIONS: Read the following paragraph from a student's character analysis of Keevan from the short story "The Smallest Dragonboy" on pages 119–132. Then, answer the questions below it on your own paper.

(1) Many people believe that Keevan is too small and too young to be chosen by a dragon, but Keevan is determined to overcome any obstacle that may prevent him from becoming a dragonrider. (2) When Beterli, the oldest candidate, begins a fight with Keevan by making him believe that Keevan is no longer eligible to be chosen by a dragon, Keevan does not back down. (3) Keevan is badly hurt in the encounter, breaking a leg and hurting his head. (4) Keevan refuses to stay in bed when he hears the humming of the dragons, signaling that the dragon eggs are hatching. (5) Keevan knows he must get to the Hatching Ground if a dragon is to choose him. (6) He pulls himself out of bed and makes his way to the Hatching Ground, sliding and stumbling in pain. (7) When he reaches the Hatching Ground, Keevan is rewarded by being chosen by a bronze dragon, the most important of all the dragons. (8) Keevan's determination definitely pays off in the end.

1. What sentence best summarizes the writer's interpretation of the character?
   A Keevan is a bully and will pick fights with anyone who disagrees with him.
   B Keevan is unsure if he wants to be a dragonrider because he is so small.
   C Keevan is unwilling to give up his dream of becoming a dragonrider.
   D Keevan is fortunate because he does not feel the pain of his broken leg.

2. What transition might the writer add to the beginning of sentence 4 to show the contrast of ideas between sentence 3 and sentence 4?
   F Nevertheless,
   G Finally,
   H Therefore,
   J Then,

3. Which of the following quotations supports the idea that Keevan is determined?
   A "The humming increased in volume and tempo . . ."
   B "Keevan glanced upward, past the black mouths of the Weyr caves . . ."
   C "more riders were favoring eliminating the youngest . . ."
   D "Keevan was constantly working, twice as hard as any other boy . . ."

4. To present an oral summary of a short story to your class, you should
   F focus on the main ideas of the story
   G present your opinion of the story
   H persuade others to read the story
   J read the entire story to your class

5. In giving an oral summary of a short story, the speaker should
   A read the summary from a piece of paper
   B speak quickly to finish in two minutes or less
   C use his or her own words except when quoting from the story
   D talk quietly so as not to disturb others in the room

Persuasion

Y ou have probably come across many forms of *persuasion*, from a friend's CD recommendation to a newspaper editorial. **Persuasion** is a type of communication that tries to convince people to believe or do something. In this workshop you will take a position on an issue of importance to you by writing a persuasive essay and giving a persuasive speech. In the process you will practice the following language arts content standards.

WRITING WORKSHOP

Writing a Persuasive Essay Page 598

LISTENING AND SPEAKING WORKSHOP

Giving and Listening to a Persuasive Speech Page 616

GO TO: go.hrw.com
KEYWORD: HLLA7 W-3
FOR: Models, Writers' Guides, and Reference Sources

 California Standards

Writing

1.0 Students write clear, coherent, and focused essays. The writing exhibits students' awareness of the audience and purpose. Essays contain formal introductions, supporting evidence, and conclusions. Students progress through the stages of the writing process as needed.

1.1 Create an organizational structure that balances all aspects of the composition and uses effective transitions between sentences to unify important ideas.

1.2 Support all statements and claims with anecdotes, facts and statistics, and specific examples.

1.3 Use strategies of notetaking, outlining, and summarizing to impose structure on composition drafts.

1.6 Create documents by using word-processing skills and publishing programs.

1.7 Revise writing to improve organization and word choice after checking the logic of the ideas and the precision of the vocabulary.

2.0 Students write persuasive texts of at least 500 to 700 words. Student writing demonstrates a command of standard American English and the research, organizational, and drafting strategies outlined in Writing Standard 1.0.

2.4 Write persuasive compositions:

   a. State a clear position or perspective in support of a proposition or proposal.

b. Describe the points in support of the proposition, employing well-articulated evidence.

   c. Anticipate and address reader concerns and counter-arguments.

Listening and Speaking

1.0 Deliver focused, coherent presentations that convey ideas clearly and relate to the background and interests of the audience. Students evaluate the content of oral communication.

1.1 Ask probing questions to elicit information, including evidence to support the speaker's claims and conclusions.

1.2 Determine the speaker's attitude toward the subject.

1.3 Respond to persuasive messages with questions, challenges, or affirmations.

1.4 Organize information to achieve particular purposes and to appeal to the background and interests of the audience.

1.5 Arrange supporting reasons and examples effectively and persuasively in relation to the audience.

1.6 Use speaking techniques, including voice modulation, inflection, tempo, enunciation, and eye contact, for effective presentations.

1.7 Provide constructive feedback to speakers concerning the coherence and logic of a speech's content and delivery and its overall impact upon the listener.

2.0 Students deliver well-organized formal presentations employing traditional rhetorical strategies (e.g., persuasion). Student speaking demonstrates a command of standard American English and the organizational and delivery strategies outlined in Listening and Speaking Standard 1.0.

2.4 Deliver persuasive presentations:

   a. State a clear position or perspective in support of an argument or proposal.

   b. Describe the points in support of the argument and employ well-articulated evidence.

Writing a Persuasive Essay

WHAT'S AHEAD?

In this workshop you will write a persuasive essay. You will also learn how to

- state a clear position on an issue
- support the position with reasons and evidence
- address reader counterarguments
- use transitions to connect ideas
- eliminate clichés

"That is *not* fair!" "We shouldn't let that happen!" Have you ever said or thought those words? When you feel strongly about an issue, you want to *do* something about it. One way you might change a situation is to write about it. You can write something that might persuade other people to share your opinion. You may even convince people to help you bring about the change you want.

Here is your chance to make the world a better place. In this workshop you will write a **persuasive essay** on an issue about which you feel strongly. Using reasons and evidence to support your position, you will try to convince your readers to believe as you do and to take action on the issue.

Professional Model: A Persuasive Essay

Just as watching professional athletes can help you improve your own athletic skills, reading the work of published writers can help you become a better writer. For instance, notice how the author of the following article, "A Veto on Video Games," uses a variety of evidence, including anecdotes, facts, and specific examples, to support his position.

As you read the article, create a **think sheet.** Note your responses to the writer's ideas and write down any questions you may have about the article. Answer the analysis questions that appear next to the article.

DO THIS

Reference Note

For more on **think sheets,** see page 529.

Writing 2.4 Write persuasive compositions.

from Newsweek®

A Veto on Video Games

A parent speaks out on why he has barred
TV video games from his home.

BY LLOYD GARVER

My wife and I are the kind of mean parents whom kids grumble about on the playground. We're among that ever-shrinking group of parents known as video game holdouts. We refuse to buy a video game set. Around Christmastime, my son made a wish list, and I noticed that Nintendo was No. 1. I said, "You know you're not going to get Nintendo." He said, "I know I'm not going to get it from *you.* But I might get it from *him.*" Alas, Santa, too, let him down.

> **1. What is the author for or against? What specific words tell you?**

I don't think that playing a video game now and then is really harmful to children. But the children I know are so obsessed with these games that they have prompted at least one second-grade teacher (my son's) to ban the word *Nintendo* from the classroom. When I asked my seven-year-old if the teacher wouldn't let the kids talk about the games because that's all they were *talking* about, he said, "No. That's all we were *thinking* about."

Our society is already so computerized and dehumanized[1] that kids don't need one more reason to avoid playing outside or going for a walk or talking with a friend. I'd still feel this way even if there were nothing wrong with games whose objectives[2] are to kill and destroy.

> **2. What reason for his position does the writer give in this paragraph?**

I know, I know. There are games other than those like Rampage, Robocop, Motor Cross Maniacs, Bionic Commando, Dr. Doom's Revenge, Guerrilla War, and Super Street Fighter. But aren't the violent games the ones the kids love to play for hours? And hours. And hours. My son told me he likes the "killing games" the best, hasn't had much experience with "sports games," and likes "learning games" the least because they are "too easy." (Manufacturers take note.) My five-year-old daughter told me she enjoyed playing Duck Hunt at a friend's house. The beauty of this game is that even very young players can have the

> **3. What audience concern does the writer address in this paragraph?**

---

1. dehumanized: machinelike; lacking emotion or individuality.
2. objectives: aims or goals.

fun of vicariously[3] shooting animals. And then there's the game with my favorite title—an obvious attempt to combine a graceful sport with exciting action— Skate or Die.

'Promote habituation'[4]: The January issue of the Journal of the American Academy of Child and Adolescent Psychiatry featured an article entitled "Pathological Preoccupation with[5] Video Games." The author believes that some game manufacturers try to develop programs that "deliberately promote habituation," and the goal of some of the people who make up these games is "to induce[6] an altered level of concentration and focus of attention in the gamester."

> **4. Why do you think the writer includes these quotations?**

If you have children, or know any, doesn't this "altered level of concentration and focus" sound familiar? If not, try talking to a child while he is staring at that screen, pushing buttons. He won't hear you unless the words you happen to be saying are, "I just bought a new game for you."

In case you couldn't tell, I'm worried that electronic games are dominating children's lives. There are games that simulate sports like baseball and basketball, and that's all some kids know about the sports.

> **5. What point is the writer trying to make in this paragraph?**

Someday soon, a young couple will take their children to their first baseball game and hear the kids exclaim, "This is great. It's almost like the *real baseball* we play on our home screen." When I took my son to a recent Lakers basketball game, the thing that seemed to excite him most was a video game in the lobby. You see, if a kid didn't want to be bored watching some of the greatest athletes in the world play, he could just put a quarter in the machine and watch lifeless electronic images instead.

> **6. Why do you think the writer includes this story about his son?**

My son's teacher was right. Kids do play and talk about these games too much. They even have books and magazines that kids can study and classes so they can get better at the games. And that's what's got me worried. I'm just concerned that this activity is so absorbing, kids are going to grow up thinking that the first people to fly that airplane at Kitty Hawk were the Super Mario Brothers.

I don't like to discourage children from doing something they're good at; in this case, I must. And believe me, my desire to see them play the games less does not diminish how impressed I am by their skill—they seem to be getting better and better at these games at a younger and younger age.■

---

3. vicariously: experienced in one's imagination by watching someone else.
4. 'Promote habituation': cause addiction.
5. "Pathological Preoccupation with . . .": total focus of attention on, to the point of obsession.
6. induce: to cause.

Think About the Model

Working with a partner, discuss the following questions and write down your responses.

1. Who do you think is the audience for "A Veto on Video Games"? What clues helped you identify this audience?

2. Do you agree with the writer's position? Why or why not?

3. Which of the writer's ideas was most persuasive? Why?

4. Which ideas in the article do you think would be most persuasive to the article's primary audience? Why?

5. Create for the article a diagram like the one below. List at least three ideas the author provides to support his position.

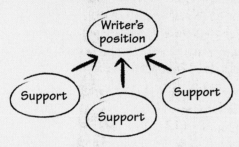

Prewriting

Choose an Issue

Picking Your Battles   The **purpose** of persuasive writing is to convince your readers to share your point of view on an issue. So, the first step in writing a persuasive essay is to choose an issue. **An issue is a subject, situation, or idea about which people disagree,** such as the best way to raise money for the band trip, whether television is harmful to children, or whether the city should build a park or a garage on an empty lot.

Your issue should be important to you. It should also be important enough for other people to have strong feelings and opinions about it. Avoid matters of personal preference, such as clothing styles or food. **Focus** on issues that have a real impact on people's lives, such as school rules or current social issues.

> **KEY CONCEPT**

> **TIP**   To help you think of issues that you can write about in your essay, read published persuasive essays, such as the professional model "A Veto on Video Games," on page 599.

Writing 1.0 Write focused essays. The writing exhibits students' awareness of the purpose. Students progress through the stages of the writing process as needed.

Choosing an Issue

Here is how to choose an issue for your persuasive essay.

STEP 1 Brainstorm issues about which you feel strongly. To discover an issue, **quickwrite** using the starter sentences below.

If I were president, the first thing I'd change is _____.

One thing that really bothers me about _____ is _____.

STEP 2 Decide which issues are most important to you and create strong feelings and opinions in others.

STEP 3 Check off the single issue you want to address.

Example

> ✓ having to pay for athletes' autographs
> chores—should parents pay kids?
> bad-tasting school lunches

> **TIP** Be sure the issue you select is one about which you can find enough information to write a 500- to 700-word composition. The issue should also be interesting enough to keep your audience's attention for an essay of this length.

State Your Opinion

Taking a Stand Every issue has at least two sides—for it and against it. As a writer, you need to adopt a **position** and tell your reader which side of the issue you support. In other words, **state your point of view, or *perspective*, clearly in an *opinion statement*.**

An **opinion statement** is made up of an issue plus a writer's point of view on the issue.

| KEY CONCEPT

> **Issue:** having to pay for athletes' autographs
> **+ Point of view:** fans shouldn't have to
> _____
> **Opinion statement:** Fans shouldn't have to pay for athletes' autographs.

> **TIP** An opinion statement serves the same purpose as a **main idea statement,** or **thesis.** It tells your readers the topic of your essay and what you are going to say about the topic.

Often an opinion statement will include a *proposition* or *proposal*. A **proposition** is a statement that can be argued, such as, "Dogs make the best pets." A **proposal** is a call to action, such as "Everyone should register to vote."

Writing 2.0 Students write persuasive texts of at least 500 to 700 words. **2.4a** State a clear position or perspective in support of a proposition or proposal.

PRACTICE & APPLY 1

Choose an Issue and State Your Opinion

Use the Thinking It Through steps on page 602 to choose an issue for your persuasive essay. Then, write an opinion statement. Make sure your opinion statement reflects your purpose by showing your readers the stand you have taken—for or against the issue.

Consider Your Audience

Who Cares?   You probably would not write a persuasive essay about the school cafeteria to your college-age brother. Since problems with the school cafeteria don't affect his life, he probably would not be very interested in them. Persuasive writing works best when it is directed at the right group, or **audience.** You can identify the audience for your persuasive essay in two steps.

1. Figure out what groups of people are interested in your issue.
2. Choose one group to focus on, and analyze that group.

Finding Your Audience   To identify the right audience for your essay, think about the issue you have chosen. Remember that any issue is likely to affect more than one group of people. Ask yourself,

■ **Who is interested in this issue?**

After identifying at least two of the groups who might care about your issue, ask,

■ **For which group do I want to write?**

The student writing about athletes charging for autographs identified sports card collectors and professional athletes as groups interested in that issue. He then decided to write to sports card collectors. As a collector himself, he feels he understands them and knows what is important to them.

Putting Your Audience in Focus   Now you can zero in on the group you picked. **Focus on the members of that group who might be undecided or might disagree with you, because they are the ones you have to convince.** (You don't need to convince people who already share your opinion.) To get them on your side, you will have to understand their concerns. To do this, answer the questions on the next page.

 KEY CONCEPT

 Writing 1.0 The writing exhibits students' awareness of the audience and purpose.

What group am I addressing? sports card collectors

How old are people in this group? They are all ages, but I know more about the ones my age.

What else do I know about this group? They all have their favorite players, but most of them love Hank Aaron.

Who will be my specific audience? sports card collectors my age who admire Hank Aaron and think it's okay for athletes to charge money for autographs

What counterarguments might people in this group have? They might think that signed cards aren't that expensive. They may get a bigger allowance than I do, so the price of the cards won't matter.

TIP Addressing **counterarguments**—the reasons people might disagree with you—is persuasive. When you show your audience that you have considered their concerns, they may take your argument more seriously, even if they disagree.

PRACTICE & APPLY 2 **Identify Your Audience**

Think of at least two groups interested in your issue; then, choose a group to address. Finally, answer the questions above.

Gather Support

| KEY CONCEPT

Back It Up You must convince your reader that your opinion is logical, or that it makes sense. To do this, **you must support your reasons for your opinion with evidence. Reasons** tell why you believe as you do. **Evidence**—in the form of anecdotes, facts, statistics, examples, or expert opinions—backs up each reason.

- An **anecdote** is a brief story that illustrates a point. *My friend spent his entire month's allowance on an autographed card.*

- A **fact** is a statement that can be proven true. *Popular players already make millions of dollars a year.* A **statistic** is information in numeric form. *The average allowance of the twenty-five Eagle Middle School students I surveyed is five dollars a week.*

- An **example** is a specific instance or illustration of a general idea. *There are better ways to outsmart professional autograph seekers . . . **For example,** a player can simply personalize the autograph.*

- An **expert opinion** is a statement made by an authority on a subject. *Some dealers feel that a signed card has been defaced.*

Writing **1.0** Essays contain supporting evidence. **1.2** Support all statements and claims with anecdotes, facts and statistics, and specific examples. **2.4b** Describe the points in support of the proposition, employing well-articulated evidence. **2.4c** Anticipate and address reader concerns and counterarguments.

To find support for your opinion, try the following suggestions:

- **Interview experts, friends, or other people who are interested in the issue.** For example, if you are writing about the school lunchroom, you might interview students, teachers, or cafeteria workers.

- **Research the issue.** For example, find magazine articles or Web pages about other young people who are vegetarians, or take a poll to see how many students at a school are vegetarian.

Seeing Is Believing **Remember that your reasons and evidence should support your opinion statement.** Notice how the reason and evidence listed below support the opinion statement "The school lunchroom should offer vegetarian meals."

◄ KEY CONCEPT |

Reason: Many students at King Middle School are vegetarians.

Evidence: A poll shows that 30% of the students here do not eat meat. (statistic)

Designing Your Writing

Using Numbers **Statistical evidence**—numbers—can be very persuasive. You can create visuals to show graphically the statistical evidence in your essay. A pie chart is a good choice when you want to show how a whole breaks down into percentages or parts. For example, the pie chart below shows the percentages of all students at one school who do and do not eat meat.

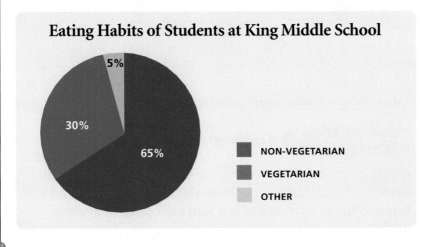

Eating Habits of Students at King Middle School

5%
30%
65%

- NON-VEGETARIAN
- VEGETARIAN
- OTHER

COMPUTER TIP

Many software programs allow you to create visuals such as pie charts on your computer. If you have access to a color printer, you can make each section of your pie chart a different color.

In addition, you may need to change the document's **page orientation**, printing large visuals sideways to allow them to fit on your paper. You can change page orientation by looking for page setup in the file menu of most word-processing programs.

Writing 1.6 Create documents by using word-processing skills and publishing programs. **2.0** Student writing demonstrates a command of the research strategies outlined in Writing Standard 1.0.

TIP A support chart can act as an **informal outline** to help you organize your ideas and structure your composition draft. For more on creating an **outline**, see page 639.

In his **notes** below, a student begins a support chart in which he lists several reasons why professional athletes should not charge fans for autographs. In the second column, he **summarizes** evidence to support each reason. In the third column, the writer evaluates his evidence, and in the fourth column, he rates the strength of each item ("Good," "Best," "Okay"), based on his audience's concerns. Knowing which evidence is strongest will help you organize your support before you write.

SUPPORT CHART

Reasons	Supporting Evidence	How Strong?	Rating
Players should be grateful for their fans' interest.	**Expert Opinion:** Hank Aaron's biographer says he was flattered to have kids look up to him.	Pretty strong. My audience still thinks of Hank Aaron as the greatest.	Good
The fans help the players get huge salaries.	**Fact:** The most popular professional athletes earn millions of dollars a year in salaries.	Very strong. Readers may think, "Players make so much money. They shouldn't take any more from us."	Best
Kids don't have enough money to spend on autographs. (response to counterargument that autographs are not expensive)	**Anecdote:** A friend of mine spent his entire month's allowance on one card.	Not as strong as the other support—it depends on who's paying for the card.	Okay

PRACTICE & APPLY 3 **Gather Support**

- Create a support chart like the one above, listing **reasons** and **evidence** to support your opinion statement. Use the third and fourth columns to evaluate and rate each piece of evidence.

- Replace any evidence you decide is too weak to convince your audience. You should have at least two strong reasons.

Writing 1.3 Use strategies of notetaking, outlining, and summarizing to impose structure on composition drafts. 2.0 Student writing demonstrates the organizational strategies outlined in Writing Standard 1.0.

THE WRITER'S LANGUAGE

Organization: Transitions

Transitions are words and phrases that show how ideas are related to each other. Writers may use a variety of types of transitions within a single composition.

The following chart shows some common transitional words and phrases.

Quick guide!

COMMON TRANSITIONAL WORDS AND PHRASES

Showing Sequence	after at last	before finally	first later	meanwhile when
Showing Cause and Effect	as a result because	since for	consequently so	so that therefore
Showing Order of Importance	first then	last mainly	to begin with furthermore	more important
Showing Comparison and Contrast	although and	but yet	instead similarly	still however

Transitions give your writing **coherence,** or connectedness, by helping you bridge the ideas between paragraphs and connect the ideas within a paragraph. For example, in "A Veto on Video Games" on page 599, the writer uses transitions such as *when* (paragraph 2) to identify the sequence of events.

PRACTICE

Write down and identify the type of each transition you find in the following paragraph. The first transition has been identified for you.

> Adults sometimes wrongly view young people as too self-involved. Sadly, some young people live up to this expectation. We must change this view ourselves. To begin with, volunteer in your community. When you volunteer, you prove yourself to be a caring and responsible member of the community. Consequently, you change attitudes about young people. Furthermore, you will change your own attitude. Instead of thinking you have little experience to offer, combine volunteer opportunities with your own interests; as a result, you will be a more effective volunteer.

Writing 1.0 Students write clear, coherent essays. 1.1 Create an organizational structure that uses effective transitions between sentences to unify important ideas.

Writing

A Writer's Framework

Persuasive Essay

Introduction

- Attention-grabbing opening
- Opinion statement

Grab your reader's attention with an **interesting beginning,** such as a startling statistic or quotation. Also, include a **clear opinion statement** so your audience knows your position. (For more information on writing **introductions,** see page 690.)

Body

- Reason #1 with evidence
- Reason #2 with evidence and so on

Choose the most convincing reasons and evidence from your support chart. Here is one effective way to organize your reasons.

- Start with your **second strongest reason** to attract your reader to your side.
- Leave your audience with a strong impression by using your **strongest reason last.**
- Sandwich any **other reasons in the middle.**

In addition, remember to use **transitions** to connect your reasons and evidence so that your essay has **coherence.** Also, address **counterarguments,** the objections readers may have to your opinion.

Conclusion

- Restatement of opinion
- Summary of reasons and/or call to action

Leave your audience convinced that you are right. **Restate your opinion in a new way.** Then, **summarize your reasons** in a single sentence and (if appropriate) **call on your audience** to take action. (For more information on **conclusions,** see page 690.)

PRACTICE & APPLY 4 **Write Your Persuasive Essay**

Now it is your turn to write a persuasive essay. As you write,

- keep your audience in mind
- use the strongest reasons and evidence from your chart
- refer to the framework above and the Writer's Model on page 609

Writing 1.0 Essays contain formal introductions, supporting evidence, and conclusions. **1.1** Create an organizational structure that balances all aspects of the composition and uses effective transitions between sentences to unify important ideas. **2.0** Student writing demonstrates a command of the drafting strategies outlined in Writing Standard 1.0. **2.4** Write persuasive compositions.

A Writer's Model

The final draft below closely follows the framework for a persuasive essay on the previous page.

GO TO: go.hrw.com
KEYWORD: HLLA7 W-3
FOR: A Student Model

What Is a Fan's Loyalty Worth?

Last week at a sports card show, I asked a well-known baseball player for his autograph. Imagine my surprise when his agent said I would have to pay fifteen dollars before the player would sign his name! Fans should not have to pay to get an athlete's autograph.

First of all, athletes should be satisfied that their fans love them. The biographer of Hank Aaron, baseball's home run king, states that Aaron was flattered just to have kids look up to him. He would not have dreamed of asking a young fan to pay for his autograph. Today's athletes should follow Hank Aaron's example.

At the card show, I told the agent that fans should not have to pay for autographs. "Come on, kid," he said. "Fifteen dollars is not very much money." Fifteen dollars may not be much to a millionaire agent, but it is to most younger fans. For example, a friend of mine spent his entire month's allowance on a single autographed card. His experience is not unusual. The average allowance of the twenty-five Eagle Middle School students I surveyed is five dollars a week. For an average student, paying for one autograph would leave little money for anything else for the rest of the month.

Sports figures and their agents say that some autograph seekers are really "runners." Runners are people who get paid by sports memorabilia companies to collect autographs, which the company then sells for a profit. True, some autograph collectors are dishonest, but most are not. Arnold Palmer, the legendary golfer, estimates that 25 to 30 percent of the people who ask for his autograph are "runners." The rest are true fans who would never sell their prized autographs. Besides, a signed sports card is not necessarily worth more than an unsigned card. Some dealers feel that a signed card has been defaced. Therefore, the card is worth less money. There are better ways to outsmart professional autograph seekers than setting a price that even honest fans have to pay. For example, a player can

(continued)

INTRODUCTION
Attention-grabbing opener

Opinion statement

BODY
Reason #1
Evidence (expert opinion)

Counterargument
Reason #2 (response to counterargument)

Evidence (anecdote)
Evidence (statistic)

Counterargument

Reason #3 (response to counterargument)

Evidence (example)

(continued)

simply personalize the autograph. A signature preceded by "To Tom" is worth up to a third less, according to experts.

Reason #4

Most important, athletes who insist on being paid for autographs are being short-sighted. One small autograph can create a lifelong fan. In the long run that will put a lot more than fifteen dollars into an athlete's pocket. Popular players—the ones fans ask for autographs most—already make millions of dollars a year. According to ESPN's Internet site, New York Mets star catcher Mike Piazza will make $91 million over six years. St. Louis Rams quarterback Kurt Warner got an $11,500,000 bonus just for signing a new contract. Venus Williams made $650,000 for winning one tennis tournament. Top athletes make more money in a year than most of us will make in a lifetime, and they make that money because of the support of fans.

Evidence (fact)

CONCLUSION
Restated opinion
Call to action

Instead of taking our money for autographs, athletes should repay our loyalty by freely signing their beloved names to our tattered cards. Do not pay for autographs. Show players that an autograph should be a way of saying "thank you" to a loyal fan, and *thank yous* should not cost money.

Evaluate and Revise Content, Organization, and Style

Giving Your Essay the Twice Over As you evaluate a peer's paper or evaluate and revise your own draft, you should do at least two readings. In the first reading, consider the content and organization using the guidelines below. In your second reading, check the style using the Focus on Word Choice on page 613.

▶ **First Reading: Content and Organization** Use this chart to evaluate and revise your paper so your message is persuasive.

Persuasive Essay: Content and Organization Guidelines

Evaluation Questions	▶ Tips	▶ Revision Techniques
❶ Does the introduction have a clear opinion statement?	**Underline** the opinion statement. Ask a friend to read it and to identify the point of view.	**Add** an opinion statement, or, if necessary, **replace** the opinion statement with a clearer one.
❷ Are there at least two reasons that logically support the opinion statement?	With a colored marker, **highlight** the reasons that support the opinion statement.	**Add** reasons that support the opinion statement as needed.
❸ Does at least one piece of evidence support each reason?	**Circle** evidence that supports each reason in the essay. **Draw a line** from the evidence to the reason it supports.	If necessary, **add** evidence to support each reason. **Elaborate** on evidence by adding details or explaining its meaning.
❹ Does the essay address counterarguments?	**Put stars** next to each counterargument. If there is not at least one star, revise.	**Add** discussion of at least one counterargument in a body paragraph.
❺ Are the reasons in an order that makes sense?	**Number** in the margin the reasons in the essay. **Rank** the reasons by their strength and check their order.	**Reorder** ideas, following the suggested order in the Framework on page 608.
❻ Does the conclusion include a restatement of the opinion and a summary of reasons or a call to action?	**Put a check mark** next to the restatement. **Draw a wavy line** under the summary of reasons or call to action.	**Add** a restatement of the opinion if it is missing. **Add** a summary of reasons, a call to action, or both.

Writing **1.7** Revise writing to improve organization after checking the logic of ideas.

ONE WRITER'S REVISIONS This revision is an early draft of the essay on pages 609–610.

add

First of all, athletes should be satisfied that their fans love them⊙
∧ The biographer of Hank Aaron, baseball's home run king, states that Aaron was flattered just to have kids look up to him. He would not have dreamed of asking a young fan to pay for his autograph. Today's athletes should follow Hank Aaron's example.

At the card show, I told the agent that fans should

elaborate
"Come on, kid," he said⊙ "Fifteen dollars is not very much money⊙"
not have to pay for autographs. ~~He did not agree.~~ Fifteen

elaborate
dollars may not be much to ~~an~~ *a millionaire* ∧ agent, but it is to most younger fans.

PEER REVIEW

As you evaluate a peer's persuasive essay, ask yourself these questions.

- What is the *most* convincing part of this essay? Why?
- What is the *least* convincing part? Why?

Responding to the Revision Process

1. Why do you think the writer added a sentence to the first paragraph?
2. Explain why you think the writer's choice to elaborate with a quotation is or is not effective.
3. How did elaborating the evidence improve the writing?

> **Second Reading: Style** Now you will look at *how* you say what you say, and that means looking closely at each of your sentences. One way to improve sentence style is to eliminate *clichés*. **Clichés** are expressions that have been overused to the point that they have lost their impact. Use the following guidelines.

Style Guidelines

Evaluation Question	▶ Tip	▶ Revision Technique
Have I used any expressions I have heard many times?	▶ **Put an X** through every word or phrase you think is a cliché.	▶ **Delete** each cliché and **replace** it with your own original words.

 Writing 1.7 Revise writing to improve word choice after checking the precision of the vocabulary.

Clichés

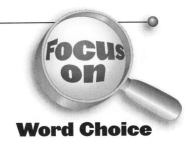

Word Choice

When you are writing persuasively, it is easy to reach for a familiar expression—called a **cliché**—to help you make your point. Clichés, though, are expressions that have been used so many times they have lost their meaning and freshness. If you use clichés in a persuasive paper, you run the risk of weakening your position.

Examples: cool as a cucumber   tough as nails
                        to run like the wind   on top of your game

   Replacing clichés with your own original, forceful words will help you get your opinion across in a more convincing way. Remember: that is the purpose of persuasive writing.

ONE WRITER'S REVISIONS

> Instead of taking our money for autographs, athletes
> *beloved names to our tattered cards.*
> should repay our loyalty by freely signing their ~~John~~
>
> ~~Hancocks.~~

Responding to the Revision Process

How did replacing "John Hancocks" with another phrase improve the sentence above?

PRACTICE & APPLY 5

Evaluate and Revise Your Essay

- First, evaluate and revise the content and organization of your essay, using the guidelines on page 611.
- Next, use the Focus on Word Choice above to see if you need to eliminate any clichés from your paper.
- If a peer evaluated your paper, think carefully about each of your peer's comments as you revise.

Writing 1.7 Revise writing to improve word choice after checking the precision of the vocabulary.

Publishing

Proofread Your Essay

Reference Note

For more on **proofreading** for common errors, see Chapter 17 in the *Holt Handbook.*

A Finishing Touch   Errors in your final essay will distract your reader from the persuasive point you are trying to make. If you have another person help proofread your essay, checking for **standard American English,** you will be less likely to miss mistakes.

Grammar Link

Using Comparatives

When you write a persuasive paper, you sometimes want to compare one thing with another. For example, you may want to convince your readers that your candidate for class president is *more experienced* than other candidates.

Most one-syllable words and many two-syllable modifiers form the comparative by adding *–er.*

> closer   cheaper   likelier

Some two-syllable modifiers (and all modifiers with more than two syllables) form the comparative by using *more.*

> more polite   more recklessly

Do not use the word *more* if the modifier is already in the comparative form.

Incorrect   Powermax batteries last **more longer** than batteries from other companies. [The word *longer* doesn't need *more* added to it, because longer already means "more long."]

Correct   Powermax batteries last **longer** than batteries from other companies.

Some words, such as *good* and *bad,* have special comparative forms.

> good ➤ better   bad ➤ worse

PRACTICE

For each of the following sentences, identify the incorrect modifier. Then, give the correct form of the modifier.

Example:

1. Video games are more cheaper than ever.

1. cheaper

1. Some video games are more harder than others.

2. Is a video game more bad than a TV crime drama?

3. Playing real basketball is more slower than playing the video game version.

4. The more I play this video game, the more better I get.

5. The more I play real sports, the more good I get.

Reference Note

For more information and practice on **comparatives,** see pages 224–228 in the *Holt Handbook.*

Writing 2.0 Student writing demonstrates a command of standard American English.

Publish Your Essay

Get the Word Out   Now is the time for your essay to do what it was written to do—persuade people. Think about the audience you identified before you wrote your first draft. What are some ways to get your persuasive essay in front of that audience?

- Send your essay to the opinion page editor of a magazine, your local or school newspaper, or another publication.
- Think about other ways to go public with your work. You might convert your essay to a speech and present it to your audience directly. (For more on **giving a persuasive speech,** see page 616.)
- Create an "Opposing Views" bulletin board by pairing your essay with one favoring a different opinion on your topic.

Reflect on Your Essay

Building Your Portfolio   Take time to reflect on your essay. Think about *what* you wrote and *how* you wrote. Reflecting will help you improve your next persuasive essay.

- What was the strongest piece of support in your essay? Why was it the strongest?
- What was your purpose for writing your essay? Do you think you achieved your purpose? Why or why not?
- How did you organize your ideas and why did you choose this order? In what other types of writing might you organize ideas in this way?

PRACTICE & APPLY 6
Proofread, Publish, and Reflect on Your Essay

Wrap up your persuasive essay by following these steps.

- First, correct grammar, usage, and mechanics errors after proofreading with a partner.
- Then, using one of the suggestions above, publish your essay to your target audience.
- Finally, look back on the process of writing a persuasive essay by answering the Reflect on Your Essay questions above. Write down your responses, and consider including them in your portfolio.

Writing 1.0 The writing exhibits students' awareness of the purpose.

Talk   Listen

WHAT'S AHEAD?

In this workshop you will give and listen to a persuasive speech. You also will learn how to

- address your audience's backgrounds and interests
- use effective visuals
- practice speaking techniques
- evaluate a speaker's persuasive techniques, delivery, and credibility

Reference Note

If you want to develop a speech about a new topic, see pages 601–607.

Giving and Listening to a Persuasive Speech

The persuasive essay you wrote in the Writing Workshop is complete, and you think that it is extremely convincing. However, if you read your essay aloud, it would probably not be as effective and persuasive. In this workshop you will learn how to adapt your persuasive essay for use as a persuasive speech. You will also have an opportunity to listen to and evaluate persuasive speeches delivered by your classmates.

Adapt Your Persuasive Essay

When giving a persuasive speech, your purpose is to convince the people to whom you are speaking that your position on the issue is correct. These may not be the same people for whom you wrote your essay. Like your written essay, your speech needs to have strong content and appeal to your audience.

To adapt your essay into a speech, begin with a copy of your written essay. Identify your essay's **position** (your opinion statement), **reasons** and **evidence,** and **proposal** or **proposition.** Next, make notes on the copy using the instructions on the following pages. Keep in mind that you may need to change some of your reasons and evidence to match your purpose and audience as well as the time you are given to make your speech. Then, create note cards to remind you of the ideas your speech should include to use as you rehearse and, if necessary, as you give your speech.

Listening and Speaking 1.0 Deliver focused, coherent presentations that convey ideas clearly and relate to the background and interests of the audience. Students evaluate the content of oral communication. **2.4** Deliver persuasive presentations. **2.4a** State a clear position or perspective in support of an argument or proposal.

We Understand Each Other For a successful persuasive speech, you must consider your **audience.** What is the point of view of the people who will hear your message? What are their feelings on the issue? Is your audience likely to agree with your position, or will they disagree? Since your listening audience may be different from your essay's audience, you will need to reconsider the reasons, evidence, and background information you include in your message.

Reasons and Evidence As you choose **reasons** for your opinion and the **evidence** (anecdotes, facts, statistics, examples, and expert opinions) that supports your reasons, consider how they relate to your listeners. For example, imagine you are writing a speech in support of a better lunch menu in your school cafeteria. If your audience were your classmates, you might give evidence such as descriptions of better tasting food. If your audience were school administrators, you might use evidence such as statistics that show how an improved menu would improve attentiveness in after-lunch classes. By considering the **interests** of your audience, you can choose the type of support that would most appeal to them.

Background Information Even the most persuasive argument can fall flat if your audience knows very little about your topic. Remember that your audience may not have the same **background information** as you do, particularly since you have researched your topic. Be sure that you explain in your speech any terms or ideas that may be unfamiliar to your listeners, even if you did not explain these terms or ideas for your essay's audience. Matching your content to your listening audience will help them understand what you have to say.

A Place for Everything A reading audience can look back at and re-read your essay, but your listening audience cannot. Therefore, you must organize your speech in a clear and persuasive manner. The most persuasive order for the ideas in your speech depends on your audience and your purpose.

Suppose you are making a speech proposing that the school needs to beautify a nearby empty lot by planting a garden. Most students are excited about the idea. The school staff, however, wants the lot to be paved to provide extra parking. Naturally, you would present your ideas to the two different audiences in different ways because the school staff will require more convincing.

TIP When you deliver your speech, you should match your spoken language to your audience, using a vocabulary and style that they can readily understand. However, it is important to use **standard American English,** language that is grammatically correct.

Listening and Speaking 1.5 Arrange supporting reasons and examples effectively and persuasively in relation to the audience. **2.4b** Describe the points in support of the argument and employ well-articulated evidence.

To organize your persuasive speech effectively, consider the following organizational strategies for persuading different audiences and achieving various purposes.

ORGANIZING IDEAS PERSUASIVELY

If your audience . . .	Your purpose is to . . .	Use this strategy:
opposes your ideas	get them to consider your ideas	Acknowledge their point of view and then list reasons that lead up to your opinion.
agrees with your ideas	get them to take action	Strengthen their existing opinion by beginning with your opinion and then by listing reasons. Close with your proposal, or call to action.
is unsure about your ideas	convince them to agree with you	Open their minds to your position by beginning with reasons that lead up to your opinion.
does not care about your ideas	get them to consider your ideas	Start with background information showing them how the issue affects them before giving your opinion and listing reasons.

As you organize your speech, remember that the order of your reasons and supporting evidence also has an impact on your audience. If you put your strongest argument at the beginning of your speech, you will make a good first impression on your audience. However, if you save the strongest argument for last, you will leave your audience with a lasting impression.

Deliver a Persuasive Speech

In persuasion, *how* you say something is often as important as *what* you say. A strong presenter can often make any argument more persuasive by using certain *speaking techniques*.

A Way with Words How well can you pay attention to a speaker who quietly mumbles and stumbles over words, who looks down while talking in a flat voice, or who races through a speech barely breathing? You probably have a difficult time following a speaker with any of these characteristics. To persuade your listeners, practice delivery techniques that will hold their attention, not distract them from your message.

TIP When practicing your speech, choose a partner or a group of classmates to be your audience, and use your note cards just as you will on the day you deliver your speech. You may also want to use a timer or watch to make sure that you stay within your time limit. Refer also to the **evaluation questions** on page 622.

Listening and Speaking 1.4 Organize information to achieve particular purposes and to appeal to the background and interests of the audience. **1.5** Arrange supporting details, reasons, descriptions, and examples effectively and persuasively in relation to the audience. **2.0** Student speaking demonstrates the organizational and delivery strategies outlined in Listening and Speaking Standard 1.0.

To help audience members focus their attention on hearing your ideas, consider the speaking techniques below and the tips for how to work them into your persuasive speech.

SPEAKING TECHNIQUES

Technique	Explanation	Tips
Enunciation	Words pronounced carefully and clearly	Practice your speech with a partner. Ask your partner to note any words that he or she does not understand. Look up in a dictionary or ask your teacher how to pronounce words that are unfamiliar to you.
Vocal Modulation	The stress you place on certain words and phrases through the volume of your voice	To stress certain points, speak more loudly or softly. Ask a partner if your volume is varied enough and if you can be heard clearly no matter what your volume.
Inflection	The high and low tones of your voice (your voice may go up at the end of a question and down at the end of a statement)	Avoid speaking in a monotone. Emphasize important ideas by making your inflection higher or lower. Ask a partner if you sound convincing and reasonable. The sound of your voice should fit your audience and suit your purpose.
Tempo	The speed and rhythm of your speech	Speak slowly enough for your audience to keep up. Use pauses to emphasize major points; a pause shows your audience that the idea was important, and it gives people time to think about your point. Remember to stop and catch your breath if necessary.
Eye Contact	A way of keeping the audience involved by looking at them	Practice being able to glance at your note cards, if needed, and then make eye contact with your partner again. Also, look at different places in the room so you can practice engaging as much of the audience as possible.

PRACTICE & APPLY 7 — Deliver a Persuasive Speech

As you adapt your persuasive essay for use as a persuasive speech,

- choose the evidence that best supports your opinion, and plan background information your audience will need
- organize your ideas clearly and persuasively
- practice your delivery using effective speaking techniques

Listening and Speaking **1.0** Deliver focused, coherent presentations that convey ideas clearly and relate to the background and interests of the audience. **1.6** Use speaking techniques, including voice modulation, inflection, tempo, enunciation, and eye contact, for effective presentations. **2.0** Deliver well-organized formal presentations employing traditional rhetorical strategies (e.g., persuasion).

Listen to and Evaluate a Speech

You may often listen while doing other things: The TV is on while you do chores, or the radio is on while you talk on the phone. For many activities this split attention is not a problem; however, when the purpose of listening is to **evaluate,** or judge, you should listen actively, giving the speaker your undivided attention.

Stay Focused   If your mind wanders while you are reading an essay, you can always re-read a section. However, if you miss something that a speaker says, you may not get another chance to hear that information. While you listen to speeches, consider these tips to help you focus on the speech and absorb the message.

- Devote your attention to the speaker by facing him or her and listening quietly and attentively.

- Keep an open mind, putting aside your own ideas in order to weigh the reasons and evidence in the speech.

- Pay attention to your understanding of the speaker's message by asking yourself if you understand the speaker's position.

- Take notes, writing down main ideas or details in your own words.

Give Feedback   Remember that, as a member of the audience, you can give the speaker **feedback.** For instance, after a speech you could ask for more information, politely counter a speaker's claim with your own ideas or experiences, or tell the speaker that you agree with his or her opinion. A student listening to a speech supporting a school garden asked the following questions.

> **To get more evidence:**
> Could you explain what you meant when you said a community garden could help students who are taking science classes?
>
> **To challenge the speaker's claims:**
> Although you said that a garden would improve the school's appearance, what will happen if the garden becomes neglected and overgrown?
>
> **To elaborate on points of agreement:**
> From your tone as you talked about the neighborhood, I understand that people in the community would like to see a garden at the school. How do you think we could best get the community involved in this type of project?

Listening and Speaking 1.1 Ask probing questions to elicit information, including evidence to support the speaker's claims and conclusions. 1.3 Respond to persuasive messages with questions, challenges, or affirmations.

One of the best ways for speakers to improve their speeches is to receive evaluations from their peers. When you are an audience member, the most useful thing you can do for your classmates is to give them honest, thorough, polite feedback about their speeches. In other words, provide your peers with useful information that will help them become more effective speakers. Remember that evaluating a speech differs from evaluating an essay; you have to consider not only the effectiveness of the words and ideas in a speech, but also the performance of the speaker.

Content and Organization When evaluating a speech's content, you are addressing its verbal message, including the speaker's reasons and evidence. The evidence the speaker provides should be **logical.** For example, evidence used as support should be relevant, or closely tied to the issue. To evaluate the organization of a speech, consider how easily you were able to follow the speaker's ideas. The organization of ideas should be **coherent,** or clearly connected.

Believability and Attitude One of the most important elements of a persuasive speech is its **believability.** As you listen to any persuasive message, you should consider how knowledgeable and sincere the speaker seems. Think about not only the strength of the speaker's reasons and evidence, but also about his or her *attitude* about the issue being addressed.

By examining a speaker's **attitude**—his or her feelings toward the subject—you may find reasons to reject the speaker's position. You might discover a **bias,** or prejudice, the speaker holds. A biased speaker might present only one side of an issue, downplay information in favor of the other side, or keep his or her true purpose hidden from the listener. For example, a speaker who strongly supports building a garden at the school could be hoping to make money selling the vegetables grown there. If so, the speaker has a **hidden agenda**—in this case, a motivation to make money. A speaker with a hidden agenda is not as credible as one who makes his or her attitudes and agendas clear from the beginning.

> **TIP** One simple way to identify a speaker's **attitude** is to ask yourself: "Why is the speaker so interested in this topic? Why does he or she want to persuade me?"

Delivery Criteria to consider when evaluating delivery are the speaker's use of speaking techniques, such as enunciation, voice modulation, inflection, tempo, and eye contact. You should consider how effectively the speaker uses each of these techniques to share his or her ideas.

Reference Note

For more on **speaking techniques,** see page 619.

Listening and Speaking 1.2 Determine the speaker's attitude toward the subject. **1.7** Provide constructive feedback to speakers concerning the coherence and logic of a speech's content and delivery and its overall impact upon the listener.

All Together Now   The questions in the following chart can help you evaluate a classmate's speech. Before you listen to a classmate's speech, you may want to make your own chart with the evaluation questions in one column and space for notes in another.

QUESTIONS FOR EVALUATING A PERSUASIVE SPEECH

Content and Organization	• What issue does the speech discuss?
	• What is the speaker's position on the issue?
	• How convincing and well supported are the speaker's reasons for his or her position?
	• How coherent and logical is the speech? Can you easily follow ideas as they flow from one to another? Or does the speech seem to jump around without logical connections or transitions?
Believability and Attitude	• How knowledgeable does the speaker seem about the issue?
	• How believable are the reasons and evidence that support the speaker's ideas?
	• How genuine and sincere does the speaker seem?
Delivery	• How clear is the speaker's delivery? Does he or she speak loudly and slowly enough? Are words pronounced carefully and clearly?
	• Does the speaker change the inflection of his or her voice to fit the audience and purpose? Explain.
	• Does the speaker pause to emphasize important ideas? Explain.
	• How often does the speaker make eye contact?

PRACTICE & APPLY 8

Evaluate a Persuasive Speech

- Use the instructions on pages 620–621 and the questions in the chart above to help you evaluate a few of the persuasive speeches given in your class.

- When you have finished, compare your evaluations with those of your classmates. In what areas did your evaluations agree or disagree? As a group, decide on an overall rating for the speaker.

- Give each speaker a chance to read and respond to your evaluation of his or her speech.

Listening and Speaking 1.0 Students evaluate the content of oral communication. **1.7** Provide constructive feedback to speakers concerning the coherence and logic of a speech's content and delivery and its overall impact upon the listener.

DIRECTIONS: Read the following draft of a paragraph from a student's persuasive essay. Then, read the questions below and choose the best answer for each question. Write your answers on your own paper.

> (1) Movies are an important part of our culture and an important part of my Saturday afternoons. (2) However, I think movies are beginning to affect people's health. (3) My friends and I like to have snacks at the movies, but we don't like to eat junk food. (4) Movie theater snacks consist of candy and popcorn popped in oil, which is more fattening than air-popped popcorn. (5) I want the option of carrot sticks, or dried fruit, or at least more-healthful air-popped popcorn. (6) Last week my friend Jake and I passed up the movie concession stand, and I could hear his stomach roar over the movie soundtrack. (7) Movie theaters don't allow you to bring your own food. (8) Once you are there you are stuck with what they offer. (9) In our town there are four movie theaters, and none of them offers a healthy snack option at its concession stand. (10) We should petition movie theater owners to provide us with healthier choices.

1. Whom is this paragraph trying to persuade?
   A movie theater owners
   B moviegoers
   C moviemakers
   D movie concession-stand workers

2. Where does the writer first state his position?
   F "Movies are an important part of our culture . . ."
   G "I want the option of carrot sticks, or dried fruit, or at least more-healthful air-popped popcorn."
   H "Movie theaters don't allow you to bring your own food . . ."
   J "We should petition movie theater owners to provide us with healthier choices."

3. Which of the following types of support is used in sentence 6?
   A fact
   B statistic
   C anecdote
   D specific example

4. Which of the following transitions might be added to the beginning of the eighth sentence to show the relationship between the ideas in the seventh and eighth sentences?
   F However,
   G To begin with,
   H After,
   J Therefore,

5. How would the following statement strengthen the writer's argument? "I took a survey of students who go to the movies at least twice a month; 70 percent said they would regularly buy healthy options."
   A It addresses the concern that no one would buy healthy food.
   B It supports the argument with an anecdote.
   C It supports the argument with a statistic.
   D It provides information about how much students like movies.

Research

Questions probably run through your mind all the time. To find answers to those questions often requires some form of research. In this workshop you will explore and share answers to questions about a topic that interests you. In the process you will practice these language arts content standards.

WRITING WORKSHOP

Writing a Research Report Page 626

LISTENING AND SPEAKING WORKSHOP

Giving and Listening to an Informative Speech Page 654

GO TO: go.hrw.com
KEYWORD: HLLA7 W-4
FOR: Models, Writer's Guides, and Reference Sources

 California Standards

Writing

1.0 Students write clear, coherent, and focused essays. The writing exhibits students' awareness of the audience and purpose. Essays contain formal introductions, supporting evidence, and conclusions. Students progress through the stages of the writing process as needed.

1.1 Create an organizational structure that balances all aspects of the composition and uses effective transitions between sentences to unify important ideas.

1.2 Support all statements and claims with anecdotes, descriptions, facts and statistics, and specific examples.

1.3 Use strategies of notetaking, outlining, and summarizing to impose structure on composition drafts.

1.4 Identify topics; ask and evaluate questions; and develop ideas leading to inquiry, investigation, and research.

1.5 Give credit for both quoted and paraphrased information in a bibliography by using a consistent and sanctioned format and methodology for citations.

1.6 Create documents by using word-processing skills.

1.7 Revise writing to improve organization after checking the logic of the ideas.

2.0 Students write expository texts of at least 500 to 700 words. The writing demonstrates a command of standard American English and the research, organizational, and drafting strategies outlined in Writing Standard 1.0.

2.3 Write research reports:

    a. Pose relevant and tightly drawn questions about the topic.

    b. Convey clear and accurate perspectives on the subject.

    c. Include evidence compiled through the formal research process.

    d. Document reference sources by means of footnotes and a bibliography.

Listening and Speaking

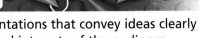

1.0 Deliver focused, coherent presentations that convey ideas clearly and relate to the background and interests of the audience. Students evaluate the content of oral communication.

1.1 Ask probing questions to elicit information, including evidence to support the speaker's claims and conclusions.

1.2 Determine the speaker's attitude toward the subject.

1.4 Organize information to achieve particular purposes and to appeal to the background and interests of the audience.

1.5 Arrange supporting details, descriptions, and examples effectively in relation to the audience.

1.6 Use speaking techniques, including voice modulation, inflection, tempo, enunciation, and eye contact, for effective presentations.

1.7 Provide constructive feedback to speakers concerning the coherence and logic of a speech's content and delivery and its overall impact upon the listener.

2.0 Students deliver well-organized formal presentations employing traditional rhetorical strategies (e.g., exposition). Student speaking demonstrates a command of standard American English and the organizational and delivery strategies outlined in Listening and Speaking Standard 1.0.

2.3 Deliver research presentations:

    a. Pose relevant and concise questions about the topic.

    b. Convey clear and accurate perspectives on the subject.

    c. Include evidence generated through the formal research process.

    d. Cite reference sources appropriately.

Writing a Research Report

WHAT'S AHEAD?

In this workshop you will write a research report. You will also learn how to

- focus a subject
- find and evaluate sources
- take notes
- add sentence variety to your writing
- treat titles correctly

I f you have ever sought answers to the questions *Who? What? When? Where? Why?* or *How?* you have done research. After all, seeking answers to questions is the whole point of doing research. In this workshop you will write a research report. The subject of your report is up to you, but it should be something that sparks your curiosity. Finding information and writing a report about it is your chance to answer your own questions about your subject, as well as the questions of your readers.

Professional Model: A Research Report

You can find examples of published research in books, magazine and newspaper articles, and on the Internet, among other places. On the following pages you will find research information from a science textbook. The authors of this selection began with a simple question: How does the human body protect itself? You will notice as you read "The Body's Defenses" that the authors found more than one answer to that question.

As you read, create a **think sheet,** by noting important passages and recording connections you make to your own knowledge and experience. Also, jot down on your think sheet any questions you may have, and answer the analysis questions that appear next to the model.

DO THIS

Reference Note

For more on **think sheets,** see page 529.

Writing 2.3 Write research reports.

from **SciencePlus**

THE BODY'S DEFENSES

The boy in the photo to the right has spent his entire life inside a plastic bubble. He is not allowed to touch anyone, not even his mother or father, because he was born with no natural defense against infectious diseases. As a result, even a simple cold could endanger his life. Fortunately, most of us have a defense system that automatically fights off most of the bacteria and viruses that could harm us. This system consists of several lines of defense.

1. Which sentence in this paragraph indicates the main idea of this selection?

The First Line of Defense
Skin and Mucus

Under normal conditions, the skin stops microorganisms from entering the body. However, when the skin is broken, cut, or damaged, germs can enter. That is why it is very important to clean cuts and scrapes. But skin does not cover every surface of the body.

2. What role does skin play in your body's defense system?

Mucus stops germs from attacking tissue not covered by the skin. For example, the inside of the nose is covered by tiny hairs and mucus. These hairs and mucus trap dust and germs from the air you breathe.

Sometimes extra mucus is made by the body in response to the presence of foreign substances such as dust, pollen, or germs. . . . Blowing your nose and sneezing help remove trapped microorganisms. It is important to cover your mouth and nose when you sneeze to prevent the spread of these microorganisms. . . .

3. What precise words are used in this paragraph to explain clearly the function of mucus?

4. What is your body doing when you sneeze?

Mucus: A thick, sticky fluid covering many surfaces inside the body and its natural openings.

The Second Line of Defense
White Blood Cells

What happens if you cut your skin and germs enter the cut? Then your second line of defense, the *white blood cells,* becomes active.

White blood cells are one part of your blood. They are made inside some of your bones. Many of them are found in structures called lymph nodes and in the tonsils.

It is believed that damaged tissue, such as a cut, and invading germs both release chemicals. These chemicals attract white blood cells. At the same time, the area around the cut becomes warm and appears red, indicating that the cut has become infected.

White blood cells surround and destroy germs and damaged tissue. This action is similar to the way that an amoeba surrounds its food. The activity of white blood cells stops infection and cleans the area so that proper healing can take place.

5. List in your own words the most important details in this paragraph.

White blood cells, like the one shown here, are the body's second line of defense.

The Third Line of Defense
The Immune System

. . . Some kinds of white blood cells make special chemicals called **antibodies.** Antibodies help in the destruction of microorganisms and other foreign substances. Your body is capable of producing antibodies for just about every kind of germ or foreign substance that exists on earth.

The production of antibodies is a relatively quick process. A few days after an invader has entered the body, a large number of antibodies can usually be found in the blood. This process of antibody production is a function of the **immune system,** the body's third line of defense.

6. Explain the sequence of events by which the immune system develops resistance to a disease. What words or phrases give you clues to the sequence?

Soon after a disease is successfully stopped, the level of the antibody that fought against it drops. For example, a person who has recovered from chickenpox will have only a small amount of chickenpox antibody left in his or her bloodstream. But a few of the white blood cells that made the chickenpox antibody remain in the bloodstream to fight the chickenpox virus if it returns. These white blood cells "remember"

Antibodies: Chemicals that are made by the body and that fight germs or other foreign substances.

Immune system: Body system that uses antibodies to seek out and destroy invading microorganisms.

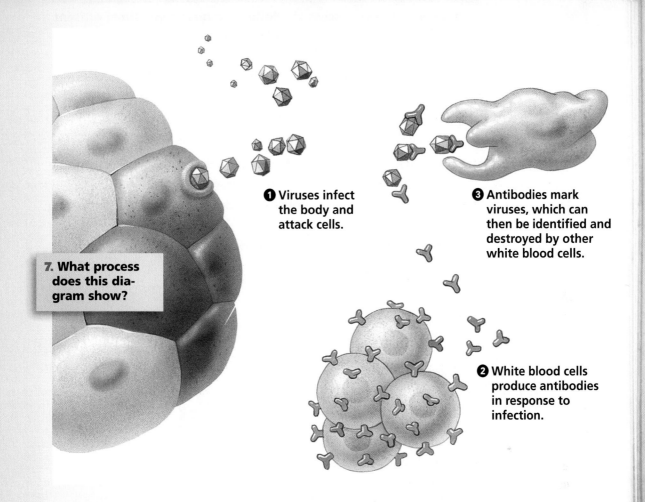

❶ Viruses infect the body and attack cells.

❸ Antibodies mark viruses, which can then be identified and destroyed by other white blood cells.

7. What process does this diagram show?

❷ White blood cells produce antibodies in response to infection.

how to make the antibody for chickenpox. If the virus that causes chickenpox enters the body again, these cells will make a lot of new antibodies in a very short time. They will eliminate the virus before it can do any damage and before you become ill. That is why a person usually gets diseases like measles, mumps, whooping cough, scarlet fever, and chickenpox only once. This resistance to a disease is called **acquired immunity**. Acquired immunity to some diseases lasts a lifetime.

8. Why is "acquired immunity" in color?

Acquired immunity: Resistance to reinfection by a disease after the body has recovered from the original infection.

Reference Note

For more information on **summarizing,** see page 530.

Prewriting

Choose and Focus a Subject

I Wonder . . . What will you write about in your research report? If you have ever said, "I wonder," about something, that something might be a good subject for research. After all, the best subject for a research report is one that really interests you.

You may already know what you want to research. However, if you still need a subject, try one of the following ideas and see if you become inspired.

- Thumb through an informative magazine to get ideas. Scientific discoveries and historical events make good research subjects.

- Think about your favorite class. Then, list the subjects from this class that you like. Choose one of these subjects to explore.

The notes on the following page show how one student developed ideas and identified a subject for a research report.

Writing **1.0** Students progress through the stages of the writing process as needed. **1.4** Identify topics and develop ideas leading to inquiry, investigation, and research.

Favorite classes: (science,) math, history, English

I like when we talk about (animals,) volcanoes, and inventions.

Animals that interest me: elephants, wolves, tigers, (eagles)

Get Focused   From avalanches to zebras, you can choose almost anything for a subject. However, unless you plan on pitching a tent and living in the library for the next year or two, **you should limit your subject. You can do this by focusing on something specific.** For example, instead of writing everything on the subject of zebras, you could limit your report to the **topic** of how zebras raise their young.

KEY CONCEPT

Begin focusing your subject by making a **conceptual map.** Draw an oval in the center of a piece of paper and fill in your subject. As you think of specific topics, write them in connecting ovals.

bald eagles as endangered animals

how they raise their young

types of eagles

Subject: Eagles

nesting habits

how they hunt

physical features

TIP   Once you start researching, you may not be able to find enough information on your specific topic to write a 500- to 700-word report. If so, you might have focused your subject too narrowly. Talk to your teacher about getting the best focus.

PRACTICE & APPLY 1   **Choose and Focus a Subject**

Choose a subject and focus it by making a map like the one above. Then, choose the specific topic that is most interesting to you.

Think About Purpose and Audience

What's My Motivation?   Every time you write, you should remind yourself why you are writing. **The purpose of a research report is to find information on a specific topic and share your perspective on it with other people.** Who are those people? Your

KEY CONCEPT

Writing   **1.0** Students write focused essays. The writing exhibits students' awareness of the audience and purpose.   **2.0** Write expository texts of at least 500 to 700 words.

audience will probably include your teacher and classmates, but anyone who is interested in your topic could be your audience. Ask yourself the following questions about the audience you identify.

CONSIDERING YOUR AUDIENCE	
Question	**Explanation**
What do my readers already know about my topic?	If you repeat information that your readers already know, they might become bored with your report.
What do my readers need to know about my topic?	Give your readers enough information to understand your topic by thoroughly explaining important ideas.
What can they do with the information?	Explain why the information is important for readers to know.

Ask Questions

What Do You Know? To think about the information you need for your report, start with what you already know about your topic. Use a graphic organizer, or make a list like the one below.

- There are fewer bald eagles now than there used to be.
- I know that there are laws to protect other animals.
- I think bald eagles used to be hunted.

What Do You Need to Know? After brainstorming what you already know about your topic, make a list of the questions you still have. **These questions will guide your research later.** Also, write down **relevant** questions—questions closely related to your topic—that your audience might have. Start with the *5W-How?* questions: *Who? What? Where? When? Why?* and *How?*

| KEY CONCEPT

TIP Your list of research questions may change as you do your research. As more questions occur to you, add them to your list.

Who is trying to help endangered eagles?

What are they doing to help endangered eagles?

Where are bald eagles most endangered?

When did bald eagles first become endangered?

Why are they endangered?

How many bald eagles are living today?

Writing 2.3a Pose relevant and tightly drawn questions about the topic.

Why Do You Ask? After making a list of questions, take a few minutes to **evaluate,** or judge, each question. Eliminating unsuitable questions now will save you time and energy later. To evaluate your research questions, ask yourself these questions.

- **Does this question serve my purpose—to inform?** Steer clear of questions that are aimed inward, toward your feelings or your opinions. Your feelings and opinions are important, but they are out of place in a research report.

- **Will this question lead to information that will interest my audience?** You do not want to bore your readers with information they already know or to confuse them with information that they do not need to understand your topic.

PRACTICE & APPLY 2 **Think About Purpose and Audience, and Ask Questions**

- Think about your purpose and audience. Answer the questions in the chart on page 632 to identify your audience's needs.

- List what you already know about your topic. Then, write a list of questions that you still have or that your audience might have.

- Evaluate each question on your list and eliminate unsuitable research questions.

Find Sources

Get the Facts! Start finding answers to your questions by researching sources. A source gives you information about your topic. Where can you find sources?

The Library The library is a great resource for **print sources,** such as books, encyclopedias, magazines, and newspapers. It is also a resource for **nonprint sources,** such as videotapes and audiotapes, CD-ROM encyclopedias and dictionaries, electronic databases, and the Internet. To begin your research, use the following items.

- **Card catalog** In many libraries the card catalog is a set of drawers with note cards listing the library's collection. For each work, the catalog contains a **title card** and an **author card.** For nonfiction works, **subject cards** will tell you where to look for more information on particular subjects. Some libraries also have **online** versions of their card catalogs. Online card catalogs usually let you

Reference Note
For information on **evaluating sources,** see page 636.

Writing 1.4 Ask and evaluate questions. **2.0** The writing demonstrates the research strategies outlined in Writing Standard 1.0.

search by title, author, keyword, and subject. Your librarian can explain how to use this **database.**

- **Magazines and magazine indexes** To find articles on a specific subject in recent and past issues of magazines, use the *Readers' Guide to Periodical Literature,* an alphabetical index organized by both subject and author. For listings of current magazine articles, use an online database.

- **Newspapers and newspaper indexes** Your school or community library may also carry current and past issues of local, state, and national newspapers. Look in the *National Newspaper Index,* an index of useful newspaper articles from major U.S. newspapers.

- **Dictionaries** An important source of information about vocabulary or specialized terms is the dictionary. Usually libraries contain abridged (condensed) and unabridged English dictionaries, foreign-language dictionaries, and specialized dictionaries, such as dictionaries of terms used in geography, medicine, and art.

The Web The World Wide Web is a resource for information on almost any subject. Web pages can serve many different purposes, such as to persuade and to inform. If you use a Web site, be sure it is a **reliable,** or trustworthy, source of information. A reliable Web site should include information on the author's professional background, when the site was last updated, and a list of the sources the author used.

Other Resources Check for informative documentaries, biographies, and science and nature programs on TV or video. You might also try interviewing experts from a local museum, university, or government office. Interview experts in person or by phone, mail, or e-mail. Prepare a list of questions in advance, and take notes on the answers you receive.

Make a Source List

Hey, Where Did You Get That?   After you find sources likely to be helpful for your report, you need to make a *source list.* A **source list** is a sheet of paper on which you identify all of the sources you may use for your report. There are several different styles for listing sources. The chart on the next page shows the style the Modern Language Association recommends for listing sources.

Writing 2.3c Include evidence compiled through the formal research process (e.g., use of a card catalog, *Readers' Guide to Periodical Literature,* a computer catalog, magazines, newspapers, dictionaries).

Book	Author/editor. <u>Title</u>. City (and state, if city is unfamiliar): Publisher, year.
	Grambo, Rebecca L., ed. <u>Eagles: Masters of the Sky</u>. Stillwater, OK: Voyageur Press, 1997.
Electronic Sources	**Online:** Author (if known). "Document Title." <u>Web Site or Database Title</u>. Date of electronic publication. Name of Sponsoring Institution. Date information was accessed \<url\>.
	Martell, Mark, and MaryBeth Garrigan. "Bald Eagle." <u>The Raptor Center</u>. Sept. 1994. U of Minnesota. 18 Nov. 2003 \<http://www.raptor.cvm.umn.edu/\>.
	CD-ROM: Author (if known). "Title of Article." <u>Title of Database</u>. Title of Medium (CD-ROM). City of Electronic Publication: Electronic Publisher, Date of electronic publication.
	"Eagle." <u>2001 Grolier Multimedia Encyclopedia</u>. CD-ROM. Danbury: Grolier Interactive, 2001.
Encyclopedia Article	Author (if known). "Title of Article." <u>Name of Encyclopedia</u>. Edition (if known) and year.
	Grier, James W. "Eagle." <u>The World Book Encyclopedia</u>. 1998.
Interview	Speaker. The words *Personal interview, Telephone interview,* or *Guest speaker.* Date.
	Sullivan, Vanessa. Personal interview. 17 Nov. 2003.
Magazine or Newspaper Article	Author. "Title of Article." <u>Publication Name</u> Date: page number(s).
	Gerstenzang, James. "Eagle May Fly from Nest of Endangered." <u>Los Angeles Times</u> 6 May 1998: A1.
Movie or Video Recording	<u>Title</u>. Name of Director or Producer. Name of Distributor, year released.
	<u>Amazing Birds of Prey</u>. Dir. Ann Neale. DK Vision, 1997.
Television or Radio Program	<u>Title of Program</u>. Name of Host (if any). Network. Station Call Letters, City. Date of broadcast.
	<u>The Amazing Eagle</u>. Discovery Channel. DISC, Austin. 26 Nov. 2003.

PRACTICE & APPLY 3

Find Sources, and Make a Source List

Find at least three different types of sources for your research report. Then, make a source list, and number each source on your list. You will need these numbers when you take notes.

Writing 1.5 Give credit for both quoted and paraphrased information in a bibliography by using a consistent and sanctioned format and methodology for citations. 2.3d Document reference sources by means of a bibliography.

Evaluating Sources

Newspapers, magazines, books, the Internet, and television shower us with information every day. Unfortunately, not all of the information available is reliable. Use the following guidelines to evaluate the sources you find.

- **Identify the writer or creator of the source.** Look for information on the writer's qualifications. In general, the more experience and education a writer has on the subject, the more reliable he or she will be. Also, sources that are endorsed by reputable nonprofit or educational organizations are generally reliable.

  Preferred source: *a book on endangered animals by an environmental scientist*

  Less reliable source: *a Web page created by a nine-year-old as a class project*

- **Locate the date the information was published.** Although older sources can be helpful for historical topics, up-to-date information is usually best for a report, especially one on a scientific topic.

- **Identify the purpose of the source.** Some books and articles are written to inform and do not include many of the author's opinions or feelings. If a source includes many opinions and few facts, don't use it as a main source.

  Preferred source: *a newspaper article citing statistics on endangered animals*

  Less reliable source: *a fund-raising brochure describing the plight of a certain species*

- **Look for different perspectives.** Sources sometimes present their findings in different ways. For example, one source may include material that another does not. Two sources may also have opposite viewpoints. Include a variety of perspectives so that your report is complete and accurate.

  Preferred sources: *two magazine articles that have opposite perspectives on the value of gray wolves for the environment*

  Less valuable sources: *two television programs with similar information about gray wolves as harmful predators*

PRACTICE

Below are several descriptions of sources for a research paper on the moon. Identify each description as either a **preferred** source or a **less reliable** source. Then, rank the preferred sources to identify which you would consult first. Be prepared to defend your answers.

1. a book published in 1910 on the geography of the moon

2. a NASA Web page on moon rocks

3. a 1999 edition encyclopedia article on geographical formations on the moon

4. a report on the moon published on the Web by a high school student

5. a 2002 edition CD-ROM encyclopedia article on geographical formations on the moon

Writing 2.3b Convey clear and accurate perspectives on the subject.

Take Notes

What Are You Looking For? As you read, view, and listen to your sources, search for **evidence,** information that answers the research questions you listed in Practice and Apply 2. Look for these kinds of evidence (examples are provided).

- **Anecdotes** are brief stories that illustrate a point. *Charles Broley, a volunteer eagle watcher, documented the decline of eagles in Florida. His experience in counting eagles over the years led him to suspect that adult eagles were not able to raise babies.*

- **Descriptions** create a mental picture of a person, animal, scene, or object by giving details and appealing to readers' senses. *Eagles that consumed DDT laid thin-shelled eggs that broke when the parent sat on them.*

- **Examples** are specific instances or illustrations of a general idea. *Laws, such as the Bald Eagle Protection Act, have helped protect the bald eagle.*

- **Facts** are statements that can be proven true. *The bald eagle has served as a symbol of the United States since 1782.* A **statistic** is information in the form of numbers. *Less than 10,000 nesting pairs of bald eagles lived in the continental United States in the 1950s.*

Unforgettable So many facts and ideas can be hard to remember. To remember the evidence you find while researching, you should write it down.

Use note cards, sheets of paper, or computer files to record your notes. Here are some suggestions for taking notes.

- Write each research question on the top line of each card, sheet of paper, or computer file to identify the subject of the note.

- **Summarize** information, using your own words. If you do write an author's exact words, use quotation marks. Using an author's words or ideas without giving credit is called *plagiarism.* **Plagiarism** is a form of cheating and can result in disciplinary action.

- Write the source number you are using in the top right corner of your card, file, or piece of paper. For example, if you are using source five from your source list, write "5" in the top right corner.

- Write the number of the page where you found the information at the bottom of your card, file, or piece of paper.

TIP Sometimes a quotation from a writer or speaker lends interest and believability to your report. Including a source's job or position title, if relevant to the topic, often adds credibility to his or her opinions.

Example:
In an interview, then Secretary of the Interior Babbitt said, "The eagle is doing splendidly. It's making a wonderful comeback everywhere."

Writing **1.0** Essays contain supporting evidence. **1.2** Support all statements and claims with anecdotes, descriptions, facts and statistics, and specific examples. **1.3** Use strategies of notetaking and summarizing to impose structure on composition drafts. **2.3c** Include evidence compiled through the formal research process.

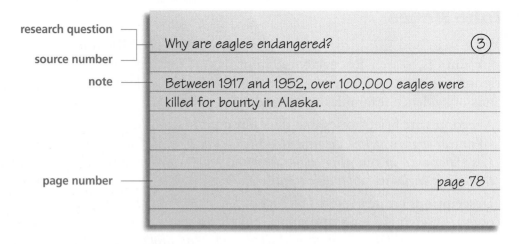

research question — Why are eagles endangered?   ③

source number —

note — Between 1917 and 1952, over 100,000 eagles were killed for bounty in Alaska.

page number — page 78

PRACTICE & APPLY 4   ## Take Notes

Read your sources to find answers to your research questions. Take notes when you find useful information. Refer to the suggestions for taking notes on page 637, if necessary.

Plan Your Report

Get It Together   Making an early plan and an outline can help you make sure none of the information you gathered falls through the cracks.

Early Plan   First, group notes that answer the same question. Then, change each question to a **heading**—a word or phrase that describes the information in that set. **The headings for your groups are the main ideas of your report.** Here is a list of headings for a student's report on bald eagles. Notice that each of her headings represents a single idea. In what order would you discuss the following headings?

| KEY CONCEPT

- General facts about endangered eagles
- Reasons eagles were endangered
- Eagles' recovery
- Ways eagles were helped

   Writing 1.3 Use strategies of outlining to impose structure on composition drafts.

Make an Early Plan

> Sort your notes into sets and give each set a heading. Then, decide
> the order in which you will discuss each heading in your report.

Mapping It Out Before you begin writing your report, you should
make an *outline* using the headings you created for your early plan.
Making an **outline** can give your report **coherence,** or connectedness, by helping you organize the ideas in the report in a way that
makes sense. Study the following excerpt from a student's outline.
Notice that she listed related details beneath her heading.

> **TIP** Look at the
> professional model on
> pages 627–629 for ideas
> on how to divide your
> topic into subtopics and
> organize those subtopics
> using subheadings.

II. Reasons eagles were endangered
  A. Hunters
  B. Demand for lumber and land
  C. Pesticides

The main heading in the example above is "Reasons eagles were
endangered." The specific causes for their low numbers are underneath the heading. These are called **subheadings.**

> **TIP** When making your outline, you may notice that some of your subhead-
> ings can be grouped together. If this happens, think of a word or phrase that
> describes these subheadings. This word or phrase will become your new sub-
> heading. Compare Roman numeral two in the example above with the Roman
> numeral two in the outline on the next page.

To make your own outline, use the following steps. If you have
trouble, study the partial outline on the next page.

- Write your main headings on a sheet of paper in the order you
  want to discuss them. Label each heading with a Roman numeral.
- Under each main heading, write subheadings. Label each subheading with a capital letter. Number each detail that explains a
  subheading.
- Your outline should have at least three Roman numeral headings
  with two subheadings each.

Writing **1.0** Students write clear and coherent essays. **1.1** Create an organizational structure that balances all aspects of the composition. **1.3** Use strategies of outlining to impose structure on composition
drafts.

I. General facts about endangered eagles
   A. Drop in numbers in the 1940s and '50s
   B. Enormous decline in 1960s

II. Reasons eagles were endangered
   A. Hunters
      1. Belief that eagles were destroying crops and livestock
      2. Bounties that encouraged hunting
   B. Demand for lumber and land
      1. Lumber mills
      2. New homes and businesses
   C. Pesticides
      1. Effect on eagles' food
      2. Effect on offspring

III. Ways eagles were helped
   A. Laws
      1. 1940—the Bald Eagle Protection Act
      2. 1972—banning of DDT
      3. 1973—the Endangered Species Protection Act
   B. Scientists

TIP Since the Roman numerals from your outline will be the main sections of your report, you might want to include these headings in your final draft. Providing a clear heading before each major part of your report can help the reader understand the organization of your report.

A Wide-Angle Lens As you review your outline, keep in mind that your aim is to help your readers gain a clear and accurate understanding of your topic. Check to see that your outline reflects a variety of **perspectives,** or points of view on the topic.

In section II of the outline above, the student lists three different reasons that eagles were endangered. To create the outline, she gathered information from three sources. Only one source, however, mentioned that Alaska at one time paid bounties on slaughtered eagles. If the student had not read and included this perspective, she would not have been able to present a fully accurate explanation of why eagles became endangered.

 PRACTICE & APPLY **6**   **Outline Your Report**

> Create an outline for your report based on your notes and on the headings you created in Practice and Apply 5. For help, refer to the example outline above and the instructions on pages 639–640.

 Writing 2.3b Convey clear and accurate perspectives on the subject.

Write Your Main Idea Statement

What's the Big Idea?   Now that you have done your research and taken notes, you are ready to write a main idea statement about your specific topic. **The main idea statement, also known as a *thesis statement,* appears in the introduction of your report and tells what you will say about your topic.** A good main idea statement serves as an umbrella for the main headings from your outline.

Focused Topic: Eagles as Endangered Animals

Headings from outline:

I. General facts about endangered eagles

II. Reasons eagles were endangered

III. Ways eagles were helped

IV. Eagles' recovery

Main idea statement: Although people almost caused bald eagles to become extinct by the 1960s, the efforts of many have since helped them make an amazing comeback.

Your main idea statement should tell readers what your report will be about. From the main idea statement above, the reader could guess that the report would cover eagles as endangered animals, the reasons eagles were once endangered, and how people helped them to recover.

Once you have developed a main idea statement, think about how you might use the rest of your report's introduction to lead up to that statement. In most cases the main idea statement will come at the end of the introduction.

> **PRACTICE & APPLY 7** ## Write Your Main Idea Statement
>
> Use the example above to help you write your main idea statement. Remember that this statement should serve as an umbrella for the Roman numeral headings of your outline.

Writing 1.0 Essays contain formal introductions.

Writing

A Writer's Framework

Research Report

Introduction

- Attention-grabbing beginning
- Main idea statement

To catch the reader's interest, start with an **attention-grabber,** or hook, such as an interesting fact, quotation, or question. Then, state the **main idea,** or **thesis,** of your paper. (For more on **writing introductions,** see page 690.)

Body

- Heading #1
  Supporting details
- Heading #2
  Supporting details
  and so on

- Use your outline and notes to write the body of your report. In general, each paragraph should address one heading or subheading from your outline. Connect ideas between sentences with **transitions,** such as *first, therefore, however, in addition,* and *since.* (For a list of transitions, see page 688.)

- Provide **supporting evidence** for the main point in each paragraph by including relevant details (facts, examples, and statistics) from your research. Elaborate on each detail by asking yourself, "Why is this detail important?" or "What does this detail mean?"

Conclusion

- Restatement of main idea

In your conclusion, sum up the ideas in your report. **Restate your main idea** and bring your report to a close. (For more on **writing conclusions,** see page 690.)

Works Cited

- List of sources used

End with a list of the works you used, in alphabetical order by the author's last name. If there is no author for a source, alphabetize by the first word in the title. If you use only print sources, your teacher may ask you to title your list "Bibliography" rather than "Works Cited." (For more on **documenting reference sources,** see page 697.)

Writing **1.0** Essays contain formal introductions, supporting evidence, and conclusions. **1.1** Create an organizational structure that balances all aspects of the composition and uses effective transitions between sentences to unify important ideas. **1.5** Give credit for both quoted and paraphrased information in a bibilography. **2.3d** Document reference sources by means of a bibliography.

The final draft below closely follows the framework for a research report on the previous page and the MLA guidelines for research report format.

Flying High—Again

You see its picture every time you look at a dollar bill. You even see it when the letter carrier delivers your mail. The bald eagle has symbolized the United States since 1782. Not long ago, though, the bald eagle seemed headed for extinction. Although people almost caused bald eagles to become extinct by the 1960s, the efforts of many have since helped them make an amazing comeback.

People were noticing a decline in bald eagle populations as early as the mid-nineteenth century (Tucker 65). However, it wasn't until the late 1930s and early 1940s that the threat of extinction became very real and obvious. Charles Broley, a volunteer eagle watcher, documented the decline of eagles in Florida. In 1939, Broley counted 150 eaglets, or baby eagles. In 1952, he counted only 15 eaglets in the same area. Broley thought something, possibly pesticides, was keeping adult birds from raising babies (Grambo 82).

INTRODUCTION
Attention-grabbing beginning

Main idea statement

BODY
Heading #1:
General facts about eagles

GO TO: go.hrw.com
KEYWORD:
HLLA7 W-4
FOR: A Student Model

(continued)

(continued)

Broley was right. The National Foundation to Protect America's Eagles estimated that less than 10,000 nesting pairs of eagles lived in the continental United States in the 1950s. Then, in the 1960s, the number of eagles fell to fewer than 500 pairs. Eagles moved closer to extinction every day (Bald).

Many things caused the decline of the bald eagle. One of the most obvious was hunting. Farmers once thought of eagles as pests. They believed that bald eagles harmed livestock and crops (Tucker 58). To decrease its number of eagles, the territory of Alaska (before Alaska became a state) paid a bounty for every eagle that was shot. It is estimated that more than 100,000 bald eagles were shot while this policy was in effect between 1917 and 1953 (Grambo 76–78).

The demand for lumber and land also hurt eagles. When America was first being settled, it had over a billion acres of forest land where eagles and other animals could make their homes. However, as lumber mills cut more and more trees, eagles lost their forest homes. Eagles also suffered as people built houses, roads, and businesses in the birds' nesting

Statistic

Heading #2: Reasons eagles were endangered

Fact

Statistic

areas. As early as 1930, much of America's forest land was becoming unsuitable for many animals (Tucker 62–69).

However, the major cause of the eagles' endangerment was the use of pesticides such as DDT. Farmers used pesticides to kill unwanted insects and plants. Sadly, other animals and plants also absorbed the poisons. When bald eagles ate the poisoned animals, they became poisoned too. Eagles that consumed DDT laid thin-shelled eggs that broke easily when the parent sat on them (Dudley 54–55).

Description

Fortunately, lawmakers realized that eagles could become extinct. In 1940, Congress passed a law to protect bald eagles: the Bald Eagle Protection Act. Under this act, people who killed eagles could be punished by a fine and time in jail (Tucker 69). This act was a good beginning, but alone it was not enough to halt the danger to the eagles. Protection of habitat and restrictions on harmful pesticides were also needed. The bald eagle was helped further by the Endangered Species Act of 1973. Under this act, the government protected millions of acres where bald eagles could live without being threatened

Heading #3:
Ways eagles
were helped
Example

Example

Fact

(continued)

(continued)

by hunting or construction. The passage of these laws, along with the banning of the pesticide DDT in 1972, provided much-needed protection for the bald eagle (Bald).

Scientists also helped bald eagles. To help increase the number of mature eagles, scientists developed a captive breeding program. In this program, injured eagles that could not survive in the wild laid eggs in a laboratory. After hatching, the eaglets were returned to the wild. Captive breeding successfully increased the number of bald eagles (Tucker 85).

**Heading #4:
Eagles' recovery**

With the help of many people all over the United States, eagles are slowly recovering. From a low point of fewer than 500 nesting pairs in the 1960s, the numbers have grown to an estimated 4,500 nesting pairs in the continental United States. If you count eaglets and young adults, there are about 55,000 bald eagles in the United States today (Bald). In 1998, Secretary of the Interior Bruce Babbitt took steps to remove the bald eagle from the endangered species list. In an interview, Babbitt said, "The eagle is doing splendidly. It's making a wonderful comeback everywhere" (qtd. in Gerstenzang).

The bald eagle is not completely out of danger yet, but its future looks better every day. If eagles keep making a comeback, our national symbol should be around for a long time to come.

Works Cited

Bald Eagle: The U.S.A.'s National Symbol. 1997. American Eagle Foundation. 16 Nov. 2003 <http://www.eagles.org/moreabout.html>.

Dudley, Karen. Bald Eagles. Austin: Raintree Steck-Vaughn, 1998.

Gerstenzang, James. "Eagle May Fly from Nest of Endangered." Los Angeles Times 6 May 1998: A1.

Grambo, Rebecca L., ed. Eagles: Masters of the Sky. Stillwater, OK: Voyageur Press, 1997.

Tucker, Priscilla. The Return of the Bald Eagle. Mechanicsburg, PA: Stackpole Books, 1994.

CONCLUSION
Restatement of main idea

TIP If your teacher asks you to show your sources in the body of your paper,
you can use **parenthetical citations** or **footnotes.** A parenthetical citation
includes the author's last name or, if no author is given, the source title followed
by the page number. This Writer's Model uses parenthetical citations.

PRACTICE & APPLY 8 ## Write Your Research Report

Write the first draft of your research report. Be sure to

- put information you gathered from sources into your own words
- write each paragraph using a separate heading or subheading
  from your outline
- support each paragraph with details, such as facts and statistics
- refer to the Writer's Model on pages 643–647 and framework on
  page 642

Writing **2.0** The writing demonstrates a command of the organizational and drafting strategies outlined in Writing Standard 1.0.   **2.3** Write research reports.   **2.3d** Document reference sources by means
of footnotes and a bibliography.

Evaluate and Revise Content, Organization, and Style

Double-Check Whether you are evaluating a peer's paper or revising your own report, it is a good idea to read the paper twice. First, consider the content and the organization of the draft, using the guidelines below. Then, add sentence variety, using the Focus on Sentences on page 651.

First Reading: Content and Organization Use this chart to evaluate a peer's report or to evaluate and revise your own paper.

Research Report: Content and Organization Guidelines

Evaluation Questions	▶ Tips	▶ Revision Techniques
❶ Does the main idea statement cover all of the report's important ideas?	▶ **Match** each part of the main idea statement with a paragraph or section of the report.	▶ **Revise** the main idea statement so that it covers the important ideas of the report.
❷ Is the main point in each paragraph clear? Does all the information in the paragraph support that main point?	▶ **Write** each paragraph's main point in the paper's margin. **Write** *N* next to information that does not support the main point.	▶ If needed, **add** a sentence that states the main point. **Delete** or **rearrange** information that does not support the main point.
❸ Is the information in each paragraph properly summarized or quoted?	▶ **Circle** sentences that sound as if someone else wrote them. **Underline** information in quotation marks.	▶ **Revise** by summarizing information or adding quotation marks.
❹ Does the conclusion restate the report's main idea?	▶ **Put a check** next to the restatement of the main idea.	▶ **Add** a restatement of the report's main idea, if needed.
❺ Do transitions give the report coherence?	▶ **Highlight** transitional words and phrases.	▶ **Add** transitional words and phrases to paragraphs with fewer than two transitions to increase coherence.
❻ Does the report end with a list of sources in the correct form? Are there at least three different types of sources?	▶ **Count** the number of different types of sources on the list. **Check** the format and punctuation by referring to the guide on page 635.	▶ **Add** correct format and punctuation as needed. **Add** information from another reliable source to the report, if needed.

Writing 1.7 Revise writing to improve organization after checking the logic of the ideas.

ONE WRITER'S REVISIONS Study this revision of an early draft of the report on pages 643–647.

rearrange

add

To decrease its number of eagles, the territory of Alaska (before Alaska became a state) paid a bounty for every eagle that was shot. It is estimated that more than 100,000 bald eagles were shot while this policy was in effect between 1917 and 1953 (Grambo 76–78). Eagles also suffered as people built houses, roads, and businesses in the birds' nesting areas.

The demand for lumber and land also hurt eagles.
When America was first being settled, it had over a billion acres of forest land where eagles and other animals could make their homes. However, as lumber mills cut more and more trees, eagles lost their forest homes. As early as 1930, much of America's forest land was becoming unsuitable for many animals (Tucker 62–69).

PEER REVIEW

As you read your classmate's report, ask yourself these questions.

■ What part of the report is the best? Why?

■ What new information did I learn about the report's topic?

Responding to the Revision Process

1. Why do you think the writer moved a sentence from the first paragraph to the second paragraph?

2. Why do you think the writer added a new sentence to the second paragraph?

▶ **Second Reading: Style** One thing you can do to make sure your report flows smoothly is to vary how your sentences begin. Adding variety to your sentence beginnings can also help ensure that the reader will remain interested in what you are saying.

Style Guidelines

Evaluation Question	▶ Tip	▶ Revision Technique
Does the report contain a variety of sentence beginnings?	▶ **Draw a wavy line** under the first five words of each sentence.	▶ If several sentences begin the same way, **revise** one or more of these sentences by moving a phrase from the end to the beginning.

Varying Sentence Beginnings

To add variety to your writing, look for places where you can move a phrase from the end of the sentence to the beginning. When you move a phrase to the beginning of a sentence, you may need to add a comma after the phrase. The following chart gives some examples of ways to move phrases.

Original Sentence	Revision Strategy	Revised Sentence
People depended on candlelight *before the invention of the light bulb.*	Move the *prepositional phrase* to the beginning.	*Before the invention of the light bulb,* people depended on candlelight.
You need skill *to repair a watch.*	Move the *infinitive phrase* to the beginning.	*To repair a watch,* you need skill.

Reference Note

For more information and practice on **prepositional phrases** and **infinitive phrases**, see pages 90 and 103 in the *Holt Handbook.*

ONE WRITER'S REVISIONS

Scientists also helped bald eagles. Scientists developed a captive breeding program to help increase the number of mature eagles.

Responding to the Revision Process

How did the revision above affect the flow of the passage?

PRACTICE & APPLY 9

Evaluate and Revise Your Research Report

Use the guidelines on page 649 to revise the content and organization of your report. Next, add variety by using the Focus on Sentences above. Finally, consider feedback from your peers as you revise your report.

 Written and Oral English Language Conventions 1.2 Identify and use infinitives.

Publishing

Proofread Your Report

Get It Right Before you write your final draft, proofread your paper for mistakes in spelling, usage, and punctuation. Having a peer edit your report will help you find and correct errors that might distract your readers.

Grammar Link

Title Treatments

One important step in formatting the sources on your Works Cited list is the treatment of their titles. Adding italics, underlining, or quotation marks to a title lets your readers know what type of source you are citing. Here are two rules to follow when writing titles.

- **Titles of books, magazines, newspapers, encyclopedias, television or radio programs, and Web sites:** These titles are <u>underlined</u> if handwritten or typed on a typewriter and usually *italicized* if typed on a word processor.

EXAMPLE (Book):

Horton, Casey. <u>Eagles</u>. Tarrytown, N.Y.: Benchmark Books, 1996.

- **Titles of magazine, newspaper, or encyclopedia articles, and Web pages that are part of a larger Web site:** These titles are placed in quotation marks.

EXAMPLE (Newspaper article):

Gerstenzang, James. "Eagle May Fly from Nest of Endangered." <u>Los Angeles Times</u> 6 May 1998: A1.

PRACTICE

Rewrite the following titles on your own paper. Use underlining or quotation marks to punctuate the titles correctly.

Example:

1. The New York Times (newspaper)

1. *The New York Times*

1. Baseball's Favorite Heroes (book)
2. Watch Out for the Bird Lady (magazine article)
3. Ancient Egypt (Web site)
4. Mummies (Web page)
5. Fresh Air (radio program)
6. That's Amazing (television program)
7. World of Wonders (magazine)
8. Dreams: What They Are (encyclopedia article)
9. The Daily Press (newspaper)
10. Blue Whales (Web page)

Reference Note

For more information and practice on **punctuating titles,** see pages 320–327 in the *Holt Handbook.*

Writing 2.0 The writing demonstrates a command of standard American English.

Designing Your Writing

Text features If you have access to a word-processing program, you can use text features to help you create interesting, eye-catching reports.

    Fonts: Use a text font, such as Times or Palatino, for formal papers. Decorative fonts, such as *Mistral*, are often difficult to read.

    Size: For your report, make sure your print size is set at twelve points. Experiment with larger sizes for headings, if your teacher allows.

    Boldfacing: Boldface headings or subheadings if you choose to use them in your report. Boldfacing these features makes them stand out from the rest of your report.

TIP Your teacher might ask you to create a *title page* for your report. A **title page** tells your name, the title of the report, and the date. Your teacher may want you to include other information, too.

Publish Your Report

Spread the News Now is the time to teach others what you have learned. Here are some publishing ideas.

- Publish your report on a personal or school Web page.
- Turn your report into an illustrated book for children.
- Send your report to a teacher with an interest in your topic.

Reflect on Your Report

Building Your Portfolio Think back on the process of researching and writing your report. Reflect on what you wrote and how you wrote it by answering the questions below.

- What information did you not include in your paper? Why? What information was the most difficult to find?
- What research techniques would you use again?

PRACTICE & APPLY 10   **Proofread, Publish, and Reflect on Your Report**

- Correct grammar, usage, and mechanics errors.
- Publish your report for your target audience.
- Answer the Reflect on Your Report questions above. Record your responses, and include them in your portfolio.

Writing 1.6 Create documents using word-processing skills.

Talk Listen

WHAT'S AHEAD?

In this workshop you will give and listen to an informative speech. You will also learn how to

- plan content and organization to fit your audience and purpose
- create note cards for effective speaking
- use audiovisual materials as part of a presentation
- respond appropriately to a speech

Reference Note

For more on **choosing and focusing a topic,** see pages 630–631.

Giving and Listening to an Informative Speech

A hush falls over the crowd as you approach the podium and everyone waits for you to begin. Delivering a speech can be a nerve-racking experience. If you prepare well, however, delivering a speech can also be fun. After all, when you give a speech, you are the center of attention. All eyes—and ears—are on *you*.

Give an Informative Speech

Use the guidelines in this section to plan and deliver an informative speech, either by adapting a written report or by exploring a topic new to you.

The Big Idea   To get ideas and information for planning your speech, follow these steps.

1. **Choose a focused topic.** You may want to speak about the topic of your written research report, or you might be ready to explore a different subject. Either way, make sure you **focus** your topic to keep your speech down to a manageable length. To focus your topic, ask yourself questions that are **relevant** (closely tied to the topic) and **concise** (brief and to the point).

2. **Think about your purpose and audience.** For this speech, your general purpose is to share information with listeners. You should also know your specific purpose—what you hope to achieve through speaking. Ask yourself, "What do I want my audience to gain from my speech?" Then, write a sentence that

Listening and Speaking 1.0 Deliver focused presentations that relate to the background and interests of the audience.   2.0 Students deliver well-organized formal presentations employing traditional rhetorical strategies (e.g., exposition).   2.3a Pose relevant and concise questions about the topic.

answers your question. For example, one student stated her purpose this way: "I want my audience to understand how people helped the endangered bald eagle recover." To make sure your listeners understand your purpose, plan to include a **thesis statement** at the beginning of your speech.

As you plan your speech, think about what your audience may already know about your topic and what they might wonder about it. Thinking carefully about your listeners' backgrounds and interests will help you decide how to catch and hold their attention throughout your presentation.

3. **Gather support.** You can search the library for printed information on your topic by looking in the card catalog, the *Readers' Guide to Periodical Literature,* magazines, newspapers, and dictionaries. At many libraries you will also find videotapes, audiotapes, slides, microfiches, CD-ROMs, and Internet access. Some libraries offer access to **databases,** collections of specific types of information.

Reference Note

For more on **using library resources,** see pages 633–634.

In order to give your audience a clear and accurate understanding of your topic, you will need to track down sources that offer a variety of **perspectives.** Take notes from your sources using the guidelines on pages 637–638, and note the source of each piece of information you find.

A Fine Organization   Once you have collected ideas about your topic, you need to organize them in a way that will appeal to your **audience** and help you achieve your **purpose.** As you organize your ideas, you should plan the types of information, including details, descriptions, and examples, that you will use in each section of your informative speech.

Introduction   Your introduction is the audience's first impression of you *and* your topic, so plan it carefully. It should be just a few sentences and should

- catch your listeners' interest
- focus attention on your topic
- make your listeners feel comfortable with you and your topic
- end with a thesis statement that makes your purpose clear

Listening and Speaking 1.4 Organize information to achieve particular purposes and to appeal to the background and interests of the audience.   **1.5** Arrange supporting details, descriptions, and examples effectively in relation to the audience.   **2.0** Students deliver well-organized presentations employing traditional rhetorical strategies (e.g., exposition).   **2.3b** Convey clear and accurate perspectives.

Quick guide!

As you plan your introduction, consider using one of the following methods. Notice that each example ends with a sentence that serves as the speaker's thesis statement.

TECHNIQUES FOR DEVELOPING INTRODUCTIONS

Technique	Student Example
Begin with a question.	What do a dollar bill and a letter carrier's car have in common? Both display the bald eagle, the symbol of the United States. Bald eagles almost became extinct in the 1960s. You can see a real eagle today, however, because many people have worked hard to help eagles make an amazing comeback.
Begin with a personal anecdote.	On a recent vacation, I visited an area where eagles often nest. I spotted a bald eagle swooping down and grabbing a fish out of the water with its talons. Fortunately, that sight is one people can still hope to see in person. Bald eagles almost became extinct in the 1960s, but thanks to the hard work of many people, eagles have made an amazing comeback since then.
Begin with a startling fact.	The bald eagle has symbolized the United States since 1782—seven years longer than our Constitution has been in effect. Yet in the 1960s this majestic national symbol almost became extinct. Fortunately, thanks to the hard work of many people, bald eagles have made an amazing comeback since then.

Reference Note

For information on **organizational structures,** see page 687.

Body To plan the body of your speech, you will need to choose an effective organizational structure and then create an outline. Thinking about your audience and your specific purpose will help you decide how to arrange the main ideas and support (details, descriptions, examples) in the body of your speech. For example, the student who wrote the report about bald eagles on pages 643–647 adapted her paper for a speech to a class of fourth-graders. She decided that her audience would better understand her ideas if she arranged them exclusively in chronological (time) order, rather than in categories.

Once you have chosen an organizational pattern that will help your audience understand your ideas, create an outline of your speech. If you are adapting a written report, revise the report outline to fit the audience and the time available.

Conclusion Like your introduction, your conclusion might be only a few sentences long. Those few sentences serve an important purpose—to re-emphasize your main idea in a memorable way. Your audience should recognize immediately that you are ending your speech, not adding to it. See the chart on the next page for two effective ways to conclude an informative speech.

Listening and Speaking 1.5 Arrange supporting details, descriptions, and examples effectively in relation to the audience. 2.0 Student speaking demonstrates the organizational and delivery strategies outlined in Listening and Speaking Standard 1.0. 2.3c Include evidence generated through the formal research process.

TECHNIQUES FOR WRITING CONCLUSIONS

Technique	Student Example
End with a summary of your findings.	Sadly, it was human factors—the need for lumber and land, the misunderstanding of the birds' role in nature, and the use of hazardous chemicals—that brought the bald eagle to the brink of extinction. Other human actions, such as enacting legislation and breeding programs, are now giving these great birds new hope.
End with an echo of your introduction.	The bald eagle is not completely out of danger yet, but its future looks brighter every day. If the eagles continue their comeback, future generations will see our national symbol as more than just a picture on a dollar bill or on a mail truck.

Hitting the Perfect Note   To turn your ideas and outline into an effective speech, create **note cards.** Speaking from note cards allows you to sound natural and make eye contact with your listeners. Review your revised outline and your research notes to decide what information you will include on your note cards. Number your note cards to make sure you present ideas in order. For a direct quotation, you can use the card you prepared as you took notes. Your other note cards should contain single words or phrases set up in outline form, like the sample note card below.

2

Up to 1950s

Loss of much forest by 1930 (lumber)

Bounty in Alaska for shooting eagles 1917–1953

Despite 1940 B.E. Protection Act, still harmed by pesticides

Broley—decline in eaglets 1939–1950

Crediting Sources   Just as you listed your sources of information in your written research report, you will also need to give your sources

Listening and Speaking **1.4** Organize information to achieve particular purposes and to appeal to the background and interests of the audience.   **2.0** Students deliver well-organized formal presentations employing traditional rhetorical strategies (e.g., exposition).   **2.3b** Convey clear and accurate perspectives on the subject.   **2.3d** Cite reference sources appropriately.

credit in your speech. When you back up your comments with source material, your speech becomes more believable to your audience. Crediting sources also lets your audience know that you have included more than one perspective on your topic. You should credit each source by mentioning its author, title, or both.

According to the National Foundation to Protect America's Eagles, there are now about 55,000 bald eagles in the United States.

As Secretary of the Interior Bruce Babbitt said in an interview published in the <u>Los Angeles Times</u>, "The eagle is doing splendidly."

In her book <u>Bald Eagles</u>, Karen Dudley explains that eagles that ate DDT laid thin-shelled eggs that broke easily.

TIP When you choose the words you will use in your speech, be sure to use only **standard American English,** the kind of English you hear spoken in newscasts. For example, do not use contractions or slang.

Get It Together Even with note cards to remind you of information to include and sources to credit, your speech content will need one more ingredient: **coherence.** Your speech will have coherence when listeners can tell how and why ideas are connected. Use **transitional words** and **phrases** to connect ideas. Transitions can compare and contrast ideas, show cause and effect, show time, show place, and show support. (For more on **transitions,** see page 687.)

Stand and Deliver Using your note cards, practice your speech until you can get through it comfortably without stopping. Try rehearsing in front of a few friends or family members. As you practice, pay attention to the way you use your hands, your eyes, and your voice. Use natural gestures, and make **eye contact** with your listeners. Practice using these **speaking techniques** effectively.

Reference Note

For more on **speaking techniques,** see page 619.

- **enunciation**—speak clearly and carefully
- **tempo**—talk at a slower **rate** than you would normally
- **voice modulation**—stay calm to control your **pitch**
- **inflection**—stress, or **emphasize,** important words and phrases

Consider including **audiovisual materials,** such as *charts, graphs, illustrations,* and *audio* or *video recordings,* in your speech. Audiovisual materials can make your ideas clearer and easier to remember for listeners or provide extra information in your speech.

Be sure that all materials can be heard and seen by all members of your audience. Always explain to your audience what the audiovisual material means, and continue to face the audience. Be sure to cue any audiotape or videotape before you speak to avoid wasting time rewinding or fast-forwarding during your speech.

Listening and Speaking 1.0 Deliver focused, coherent presentations that convey ideas clearly. **1.6** Use speaking techniques, including voice modulation, inflection, tempo, enunciation, and eye contact, for effective presentations. **2.0** Student speaking demonstrates a command of standard American English.

Prepare an original speech, or adapt your research report, using the suggestions on pages 654–658. Then, practice your speech until you are completely comfortable with the material. If you plan to use audiovisual materials, be sure to include them in your practice sessions.

Listen to an Informative Speech

To get the most out of the informative speeches you hear, follow these guidelines.

Before the Speech

- **Determine your purpose.** Identify what you want to learn from the speech.
- **Make predictions.** Identify two or three points you expect the speaker to cover, once you know the title of the speech.

During the Speech

- **Determine the speaker's attitude toward the topic.** The speaker's word choice or tone of voice may reveal his or her **attitude,** or feelings about the topic. For example, does the speaker use mostly positive or negative terms to refer to the topic?

  Reference Note
  For more on **determining a speaker's attitude,** see page 621.

- **Listen for cues that signal main points,** such as changes in volume or tone of voice. Cues can also include transitional words and phrases such as *first, there are many reasons, most important,* and *in conclusion.* Noticing these cues will help you understand, interpret, and organize the information you hear.

- **Monitor your understanding.** Ask yourself whether you understand what is being said well enough to explain the ideas to someone else. If not, try creating a rough outline or cluster diagram of the main idea and important points in the speech as you hear them.

- **Summarize the main points of the speech.** As you listen, take notes by summarizing the speaker's message. When you summarize, you restate the speaker's main points and supporting details in your own words.

  Reference Note
  For more on **summarizing,** see page 530.

Listening and Speaking 1.2 Determine the speaker's attitude toward the subject.

After the Speech

- **Ask probing questions.** Ask the speaker to clarify any points in the speech that you did not understand. If any points you expected to be covered were left out, ask the speaker to address them. Ask for specific evidence to support any unsupported claims and conclusions the speaker may have made. For example, following the speech about the bald eagle, a student might ask, "You said eagles became endangered in part because they lost some of their habitat, but now they're making a comeback. It seems like they would have even less habitat now, so how are the eagles dealing with that?"

- **Provide constructive feedback.** Be specific. Base your feedback on your responses to questions such as these.

FEEDBACK QUESTIONS

Content and Organization	Delivery
• Did the speech offer a variety of perspectives on the topic?	• How well could you hear the speaker from where you sat?
• How directly did the information support the speaker's main idea?	• How effectively did the speaker make eye contact with various audience members and use appropriate gestures?
• How logical was the order in which the ideas were presented?	• If audiovisual materials were part of the presentation, how clear and easy were they to understand?
• Did the speaker credit his or her sources?	

Overall: What impact did the speech have on you? What was your overall impression of the topic and the speaker?

Whenever possible, begin by complimenting specific things that you thought the speaker did well. When you ask questions or offer suggestions for improvement, be sure to phrase them politely.

> **PRACTICE & APPLY** 12 **Listen to an Informative Speech**
>
> Practice your listening skills when classmates present their speeches, and provide specific, constructive feedback on the content and organization, delivery, and overall impact of each presentation.

Listening and Speaking **1.0** Students evaluate the content of oral communication. **1.1** Ask probing questions to elicit information, including evidence to support the speaker's claims and conclusions. **1.7** Provide constructive feedback to speakers concerning the coherence and logic of a speech's content and delivery and its overall impact upon the listener.

DIRECTIONS: Read the following paragraph from a student's research report on mongooses. Then, read the questions below it. Choose the best answer for each item, and mark your answers on your own paper.

(1) Because of the popularity of Rudyard Kipling's "Rikki-tikki-tavi," mongooses are well known for attacking and killing poisonous snakes. (2) Not all mongooses attack snakes, and those who do are not, as some believe, immune to venom. (3) Instead, the mongoose uses its speed and agility to strike the snake's skull with its sharp teeth. (4) Mongooses are small, with short legs and long, furry tails. (5) Though fierce, mongooses can be tamed and are often kept as pets in countries, such as India, where poisonous snakes are a threat.

1. Which of the following research questions does this paragraph best answer?
   A   What do mongooses eat?
   B   Do mongooses really kill snakes, and if so, how?
   C   How do mongooses raise their young?
   D   Could I keep a mongoose as a pet?

2. If you were revising this paragraph to make it more coherent, which sentence might you delete or move to another paragraph?
   F   1
   G   3
   H   4
   J   5

3. Which of the following transitions might be added to the beginning of sentence 2 to show the relationship between the ideas in sentences 1 and 2?
   A   However,
   B   First,
   C   Consequently,
   D   In addition,

4. Which of the following research questions might help you find additional relevant information for a report on mongooses?
   F   In India, how serious a threat to humans are poisonous snakes?
   G   What other books did Rudyard Kipling write?
   H   Why is snake venom poisonous?
   J   What are the different varieties of mongooses?

5. If you were asked to give a presentation based on the paragraph above, which of the following visuals would best help you to share the information in the paragraph with your audience?
   A   a map of India
   B   an enlarged photograph of a mongoose striking a snake
   C   a drawing of a mongoose
   D   a chart showing mongoose populations in various regions

Writing to Learn

Although you usually write to show what you already know, you can also use writing to aid your own learning. For example, the act of writing something down may help you remember it better. When you make a list of supplies needed for your soccer team party, the act of writing will help you remember what to buy—even if you forget to bring the list to the store.

When you deal with several related ideas, writing can help you organize them in your mind. For instance, creating a Venn diagram could help you plan a comparison-contrast paper for school. Finally, writing can help you learn new information by connecting it to what you already know. If you read a book about basketball strategies, for example, you can more thoroughly understand those strategies by writing about how you saw them used in a televised game.

In this workshop you will learn how creating summaries, spreadsheets, and databases can help you learn. You will also learn how to use word-processing features to publish information. In the process you will practice the language arts standards below.

GO TO: go.hrw.com
KEYWORD: HLLA7 W-5
FOR: Models, Writer's Guides, and Reference Sources

California Standards

Writing

1.3 Use strategies of notetaking and summarizing to impose structure on composition drafts.

1.6 Create documents by using word-processing skills and publishing programs; develop simple databases and spreadsheets to manage information and prepare reports.

2.5 Write summaries of reading materials:

    a. Include the main ideas and most significant details.

    b. Use the student's own words, except for quotations.

    c. Reflect underlying meaning, not just the superficial details.

Learning Through Writing

The more information you need to manage, the more you will find it helpful to get your ideas down on paper (or into a computer). When you write to learn, you use writing strategies and tools to help you remember, organize, and understand information. Four ways you can learn more about nearly any subject are by writing summaries, creating databases, creating spreadsheets, and using word-processing skills and publishing features.

WHAT'S AHEAD?

In this workshop you will create a summary, a database, and a spreadsheet, and you will use word-processing skills and publishing features. You will also learn how to

■ reflect the underlying meaning of a reading selection

■ choose relevant fields for creating and sorting database records

Summaries

Sum It Up   When your friend asks you to "sum up" what a new movie is about, she wants you to tell her briefly the important information about that movie. In other words, your friend wants you to create a *summary*. A **summary** is a short restatement of the main idea and important details in a piece of writing or another work. Writing a summary can help you learn in the following three ways.

Summaries Help You Understand What You Read. When you write a summary, you rewrite the important information in a shorter form. Condensing the information in your own words helps you better understand the ideas in a selection. Here are two examples.

■ Creating a summary can help you better understand unfamiliar material or complex ideas, such as a complicated section of a science textbook.

■ Summarizing can also help you develop ideas for your own writing, such as when you summarize a short story about which you are writing a literary analysis.

Writing 2.5 Write summaries of reading materials.

Summaries Help You Organize Information Before You Write.
Writing a summary can help you plan a certain type of writing by giving you an organizational pattern to follow. For example, you might read and summarize a cause-and-effect article to help you plan the organization of your own cause-and-effect essay. Your summary might show you that the author of the article organized ideas using a cause-and-effect chain. You could then see how to organize your own ideas using a cause-and-effect chain.

Summaries Help You Review and Study Information. Sometimes the things we hear go "in one ear and out the other." Likewise, we may easily forget things we read. If you have a test coming up, writing a summary can help you study. For example, you could create a summary of a textbook chapter to help you review the important information in that chapter.

As Easy as 1, 2, 3 . . . To create a summary, use the following steps.

CREATING A SUMMARY

1. **Read the passage at least twice.** Reading the passage two times or more can help you better understand it.

2. **Identify the main idea and restate it in your own words.** The main idea is the most important idea in the passage. It may be directly stated, but if it is not, you can use these steps to identify the main idea.
   - Re-read the passage to identify its general topic.
   - Look at the details included to decide what point the author is making about the general topic.
   - Sum up the details in a statement that tells what the author's point is, and confirm the statement by re-reading the passage to make sure all details support the statement.

3. **Identify important details to include in the summary.** Not every detail you used to identify the main idea will be important enough to include in your summary. Use only the details from the passage that directly support the author's point, not information that elaborates on the support. After you have listed only the important details, combine related ideas on your list.

4. **Write the condensed information, in order and in your own words, in a paragraph.** Use the combined ideas on your list, and eliminate repeated words and phrases. Use transitions to show the connections between ideas. If you quote a sentence that expresses an idea particularly well, put the exact words in quotation marks and credit the writer.

Writing 1.3 Use strategies of summarizing to impose structure on composition drafts.   **2.5a** Include the main ideas and most significant details.   **2.5b** Use the student's own words, except for quotations.

What Do You Really Mean?   To summarize a passage effectively, you should identify its *underlying meaning*. The **underlying meaning** of a passage is its unstated message, point, or theme. You can determine this meaning by understanding the author's purpose for writing a piece and by recognizing his or her point of view about the topic. To identify the underlying meaning, consider the ideas, details, and words the author uses.

Use the following steps to identify the underlying meaning of this passage from "A Veto on Video Games," on page 599.

> I don't think that playing a video game now and then is really harmful to children. But the children I know are so obsessed with these games that they have prompted at least one second-grade teacher (my son's) to ban the word *Nintendo* from the classroom. When I asked my seven-year-old if the teacher wouldn't let the kids talk about the games because that's all they were talking about, he said, "No. That's all we were *thinking* about."

THINKING IT THROUGH   **Identifying the Underlying Meaning**

▷ **STEP 1 Read the passage carefully.**

▷ **STEP 2 Look for emotional words or phrases that communicate strong feelings.** *The writer uses words like "harmful," "obsessed," and "ban" to talk about the effects of video games.*

▷ **STEP 3 Look for words that communicate the author's point of view about the topic.** *The writer starts out saying that occasionally playing video games is OK, but that is only to make the point that some kids can't just play them every once in a while. He uses the example of second-grade students who can't think about anything else.*

▷ **STEP 4 Write a statement that expresses the underlying meaning of the passage, and include it in your summary.** *The writer of this passage uses the example of his son's classroom to point out that video games have taken over the lives of some children.*

 Writing 2.5c Reflect underlying meaning, not just the superficial details.

Read the passage below. Then, read the notes and summary that follow the passage. Answer the questions on page 667 to help you understand the process of creating a summary.

Confucius' Legacy

He lost his father at the age of three. As a boy, he did not attend school but was taught at home by his mother. His political career was unremarkable. In spite of these difficulties, however, Confucius became one of the most influential teachers and philosophers who ever lived.

Confucius was born in China in 551 B.C. By the time he was a teenager, Confucius knew he wanted to devote his life to learning. Eventually, he mastered all six traditional Chinese arts: music, archery, chariot driving, calligraphy, basic math, and Chinese rituals.

Confucius became a teacher when he was in his thirties. At the time, education was available only to the wealthy or to civil servants. However, Confucius supported extending education beyond these groups in order to benefit society. Hoping to gain broader acceptance of his policies, Confucius entered the Chinese government. However, he soon realized that China's leaders did not agree with him, and he left government service to return to his cause. Confucius became well known as a champion of education and self-improvement. His achievement, dedication, and vision make him one of history's outstanding figures.

Here are notes one student made while reading the passage above. Notes added later show how the student planned to combine and show the relationships between ideas to create a summary.

Main idea: The Chinese teacher and philosopher Confucius overcame many difficulties to become an influential historical figure.
Important details:
Even though
∧He had little early schooling,
He mastered the traditional arts of China, and
He became a teacher.

 Writing 1.3 Use strategies of notetaking to impose structure on composition drafts.

He wanted people besides wealthy people and civil servants to be able to get an education because it would improve society.

He worked for the Chinese government, *but*

~~He left government~~ because leaders did not accept his policies.

He went back to teaching and became well known.

Underlying meaning: The writer admires Confucius and considers him inspirational.

Here is the summary the student created using the notes above.

The Chinese teacher and philosopher Confucius overcame many difficulties to become an influential historical figure. Even though he had little early schooling, he mastered the traditional arts of China and became a teacher. In ancient China, only the wealthy and civil servants got education, but Confucius wanted education for more people because it would improve society. He worked for the Chinese government but left when he saw that the leaders did not support his education policies. He returned to teaching, becoming an inspirational and well-known educator and, according to the writer, "one of history's outstanding figures."

DO THIS

Answer these questions about how the student developed a summary of the passage on page 666.

- What details from the original passage support the main idea the writer of the summary identified?
- What details from the original passage did the student not include in the summary? Why do you think these details were left out?
- Why did the summary writer combine into one sentence the first three ideas in his notes?

TIP Use these guidelines to plan the lengths of your own summaries.

- If you are summarizing a passage of just a few paragraphs, your summary should be about one third as long as the original passage.
- If you are summarizing a long selection, such as an article or a chapter from a textbook, write no more than one sentence for each paragraph of the original selection. In other words, if the selection is twenty paragraphs long, your summary should be no more than twenty sentences long.

Here is an example of a summary of a longer piece of writing, the science article "When the Earth Shakes" on pages 371–376. In this case, the writer has condensed material from forty-four paragraphs into three paragraphs.

Main idea of selection **Main ideas from paragraphs 1–23**	"When the Earth Shakes," an article by Patricia Lauber, explains the causes and effects of earthquakes. In Anchorage, Alaska, in 1964, a rumbling started. It eventually grew to shake houses, tilt the ground, cause landslides, and open huge holes in the ground. Other parts of Alaska suffered similar damage, all of it caused by an earthquake. The earthquake damaged towns along Alaska's coast because the land there is unstable. It hit the port town of Seward especially hard because it split oil tanks, causing a huge fire. Despite all of the damage it did, the earthquake lasted only five minutes. Some parts of Alaska's landscape rose, other areas sank, some moved sideways, and some fell into the ocean. A mountain even split apart. The earthquake was one of the most powerful ones ever recorded.
Main ideas from paragraphs 24–32	A sudden movement of rock inside the earth causes an earthquake. The earth's rock has three layers: the core (the center), the mantle, and the crust. The crust, or top, contains two kinds of rock. The granite-like rock that forms continents, which is about twenty-five miles thick, also extends out under part of the ocean near each continent. Under the ocean is the other part of the crust: a layer of dark rock called basalt about five miles thick. The rock gets hotter the deeper it is. The mantle, the layer underneath the crust, is about eighteen hundred miles thick, very hot, and under a lot of pressure. This rock can be soft and gummy or it can shift or break because of pressure. When rock in the mantle or the crust shifts or breaks, the movement causes earthquakes.
Main ideas from paragraphs 33–44 **Underlying meaning of selection**	Rock shifts or breaks because pressure stores energy in it, the way the energy stored in a tight bowstring makes an arrow fly. Earthquakes release energy in waves, with the energy from one piece of rock pushing on the next one, and so on. Waves of energy that move from rock into the air create rumbling sounds. Waves that move deep inside the earth are usually not felt, but waves that move along the surface can be very destructive. The writer seems to find earthquakes interesting because they are so complex in their causes and unpredictable in their effects.

Using the steps in the chart on page 664 and the Thinking It Through on page 665, write a summary for "A Veto on Video Games" on pages 599–600. Make sure your summary includes the main idea and important details, is written in your own words, and includes a statement of the selection's underlying meaning.

Databases

You Could Look It Up   If you need to find information quickly, where do you look? One place to look is in a *database* on the subject of interest. A **database** is a collection of information on a particular subject, organized in categories. Every database consists of *records*, and each record usually has several *fields*. The example below comes from a database of information about important historical documents. Each **record** in the database represents a different document, while the **fields** are the categories of information about that document.

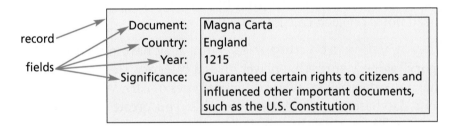

Document:	Magna Carta
Country:	England
Year:	1215
Significance:	Guaranteed certain rights to citizens and influenced other important documents, such as the U.S. Constitution

record → fields →

In a computer database, you can access, or look up, information in any field. When you use an online card catalog or encyclopedia, you are using a database. You can also create your own databases to help you learn.

An Information Storehouse   Although most people think of using databases to access information, creating your own databases can help you as a writer. Think about your last research project. Chances are that at some point you felt overwhelmed by the amount of information you found. Had you created a database of that information, though, it could have helped you organize the ideas to understand better how all the information on the topic fit together.

Writing 1.6 Develop simple databases to manage information and prepare reports.

For example, if you researched famous composers, your database could contain a separate record for each composer. Each record might contain fields for notable works, biographical information, and quotations about the composer's significance. By creating a database during prewriting, you could easily identify composers about whom you still needed to gather more information.

Creating a database can help you in two important ways: sorting and searching.

Sorting First, you can *sort* the information in your database. **Sorting** involves reorganizing the database records into an order that is more useful. In the composer database, for example, you could sort the composers by birth date in order to arrange them in chronological order. Doing this would make it easier to draft a clearly organized essay on the topic.

Searching Another useful function of databases is *searching*. To **search** a database, you type in a word located anywhere in the record. For example, you could search your database for all information on Johann Sebastian Bach by typing in "Bach" instead of looking at every record you created. Quickly finding the record you need can not only help you complete your research, but also help you write a draft more effectively by making it easy to see your organized notes on each category of your topic.

Play a Game of Categories You may have played the "Category" game before. One player gives a category, such as "cars," and then the other players name different types of cars. When you create your database, the categories, or fields, you create will determine how useful your database is. Follow the steps below to create your own database.

Quick guide

CREATING A DATABASE
1. Identify the records you will include in your database. Databases work best for detailed information on a number of related topics. If you were studying native plants of your region, you might create a database of records about specific plants.
2. Identify the fields, or categories, you need for each record. Keep in mind that you will be able to search by categories, so include any fields you think may be helpful. Begin with the basics, such as the name of the item or a description. Additional fields for a database of plants might include where each plant grows and how each plant is helpful or harmful to humans. Start with many fields; it will be easier to delete fields later than to add them.

3. **Begin entering your information in your own words.**
Once you have your database fields set up, start entering the information you have found. Do not copy ideas word-for-word from your source.

4. **Revise your fields as necessary.**
You can always go back and add, change, or delete fields. As you enter information you will probably find ways to make the fields in your records more useful.

Imagine that you are writing a report on fish and that you have created the four records below as part of a database. Study the records, and answer these questions.

DO THIS

■ If you were writing a section of your report on how different fish reproduce, by what field would you sort the database? Which records would be grouped together after this sort?

■ If you wanted to focus a section of your report on bony fish, how would you use your database to find this information?

■ Which of the four records below would be included in a search for fish that live in oceans and also lay eggs?

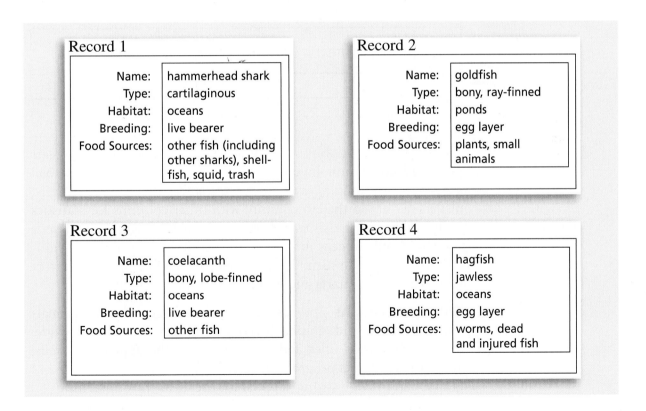

Record 1

Name:	hammerhead shark
Type:	cartilaginous
Habitat:	oceans
Breeding:	live bearer
Food Sources:	other fish (including other sharks), shell-fish, squid, trash

Record 2

Name:	goldfish
Type:	bony, ray-finned
Habitat:	ponds
Breeding:	egg layer
Food Sources:	plants, small animals

Record 3

Name:	coelacanth
Type:	bony, lobe-finned
Habitat:	oceans
Breeding:	live bearer
Food Sources:	other fish

Record 4

Name:	hagfish
Type:	jawless
Habitat:	oceans
Breeding:	egg layer
Food Sources:	worms, dead and injured fish

TIP If you do not have access to a computer database program, create a separate index card for each record in your planned database.

PRACTICE & APPLY 2 **Create a Database**

Using the steps on pages 670–671, create a database of the movies you have seen this year. Each movie will be a separate record. Create at least four fields for your database, and begin entering each movie. Add, change, or delete fields as necessary. Include a *summary* field for each movie in your database.

Spreadsheets

Not Just for Math If the information you will write about is more easily expressed in numbers than in words, a *spreadsheet* may be a more helpful prewriting tool than a database. A **spreadsheet** is a table that uses **cells** arranged in **rows** and **columns** to organize and display information. Spreadsheets are often used in math and science to display information and make calculations, but you can also use them to write to learn.

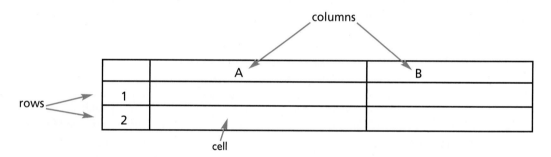

Uses of Spreadsheets Spreadsheets can be used to create tables of information. If you want to display your school's basketball statistics, for example, you can create a spreadsheet. You might list players' names in the left column, with other columns for statistics such as rebounds, assists, and free-throw percentage. Each player's statistics would appear in the same row as his or her name. In addition to displaying information, spreadsheets can help you use information to create charts and graphs and to make calculations.

Charts and Graphs Spreadsheet programs can create professional-looking charts and graphs based on information you provide. Simply enter your titles and information in the appropriate cells, and the spreadsheet program will create your graph. Such charts and graphs can provide strong support for the ideas in your writing.

Writing 1.6 Develop simple spreadsheets to manage information and prepare reports.

Calculations   Spreadsheet programs can do mathematical functions for you. Programs normally include common functions such as adding and averaging as well as more advanced functions. By selecting the data to calculate and then choosing the appropriate menu option, you can make your spreadsheet perform calculations using your data. For example, if you were writing a report on the plant species found in California forests, you might want to know the total number of plant species. You could simply select the column listing the plant species and have the spreadsheet add them up.

Fill in the Blanks   To create a spreadsheet, use the steps below.

CREATING A SPREADSHEET

1. **Identify the information for the spreadsheet.**
   Spreadsheets are most useful for numerical information, so consider what parts of your topic might be explained in number form.

2. **Identify any math functions that are necessary.**
   Think about how you want to use the numeric information in the spreadsheet, and identify the computations you want the spreadsheet program to perform for you.

3. **Choose the chart or graph that best supports your ideas.**
   Use a **bar graph** to compare amounts—for example, the number of trees planted in your community each year. Use a **line graph** to show change over time, such as the growth in centimeters of a seed into a tall, mature plant. Use a **pie chart** to divide a subject into parts—for example, the percentage of old-growth trees in a forest versus the percentage of younger, smaller trees there. (For more on **pie charts** see page 605.)

4. **Follow the program's instructions for creating the spreadsheet and charts or graphs.**
   All spreadsheet programs are a little different, so you will need to use the instructions for the software you are using. Most programs also have a "help" feature if you need assistance.

Designing Your Writing

Embedding Charts and Graphs   To embed an object created in a spreadsheet program in a piece of your writing,

- use a computer with both spreadsheet and word-processing programs
- first, create the graph in the spreadsheet program (though some programs may allow you to create your graph while you are inserting it into your document)
- then, select the location for the object in your text document, and follow the embedding instructions for your program

Look at the spreadsheet and its related bar graph below. As you do so, answer the following questions.

- How does the spreadsheet organize the information on U.S. volcanoes?

- What calculations might be made using the information in this spreadsheet?

- How could you use the bar graph to support a paper about volcanoes in the United States?

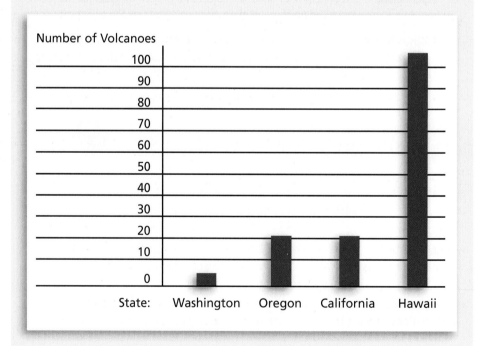

Volcanoes in the U.S.

	A	B
1	State	Number of Volcanoes
2	Washington	7
3	Oregon	21
4	California	21
5	Hawaii	107

Number of Volcanoes

PRACTICE & APPLY 3 **Create a Spreadsheet**

Imagine that you have been assigned to write a research paper analyzing how students spend their time. Ask five friends how much time they have spent each evening on homework over the past three weeks. Then, follow these steps.

- Make a spreadsheet to display the data.

- Then, think about what calculations you can use to learn from this data. For example, how would you figure the average amount of time each student spent doing homework each evening? Think of three ways to analyze this data using calculations, and perform those calculations.

- Finally, use the results of your calculations to create a bar graph that represents part of your data.

TIP If you do not have access to a computer spreadsheet program, create your spreadsheet and bar graph on notebook paper or graph paper.

Word-Processing and Publishing Features

Presenting What You Know   You probably already know that **word-processing** and **publishing programs**—computer software that helps you compose and design documents—can make your writing easy to read and eye-catching. Formatting your ideas by using word-processing or publishing features will also help you confirm your understanding of a topic in the following ways.

- Creating section headings for a report can help you group details into categories.

- Developing a numbered or bulleted list can help you see the steps in a process.

- Making choices about fonts, sizes, and styles of type can help you identify important ideas.

Using a Professional Look   **Desktop publishing** is a way of using a computer to design documents with neatly arranged text and graphics. However, all word-processing and publishing programs used in desktop publishing are not alike. While most have the same basic features, commands and options will vary. Consult your teacher, your computer lab instructor, your media specialist, or the

COMPUTER TIP

In most cases, you can create an attractive document with the same word-processing program that you used to write your composition. If you want your document to include more complex formatting, you may need to use a desktop publishing program.

Writing 1.6 Create documents by using word-processing skills and publishing programs.

software manual for specific help with the program you are using. Whenever you use software to publish your work, you will need to consider *page layout, organizational features,* and *type style.*

Page Layout The **page layout** is the design of the text and graphics on the printed page, including the balance between the white and dark spaces. (The text and graphics are called "dark spaces" because they are printed in ink.) When you decide upon your page layout, you make choices about the *alignment* of your text, the size of the *margins,* and how much *spacing* you will use between lines and paragraphs. To help you make those choices, look at the following elements of page layout.

■ **Alignment Alignment** refers to where the lines of your text line up on the page. *Center-align* your title and any information on your cover sheet, if you use one. **Center-aligned** text lines up along an imaginary vertical line down the middle of the page, as in this example:

Goddard's Rockets

by Lisa Minter

Here are three other types of alignment you might use.

TYPES OF TEXT ALIGNMENT	
Type	**Definition and Example**
left	The body of your text will usually be **left-aligned,** with each line beginning on the left margin. A left-aligned document may have **ragged,** or uneven, alignment on the right-hand side because lines of text will vary in length. The space between letters and words remains consistent. This text is left-aligned.
right	**Right-aligned text,** which lines up on the right-hand side of the page, is harder to read. Avoid overusing this technique, but consider right-aligning some portions of your document, such as your name and the page numbers. This text is right-aligned.
justified	With **justified alignment,** text lines up on both the right-hand and left-hand sides of the page. Because justified text presents a neater appearance than ragged text, books, magazines, and newspapers are set justified. The disadvantage of justified alignment is that it can lead to word-spacing and letter-spacing problems. This text is justified.

- **Margins** The blank, or white, spaces at the top, bottom, and sides of your page are called the **margins.** Most word-processing programs have a *default margin*—one inch for the top and bottom of a page and 1.25 inches for the sides—but you can adjust margins if necessary. The size of your margins will affect how "heavy" with text your pages look.

- **Spacing Spacing** refers to the blank, or white, areas between lines of text. Spacing is also known as *leading* (rhymes with *heading*). Because double-spaced documents are easier to read and mark for grading than single-spaced documents, most of the documents you create for school will be double-spaced. Most published books, magazines, and newspapers are single-spaced.

Organizational Features In addition to making decisions about page layout, you should consider using features in your word-processing program that will help you organize your manuscript in an appealing way and emphasize important information. The following chart explains how to use features to organize your text.

WAYS TO ORGANIZE A MANUSCRIPT

Feature	Definition	Tips
Bullet	A large dot or other symbol used to separate items in a list	Use at least two items, and use parallel wording in all items. In other words, if the first item is a question, every item should be a question. If the text is more than one line, start the second line beneath the first word of the first line, not beneath the bullet. Most word-processing programs have an automatic bullet-list function.
Emphasis	The use of color, shading, graphics, or type size to emphasize text	Emphasize only the most important items so that the technique does not lose its effectiveness.
Header or Footer	Text at the top (header) or bottom (footer) of each page that gives information about a document	Include important identifying information, such as the writer's name, document title, date, and page number.
Headings and Subheadings	Titles of sections within a document	• Use a heading at the beginning of each major section of text to describe its contents. Consider using larger, bold, or capital letters for headings. • Use subheadings for more specific portions within a major section of text. Consider using a different style or size of type for subheadings.

(continued)

(continued)

Title and Subtitle	• Title: The name of a document • Subtitle: A secondary, more descriptive title	Use a colon after the title, if the subtitle appears on the same line. You also may use a subtitle on a separate line and omit the colon.
Tabs	Preset points across the page at which the cursor will stop when the Tab key is pressed	Set a tab at half an inch from the left margin to create uniform indents at the beginnings of paragraphs.
Rules and Borders	• Rules: Vertical and horizontal lines • Borders: Rules that surround a graphic or portion of text	Use rules or borders to separate columns or other text, such as a headline or graphic, from the main body of a document.

Type Style **Type** refers to the letters, numbers, and other characters in a printed text. A **type font** is a particular set of letters, numbers, and punctuation marks of a specific design. For example, Palatino, Chancery, and Helvetica are all names of fonts. (See the examples below.) Usually a word-processing program has a number of type fonts from which to choose, as well as the ability to make these fonts bold or italic, and to enlarge or reduce the size of the type.

Reference Note

For information and practice on using **italics,** see pages 320–321 in the *Holt Handbook.*

- **Bold type** and *italic type* are used for emphasis. You may see bold type used in titles and headings and for vocabulary words in a textbook. Italic type can make important words stand out or show that a word is being used as a word, as in this sentence:

  The word *font* comes from a French word meaning "to cast."

- The size of type is measured in *points*. A **point** is $\frac{1}{72}$ of an inch. The main text of a school assignment is usually printed in 10- or 12-point type. Titles or headlines may appear in a larger point size, and captions may appear in a smaller point size.

  Choose a type style based on **legibility.** Your document should be clear, uncluttered, and easy to read.

A	A	A
B, C, D, E	B, C, D, E	B, C, D, E
a, b, c, d, e	a, b, c, d, e	a, b, c, d, e
1, 2, 3, 4, 5	1, 2, 3, 4, 5	1, 2, 3, 4, 5
Palatino	*Chancery*	Helvetica
Palatino Bold	***Chancery Bold***	**Helvetica Bold**
Palatino Italic	*Chancery Italic*	*Helvetica Italic*

A Writer's Model

Read the following excerpt from a longer essay. Watch for the word-processing and publishing strategies the writer used to make the essay's information easier to understand.

Baghdad and Beyond: Islamic Scholars in the Middle Ages

In A.D. 750, Islamic scholars began to translate ancient Greek manuscripts of science and philosophy into Arabic, beginning an era of significant scientific investigation. Baghdad became a center of learning, attracting mathematicians, astronomers, geographers, and physicians to Bayt al-Hikmah, its House of Wisdom. There, from A.D. 750 to 950, Islamic scholars gathered, first translating, then discussing, and finally developing their own theories based on the information found in the Greek manuscripts.

The Mathematical Sciences

The work of a ninth-century Islamic mathematician brought to the West the Arabic numerals we use today. The very first algebra book was the work of another Islamic mathematician. In fact, our English word *algebra* comes from the Arabic word *al-jabr*. Other Islamic mathematical developments during the Golden Age included

- the development of *geometry* based on translations of Greek works and further efforts by Islamic mathematicians
- the beginnings of what would become *integral calculus*
- the establishment of *trigonometry* as a separate branch of mathematics
- the development of *spherical astronomy* to solve problems in astronomy

On to the Stars

For Islamic scholars in the Middle Ages, mathematics included astronomy. The scholars carefully observed the heavens and discovered new stars. They gave names to Aldebaran,

(continued)

Annotations (right margin):

- Title separated from subtitle by colon; large, boldface type; center-aligned
- Left-aligned margins
- Times type font; 12-point type size
- Extra white space
- Subheading #1—boldface
- Italics for words used as words
- Bulleted list
- Italics for special emphasis
- Subheading #2—boldface

(continued)

Betelgeuse, Deneb, and Altair. The astronomers, both in Baghdad and in the great Islamic center of learning at Córdoba, Spain, studied the heavens and collected their findings in astronomical tables, charting the movements of stars and planets. They invented the *astrolabe,* an instrument for measuring the altitude of a star. They built an astronomical observatory at Maragha, Persia, and applied their knowledge of astronomy to the development of a solar calendar and an almanac.

Think About the Model

Working with a partner, discuss the following questions and write down your responses.

1. What is the purpose of the larger type size and style of the title?

2. How do the two subheadings help you understand the excerpt? Why are they printed in a different font style from the regular text?

3. Why do you think the writer used a bulleted list in the second paragraph?

4. What is the purpose of the writer's use of italics? Is it effective? Why or why not?

5. Does the writer's use of white space help make the excerpt easy to read? Why or why not?

PRACTICE & APPLY 4

Use Word-Processing or Publishing Software

Choose your favorite essay that you wrote for a workshop in this book, and use a word-processing or publishing program to prepare the essay for publication. Remember to rethink the organization of your essay and consider adding headings and subheadings, bullets, varied type styles, and other publishing features to present your ideas clearly.

DIRECTIONS: Read the following paragraph from a student's summary of a magazine article. Then, read the questions below it. Choose the correct answer for each, and mark your answers on your own paper.

An Inspirational Story

The article "Tri It!" in the May 2001 issue of *Sports for All* is about how unathletic people can get into shape for a short triathlon. Using the story of an overweight high school student's journey "from couch potato to tri guy," the author inspires readers to see themselves as athletes no matter what shape they are in. Training for a triathlon, which involves swimming, cycling, and running, takes time, as the sample training schedule in the article shows. The article includes tips for completing each part of the race and the two transitions between race segments. Judging from the student's story, the feeling of crossing the finish line is worth all this effort, because at the end of the article the student himself urges others to follow his example.

1. Based on the summary above, what is the main idea of the magazine article?
   A Overweight high school students can become accomplished athletes.
   B Ordinary people can complete a short triathlon with proper training.
   C A triathlon consists of swimming, cycling, and running.
   D Readers must use the training schedule to complete a short triathlon.

2. Why are the words "from couch potato to tri guy" in quotation marks?
   F because the phrase contains two slang terms
   G because it is the title of the article
   H because it shows the student's opinion
   J because these words come from the original article

3. How might the student use this summary to plan his own triathlon essay?
   A He might use the article's chronological order as a model for organizing his own essay.

B He might use the underlying meaning of the article as his thesis.
   C He might better understand the topic after summarizing information about it.
   D all of the above

4. What information below would probably be included in the "triathlon" record in a database on endurance sports?
   F other endurance sports
   G a sample training schedule
   H the definition of "endurance"
   J biographies of runners

5. Why are the words *An Inspirational Story* printed in boldface?
   A because this is the name of the magazine where the article appeared
   B because this is the name of the article the student summarized
   C because this is the title the student has given to the summary
   D because this is the main idea of the student's summary of the article

Learning About Paragraphs

A paragraph is a section of text focused on a single idea. Usually a paragraph is part of a longer piece of writing. In an essay about summer camp, for example, one paragraph might focus on the meals. Each of the other paragraphs in the essay would focus on another aspect of camp, such as the outdoor activities. Together, the paragraphs create an overall picture of the experience of summer camp.

In everything from an essay question on a social studies test to a letter to a friend, you write paragraphs. To make your paragraphs more effective and easier for your readers to understand, you should practice using the techniques explained in this workshop. In this workshop you will learn how to develop focused, coherent paragraphs. In the process you will practice these language arts standards.

California Standards

Writing

1.0 Students write clear, coherent, and focused essays. Essays contain formal introductions, supporting evidence, and conclusions.

1.1 Create an organizational structure that balances all aspects of the composition and uses effective transitions between sentences to unify important ideas.

1.2 Support all statements and claims with descriptions, facts, and specific examples.

GO TO: go.hrw.com
KEYWORD: HLLA

The Paragraph

The Parts of a Paragraph

Most paragraphs have the same parts. Paragraphs that stand alone usually focus on a *main idea* that is made clear through a *topic sentence* and *supporting sentences.*

The Main Idea   Whether they stand alone or are part of a longer piece of writing, paragraphs usually have a main idea. The **main idea** is the overall point of the paragraph. In the following paragraph the main idea is in the first sentence.

> Personally, I thought Maxwell was just about the homeliest dog I'd ever seen in my entire life. He looked like a little old man draped in a piece of brown velvet that was too long, with the leftover cloth hanging in thick folds under his chin. Not only that, his long droopy ears dragged on the ground; he had sad wet eyes and huge thick paws with splayed toes. I mean, who could love a dog like that, except my brother Joji, aged nine, who is a bit on the homely side himself.
>
> Yoshiko Uchida, *A Jar of Dreams*

TIP There are four types of paragraphs. **Descriptive** paragraphs, such as the model above, describe a scene or object. **Narrative** paragraphs tell a story or explain a sequence of events. **Expository** paragraphs provide information, including facts, instructions, and definitions. **Persuasive** paragraphs attempt to convince others to accept the writer's opinion or to take action.

The Topic Sentence   The main idea of a paragraph is often stated in a **topic sentence.** You may find a paragraph's topic sentence at the beginning of the paragraph, in the middle, or even at the end.

WHAT'S AHEAD

In this workshop you will develop coherent, focused paragraphs. You will also learn how to
- write a topic sentence that expresses a main idea
- develop and arrange supporting details
- use transitional words and phrases
- write introductions and conclusions

In the following paragraph, the topic sentence is last. This sentence makes it clear that the villagers are preparing for a battle. The other sentences lead up to that point.

Quickly, quickly we gathered the sheep into the pens. Dogs barked, and people shouted out orders to one another. Children rushed through the village gathering firewood to pile inside the homes. Men and women scooped up pots and pots of water, filling cisterns and containers as rapidly as possible. People pulled the last ears of corn from the fields and turned their backs on the dry stalks. Finally, we all stood together in the plaza in the center of the village for just a moment before the fighters went to stand near the walls and the wide-eyed children were coaxed inside the houses. We were prepared for the coming battle.

Although not all paragraphs have topic sentences, it is helpful to use them when you are writing. A topic sentence may help you **focus** on your main idea as you develop a paragraph. It also tells the reader the main idea. Given the main idea, the reader knows what to expect from the rest of the paragraph. However, paragraphs that relate a series of events or that tell a story often lack a topic sentence. Read the following paragraph. Although it has no topic sentence, all the sentences focus on one main idea—the unexpected reactions of a poor woman toward her wealthy friend.

"Oh, Lottie, it's good to see you," Bess said, but saying nothing about Lottie's splendid appearance. Upstairs Bess, putting down her shabby suitcase, said, "I'll sleep like a rock tonight," without a word of praise for her lovely room. At the lavish table, top-heavy with turkey, Bess said, "I'll take light and dark both," with no marveling at the size of the bird, or that there was turkey for two elderly women, one of them too poor to buy her own bread.

Dorothy West, *The Richer, the Poorer*

TIP When a writer includes no topic sentence, readers must determine the main idea of a paragraph from its supporting details. In paragraphs like the one above from *The Richer, the Poorer,* the main idea is *implied,* rather than directly stated.

Writing 1.0 Students write focused essays.

PRACTICE & APPLY 1   **Write a Topic Sentence**

For the following paragraph, write a topic sentence that communicates the main idea.

> This movie is packed with action. I have never seen so many chases and explosions before. It also has an important lesson about friendship. The two main characters always look out for each other. Maybe the best thing about it is the music. The soundtrack will certainly be a bestseller.

COMPUTER TIP

Use a word-processing program's cut and paste commands to find the best placement of a topic sentence within a paragraph. You can always move or replace the sentence if you change your mind.

Supporting Sentences   **Supporting sentences** contain the details that elaborate on, explain, or prove a paragraph's main idea. These details can include

- **sensory details,** or what we experience through the senses of sight, hearing, touch, taste, and smell

- **facts,** or information that can be proved true by direct observation or by checking a reliable reference source

- **examples,** or typical instances of an idea

Here are examples of these kinds of details.

USING DETAILS TO ELABORATE	
Kinds of Details	**Supporting Sentences**
Sensory Details	
Sight	The bright sun glared off the front windshield of the car.
Hearing	Thunder boomed down the canyon, echoing off the walls.
Touch	My hands felt frozen to the cold, steel handlebars.
Taste	Thirstily, she gulped down the sweet orange juice.
Smell	The sharp, unpleasant odor of asphalt met his nose.
Facts	In 1998, Mark McGwire slammed seventy home runs in one season to break the record of sixty-one held by Roger Maris.
Examples	Some windstorms generate awesome wind speeds. For example, tornadoes can have wind speeds over 200 miles per hour.

 Writing 1.0 Essays contain supporting evidence. 1.2 Support all statements and claims with descriptions, facts, and specific examples.

TIP To brainstorm details for the practice items, picture specific instances or events relating to each. For example, imagine specific activities you enjoy with your friends, a specific person who has had an observable effect on someone else's life, and the specific parts of a favorite meal.

PRACTICE & APPLY 2 **Collect Supporting Details**

When you write paragraphs, you have to collect details that support your main idea. You can practice with the following topic sentences. List at least two details to support each topic sentence.

1. The time I spend with my friends on Saturday nights is my favorite time of the week.

2. One person's actions can make a difference in the lives of others.

3. When I feel hungry, I can just imagine my favorite meal.

The Makings of a Good Paragraph

Planning the parts of a paragraph alone will not create a clear piece of writing. To hang together, a paragraph must have *unity* and *coherence.*

Unity A paragraph has **unity** when all the sentences relate to the central focus, or main idea. A paragraph that does not have unity may confuse your readers. For example, suppose the main idea of a paragraph about Bonnie St. John Deane is that she became a skiing champion despite losing a leg. If you included a sentence about a friend who is also a skier, you would destroy the unity of the paragraph. The information about the friend is not related to your main idea.

Notice that all the sentences in the following paragraph tell something more about the paragraph's main idea.

People Weekly/Time Inc., ©1986 Richard Howard.

> Technology has changed the ways of the ranch. While cowboys continue to drive cattle to the corral on horseback, a pickup truck—air-conditioned, of course—also helps. And though they don't plug branding irons into electrical outlets, propane tanks make lighting fires and heating branding irons easier. Computers log inventory and keep track of wildlife. Hal Hawkins, King Ranch's animal physiologist, monitors herd research and development with a laptop computer.
>
> Johnny D. Boggs, "Home on the Range," *Boys' Life*

Writing **1.0** Students write focused essays.

Identify a Sentence That Destroys Unity

The following paragraph has one sentence that destroys the unity. Try your skill at finding the unrelated sentence.

> Canoes are made for many purposes. White-water canoes are made for use in fast, rock-filled streams. They can turn quickly to avoid obstacles. Other canoes are made for lakes and quiet rivers. Unable to turn quickly, they are a poor choice for use on a river with lots of rapids. On the other hand, they are easy to paddle in a straight line. White-water canoes can be very expensive. Before choosing a canoe, think about what kind of water you will ride.

TIP The first step in completing Practice & Apply 3 is to decide what the main idea is. Next, find the sentence that is not closely connected to the main idea.

Coherence   What goes into a paragraph is only part of the picture. Supporting details need to be clearly connected and arranged. A paragraph has **coherence** when readers can tell how and why ideas are connected. One way to create coherence is to arrange your details in an *organizational structure* that makes sense to the reader. Another is to use *transitional words* and *phrases*.

Organizational Structures   An **organizational structure** is a way of arranging ideas. Three common arrangements of supporting details are *chronological order*, *spatial order*, and *order of importance*. **Chronological order,** which presents details in the order in which they happen, is the order usually used to tell a story, to explain a process, or to show causes and effects. **Spatial order,** which presents details according to their location, is most often used in writing descriptions. **Order of importance,** in which the most important idea is located either at the beginning or at the end of a series of ideas, is often used in persuasive writing.

Reference Note

For more on **chronological order** and **order of importance,** see page 573. For more on **spatial order,** see page 701.

Transitional Words and Phrases   Another way to create coherence within and between paragraphs is to use **transitional words** or **phrases,** such as *for example, mainly,* and *in addition,* to connect ideas and tell why and how they are related. The chart on the next page shows examples of transitional words and phrases that help to create coherence.

Writing **1.0** Students write clear, coherent essays. **1.1** Create an organizational structure that balances all aspects of the composition and uses effective transitions between sentences to unify important ideas.

Depending upon how you have organized details, some transitions may be more effective than others at creating coherence. Refer to the appropriate section of this chart when you write.

TRANSITIONAL WORDS AND PHRASES

Comparing and Contrasting Ideas	also	however	on the other hand
	although	in the same way	similarly
	and	like	too
	another	likewise	unlike
	but	moreover	yet
Showing Cause and Effect	as a result	for	so
	because	for this reason	so that
	consequently	since	therefore
Showing Time	about	eventually	often
	after	finally	soon
	at	first, second, etc.	then
	at last	immediately	thereafter
	at the same time	later	until
	before	meanwhile	when
	during	next	while
Showing Place	above	beside	into
	across	between	near
	among	beyond	next to
	around	by	over
	before	down	there
	behind	here	to the left
	below	in	to the right
	beneath	inside	under
Showing Support	for example	furthermore	mainly
	for instance	in fact	most important

Writing 1.1 Create an organizational structure that uses effective transitions to unify important ideas.

In the following paragraph, the writer uses transitional words to show how ideas are connected. Notice, for example, how "at first" kids pretend not to see him. "Then," they turn and look.

> <u>When</u> I go someplace, most of the time those little people see me. <u>At first</u> they'll pretend not to see me. They go past me a little ways, and <u>then</u> they will turn back and look at me. <u>Then</u> they'll nudge their mama or daddy or grandma or grandpa, and I'll hear them say, "There's an Indian back there." So the Indians are still here. We never phased away. We didn't just blend into society and vanish. <u>In fact,</u> we're appearing more and more and more.
>
> Wallace H. Black Elk and William S. Lyon,
> *Black Elk: The Sacred Ways of a Lakota*

PRACTICE & APPLY 4 **Identify Transitional Words and Phrases**

Using the chart on page 688 as a guide, make a list of all the transitional words and phrases in the paragraph below.

> When she was elected principal chief of the Cherokee Nation in 1987, Wilma Mankiller took on a huge job. She was used to challenges, though. For example, she had developed many needed projects for Cherokees in rural Oklahoma in 1977. First, she helped people learn how to build their own homes. Next, she organized the installation of new water supply lines. Finally, she started new health clinics. While others were impressed with the new chief's dedication, no one who knew her well found her leadership ability surprising. Once elected chief, Mankiller continued her work to improve Cherokee communities. She focused on housing and education needs, and she encouraged her people to be proud of their language and culture. After serving two terms as chief, Wilma Mankiller continued to work for the Cherokee Nation by speaking across the country.

Writing 1.0 Students write coherent essays. 1.1 Create an organizational structure that uses effective transitions between sentences to unify important ideas.

Other Types of Paragraphs

Most paragraphs do not stand on their own, but work as part of the body of a longer piece of writing. **Introduction** and **conclusion** paragraphs connect the ideas in the body of a composition and clearly state the composition's main idea.

Introductions   An introduction must catch readers' attention and prepare them to read. To catch readers' attention,

- ask a question (*Have you ever found yourself bored during summer and wondered what your neighbor was doing at summer camp?*)

- start with an anecdote, or brief story (*As I packed for camp, I thought of the fun I would have and the friends I would make.*)

TIP For information on stating a **main idea,** see pages 683–684.

- begin with a surprising fact (*For over one hundred years YMCA summer camps have helped young people learn new skills.*)

Conclusions   A conclusion should give readers the sense that a composition is complete and tie together the supporting ideas from the body of the piece. Try one of these techniques.

- Refer to your introduction by answering the question, wrapping up the anecdote, or summing up the explanation of the surprising fact you used to catch readers' attention.

- Restate your main idea in a different way.

- Follow up on the ideas in the piece—for example, by stating what you will do as the result of an experience you have described.

PRACTICE & APPLY 5   Write an Original Paragraph

Write a paragraph on the topic of your choice.

- Choose the type of paragraph will you write—narrative, descriptive, expository, or persuasive. (See page 683 for definitions, or refer to the Writing Workshops in this book for instruction.)

- Express your main idea in a topic sentence. (See pages 683–684.)

- Choose details that support your main idea. (See page 685.)

- Organize your details in chronological order, spatial order, or order of importance. (See page 687.) Use transitions to connect your ideas. (See pages 687–688.)

Writing   **1.0** Students write clear, coherent, and focused essays. Essays contain formal introductions, supporting evidence, and conclusions. **1.1** Create an organizational structure that balances all aspects of the composition and uses effective transitions between sentences to unify important ideas. **1.2** Support all statements and claims with anecdotes, descriptions, facts, and specific examples.

DIRECTIONS: Read the following paragraph. Then, read the questions below it. Mark the best answer for each question on your own paper.

> (1) Helping homeless people helps the community. (2) In many cases, homeless people only need a chance to improve their living conditions. (3) When homeless people are given housing assistance and job training, they can become our neighbors, co-workers, and friends. (4) In fact, not only do they find work and learn to support themselves, but they also pay taxes and share their skills with others. (5) We must help people out of homelessness because each person we help can enrich our community.

1. Which of the following would best support the ideas in sentence 4?
   A an anecdote about a time when the writer's family, lost on vacation, got helpful directions from a friendly homeless person
   B facts about increased tax income and decreased aid costs in a community where homeless people have found housing and jobs
   C descriptions of the difficult conditions under which some homeless people live, including problems with weather and crime
   D examples of the problems homeless people face in finding jobs when they have no address, transportation, or clean clothing

2. What organizational structure did the writer of the paragraph above use?
   F chronological order
   G spatial order
   H order of importance
   J all of the above

3. Where should the writer add the transitional phrase *for these reasons* to make the paragraph more coherent?
   A at the beginning of sentence 2
   B at the beginning of sentence 3
   C at the beginning of sentence 4
   D at the beginning of sentence 5

4. If this paragraph were part of a longer composition about solving problems in the writer's community, which of the following statements would most likely appear in the introduction?
   F We can work together to reduce the problems caused by pollution and homelessness in our community.
   G Some people become homeless as a result of job loss, divorce, or even natural disasters such as earthquakes.
   H Pollution is another problem facing our community, a problem that each of us can do a little bit to improve.
   J Solving our problems, such as those I have explained in this essay, can set an example for larger towns.

5. In a longer composition about solving problems in the writer's community, which of the following statements would most likely appear in the conclusion?
   A Did you know that even a town as small as ours creates significant pollution from vehicles and factories?
   B Here are some solutions to pollution and homelessness in our community.
   C A surprising number of people in our town are just one paycheck away from becoming homeless themselves.
   D Every effort we make will create progress toward solving these problems.

Mini-Workshops

This section contains several short workshops on a variety of topics. The mini-workshops in this section will help you learn to

- analyze causes and effects in literature
- document reference sources
- write a descriptive essay
- write an autobiographical narrative
- analyze a documentary

As you work through each of these mini-workshops, you will practice the following language arts standards.

 California Standards

Analyzing Cause and Effect, pages 694–696

Writing

1.1 Create an organizational structure that uses effective transitions between sentences to unify important ideas.

1.2 Support all statements and claims with specific examples.

1.3 Use strategies of outlining to impose structure on drafts.

2.0 Students write expository texts.

2.2 Write responses to literature:

   a. Develop interpretations exhibiting careful reading, understanding, and insight.

   b. Organize interpretations around several clear ideas, premises, or images from the literary work.

   c. Justify interpretations through sustained use of examples and textual evidence.

Documenting Reference Sources, pages 697–699

Writing

1.5 Give credit for both quoted and paraphrased information by using a consistent and sanctioned format and methodology for citations.

2.3d Document reference sources by means of footnotes and a bibliography.

GO TO: go.hrw.com
KEYWORD: HLLA

Writing a Descriptive Essay, pages 700–703

Writing

1.0 Students write clear, coherent, and focused essays. The writing exhibits students' awareness of the audience and purpose. Essays contain formal introductions, supporting evidence, and conclusions.

1.1 Create an organizational structure that balances all aspects of the composition and uses effective transitions between sentences to unify important ideas.

1.2 Support all statements and claims with descriptions.

1.7 Revise writing to improve organization and word choice after checking the logic of the ideas and the precision of the vocabulary.

2.0 Students write descriptive texts of at least 500 to 700 words.

Writing an Autobiographical Narrative, pages 704–706

Writing

1.1 Create an organizational structure that balances all aspects of the composition and uses effective transitions between sentences to unify important ideas.

1.2 Support all statements with descriptions and specific examples.

2.0 Students write narrative texts.

2.1 Write autobiographical narratives:
   a. Develop a standard plot line (having a beginning, conflict, rising action, climax, and denouement) and point of view.
   b. Develop complex characters and a definite setting.
   c. Use a range of appropriate strategies (e.g., dialogue; suspense; naming of specific narrative action, including movement, gestures, and expressions).

Analyzing a Documentary, page 707

Listening and Speaking

1.2 Determine the speaker's attitude toward the subject.

1.8 Analyze the effect on the viewer of images, text, and sound in electronic journalism; identify the techniques used to achieve the effects in each instance studied.

Analyzing Cause and Effect

Have you and a friend ever left a theater arguing about a villain's motives in a film? Have you ever discussed the surprise ending of a short story with classmates? If you have picked apart the sequence of events in a film, story, or novel, then you have analyzed *cause and effect*. In this workshop you will learn how to write a brief (one or two paragraphs) **literary response** about the causes and effects in a short story.

Cause-and-Effect Relationships A **cause** is an action or situation that makes something else happen. An **effect** is the result of the cause. For example, hitting a home run (cause) might result in a win for your softball team (effect). As you read a short story, you may notice that some of the events in the **plot** are arranged in a cause-and-effect chain. In a cause-and-effect chain, one action leads to another, which leads to another, and so on. Identifying the causes and effects in the short story requires some **interpretation,** or exploration of the meaning of events. As you read the short story of your choice, ask yourself not only what hap-

pened first and what happened next but also why.

To keep track of the causes and effects in your short story as you read, organize them in a **flowchart**—a graphic outline. A student drew the flowchart below while reading the short story "User Friendly" on pages 186–195. The story features an unruly computer named Louis. Then, the student chose to explore the causes and effects of three events in the story. These events are marked with a check in the flowchart below.

Contributing Factors After you read your story and choose a few events to analyze for cause and effect, consider the *contributing factors* of these events. **Contributing factors** are the situations or actions that helped cause an event. Some contributing factors are also causes that are part of the cause-and-effect chain. Other contributing factors are other events or situations in the story. For example, look at the first row of contributing factors in the student's chart on the next page. You can see that Kevin talks to

Writing **1.3** Use strategies of outlining to impose structure on drafts. **2.2** Write responses to literature. **2.2a** Develop interpretations exhibiting careful reading, understanding, and insight. **2.2b** Organize interpretations around several clear ideas, premises, or images from the literary work.

Events	Contributing Factors
• Kevin talks to his computer, Louis, about his hurt feelings.	• Ginny hurts Kevin's feelings when Kevin tries to talk to her. Kevin doesn't have any friends so he talks to his computer.
• Louis begins to harass Ginny's family.	• Kevin's happiness means everything to Louis. When Kevin tells Louis that he is unhappy, Louis begins to harass the person who caused Kevin's unhappiness.
• Kevin considers disconnecting Louis.	• When Louis causes trouble for Ginny's family, Kevin realizes that Louis is dangerous. Even though Kevin feels that Louis is a friend, he thinks it would be best if Louis were disconnected.

Louis for two reasons. The first reason was already identified in the student's flowchart—Ginny hurt Kevin's feelings. The second reason, though, is not part of the flowchart, but it is still a contributing factor. Kevin talks to Louis because he does not have any friends. To find contributing factors that help explain the events in your short story, choose a particular event and ask yourself why this event happened.

From the Top   Once you have chosen, read, and analyzed a short story, you are ready to write your literary response.

Introduction   To start your draft, write a *main idea statement*. The **main idea statement** will tell readers your **purpose**—to illustrate the cause-and-effect relationships among the events of a short story. It will also tell the readers the title of the short story and the author's name.

Body   The middle of your literary response will explain the cause-and-effect relationships among events in the short story, including any contributing factors. Support each statement you make about causes, contributing factors, or effects with specific **examples** and **evidence** from the short story.

Conclusion   End your literary response with a *concluding sentence*. The **concluding sentence** will either summarize your ideas or restate the main idea statement.

All Together Now   Look at the following cause-and-effect analysis in response to the short story "User Friendly." Notice that the student used transitional words and phrases to show the cause-and-effect relationships. (For more on **transitions,** see page 687.)

Writing **1.1** Create an organizational structure that uses effective transitions between sentences to unify important ideas. **1.2** Support all statements and claims with specific examples. **2.2c** Justify interpretations through sustained use of examples and textual evidence.

Writer's Model

Main idea statement

Although amazing things happen in the short story "User Friendly" by T. Ernesto Bethancourt, actions and situations within the story can explain why events happen the way they do. One event that seems unbelievable is Kevin's decision to talk to his computer, Louis. At the beginning of the story, Kevin is cautious about talking to Louis, but after Ginny hurts his feelings, he discusses his problem with Louis. Kevin decides to talk to Louis partly because he has no other friends. Even though it might seem strange that a boy would talk to a computer about his feelings, causes and contributing factors in the story explain why Kevin does so.

Cause/Contributing factor

Effect

Contributing factor

Cause/Contributing factor

The actions Louis takes against Ginny's family can also be explained. After Kevin tells Louis about his hurt feelings, Louis begins to harass Ginny's family because Kevin's happiness means everything to Louis. Finally, Kevin's wish to disconnect Louis is caused by the computer's behavior toward Ginny's family. Even though Kevin feels that Louis is a friend, he understands that Louis can be very dangerous. While the events in "User Friendly" are incredible, the cause-and-effect relationships among them explain why they happened and make the story believable.

Effect

Cause

Concluding sentence

PRACTICE & APPLY   ## Analyze Cause and Effect

Now it is your turn to write a literary response analyzing the causes and effects in a short story.

- First, select and read a short story, making a flowchart of causes and effects as you read.

- Then, identify contributing factors to the causes and effects in the plot of the short story.

- Finally, write a one- or two-paragraph response that includes a main idea statement, an explanation of the cause-and-effect relationships among events in the story that includes contributing factors, and a concluding sentence.

Writing 2.0 Students write expository texts.

Documenting Reference Sources

When you write a research report, you build on the work of other researchers who share your interest in your topic. **Documenting sources,** or giving credit to sources of information that you use in your report, is important. Documenting sources makes your report more believable and tells readers where to learn more about the topic.

To document your sources, you need to mention, or **cite,** them in two places:

- in notes within the body of the report
- in a separate list at the end of the report, called *Works Cited.* (If you use print sources only, this listing is called the *Bibliography.*) For more on creating a **source list,** see pages 634–635.

To Cite or Not to Cite? You must give credit any time you draw on someone else's work, whether you quote the person's words exactly or summarize or paraphrase the ideas. If you fail to give proper credit for borrowed material, you are **plagiarizing,** or leading the reader to believe someone else's work is your own.

Still, not every fact in your report needs to be documented. Some facts are considered *common knowledge.* **Common knowledge** is information that can easily be found in several sources (for example, *Washington, D.C., is the capital of the United States*) or that most people know from their own experience (for example, *The U.S. Postal Service uses the image of an eagle on its cars and trucks*).

Way to Go Two ways of documenting sources within the body of a report are **parenthetical citations** and **footnotes.** Your teacher will tell you which type of citation you should use. Both types show the same kind of information—what sources you have used and where a reader may locate specific information within a source. However, parenthetical citations and footnotes differ in form.

Parenthetical Citations Most reports, including the Writer's Model on pages 643–647, cite sources using parenthetical citations. Using parenthetical citations creates an uncluttered look. Follow these steps.

- Draw the information for your parenthetical citations from the source list and notes you made as you researched your topic. (See pages 634–638.)
- Place each citation in parentheses right before the period at the end of the sentence(s) in which you used the material.
- Within the parentheses, provide just enough information for readers to be able to find the source on your *Works Cited* list. Usually you will need to list only the author's last name and the page numbers where you found the information.

  The guidelines on the next page show what information to include in your parenthetical citations and how to punctuate them. Information provided in a parenthetical citation should clearly refer to a corresponding *Works Cited* entry.

Mini-Workshop 2 • Documenting Reference Sources

GUIDELINES FOR USING PARENTHETICAL CITATIONS

Print Source with One Author or Editor Author's or editor's last name followed by the page number(s): (Dudley 54–55).

Print Source with Two or More Authors or Editors All authors' or editors' last names followed by the page number(s), or if there are more than three authors, the first author's last name followed by the words *et al.* and the page number(s): (Barghusen and Hitzeroth 79).

Print Source, When Report Includes More Than One Source by the Same Author(s) Author's last name, followed by the title (or a shortened form of it), followed by the page number(s): (Grambo, <u>Eagles: Masters of the Sky</u> 46).

Print Source with No Author Given Title, or a shortened form of it, followed by the page number(s): ("Bald Eagle" 1).

Nonprint Source (Interview, Audiotape, Web page, etc.) Speaker or title (or a shortened version of it): (<u>Bald</u>).

Material Quoted from a Source Other Than the Original The abbreviation *qtd. in* ("quoted in") followed by the name of the author (or, if no author is given, the title) of the source you used. If the source is more than one page long, include the page number: (qtd. in Gerstenzang).

TIP If you use the name of the author or the title of the source in your own sentence, you do not need to repeat it in your parenthetical note. For example, *As early as 1930, Tucker points out, much of America's forest land was becoming unsuitable for many animals (62–69).*

Footnotes As the name suggests, a footnote is placed at the bottom of a page on which information from a source is used. To create footnotes, do the following.

- Place the footnote number in the text just after, and slightly above, the period at the end of the sentence(s) in which you are using source material.

- Then, at the bottom of the page, four lines below the last line of text on that page, begin the footnoting. Indent five spaces, or one-half inch, and repeat the footnote number, placing it slightly above the line on which you will type the source information. Single-space the information in each footnote, and leave a blank line between footnotes on the same page.

- The first time you cite a source, give full information for it, including the author's name, the title, the facts about the source's publication, and the page numbers. (See the examples on the next page.)

- For later footnotes to the same source, you may use a shortened form; usually, just the author's last name and the page number(s) are enough.

The guidelines on the next page show specific information to include in your footnotes and how to punctuate them.

Writing 2.3d Document reference sources by means of footnotes.

Mini-Workshop 2 • Documenting Reference Sources

GUIDELINES FOR USING FOOTNOTES

Book with One Author or Editor *First Note:* Author's or editor's full name (first name first) followed by the title, city of publication, publisher, year, and page number(s):

> [1] Karen Dudley, <u>Bald Eagles</u> (Austin: Raintree Steck-Vaughn, 1998) 54–55.

Later Notes: [7] Dudley 37.

More Than One Source by the Same Author(s) *First Note:* See the style in the example above.

Later Notes: Author's last name followed by title (or a shortened form of it) and page number(s):

> [4] Grambo, <u>Eagles: Masters of the Sky</u> 46.

Book with Two or More Authors or Editors *First Note:* All authors' or editors' names (first name first, abbreviating "editors" as "eds.") followed by title, city, publisher, year, and page number(s):

> [2] Joan D. Barghusen and Deborah Hitzeroth, eds., <u>The Bald Eagle</u> (San Diego: Lucent Books, 1998) 66–67.

Later Notes: [8] Barghusen and Hitzeroth 47.

Newspaper or Magazine Article *First Note:* Author's full name followed by the title of the article, the title of the magazine or newspaper where the article appeared, date of publication, and page number:

> [3] James Gerstenzang, "Eagle May Fly From Nest of Endangered," <u>Los Angeles Times</u> 6 May 1998: A1.

Later Notes: [9] Gerstenzang A1.

Nonprint Source: Personal Interview *First Note:* Full name of speaker followed by *personal interview* and the date the interview took place:

> [5] Vanessa Sullivan, personal interview, 17 Nov. 2003.

Later Notes: [10] Sullivan.

Nonprint Source: Web Site *First Note:* Title followed by date of electronic publication, name of site sponsor, date you accessed the site, and Web site address:

> [6] <u>Bald Eagle: The U.S.A.'s National Symbol</u>, 1997, American Eagle Foundation, 16 Nov. 2003 <http://www.eagles.org/moreabout.html>.

Later Notes: [11] <u>Bald</u>.

PRACTICE & APPLY **Document Reference Sources**

Use the method of documenting reference sources that your teacher prefers to create source citations within the research report you wrote for the Writing Workshop on pages 626–653.

Writing a Descriptive Essay

If you have written a short story, you have probably written brief descriptions of settings and characters. When you write a **description,** your main **purpose** is to paint a detailed, vivid picture of an object, place, animal, or person. You use words to help your audience see, hear, smell, taste, and touch the subject of your description. You might also choose to share with readers your thoughts, memories, and feelings about your subject.

In this section you will choose and observe a subject, organize a description of that subject, and use sensory details to elaborate your description.

Decisions, Decisions Look around you. You can probably see more objects, places, or people than you can count. How do you decide which one to describe? Here are some qualities to look for in choosing the subject of a description.

- **Sense-able** Choose something that appeals to several of your senses. For example, you might choose a place that not only *looks* interesting, but also contains a variety of sounds, smells, tastes, or textures, such as a kitchen.

- **Observable** Choose something that you can spend at least twenty minutes observing. For example, don't write about a rabbit that you caught a glimpse of this morning. Write instead about your neighbor's pet rabbit that you are allowed to hold and play with.

- **Manageable** Choose something that can be fully described in a 500- to 700-word essay. For example, you could not describe the whole Pacific Ocean, but you could describe one small cove.

- **Meaningful** Choose something that is important or interesting to you.

- **Comfortable** Choose a topic you will feel comfortable sharing with readers.

What You See Is What They'll Get Close, accurate observation is essential to writing a description. Once you choose a subject, spend at least twenty minutes observing it. As you observe, take notes, paying particular attention to the **specific details** that make your subject unique.

Here are some questions to help you develop details for your description.

- What color(s) is your subject?
- What size is the subject?
- What shape or shapes do you see?
- What sounds do you hear?
- Does the subject have a particular smell?
- What does your subject feel like—soft, gritty, moist, cold, silky?
- What memories do you associate with the subject?
- How do you feel about the subject?
- Can you use a simile or metaphor to compare the subject to something else? (For information on **similes** and **metaphors,** see page 701.)

Writing **1.0** The writing exhibits students' awareness of the audience and purpose. **1.2** Support all statements and claims with descriptions.

An Orderly Choice When you have observed your subject thoroughly and have recorded as many details about it as possible, you must decide how to organize those details. Two effective ways to organize details in a description are *spatial organization* and *order of importance*.

When you describe items according to their location, you are using **spatial organization.** Using this technique, you start your description at a certain point and then move in a logical way around your subject. For example, if you were describing a dog, you might start with the dog's face and then move along his body to his tail. You could organize the description in your essay so that it moves

- from top to bottom or bottom to top
- from near to far or far to near
- from left to right or right to left
- from inside to outside or outside to inside

When you use spatial organization for your description, it is important that your readers be able to follow your movements around your subject. The following chart gives **transitions** you can use to show the relationships among details and to help readers follow your essay.

Words Showing Spatial Organization		
across from	close	near
around	down	next to
between	far	up

Another way to organize your description is by **order of importance,** starting with what you consider to be the most important element of your subject and finishing with the least important element, or vice versa. For example, if you were describing a photograph of someone, you might first describe the person and then the background (most important to least important), or you could first describe the background and then the person (least important to most important).

Beef It Up Elaborate on the details about your subject by using **descriptive language**—sensory details, figures of speech, and precise words. Descriptive language helps you *show* your subject rather than just *tell* about it.

- **Sensory details** appeal to the senses of sight, smell, touch, taste, and hearing.

  Example: The yellow cat, purring loudly, curled up on the soft pillow.

- **Figures of speech** make comparisons between two different things. A **simile** uses the words *like* or *as* to make the comparison, while a **metaphor** makes the comparison directly.

  Examples: The cat purred *like distant thunder.* (simile)

  The cat *is the queen* of the household. (metaphor)

- **Precise words** give readers an exact picture of your subject.

  Example: The cat folded its paws and then dreamily closed its eyes.

Writing 1.1 Create an organizational structure that balances all aspects of the composition and uses effective transitions between sentences to unify important ideas.

Picture This   As you read the following description, notice how author Jamaica Kincaid uses specific details, spatial organization, and descriptive language to describe her narrator's friend Gwen. Notice also that she includes the narrator's thoughts and feelings about Gwen.

Professional Model

Specific details

Spatial organization— head to toe

Precise words

Sensory details

Figure of speech

Figure of speech

Gwen and I were soon inseparable. If you saw one, you saw the other. For me, each day began as I waited for Gwen to come by and fetch me for school. My heart beat fast as I stood in the front yard of our house waiting to see Gwen as she rounded the bend in our street. The sun, already way up in the sky so early in the morning, shone on her, and the whole street became suddenly empty so that Gwen and everything about her were perfect, as if she were in a picture. Her panama hat, with the navy blue and gold satin ribbon—our school color—around the brim, sat lopsided on her head, for her head was small and she never seemed to get the correct-size hat, and it had to be anchored with a piece of elastic running under her chin. The pleats in the tunic of her uniform were in place, as was to be expected. Her cotton socks fit neatly around her ankles, and her shoes shone from just being polished. If a small breeze blew, it would ruffle the ribbons in her short, shrubby hair and the hem of her tunic; if the hem of her tunic was disturbed in that way, I would then be able to see her knees. She had bony knees and they were always ash-colored, as if she had just finished giving them a good scratch or had just finished saying her prayers. The breeze might also blow back the brim of her hat, and since she always walked with her head held down I might then be able to see her face: small, flattish nose; lips the shape of a saucer broken evenly in two; wide, high cheekbones; ears pinned back close against her head—which was always set in a serious way, as if she were going over in her mind some of the many things we had hit upon that were truly a mystery to us. (Though once I told her that about her face, and she said that really she had only been thinking about me. I didn't look to make sure, but I felt as if my whole skin had become covered with millions of tiny red boils and that shortly I would explode with happiness.) When finally she reached me, she would look up and we would both smile and say softly, "Hi." We'd set off for school side by side, our feet in step, not touching but feeling as if we were joined at the shoulder, hip, and ankle, not to mention heart.

Feelings

Jamaica Kincaid, *Annie John*

Now You Try The framework below will help you write the first draft of your descriptive essay.

Quick guide

Introduction
Introduce your subject, giving any necessary background information.

Body
- Begin your detailed description of the subject, using sensory details, figures of speech, and precise words.
- For spatial organization, move from one point to another, such as from top to bottom. For order of importance, begin with the most important detail and move to the least important, or vice versa.

Conclusion
Close with your final thoughts or feelings or with a question about what you have observed. Leave your reader with an understanding of the importance or uniqueness of your subject.

Finishing Touches After you have written a first draft, review your description and revise where necessary by following these suggestions.

- Add **details** about the subject's shape, size, color, texture, sound, smell, or taste.
- Add **figures of speech** and **precise words.**
- Include your **thoughts** or **feelings** about your subject.
- Rearrange information to make the **organization** of your description clearer.

After you revise your description, proofread it and consider how you would like to publish it. You might read your description to family members and friends or turn your description into an illustrated booklet for children.

PRACTICE & APPLY   Write a Descriptive Essay

Use the steps on pages 700–703 to develop a description of at least five hundred words. Revise your description to make it clearer and more vivid. Finally, proofread your essay and choose a way to publish it.

Writing **1.0** Students write clear, coherent, and focused essays. Essays contain formal introductions, supporting evidence, and conclusions. **1.7** Revise writing to improve organization and word choice after checking the logic of the ideas and the precision of the vocabulary. **2.0** Students write descriptive texts of at least 500 to 700 words.

Writing an Autobiographical Narrative

Writing an autobiographical narrative is similar to writing a short story. Like a short story, an autobiographical narrative includes a **setting**, a **plot**, a **point of view**, and **characters**. However, when you write an autobiographical narrative, the point of view is your own and the main character is *you*. In autobiographical writing your **purpose** for writing will be partly to express your own thoughts and feelings. In this section you will write about an incident from your life that has had an effect on you or is meaningful to you.

The Big Event Since an autobiographical narrative focuses on only one event from your life, your first task is to choose an incident that

- you remember clearly
- you feel comfortable sharing with your **audience**
- had a significant impact on you

The Details Once you have chosen an incident, ask yourself what happened first, next, and so on. Jot down as many **action details**, details that tell what happened and what people did and said, as you can recall. Action details include

- **specific movements** (He threw his newspaper.)
- **gestures and expressions** (I hung my head.)

- **dialogue and thoughts** ("What are you doing?" he said.)

Including characters' movements, gestures, expressions, dialogue, and thoughts will help you create more **complex characters.**

Next, look over your action details and make sure that they are in **chronological order**—the order in which they actually occurred. Telling your story in chronological order will help readers imagine your experience exactly as it happened to you. To help you organize action details in chronological order, you might create a time line like the one below.

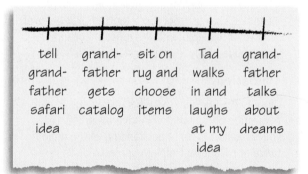

TIP To show the order of events in your narrative clearly and to create **coherence**, use *transitional words and phrases*. **Transitional words and phrases** that show chronological order include *first, then, next, just then, after, the next day, later, finally, before, at the same time,* and *meanwhile.*

Writing 1.0 Students write clear, coherent, and focused essays. The writing exhibits students' awareness of audience and purpose. Essays contain formal introductions, supporting evidence, and conclusions. 1.1 Create an organizational structure that uses effective transitions between sentences to unify important ideas. 1.2 Support all statements with descriptions and specific examples.

As you choose and arrange the action details that make up the sequence of events in your narrative, keep in mind that even though you are telling a true story, your narrative should have a **plot**. A standard plot includes a **conflict** that builds to a **climax**. As you plan your narrative, consider these questions about its plot.

■ **Conflict** Did someone or something cause problems or tension?

■ **Rising Action** What happened to complicate things and increase the problem, creating **suspense**?

■ **Climax** Which part of the incident was most tension-filled, scary, or exciting?

■ **Denouement** How did the conflict resolve itself? What was the final outcome?

Next, use **descriptive details** to describe the people involved and the **setting** and to elaborate on all of the actions that make up the incident. For example, look at the following two sentences. The first describes an action. The second adds descriptive details to fill out the picture.

He threw his newspaper. [action detail]

He tossed aside his rumpled newspaper. [action detail with descriptive details]

Notice that the second sentence gives the reader a better idea of what the event was like. To bring your own experience to life, jot down descriptive details next to each action detail you noted.

What Does It All Mean? Finally, write a sentence or two reflecting on the meaning of the incident. Did it change your life? Did you learn something important about yourself or another person? Did you learn what *not* to do next time? End your autobiographical narrative by making it clear why this incident is important to you—why it is so meaningful that you chose to write about it.

As you read the following autobiographical narrative, notice the details that bring the events, characters, and setting to life.

Writer's Model

> ### On Safari
>
> "Africa!" I said to my grandfather, waving my book at him like a flag. "I want to go on a safari to Africa!" I was ten years old, and I had just read a book about explorers in Africa.
>
> "Well," he said in a gravelly voice, "we'd better decide what you'll need to take along." He tossed aside his rumpled newspaper and reached for a fat department store catalog.
>
> *(continued)*

Action details

Dialogue

Writing 2.1 Write autobiographical narratives. **2.1a** Develop a standard plot (having a beginning, conflict, rising action, climax, and denouement) and point of view. **2.1b** Develop complex characters and a definite setting. **2.1c** Use a range of appropriate strategies (e.g., dialogue; suspense; naming of specific narrative action, including movement, gestures, and expressions).

(continued)

Setting Descriptive details	For the next hour, we sat on the rug in front of his potbellied stove, warm and cozy, while snow whirled and swirled past the windows. We made a list, imagining exactly what a ten-year-old boy would need on a safari to Africa.
Dialogue	"I think you might want the biggest of these tents," my grandfather said, pointing with a gnarled finger. "You might make some friends over there, you know." He added the tent to the growing list, which included a cookstove, hiking shoes, a
Descriptive details Action details	portable TV, frying pans, rain gear, and a collapsible microscope. Just then my older brother, Tad, walked in. "What are you doing?" he said.
Conflict Thoughts	After I explained, Tad laughed at the idea. "Don't be silly," he said. "You'll never get to Africa." I hung my head. Maybe he was right. How was I ever going to get as far as Africa? It *was* silly.
Denouement	"I know one thing for sure, boys," said Grandfather, stroking his beard. "Nobody ever gets anywhere worthwhile without first going there in dreams. Don't be afraid to dream."
Meaning of incident	I have always remembered my grandfather's words on that snowy afternoon, and when I do go on a safari to Africa, I'll be sure to take along a picture of him. After all, my safari will be proof of the important lesson my grandfather taught me—that the first step toward making your dreams come true is to dare to dream in the first place.

Thinking It Over Before you share your narrative with others, have a classmate read it and retell the narrative to you. Add details at any point where his or her retelling seems uncertain or dull. Add more transitions where the narrative's events seem unconnected. (For more on **transitions,** see page 687.)

PRACTICE & APPLY ### Write an Autobiographical Narrative

Use the steps on pages 704–706 to write an autobiographical narrative. Then, consider publishing your narrative by reading it aloud or posting it on a class author's wall.

Writing 2.0 Students write narrative texts.

Analyzing a Documentary

Several decades ago, CBS aired Edward R. Murrow's *Harvest of Shame*. This documentary led to legislation that improved the lives of migrant farm workers, who travel from place to place to harvest crops.

Murrow followed the workers for a season, showing viewers what life was like for them. One **technique** that he used effectively was the **interview**—letting the workers speak for themselves. One woman he interviewed had been working in the fields since she was eight years old. She had worked ten hours that day and earned only one dollar. She had fourteen children to feed.

Media critics say that this documentary triggered changes in federal policy toward migrant workers. What made the documentary so effective in influencing and informing viewers?

- **A timely topic.** CBS aired the program on Thanksgiving Day, forcing viewers to connect the food they ate with the migrant workers who had harvested it.

- **Powerful images, words, and sounds.** Part of what gives images, words, and sounds power is their arrangement. For example, an image of cattle being shipped was placed next to an image of workers jammed into trucks. This technique, **juxtaposition** (side-by-side arrangement), showed viewers that the workers were treated like cattle. Filmmakers can also use sound techniques, such as **music** and **background noise,** to add to the messages they present.

- **A bias, or point of view.** The filmmaker's **attitude,** or **bias,** toward the subject can reflect the documentary's **purpose.** The creators of *Harvest of Shame* revealed their bias indirectly through the selection and arrangement of images and interviews. Clearly, they intended to influence, not just inform. Murrow revealed his bias directly by urging viewers to help pass legislation to improve conditions for migrant workers.

PRACTICE & APPLY **Analyze a Documentary**

- View a documentary. As you watch, take notes on the topic; powerful images, words, and sounds; and the filmmaker's point of view and purpose.

- Also note techniques, such as interviews, juxtaposition, and music or background noise, used for effect.

- Using your notes, write a one-paragraph analysis of the documentary.

Listening and Speaking **1.2** Determine the speaker's attitude toward the subject. **1.8** Analyze the effect on the viewer of images, text, and sound in electronic journalism; identify the techniques used to achieve the effects in each instance studied.

Resource Center

Test Smarts *by* Flo Ota De Lange and Sheri Henderson

Strategies for Taking a Multiple-Choice Test

If you have ever watched a quiz show on TV, you know how multiple-choice tests work. You get a question and (usually) four choices. Your job is to pick the correct one. Easy! (Don't you wish?) Taking multiple-choice tests will get a whole lot easier when you apply these Test Smarts:

T rack your time.

E xpect success.

S tudy the directions.

T ake it all in.

S pot those numbers.

M aster the questions.

A nticipate the answers.

R ely on 50/50.

T ry. Try. Try.

S earch for skips and smudges.

Track Your Time

You race through a test for fear you won't finish, and then you sit watching your hair grow because you finished early, or you realize you have only five minutes left to complete eleven zillion questions. Sound familiar? You can avoid both problems if you take a few minutes before you start to estimate how much time you have for each question. Using all the time you are given can help you avoid making errors. Follow these tips to set **checkpoints:**

- How many questions should be completed when one quarter of the time is gone?
- What should the clock read when you are halfway through the questions?
- If you find yourself behind your checkpoints, you can speed up.
- If you are ahead, you can—and should—slow down.

Expect Success

Top athletes know that attitude affects performance. They learn to deal with their negative thoughts, to get on top of their mental game. So can you! But how? Do you compare yourself with others? Most top athletes will tell you that they compete against only one person: themselves. They know they cannot change another person's performance. Instead, they study their own performance and find ways to improve it. That makes sense for you too. You are older and more experienced than you were the day you took your last big test, right? So review your last scores. Figure out just what you need to do to top that "kid" you used to be. You can!

What if you get anxious? It's OK if you do. A little nervousness will help you focus. Of course, if you're so nervous that you think you might get sick or faint, take time to relax for a few minutes. Calm bodies breathe slowly. You can fool yours into feeling calmer and thinking more clearly by taking a few deep breaths—five slow counts in, five out. Take charge, take five, and then take the test.

Study the Directions

You're ready to go, go, go, but first it's wait, wait, wait. Pencils. Paper. Answer sheets. Lots of directions. Listen! In order to follow directions, you have to know them. Read all test directions as if they contain the key to lifetime happiness and several years' allowance. Then, read them again. Study the answer sheet. How is it laid out? Is it

1

2

3

4

or

1   2   3   4 ?

What about answer choices? Are they arranged

A   B   C   D

or

A   B

C   D ?

Directions count. Be very, very sure you know exactly what to do and how to do it before you make your first mark.

Take It All In

When you finally hear the words "You may begin," briefly **preview the test** to get a mental map of your tasks:

- Know how many questions you have to complete.

- Know where to stop.

- Set your time checkpoints.

- Do the easy sections first; easy questions are worth just as many points as hard ones.

Spot Those Numbers

"I got off by one and spent all my time trying to fix my answer sheet." Oops. Make it a habit to

- match the number of each question to the numbered space on the answer sheet every time

- leave the answer space on your answer sheet blank if you skip a question

- keep a list of your blank spaces on scratch paper or somewhere else—but *not* on your answer sheet. The less you have to erase on your answer sheet, the better.

Master the Questions

"I knew that answer, but I thought the question asked something else." Be sure—very sure—that you **know what a question is asking you.** Read the question at least twice before reading the answer choices. Approach it as you would a mystery story or a riddle. Look for clues. Watch especially for words like *not* and *except*—they tell you to look for the choice that is false or different from the other choices or opposite in some way. If you are taking a reading-comprehension test, read the selection, master all the questions, and then re-read the selection. The answers will be likely to pop out the second time around. Remember: A test isn't trying to trick you; it's trying to test your knowledge and your ability to think clearly.

Anticipate the Answers

All right, you now understand the question. Before you read the answer choices, **answer the question yourself. Then, read the choices.**

If the answer you gave is among the choices listed, it is probably correct.

Rely on 50/50

"I . . . have . . . no . . . clue." You understand the question. You gave an answer, but your answer is not listed, or perhaps you drew a complete blank. It happens. Time to **make an educated guess**—not a *wild* guess, but an *educated* guess. Think about quiz shows again, and you'll know the value of the 50/50 play. When two answers are eliminated, the contestant has a 50/50 chance of choosing the correct one. You can use elimination too.

Always read every choice carefully. **Watch out for distracters**—choices that may be true but are too broad, too narrow, or not relevant to the question. Eliminate the least likely choice. Then, eliminate the next, and so on until you find the best one. If two choices seem equally correct, look to see if "All of the above" is an option. If it is, that might be your choice. If no choice seems correct, look for "None of the above."

Try. Try. Try.

Keep at it. **Don't give up.** This sounds obvious, so why say it? You might be surprised by how many students do give up. Think of tests as a kind of marathon. Just as in any marathon, people get bored, tired, hungry, thirsty, hot, discouraged. They may begin to feel sick or develop aches and pains. They decide the test doesn't matter that much. They decide they don't care if it does—there'll always be next time; whose idea was this, anyway? They lose focus. Don't do it.

Remember: The last question is worth just as much as the first question, and the questions on a test don't get harder as you go. If the question you just finished was really hard, an easier one is probably coming up soon. Take a deep breath, and keep on slogging. Give it your all, all the way to the finish.

Search for Skips and Smudges

"Hey! I got that one right, and the machine marked it wrong!" If you have ever—ever—had this experience, pay attention! When this happens in class, your teacher can give you the extra point. On a machine-scored test, however, you would lose the point and never know why. So, listen up: All machine-scored answer sheets have a series of lines marching down the side. The machine stops at the first line and scans across it for your answer, stops at the second line, scans, stops at the third line, scans, and so on, all the way to the end. The machine is looking for a dark, heavy mark. If it finds one where it should be, you get the point. What if you left that question blank? A lost point. What if you changed an answer and didn't quite get the first mark erased? The machine sees two answers instead of one. A lost point. What if you made a mark to help yourself remember where you skipped an answer? You filled in the answer later but forgot to erase the mark. The machine again sees two marks. Another lost point. What if your marks are not very dark? The machine sees blank spaces. More lost points.

To avoid losing points, take time at the end of the test to make sure you

- did not skip any answers
- gave one answer for each question
- made the marks heavy and dark and within the lines

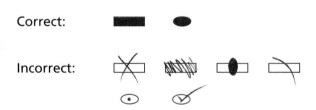

Get rid of smudges. Make sure there are no stray pencil marks on your answer sheet. Cleanly erase those places where you changed your mind. Check for little stray marks from pencil tapping. Check everything. You are the only person who can.

Reading Comprehension

Many tests have a section called **reading comprehension.** The good news is that you do not have to study for this part of the test. Taking a reading-comprehension test is a bit like playing ball. You don't know where the ball will land, so you have to stay alert to all possibilities. However, just as the ball can come at you in only a few ways, there are only a few kinds of questions on reading-comprehension tests. This discussion will help you identify the most common ones. Two kinds of texts are used here. The first one is an informational text. The second is an updated fairy tale.

DIRECTIONS: Read the following selection. Then, choose the best answer for each question. Mark each answer on your answer sheet in the square provided.

Night Lights on the High Seas

For centuries, lighthouses have been used to alert sailors that land is near, to point out dangerous rocks and reefs, and to cast a bright light into the night to guide ships on their way. Seafarers have relied on these structures since the days of ancient Egypt. The lighthouse built in 300 B.C. on Pharos, an island near Alexandria, was regarded as one of the Seven Wonders of the World.

Lighthouses help to guide ships at night by giving off an intense beam that flashes every few seconds. Until the eighteenth century, the source of light was an oak-log fire. Coal fire was used for many years after that, until electricity became common in the early twentieth century. Some modern lighthouses also send out radio signals to help ships find their way in foggy weather. Even in their modern form, lighthouses serve their ancient purpose as guiding lights, flashing specks of civilization in the dark, lonely waters of night.

ITEM 1 asks for vocabulary knowledge.

1. In the first paragraph, the word seafarers means —

    A oceans

    B sailors

    C fish

    D ships

Answer: Look at the surrounding sentences, or **context,** to see which definition fits.

A is incorrect. The word *ocean* is another word for "sea," but oceans do not rely on lighthouses.

B is the best answer. In the context of the passage, it makes sense that *sailors* have relied on lighthouses for centuries.

C is incorrect. Fish live and travel in the sea, but nothing in the passage indicates that they depend on lighthouses.

D is incorrect. The safety of ships on the ocean depends on lighthouses. However, it is the *sailors* on the ships who have "relied on these structures for centuries."

ITEM 2 asks for close reading. Read carefully to see if the answer is stated directly in the text.

2. What was used to produce the light in lighthouses before the eighteenth century?

    F Wood

    G Coal

    H Gas

    J Electricity

Answer: Read the passage carefully to find the answer.

F is the correct answer. The second sentence of the second paragraph indicates that "until the eighteenth century, the source of light was an oak-log fire." The words *oak* and *log* clearly indicate that "wood" is the right choice.

3. What is the main idea of this passage?

   A Working in a lighthouse is a dangerous job.

   B Modern lighthouses are very different from those of long ago.

   C The first lighthouse was built in 300 B.C. on the island of Pharos.

   D Lighthouses have helped guide ships for thousands of years.

Answer: Think about which statement covers the passage as a whole.

A is incorrect. The passage does not provide an explanation of working in a lighthouse.

B is incorrect. Lighthouses have not changed that much over the years.

C is incorrect. It is only one detail in the passage.

D is the best answer. It covers most of the details in the passage.

4. As more and more ships become equipped with navigational computers, what will probably happen?

   F More lighthouses will be built.

   G There will be more shipping accidents.

   H The number of lighthouses will be reduced.

   J Different energy sources will be used in lighthouses.

Answer: Find the information in the passage that supports a probable future outcome.

F is incorrect. Navigational computers will most likely reduce the need for lighthouses.

G is incorrect. The navigational computers will protect the ships from accidents.

H is the best answer. Navigational computers mean that ships will no longer need to rely on lighthouses for guidance.

J is incorrect. The passage does not say anything about new or different energy sources.

5. Which is an **opinion** expressed in the passage?

   A The beam from a lighthouse flashes every few seconds.

   B Modern lighthouses send out radio signals.

   C Pharos is an island near Alexandria.

   D The ocean waters are lonely at night.

Answer: A **fact** can be proved true or false. An **opinion,** a personal feeling or belief, cannot be proved true or false. **A, B,** and **C** are facts that can be proved true or false. **D is correct** because it is the only opinion.

6. What is the author's main **purpose** for writing this passage?

   F To entertain readers with an exciting story

   G To inform readers about the history of lighthouses

   H To persuade readers to visit a lighthouse

   J To describe what life in a lighthouse is like

Answer: Look at the information given in the passage, and decide what the writer's purpose was in writing.

F is incorrect. The writer does not tell a story.

G is the best answer. The writer presents information about the function of light-houses over time.

H is incorrect. The writer's purpose is not to persuade readers to visit a lighthouse.

J is incorrect. The writer never tells what it's like to live in a lighthouse.

DIRECTIONS: Read the following selection. Then, choose the best answer for each question. Mark each answer on your answer sheet in the space provided.

A Technologically Correct Fairy Tale:

Jack and the Beanstalk

There once was a poor widow who lived in a small cottage with her son, Jack. Jack was a good-hearted fellow who devoted all his time to a mega-computer game. Since Jack did not have a paying job, he and his widowed mother were very poor.

The day arrived when the widow had sold all her possessions via the Internet, except for an elderly cow. Jack was to sell the cow at the market since his mother was too frail to make the trip.

"Get a good price for her," the widow instructed.

"Yes, Mother," Jack answered.

Off he went with the cow in tow.

Out on the highway, Jack was stopped by a man who offered to trade him a handful of oddly shaped, brightly colored beans for the cow. "These are turbo-beans," the man whispered. While Jack didn't know exactly what that meant, he did know that the word *turbo* made the beans sound special, so he agreed to the trade. When he got home, he proudly handed the beans to his mother. She promptly tossed them out the window, declaring she didn't know what he could have been thinking. . . .

ITEM 1 is a vocabulary question. To answer it, consider the surrounding words, or **context,** to identify the best definition.

1. In the first paragraph the underlined word devoted means —

   A donated

   B avoided

   C captured

   D dedicated

A is incorrect. *Donated* means "gave someone something of value." It doesn't fit in this context.

B is incorrect. It doesn't fit the context, which shows what Jack did with his time, not what he didn't do.

C is incorrect. It doesn't fit in the context.

D is the best answer. In this context, *devoted* means "dedicated" or "gave one's time to a particular pursuit."

ITEM 2 is another vocabulary question.

2. In the second paragraph of the fairy tale, frail means —

   F proud

   G weak

   H stubborn

   J forceful

The best answer is G, since it offers the only reason why the widow would not be able to make the trip herself.

ITEM 3 is a factual question. Re-read the fairy tale, and you'll find the answer.

3. How did the widow sell all of her possessions, except for the old cow?

   A She sold them via the Internet.

   B She set up a shop on the highway.

   C She sold them to her neighbors.

   D She sold them to the man with the beans.

A is the best answer. The fairy tale clearly states that she sold her possessions on the Internet.

B is incorrect. Jack met the man with the beans on the main highway. The widow did not go there.

C is incorrect. Neighbors are not mentioned in the selection.

D is incorrect. Jack, not the widow, traded the cow for the beans.

ITEM 4 asks you to analyze a cause-and-effect relationship. Don't worry, though. The answer is in the text.

4. Because Jack didn't have a paying job, he and his mother were —

    F supported by an uncle

    G very poor

    H reduced to stealing

    J very angry

F is incorrect. An uncle is not mentioned in the story.

G is the best answer. The fairy tale says that they were poor.

H is incorrect. Stealing is not mentioned in the story.

J is incorrect. Anger is not mentioned in the story.

ITEM 5 requires that you make an **inference** based on the text.

5. Jack's mother didn't think beans for a cow was a good trade. How do you know this?

    A She explains that a cow is worth more than a handful of beans.

    B Jack was supposed to sell the cow.

    C The man cheated Jack.

    D She tossed the beans out the window.

A is incorrect. Jack's mother doesn't say this in the story.

B is incorrect. This is true, but it doesn't explain why his mother didn't think it was a good trade.

C is incorrect. This may be true, but it doesn't tell us how we know what Jack's mother thought of the trade.

D is the best answer. Her actions show what she thought of the trade.

ITEM 6 asks you to use your **prior knowledge** about fairy tales to predict the outcome of this tale.

6. If this story ended like a typical fairy tale, which of the following predictions would you make?

    F The beans do, indeed, prove worthless.

    G The beans become the key to lifelong happiness for Jack and his mother.

    H The beans end up in a stew.

    J The cow comes home.

F is incorrect. The fairy tale cannot have its "happily ever after" ending if the beans are worthless.

G is the best answer. In fairy tales, magical gifts from strangers often bring great rewards in the end.

H is incorrect. This is too ordinary an ending for a fairy tale.

J is incorrect. This ending is also too ordinary for a fairy tale.

Strategies for Taking Writing Tests

Writing a Fictional or Autobiographical Narrative

Some tests may include writing prompts that ask you to write a narrative, or story. The following steps will help you write a **fictional** or **autobiographical narrative**. The responses are based on this prompt.

> ### Prompt
>
> Write a short fictional narrative. The story should include major and minor characters, a thoroughly developed plot, and a definite setting.

THINKING IT THROUGH

Writing a Fictional or Autobiographical Narrative

STEP 1 Read the prompt carefully. Does the prompt ask you to write a fictional story (a made-up story) or an **autobiographical story** (a story of something that really happened to you)?

The word "fictional" tells me that the prompt is asking for a made-up story.

STEP 2 Outline the plot of your narrative. Explain the conflict, the climax, and the resolution.

Conflict—the main character, Sue, wants to win the fencing tournament. Climax—Sue fences against the champion. Resolution—Sue wins but feels bad when she sees her opponent crying.

STEP 3 Identify the major and minor characters. What do they look and act like? How do they sound when they speak?

Major character—Sue is tall and lanky; she is shy; she is very competitive. Minor character—Sue's competitor, Tory, is tall; she is confident and sometimes rude.

STEP 4 Identify the setting of your narrative. Where and when does your story take place?

The story takes place in January during the state fencing championships in a gymnasium.

STEP 5 Draft your narrative, adding dialogue, suspense, and sensory details.

I plan to create suspense by drawing out the moment when Sue must decide what to do when she sees Tory crying. I will use sensory details to describe how she feels. I will also include dialogue of her conversation with Tory.

STEP 6 Revise and proofread your narrative. Make sure that you have organized the events in your story in a logical order. Add transitions that show time, such as *earlier, afterward, at the same time,* and *later.*

Writing a Summary

Some tests include writing prompts like the one to the right.

To write a **summary** of a passage, you rewrite in your own words the passage's main idea and significant details. The summary should both paraphrase and condense the original. A summary of a short passage should be about one-third as long. For a longer selection, a summary should include no more than one sentence for each paragraph.

The following steps will help you write an effective summary in response to a prompt. The student responses are based on only two paragraphs from the reading selection "The Body's Defenses" on pages 627–629. On a test, though, the student would summarize the entire selection.

Prompt

Read the article "The Body's Defenses," and then summarize it. In your summary, include the main idea and significant details of the article.

THINKING IT THROUGH · **Writing a Summary**

STEP 1 Read the passage carefully. Identify the main idea, and restate it in your own words. What is the most important point the writer is making about the topic? How would *you* say it?

Main idea: Skin and mucus are the first parts of the immune system to fight germs.

STEP 2 Identify significant details to include in the summary. Which details directly support the main idea? List at least one key idea or detail from each paragraph.

Significant details: Microorganisms are stopped by skin unless it is damaged, so you should wash cuts; mucus protects tissue not covered by skin, like the inside of your nose; mucus traps germs from the air—sneeze or blow your nose to get rid of them.

STEP 3 Write the main idea and most significant details in a paragraph, using your own words. Give details in the same order they are presented in the passage.

Skin and mucus are the first parts of the immune system to fight germs. Skin stops germs unless it is damaged, so it is important to wash cuts. Mucus protects tissue, like the inside of your nose, that is not covered by skin. Nose mucus traps germs from the air, which are removed by blowing the nose or sneezing.

Writing a Response to Literature

On a writing test, you may be asked to write a **literary response.** Often on such tests, you will be given a literary selection to read and a prompt such as the one on the right.

Prompt

What sort of character is Andrew from the short story "Duffy's Jacket"? Analyze his thoughts, actions, and words.

The following steps and the partial student responses will help you respond to a prompt like the one above. The short story "Duffy's Jacket" can be found on pages 7–11.

THINKING IT THROUGH ○ ○ Writing a Response to Literature

▶ **STEP 1 Read the prompt carefully, noting key words.** Key words might include a verb—such as *analyze, identify,* or *explain*—and a literary element—such as *plot, character, setting,* or *theme.*

The key words are "analyze" and "character."

▶ **STEP 2 Read the selection at least twice.** Read first for the overall meaning of the work. Then, read the selection a second time, keeping the key words from the prompt in mind.

▶ **STEP 3 Write a main idea statement.** Your main idea statement should give the title and author of the work and should directly address the prompt.

Andrew, the narrator of "Duffy's Jacket" by Bruce Coville, is similar to my friend Joss; both are easygoing and funny.

▶ **STEP 4 Find specific examples and details from the selection to support your main idea.** If you include quotations from the literary work, remember to enclose them in quotation marks.

When Andrew's mom gets mad at Andrew for not reminding Duffy to get his jacket, Andrew thinks to himself, "What do I look like, a walking memo pad?"

▶ **STEP 5 Draft, revise, and proofread your response.** To create coherence, use transitions between ideas, such as *for example, however,* and *finally.* When you have written your draft, re-read it to make sure you have presented your ideas clearly. Also, check to see that you have fully addressed all the key words in the prompt. Finally, proofread to correct mistakes in spelling, punctuation, and capitalization.

Using the T.H.E.M.E.S. Strategy on a Writing Test

Writing tests often ask you to write a **persuasive essay** in response to a prompt. Most of these prompts give you a topic, but you must identify your position and generate support for your position. Thinking of what to say in a limited amount of time is one of the most difficult parts of such a test.

Use the T.H.E.M.E.S. strategy, explained in the steps below, to generate support for a position quickly. The student responses are based on this prompt.

Prompt

The city council is considering building a parking garage or a park on an empty lot. Write an essay that takes a position on the issue and defends the position with relevant support.

THINKING IT THROUGH

Using the T.H.E.M.E.S. Strategy on a Writing Test

Each letter in T.H.E.M.E.S. stands for a category you could use to trigger ideas for supporting your position in a persuasive essay.

T=Time   H=Health   E=Education   M=Money   E=Environment   S=Safety

STEP 1 Identify your position on the topic given in the prompt.

The city council should build a park.

STEP 2 Use T.H.E.M.E.S to list benefits for your position.

T = A park would take less time to build than a garage. H = People could use the park to exercise and remain healthy. E = People might become more aware, or educated, about the wildlife and plants that occupy the area. M = The city would save money because constructing playscapes and jogging trails is less expensive than clearing the land and building a garage. E = The environment would benefit because the trees and homes of animals are not destroyed. S = Without a garage, fewer cars may drive in the area, reducing the safety hazard of automobile accidents.

STEP 3 Identify the three strongest reasons you developed using T.H.E.M.E.S. Your strongest reasons will be those for which you have the most evidence and those that address readers' concerns about the topic.

My three strongest reasons for building a park are health benefits, reduced costs, and environmental benefits. These are the issues that I think concern my readers the most.

Handbook of Reading and Informational Terms

For more information about a topic, turn to the page(s) in this book indicated on a separate line at the end of the entry. To learn more about *Cause and Effect,* for example, turn to page 170.

On another line are cross-references to entries in this handbook that provide closely related information. For instance, the entry *Chronological Order* contains a cross-reference to *Text Structures.*

ANALOGY

1. An **analogy** is a point-by-point comparison made between two things to show how they are alike. An analogy shows how something unfamiliar is like something well-known. Writers of scientific texts often use analogies. In "When the Earth Shakes" (page 371), Patricia Lauber uses an analogy to compare the strain inside a rock before an earthquake to the strain in a bent ruler.

> Rock shifts or breaks for the same reason that anything else does: because it has been put under great strain. If you take a ruler and bend it, you are putting it under strain. If you bend, or strain, it too much, it will break.

2. Another kind of analogy is a **verbal analogy.** A verbal analogy is a word puzzle. It gives you two words and asks you to identify another pair of words with a similar relationship. In an analogy the symbol ":" means "is to." The symbol "::" means "as."

> Select the pair of words that best completes the analogy.
>
> Toe : foot :: _____
>
> A house : barn
>
> B finger : hand
>
> C road : path
>
> D light : darkness
>
> The correct answer is B: Toe : foot :: finger : hand, or "Toe is to foot as finger is to hand." The relationship is that of part to whole. A toe is part of the foot; a finger is part of the hand.

Another relationship often represented in verbal analogies is that of opposites:

> clear : cloudy :: bright : dark

Both sets of words are opposites. Clear is the opposite of cloudy, and bright is the opposite of dark.

Verbal analogies are often found in tests, where they are used to check vocabulary and thinking skills.

See pages 179, 202, 356.

ARGUMENT An **argument** is a position supported by evidence. Arguments are used to persuade us to accept or reject an opinion on a subject. Arguments are also used to persuade us to act in a certain way.

Supporting evidence can take the form of facts, statistics, anecdotes (brief stories that illustrate a point), and expert opinions. Not all arguments are logical. **Emotional appeals** find their way into most arguments, and you should learn to recognize them. Details that appeal to your feelings make an argument more interesting and memorable—but you should not accept an argument that is based only on an emotional appeal.

Athletes should not charge kids for autographs. The most popular players are the ones that fans ask for autographs. These players don't need extra money. They already earn millions of dollars. Kids are much poorer than star athletes. I had to spend six weeks of my allowance and borrow twenty dollars from my brother to attend a game. After the game I started waiting in line to get an autograph. The line broke up quickly when we heard that the player was charging fifty dollars for each autograph. We were all disgusted. After all, the athletes' fans make them famous. My soccer coach says players should see that an autograph is a way of saying "thank you" to a loyal fan. Signing a name isn't hard. It takes less than a minute. To be asked to pay for an autograph is an insult.	*Position* *Opinion* *Fact* *Anecdote* *Emotional appeal* *Expert opinion* *Fact* *Emotional appeal*

See pages 257, 432.
See also *Evidence*.

BIAS (bī′əs) A leaning in favor of or against a person or issue is called a **bias.** Sometimes a writer's bias is obvious. For instance, Rudyard Kipling in "Rikki-tikki-tavi" (page 21) reveals his bias against snakes. In the conflict between the cobras and a mongoose, Kipling is clearly biased in favor of the mongoose. People are often not upfront about their biases. You should look for bias whenever writers or speakers make claims and assertions that they don't (or can't) support with logical reasons and facts. When people ignore, distort, or hide the facts that oppose their bias, they may be guilty of prejudice.

See page 463.

CAUSE AND EFFECT A **cause** is the event that makes something happen. An **effect** is what happens as a result of the cause. Storytellers use the cause-and-effect organizational pattern to develop their plots. Writers of historical texts use this organizational pattern to explain things like the causes and effects of war. Scientific writers use this organizational pattern to explain things like the causes and effects of an epidemic. Some of the words and phrases that point to causes and effects are *because, since, therefore, so that,* and *if . . . then.* Notice the cause-and-effect chain in the following summary of the Midas myth:

Because he did a favor for a god, Midas was granted the golden touch. Since everything he touched turned to gold, his daughter also turned to gold. Because of that, he asked to be released from the golden touch. Since gold had brought him such trouble, he then turned to nature and rejected riches.

See pages 170, 185, 198, 370.
See also *Text Structures*.

CHRONOLOGICAL ORDER Most narrative texts, true or fictional, are written in **chronological order.** Writers use chronological order when they put events in the sequence, or order, in which they happened in time, one after the other. Recipes and technical directions are usually written in chronological order. When you read a narrative, look for words and phrases like *next, then,* and *finally.* Writers use such words as transitions to signal the order in which events or steps occur.

See page 15.
See also *Text Structures.*

COMPARE-AND-CONTRAST PATTERN

When you **compare,** you look for similarities, or likenesses. When you **contrast,** you look for differences. You've used comparison and contrast many times. For instance, you might compare and contrast the features of several dogs when you choose a puppy that is like the dog you used to have. When writers compare and contrast, they organize the text to help readers understand the **points of comparison,** the features that they're looking at.

A Venn diagram can help you tell similarities from differences. The one below compares and contrasts two stories: "Yeh-Shen" (page 251) and the Cinderella folk tale. Where the circles overlap, note how the stories are alike. Where there is no overlap, note differences.

Venn Diagram

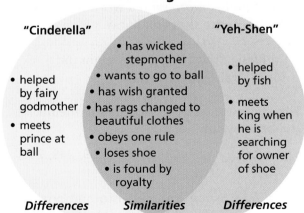

An effective comparison-and-contrast text may be organized in the block pattern or the point-by-point pattern.

Block pattern. A writer using the block pattern first discusses all the points of subject 1, then goes on to discuss all the points of subject 2.

> **Subject 1—"Yeh-Shen":** In the Chinese folk tale "Yeh-Shen" a magic fish dies, but its spirit gives Yeh-Shen, a kind orphan, advice and help. It changes her rags into beautiful clothes. Her wicked stepmother treats Yeh-Shen badly. [*And so on*]
>
> **Subject 2—"Cinderella":** American children probably know best the Cinderella story in which a fairy godmother changes Cinderella's rags into beautiful clothes. Cinderella also has a wicked stepmother. [*And so on*]

Point-by-point pattern. A writer who uses the point-by-point pattern goes back and forth between the two things being compared and contrasted.

> In "Yeh-Shen" a magic fish helps the orphan girl. In "Cinderella," however, a fairy godmother helps the girl. In both stories, there is a wicked stepmother. [*And so on*]

Some of the words that signal comparison and contrast are *although, but, either . . . or, however,* and *yet.*

See pages 136, 308, 320.
See also *Text Structures.*

CONCLUSIONS A **conclusion** is a general summing up of the specific details in a text. The text below is from "Buddies Bare Their Affection for Ill Classmate" (page 368). One reader's conclusion based on these details follows the text.

> In Mr. Alter's fifth-grade class, it's difficult to tell which boy is undergoing chemotherapy. Nearly all the boys are bald. Thirteen of them shaved their heads so a sick classmate wouldn't feel out of place.
>
> **Conclusion:** These boys care a lot about their sick classmate.

See also *Evidence.*

CONNOTATION AND DENOTATION The **connotation** of a word is all the feelings and associations that have come to be attached to the word. The **denotation** of a word is its strict dictionary definition. Not all words have connotations. Words like *the, writer,* and *paper* do not have connotations. Words like *Democrat, Republican, conservative,* and *liberal* are loaded with associations and feelings.

The words *skinny, slender, gaunt,* and *lean* have approximately the same denotation. They all mean "thin; having little fat." There are important shades of meaning among those words, however. If a relative said you were skinny or gaunt, you'd probably feel hurt or angry. *Skinny* and *gaunt* have negative connotations. They suggest that the thin person may have been sick and is now unattractive. *Slender* and *lean,* on the other hand, have positive connotations. They suggest a healthy, athletic body.

See page 349.

CONTEXT CLUES When you don't know the meaning of a word, look for a clue to its meaning in the **context,** the words and sentences surrounding the unfamiliar word. Here are some common types of context clues. In each sentence, the unfamiliar word appears in boldface type; the clue is underlined.

Definition clue. Look for a familiar word that defines the meaning of the unfamiliar word.

> Keevan was rarely <u>bothered</u> by rivals, but he was **perturbed** to see Beterli wandering over to him.

The word *bothered* tells you that *perturbed* also means "something like bothered."

Example clue. Look for examples of the unfamiliar word. In the context of the sentence, the examples reveal the meaning of the unfamiliar word.

> **Tugs** and <u>other</u> <u>boats</u> were washed ashore by the tidal wave.

The words *other boats* tell you that a tug is a kind of boat.

Restatement clue. Look for words that restate the meaning of the unfamiliar word.

> We **delved** into the criminal's past—we <u>searched through</u> hundreds of pieces of evidence.

The restatement clue that helps you guess the meaning of *delved* is *searched through.* (*Delved* means "dug into; searched; investigated.")

Contrast clue. Look for words that contrast the unfamiliar word with a word or phrase in the sentence that you know.

> Although Helen wanted to **detain** the visitors, she had to <u>let</u> them <u>go.</u>

This sentence tells you that *detain* means the opposite of "let go."

See pages 203, 209, 249, 295.

EVIDENCE When you read informational and persuasive texts, you need to **assess,** or judge, the **evidence** that a writer uses to support a position. That means you need to read carefully, looking critically at the writer's claims and assertions. You need to evaluate the writer's sources. You also need to look at the writer's own background and expertise. One way to assess evidence is to give it the **3As test.** The *As* stand for *adequate, appropriate,* and *accurate.*

Adequate means "sufficient" or "enough." You have to see if the writer has provided enough evidence to support his or her position. For some positions, one or two supporting facts may be adequate. For others a writer may need to provide many facts, maybe even statistics. Sometimes a direct quotation from a well-respected expert, an authority on the subject, will be convincing.

You must make sure that the writer's evidence is **appropriate,** that it has direct bearing on the conclusion. Sometimes a writer presents a lot of flashy evidence, such as details loaded with emotional appeals. When you look at this kind of evidence closely, you realize that it doesn't have much, if anything, to do with the writer's conclusions.

To make sure that the evidence is **accurate,** or correct, check to see that it comes from a source you can trust. Don't assume that everything (or anything) you see online or even printed in a newspaper or book is accurate. If a fact, example, or quotation doesn't sound accurate, check it out. Look for the title of the magazine or book that the quotation comes from. Is it a reliable source? Look up the writer's background. Does the writer have the background and education to qualify him or her as an expert on the subject? Is the writer biased in some way?

See pages 463, 467.
See also *Argument.*

FACT AND OPINION A **fact** is a statement that can be proved true. Some facts are easy to prove by **observation.** For instance, *Cats make different vocal sounds* is a fact you can prove by listening to cats meow and purr. Other facts can be **verified,** or proved, if you look them up in a reliable source. You need to be sure that the source is **authoritative**—an official source that can be trusted, such as an encyclopedia. In fields where new discoveries are being made, you need to check facts in a *recently* published source.

An **opinion** expresses a personal belief or feeling. Sometimes strongly held opinions look and sound like facts. Dog lovers would never question the statement *Dogs are smarter than cats.* Cat lovers, however, would express the opposite opinion, *Cats are smarter than dogs,* and believe it just as strongly. Even if a statement sounds as if it's true, it's not a fact unless it can be proved. Here are some opinions:

> Travel to other planets will happen in my lifetime.
>
> We have the best football team in the United States.
>
> Every teenager should receive an allowance.

A **valid opinion** is a personal belief that is supported by facts. An **invalid opinion** is a belief that is either not supported by facts or is supported by illogical and wishful thinking.

Remember that what you see in print or on the Internet may or may not be true. If a statement looks like a fact but you suspect it's an opinion, check it out in a reliable source. Ask: Can this be proved true?

See pages 146, 257, 270, 323.

FALLACIOUS REASONING
Fallacious (fə·lā′shəs) means "false." **Fallacious reasoning** is false reasoning. Here are four major types of false reasoning:

1. **Hasty generalizations** are reached without considering enough facts. A

generalization is a conclusion drawn after considering as much of the evidence as possible. (See page 332.) If there is even one exception to the conclusion, your generalization is not true or valid.

> **Fact:** "User Friendly" is a story with a surprise ending.
>
> **Fact:** "After Twenty Years" is a story with a surprise ending.
>
> **Hasty generalization:** All stories have surprise endings.

That conclusion is a hasty generalization. You could name many stories that do not have a surprise ending. Sometimes hasty generalizations can be corrected by using a qualifying word such as *most, usually, some, many,* or *often.* It is especially important to watch out for hasty generalizations when you're reading a persuasive text.

2. With **circular reasoning** a writer tries to fool you by restating the opinion in different words.

> Hungry students can't study because they haven't had enough to eat.
>
> Jean is the best candidate for student-council president because she's better than all the other candidates.

3. **Cause-and-effect fallacies.** One common **cause-and-effect fallacy** assumes that if something happens right before another event, the first event caused the next event.

> I wasn't wearing my lucky shirt, so I failed my history test.

Another **cause-and-effect fallacy** names a single cause for a complicated situation that has many causes.

> Popularity in middle school depends on wearing the right clothes.

4. The **either-or fallacy** suggests that there are only two sides to an issue.

> Either you get a summer job, or you waste the whole summer.

See also *Argument, Evidence, Persuasion.*

5W-HOW? The first paragraph of a news story, called the **lead** (lēd) paragraph, usually answers the questions *who? what? when? where? why?* and *how?* Look for the answers to these **5W-How?** questions when you read a newspaper story or any eyewitness account.

See page 62.

GENERALIZATION A **generalization** is a broad statement that covers several particular situations. Scientists and detectives, for instance, begin their investigations by amassing many specific facts. Then they put the facts together and draw a conclusion about what all this evidence tells them, what it adds up to.

> **Fact:** Cobras are poisonous.
>
> **Fact:** Rattlesnakes are poisonous.
>
> **Fact:** Garter snakes are not poisonous.
>
> **Generalization:** Some snakes are poisonous.

The generalization *Most snakes are poisonous* would have been incorrect. Only three species out of a population of more than 2,500 species of snakes were considered. About four fifths of all snakes are not poisonous. To be valid, a generalization must be based on all the evidence (the facts) that can be gathered.

See page 332.
See also *Stereotyping.*

GRAPHIC FEATURES **Graphic features** are design elements in a text. They include things like headings, maps, charts, graphs, and illustrations. Graphic features are visual ways of communicating information.

Some design elements you may find in a text are **boldface** and *italic* type; type in different styles (called fonts), sizes, and colors; bullets (dots that set off items in a list); and logos (like computer icons). For example, the Quickwrite heading in this book always appears with the pencil logo. Design elements make a text look more attractive. They also steer your eyes to different types of information and make the text easier to read.

A **heading** serves as a title for the information that follows it. Size and color set off from the rest of the text the type used for a heading. A repeated heading, like "Bonus Question" in this textbook, is always followed by the same type of material. Skimming the headings is one way to preview a text.

Graphic features such as **maps, charts,** and **graphs** display and sometimes explain complex information with lines, drawings, and symbols. Graphic features usually include these elements:

1. A **title** identifies the subject or main idea of the graphic.

2. **Labels** identify specific information.

3. A **caption** is text (usually under an illustration) that explains what you're looking at.

4. A **legend,** or **key,** helps you interpret symbols and colors, usually on a map.

Look for a **scale,** which relates the size or distance of something on a map to the real-life size and distance.

5. The source tells where the information in the graphic comes from. Knowing the source helps you evaluate the accuracy.

Different types of **maps** present special information. **Physical maps** show the natural landscape of an area. Shading may be used to show features like mountains and valleys. Different shades of color are often used to show different elevations (heights above sea level). **Political maps** show political units, such as states, nations, and capitals. The map of Canada, the United States, and Mexico shown here is a political map. **Special-purpose maps** present information such as the routes of explorers or the location of earthquake fault lines.

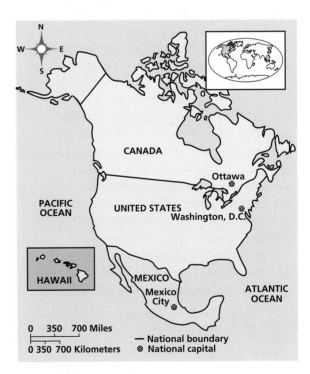

A **flowchart** shows a sequence of events or the steps in a process. Flowcharts are often used to show cause-and-effect relationships. See page 170 for an example of a flowchart. **Pie charts,** also called **circle graphs,** show how parts of a whole are related. A pie chart is a circle divided into different-sized sections, like slices of a pie. The emphasis in a pie chart is always on the proportions of the sections, not on the specific amounts of each section.

Pie Chart

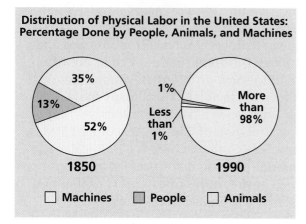

Distribution of Physical Labor in the United States: Percentage Done by People, Animals, and Machines

☐ Machines ■ People ☐ Animals

A **diagram** is a graphic that outlines the parts of something and shows how the parts relate to one another or how they work. You'll often find diagrams in technical directions, to show how a mechanical device works. Diagrams prove that a picture can be worth more than a thousand words. See page 502 for an example of a diagram.

A **time line** identifies events that take place over the course of time. In a time line, events are organized in chronological order, the order in which they happened.

Graphs usually show changes or trends over time. In line graphs, dots showing the quantity at different times are connected to

create a line. **Bar graphs** generally compare various quantities.

Bar Graph

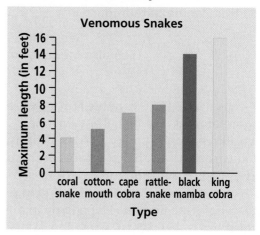

Line Graph

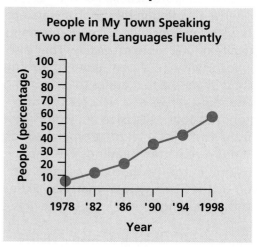

A **table** presents information arranged in rows and columns. There are many different types of tables. See page 499 for an example of a table showing a train schedule.

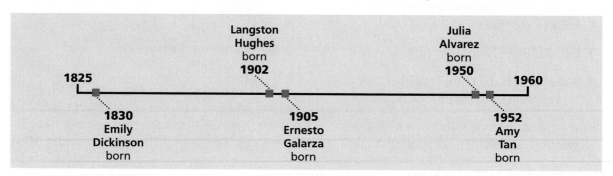

Tips for Understanding Graphic Features

1. Read the title, labels, and legend before you try to analyze the information.

2. Read numbers carefully. Note increases or decreases in sequences. Look for the direction or order of events and for trends and relationships.

3. Draw your own conclusions from the graphic. Then, compare your conclusions with the writer's conclusions.

See pages 42, 62, 139, 367, 370.

IMAGES Descriptive writing appeals to the senses to create **mental images,** pictures in the reader's mind. Most description appeals to the sense of sight, but description can also appeal to one or more of the other senses. When you read a description, use the details to *visualize,* or form mental pictures of, the characters, settings, and events. Forming mental images is especially important when you read description in scientific texts.

See page 351.

INFERENCE An **inference** is an educated guess, a conclusion that makes sense because it's supported by evidence. The evidence may be a collection of **facts,** information that can be proved, or it may come from experiences in your own life. However, the evidence must provide some reason for believing that the conclusion is true if the inference is to be valid, or based on sound, logical thought. Nevertheless, people may draw different conclusions from the same evidence—especially if there isn't much evidence to go on.

> Bobby has recently transferred to your school. You ask Bobby to join you and a couple of other friends, Sam and Ali, at your house after school on Thursday. Bobby says, "Sorry. I have to go home right after school."

> **Inferences:** Sam infers that Bobby's parents are really strict. Ali infers that Bobby is stuck-up. You infer that Bobby doesn't like you.

As you read, you make inferences based on clues that the writer provides. For example, when you read a narrative, you **infer,** or guess, what will happen next based on what the writer has told you and on your own knowledge and experience. Sometimes a writer deliberately gives clues that lead you to different—and incorrect—inferences. That's part of the fun of reading. Until you get to the end of a suspenseful story, you can never be completely sure about what will happen next.

In O. Henry's short story "After Twenty Years" (page 225), a policeman speaks to a well-dressed man waiting in a doorway in New York City. The man is waiting for his boyhood friend, Jimmy. He hasn't seen Jimmy for more than twenty years. Read the following dialogue, and the inferences that follow it.

> "Did pretty well out West, didn't you?" asked the policeman.
>
> "You bet! I hope Jimmy has done half as well. He was a kind of plodder, though, good fellow as he was. I've had to compete with some of the sharpest wits going to get my pile. A man gets in a groove in New York. It takes the West to put a razor edge on him."
>
> **Inferences:** The policeman seems to be impressed by the man in the doorway. The well-dressed man thinks a lot of himself and looks down on his old friend Jimmy, who may have been too "good" to be successful.

See pages 67, 108, 118, 140, 146, 261.
See also *Evidence, Fact and Opinion.*

INSTRUCTIONAL MANUALS Instructional manuals tell you how to operate a specific device, such as a VCR or a car. Instructional manuals contain detailed directions, usually organized in chronological steps. Drawings and diagrams, such as flowcharts, might be included to help you understand the different parts of the device.

See page 91.

KWL CHART Using a **KWL chart** is a way to focus your reading and record what you learn. KWL means "What I **k**now, what I **w**ant to know, and what I **l**earned." When you use a KWL strategy, you first skim the text, looking at headings, subtitles, and illustrations. You decide what the topic of the text is. Then, on a blank sheet of paper, you draw a KWL chart. In the K column you note what you already know about the subject. In the W column you write down what you'd like to find out. After you finish reading the text, you write the answers under the L column to the questions you asked in the W column. Here is the beginning of a KWL chart based on "Sir Gawain and the Loathly Lady" (page 452).

K	W	L
What I **K**now	What I **W**ant to Know	What I **L**earned
Sir Gawain was a knight.	Why was the lady loathly?	

See also *Graphic Features.*

MAIN IDEA The most important point or focus of a passage is its **main idea.** Writers of essays, nonfiction narratives, and informational articles have one or more **main ideas** in mind as they write a text. The writer may state the main idea directly. More often the main idea is suggested, or implied. Then it's up to you, the reader, to **infer,** or guess at,

what it is. To infer the main idea, look at the key details in the text. See if you can create a statement that expresses a general idea that covers all these important details. When you are deciding on the main idea, look especially for a key passage at the beginning or end of the text. That's where a writer often refers to a key idea.

See pages 38, 62, 180, 261, 367.

NEWSPAPERS Newspapers are informational texts that present facts about current events. Newspapers may also contain feature articles that aim to entertain as well as inform. Newspapers often contain editorials that support a *position* for or against an issue. **Headlines** at the top of each story indicate the topic of the story. They are worded to catch your attention. The writer of a **news story** usually organizes the details in order of importance. If the article is running too long, the less important details can easily be cut from the end of the story.

See pages 15, 62.

OBJECTIVE WRITING Objective writing sticks to the facts. It does not reveal the writer's feelings, beliefs, or point of view about the subject. In a newspaper, news articles are usually written objectively. Readers of news articles want to get a true and accurate account of what happened. If they want to know a writer's point of view or perspective on the news, they turn to the **editorial page.** Editorials and letters to the editor are usually *not* written objectively. They are examples of **subjective writing.** See page 469 for an example of a letter to the editor.

See pages 261, 282.

OUTLINING Outlining an informational text can help you identify main ideas and understand how they are related to one another. Outlining also shows you the important details that support each main idea. When you have an outline, you have a visual summary of the text.

Many readers start an outline by taking notes. Note taking is an especially good idea if you're reading a text with many facts, such as names and dates, that you want to remember.

Tips for Taking Notes

1. You can jot down notes in a notebook or on note cards. Put your notes in your own words, writing each main idea on its own note card or page.

2. As you continue to read, add details that relate to the important idea you have on each card.

3. Whenever you copy the writer's exact words, put quotation marks around them. Write down the page number for the source of each note.

After you have your notes on the text, you're ready to make an outline. Many outlines label the main ideas with Roman numerals. You need to have at least two headings at each level. This is how an outline might begin:

I. Main idea

  A. Detail supporting main idea I

    1. Detail supporting A

      a. Detail supporting 1

      b. Detail supporting 1

    2. Detail supporting A

  B. Detail supporting main idea I

II. Main idea

See page 180.

PERSUASION Persuasion is the use of language or pictures to convince us to think or act in a certain way. Recognizing **persuasive techniques** will help you evaluate the persuasion that you read, hear, and see all around you today. Here are some persuasive techniques to watch for:

1. **Logical appeals** are based on correct reasoning. Logic appeals to reason with opinions supported by strong factual evidence, such as facts, statistics, or statements by experts on the issue being considered.

2. **Emotional appeals** get your feelings involved in the argument. Some writers use vivid language and supporting evidence that arouse basic feelings, such as pity, anger, and fear. Persuasion tends to be most effective when it appeals to both your head and your heart. However, it's important to be able to recognize emotional appeals—and to be suspicious of how they can sway you.

3. **Logical fallacies** (fal′ə·sēz) are mistakes in reasoning. If you're reading a text quickly, fuzzy or dishonest reasoning may look as if it makes sense. See the entry for *Fallacious Reasoning* for examples of specific logical fallacies.

See pages 257, 463.
See also *Argument.*

PREDICTIONS Guessing what will happen next in a narrative text is a reading skill called **making predictions.** To make predictions, you look for clues that **foreshadow,** or hint at, future actions. You try to connect those clues with past and present actions in the story. You quickly check your memory for other things you've read that are in any way like the story you're reading. You recall your real-life experiences. Then you make your predictions. As you read, you'll continuously revise your guesses, adjusting your predictions as new clues crop up.

See pages 6, 48, 160, 224, 236.

PROPAGANDA **Propaganda** is an organized attempt to influence a large audience of readers, listeners, or TV watchers. Propaganda techniques are used in all kinds of persuasive texts. You see them especially in advertisements, speeches, and editorials. Some writers use propaganda to advance good causes—for instance, to persuade people to recycle, to exercise, or to join together to fight a terrible disease. However, many writers of propaganda use emotional appeals to confuse readers and to convince them that the writer's biased opinions are the only ones worth considering.

Common propaganda techniques include the following:

- The **bandwagon** appeal urges you to do or believe something because everyone else does.

> "Shop where the action is! Join the parade to Teen-Town Mall."

- The **testimonial** uses a famous person, such as an actor or an athlete, to testify that he or she supports the issue or uses the product.

> "I'm professional basketball player Hank Smith, and I drink Starade every day for quick and long-lasting energy."

- **Snob appeal** suggests that by using this product you can be superior to others—more powerful, wealthy, or beautiful.

> "You deserve this car. Don't settle for less than the best."

- **Stereotyping.** Writers who use stereotyping refer to members of a group as if they were all the same. (See also page 463.)

> Teenagers are bad drivers.
>
> Didn't I tell you that Martians can't be trusted?

- Writers using **name-calling** avoid giving reasons and logical evidence for or against an issue. Instead, they attack people who disagree with them by giving those people negative labels.

> That's just what I'd expect a nerd like you to say.
>
> I won't waste time listening to a puppet-politician whose strings are controlled by ill-informed special-interest groups.

PURPOSES OF TEXTS Texts are written for different **purposes:** to inform, to persuade, to express feelings, or to entertain. The purpose of a text, or the reason why a text is written, determines its **structure,** the way the writer organizes and presents the material.

READING RATE The speed at which you read a text is your **reading rate.** How quickly or slowly you should read depends on the type of text you are reading and your purpose for reading it.

Reading Rates According to Purpose

Reading Rate	Purpose	Example
Skimming	Reading for main points	Glancing at newspaper headlines; reviewing charts and headings in your science textbook before a test
Scanning	Looking for specific details	Looking for an author's name in a table of contents; looking in a geography book for the name of the highest mountain in North America
Reading for mastery	Reading to understand and remember	Taking notes on a chapter in your science textbook to study for a test; reading a story or poem for understanding

RETELLING The reading strategy called **retelling** helps you identify and remember events that advance the plot of a story. Retelling is also useful when you read informational texts, such as science or history texts. From time to time in your reading, stop for a moment. Review what's gone on before you go ahead. Focus on the important events or key details. Think about them, and retell them briefly in your own words. When you read history or science texts, you should stop after each section of the text and see if you can retell the key details to yourself.

See page 20.

SQ3R The abbreviation **SQ3R** stands for a reading and study strategy that takes place in five steps: **s**urvey, **q**uestion, **r**ead, **r**etell, **re**view. The SQ3R process takes time, but it helps you focus on the text—and it works.

- *S—Survey.* Glance through the text. Skim the headings, titles, charts, illustrations, and vocabulary words in boldface type. Read the first and last sentences of the major sections of the text, if they are indicated by headings.

- *Q—Question.* List the questions that you have. These may be questions that came out of your survey, or they may be general questions about the subject. Ask the questions that you hope to find answers to in the text.

- *R—Read.* Read the text carefully, keeping your questions in mind. As you read, look for answers. Take brief notes on the answers you find.

- *R—Retell.* Use your notes to write down the main ideas and important details in the text. Before you write, say your answers out loud. Listen to your answers to hear if they make sense.

- *R—Review.* Look back over the text. See if you can answer your questions without using the notes and answers you wrote down. Write a brief summary of the text so you'll be able to remember it later.

See page 283.

SIGNS Signs are probably the briefest informational texts you see. A sign displays specific information, often using eye-catching colors and shapes to send its message. Signs give drivers information about road conditions, speed limits, and distances. Signs are essential in airports and bus and train stations. Signs are also used in parks and stores and even in schools.

See page 94.

STEREOTYPING (ster′ē·ə·tīp′iŋ) Referring to all members of a group as if they were all the same is called **stereotyping.** Stereotyping ignores the facts about individuals. The most important fact about members of a group is that each individual person is *different* from all the others. Stereotyping does not allow for individual differences. Whenever you assess a writer's evidence, be on the lookout for stereotyping. When a writer makes a claim about an individual or a group and supports the assertion with a stereotype, you know that the writer is guilty of faulty reasoning. Here are some examples of stereotyping:

> All teenagers are lazy.
>
> Senior citizens have more money than they need.
>
> All lawyers are dishonest.
>
> All football players are dumb.

See page 463.
See also *Propaganda.*

SUBJECTIVE WRITING Writing that reveals and emphasizes the writer's personal feelings and opinions is called **subjective.** Subjective and objective writing are opposites. *Subjective* means "personal; resulting from feelings; existing only in the mind." *Objective* means "real; actual; factual; without bias." Writers may combine subjective and objective details in the same text. As a reader you must figure out which statements are based on subjective impressions and which are based on factual, objective evidence.

We expect subjectivity in some writing. We would expect an autobiography to reveal the writer's personal feelings. In a historical text, however, we expect objectivity—we want facts, not the writer's personal feelings.

SUMMARIZING Restating the main ideas or major events in a text is called **summarizing.** A summary of text is much shorter than the original. To summarize an informational text, you must include the main ideas and the important details that support those main ideas. To summarize a narrative, you must include the main events and be certain you have indicated cause and effect. In a summary, except for direct quotations from the text, you put the writer's ideas into your own words. (Every time you jot down a direct quotation, be sure to put quotation marks around it and write down the source.) Here is a summary of the selection from *Barrio Boy* by Ernesto Galarza (page 324):

Ernesto's family had recently moved to Sacramento from Mazatlán, Mexico. This true account begins with Ernesto's mother taking him to school. The new school seems strange to Ernesto, who speaks no English. Ernesto finds out that many of his first-grade classmates are from other countries or have different ethnic backgrounds. Several of them, along with Ernesto, receive private English lessons from their teacher. The teachers at the school help Ernesto learn that he can be proud of being American while still feeling proud of his Mexican roots.

See page 367.
See also *Main Idea.*

TEXT STRUCTURES There are some basic ways in which writers structure informational texts: **cause and effect, chronological order,** and **comparison-and-contrast.** Sometimes a writer will use one pattern throughout a text. Many writers will combine two or more patterns. These guidelines can help you analyze text structure:

1. Search the text for the main idea. Look for words that signal a specific pattern of organization.

2. Study the text for other important ideas. Think about how the ideas are connected to one another. Look for an obvious pattern.

3. Draw a graphic organizer that shows how the text seems to be structured. Your graphic organizer may look like one of the common text structures shown below.

The **cause-and-effect pattern** presents a series of causes and their effects. This example shows the effect of an earthquake, which led to another effect, which became the cause of another effect, and so on:

Causal Chain

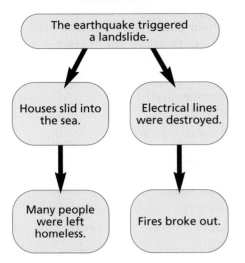

The earthquake triggered a landslide.

↓ Houses slid into the sea. → Many people were left homeless.

↓ Electrical lines were destroyed. → Fires broke out.

Chronological-order pattern shows events or ideas happening in time sequence. The example below gives directions for getting from school to a student's home:

Sequence Chain

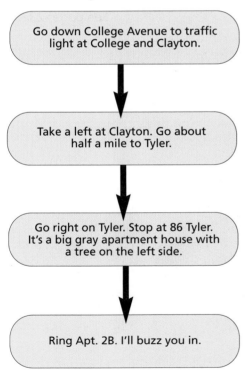

Go down College Avenue to traffic light at College and Clayton.

↓

Take a left at Clayton. Go about half a mile to Tyler.

↓

Go right on Tyler. Stop at 86 Tyler. It's a big gray apartment house with a tree on the left side.

↓

Ring Apt. 2B. I'll buzz you in.

The **comparison-and-contrast pattern** points out similarities and differences. A Venn diagram can help you see how two subjects are alike and how they are different. Similarities are listed where the two circles overlap. Differences are shown where the circles don't overlap. This example compares a middle school with a high school.

Venn Diagram

Middle School
- smaller—500 students
- students from four K–5 schools
- everyone knows everyone else

- classes same length
- many electives
- three foreign languages to choose from

High School
- Big school—2000 students
- Students from four middle schools
- More cliques; hard to get to know people

Differences   *Similarities*   *Differences*

Another kind of graphic organizer focuses on points of comparison (the features being compared).

Comparing and Contrasting

	Middle School	High School
Size of school		
Length of school day		
Sports program		

See pages 15, 320, 364, 370.
See also *Cause and Effect, Chronological Order, Compare-and-Contrast Pattern.*

TEXTBOOKS **Textbooks** are informational texts written to help students learn about a subject. This textbook is quite different in structure from a geography textbook. Nonetheless, both kinds of textbooks have certain elements in common. For example, they have the same general purpose. In addition, most textbooks present information followed by questions that help students determine whether they have learned the material. Finally, most textbooks contain a table of contents, an index, illustrations, charts, and other graphic features.

See page 42.

WRITER'S PERSPECTIVE **Perspective** is the way a person looks at a subject. Some people have a negative perspective, for instance, on violent computer games. They believe that such games may influence children to become violent. Other people have a positive perspective on violent computer games. They say that when children play such games, they may rid themselves of some of their aggressive feelings. Figuring out a writer's perspective can help you understand and evaluate what you are reading. The following paragraph is from Clifton Davis's "A Mason-Dixon Memory" (page 358). A statement describing Davis's perspective follows:

In his words and in his life, Lincoln had made it clear that freedom is not free. Every time the color of a person's skin keeps him out of an amusement park or off a country-club fairway, the war for freedom begins again. Sometimes the battle is fought with fists and guns, but more often the most effective weapon is a simple act of love and courage.

Writer's perspective: Prejudice still exists today, and it can be fought best with simple, nonviolent actions.

See pages 232, 278.

Handbook of Literary Terms

For more information about a topic, turn to the page(s) in this book indicated on a separate line at the end of the entries. To learn more about *Alliteration,* for example, turn to page 391.

On another line are cross-references to entries in this handbook that provide closely related information. For instance, at the end of *Autobiography* is a cross-reference to *Biography.*

ALLITERATION **The repetition of the same or very similar consonant sounds in words that are close together.** Though alliteration usually occurs at the beginning of words, it can also occur within or at the end of words. Among other things, alliteration can help establish a mood, emphasize words, and serve as a memory aid. In the following example the *s* sound is repeated at the beginning of the words *silken* and *sad* and within the words *uncertain* and *rustling:*

> And the silken sad uncertain rustling of each purple curtain
>
> —Edgar Allan Poe, from "The Raven"

See page 391.

ALLUSION **A reference to a statement, a person, a place, or an event from literature, history, religion, mythology, politics, sports, or science.** Allusions enrich the reading experience. Writers expect readers to recognize an allusion and to think, almost at the same time, about the literary work and the person, place, or event that it refers to. The following lines, describing a tunnel in the snow, contain an allusion to Aladdin, a character in *The Thousand and One Nights:*

> With mittened hands, and caps drawn low,
> To guard our necks and ears from snow,
> We cut the solid whiteness through.
> And, where the drift was deepest, made
> A tunnel walled and overlaid
> With dazzling crystal: we had read
> Of rare Aladdin's wondrous cave,
> And to our own his name we gave.
>
> —John Greenleaf Whittier,
> from "Snow-Bound"

The cave in the tale contains a magic lamp that helps Aladdin discover vast riches. By alluding to Aladdin's cave, Whittier makes us see the icy tunnel in the snow as a magical, fairy-tale place.

The cartoon below makes an allusion to a popular fairy tale.

"Now, this policy will cover your home for fire, theft, flood and huffing and puffing."
Reprinted from The Saturday Evening Post © 1993.

ATMOSPHERE **The overall mood or emotion of a work of literature.** A work's atmosphere can often be described with one or two adjectives, such as *scary, dreamy, happy, sad,* or *nostalgic.* A writer creates atmosphere by using images, sounds, and descriptions that convey a particular feeling.

See also *Mood.*

AUTOBIOGRAPHY **The story of a person's life, written or told by that person.** Maijue Xiong wrote an autobiography called "An Unforgettable Journey" (page 271) about her escape from war-torn Laos as a child. Another well-known autobiographical work is Maya Angelou's *I Know Why the Caged Bird Sings.*

See pages 271, 306–307, 323.
See also *Biography.*

BIOGRAPHY **The story of a real person's life, written or told by another person.** Milton Meltzer has written a number of biographies of historical figures, such as George Washington and Mark Twain. "Elizabeth I" (page 284) is his biography of the remarkable queen of England who reigned in the sixteenth century. Frequent subjects of biographies are movie stars, television personalities, politicians, sports figures, self-made millionaires, even underworld figures. Biographies are among the most popular forms of contemporary literature.

See pages 282, 306–307, 323.
See also *Autobiography.*

CHARACTER **A person or animal who takes part in the action of a story, play, or other literary work.** In some works, such as Aesop's fables, a character is an animal. In myths and legends a character may be a god or a superhero. Most often a character is an ordinary human being, such as Kevin in "User Friendly" (page 187).

The process of revealing the personality of a character in a story is called **characterization.** A writer can reveal a character in the following ways:

1. by letting you hear the character speak

2. by describing how the character looks and dresses

3. by letting you listen to the character's inner thoughts and feelings

4. by revealing what other people in the story think or say about the character

5. by showing you what the character does—how he or she acts

6. by telling you directly what the character's personality is like (cruel, kind, sneaky, brave, and so on)

When a writer uses the first five ways to reveal a character, you must make an inference, based on the evidence the writer provides, to decide what the character is like. When a writer uses the sixth method, however, you don't make a decision but are told directly what kind of person the character is.

Characters can be classified as static or dynamic. A **static character** is one who does not change much in the course of a work. Mr. Andersen in "Song of the Trees" (page 333) is a static character. By contrast, a **dynamic character** changes as a result of the story's events. Keevan in "The Smallest Dragonboy" (page 119) is a dynamic character.

A character's **motivation** is any force that drives or moves the character to behave in a particular way. Many characters are motivated by the force of fear or love or ambition.

See pages 106–107, 108, 118, 140, 159, 160, 308, 412–413, 432.

CONFLICT **A struggle or clash between opposing characters or opposing forces.** In an **external conflict** a character struggles against some outside force. This outside force may be another character or society as a whole or a storm or a grizzly bear or even a machine. In "Three Skeleton Key" (page 49), the characters have an external conflict with a swarm of sea rats. An **internal conflict,** on the other hand, takes place within a character's mind. It is a struggle between opposing needs, desires, or emotions. In "After Twenty Years" (page 225), Officer Wells must resolve an internal conflict: Should he arrest an old friend or let him go?

See pages 4–5, 20.

CONNOTATION **The feelings and associations that a word suggests.** For example, *tiny*, *cramped*, and *compact* all have about the same dictionary definition, or **denotation,** but they have different connotations. A manufacturer of small cars would not describe its product as tiny or cramped. Instead, the company might say that its cars are compact. To grasp a writer's full meaning, you must pay attention not only to the literal definitions of words but also to their connotations. Connotations can be especially important in poetry.

See page 349.

DENOTATION **The literal, dictionary definition of a word.**

See page 349.
See also *Connotation*.

DESCRIPTION **The kind of writing that creates a clear image of something, usually by using details that appeal to one or more of the senses: sight, hearing, smell, taste, and touch.** Writers use description in all forms of fiction, nonfiction, and poetry. In "Fish Cheeks" (page 352), Amy Tan vividly describes the colors, sounds, and tastes of her family's Christmas celebration.

See page 370.

DIALECT **A way of speaking that is characteristic of a particular region or group of people.** A dialect may have a distinct vocabulary, pronunciation system, and grammar. In a sense, we all speak a dialect. One dialect usually becomes dominant in a country or culture and is accepted as the standard way of speaking. In the United States, for example, the formal written language is known as standard English. This is the dialect used in most newspapers and magazines.

Writers often reproduce regional dialects, or speech that reveals a character's economic or social class, in order to give a story local color. Mr. Baumer in "Bargain" (page 237) speaks in a dialect that reveals that his first language is German. The poem "Madam and the Rent Man" (page 393) is written in a dialect spoken in some urban African American communities in the northeastern United States.

See page 379.

DIALOGUE **A conversation between two or more characters.** Most stage dramas consist of dialogue together with stage directions. (Screenplays and teleplays sometimes include an unseen narrator.) The dialogue in a drama, such as *The Monsters Are Due on Maple Street* (page 69), must move the plot along and reveal its characters almost single-handedly. Dialogue is also an important element in most stories and novels as well as in some poems and nonfiction. It is one of the most effective ways for a writer to show what a character is like. It can also add realism and humor.

In the written form of a play, dialogue appears without quotation marks. In prose or poetry, however, dialogue is usually enclosed in quotation marks.

A **monologue** is a part of a drama in which one character speaks alone.

See page 319.

DRAMA **A story written to be acted for an audience.** (A drama can also be appreciated and enjoyed in written form.) In a drama, such as *The Monsters Are Due on Maple Street* (page 69), the action is usually driven by characters who want something very much and take steps to get it. The related events that take place within a drama are often separated into **acts.** Each act is often made up of shorter sections, or **scenes.** Most plays have three acts, but there are many, many variations. The elements of a drama are often described as **introduction** or **exposition, complications, conflict, climax,** and **resolution.**

ESSAY **A short piece of nonfiction prose that examines a single subject.** Most essays can be categorized as either personal or formal.

The **personal essay** generally reveals a great deal about the writer's personality and tastes. Its tone is often conversational, sometimes even humorous. In a personal essay the focus is the writer's feelings and response to an experience.

The **formal essay** is usually serious, objective, and impersonal in tone. Its purpose is to inform readers about a topic or to persuade them to accept the writer's views.

See pages 307, 357.

FABLE **A brief story in prose or verse that teaches a moral or gives a practical lesson about how to get along in life.** The characters of most fables are animals that behave and speak like human beings. Some of the most popular fables are attributed to Aesop, who is thought to have been a slave in ancient Greece.

See also *Folk Tale, Myth.*

FICTION **A prose account that is made up rather than true.** The term *fiction* usually refers to novels and short stories. Fiction may be based on a writer's experiences or on his-

torical events, but characters, events, and other details are altered or added by the writer to create a desired effect. "A Rice Sandwich" (page 141) is a fictional account based on an episode in the writer's childhood.

See pages 306–307.
See also *Nonfiction.*

FIGURE OF SPEECH **A word or phrase that describes one thing in terms of something else and is not literally true.** Figures of speech always involve some sort of imaginative comparison between seemingly unlike things. The most common forms are **simile** ("The stars were like diamonds"), **metaphor** ("My soul is an enchanted boat"), and **personification** ("The sun smiled down on the emerald-green fields").

See pages 380–381, 382, 412–413.
See also *Metaphor, Personification, Simile.*

FLASHBACK **An interruption in the action of a plot to tell what happened at an earlier time.** A flashback breaks the usual movement of the narrative by going back in time. It usually gives background information that helps the reader understand the present situation. "A Mason-Dixon Memory" (page 358) contains a long flashback.

A break in the unfolding of a plot to an episode in the future is known as a **flashforward.**

See page 357.

FOLK TALE **A story with no known author that originally was passed on from one generation to another by word of mouth.** Folk tales tend to travel, so similar plots and characters are found in several cultures. For example, "Yeh-Shen" (page 251) is a Chinese folk tale that is almost identical to the European story of Cinderella. Folk tales often contain **fantastic** elements, or events that could not happen in the world as we know it.

See also *Fable, Myth, Tall Tale.*

FORESHADOWING **The use of clues to suggest events that will happen later in the plot.** Foreshadowing is used to build suspense or create anxiety. In a drama a gun found in a bureau drawer in Act One is likely to foreshadow violence later in the play. In "Three Skeleton Key" (page 49), the story of three convicts who perished on the key foreshadows the danger the three lighthouse keepers will face.

See pages 4–5, 6, 48, 224.
See also *Suspense.*

FREE VERSE **Poetry without a regular meter or a rhyme scheme.** Poets writing in free verse try to capture the natural rhythms of ordinary speech. To create their music, poets writing in free verse may use internal rhyme, repetition, alliteration, and onomatopoeia. Free verse also frequently makes use of vivid imagery. The following poem in free verse effectively uses images and the repetition of words to describe the effects of a family's eviction for not paying rent:

The 1st

What I remember about that day
is boxes stacked across the walk
and couch springs curling through the air
and drawers and tables balanced on the curb
and us, hollering,
leaping up and around
happy to have a playground;

nothing about the emptied rooms
nothing about the emptied family

—Lucille Clifton

See pages 390–391.
See also *Poetry, Rhyme, Rhythm.*

IMAGERY **Language that appeals to the senses.** Most images are visual—that is, they create pictures in your mind by appealing to the sense of sight. Images can also appeal to the sense of hearing, touch, taste, or smell or to several senses at once. The sensory images in "The Highwayman" (page 161) add greatly to the enjoyment of the poem. Though imagery is an element in all types of writing, it is especially important in poetry.

See pages 380–381, 413.
See also *Poetry.*

IRONY **In general, a contrast between expectation and reality.** Irony can create powerful effects, from humor to strong emotion. Here are three common types of irony:

1. **Verbal irony** involves a contrast between what is said or written and what is meant. If you were to call someone who failed a math test Einstein, you would be using verbal irony.

2. **Situational irony** occurs when what happens is very different from what is expected to happen. The surprise ending of "After Twenty Years" (page 225) involves situational irony.

3. **Dramatic irony** occurs when the audience or the reader knows something a character does not know. In Part 2 of "The Highwayman" (page 161), the reader feels an anxious sense of irony when King George's soldiers have Bess tied up. Although the highwayman doesn't yet know it, *we* know that a trap is set for him.

MAIN IDEA **The most important idea expressed in a paragraph or in an entire essay.** The main idea may be directly stated in a **topic sentence,** or you may have to look at all the details in the paragraph and make an **inference,** or educated guess, about its main idea.

See page 261.

Handbook of Literary Terms

METAMORPHOSIS **A marvelous change from one shape or form to another one.** In myths the change is usually from human to animal, from animal to human, or from human to plant. Greek and Roman myths contain many examples of metamorphosis. The myth of Echo and Narcissus (page 204) tells how the vain youth Narcissus pines away for love of his own reflection until he is changed into a flower.

See page 203.
See also *Myth.*

METAPHOR **An imaginative comparison between two unlike things in which one thing is said to be another thing.** A metaphor is an important type of figurative language. Metaphors are used in all forms of writing and are common in ordinary speech. If you were to say someone has a heart of gold, you would not mean that the person's heart is actually made of metal. You would mean, instead, that the person is warm and caring. You would be speaking metaphorically.

Metaphors differ from similes, which use specific words (notably *like, as, than,* and *resembles*) to state comparisons. William Wordsworth's famous comparison "I wandered lonely as a cloud" is a simile because it uses *as.* If Wordsworth had written "I was a

lonely, wandering cloud," he would have been using a metaphor.

See pages 169, 382.
See also *Figure of Speech, Personification, Simile.*

MOOD **The overall emotion created by a work of literature.** A work of literature can often be described with one or more adjectives: *sad, scary, hopeful, exciting,* and so on. These are descriptions of the work's mood—its emotional atmosphere. For example, the mood of "Annabel Lee" (page 175) could be described as haunting or romantic. That mood has a lingering effect on its readers.

See also *Atmosphere.*

MOTIVATION See *Character.*

MYTH **A story that explains something about the world and typically involves gods or other superhuman beings.** Myths, which at one time were believed to be true, reflect the traditions of the culture that produced them. Almost every culture has **origin myths** (or **creation myths**), stories that explain how something in the world (perhaps the world itself) came to be. Myths may also explain many other aspects of nature. The ancient Greek myth of Echo and Narcissus (page 204), for example, explains the origins of a flower. Most myths are very old and were handed down orally long before being put in written form. In some of the world's greatest myths, a hero or even a god embarks on a **quest,** a perilous journey taken in pursuit of something of great value.

See pages 203, 208, 451.
See also *Fable, Folk Tale.*

NONFICTION **Prose writing that deals with real people, events, and places without changing any facts.** Popular forms of nonfiction are the **autobiography,** the **biography,**

PEANUTS

The curtain of night enveloped the fleeing lovers.

Though fiery trials had threatened, oceans of longing had kept them together.

Now, a new icicle of terror stabbed at the embroidery of their existence.

JOE METAPHOR!

PEANUTS reprinted by permission of United Feature Syndicate, Inc.

and the **essay.** Other examples of nonfiction include newspaper stories, magazine articles, historical writing, scientific reports, and even personal diaries and letters.

Nonfiction writing can be subjective or objective. **Subjective writing** expresses the feelings and opinions of the writer. **Objective writing** conveys the facts without introducing any emotion or personal bias.

See pages 306–307.
See also *Autobiography, Biography, Fiction.*

NOVEL **A fictional story that is usually more than one hundred book pages long.** A novel uses all the elements of storytelling—**plot, character, setting, theme,** and **point of view.** A novel, because of its length, usually has more characters, settings, and themes and a more complex plot than a short story. Modern writers sometimes do not pay much attention to one or more of the novel's traditional elements. Some novels today are basically character studies that include only the barest story lines. Other novels don't look much beyond the surface of their characters and concentrate instead on plot and setting. A novel can deal with almost any topic. Many of the books recommended in the Read On sections of this text are novels. A **novella** is shorter than a novel and longer than a short story.

See pages 306–307, 332.

ONOMATOPOEIA **The use of words whose sounds echo their sense.** Onomatopoeia (ăn′ō·mat′ō·pē′ə) is so natural to us that we use it at a very early age. *Buzz, rustle, boom, ticktock, tweet,* and *bark* are all examples of onomatopoeia. Onomatopoeia is an important element in creating the music of poetry. In the following lines the poet creates a frenzied mood by choosing words that imitate the sounds of alarm bells:

> Oh, the bells, bells, bells!
> What a tale their terror tells
> Of Despair!

> How they clang, and clash, and roar!
> What a horror they outpour
> On the bosom of the palpitating air!
> Yet the ear, it fully knows
> By the twanging
> And the clanging
> How the danger ebbs and flows.
>
> —Edgar Allan Poe, from
> "The Bells"

See pages 390–391.
See also *Alliteration.*

PERSONIFICATION **A figure of speech in which a nonhuman or nonliving thing or quality is talked about as if it were human or alive.** In the following lines, sleep is spoken of as a human weaver:

> The soft gray hands of sleep
> Toiled all night long
> To spin a beautiful garment
> Of dreams
>
> —Edward Silvera, from
> "Forgotten Dreams"

See page 386.
See also *Figure of Speech, Metaphor, Simile.*

PLOT **The series of related events that make up a story.** Plot is what happens in a short story, novel, play, or narrative poem. Most plots are built on these bare bones: An **introduction,** or **exposition,** tells us who the characters are and what their **conflict** is. **Complications** arise as the characters take steps to resolve the conflict. The plot reaches a **climax,** the most emotional or suspenseful moment in the story, when the outcome is decided one way or another. The last part of a story is the **resolution,** when the characters' problems are solved and the story ends.

Not all works of fiction or drama have this traditional plot structure. Some modern writ-

Handbook of Literary Terms

ers experiment, often eliminating parts of a traditional plot in order to focus on elements such as character, point of view, or mood.

See pages 4–5, 20, 67, 158–159, 160, 412–413, 438.
See also *Conflict.*

POETRY A kind of rhythmic, compressed language that uses figures of speech and imagery designed to appeal to emotion and imagination. We know poetry when we see it because it is usually arranged in a particular way on the page. Traditional poetry often has a regular pattern of rhythm (**meter**) and may have a regular **rhyme scheme. Free verse** is poetry that has no regular rhythm or rhyme. The major forms of poetry are the **lyric** (a songlike poem that expresses a speaker's feelings) and the **narrative** (a poem that tells a story). Two popular narrative forms are the **epic** and the **ballad.**

See pages 160, 390–391.
See also *Figure of Speech, Free Verse, Imagery, Refrain, Rhyme, Rhythm, Speaker, Stanza.*

POINT OF VIEW The vantage point from which a story is told. The most common points of view are the **omniscient,** the **third-person limited,** and the **first person.**

1. In the **omniscient** (äm·nish′ənt), or all-knowing, **point of view** the narrator knows everything about the characters and their problems. This all-knowing narrator can tell about the characters' past, present, and future. This kind of narrator can even tell what the characters are thinking or what is happening in other places. This narrator is not in the story. Instead, he or she stands above the action, like a god. The omniscient is a very familiar point of view; we have heard it in fairy tales since we were very young. "Yeh-Shen" (page

251), a Chinese Cinderella story, is told from the omniscient point of view.

> Her loveliness made her seem a heavenly being, and the king suddenly knew in his heart that he had found his true love.

2. In the **third-person limited point of view,** the narrator focuses on the thoughts and feelings of only one character. From this point of view, you observe the action through the eyes and feelings of only one character in the story. "The Smallest Dragonboy" (page 119) is told from the third-person limited point of view.

> There was such a lot to know and understand about being a dragonrider that sometimes Keevan was overwhelmed. How would he ever be able to remember everything he ought to know at the right moment?

3. In the **first-person point of view,** one of the characters, using the personal pronoun *I,* is telling the story. You become very familiar with this narrator but can know only what he or she knows and can observe only what he or she observes. All information about the story must come from this character. In some cases the information is incorrect. "User Friendly" (page 187) is told from the first-person point of view of the boy whose computer starts acting funny.

> As I walked by the corner of my room, where my computer table was set up, I pressed the *on* button, slid a diskette into the floppy drive, then went to brush my teeth. By the time I got back, the computer's screen was glowing greenly, displaying the message: *Good morning, Kevin.*

See pages 222–223, 250, 261.

REFRAIN A group of words repeated at intervals in a poem, song, or speech. Refrains are usually associated with songs and poems, but they are also used in speeches and other forms of literature. Refrains are most often used to create rhythm, but they may also provide emphasis or commentary, create suspense, or help hold a work together. Refrains may be repeated with small variations in a work in order to fit a particular context or to create a special effect.

See page 174.

RHYME The repetition of accented vowel sounds and all sounds following them in words close together in a poem. *Mean* and *screen* are rhymes, as are *crumble* and *tumble*. Rhyme has many purposes in poetry: It creates rhythm, lends a songlike quality, emphasizes ideas, organizes the poem (for instance, into stanzas or couplets), provides humor or delight, and makes the poem memorable.

Many poems—for example, "The Runaway" (page 397)—use **end rhymes,** rhymes at the end of a line. In the following stanza, *walls/calls/falls* form end rhymes, as do *hands/sands.* The pattern of end rhymes in a poem is called a **rhyme scheme.** To indicate the rhyme scheme of a poem, use a separate letter of the alphabet for each rhyme. For example, the rhyme scheme below is *aabba.*

> Darkness settles on roofs and walls,
> But the sea, the sea in the darkness calls;
> The little waves, with their soft,
>   white hands,
> Efface the footprints in the sands,
> And the tide rises, the tide falls.
>
> —Henry Wadsworth Longfellow,
>   from "The Tide Rises, the Tide Falls"

Internal rhymes are rhymes within lines. The following line has an internal rhyme (*turning/burning*):

> Back into the chamber turning, all my soul within me burning
>
> —Edgar Allan Poe, from "The Raven"

Rhyming sounds need not be spelled the same way; for instance, *gear/here* forms a rhyme. Rhymes can involve more than one syllable or more than one word; *poet/know it* is an example. Rhymes involving sounds that are similar but not exactly the same are called **slant rhymes** (or **near rhymes** or **approximate rhymes**). *Leave/live* is an example of a slant rhyme. Poets writing in English often use slant rhymes because English is not a very rhymable language. It has many words that rhyme with no other word (*orange*) or with only one other word (*mountain/fountain*). Poets interested in how a poem looks on the printed page sometimes use **eye rhymes,** or **visual rhymes**—rhymes involving words that are spelled similarly but are pronounced differently. *Tough/cough* is an eye rhyme. (*Tough/rough* is a "real" rhyme.)

See pages 380–381, 390–391, 396, 400, 413.
See also *Free Verse, Poetry, Rhythm.*

RHYTHM A musical quality produced by the repetition of stressed and unstressed syllables or by the repetition of certain other sound patterns. Rhythm occurs in all language—written and spoken—but is particularly important in poetry.

The most obvious kind of rhythm is the regular pattern of stressed and unstressed syllables that is found in some poetry. This pattern is called **meter.** In the following lines describing a cavalry charge, the rhythm echoes the galloping of the attackers' horses:

> The Assyrian came down like the wolf on the fold,

> And his cohorts were gleaming in purple and
>   gold;
> And the sheen of their spears was like stars on
>   the sea,
> When the blue wave rolls nightly on deep
>   Galilee.
>
> —George Gordon, Lord Byron,
>   from "The Destruction of Sennacherib"

Marking the stressed (´) and unstressed (˘) syllables in a line is called **scanning** the line. Lord Byron's scanned lines show a rhythmic pattern in which two unstressed syllables are followed by a stressed syllable. Read the lines aloud and listen to this rhythmic pattern. Also, notice how the poem's end rhymes help create the rhythm.

Writers can also create rhythm by repeating words and phrases or even by repeating whole lines and sentences.

See pages 380–381, 390–391, 413.
See also *Free Verse, Poetry, Rhyme.*

SETTING **The time and place in which the events of a work of literature take place.** Most often the setting of a narrative is described early in the story. Setting often contributes to a story's emotional effect. In "Song of the Trees" (page 333), the forest setting helps create a soothing (yet mysterious) mood. Setting frequently plays an important role in a story's plot, especially one that centers on a conflict between a character and nature. In "Three Skeleton Key" (page 49), the characters must fight elements of a deadly setting to survive—they are threatened by a vast army of rats. Some stories are closely tied to particular settings, and it is difficult to imagine them taking place elsewhere. By contrast, other stories could easily take place in a variety of settings.

See pages 160, 236.

SHORT STORY **A fictional prose narrative that is usually ten to twenty book pages long.** Short stories were first written in the nineteenth century. Early short story writers include Sir Walter Scott and Edgar Allan Poe. Short stories are usually built on a plot that consists of at least these bare bones: the **introduction** or **exposition, conflict, complications, climax,** and **resolution.** Short stories are more limited than novels. They usually have only one or two major characters and one important setting.

See pages 306, 308, 332.
See also *Conflict, Fiction, Plot.*

SIMILE **A comparison between two unlike things, using a word such as *like, as, than,* or *resembles.*** The simile is an important type of figure of speech. In the following lines a simile creates a clear image of moths in the evening air:

> When the last bus leaves, moths stream
>   toward lights like litter in wind.
>
> —Roberta Hill, from "Depot in Rapid City"

This example shows that similes can generate a strong emotional impact. By choosing to compare the moths to litter, the poet not only creates a picture in the reader's mind but also establishes a lonely, dreary mood.

See pages 169, 382.
See also *Figure of Speech, Metaphor.*

SPEAKER **The voice talking in a poem.** Sometimes the speaker is identical to the poet, but often the speaker and the poet are not the same. The poet may be speaking as a child, a woman, a man, an animal, or even an object.

See also *Poetry.*

STANZA **In a poem a group of consecutive lines that forms a single unit.** A stanza in a poem is something like a paragraph in prose; it often expresses a unit of thought. A stanza may consist of any number of lines. "I'm Nobody!" (page 383) consists of two four-line stanzas, each expressing a separate idea. In some poems each stanza has the same rhyme scheme.

See pages 380–381.
See also *Poetry, Rhyme.*

SUSPENSE The uncertainty or anxiety you feel about what will happen next in a story. In "Three Skeleton Key" (page 49), the narrator hooks your curiosity in the first sentences when he says he is about to describe his "most terrifying experience."

See pages 48, 224, 236.
See also *Foreshadowing.*

SYMBOL A person, a place, a thing, or an event that has its own meaning *and* stands for something beyond itself as well. Examples of symbols are all around us—in music, on television, and in everyday conversation. The skull and crossbones, for example, is a symbol of danger; the dove is a symbol of peace; and the red rose stands for true love. In literature, symbols are often more personal. For example, in "Names/Nombres" (page 262), Julia Alvarez's name is a symbol of her cultural identity.

TALL TALE An exaggerated, fanciful story that gets "taller and taller," more and more far-fetched, the more it is told and retold. The tall tale is an American story form. Two famous tall-tale characters are Pecos Bill and Paul Bunyan. Here is a short tall tale:

This artist was so talented that when he painted a dog it bit him. But he should have known better. Earlier he had painted a snowstorm and caught cold.

See also *Folk Tale.*

THEME The truth about life revealed in a work of literature. A theme is not the same as a subject. The subject of a work can usually be expressed in a word or two: *love, childhood, death.* The theme is the idea that the writer wishes to convey about a particular subject. The theme must be expressed in at least one sentence. For example, the subject of *The Monsters Are Due on Maple Street* (page 69) is alien invasion. The play's theme might be this: Prejudice is the fearful, unseen enemy within each of us.

A story can have several themes, but one will often stand out from the others. A work's themes are usually not stated directly. You have to think about all the elements of the work and use them to make an **inference,** or educated guess, about what the themes are.

It is not likely that two readers will ever state a theme in exactly the same way. Sometimes readers even differ greatly in their interpretations of theme. A work of literature can mean different things to different people.

See pages 158–159, 160, 174, 185, 203, 332, 412–413.

TONE The attitude that a writer takes toward the audience, a subject, or a character. Tone is conveyed through the writer's choice of words and details. The poem "maggie and milly and molly and may" (page 401) is light and playful in tone. By contrast, the poem "Annabel Lee" (page 175) is serious in tone.

See page 392.

Handbook of Literary Terms

Glossary

The glossary that follows is an alphabetical list of words found in the selections in this book. Use this glossary just as you would use a dictionary—to find out the meanings of unfamiliar words. (Some technical, foreign, and more obscure words in this book are not listed here but instead are defined for you in the footnotes that accompany many of the selections.)

Many words in the English language have more than one meaning. This glossary gives the meanings that apply to the words as they are used in the selections in this book. Words closely related in form and meaning are usually listed together in one entry (for instance, *compassion* and *compassionate*), and the definition is given for the first form.

The following abbreviations are used:

adj.	adjective
adv.	adverb
n.	noun
v.	verb

Each word's pronunciation is given in parentheses. A guide to the pronunciation symbols appears at the bottom of this page. For more information about the words in this glossary or for information about words not listed here, consult a dictionary.

A

adaption (ad'əp·tā'shən) *n.:* in biology, a change in structure, function, or form that improves an animal's or a plant's chances of survival. The protective coloration of some animals is a form of adaptation.

alleviate (ə·lē'vē·āt') *v.:* relieve; reduce.
alliance (ə·lī'əns) *n.:* pact between nations, families, or individuals that shows a common cause.
amble (am'bəl) *v.:* walk without hurrying.
amplify (am'plə·fī') *v.:* increase in strength. —**amplified** *v.* used as *adj.*
antic (an'tik) *n.:* playful or silly act.
appalling (ə·pôl'iŋ) *adj.:* horrifying.
arrogant (ar'ə·gənt) *adj.:* overly convinced of one's own importance.
ashen (ash'ən) *adj.:* pale.
assent (ə·sent') *n.:* agreement.
assure (ə·shoor') *v.:* promise confidently.

B

bedraggled (bē·drag'əld) *adj.:* hanging limp and wet; dirty.
bluff (bluf) *n.:* steep cliff.
bout (bout) *n.:* match; contest.
buckle (buk'əl) *v.:* collapse under pressure.

C

chivalry (shiv'əl·rē) *n.:* code that governed knightly behavior, such as courage, honor, and readiness to help the weak.
churn (churn) *v.:* shake; stir. —**churning** *v.* used as *adj.*
clamor (klam'ər) *n.:* loud, confused noise.
coexist (kō'ig·zist') *v.:* live together peacefully.
commotion (kə·mō'shən) *n.:* disturbance.
confrontation (kän'frən·tā'shən) *n.:* face-to-face meeting between opposing sides.

---

at, āte, cär; ten, ēve; is, īce; gō, hôrn, look, tool; oil, out; up, fur; ə *for unstressed vowels, as* a *in* ago, u *in* focus; ' *as in* Latin (lat''n); chin; she; zh *as in* azure (azh'ər); thin; *the*; ŋ *as in* ring (riŋ)

---

congregation (käŋ'grə·gā'shən) *n.:* gathering.

consolation (kän'sə·lā'shən) *n.:* comfort.

contraption (kən·trap'shən) *n.:* strange machine or gadget.

converge (kən·vʉrj') *v.:* close in.
—**converging** *v.* used as *adj.*

convoluted (kän'və·lōōt'id) *adj.:* complicated.

countenance (koun'tə·nəns) *n.:* face; appearance.

cower (kou'ər) *v.:* crouch and tremble in fear.

curt (kʉrt) *adj.:* rude, using few words.
—**curtly** *adv.*

D

descent (dē·sent') *n.:* ancestry.

defiant (dē·fī'ənt) *adj.:* boldly resisting authority.

delve (delv) *v.:* search.

deprivation (dep'rə·vā'shən) *n.:* loss; condition of having something taken away by force.

derisive (di·rī'siv) *adj.:* scornful and ridiculing.

detain (dē·tān') *v.:* hold back; delay.

dismal (diz'məl) *adj.:* miserable; gloomy.
—**dismally** *adv.*

dispel (di·spel') *v.:* drive away.

dispute (di·spyōōt') *n.:* argument.

E

edible (ed'ə·bəl) *adj.:* fit to be eaten.

egotism (ē'gō·tiz'əm) *n.:* conceit; talking about oneself too much.

elude (ē·lōōd') *v.:* escape cleverly.

elusive (ē·lōō'siv) *adj.:* hard to detect.

erupt (ē·rupt') *v.:* burst forth.

eternity (ē·tʉr'nə·tē) *n.:* very long time; forever.

ethnicity (eth·nis'ə·tē) *n.:* common culture or nationality.

exotic (eg·zät'ik) *adj.:* foreign; not native.

explicit (eks·plis'it) *adj.:* definite; clearly stated.

F

fathom (fath'əm) *v.:* understand.

finicky (fin'ik·ē) *adj.:* fussy and extremely careful.

forfeit (fôr'fit) *v.:* lose the right to compete.

formidable (fôr'mə·də·bəl) *adj.:* awe-inspiring; impressive.

frenzied (fren'zēd) *adj.:* wild.

fumigate (fyōō'mə·gāt') *v.:* clean out by spraying with chemical vapors.
—**fumigating** *v.* used as *n.*

G

goad (gōd) *v.:* push or drive.

H

habitual (hə·bich'ōō·əl) *adj.:* done or fixed by habit.

heritage (her'ə·tij) *n.:* traditions that are passed along.

horde (hôrd) *n.:* large, moving crowd.

huddle (hud''l) *v.:* nestle close together.

I

idiosyncrasy (id'ē·ō·siŋ'krə·sē) *n.:* peculiarity.

immense (i·mens') *adj.:* enormous.
—**immensely** *adv.*

imminent (im'ə·nənt) *adj.:* about to happen.

impotent (im'pə·tənt) *adj.:* powerless.

incredulous (in·krej'ōō·ləs) *adj.:* unbelieving.
—**incredulously** *adv.*

insolence (in'sə·ləns) *n.:* disrespect.

integrity (in·teg'rə·tē) *n.:* honesty; uprightness.

intelligible (in·tel'i·jə·bəl) *adj.:* understandable.

intent (in·tent') *adj.:* concentrating deeply.
—**intently** *adv.*

intimidate (in·tim'ə·dāt') *v.:* frighten with threats.

intolerable (in·täl'ər·ə·bəl) *adj.:* unbearable.

intricate (in'tri·kit) *adj.:* complicated; full of detail.

L

ligament (lig′ə·mənt) *n.:* in anatomy, band of tough tissue that connects bones and holds organs in place.

loathsome (lōth′səm) *adj.:* disgusting.

M

matinee (mat′′n·ā′) *n.:* afternoon performance of a play or a movie.

meager (mē′gər) *adj.:* slight; small amount.

menace (men′əs) *n.:* danger; threat.

minority (mī·nôr′ə·tē) *n.:* small group that differs from the larger, controlling group.

monarch (män′ərk) *n.:* sole and absolute leader.

monopoly (mə·näp′ə·lē) *n.:* exclusive control of a market.

muster (mus′tər) *v.:* call forth.

O

observatory (əb·zurv′ə·tôr′ē) *n.:* building equipped for scientific observation.

ominous (äm′ə·nəs) *adj.:* threatening.

P

parch (pärch) *v.:* make very hot and dry. —**parched** *v.* used as *adj.*

particle (pärt′i·kəl) *n.:* tiny piece.

pensive (pen′siv) *adj.:* thoughtful. —**pensively** *adv.*

persecution (pur′sə·kyōō′shən) *n.:* act of willfully injuring or attacking others because of their beliefs or ethnic backgrounds.

perturb (pər·turb′) *v.:* disturb; trouble. —**perturbed** *v.* used as *adj.*

predominant (prē·däm′ə·nənt) *adj.:* main. —**predominantly** *adv.*

prey (prā) *n.:* animal hunted or killed for food by another animal. Mice are prey to owls. Gazelles are prey to lions.

profane (prō·fān′) *adj.:* not religious.

R

reassure (rē′ə·shoor′) *v.:* comfort. —**reassuring** *v.* used as *adj.*

recede (ri·sēd′) *v.:* move back. —**receding** *v.* used as *adj.*

recognition (rek′əg·nish′ən) *n.:* knowing again.

refuge (ref′yōōj) *n.:* shelter; protection.

refugee (ref′yōō·jē′) *n.:* person who flees home or country to escape war or persecution. —**refugee** *n.* used as *adj.*

resolve (ri·zälv′) *v.:* decide.

rumple (rum′pəl) *v.:* wrinkle and make untidy. —**rumpled** *v.* used as *adj.*

ruthless (rōōth′lis) *adj.:* without pity.

S

sabotage (sab′ə·täzh′) *v.:* obstruct or destroy.

sentinel (sent′′n·əl) *n.:* watchful guard.

sentry (sen′trē) *n.:* guard.

simultaneous (sī′məl·tā′nē·əs) *adj.:* occurring at the same time. —**simultaneously** *adv.*

skirt (skurt) *v.:* avoid.

sophisticated (sə·fis′tə·kāt′id) *adj.:* worldly; elegant and refined.

sovereignty (säv′rən·tē) *n.:* control; authority.

species (spē′shēz) *n.:* in biology, a naturally existing population of similar organisms that usually breed only among themselves. The human species living today is called *Homo sapiens* ("wise man").

staid (stād) *adj.:* settled; quiet.

T

tirade (tī′rād′) *n.:* long, scolding speech.

torrent (tôr′ənt) *n.:* flood or rush.

tournament (toor′nə·mənt) *n.:* series of contests.

transfix (trans·fiks′) *v.:* make to stand very still, as if nailed to the spot. —**transfixed** *v.* used as *adj.*

transition (tran·zish'ən) *n.:* change; passing from one condition to another.

turbulent (tʉr'byə·lənt) *adj.:* wild; disorderly.

U

unrequite (un'ri·kwīt') *v.:* fail to return in kind. —**unrequited** *v.* used as *adj.*

V

vain (vān) *adj.:* useless; having no result. —**vainly** *adv.*

valiant (val'yənt) *adj.:* brave and determined.

variation (ver'ē·ā'shən) *n.:* difference.

W

wedge (wej) *n.:* pie-shaped slice.

Acknowledgments

For permission to reprint copyrighted material, grateful acknowledgment is made to the following sources:

American Library Association: From Newbery Award–acceptance speech by Mildred D. Taylor, 1977.

Américas, bimonthly magazine published by the General Secretariat of the Organization of American States in English and Spanish: From "Mongoose on the Loose" by Larry Luxner from *Américas*, vol. 45, no. 4, page 3, July–August 1993. Copyright © 1993 by Américas.

Claudia Arnett: "Early Song" by Gogisgi/Carroll Arnett from *Collected Poems of Carroll Arnett/Gogisgi: Poems 1958–1995*. Copyright © 1979 by Gogisgi/Carroll Arnett. Published by Pavement Saw Press.

The Associated Press: "Buddies Bare Their Affection for Ill Classmate" from *Austin American-Statesman*, March 19, 1994. Copyright © 1994 by The Associated Press. From "Hatteras Lighthouse Completes Its Move." Copyright © 1999 by The Associated Press.

Ballantine Books, a division of Random House, Inc.: From review of *Catherine, Called Birdy* by Karen Cushman from *Great Books for Girls: More Than 600 Books to Inspire Today's Girls and Tomorrow's Women* by Kathleen Odean. Copyright © 1997 by Kathleen Odean.

Susan Bergholz Literary Services, New York: "Names/Nombres" by Julia Alvarez. Copyright © 1985 by Julia Alvarez. First published in *Nuestro*, March 1985. "A Rice Sandwich" from *The House on Mango Street*. Copyright © 1984 by Sandra Cisneros. Published by Vintage Books, a division of Random House, Inc., and in hardcover by Alfred A. Knopf in 1994. All rights reserved. From "The Tejano Soul of San Antonio" by Sandra Cisneros. Copyright © 1992 by Sandra Cisneros. First published in *The New York Times*, The Sophisticated Traveler, Part 2, May 17, 1992.

BOA Editions, Ltd.: "the 1st" from *good woman: poems and a memoir 1969–1980* by Lucille Clifton. Copyright © 1987 by Lucille Clifton.

The Estate of Gwendolyn Brooks: "Home" from *Maud Martha* by Gwendolyn Brooks. Copyright © 1993 by Gwendolyn Brooks. Published by Third World Press, Chicago.

Condé Nast on Behalf of John Updike: From "An Ode to Golf" by John Updike. Copyright © 2000 by John Updike. Originally published in *The New Yorker*. All rights reserved.

Bruce Coville c/o Ashley Grayson Literary Agency: "Duffy's Jacket" from *Oddly Enough: Stories by Bruce Coville*. Copyright © 1989 by Bruce Coville.

Dell Publishing, a division of Random House, Inc.: "User Friendly" by T. Ernesto Bethancourt from *Connections: Short Stories*, edited by Donald R. Gallo. Copyright © 1989 by T. Ernesto Bethancourt.

Dial Books for Young Readers, a division of Penguin Putnam Inc.: *Song of the Trees* by Mildred D. Taylor. Copyright © 1975 by Mildred Taylor.

Doubleday, a division of Random House, Inc.: From *The Richer, the Poorer* by Dorothy West. Copyright © 1995 by Dorothy West.

Dutton Children's Books, a division of Penguin Putnam Inc.: "Merlin and the Dragons" by Jane Yolen. Copyright © 1995 by Jane Yolen; illustrations copyright © 1995 by Li Ming.

Dutton Children's Books, an imprint of Penguin Putnam Books for Young Readers, a division of Penguin Putnam Inc.: From "Elizabeth I" from *Ten Queens: Portraits of Women of Power* by Milton Meltzer. Copyright © 1998 by Milton Meltzer.

Esquire and the Hearst Corporation: "Three Skeleton Key" by George G. Toudouze from *Esquire*, January 1937. Copyright © 1937 by Hearst Communications, Inc. All rights reserved.

Farrar, Straus & Giroux, LLC: From "Gwen" and "The Red Girl" from *Annie John* by Jamaica Kincaid. Copyright © 1985 by Jamaica Kincaid.

The Gale Group: Quotes by Patricia Lauber from "Patricia Lauber" from *Something About the Author*, vol. 33, edited by Anne Commire. Copyright © 1983 by Gale Research Inc. Quotes by Anne McCaffrey from "Anne McCaffrey" from *Something About the Author*, vol. 8, edited by Anne Commire. Copyright © 1976 by Gale Research Inc.

Lloyd Garver: From "No, You Can't Have Nintendo" (retitled "A Veto on Video Games") by Lloyd Garver from "My Turn" from *Newsweek*, June 11, 1990, p. 8. Copyright © 1990 by Lloyd Garver.

Harcourt, Inc.: "Mother and Daughter" and "The No-Guitar Blues" from *Baseball in April and Other Stories* by Gary Soto. Copyright © 1990 by Gary Soto.

HarperCollins Publishers: From *Black Elk: The Sacred Ways of a Lakota* by Wallace H. Black Elk and William S. Lyon, Ph.D. Copyright © 1990 by Wallace H. Black Elk and William S. Lyon. Quote by Hudson Talbott from jacket cover of *King Arthur: The Sword in the Stone*, written and illustrated by Hudson Talbott. Copyright © 1991 by Hudson Talbott.

Harvard University Press and the Trustees of Amherst College: "288: I'm Nobody! Who are you?" from *The Poems of Emily Dickinson*, edited by Thomas H. Johnson. Copyright © 1951, 1955, 1979, 1983 by the President and Fellows of Harvard College. Published by The Belknap Press of Harvard University Press, Cambridge, MA.

Henry Holt and Company, Inc.: "The Runaway" from *The Poetry of Robert Frost*, edited by Edward Connery Lathem. Copyright © 1951 by Robert Frost; copyright © 1923, 1969 by Henry Holt and Company, Inc.

Houghton Mifflin Company: "Bargain" from *The Big It and Other Stories* by A. B. Guthrie. Copyright © 1960 by A. B. Guthrie. All rights reserved.

International Creative Management, Inc.: "The Monsters Are Due on Maple Street" by Rod Serling. Copyright © 1960 by Rod Serling.

Alfred A. Knopf, a division of Random House, Inc.: "Epigram" and "Madam and the Rent Man" from *Collected Poems* by Langston Hughes. Copyright © 1957 by Ballantine Books, Inc.; copyright renewed © 1985 by George Houston Bass; copyright © 1994 by the Estate of Langston Hughes.

Patricia Lauber: "When the Earth Shakes" from *Earth-*

quakes: New Scientific Ideas About How and Why the Earth Shakes by Patricia Lauber. Copyright © 1972 by Patricia Lauber.

Liveright Publishing Corporation: "maggie and milly and molly and may" from *Complete Poems: 1904–1962* by E. E. Cummings, edited by George J. Firmage. Copyright © 1956, 1984, 1991 by the Trustees for the E. E. Cummings Trust.

The Los Angeles Times: "Eeking Out a Life" by Matt Surman from *The Los Angeles Times,* July 8, 2000. Copyright © 2000 by The Los Angeles Times.

Anne McCaffrey and agent, Virginia Kidd Agency, Inc.: "The Smallest Dragonboy" from *Get Off the Unicorn* by Anne McCaffrey. Copyright © 1973 and renewed © 2001 by Anne McCaffrey. First appeared in *Science Fiction Tales.*

Margaret K. McElderry Books, an imprint of Simon & Schuster Children's Publishing Division: From *A Jar of Dreams* by Yoshiko Uchida. Copyright © 1981 by Yoshiko Uchida.

Pat Mora, www.patmora.com: "Gold" by Pat Mora. Copyright © 1998 by Pat Mora. Originally published by Harcourt Brace in *Home: A Journey Through America* by Thomas Locker and Candace Christiansen.

Motorola, Inc.: "Battery Removal and Replacement" from *Premier Cellular Telephone: Owner's Manual.* Copyright © 1994 by Motorola, Inc.

NEA Today: From "Amy Tan: Joy, Luck, and Literature," an interview by Anita Merina from *NEA Today,* October 1991. Copyright © 1991 by the National Education Association of the United States.

Agate Nesaule: Commentary by Agate Nesaule from *NPR Morning Edition,* October 24, 2000. Copyright © 2000 by Agate Nesaule.

The New York Times Company: "Yeti-like Monster Gives Staid Town . . ." by Andrew Malcolm from *The New York Times,* November 1, 1973. Copyright © 1973 by The New York Times Company.

The Oryx Press, 4041 North Central Avenue, Suite 700, Phoenix, AZ 85012, 800-279-6799: "Sir Gawain and the Loathly Lady" from *The Oryx Multicultural Folktale Series: Beauties and Beasts* by Betsy Hearne. Copyright © 1993 by The Oryx Press.

Persea Books, Inc. (New York): From "Who Is Your Reader?" from *The Effects of Knut Hamsun on a Fresno Boy* by Gary Soto. Copyright © 1983 and renewed © 1988 and © 2000 by Gary Soto.

Philomel Books, an imprint of Penguin Putnam Books for Young Readers, a division of Penguin Putnam Inc.: *Yeh-Shen: A Cinderella Story from China,* retold by Ai-Ling Louie. Text copyright © 1982 by Ai-Ling Louie.

Random House UK Ltd: "Narcissus" (retitled "Echo and Narcissus") from *Tales the Muses Told* by Roger Lancelyn Green. Copyright © 1965 by Don Bolognese. Published by The Bodley Head.

The Saturday Review: "The Dinner Party" by Mona Gardner from *The Saturday Review of Literature,* vol. 25, no. 5, January 31, 1941. Copyright © 1979 by General Media Communications, Inc.

Colonel John D. Silvera, Executor of the Estate of Edward Silvera: From "Forgotten Dreams" by Edward Silvera from *The Poetry of the Negro, 1746–1970,* edited by Langston Hughes and Arna Bontemps.

Amy Tan and Sandra Dijkstra Literary Agency: "Fish Cheeks" by Amy Tan. Copyright © 1987 by Amy Tan. Originally appeared in *Seventeen Magazine,* December 1987.

Temple University Press: From "The Xiong Family of Lompoc" from *Hmong Means Free: Life in Laos and America,* edited by Sucheng Chang. Copyright © 1994 by Temple University. All rights reserved.

Piri Thomas: "Amigo Brothers" from *Stories from El Barrio* by Piri Thomas. Copyright © 1978 by Piri Thomas.

Time Inc.: "Can We Rescue the Reefs?" by Ritu Upadhyay from *Time for Kids,* vol. 6, no. 9, November 10, 2000. Copyright © 2000 by Time Inc.

University of Notre Dame Press: From *Barrio Boy* by Ernesto Galarza. Copyright © 1971 by University of Notre Dame Press.

University Press of Mississippi: From an interview with Sandra Cisneros from *Interviews with Writers of the Post-Colonial World* by Reed Dasenbrock and Feroza Jussawalla. Copyright © 1992 by University Press of Mississippi.

Anna Lee Walters: "I Am of the Earth" by Anna Walters from *Voices of the Rainbow: Contemporary Poetry by American Indians,* edited by Kenneth Rosen. Copyright © 1975 by Anna Lee Walters.

Wiley Publishing, Inc.: Pronunciation key from *Webster's New World™ College Dictionary,* Fourth Edition. Copyright © 1999, 2000 by Wiley Publishing, Inc.

Mel White: "A Mason-Dixon Memory" by Clifton Davis, slightly adapted from *Reader's Digest,* March 1993. Copyright © 1993 by Mel White.

Roberta Hill Whiteman: "Depot in Rapid City" by Roberta Hill from *A Book of Women Poets: From Antiquity to Now,* edited by Aliki Barnstone and Willis Barnstone.

Joseph D. Younger: From "The Joy Luck Writer," an interview with Amy Tan by Joseph D. Younger from *Amtrak Express Magazine,* vol. 13, no. 4, July–August 1993.

Sources Cited

From "Home on the Range" by Johnny D. Boggs from *Boys Life,* June 1998. Published by the Boy Scouts of America, 1998.

From "A Note from the Author" from *Oddly Enough: Stories* by Bruce Coville. Published by Harcourt, Inc., 1994, Orlando, FL.

Picture Credits

The illustrations and/or photographs on the Contents pages are picked up from pages in the textbook. Credits for those can be found either on the textbook page on which they appear or in the listing below.

Page 12: Courtesy of Bruce Coville; 19: Bettmann/Corbis; 21: Joe McDonald/DRK Photo; 22: Dinodia/Omni–Photo Communications; 25: Renee Lynn/Photo Researchers; 27: Michael Fogden/Animals Animals; 31: OSF/Senani/Animals Animals; 32–33: Studio Carlo Dani/Animals Animals; 34: Dr. E. R. Degginger/Color-Pic; 35: Bettmann/Corbis; 37: © PhotoDisc, Inc.; 38: Joe McDonald/Corbis; 49: Stephen Dalton/Photo Researchers; 63, 66: Joe McDonald/Corbis; 87: Bettmann/Corbis; 91: Bob Daemmrich/Stock, Boston/PictureQuest; 109: Orion Press/Black Sheep; 115: Courtesy of Gary Soto; 133: Courtesy of Anne McCaffrey; 141, 143: © PhotoDisc, Inc.; 146: Bryce Harper; 149: Pictor; 164: Amos Zezmer/Omni–Photo Communications; 170–171: British Museum/The Bridgeman Art Library; 171 (top): North Wind Pictures; 172: Christie's Images London/SuperStock; 174: (top) Lee Snider/Corbis; (bottom) Bettmann/Corbis; 177: (bottom left) Bettmann/Corbis; (bottom right) Courtesy of The Edgar Allan Poe Museum, Richmond, Va.; 180: Art Today; 181: (top left) Michael J. Deas; (top right) Art Today; (bottom) © PhotoDisc, Inc.; 182: Photographs by Michael J. Deas; 184: Art Today; 195: Tom Tondee; 196, 199, 200: © PhotoDisc, Inc.; 208: (top) Wolfgang Kaehler/Corbis; (bottom) Arte & Immagini SRL/Corbis; 225: Grace Davies/Omni–Photo Communications; 229: Corbis; 230: Grace Davies/Omni–Photo Communications; 233: Bettmann/Corbis; 234: (top) AP/Wide World Photos; (bottom) Archive Photos; 235: (top) © PhotoDisc, Inc.; (bottom) Bill Bachman/Photo Network/PictureQuest; 237: Culver Pictures; 247: © Bettmann/Corbis; 249: Culver Pictures; 255: McIntosh and Otis; 257, 258 (inset): © PhotoDisc, Inc.; 258–259: Jacqui Hurst/Corbis; 262: Courtesy of Julia Alvarez; 266: Theo Westenberger/Gamma Liaison; 268: Corbis; 271: (middle) Courtesy of Maijue Xiong; (bottom): Michael S. Yamashita/Corbis; 272, 273: Courtesy of Maijue Xiong; 273 (right): © PhotoDisc, Inc.; 275: Courtesy of Maijue Xiong; 276: Nik Wheeler/Corbis; 278: Courtesy of Agate Nesaule; 279: Peter Turnley/Corbis; 280 (top to bottom): Peter Turnley/Corbis; David Turnley/Corbis; Peter Turnley/Corbis; Liba Taylor/Corbis; 285: (top left) Francis G. Mayer/Corbis; (top middle) National Trust/Art Resource, New York; (top right) Giraudon/Art Resource, New York; (bottom right) Archivo Iconografico SA/Corbis; (bottom left) Scala/Art Resource, New York; 287: Corbis; 289: (left) Bettmann/Corbis; (middle) Joel W. Rogers/Corbis; (right) Michael Nicholson/Corbis; 290: Corbis; 291: (left) Archivo Iconografico SA/Corbis; (right) Erich Lessing/Art Resource, New York; 292: Corbis; 293: Courtesy of Milton Meltzer; 295: (top) Archivo Iconografico SA/Corbis; (bottom) The Bridgeman Art Library; 315: © PhotoDisc, Inc.; 317: Jim Pickerell/Blackstar; 320: © PhotoDisc, Inc.; 321: Chris George/Corbis; 324: (top) Randy Duchaine/The Stock Market; (bottom) Gary Conner/Photo Edit; 328: University of Notre Dame Press; 347: Jack Ackerman/Penguin USA; 354: AP/Wide World Photos; 356: © PhotoDisc, Inc.; 358–359: Saint Frederick High School Yearbook; 363: Gerardo Somoza/Outline Press Syndicate; 365: Saint Frederick High School Yearbook; 368, 369: AP/Wide World Photos; 371, 373: Steve McCutcheon; 374: Patrick Robert/Sygma; 375: Paul X. Scott/Sygma; 376: Steve McCutcheon; 377: (top) HarperCollins; (bottom) Paras Shah/Photo Archive; 378: Robert Yager/Tony Stone Images; 386–387: Kevin Fall Collection; 388: Courtesy of Anna Lee Walters, Photo by Ed McCombs; 389: Kevin Fall Collection; 392: Robert W. Kelley/Timepix; 394: Fred Stein/Black Star; 395: Bettmann/Corbis; 397: Ralph Reinhold/Animals Animals; 398: Bettmann/Corbis; 400–401: Hisanori Kondo/Photonica; 402: Corbis; 403: Donald Nausbaum/Tony Stone Images; 425: The Bridgeman Art Library; 429: Courtesy of Hudson Talbott; 448: © Jason Stemple; 455, 457: (background), PhotoAlto; 459: Courtesy of Betsy Hearne; 461: The Bridgeman Art Library; 462: Giraudon/Art Resource, New York; 463, The Bridgeman Art Library; 483: Eyewire; 485: Alan Klehr/Tony Stone Images; 486: (left) © PhotoDisc, Inc.; (right) John Sohm/Stock Boston/PictureQuest; 487: (top) Claus Meyer/Blackstar/Picture Quest; (bottom) Courtesy of Sotheby's; 490: Alon Reininger/Contact Press; 495: Baron Wolman/Tony Stone Images; 496: San Francisco Bay Area Rapid Transit District; 501: PhotoAlto; 591: (top left) © Yann Arthus-Bertrand /Corbis; (top right) © Reuters NewMedia Inc./Corbis; (bottom) AP/Wide World Photos; 592: (top) Glen E. Ellman /George Hall/Check Six; (bottom) SIPA Press; 627: Diane Gentry/Blackstar; 629: Walter Stuart/Richard W. Salzman Artist Representative; 686: People Weekly © 1986 Richard Howard; 689: UPI/Bettmann/Corbis.

Illustrations

All art, unless otherwise noted, by Holt, Rinehart & Winston.

Anderson, Paul, A32–A33, A34–A35, A36–1, 508–509, 526–527, 708–709
DiGiorgio, Mike, 502–504
Dill, Jane, 119–120, 132
Ehlert, Lois, 352, 353
Garbot, Dave, 510, 512, 516, 518, 521, 523
Geis, Alissa Imre, 109–114
Grossman, Myron, 349–350, 366, 450, 466
Haggerty, Tim, 179, 199, 200
Halbert, Michael, 21
Hovell, John, 16–17, 63–64, 92, 94–95, 98, 137, 147, 171–172, 181–182, 199–200, 321, 368

Leister, Brian, 118, 119, 123, 127, 131
Leonard, Tom, 50, 54, 56, 57, 61
Margeson, John, 232, 382, 385
Ortega, Jose, 309, 311, 318
Reagan, Mike, 60
Riedy, Mark, 67, 69–71, 73, 75, 77–78, 80, 83, 86, 88–90
Schulenburg, Paul, 2–3, 104–105, 156–157, 220–221, 304–305, 410–411, 480–481
Spransy, Tim, 186–187
Stuart, Walter, 629
Thompson, John, 333, 334, 337, 338, 339, 341, 342, 343, 344, 345
Verougstraete, Randy, 6, 7, 8, 9, 10, 11, 12
Map: pre- 1975 Laos and Southeast Asia, 271

Index of Skills

Narrative, 48, 276
   biographical, 282
Narrative poetry
   characters in, 160
   plot of, 160
   sequence chart for, 168
   setting in, 160
Narrator, 140, **222–223**, 297
   first-person, 140, 144, **222–223**, 236
   omniscient, 140, **222–223**, 224, 256
Nonfiction, 306, 413, 742–743
   characters and, 413
   objectivity and, 413
   primary sources and, 413
Novel, 306, **332**, 405, 743
Novella, 306, **332**, 743
Objective details, 276
Objective point of view, 261, 267, 276, 282, 294, 297
Objective writing, 261, 276, 282, 294, 297, 730
Objectivity, 413
Omniscient narrator, 140, **222–223**, 224, 250, 256
Omniscient point of view, **222, 224, 250**, 516, 744
Onomatopoeia, 391, 743
Origin myth, 208, 742
Paraphrasing, **389**
Personification, 348, **386**, 740, 743
Plot, **4–5**, 13, 20, 23, 25, 26, 29, 33, 36, 88, 97, 116, 332, 348, **412**, 449, **510–511**, 743–744
   character and, 512–513
   complications in, 4, **67**, 510, 511
   conflict and, 20
   diagram of, 5, 13, 36, 88, 318, 348
   in narrative poetry, 160
   theme distinguished from, 158
Poetry, 744
   alliteration in, 391, 737
   comparisons in, 381, 382
   elements of, **380**
   figurative language in, 380, 382, 413
   forms of, 380
   free verse, 390, 741
   imagery in, 380, 381, 413
   limerick, 391
   memorizing, 381
   meter in, 390
   narrative, **160**
   onomatopoeia in, 391, 743
   punctuation of, **381**
   refrain, 745
   rhyme in, 381, 390, 396, 399, 744
   rhythm in, 381, 390, 745–746
   scanning, 390, 746
   sound effects in, 380, 390, 391, 413
   speaker in, 746
   stanzas in, 380, 746–747
   theme in, 178, 413
   See also Rhyme.
Point of view, **222–223**, 224, 261, 276, 297, **516–517**, 744
   author's, 88
   first-person, **223, 236**, 248, 516, 744

objective, 261, 267, 276, 282, 294, 297
omniscient, **222, 224, 250**, 256, 516, 744
subjective, 261, 267, 270, 276, 283, 294
third-person limited, **223**, 297, 516, 744
Predict, 78
Primary source, 413
Problem, 308, 348, 510
Prose, 306
Prose chart, 307
Protagonist, 511
Punctuation, 381
Purpose, 261, 281, 299, 355, 357, 732
Quest, 438, **451**, 460, 742
Quotations, 436
Reactions, 107
Reading Comprehension (Reading Check), 13, 36, 60, 78, 88, 116, 134, 144, 168, 178, 196, 230, 248, 256, 267, 276, 294, 318, 329, 348, 355, 364, 378, 399, 430, 436, 449, 460
Reading Comprehension (Test Practice), 96–97, 150–151, 210–213, 296–297, 404–405, 472–473
Recurring themes, 203
Refrain, 745
Repetition, **174**
Resolution, **5**, 13, 97, 116, 308, 348, 511
Rhyme, 381, 390, 395, 396, 745
   end, 390, 396, 745
   exact, 400, 403
   eye, 745
   internal, 390, 745
   scheme, 391, 395, 396, 399, 744, 745
   slant, 400, 403, 745
   See also Poetry.
Rhyming sounds, 178
Rhythm, 381, 395, 745–746
   free verse and, 390
   meter and, 390
Riddle, **451**, 460
Scanning, 390, 746
Scapegoat, 78
Scientific terms, **370**
Scientific writing, **370**, 378
Screenplay, **70**
   close-up, 70
   cut to, 70
   dissolve, 70
   fade in, 70
   fade to black, 70
   long shot, 70
   opening shot, 70
   outside shot, 70
   pan, 70
Sequence chart, 168, 355
Series of events, **4**
Setting, 60, 97, 160, 168, 178, 236, 746
   in narrative poems, 160
Short-short story, 308
Short story, **306, 308, 332**, 405, 746

Simile, **169**, 378, 382, 385, 739, 746
Slant rhyme, 400, 403, 745
Somebody Wanted But So, 516–517
Sound effects, 380, **390, 391**, 413
Source, primary, 413
Speaker, 297, 746
Speech, **107**
Stanza, 380, 746–747
Static character, 738
Story map, 13, 116, 318, 348
Story pattern, **438**
Story structure, 449
Style, 400
Subject, **160**
   theme distinguished from, 160
Subjective details, 276, 282, 294
Subjective point of view, 261, 267, 270, 276, 283
Subjective writing, 261, 270, 276, 282, 283, 294, 730, 734
Subplot, 332
Summary, **367, 369**, 436, 510–511, 734
Suspense, 4, **48**, 60, 224, **378**, 747
Symbol, **89**, 747
Symbolism, 399
Tall Tale, 747
Teleplay, **70**
   close-up, 70
   cut to, 70
   dissolve, 70
   fade in, 70
   fade to black, 70
   long shot, 70
   opening shot, 70
   outside shot, 70
   pan, 70
Theme, **158–159**, 160, 168, 178, 185, 196, 213, 230, 248, 256, 332, 412, **413, 514–515**, 747
   comparison chart for, 159
   comparison of, 196
   discovery of, 185
   evaluating, 159
   as generalization, **332**
   most important word and, **514–515**
   in myths, 208
   plot distinguished from, 158
   recurring, **203**
   subject distinguished from, **160**
   title and, 174, 185
   uncovering, 514–515
Third-person limited point of view, **223**, 297, 516, 744
Thought bubbles, 223
Thoughts and feelings, **107**
Time line, 276
Title, 159, 185, 267, 355, 399
Tone, 389, **392**, 393, 403, 747
Topic Sentence, 741

READING COMPREHENSION (INFORMATIONAL MATERIALS)

Accurate evidence, **467**, 471, 475, 725
Adequate evidence, **467**, 471, 725
Advertisement, 482
Analogy, 40, 721

underlining and circling information for, 180
Number facts (statistics), 257, 260, 299
Opinion, 40, **146**, 183, 257, 276, 294, 323, 329, 725
  invalid, **146**, 725
  personal beliefs, 146
  predictions, 146
  thoughts and feelings, 146
  valid, **146**, 468, 725
Organizational patterns, 139
  cause-and-effect, 198, 201, 215, 722, 734–735
  chronological order, 15, 723, 734–735
  compare-and-contrast, 136, 139, **320**, 723, 735
Outline, 180, 183, 730–731
Personal narrative, 278, 281
Perspective, **232**, 235, 257, 260, 278, 281, 736
Persuasion, 257, 278, 731
Phone number, in an instructional manual, 91
Point-by-point pattern of organization, **136**, **320**, 723
Propaganda, 732
  bandwagon appeal, 732
  name-calling, 732
  snob appeal, 732
  stereotyping, 732
  testimonial, 732
Pseudonym, 235
Public documents, 483, **484**, 489
Pun, 65
Purpose, 261, 281, 299, 355, 357, 732
  of essays, 357
  of instructional manuals, **91**, 93
  of newspaper articles, 15, **62**, 65, 93, 99
  of nonfiction, 278, 281
  of signs, **94–95**
  of textbooks, **42–46**, 93, 99
Questions
  in textbooks, 46
  on tests, 711
Reading checks, in textbooks, 46
Reading Comprehension (Reading Check), 18, 40, 65, 93, 139, 148, 183, 201, 235, 260, 281, 322, 436, 465, 489, 494, 500
Reading Comprehension (Test Practice), 18, 40, 47, 65, 93, 139, 148, 173, 183, 201, 235, 260, 281, 322, 369, 436, 465, 470, 489, 494, 500
Reading comprehension test, 713–716
Rely on 50/50, 712
Response to literature, **432–435**
Revealing truths about life, 278
Schedule, 482
Search for skips and smudges, 712
Sharing experiences, 278
Signs, **98–99**, 732
  purpose of, **94–95**
  structure of, **94–95**
Snob Appeal, 732

Social Security number, 482
Sources, 468
Spot those numbers, 711
Statistics (number facts), 257, 260, 299
Stereotype, **463**, 465, 468, 732, 733
Strategies for taking a multiple-choice test, 710–712
Strategies for taking writing tests, 717–720
Structural features
  of instructional manuals, **91**, 93, 99
  of newspaper articles, 15, **62**, 65, 93
  of signs, **94–95**
  of textbooks, **42–46**, 93, 99
Study the Directions, 711
Subhead, in newspaper articles, 62, 65
Summary, **367**, **369**, 436, 510–511, 734
  in textbooks, 44
Summary lead, 62
Support, 299
Table, 728
Table of contents
  in instructional manuals, **91**
  in textbooks, **43**, 47
Take it all in, 711
Tax form, 482–483
Technical directions, 482, 501
Test Smarts, **710–720**
Testimonials, 732
Text Structures, 15, 42, 62, 91, 94, 320, **357**, 360, 362, 364, 732, 734–735
Textbook, **42–46**, 736
  author page in, 47
  boldface type in, 45
  caption in, 44
  copyright page in, 47
  insets in, 44
  purpose of, **42–46**, 93, 99
  questions in, 46
  reading checks in, 46
  structure of, **42–46**, 93, 99
  summary in, 44
  table of contents in, 43, 47
Time Line, 728
Title, 38, 40, 139, 727
Tone, of newspaper article, 62, 65
Topic, 257, 260, 369
Tracing a writer's argument, 258–259
Track Your Time, 710
Transitions, **198**
Try. Try. Try., 712
Valid opinion, **146**, 468, 725
Venn diagram, 139, 308, 723, 735
Warranty, 482
Web site, 487
  for instructional manual, 91
  for locating information, 497–499
Who? what? when? where? why? *and how?*, 62, 65, 726
Work permit, 482, 489
Workplace documents, 482–483, 490, 494

Workplace instructions, 492, 494
Writer's perspective, 232, 235, 257, 260, 736

READING: WORD ANALYSIS, FLUENCY, AND SYSTEMATIC VOCABULARY DEVELOPMENT

Affixes, **135**, **520–523**
  list of, 522
  prefixes, **135**, 437, 450, 520, 522
  suffixes, **135**, 450, 520, 522
Analogies, 40, **179**, **202**, **356**, 721
  verbal, 721
  See also Reading Comprehension (Informational Materials): Analogies.
Anglo-Saxon roots, **431**, 437
Borrowed words, **145**
Clarifying word meanings, 61, 231, 379
  by contrast, **37**, 231, **277**
  by definition, **79**, **90**, 231, **268–269**, 295
  by example, **61**, 231, **330**
  by restatement, **14**, 19, 231
  in sports reporting, 319
Cluster diagram, 37, 79
Comprehension strategies, 249
Connotation, **349**, 724, 739
Context clues, 40, 148, **203**, 209, 216, 249, 406, **524–525**, 724
  contrast, **525**, 724
  definition, **524**, 724
  example, **524**, 724
  restatement, **525**, 724
Contrast, 36, 231, **277**, 724
Decoding words, 249
Definitions, **79**, **90**, 231, **268–269**
  in context, 295, 724
Denotation, **349**, 724, 739
Dictionary, 117
Etymologies, **117**
Example, **61**, 231, **330**, 724
Figures of speech, **169**, 370, 380, 382, 389, 740
  metaphor, **169**, 740
  personification, 740
  simile, **169**, 740
French roots, **461**
Graphic organizers
  cluster diagram, 37, 79
  figure of speech comparison chart, 169
  for etymologies, 117
  for prefixes, 450
  similar-word chart, 14
  vocabulary tree, 523
  word tree, 135
  word web, 231
Greek roots, 117, **466**, **520–523**
Idioms, **197**
Indo-European roots, 117
Latin roots, 41, 117, **184**, 249, **431**, 437, **520–523**
Meaning, 249
Metaphor, **169**, 329, 378, 382, 385, 740, 742

Multiple-meaning words, 100, 476
Paragraph clues, **149**
Prefixes, **135,** 437, 450, 520, 522
   Anglo-Saxon, **437**
   chart of, 437, 466
   graphic organizer for, 450
   Latin, **437**
Restatement, **14,** 19, 231, 724
Roots of words, **135, 184, 520–523**
   Anglo-Saxon, **431**
   French, **461**
   Indo-European, 117
   Greek, 117, **466, 520–523**
   Latin, 117, **135, 184,** 249, **520–523**
Sentence clues, **149,** 379
Simile, **169,** 378, 382, 385, 739, 746
Suffixes, **135,** 450, 520, 522
Synonyms, 152, 300, **365**
Thesaurus, 365
Vocabulary tree, 523
Word analysis, 406
Word clues, **149**
Word context, 249, 406
Word map, 365, 450
Word origins, 117
Word parts, 249
Word roots, 117, **135, 184, 431, 461, 466, 520–523**
   list of, 521
Word tree, 135
Word web, 231

READING SKILLS AND STRATEGIES

Autobiography, facts and opinions in, 329
Basic situation
   complications in, 510
   retelling of, 510
Causal chain, **185,** 198, 217
Causal relationship, **518**
Cause and effect, 170, **185,** 189, 191, 193, 196, 198, 199–200, 201, 208, 215, 370, 372, 373, 374, 375, 376, 460, **518–519,** 722
   cause, **185,** 196, 460, 722, 734–735
   chart for, 378, 460, 518
   effect, **185,** 196, 460, 722
   identifying, **518–519**
   recognition of, **185,** 189, 191, 193
   tracking, 370
   words signaling, 519
Character, 116, 120, 121, 123, 126, 129, 144, 738
   inferring about, 108, 118, 134, 230
   motivation of, 134
   retelling, 510
   traits of, 116, 134, 196
   wants of, 510, 511
   See also Literary Response and Analysis: Character.
Clarifying, 417, 422
Comparing, **136, 308,** 320
   themes, 196
Comparison and contrast, **136,** 139, **308, 320,** 420, 436, 723, 734–735
Complications, retelling, 510

Conclusions, 723–724
Conflict, **20,** 738–739. *See also* Literary Response and Analysis: Conflict.
Context clues, **203, 524–525,** 724
   contrast, **525,** 724
   definition, **524,** 724
   example, **524,** 724
   restatement, **525,** 724
   See also Reading: Word Analysis, Fluency, and Systematic Vocabulary Development.
Contrast, **136, 308,** 320
   clues, **525,** 724
Definition clues, **524,** 724
Details, 38, 248, 261, 267, 351, 378, 731
Distinguishing fact from opinion, 270, 276, 323
Drawing conclusions, 723–724
Effect, **185,** 196, 460, 722
   words signaling, 519
Example clues, **524,** 724
Facts, 276, 323, 329, 725
   distinguished from opinions, **270,** 276, 323
   See also Reading Comprehension (Informational Materials): Facts.
Flashback, **357,** 364, 740
Foreshadow, 48, 60, 731. *See also* Literary Response and Analysis: Foreshadowing.
Generalization, **332,** 473, 725–726, 726–727
Graphic organizers
   cause-and-effect chart, 378, 460, 518
   character-traits box, 513
   hero-story chart, 430
   KWL chart, 730
   plot diagram, 36
   retelling summary sheet, 510–511
   Somebody Wanted But So box, 516, 517
   SQ3R organizer, 283
   Venn diagram, 308
If . . . then . . . , **512–513**
Images, **351,** 355, 729
Implying, 261
Independent reading, 12, 35, 87, 102–103, 115, 133, 143, 154–155, 177, 195, 218–219, 229, 247, 293, 302–303, 328, 347, 377, 394, 398, 402, 408–409, 429, 448, 459, 478–479, 506–507
Inferences, 38, 67, 72, 74, 76, 77, 78, 81, 84, 85, 86, 88, **108,** 116, **118,** 120, 121, 123, 126, 129, 134, 140, **146,** 148, 151, 153, 238, 240, 246, 261, 294, 419, 423, 425, 494, 729, 730, 741, 747
KWL chart, 730
Main idea, **38,** 40, 62, 65, 93, 139, **261,** 267, 276, 355, 357, 367, 436, 473, 730, 741
Most important word, 514–515
Narrative, 48, 276
Opinion, 40, **146,** 183, 257, 276, 294, 323, 329, 725

distinguished from facts, **270,** 276, 323
Paraphrasing, 389
Plot, 23, 25, 26, 29, 33, 36
   diagram for, 36
   See also Literary Response and Analysis: Plot.
Predicting, **6,** 7, 9, 10, **48,** 60, 78, 160, **224,** 227, 228, 230, **236,** 238, 240, 242, 243, 248, 329, 428, 731
Quotations, 267, 283
Reading rate, 732
Restatement clues, **525,** 724
Retelling, **20,** 23, 25, 26, 29, 33, 36, 283, 416, 418, **510–511,** 733
Retelling summary sheet
   antagonist, 511
   author, 511
   characters, 511
   chronology, 511
   climax, 511
   complications, 511
   conflict, 511
   introduction, 510, 511
   main events, 511
   protagonist, 511
   resolution, 511
   setting, 511
   time-order words, 511
   title, 511
Revising predictions, 236
Sensory imagery, **351**
Setting a purpose for reading (Before You Read), 6, 20, 48, 67, 108, 118, 140, 160, 174, 185, 203, 224, 236, 250, 261, 270, 282, 308, 323, 332, 351, 357, 370, 382, 386, 392, 396, 400, 414, 438, 451
Setting a purpose for reading (Reading Informational Materials), 15, 38, 42, 62, 91, 94, 136, 146, 170, 180, 198, 232, 257, 278, 320, 367, 432, 463, 467, 484, 490, 496, 501
Somebody Wanted But So, **516–517**
SQ3R, 283, 294, 733
   organizer for, 283
Suspense, **48**
Text structures, recognizing, **357,** 360, 362. *See also* Reading Comprehension (Informational Materials): Text Structures.
Theme
   as generalization, **332**
   stating, 348
   uncovering, 514
   See also Literary Response and Analysis: Themes.
Think sheets, using, 336
Venn diagram, 308

STANDARDS PRACTICE AND REVIEW

Literary Standard 3.1, 404–405
Literary Standard 3.2, 96–97
Literary Standard 3.3, 150–151
Literary Standard 3.4, 210–213
Literary Standard 3.5, 296–297

Topics, for documentary analysis, 707
Transitional words and phrases
    in informative speech, 658
    in oral summary, 585
TV news broadcasts, analyzing
    electronic journalism and, 593
TV newsmagazines, analyzing
    electronic journalism and, 593
Variety of perspectives, in
    informative speech, 655
Voice modulation
    in informative speech, 658
    in persuasive speech, **619**
    in stories, 561
Volume, in oral summary, 586

INDEPENDENT READING

Index of Authors and Titles